Investment and Portfolio Management

Investment and Portfolio Management

A practical introduction

Ian Pagdin and Michelle Hardy

Publisher's note

Every possible effort has been made to ensure that the information contained in this book is accurate at the time of going to press, and the publishers and authors cannot accept responsibility for any errors or omissions, however caused. No responsibility for loss or damage occasioned to any person acting, or refraining from action, as a result of the material in this publication can be accepted by the editor, the publisher or the authors.

First published in Great Britain and the United States in 2018 by Kogan Page Limited

Apart from any fair dealing for the purposes of research or private study, or criticism or review, as permitted under the Copyright, Designs and Patents Act 1988, this publication may only be reproduced, stored or transmitted, in any form or by any means, with the prior permission in writing of the publishers, or in the case of reprographic reproduction in accordance with the terms and licences issued by the CLA. Enquiries concerning reproduction outside these terms should be sent to the publishers at the undermentioned addresses:

2nd Floor, 45 Gee Street	c/o Martin P Hill Consulting	4737/23 Ansari Road
London	122 W 27th, 10th Floor	Daryaganj
EC1V 3RS	New York, NY 10001	New Delhi 110002
United Kingdom	USA	India

© Ian Pagdin and Michelle Hardy 2018

The right of Ian Pagdin and Michelle Hardy to be identified as the authors of this work has been asserted by them in accordance with the Copyright, Designs and Patents Act 1988.

ISBN   978 0 7494 8005 9
E-ISBN 978 0 7494 8006 6

British Library Cataloguing-in-Publication Data

A CIP record for this book is available from the British Library.

Typeset by Integra Software Services, Pondicherry
Print production managed by Jellyfish
Printed and bound in Great Britain by CPI Group (UK) Ltd, Croydon CR0 4YY

CONTENTS

Acknowledgements xi
Introduction xii
About the authors xiv

01 Financial markets 1
Introduction 1
Defining financial markets 2
History and developments of financial markets 3
Financial markets today 5
Categorization of markets 10
The key participants in a financial market 18
Cross-border transactions 22
Recent developments in financial markets 25
Financial crises 31
Summary 37
Check your understanding 37
Further reading 37

02 Global fund management industry 38
Introduction 38
The global investment management industry and its major players 39
Global issues shaping investing in 2017 45
The size of the UK investment management industry 48
Fund valuation 49
Measurement of AUM in the UK 50
Asset management house structure 57
Investment managers 59
Future developments in the fund management industry 65
Summary 69
Check your understanding 69
Further reading 69

03 Main market participants 71
Introduction 71
Central banks 72
Wholesale banking 75
Retail banking 77
Private banks 79
Investment banks 80
Private equity 82
Sovereign wealth funds 84
Hedge funds 89
Pension funds and insurance companies 91
Private investors 93
Summary 96
Check your understanding 97
Further reading 97

04 Types of risk 98
Introduction 98
Types of risk 99
Measuring risk 115
Summary 128
Check your understanding 128
Further reading 129

05 Investment theory 130
Introduction 130
Random walk theory 131
Efficient market hypothesis 132
Modern portfolio theory 135
Measurement of performance under modern portfolio theory 150
Capital asset pricing model 151
Arbitrage pricing theory 158
Behavioural finance 161
Investment returns 163
Summary 175
Check your understanding 175
Further reading 175

06 Investment classes: Fixed-interest (debt) 176
Introduction 176
Bond issuers and bond types 180

Nominal or par value of a bond 185
Types of coupon or interest rates payable on a bond 186
When will the coupon or interest be paid? 188
Maturity or other repayment of a bond 189
Identifying a bond 193
Where can investors buy bonds? 194
Bond ownership 197
Costs of buying a bond 198
Factors affecting bond prices 201
Understanding risk in bonds and its effect on bond prices 204
Measuring the return on a bond 209
The risks of investing in bonds 213
Bond taxation 218
The advantages and disadvantages of investing in bonds 220
Summary 220
Check your understanding 220
Further reading 220

07 Investment classes: Equity 222

Introduction 222
Types of shares 224
Nominal and market values of shares 230
Changes in the number of issued shares 231
Stock exchanges 238
Trading shares 242
The effect of corporate actions on the costs of buying and selling shares 245
Possible returns from holding shares as an investment 245
Measuring returns from shares 246
Risks of investing in shares 250
Factors affecting the price of shares 255
Advantages and disadvantages of equity investment 258
Are private equity and equity the same? 258
Summary 260
Check your understanding 261
Further reading 261

08 Investment classes: Collective invesments 262

Introduction 262
Advantages 264
Disadvantages 266

Different types of collective 269
Summary 293
Check your understanding 294
Further reading 294

09 Investment classes: Derivatives 295
Introduction 295
Derivative uses for investors 297
Types of derivative 299
Determining the option premium 317
Methods of ending a derivative contract 322
Trading derivatives 323
Summary 324
Check your understanding 325
Further reading 325

10 Investment classes: Alternative investments 327
Introduction 327
General risks of investing in alternative assets 328
Collectibles and chattels 332
Commodities 333
Gold 335
Crowdfunding 338
Property 340
Collective funds 352
Structured products 359
Summary 362
Check your understanding 363
Further reading 363

11 Portfolio management: The adviser and the client 364
Introduction 364
Client relationship 365
The advisory and planning process 373
Investment strategies 390
Client review process 399
Summary 403
Check your understanding 403
Further reading 404

12 Portfolio management: Utilization of retail fund management products 405

Introduction 405
Identification and setting of portfolio objectives 407
Implementation of appropriate investment strategy 410
Summary 449
Check your understanding 449
Further reading 450

13 Taxation 451

Introduction 451
Residency and domicile 455
Withholding tax 460
Income taxation 461
Trusts 465
National insurance (NI) 471
Investment income or unearned income tax 473
Capital gains tax (CGT) 479
Inheritance tax (IHT) 486
Stamp duty 498
Value added tax (VAT) 500
Corporation tax 503
Summary 504
Check your understanding 504
Further reading 505

14 Financial regulation and supervision 506

Introduction 506
The reasons for regulation: the importance of financial stability 507
Regulatory landscape in the United Kingdom 511
Regulatory landscape in the European Union 515
Regulatory landscape in the United States of America 519
Regulatory landscape in Hong Kong 525
Regulatory landscape in China 531
Regulatory landscape in Singapore 536
Regulation and supervision style 541
Anti-money-laundering and prevention of financial crime 548
Complaints and dispute resolution 554

Summary 556
Check your understanding 557
Further reading 557

Glossary 558
References 577
Index 583

ACKNOWLEDGEMENTS

Ian
To my loving wife who has patiently put up with me during the process of writing this book and who continues to be my life foundation. Without her I would be lost. Also to my sons who have provided me with much encouragement and technical support, whenever needed. UTB.

To my faithful companion Spike... who is sadly no longer with us but is never forgotten.

Michelle
To those who have helped me get to today. You know who you are.

Ian and Michelle
With particularly grateful thanks to Catherine our development editor, always available with sound advice, support and guidance and bags of enthusiasm and positivity when the road ahead seemed daunting.

We are also grateful to our reviewers for their helpful comments and suggestions, as well as to the undergraduates and postgraduate students of Sheffield Hallam University who take our courses and whose questions inspire us and develop our teaching content and methods, and our colleagues in Sheffield Business School for their friendship and support.

INTRODUCTION

Investment and Portfolio Management offers undergraduate and postgraduate students an introduction to the dynamic and fast-moving world of investment and portfolio management. It introduces and develops knowledge of key financial products, investment strategies and risks in UK and global financial markets. This book is ideal for students working towards a career in financial markets and investment, presenting both investment and portfolio management theory as well as real-world relevance and practical application in the financial workplace.

The content is based on investment and portfolio management material, which is broadly covered in the syllabi of several UK higher educational institutions. This subject matter also includes relevant material for candidates studying for professional examinations with bodies such as the Charted Insurance Institute (CII) and the Chartered Institute for Securities & Investment (CISI).

In writing this book, we are aiming to provide an accessible, practical resource that is easily navigated, enabling the reader to find the most relevant topics for their needs quickly and easily.

We feel that some of the technical language and jargon used in the financial industry can be off-putting when learning a new subject and therefore we have consciously made our book as free of jargon as possible. Where technical language is used, we have provided easy to understand definitions. We hope this will help readers to understand the theory, techniques and tools of investment and in doing so stimulate their appetite for more and deeper knowledge. We recognize that most readers will not read this type of book from cover to cover, but often prefer to use books to read about a specific topic, theory or method; as such our chapters can be read on a standalone basis. The inclusion of certain style devices such as highlighted key concepts and glossary definitions (highlighted in bold in the text) should ensure the content is a good revision resource.

As we have mentioned, our aim in publishing this book is to provide a real-life and practical source of information for students. This factor, in conjunction with years of feedback from students overwhelmed by the theoretical depth and language of some existing textbooks in the field, led to us using an abbreviated, less-weighty style which is more practical, informal and user-friendly in nature. Our book is rooted in the UK; however, many international comparisons are included together with practical real-world examples to enhance learning. Whilst this book provides a thorough grounding in the subject the reader is directed to additional relevant sources allowing them to delve more deeply into a topic or theory should they wish to.

We begin in Chapter 1 looking at the financial markets, before moving on to consider the global fund management industry in Chapter 2. Main market participants are explored in Chapter 3 and risk is a key area discussed in Chapter 4, considering different types of risk as well as ways of measuring risk. We then move on to examine various relevant investment theories in Chapter 5, followed by Chapters 6 to 10 which explore the characteristics and features of the key asset classes. Chapters 11 and 12 consider portfolio management issues starting with the relationship between the client and the adviser as well as addressing management issues. We finish with two areas often only briefly covered in many texts, but of significant importance in the real world: taxation in Chapter 13 and financial regulation in Chapter 14.

How to use this book

We want this book to be as accessible as possible, particularly considering the fact many readers will not read chapters sequentially. As such, each chapter contains the following features:

Chapter guide – each chapter starts with an overview of the key topics included to help guide you through the main themes and issues covered.

Keyword boxes – key concepts and terms are highlighted throughout each chapter where they first appear.

In practice boxes – these illustrate how the theory of investment and portfolio management relates to real-life practice. They take the form of examples, scenarios, mini-case studies or calculations to illustrate specific themes and issues.

Chapter summary – at the end of each chapter you will find a summary, pulling together the key points from the chapter.

Check your understanding – several questions are included at the end of each chapter to help check your understanding of the key topics explored within that chapter.

Further reading – details of publications and web links are provided at the end of the chapter to direct you to sources for more in-depth study, if required.

Glossary – additionally, if you come across an unfamiliar word of phrase you can look it up in the comprehensive 19-page glossary, which starts on page 557.

ABOUT THE AUTHORS

Ian Pagdin and Michelle Hardy are both senior lecturers in Finance and Banking at Sheffield Business School, which is part of Sheffield Hallam University.

Ian has worked in the finance industry for 23 years including 20 years' experience as an independent financial adviser. Ian has lecturing responsibilities for undergraduate and postgraduate students where he covers modules including Principles of Investment, Risk Management and Investment, Advanced Portfolio Management and Wealth Management. He is also a course leader for the Business Schools Masters programme, MSc Banking & Finance, MSc Finance & Investment and MSc Wealth Management Courses as well as being a core subject module leader for both undergraduate and postgraduate students.

After qualifying as a chartered accountant, Michelle worked for over 14 years in banking in the UK and Europe in both corporate and high net worth departments. After completing her MA in Legal Practice, she returned to Sheffield Hallam where she had originally obtained her Bachelor degree. Michelle is a senior lecturer and module leader for undergraduate and postgraduate modules. Her lecturing subjects include Understanding Financial Services, Financial Management, Portfolio Management, International Financial Management, Advanced Portfolio Management and Financial Business Management.

Financial markets 01

By the end of this chapter you should understand the following key areas of financial markets:

- the definition of financial markets;
- the history and development of financial markets;
- financial markets today;
- the categorization of markets;
- the key participants in a financial market;
- recent developments in financial markets;
- financial crises.

Introduction

As with the global fund management industry, which we cover in Chapter 2, the financial markets provide a critical link between the providers of capital and those looking to use capital. Providers of capital include retail and institutional investors whilst users of capital include corporations and governments. Capital itself can include both debt and equity as well as other more exotic investments. Both providers and consumers of capital want transactions to be conducted efficiently, which, as we will see in Chapter 5, includes transactions being conducted accurately, at low transaction costs, and with assets being valued at a fair price. One key aspect of financial markets over recent years is the pace of change which is being experienced due to increasing volatility in global markets, as well as developments in products, technology and investor sentiment. All of which make this industry dynamic and challenging for participants.

Defining financial markets

The term 'market' in financial literature is used inconsistently and sometimes with little thought to the context of the situation. This is not a problem when you have been studying finance for a while as you will automatically know which market is being referred to in a piece of writing or conversation. However, when you first study finance it can make the area appear confusing and impenetrable. In the first instance, it helps to understand that a financial market or marketplace, unlike traditional food markets for instance, can be both a physical place and a virtual space. Additionally, the term 'marketplace' is often shortened to market, which again can make differentiation and understanding more difficult.

'Markets' can also have a broader meaning than simply a commercial arena and may refer to a wider range of operations, potentially having all the following meanings:

1 A place of trade where buyers and sellers of a good and services, in this case financial goods and services, meet to exchange them at a suitable price. Such places can be grounded in the real world, in the form of a physical marketplace (eg New York Stock Exchange – NYSE), or the virtual world where transactions take place in an online forum and the parties to the transaction never meet. The effect is to enable buyers and sellers to interact to create demand and supply respectively within the market. Suppliers of capital transact with a view to obtaining the best possible return for the lowest level of risk whilst capital users want to raise capital at the lowest cost possible.

2 The totality of an asset class. So for example when investors say 'the housing market is down' this does not refer to any specific transaction; rather it refers more widely to the volume and value of transactions within an asset class.

3 A proxy used to represent a financial market. For instance, an index can be used to represent a market, and commentators may say 'the market is down' when referring to a drop in an index such as the FTSE 250.

4 Alternatively, markets can be referred to in aggregate. For example, when initially commentators were noting that Brexit would be bad for the markets they were referring to all types of financial markets including currency and equity amongst others.

5 The term can characterize the total number of people with an interest in or looking to transact in a market such as the diamond or gold market,

thus leading to a price determined by such transactions being referred to the market price.

6 Markets can exist on any social level and be of any size: for example the London housing market or the global copper market. As well as being designated by their geographic location and size (eg national or regional) markets can also be categorized by the designation 'developing' and 'developed'. Such developed and developing designations are dependent on many factors such as income levels, how open the specific market is to foreign trade and how efficiently the instruments traded are priced.

Individual financial markets for different financial products come in many shapes and sizes based on a range of characteristics including location, types of products sold, customer base and value and volume of transactions. Despite these different characteristics western economies largely remain market economies with mostly run under free market rules where the primary means of control are market forces.

> **Keyword**
>
> A **market economy** describes an economic system that is not controlled by government, but open to free competition where prices and services are determined by forces such as supply and demand.

The reasoning behind the use of a free market is that the operation of market forces should lead to the efficient allocation of resources with finance being directed to projects which will produce the highest level of return. However, it is possible the allocation of resources by market forces can be distorted by oligopolies and monopolies which may for instance reduce the efficiency and productivity of the market.

History and development of financial markets

The Italian city states such as Venice and Rome were probably the first places to develop and trade securities which resemble today's shares as well as governmental debt. In the UK, the first stock markets tended to be well-known meeting places, usually coffee houses, rather than traditional markets. These meeting places were within the boundaries of the Roman wall which delineates the oldest part of London. As the markets developed, this area has become known as the 'square mile' or the City of London and remains London's traditional financial centre today. Today's stock market, the London Stock Exchange (LSE) remains in the City; however, there are national financial centres in both the City and Canary Wharf.

Such concentration was not always the case. In the past, the UK had several regional stock exchanges in places such as Hull in England, Greenock in Scotland and Newport in Wales. In total, there were approximately 15 markets in England, three in Wales and five in Scotland. This number of markets supported the Industrial Revolution in the 18th and 19th centuries. However, with the advent of improved technology there was a general shift towards London, with most regional financial markets ceasing to trade or being amalgamated into the LSE by the 1970s. There have been attempts to regionalize stock markets once more to funnel funding to the regions, but to date this has not been successful.

Originally owned by its members, from 2001 the LSE became a public limited company with traded shares and in 2004 it relocated from its traditional location of Old Broad Street to Paternoster Square. When it merged with the Italian Borsa, it became the London Stock Exchange Group (LSEG). This strategic development of the Exchange began in the late 1980s when the LSE was losing business to more modern exchanges around the world due to its high commission levels (because of the lack of competition within the market) and the speed of face-to-face trading. The 'Big Bang' in 1986 liberated the stock market through a series of reforms which:

- allowed foreign companies to own market makers and brokers;
- adopted computer-based trading;
- removed fixed commission deals, over a period.

As well as leading to the rejuvenation of the LSE, the Big Bang brought the added benefits of a lower-cost trading environment, specialization of trading and an amalgamation of market makers and brokers into large financial firms, which improved levels of liquidity and investment.

In practice

Read more about the Big Bang in an article by Jamie Robertson entitled 'How Big Bang changed the City of London for ever'.[1]

Financial markets today

Companies today are larger and more complex than ever before, with some trading on a global level. This is also the case for investors, with large institutional investors trading on a global level in many financial markets rather than specializing in just one. That is not to say all companies or investors are multinational or institutions. In fact, on exchanges worldwide there will be a range of different sizes and types of companies using financial instruments to operate their business as well as listing their shares, just as there will be investors ranging from amateur or small investors to professional individuals as well as institutional investors.

Financial markets today are larger, trade at a faster pace, have more information available, utilize more complex instruments for trade and involve more individuals than ever before. There are developments in the areas of method of trading, speed of trading, and virtual and physical exchanges. In fact, whilst most buyers and sellers tend to prefer trading at larger established exchanges, where they have more options and opportunities, in recent years, there has been an increase in transactions through third-party markets which bypass stock exchanges and their related commissions altogether, which many see as a benefit but which also pose a risk in respect of payment and delivery of stock.

With the expansion of geographic reach of the markets and the fact that trade can be separated from a physical nation or geographic area, regulation has become increasingly more complex to try to maintain transparency and protect investors. This has led to an increase in domestic regulation, for example, national regulators such as the Financial Conduct Authority (FCA) in the UK, but also to a reliance on regional or international bodies to police the markets to ensure a level playing field. This can be seen with the regulations overseen within the European Union, for example, UCITS (Undertakings for the Collective Investment of Transferable Securities) allowing financial 'passporting' enabling products to be sold in any country within the Union without additional checks being required.

We will look at some of these areas in more detail in Chapter 2 where we look at the issues and potential developments in financial markets.

Where are financial markets based and how large are they?

Financial markets can be based anywhere in the world, especially with the increase in electronic trading and virtual marketplaces, although they tend to be linked to areas of economic importance. It is usual to have major regions with dominant and satellite markets in each and whilst there will be many satellite markets for different financial securities the dominant markets for each security type may differ in an area.

Whilst the LSE in the UK started trading in its earliest form in the late 18th century in a London coffee house, until the start of the 19th century the Dutch had the pre-eminent stock market. Today there are markets all over the world; however, the main trading areas are usually analysed as the Americas, EMEA (Europe, Middle East and Africa) and Asia. That is not to say other continents do not have developed financial markets; just that markets in these three regions are seen to operate more frequently on a global level. Whilst markets tend to develop in areas where there is economic development which they help to sustain, it is possible, with some strategic direction, to develop a financial market that has more global leverage than its surrounding economic area would suggest. An example of this could be Singapore which, whilst being noted for its importance as a transport and commercial area, has a stock market that carries international weight above that which could be expected from current trading levels.

Whilst such markets are seen as one, in Asia for instance there can be regional splits, for instance between the North and South Asian markets. This can be due to a number of factors such as the physical distances between some markets, with distances between some Asian markets equalling those between the UK and New York. Whilst technological advances render this less of a problem, there are still the potential difficulties of differing time zones. In addition, there may also be some cultural or historical references, as seen in the Scandinavian countries, which may also produce a regional hub. However, it should be remembered that it is possible for some players to move from one region to another or be pan-regional, for example China within the Asian market.

There has also been a development of capital markets within countries which have previously shunned capitalist economic ideas, such as Russia and Poland, and in those which still do. For instance, Vietnam has a trading market and China has two in Shanghai and Shenzen featuring over 2,000 companies with millions of shareholders in the form of Chinese citizens. Figure 1.1 from the annual review by Credit Suisse shows the domination of the US stock market in relation to most other major financial players in the world.

As with all markets, growth and developments are fluid. Based on the expanding trade within the area many commentators would describe the North American market as being dominant in the late 20th century, particularly in respect of securities trading on the New York Stock Exchange and derivatives on the Chicago Stock Exchange. In addition, this could be said to have had a knock-on effect on the regional markets in the area, with developments in both

Figure 1.1 Relative size of the world's stock markets at end 2015

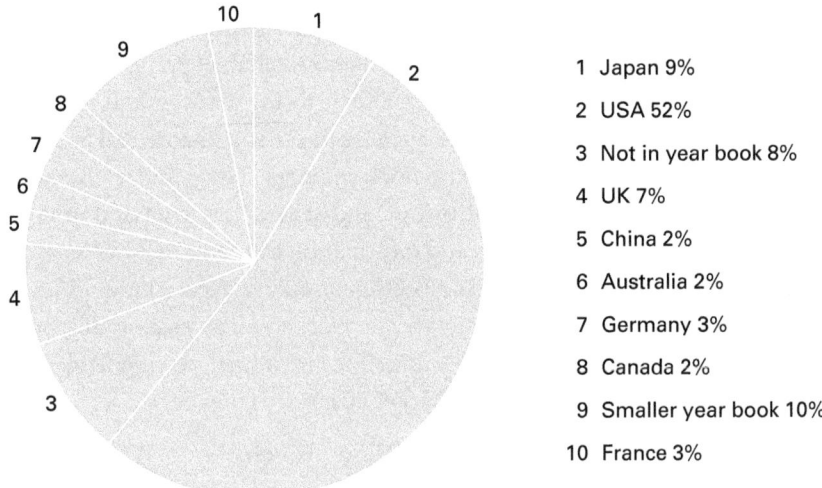

1 Japan 9%
2 USA 52%
3 Not in year book 8%
4 UK 7%
5 China 2%
6 Australia 2%
7 Germany 3%
8 Canada 2%
9 Smaller year book 10%
10 France 3%

SOURCE Elroy Dimson, Paul Mason and Mike Staunton, *Credit Suisse Global Investment Returns Sourcebook* 2016

the Canadian and Mexican stock exchanges since the 1980s. There was also the resurgence of Europe following the Big Bang of 1986 and the emergence of the European Union's focus on a single unified market. Looking forward, Asia may be the dominant marketplace for the first part of the 21st century with high rates of growth in trading in Singapore for instance. It should also be remembered that with changing demographics and political structures it is likely we will see new and emerging markets in developing nations such as India fighting for a place on the global stage in the coming years.

What types of financial instruments are traded?

Each financial market will trade some or all of a variety of financial instruments including:

- domestic and international equities;
- preference shares;
- global depository receipts;
- exchange-traded funds (ETFs) and investment funds;
- warrants and covered warrants;
- UK local and national government and foreign government bonds;
- UK and foreign (Eurobonds) corporate bonds.

Why are financial markets important?

In economic theory, a perfect market is the most efficient, with its characteristics of: free information which is immediately available; no domination of the market by individuals; free entry and exit to the market; and no transaction costs. Whilst characteristics such as these are theoretical and not available in the real world, efficient stock markets show similar characteristics including large numbers of buyers and sellers, low transaction costs, easy entry and exit to the market and information available at a low cost. All of which makes financial markets more liquid and therefore more efficient. There is also the aspect of regulation of the market which ensures all parties are treated fairly and investors make decisions on a level playing field.

An efficient and well-regulated market ensures:

- Firms can find the required funds to allow growth.
- Formation of an efficient allocation of funds mechanism, by reviewing funding requests and allocating available finance to the most efficient use.
- Shareholders hold liquid investments which allows for a flexible investment policy and for a firm's founder, flotation provides an exit route to monetize their equity holdings fully or partially.
- Takeovers can be more easily accommodated; however, in the case of a hostile takeover this may not always be appreciated by all firms.
- Where firms are growing in stature or moving into a new market a stock market listing on the local exchange can enhance their reputation.
- Minimum standards of corporate government and information disclosure from listed organizations.

What does a financial market do?

The following is a list of practical tasks which need to be undertaken for a financial market to work efficiently and in a well-regulated manner:

- Supervision of transactions.
- Authorization and regulation of market participants (such as brokers and dealers) and new and existing companies (prior to admission to the market and during their trading life).
- Settlement of transactions to ensure shares are paid for and transferred to the new owner accurately.
- Provision of information to ensure high-quality up-to-date information is available in respect of prices and relevant news to enable investors to make informed decisions.

- Provision of a liquid market ensuring trading levels are maintained and therefore promoting efficiency and future investment.

Historically the market would have undertaken all these tasks itself; however, we now see stock markets outsourcing some areas to promote cost efficiency and effectiveness. This is the case with the LSE which outsourced its transaction settlement arm to CREST several years ago. In addition, there may be multiple providers of a service moving in to a market so within the LSE for instance there is more than one provider of information with the LSE's news service competing against seven other regulatory news services.

Where are the most important financial markets in the world?

Today there are stock markets all over the world, with some commentators estimating there are over 630,000 companies traded publicly. This number continues to grow, due firstly to the growth in the number of companies; and secondly to the growth in the number of exchanges around the world, thus allowing existing companies greater access in regional areas to investors, and the trading of global securities between markets and multiple listings on different markets. The US continues as the largest market; however, there is a growing influence of the Asian markets. Before looking at some of the larger exchanges within the global market it is important to understand how markets are analysed.

Markets can be categorized in many ways:

- by the maturity period of the financial instrument, eg short term (less than one year), medium term (1–10 years) and longer term (over 10 years);
- by whether the financial instrument is being issued for the first time to the marketplace or whether it is an existing asset which is trading between holders, ie between the primary market for new issues and the secondary market.

However, one of the easiest ways to categorize different financial markets is by the type of financial security which is traded there. The following list shows the large number of different markets. These markets operate both on a standalone basis and in tandem on occasion where trades require the use of more than one type of financial instrument interacting with each other to be successful, eg a foreign exchange accommodation trade combined with a share purchase for instance.

- Capital markets: generally, for financial assets with a maturity of over one year. Commonly divided into equity and debt markets but can also be classified in relation to the type of borrower, eg government or non-government.

- Money markets: used for trading in short-term financial assets with a maturity of up to one year.
- Commodities markets: used for trading basic uniform goods, eg coffee, metals, oil etc, which are used in the production of goods. Commodities trades can be paired with derivative trades.
- Derivatives markets: here financial instruments who obtain their value from separate underlying assets, eg commodities or foreign exchange are traded.
- Depository markets: deposits from individuals and organizations are used to provide loans to business or to purchase government debt instruments.
- Non-depository markets: sometimes known as 'shadow banks', institutions such as mutual funds, insurance companies, pension firms and brokerages carry out financial functions ranging from intermediary services to insurance underwriting.

Categorization of markets

Capital markets

Keyword

Capital is used as an umbrella term for the two main types of long-term finance: equity (ordinary share or stocks in a company) and debt (lending or bonds). The capital markets allow funding from the suppliers of capital (individuals and institutional investors) to be channelled to the users of capital (governments and businesses) for medium- and long-term periods (over one year) allowing the economy to function smoothly.

Equity markets

Buyers and sellers of shares (stocks) trade through equity markets often known as exchanges, for example, the LSE. Trades through an exchange will be of the shares of public limited companies, usually ordinary shares. These companies are known as Plcs in the UK. The ordinary shares of private limited companies can also be traded by agreement between two parties (OTC) rather than in the stock market.

In practice

Stock exchanges

There are stock exchanges in almost every region of the world. These are some of the best known:

Amsterdam Stock Exchange (AEX)
The AEX was founded to trade the stocks of the Dutch East India Company in the early 17th century and was the first to operate in a format we would recognize as a stock exchange today, although prior to that there were systems of trade in regional areas.

New York Stock Exchange (NYSE)
Originating in 1792 the NYSE is now part of the NYSE EURONEXT group with exchanges in the USA and Europe and is estimated to trade approximately 33 per cent of equities worldwide representing capitalizations of approximately $10 trillion. The start and end of daily trading is known worldwide for the bell which is rung. However, the NYSE doesn't just trade shares, as filings to the Securities and Exchange Commission (SEC) show: the company has noted increased competition levels in most of its markets including cash, equities, ETFs and derivatives.

Tokyo Stock Exchange (TSE)
With approximately 2,000 firms listed on the TSE capitalizations totalling approximately $3 trillion, Tokyo Stock Exchange is ranked No 2 behind NYSE. The TSE's index, the Nikkei 225, represents the largest and most successful firms in Japan. Opening in 1878, the exchange is younger than NYSE; however, it also collaborates with other exchanges including the LSE.

London Stock Exchange (LSE)
Whilst the LSE is one of the best-known stock exchanges, it is somewhat smaller than the NYSE and TSE with trades estimated at $2.2 trillion and a total of approximately 3,000 companies on both the LSE and its affiliated exchanges. Officially founded in 1801, trading has been carried out within the City since the early 18th century.

Hong Kong Stock Exchange
Since just before 1900 the Hong Kong Exchange has been a vital player in the Asian market and was historically one of the primary avenues for global investors into China. It remains within the top 10 exchanges with approximately 1,500 companies trading at a market capitalization of about $2 trillion.

> **Shanghai Stock Exchange**
> Opening in 1990 Shanghai is one of the newest exchanges in the world. However, whilst trading volumes remain large, with circa 1,500 companies on the exchange, there has been a marked slowdown in the growth of trading volumes since 2008. This market includes two types of shares: 'A' shares which may only be traded by resident Chinese citizens; and 'H' shares open to global investors.

The box above lists only a sample of the exchanges which facilitate global daily trades; in fact, the list could be far longer, with the inclusion of the Bombay Stock Exchange highlighting India's development on the financial stage as well as exchanges in South America and Australia which are also continuing to exert greater influence and take their place in the global exchange networks.

Capital markets are regulated in the UK by the FCA and by the EU whilst other countries have their own regulators, such as the SEC in the USA. In the UK when conducting the role of regulator in the capital markets the FCA is known as the UK Listing Authority and its roles include:

- monitoring marketing material and disclosures by issuers to ensure compliance with regulations;
- reviewing and approving prospectuses produced by issuers and offers of capital;
- operating the UK listing regime to ensure all issuers comply with UK regulations.

The debt or bond market

Investors can trade debt securities, mostly bonds issued by government, banks and companies in the UK. However, until recently, unlike shares, most trades were over-the-counter (OTC).

> **Keyword**
>
> **Over-the-counter (OTC)** means a bespoke transaction between two parties rather than through an exchange.

The idea of exchange debt trading started in Italy in the late 1990s where the Italian Borsa provided government and corporate debt to European investors through its MOT market. By 2010, with UK companies finding funding difficult to secure following the banking crisis and banks looking to rebuild their balance sheets at the time UK investors were facing historically low levels of interest, the Italian model appeared very appealing allowing a new market of potential private investors for corporate debt. As a result, in 2010 the LSE group opened the ORB (Order Book for Retail Bonds) market to private investors with investing possible initially in 10 stocks. There are now over 100 companies trading debt on ORB including companies such as National Grid and the LSE itself and the market is FCA regulated and MiFID (Markets in Financial Instruments Directive) compliant.

The process requires debt issues to be underwritten by investment banks, amongst others, who advise the issuer during the selling process on matters such as setting the terms and conditions, creating a prospectus and supporting legal documentation to allow the debt to be sold in the market. Buyers of debt may include corporates, governments, individual and institutional investors. Intragovernment debt trading may also occur in part due to general day-to-day trading but also due to the investment of excess reserves of a country's currency, for instance, Japan holding US debt.

Money markets

> **Keyword**
>
> **Money markets** provide the financial oil which keeps industry moving, allowing for the day-to-day running of institutions and individuals by providing a trading place for those with surplus cash to lend to those with a current cash deficit. This can include the treasury departments of banks and companies as well as blocks of loans to finance companies to provide car loans to individuals, for instance.

Capital markets and money markets, despite their different characteristics, can be confused. However, capital markets are used for medium- and long-term funds, usually over a year, whilst money markets trade financial instruments with maturities of one year or less. Money markets also use different financial instruments. Rather than debt and equity as you would find in the capital markets, money markets use deposits, commercial paper, securitized loans, acceptances, and bills of exchange amongst others.

Due to the different nature and maturity of the assets traded in the money markets compared to those in the capital markets, both investors and organizations will use the money markets in a different way to capital markets. Investors in capital markets not only look for income-generating assets, but they are also often looking to make a capital gain due to rising asset values over time, whilst companies looking for finance are usually looking for longer-term capital. However, investors or depositors in the money market can be individuals or companies looking to make small, lower-risk returns on temporary cash surpluses.

This market is often seen as lower risk due to the types of financial instruments available, for example commercial paper, which rely on high-quality credit ratings as well as a relatively short timescale which reduces the potential for an adverse movement in risk. Companies and governments also generally use money market funds to generate smaller amounts of finance to provide ongoing liquidity for shorter periods.

Trading houses or bank dealing rooms often conduct money market transactions in million-pound multiples by telephone or electronic trading. The market is split into the domestic money market which is where both lending and borrowing are in the home currency, ie sterling in the UK and the Euromarket, where foreign currencies are used for lending or borrowing. Despite the name 'Euromarket', it does not mean the currency used is always euros, but simply that a currency is used other than the domestic currency of the country where the trade takes place. For investors, the regulation levels of euro or international money market transactions should be considered as they may not be of the same standard as domestic currency transactions, depending on which markets are invested in. Trades may be bespoke using OTC agreements or through a clearing house.

Keyword

A **clearing house** sits within an exchange and acts as an intermediary between the parties settling the transaction by adjusting their respective accounts and reducing counterparty risk due to holding security on behalf of the buyer.

Commodities markets

> **Keyword**
>
> A **commodity market** facilitates the buying, selling and trading of primary products, known as commodities. Commodities are split into two main groups: hard and soft. Hard commodities are products that are mined, such as metals or oil. Soft commodities are agricultural products such as wheat. There are currently about 50 major commodity markets around the world, trading 100 primary commodities.

Industrialists are the most prevalent participants in the commodities markets, not least because of the amount of oil, a major commodity, used in a variety of industrial processes and products. In addition to oil, there are more specialist commodities such as metals, which are important to ship and car builders for example, and 'softs' such as coffee, wheat and sugar. The cost of these primary products may constitute a considerable percentage of the overall cost of the final product to the buyer/producer and as such they need to ensure they obtain the best price possible and protect themselves against the risk of adverse price movements.

Commodities also provide an example of the interaction of the different markets as a company's need to protect its commodity price will affect not only the commodities market but also the futures market as they look to hedge their risk of price rises into the future. We will go on to talk more about this in Chapter 4.

Potential price movements also bring the potential for returns for investors; however, due to the zero-sum nature of the market, possible returns come with a high degree of possible risk. In addition, where physical delivery is required this brings additional cost factors including transport, specialist storage and quality confirmation. Professional investors tend to dominate commodities markets working through hedging a company's requirements. Despite its specialized nature, price movements in the commodities markets are seen by some commentators as 'the canary in the mine' for their potential to indicate imminent inflation and subsequent equity price moves.

Examples of commodities markets

London has a spot market for commodities requiring delivery within two days of the transaction and the costs given usually represent the physical material costs. The London market also quotes forward prices which are an agreed price for later physical delivery, as opposed to futures which are in the main paper-based transactions used to hedge price movement risk. As mentioned above, the nature of commodities and the requirement for industry to hedge prices means the markets are often intertwined with the derivatives based on the underlying asset being traded.

In practice

Key commodities markets around the world

'Soft' commodity futures markets
- LIFFE (London International Financial Futures and Options Exchange) has core trading in coffee, sugar and cocoa as well as quoting prices for other commodities traded elsewhere.
- NYBOT (New York Board of Trade) is the parent of the NYCE (New York Cotton Exchange) and the CSCE (Coffee and Sugar Exchange). The NYBOT is a physical market trading in coffee, cocoa, sugar and cotton.
- NYSE LIFFE (the New York Stock Exchange) trades in wheat including futures and options in offices in the USA and mainland Europe, eg Brussels, Paris and London.
- CBT (Chicago Board of Trade) is based in Chicago and trades in wheat, maize, soybeans, soybean oil and soybean meal.
- CME or Merc (Chicago Mercantile Exchange) trades in live cattle, lean hogs, feeder cattle and pork bellies.

Other commodities markets
- IPE (International Petroleum Exchange) trades in oil.
- The London Metals Exchange (LME) deals in non-ferrous metals which include aluminium, lead, nickel and tin. This market has a potentially higher level of physical trades than other metal markets as well as having a futures trade.
- COMEX (the Commodity Exchange, New York) trades in copper, silver and gold with the price of gold here being included in the prices recorded in the *Financial Times*.

- NYMEX (the New York Mercantile Exchange) includes trade in metals such as platinum and palladium as well as oil and natural gas.
- London Bullion Market notes the price of gold which is set twice a day when the major bullion traders meet the NM Rothschild offices to set the prices and carry out transactions.

Derivatives markets

Keyword

Derivatives are contracts between two or more parties where the contract value comes from a separate asset whose value underlies the derivative contract. Underlying assets may include shares and bonds as well as currencies, interest rates and even index movements, such as movements in the FTSE 100. Derivatives may be used by investors for speculation and hedging risk (risk minimization) and will be examined in more detail in Chapter 9.

Today, electronic trading through phone or other means has replaced the traditional 'open outcry' of the trading floor for the trading of derivatives. Such trades can occur, as with other financial instruments, in OTC markets or via an exchange, and the size of the derivatives market, whilst indisputably huge due to the fact derivatives can be created for virtually every financial instrument, is a matter of some contention. However, most of the contention derives from how the market is measured.

As with other exchange-traded markets, derivative contracts are standardized in the main with specific delivery or settlement terms. Exchange-traded transactions are publicly reported, enhancing transparency, and cleared through a clearing house. The clearing house is obliged to honour the trade if there is a seller default therefore reducing counterparty risk, whilst marking positions to the market through margin calls protects the clearing house's solvency. By contrast, derivative trades in OTC markets are bilateral in nature. All contract terms such as delivery, quality, quantity, location, date and prices are negotiable between the two parties with information about the transaction remaining between the parties. The two transaction methods provide a solution for different business requirements and different trade characteristics. The exchange-based transactions provide more transparency than the OTC market as well as small counterparty risk. Whereas the OTC markets have a higher level of flexibility for derivative transactions which are specialized in nature or have a limited number of transactions as well as providing a means to develop and test new financial products.

The key participants in a financial market

Capital markets move money from people who wish to invest to organizations who require it to allow them to produce goods and services. As such, the existence of financial markets is essential to the smooth running of the economy and can also be an indicator of the health of economies around the world. Just as the capital markets are becoming more globalized and interconnected, so also are the main participants in the markets as well as the markets themselves. Whilst this can lead to increased efficiency and effectiveness it may also lead negative ripples in one market to make waves in another.

To ensure buyers and sellers are brought together in an organized and regulated way to allow them to transact with each other, the capital markets must be able to ensure transactions between participants are fair (as parties are often unequal in size) and all parties will also require support services to facilitate the transaction. There will therefore be many participants in the market and the main ones can be summarized as:

- Buyers: these can include individuals and institutions who manage funds on their own behalf or on behalf of clients, respectively acting as both traders and investors.
- Sellers: these can include non-financial firms, institutions and governments in the primary market as well as individuals and institutions trading financial products in the secondary market.
- Support services:
  - banking:
    - buy-side banking services, eg custody and payment services;
    - sell-side banking services, eg payments and financing.
  - regulation: to ensure the market runs in a transparent and fair way;
  - intermediaries:

- brokers/dealers: intermediaries for both retail and institutional investors;
- retail broker: intermediary for retail investors;
- day trading firm: intermediary for high-frequency traders.
- trading venues: this can include the physical stock market and the clearing house which guarantees settlement on the market as well as the physical operation of the trades through computer systems.

Keyword

Buy-side refers to the fact that the buy-side is using or consuming the financial services whilst the **sell-side** is providing the financial services.

Traders versus investors

Keywords

There is the tendency to interchange the terms 'trader' and 'investor'. However, we should remember that there is vast difference between an investor, who purchases specific securities to hold for a period as they believe they will increase in value, and a **trader** who focuses on the market itself to take advantage of price movements. The largest amount of money in the financial markets in the longer term comes from investors; however, the traders will conduct the largest volume and value of trades within a day.

Investors are looking for value for money within their investments and the possibility for success within the organization they are investing in. Their analysis usually focuses therefore on the company's financial and strategic strengths and evaluates its future cashflows as this will be the channel through which the investors obtain their return through capital gains and dividend income. For instance, it is possible for investors to analyse ratios such as the P/E growth (PEG) ratio which compares the value of a company to its potential for success as well as analysing financial news and information.

The main investors in the financial markets will be:

- Investment banks who often retain a proportion of securities from companies they assist in joining the stock market, for instance through an IPO.
- Mutual funds which are legally obliged to act as an investor and provide a low-cost method for retail investors to enter the financial markets.
- Institutional investors including businesses and individuals who retain holdings such as company insiders and competitors hedging their position.
- Retail investors (individuals with holdings of less than £50,000) who often manage their own portfolios. Whilst historically this group has been small the impact of improved technology and increases in available information and analysis as well as reductions in the costs of transactions has led to this sector increasing.
- Shadow banks including insurance companies and pension funds.

Traders on the other hand can be individuals or institutions. However, when they purchase financial instruments their focus is on the market rather than the long-term holding of the instrument itself, so they are looking to profit from short-term trading volatility, with holdings lasting from seconds to weeks. The commodity market for instance has relatively uniform products so here profits are sought from small price movements caused by the interaction of supply and demand.

Often traders will look at the following areas as a basis for their transactions:

- technical analysis of price patterns looking to forecast future prices from historic price information;
- supply and demand to understand how the market is moving;
- hiring of market makers to provide liquidity through rapid trading;
- herd behaviour where they will bet against large movements in markets caused by investor panic.

The split between the two types of participant in the market is not black and white and both investors and traders are required to ensure the market functions smoothly: without traders making the market investors would not have the liquidity which makes the market attractive; whilst for the traders without the investors there would be no basis for buy and sell.

How are the buyers and sellers organized?

Whilst a buyer can and most probably will be a seller, on occasion it can be useful to split the trading activities into two areas – those related to the buyer of the transaction and those related to the seller – although some institutions will have internal departments which do both. Buying functions within institutions are often organized into three main areas, which may overlap and the departments must work together to provide an efficient and effective service to clients and a profit for their own shareholders:

- Front office: this is trading and customer-focused encompassing portfolio management and client-facing services including sales, research and trading.
- Middle office: this will include support services for front-office staff eg preparation of documentation and day-to-day running of client accounts including areas of regulation ensuring client accounts are compliant with national and market regulations and client requests are actioned efficiently.
- Back office: this department supports the functionality of the business including management of documentation, deposits and facilities management including office locations and the computer systems required to support the front and middle offices. On a day-to-day basis the back office does not normally have contact with front-office staff.

The sell-side functions relate mainly to intermediaries who act between individual or institutional investors and the market or those who act on their own behalf and the market. This highlights the difference between a broker who acts as an agent on behalf of their principal (the investor) in the principal's best interest, and a dealer who acts on their own behalf with the intention of making a profit for themselves from trading. There are some markets which allow broker/dealers where the firms may act as both brokers and dealers, although not usually in the same transaction.

Including both buy- and sell-side activities in one organization produces complex institutions, for example investment banks who, as well as buy and sell functions, will also have departments to carry out proprietary trading on their own behalf as well arbitrage and treasury functions where the firm will manage its own capital and investments to ensure it maintains the required level of capital as well as taking opportunities to produce a profit on its own behalf. Following the financial crash, it came to light that there were conflicts of interest between the client aspects of trading and investment and the institutions' own proprietary trading and in certain circumstances this has led to criminal sanctions against individuals and civil sanctions, including multimillion dollar fines, against some institutions. Since then there has been legislation and internal reviews to strengthen the corporate governance within financial businesses to ensure the businesses' own positions are separated from their clients and adequate audit trails and transparency of dealing and ownership are maintained.

Cross-border transactions

The introduction of global trading has produced another layer of decision making for portfolio managers as the markets around the globe are very fluid and dynamic and the numbers of markets being watched has increased. However, the advent of new technology has allowed new approaches to investment and portfolio management. As such, decisions now need to be made not only regarding transactions in the domestic or home market but also about how to invest in financial instruments in a foreign market either using an intermediary or going directly to the foreign market. How investors manage these decisions will depend on the size and knowledge of the investor.

For individuals, their main method of international diversification will usually be through investment in pooled investment products such as mutual funds. Where individuals do invest directly in foreign markets they will usually do this through an intermediary such as a broker. Even where investors use electronic systems to invest 'directly' in foreign markets these tend to be intermediary platforms rather than direct into the market.

For institutional investors, diversification methods will fall into three main categories. However, all will require a trading strategy to cover their relationships with both domestic and foreign markets and their respective intermediaries:

- Local firms operating in one domestic market tend to transact directly, with all orders for other markets being handled by intermediaries.
- Regional firms operating in several different markets but in one geographical area may have multiple regional offices, with trading offices which deal directly with their markets. Any orders outside the region will be handled through an intermediary.
- Global firms are active in markets worldwide across different regions; as such they have the option to trade 'in-house' within regional offices or use an intermediary.

The same problems are also faced by supply-side firms and their response will depend on the size of the firm and their availability of offices within a specific market. For most firms, sales offices will be maintained in all major financial centres in their locality or region; however, they may have fewer trading offices which are centred on several key markets. Where they do not have a trading presence they may use a 'partner' firm to conduct the business in the market. Global firms will maintain trading offices in areas where they conduct regular transactions, whilst for regions where they transact infrequently they will use partner firms.

Issues affecting global transactions

Accommodation trades: The effect of foreign exchange

Where sales or purchases of financial instruments are made in a foreign market to facilitate the trade a simultaneous foreign exchange trade will be required, this may not be an explicit currency trade but may involve incurring a currency liability for instance. Such trades make analysis of the global trading more complex as there are potentially four different outcomes in respect of total transaction (see Figure 1.2).

Where both the investment trade and the currency trade make a gain then the investors' net wealth will increase, just as when both the investment and currency trade make a loss we can guarantee the investors' net wealth will

Figure 1.2 Transaction outcomes

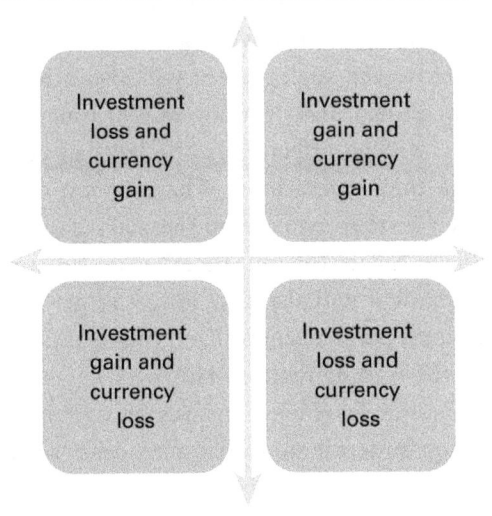

Investment loss and currency gain	Investment gain and currency gain
Investment gain and currency loss	Investment loss and currency loss

fall because of this transaction. It is not possible to assign a gain or loss to the other two scenarios as in those cases the overall gain or loss will depend on the relative gains and losses of the investment trade compared to the currency trade. The costs and gains or losses on the currency trades may be separate transactions or may be included as part of an overall transaction for the investment.

Latency

> **Keyword**
>
> **Latency** refers to the amount of time from the moment a signal (ie some form of information) is sent to the moment it is received. In financial terms this can be split into four potential areas:
>
> 1 Input latency: the time required to receive information which will lead to a reaction eg a trade.
> 2 Decision latency: the time required to assess the information received and decide.
> 3 Processing latency: the time required to formulate a response.
> 4 Implementation latency: the time required to transmit the response to where the decision can be implemented.

For high-frequency trades the lower the latency the faster the trade, so traders are co-locating their servers within the exchanges to gain a competitive edge. However, such factors will also affect decisions made between regions for global firms trading in real time. Their response to the issue of latency will be affected by the level of centralization with which they manage their operations. Where operations are centralized the decision is taken further away from the market and will take longer to arrive at the place a decision can be taken, for example head office. Once a decision is made it will also take longer to get back to the market than would be the case for a decentralized organization which can take decisions closer to the trading market. However, centralized trading may offset this higher latency level as it ensures an overall focus is retained on the trades being undertaken which may lead to a higher overall profitability.

Recent developments in financial markets

In the media, textbooks and communications, acronyms are used and discussions take place about areas which are never defined despite forming the basis for some of the cutting-edge developments within the industry. The following sections provide a basic introduction to some of the main areas of development and contention in financial markets.

Multilateral trading facilities (MTFs)

> **Keyword**
>
> A **multilateral trading facility** or **MTF** is an electronic trading facility which, in the same way as ATFs, bring eligible parties together via a search engine to trade in a variety of financial instruments including those which may not have an official market.

Whilst MTFs in Europe will be regulated by the MiFID II, such exchanges have fewer regulations and as such more exotic securities may be traded. However, traders are restricted from executing client orders against proprietary capital or matching orders to avoid a conflict of interest. The European Securities and Markets Authority (ESMA) produces a database of European MTFs and is used to identify the counterparties to a transaction. Within the EU MTFs are grouped mainly in the UK, Germany, Italy and Belgium with others in Norway and Iceland.

Markets in Financial Instruments Directive (MiFID)

The introduction of MiFID in 2008 aimed to increase transparency in financial transactions and reporting, primarily in OTC transactions, by standardizing regulatory disclosures in specific markets. This was to be done by setting pre- and post-trade transparency requirements and conduct standards for financial firms. The legislation provides the EU's framework for investment intermediaries servicing clients in the financial instruments market, including shares, bonds, UCITS and derivatives as well as the organized trading of financial instruments.

Following the shortcomings in the functioning of the financial markets and investor protection highlighted by the financial crisis, changes to MiFID are coming into force in January 2018 when MiFID II takes effect in conjunction with the new MiFIR (Markets in Financial Instruments Regulation). Whilst the original aim of MiFID was the introduction of a robust pan-European regulatory framework, this did not work in certain areas as the regulation of non-EU firms was left to individual governments, leading to competitive advantages being obtained by different levels of regulation being given to non-EU firms compared to EU firms. MiFID II will overcome this by harmonizing regulations for all firms which have EU clients whilst MiFIR will extend the code of conduct to include contract-based assets and structured products as well as existing financial instruments.

Dark pools

Keyword

Dark pools are trading areas set up by large organizations such as banks to allow them to trade with relative anonymity.

Previously large block trades of securities were advertised by the requirement on the buyer to disclose the number and price of the shares they wished to purchase. As such, the moment that a large trade or one outside an institution's normal trading parameters was made the market would be alerted and this might make the trade more difficult or expensive. This was partly overcome by the strategy of using smaller individual trades; however, even then some experts began to spot patterns in the buying which negated this practice. With dark pools, the trades must be advertised once the deal is concluded but prior to that the interested party can operate in relative obscurity. This lack of transparency has led to calls for greater regulation of dark pools.

High-frequency trading

Recently there has been a move away from physical marketplaces to e-dealing, where computers provide the best buy and sell price and execute deals. This has led to some benefits such as increased transparency, reduction in the buy–sell spread and increased liquidity amongst others.

Keyword

As investors demand ever shorter trading times there has been a development of **high-frequency** trades which uses algorithms to determine a trading strategy which can be implemented in milliseconds. This will include buying or selling when certain pre-set conditions are met.

There has been a move by some traders to co-locate their trading servers into the exchanges' data centres to save an extra microsecond. The exchanges are taking similar steps: in 2010 the LSE purchased a 51 per cent stake in Turquoise, an electronic market which trades more than 2,000 European equities, and which has a total trading time – from client inputting the order to receipt of message to confirm the deal – of 124 microseconds.

Flash crashes

Stock market crashes can be identified from a sudden and unexpected drop in overall stock market prices. This can be due to a catastrophic natural event; perceived economic change as was potentially the case in the UK after the Brexit vote; or a speculative bubble as seen in the dot.com crash of the late 1990s in the UK. Such crashes are likely to be exacerbated by the actions of individual investors. Such investors may have a psychological aspect to their trading leading them to exit the market in panic which in turn may exacerbate losses and economic instability.

Keyword

Flash crashes show the same characteristics as a crash but a flash crash is often large in scale and quicker in crash and recovery timescale.

In practice

A fall of 1,000 points in the Dow Jones was seen on 6 May 2010 following a $4.1 billion trade on the NYSE; however, the fall had been recovered in 15 minutes. Despite the best investigative efforts of the SEC and the

Commodity Futures Trading Commission (CFTC) no definitive explanation for the crash has been identified. To try to overcome such crashes the SEC introduced new rules in 2010 which stops trading for any stock in the S&P 500 whose stock value changes by more than 10 per cent in a five-minute period. In addition, on 21 April 2015, 22 criminal charges were made against individuals which included fraud, market manipulation and 'spoofing' algorithms. The case is ongoing.

Fat finger trades

Keyword

Fat finger trades or **fat finger errors** are where a human error occurs whilst a trade is being made. Such errors can occur internally within an organization as reported in 2016 when an analyst at Deutsche was reported to have transferred $6 billion dollars to an individual hedge fund customer. They can also occur at market level with a dramatic fall of the FTSE 100 index on the London stock market in September 2015 which, following investigation, was blamed on a fat finger error in a basket trade order. In this case the effects were far-reaching with trading in nine companies, including BP Plc, being suspended and a loss on the transaction for the trader of £500,000.

Such errors can take many forms but may include:

- Incorrect number of units being input as seen in October 2014 when a dealer on the Tokyo stock market placed a $622 million order to buy blue-chip shares, entering the price and volume in the same column.
- A transposition error where the numbers for eg price and volume are entered correctly but in the wrong columns eg volume where price should be. An example of this was seen when Mizuho Securities in Japan placed an order to sell 610,000 shares of J-Com for one yen each when they wanted to sell one share for 610,000 yen.

Historically, slower trading speeds made it easier to correct errors. However, there is still potential for errors to be corrected. For example, the NYSE has a 30-minute review and cancellation policy. In some cases it has also been possible to stop an error; for instance in 2001 an input error was made which would have led to an £81 billion order being requested for a company (which was approximately four times the company's market capitalization) and this was stopped before the trade could take place. However, with the introduction of electronic and algorithmic trading and decisions being made in microseconds, there is huge potential for mistakes to trigger large-scale trading and move markets.

For a portfolio manager and traders, such trades can be catastrophic and therefore institutions and organizations look to include processes and procedures to reduce such transactions to a minimum. These include:

- ongoing analysis of trading in the market to identify unexpected trends or large sudden movements in the markets;
- automatic limits for volume and value within computer systems to prevent trades of unusual size or value;
- second person authorization and review policies required before the trade can take place eg Deutsche Bank's 'four eyes' policy.

Day trading

Keyword

Day trades, which entail buying and selling the same financial instrument within one trading day, can occur in any financial instrument market. The idea behind the trade is to profit from small movements in high liquid securities. The inclusion of day trades ensures both a liquid market and that the market runs efficiently due to arbitrage trading. That said, the practice is not without controversy and has been subject to several get rich quick 'scams' which have hit retail investors.

To be successful within this market traders need several characteristics:

- Market knowledge is essential to try to avoid the losses.
- Capital is required to allow trading in sufficient volumes to make a meaningful profit. Successful traders often use capital they can afford to lose thereby eliminating emotion from their trades. That said, they will also utilize high amounts of leverage.

- A strategy is required to ensure consistent profits and limit losses. Several different strategies can be used including swing trading (which is high risk and reward) and arbitrage which is relatively low risk with the potential for a medium-level reward.

Day traders who are self-employed could be said to face disadvantages compared to those employed by large institutions who have access to large amounts of capital, direct lines to dealing desks and analytical software making their chances of success much higher.

Alternative trading systems (ATS) and electronic communication networks (ECN)

ATSs originated in the USA and historically have been mainly unregulated exchanges (the SEC introduced the regulated ATS in 1998 with stricter rules on trading). They include electronic communication networks (ECNs) and crossing networks.

Many ATSs have been set up to trade large volumes mostly for professional traders and investors. However, institutions may also use an ATS to find counterparties for trade rather than using established exchanges, mainly to reduce costs. The effect is that such systems account for a growing amount of liquidity in the market and can skew the market in certain circumstances.

The SEC sanctions ECNs and allows direct connections between buyers and sellers, including retail investors. Such connections bypass market makers (brokers and investment banks) and allow stock from exchanges such as the NASDAQ and other European markets to be traded. Current ECNs include INET and Archipelago. An ECN is an intermediary and earns income from a transaction fee on each trade or a margin on the spread; however, the additional competition plus the ECN's electronic nature pushes down transaction costs and as such are a threat to traditional exchanges. That said, the ability to continue to trade outside normal market hours and trade between geographical locations has increased the level of trading and globalization of the financial markets.

As well as shares, currency trades can also take place on ECNs with almost immediate transactions available for spot trades as well as transparency of information regarding available currency and price movements.

Matching and call systems are also seen as forms of ATS with the former receiving orders and directing them through a search engine to match them against current resting orders. If a match is unavailable, the order is placed in the book as a quote. The latter accepts one order at a time with the price determined based on activity in the exchange following an order.

Auction exchanges and electronic exchanges

An auction exchange, such as the NYSE, has a physical trading floor where specialists buy and sell the stock in an auction. The auction system is called 'open outcry' which is often depicted in the media with shouting and hand signals with a floor broker earning a commission for filtering the different trades required in a stock. Such trading floors are under threat from electronic-only exchanges which claim to trade more quickly and with smaller bid–ask spreads and therefore may be assessed as being more efficient. In fact, there is an option to trade online from the NYSE as well – as such it should technically be referred to as a hybrid market. The NASDAQ is an electronic or 'screen-based' exchange as participants carry out all transactions through computers. Despite its virtual nature, the main participants are still seen with market makers or dealers who carry a stock of financial instruments and post bid and ask prices.

Over the counter (OTC)

OTC describes bilateral trades, ie between two parties, for whatever financial instrument or company is being traded. Such instruments or companies are not usually listed on an exchange and therefore the transaction may potentially be riskier than exchange-traded stocks and more difficult to value. That said, some firms may have delisted due to the cost of regulation, for example compliance with Sarbanes–Oxley; however, this does not lower the risk for the potential investor.

In the USA, there are two major OTC markets: 1) The OTC Bulletin Board (OTCBB) which is an electronic market of firms who have failed to meet the requirements for the NASDAQ, for example by not reaching required turnover levels or asset values to list – such firms are said to have 'fallen off' the exchange; 2) The OTC Pink where companies are not required to register with the SEC or submit the normal reports required in the US market, leading to potential transparency issues as well as having potentially low levels of liquidity.

Financial crises

The general buoyancy of a domestic stock market should, in most cases, reflect a growing economy. This is because rising prices reflect investors' belief that companies will generate higher levels of cashflow in the future, justifying higher buying prices for financial instruments. This is because the price of the financial instrument is determined by the required level of return for the level of risk identified. As such, if additional cash will be generated in future a higher price can be maintained. However, this analysis by traders and in some cases the levels of supervision and regulation seen in the market have not been sufficient to protect investors who have suffered potentially huge losses due to several financial crises during the 20th and 21st centuries. These periods of crisis saw markets around the world fall or stagnate for different reasons and we must be aware of such possibility when investing on our own or our client's behalf:

- The 1920s and 30s saw the Great Depression triggered by the Wall Street crash of 1929 and exacerbated by poor US government policy decisions with widespread public panic and distrust of banks causing chaos in the banking market. The Depression lasted almost 10 years and resulted in massive loss of income, record unemployment rates, and output loss in industrialized nations in Europe and the US with unemployment for example peaking at almost 25 per cent in the USA in 1933.
- The 1970s saw the OPEC crisis with OPEC (Organization of the Petroleum Exporting Countries) members retaliating against the USA in response to its supply of arms to Israel during the Fourth Arab–Israeli War. OPEC launched an oil embargo against the USA and its allies leading to large price rises and shortages. The following period of economic crisis included stagflation with high levels of inflation combined with economic stagnation.
- During the 1990s speculative cashflows were invested by developed countries into emerging Asian economies known collectively as the 'Asian Tigers' (Thailand, Indonesia, Malaysia, Hong Kong and South Korea). The crisis erupted due to an over-extension of credit and accumulated debt. Originating in Thailand in July 1997 when Thailand had to abandon its fixed exchange rate against the US dollar due to a lack of available foreign currency, the crisis started a wave of panic amongst investors in the region leading to the withdrawal of billions of dollars of foreign investment as they feared possible bankruptcies of East Asian governments and a worldwide financial meltdown. Recovery for the regions took years and included relief funding from the International Monetary Fund for the most badly affected countries to help them to avoid debt default.
- 2008 saw the Great Recession triggered by the collapse of the US housing market and which resulted in the collapse of Lehman Brothers, a global investment bank, amongst others which included Bank of Scotland in the UK. Many financial institutions and businesses were taken to the point of collapse and required government intervention to ensure their survival, for example, Royal Bank of Scotland. This was the most severe financial crisis since the Great Depression, taking nearly a decade for most financial markets to return to pre-recession positions.

Table 1.1 2008 financial crisis timeline

May 2000–December 2001	Following the dot.com bubble, the accounting scandals of Enron and the terrorist attacks of 9/11, the fear in government was of a potential recession. In response to this the US Federal Reserve lowered the federal funds rate from 6.5% in May 2000 to 1.75% in December 2001. Vast amounts of cash were generated which banks needed to invest, encouraging them to lend money to mortgage customers who would historically not have been able to obtain mortgages due to a lack of assets and stable incomes. This was the start of the push to provide what became known as subprime mortgages.
2003	The Federal Reserve lowered the federal funds rate to 1% which was the lowest rate since the 1950s. Collateralized debt obligations also started to appear where subprime mortgages were packaged and sold to investors.
2004: June–October	The Federal Reserve started to raise the federal funds rate. The Securities and Exchange Commission relaxed the capital requirements for five banks allowing them to leverage their investments up to 30–40 times. The banks allowing this increased liquidity included Goldman Sachs, Merrill Lynch, Bear Stearns, Morgan Stanley and Lehman Brothers. US home ownership peaked at 70%.
2005: September–December	There was a fall in US house prices and a 40% fall in the US Home Construction Index. Subprime borrowers could not pay the higher interest rates and started to default on their loans.
2006	During the 20th century, the US Congress established Fannie Mae and Freddie Mac to assist in providing a liquid, stable and affordable mortgage market in the USA. They did this by buying mortgages from lenders which they either securitize and sell, or hold to expiry. However, unlike private organizations they were regulated by Congress. By 2006 Fannie Mae and Freddie Mac were eclipsed as mortgage originators with their market share falling from 57% of all new mortgage originations in 2003 to 37% in 2005/06. They had been replaced by private organizations, unregulated by Congress, who sold most of their mortgages to Wall Street. This left Freddie and Fannie to chase growth rather than good lending practices as private securitizers grew from 10% of the market in 2002 to nearly 40% in 2006.

(continued)

Table 1.1 *(Continued)*

2007:	
January–March	25 subprime lenders filed for insolvency. News reports suggested financial firms and hedge funds had investments of $1 trillion in subprime mortgages.
June	Bear Stearns stopped investors in two of its hedge funds redeeming funds and Merrill Lynch seized $800 million of assets from two Bear Stearns hedge funds.
9 August	BNP Paribas suspended activity in three US hedge funds which specialized in subprime mortgages. A lack of information about potential levels of losses in mortgage markets led to a breakdown of trust between banks and a cessation of interbank lending. The effect on the UK bank Northern Rock was immediate due to its reliance on interbank loans to maintain liquidity. Hearing the news from the US, UK banks wanted to retain their own cash for emergencies and because they feared defaults by other banks.
13 September	Following the first run on a UK bank for more than a century Northern Rock requested emergency funding from the Bank of England in its role as 'lender of last resort'.
2008:	
17 February	The UK government nationalized Northern Rock.
14 July	US financial authorities took control of Fannie Mae and Freddie Mac who are lenders for or guarantee $5 trillion of home loans including subprime mortgages.
15 September	Lehman Brothers filed for bankruptcy due to its exposure to the subprime mortgage market. At this point the markets realized governments would not always step in to bail out failing banks.
17 September	Lloyds Bank agreed to acquire HBOS which faced insolvency due to its inability to source new funds from the interbank market.
21 September	Goldman Sachs and JP Morgan changed their status to bank holding companies to protect themselves from the turmoil in the market.
28 September	Fortis, a European banking and insurance organization, was partly nationalized by the Belgian government to prevent its collapse.
	Bradford and Bingley's £50 billion of home loans were hived from the main business by the UK government, with its savings and deposits

(continued)

Table 1.1 *(Continued)*

	operations, including its branches, sold to Santander.
October	The federal funds rate reduced to 1%. Rates were also cut by central banks in Europe, China, the UK and Switzerland.
	The US passed the National Economic Stabilization Act which created a $700 billion fund (Troubled Asset Relief Programme – TARP) which could be used to purchase distressed securities from financial institutions to allow them to improve their liquidity position.
7 October	Glitnir, Kaupthing and Landsbanki, Iceland's three largest commercial banks collapsed. The UK prime minister, Gordon Brown, used legislation more commonly used to freeze terrorists' assets to protect UK investors. Whilst individual investors were protected from losing amounts up to £75,000, UK local authorities who had invested reserves with the banks lose everything.
8 October	The Bank of England, the European Central Bank and the Federal Reserve cut interest rates to 0.5% to help borrowers.
	Quantitative easing, like the TARP programme in the USA, was also carried out in the UK by the Bank of England and in Europe by the European Central Bank. In addition, there was nationalization of some banks such as Royal Bank of Scotland in the UK as well as other forms of bailout and guarantees put in place.
November	Unemployment reports in the USA showed 240,000 Americans had lost their jobs. There was a change in policy with the Federal Reserve moving from purchasing toxic assets from banks to release liquidity to a policy of direct cash injections.
2009: April	The G20 nations agreed a package of measures worth £5 trillion to stimulate the global economy
October	A new socialist government was elected in Greece and revealed the country's financial deficit was twice what had been reported previously.

(continued)

Table 1.1 (Continued)

2010:	
April	Credit Agencies down-rated Greek debt to 'junk' status.
May	The European Central Bank agreed loans to Greece of €110 billion to avert financial crisis; however, the agreement included stringent austerity measures leading to civil unrest in Greece. By now focus had switched from the solvency of banks to the solvency of governments.
November	The European Central Bank and EU ministers agreed loans to Ireland of €85 billion; this agreement also included stringent austerity measures.
2011:	
May	The European Central Bank agreed loans to Portugal totalling €78 billion.
June	Greece failed to implement austerity measures and an additional financial package worth €109 billion was agreed. In addition, €37 billion of private bonds were rolled over to new debt with a 30-year maturity and €12.6 billion of bonds were sold at a reduced price.
5 August	Standard and Poor downgraded the USA from AAA to AA+.

In practice

Table 1.1 presents the timeline for the key events leading up to the 2008 financial crisis. Whilst the table shows some of the highlights of the crisis there are additional nuances not reflected in the timeline including credit rating downgrades for the UK in 2013 and continuing economic instability in Europe.

You can read more about the financial crisis in the *Forbes* article, 'Lest we forget why we had a financial crisis' by Steve Denning.[2] The role played by the credit rating agencies is covered in an article in the *Financial Times* by Kevin Sieff and Stephanie Kirchgaessner,[3] and *The Guardian* has an article about the financial penalties faced by the credit rating agencies.[4]

Summary

In this chapter we have discussed the organization of different types of financial markets whilst highlighting some of the general issues which those markets and financial transactions face. An increasing globalization of the markets, in conjunction with an increasing use of technology, is leading to ever faster trades and potentially larger values and volumes of trading, with implications for both buyers and sellers as well as the economies in which the markets operate. We are also seeing movements in established markets due to developments of new financial centres both organically, as part of a natural financial development of individual countries, and also as a strategic decision to provide higher economic leverage than would be expected based on the countries' size.

Check your understanding

1 In which London square is the LSEG now based?
2 Which Asian nation has developed its financial markets to punch above its weight as a financial player?
3 Which UK banks were nationalized by the government during the financial crisis?
4 When does MiFID II come into force?
5 Which French bank was the first to suspend trading in US hedge funds which were specializing in subprime mortgages in 2007?

Further reading

Useful and up-to-date information can be found on the websites of the London Stock Exchange and the UK Listing Agency: www.londonstockexchange.com and https://www.fca.org.uk/markets/ukla

An in-depth discussion of financial markets and institutions can be found in: Mishkin, FS and Eakins, S (2015) *Financial Markets and Institutions*, global edition, Pearson

Global investment management industry

02

By the end of this chapter you should have an understanding of the following:

- the size of the global investment management industry and the major players within the industry;
- some of the global issues faced by the investment management industry;
- the size of the UK investment management industry and the current issues faced;
- fund valuation and the factors affecting their valuation in the UK including regulatory returns;
- asset management house structures;
- the types of investment manager and their day-to-day activities;
- potential future developments in the industry.

Introduction

Investment management is concerned with managing clients' funds, whether clients are individual retail investors or institutional investors. The investment industry provides the conduit between capital providers (investors) and capital seekers (companies and other organizations). Investment management, especially in Western economies, is a highly competitive market facing a dynamic and changing environment.

In future chapters, we will look at how investors, with the help of a portfolio manager, decide on an investing strategy and the different asset types investors can purchase to achieve their strategy.

It is very easy to become engrossed in asset classes, rules of investment and asset allocation and to lose sight of the context in which investment decisions are made:

- the industry which functions to support the investments;
- the people and organizations who are making the decisions;
- and the factors which may shape the industry in the future in the UK and globally.

In this and the previous chapter, we look at the investment industry to determine its size, nature, major players and where commentators believe it will develop in future years, as well as looking in more detail at financial markets to provide background and context to those starting their studies of portfolio management.

The global investment management industry and its major players

The terms 'investment', 'asset' or 'fund' management/manager are used interchangeably in everyday language to refer to both individuals and organizations who manage investment funds for clients. There are a multitude of organizational types which have evolved to serve the diverse range of investment clients, from multinational organizations responsible for the investment of pension liabilities to those servicing individual investors looking to provide for the future or manage saving aspirations.

The investment management industry forms part of a cycle to provide finance for organizations through investment products, accessed using intermediaries and asset managers to feed into capital markets and ultimately to recycle funds to investors in the form of income and/or capital gains leading to wealth maximization, as summarized in Figure 2.1.

The major players in this investment cycle are:

1 Investors: these are the legal owners of the assets and may include institutions and individuals.
2 Intermediaries: these include consultants and financial advisers who manage asset selection and allocation and financial planning.

Figure 2.1 Investment management relationships

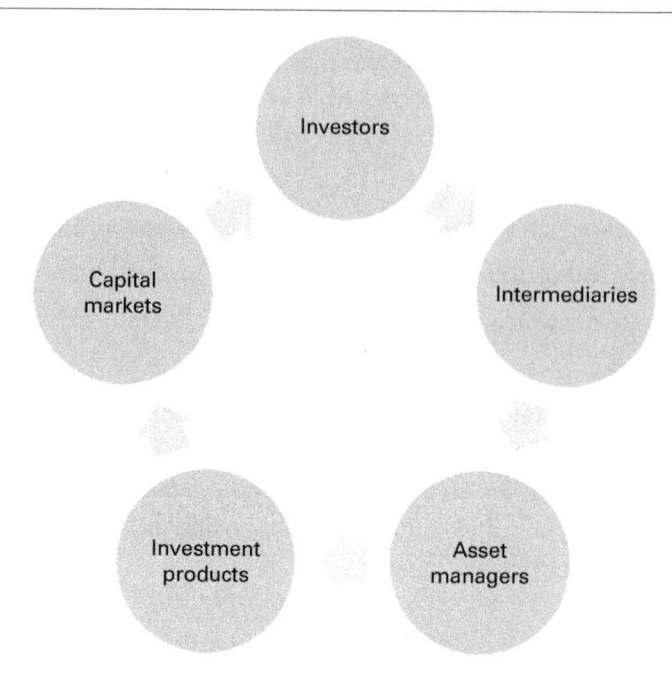

```
                    Investors

   Capital                           Intermediaries
   markets


       Investment              Asset
       products               managers
```

3 Asset managers: these provide traditional and alternative asset management strategies leading to investment management and asset management solutions.

4 Investment products: these include mutual funds, UCITSs (undertakings for the collective investment in transferable securities); ETFs (exchange-traded funds) and LPs (limited partners) as well as separately managed accounts.

5 Capital markets: these include equities, debt, securitizations, derivatives and commodities, with monies returned to investors through income (dividends, interest etc) and capital gains.

Asset management includes:

- analysing and assessing client requirements in respect of financial goals;
- creating an investment plan to achieve those goals;
- actioning the strategy required to deliver those goals.

This analysis then allows the manager to offer a range of strategies or products. These can be specific as seen in boutique management firms which may specialize in one market or type of product or more diverse where 'full service' managers offer a continually evolving suite of products to suit a variety of investment requirements.

Fund management organizations

These may be characterized by the type of client, the management method or the type of investment made and can range from individuals to teams of fund managers and may also include hedge fund managers. As we can see below, they may also take different forms and the form may influence assessment of the firm by analysts:

- Private organizations: these may take the form of limited companies or limited partnerships. They often retain the services of the original founders within day-to-day management. Some organizations such as ORIX (private equity firm) and AMG (publicly listed on the NYSE) may also have holdings in private asset management firms.
- Public companies: listed companies can include those who purely trade in asset management and financial services companies with a significant asset management division (eg State Street, see p 44).
- Shareholder owned: by this we mean the organization is run and owned by the clients. Vanguard, which we talk about later in the chapter (p 44), is the only organization run on this basis.

Retention of key investment managers is critical to a financial firm's success, as they are the basis of the investment decisions made. The outcome of such decisions is measured by both the organization's stakeholders and by the wider investment industry who use metrics to assess a firm's strength. This is because an investment manager with a strong record of accomplishment and confidence in their future predictions will enhance their firm by drawing in investor funds. This confidence in their future stock-picking abilities has additional credibility where managers' own funds are invested in their investment choices, so part of a manager's remuneration is often in the form of investments in their own managed funds.

The size of the global asset management industry

Investment and Pensions Europe (www.ipe.com) produces an annual analysis of the 400 largest global asset management organizations. Their figures, graphed in Figure 2.2, show the investment industry continues to grow and is relatively concentrated with the top 10 managers controlling c33 per cent of all assets and the largest, BlackRock, controlling €4.4 trillion or 7.8 per cent individually.

The top five asset management firms (see Figure 2.3) show a growth in the level of assets managed between 2015 and 2016, the latest figures available, with all five based in both the US and UK markets except Fidelity Investments, which is US-based although it sells in the UK.

Figure 2.2 Size of the investment management industry by assets under management (AUM)

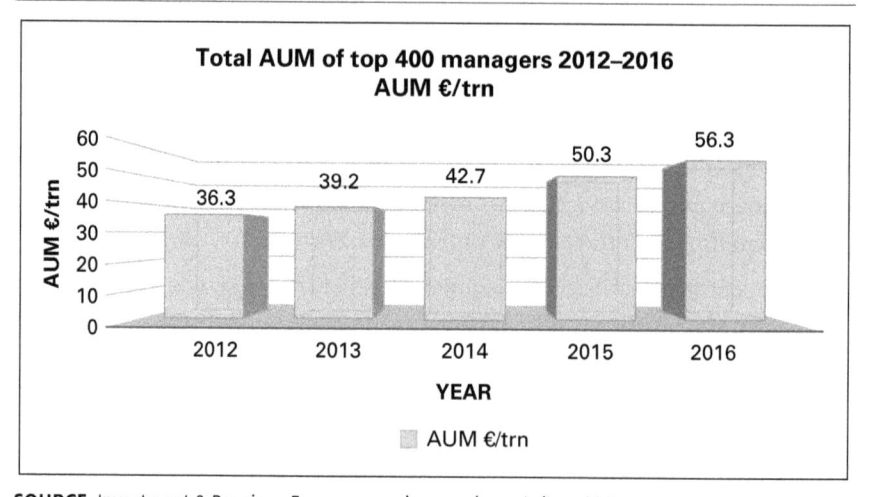

Total AUM of top 400 managers 2012–2016
AUM €/trn

Year	AUM €/trn
2012	36.3
2013	39.2
2014	42.7
2015	50.3
2016	56.3

SOURCE Investment & Pensions Europe, www.ipe.com/reports/top-400-asset

Figure 2.3 Top five asset managers 2015 (€m)

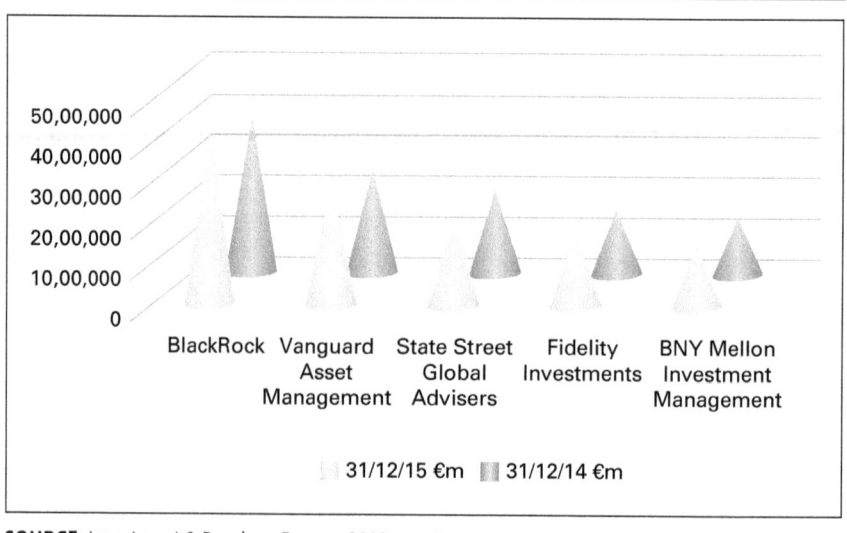

Top five asset managers: BlackRock, Vanguard Asset Management, State Street Global Advisers, Fidelity Investments, BNY Mellon Investment Management

31/12/15 €m   31/12/14 €m

SOURCE Investment & Pensions Europe, 2016 report

In practice

A short history of the top five asset management firms

It is easy to see global investment organizations as being very distant from ourselves as retail investors, students and even portfolio managers; however, it is important when looking after clients' funds that you understand the organizations your clients are investing with. This ensures a client's objectives are met by the organization, as these objectives may not just be financial but may encompass the philosophy of the firm itself and its manner of ownership and operation. As such it is useful to know about the origins and management of individual firms. Below we include some background information on five asset management firms, although more detailed information can be found on their websites.

BlackRock

The Blackstone Group was founded in 1988 by Lawrence D Fink, one of eight original founders. Four founders remain at the company including Fink, the chairman and CEO; Robert Kapito, president and director of BlackRock; Barbara Novak, vice chairman amongst other roles; and Dr Ben Goulab, chief risk officer.

The company, which is at the time of writing the largest asset management company in the world, changed its name to BlackRock in around 2003 and now has over 12,000 employees located in 30 countries. Clients include governments, pension funds, sovereign wealth funds and endowment providers who make up 65 per cent of clients. Some 62 per cent of **assets under management (AUM)** originate in the Americas and 29 per cent from EMEA countries. AUM includes mutual funds, exchange-traded funds, closed-end funds, and products focusing on providing retirement income, under their own brand CoRI as well as university saving plans in the UK. Whilst BlackRock did not invent ETFs, they are parent to iShares, the largest ETF provider in the world which invests in many areas from emerging markets to pharmaceuticals.

Despite its size, BlackRock has continued to grow, with commentators noting revenue increases of approximately 9 per cent in 2015 and 2016 and operating margin growth up to approximately 40 per cent in 2016. Analysts find it hard to pinpoint one factor which accounts for the firm's success; however, they note clients have increased investment in debt due to volatility of markets as well as increasing the level of funds invested, amongst other factors.

Vanguard Asset Management

Vanguard, founded in 1975 by John Bogle, is named after an 18th-century sailing ship which features as their logo. They are unique in the industry as a client-owned mutual fund with no external owners. The owners of the funds own the organization and Vanguard believe this has allowed them to promote high levels of customer service at low cost whilst eliminating any conflict of interest between owners and clients. By 2015 its fund expense ratio was 0.18 per cent. This low-cost philosophy allowed them to develop the first index tracker fund although they also undertake active management. The company currently has offices in several international locations including London, which houses its European headquarters.

State Street Global Advisors (SSGA)

SSGA is part of the Boston-based State Street Corporation with offices in more than 16 countries and over 2,500 employees. SSGA was responsible for developing the first EFT in 1993 (S&P 500 SPDR ETF) as well as having a high proportion of AUM for clients based outside the USA.

Fidelity International

Fidelity was founded in 1946 by Edward C Johnson and under its current CEO, Abigail Johnson, it is one of the top five financial services groups in the world with over 45,000 employees and a Boston-based headquarters. Fidelity's investment base was developed under its founder 'Mister Johnson' who focused on long-term strategies incorporating technical research and a belief in active management. The company embraced technology, being the first to use free telephone numbers to encourage direct sales as well as being the first financial services company to develop a website in 1995.

BNY Mellon

BNY Mellon, founded in 1784 by Alexander Hamilton, one of the USA's founding fathers, was originally known as the Bank of New York. From its original premises, in a house near Wall Street, the business has grown, now trading in 35 countries and 100 markets. The Bank of New York was the first stock traded on the NYSE and provided the US government's first loan. Now over 80 per cent of its clients are Fortune 500 companies. Its current chairman and CEO Gerald Hassell has held the post since 2011, originally joining the business as a graduate trainee in 1973 after graduating in economics from Duke University.

Barriers to entry in the market

Whilst it may not appear likely to be the case with an industry based around individuals and their skills, there are several barriers to entry facing new managers, and the strength of these barriers has grown in recent years with the increasing size and complexity of financial services firms:

- Past performance: the most important attribute for any asset manager is a performance track record, with a minimum of three years' records often being expected. Breaking into the market without a performance record can be difficult, especially in today's competitive market; however, it can sometimes be possible to start new funds when backed by an existing investment manager.
- Economies of scale: economies of size can assist in lowering costs in areas such as technology and compliance by allowing favourable contracts to be negotiated. Such cost reductions impact directly on investor returns and as such can bring advantages to larger and established firms/managers when looking to maximize profits in conjunction with investor returns.
- Brand: where managers are operating as part of a larger brand it may be possible to leverage off that relationship; in addition it may be possible to provide a multifaceted investment solution to a client in-house, due to the breadth of investment products available, in a way a smaller organization could not achieve.
- Product differentiation: larger and more diverse companies have both the budget and back-office capabilities to research and develop new products to fulfil client requirements; smaller firms and individuals may not have the time or resources to achieve this.
- Regulation: increasing regulation levels since the financial crash in 2008 lead to additional costs. Such costs are more easily spread between larger numbers of clients as well as larger organizations having the operational support and processes in place to ensure compliance.

Global issues shaping investing in 2017

Many firms produce their opinions on the biggest influences facing the investment industry each year. For example, Goldman Sachs (GS) produced their *Investment Outlook 2017* report. Overall, GS believes growth will become more widespread amongst economies and they retain their preference for risk assets, ie equities over debt; however, they believe returns will be low due to their perception of the current high valuation being attributed to assets as well as limited potential for economic growth and corporate earnings. From this base position, the report looks to focus on the most important trends based on analysis of staff views from around the world and they do this by focusing on four key areas: rising populism, inflation, interest in fiscal policy and deregulation.

Rising populism and anti-global sentiment

GS perceives populism as a political message, underpinned by a combination of ideas, in individual countries. This combination of ideas, they believe, is centred around immigration, protectionist trade measures and fiscal policy. At the time of writing GS are monitoring the first 100 days of Donald Trump's presidency in the USA as well as the elections in Europe, which, over the spring and summer 2017 will include France and Germany. Whilst GS doesn't foresee the eurozone disintegrating, they feel that the results of these elections will indicate the strength of relationships within Europe which may affect future direction. They also feel the US may take a more protectionist stance, with the economic effects of this being determined by other countries' responses. This area highlights the need for portfolio managers to stay abreast of all areas of economic and political life as such factors can affect the value of assets and investment decisions as well as a wider economic outlook.

Rising inflation following a period of stagflation

Keyword

Stagflation is high unemployment combined with stagnant economic demand within a country's economy and persistent high inflation.

In recent history, there has been a period of low growth and inflation which it was feared would lead to a period of stagflation. However, with the recent rise in commodity prices and wages the risk of this is felt to be over, with price and inflation expectations expected to rise. Overall, it is felt this should be good for assets but only if carefully managed by central banks to avoid volatility, and bearing in mind not all companies will benefit equally from an inflationary landscape with those which cannot pass on price increases potentially feeling squeezed.

Rising interest in fiscal rather than monetary policies

> **Keywords**
>
> **Fiscal policy** is a means for government to influence an economy using taxation and government spending. Its sister is monetary policy which is a means for government to influence an economy using the money supply and interest rates.

GS feels it is unlikely that the asset purchase levels by the European Central Bank and the Bank of Japan seen recently can continue in the long term and they believe there are already signs of a move towards fiscal spending to overcome low growth rates, for example as outlined by Donald Trump in his election campaign. Predicting the effect of such actions is felt to be difficult as they may lead to either increased growth and company earnings or potentially a rise in inflation and volatility in investment assets.

Rising deregulation rather than new regulation

Regulation, as can be seen in Figure 2.4, is one of the most important problems identified by independent businesses in 2016. Whilst the potential for fiscal spending has a higher media profile, GS believes the potential for deregulatory moves proposed by President Trump, with a view to improving capital access and removing barriers to business start-ups, may have more effect on growth. GS are waiting to assess the potential for deregulation based on President Trump's appointments as US Regulators. This may also have a knock-on effect on EU and UK regulation levels. Later in autumn 2017, China is due to hold its National Congress and it is expected that, prior to this, any regulatory amendments will be aimed at stability.

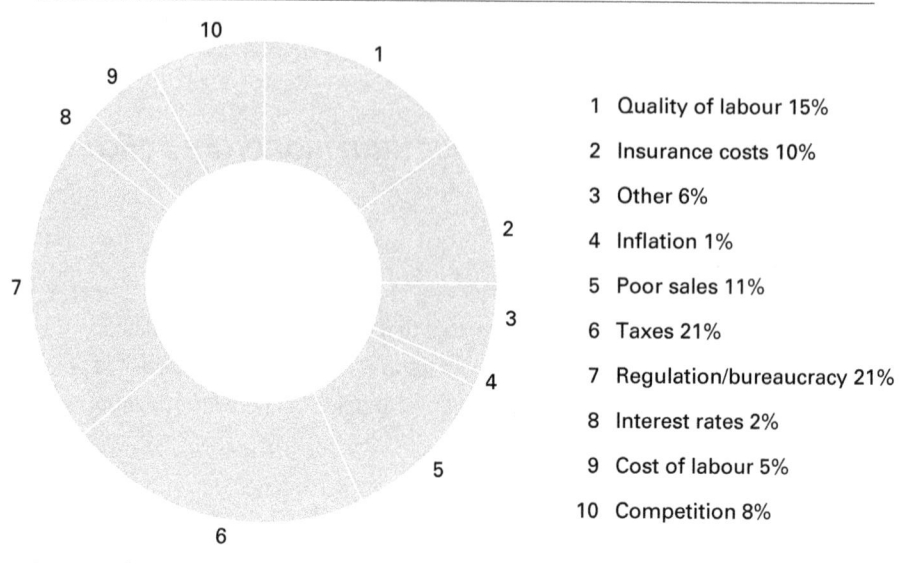

Figure 2.4 Single most important independent business concerns (%) (November 2016)

1. Quality of labour 15%
2. Insurance costs 10%
3. Other 6%
4. Inflation 1%
5. Poor sales 11%
6. Taxes 21%
7. Regulation/bureaucracy 21%
8. Interest rates 2%
9. Cost of labour 5%
10. Competition 8%

SOURCE Bloomberg, National Federation of Small Businesses

The size of the UK investment management industry

The Investment Association (IA) is the trade body representing UK investment managers worldwide, with over 200 member firms collectively managing funds of £5.7 trillion (at the time of writing) on behalf of UK and global clients. Their annual survey provides a comprehensive analysis of the value of assets under management (AUM) in the UK as it estimates it reports on over 83 per cent of all UK AUM. That said, there is a wider market of firms who do not report to the IA and which are summarized with estimated variations at 31 December 2015 as:

- discretionary private client management – £417 billion;
- UK commercial property management – £480 billion;
- hedge funds – £245 billion;
- private equity firms – £210 billion;
- other asset management firms managing assets in the UK – £6.9 trillion.

Fund valuation

> **Keyword**
>
> Funds are valued using **assets under management (AUM)** which equals the total market value of assets that are managed or controlled by a fund manager or institution either for all their clients or for specific subsets of clients depending on what analysis is being undertaken.

AUM valuation is important to fund managers because: a) management fees are often a fixed percentage of AUM, and fund managers will therefore be looking to increase the value of AUM so investors need to ensure they understand fee charges; and b) AUM may also be used within marketing and promotional material to validate fund performance.

Broadly there are two subsections within AUM:

- Pooled vehicles: for example, authorized unit trusts, open-ended investment companies (OEICs), unauthorized investment vehicles, closed-ended investments such as investment trusts, exchange-traded funds and life funds. Here the funds of many individual clients are joined together, invested and managed in one investment vehicle.
- Segregated mandates: this is a bespoke service where portfolios are developed to fulfil individual client needs and managed by fund managers.

As there are different valuation methods it is important to understand the context of the measurement as well as the calculation itself. What is included in AUM may vary between organizations with some including bank deposits, mutual funds and cash whilst others only include assets under discretionary management (where investors authorize fund managers to make investment decisions on their behalf). AUM is a fluid figure as the total amount will increase and decrease due to different factors.

From an investor's perspective AUM is only one aspect of fund assessment and needs to be seen in context. It isn't always better to have a larger fund which may be unwieldy to manage and lose focus on key areas. In addition, AUM may not be the most appropriate metric with others, such as AUM compared to market capitalization, potentially providing a clearer view of the current fund position.

Measurement of AUM in the UK

Investment Association

Twice a year in the UK, each IA member firm provides their AUM figure, once, at 30 June, as part of the subscription call and once at 31 December as part of the asset management survey. The AUM figure used by the IA includes the value of assets under the discretionary management of managers within member firms, ie those people who carry out day-to-day investment management as opposed to the client management role. As such, the relevant factor is the fund manager's location rather than the location of the client, the fund, or the relationship manager, and the following types of assets should be included:

- assets managed by the firm in the UK irrespective of where the client is based;
- assets managed by UK asset managers after management is delegated by third-party asset managers or overseas offices within their company or group;
- worldwide pooled investment assets managed in the UK;
- UK-managed assets using fund of funds or manager of manager products.

The Investment Association figures do not include:

- assets managed by third-party managers or group overseas offices;
- UK domiciled assets where day-to-day investment decisions are taken overseas, even where relationship and operations management are undertaken in the UK;
- fund of fund or manager of manager products which do not fulfil the conditions above.

In practice

To show which assets will be included in the AUM asset figure given to the Investment Association, let us consider the following case study.

XYZ Asset Management (XYZ) is an asset management firm and we know the following information about it:

Global fund management industry

- 90 per cent of XYZ discretionary investment decisions are taken at its head office in Leeds, with the other 10 per cent taken from its office in Tokyo.
- XYZ's client relationship managers operate from regional offices in Paris, London, Dublin and Tokyo. Relationship managers do not make asset investment decisions.
- ABC Asset Management based in New York may sometimes delegate assets to XYZ and vice versa but the two companies are independent of each other.
- This is also the case with another firm, CDE Asset Management.

XYZ are completing their latest return to the Investment Association and must decide whether to include the assets in each of the following scenarios:

1. XYZ clients include a French pension fund (assets managed £35 billion) and a UK insurance firm (assets managed £10 billion) with investment decisions made in Leeds.
   Decision: The relevant rule here is: assets managed in the UK should be included in the AUM figure irrespective of where the asset or relationship is based. From the information above we know that XYZ's investment decisions are taken in the UK even though the relationship is managed from regional offices; as such both the client's assets should be included in the AUM figure.

2. ABC have contracted £10 billion of Client A's assets to XYZ for management in the UK, whilst XYZ has delegated £15 billion of their client T's total assets of £30 billion to ABC for management in the US.
   Decision: Assets which are managed in the UK irrespective of whether they are the firm's own assets or delegated should be included. However, those assets which UK firms delegate overseas should not be included. In the above example, the £10 billion of assets ABC delegates to XYZ to manage in the UK should be included; however, the proportion of XYZ's client T's assets which are being managed by ABC, £15 million, should not be included.

3. XYZ manages £15 billion of assets in the UK, which form part of a worldwide pool totalling £50 billion domiciled in Germany. The remaining assets are managed and investment decisions made in Japan by XYZ.
   Decision: Assets which are managed within the UK, even though they form part of a worldwide pool of assets domiciled in another country, should be included in AUM figures. As such, the £15 billion of

assets within the pooled fund which are managed in the UK should be included; however, the remaining £35 billion of assets should not.

4 XYZ manages a £10 billion manager of manager fund; however, £6 billion of the fund is managed by firm CDE in their in-house products.
Decision: Assets should be included in the AUM figure where they are managed in-house by the reporting firm. As such XYZ should include the £4 billion it manages itself but not the remaining £6 billion which were managed by firm CDE. This avoids double counting.

The Financial Conduct Authority (FCA) Return

In addition to the Investment Association return, the FCA requires firms to calculate the A007 and I005 figures annually to be able to calculate a firm's contribution to the Money Advice Service (MAS) and the Financial Ombudsman Service (FOS) respectively. The FCA calculation should match with the IA calculation in all but two areas:

- Group assets, as the FCA figure excludes assets managed within the firm's group under certain conditions which are outside the scope of this book.
- Only UK asset managers are included in the Investment Association figures whereas manager location may not be relevant for the FCA figures subject to certain conditions which are outside the scope of this book.

Keyword

UK investment bodies

The Financial Conduct Authority replaced the Financial Services Authority. It is based in Canary Wharf, London and is an independent financial regulatory body for the financial services industry. Its budget of approximately £450 million is funded by member firms' fees.

The Money Advice Service (MAS) was a government initiative to help educate individuals in respect of their finances which, following the 2016 budget, looks set to be replaced.

The Financial Ombudsman Service (FOS) was set up by Parliament to resolve consumer financial complaints. The FOS will be used where a financial institution and a customer cannot resolve the matter using internal customer complaint procedures. The FOS provides unbiased answers to situations and where there has been unfair treatment they can legally enforce restitution.

The UK fund management industry 2016

In their 2016 analysis of member data the Investment Association highlighted several areas they felt were of importance in respect of the current UK investment management industry.

The importance of UK asset management within the global market

Within Europe the UK remains the largest centre of the asset management industry, exceeding the combined French, Italian and German markets, and accounting for 37 per cent of AUM in Europe in 2012 (the latest figures available). The UK remains much smaller than the USA which is the largest centre with approximately £24.5 trillion of the total global AUM of £48.5 trillion. Japan, one of the larger markets, has also seen an increase of approximately 14.5 per cent in 2015 to £2.75 trillion. Japan's increased AUM levels are partly due to a physical increase in AUM but also shows the influence of exchange rate movements and the effect this has on the valuation of the funds.

The importance of UK asset management to the domestic economy

Within the UK, the value of AUM was £5.7 trillion at the beginning of 2016 with approximately 39 per cent of this managed for overseas clients based not only in the USA and Europe (particularly Luxembourg and Dublin) but also the rest of the world. Fund values continue to grow, up 8 per cent over the last 10 years; however, the value of financial exports, in relation to investment management, highlights the industry's importance to the UK economy, currently representing 6 per cent of the net services exports. The UK economy continues to retain its concentration around financial services: based on Investment Association figures at the end of 2015, AUM totalled £5.7 trillion which equates to 320 per cent of the GDP of the UK at that time. In turn, this can be compared to the markets of European countries of c114 per cent. Whilst such concentation can provide specialisms, assisting the domestic economy

Figure 2.5 Percentage of staff directly employed by asset managers in the UK by function

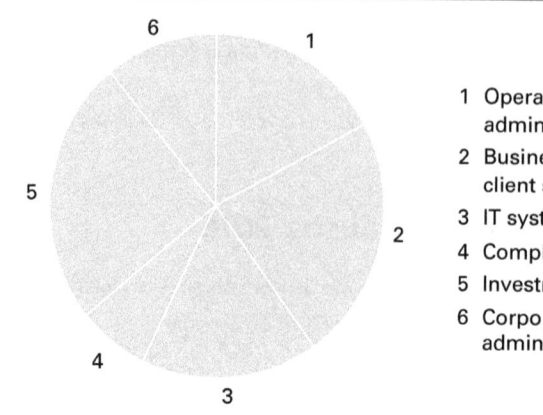

1 Operation & funds administration 17%
2 Business development & client services 23%
3 IT systems and other 17%
4 Compliance, legal & audit 7%
5 Investment management 25%
6 Corporate finance & corporate administration 11%

SOURCE The Investment Association, 2016 survey report

and company growth, over-reliance on one industry may prove disastrous in the event of an economic downturn or change in circumstances.

Levels of employment in the UK asset management industry

The IA estimates approximately 37,000 individuals are employed directly within asset management with 55,000 individuals in supporting roles, as detailed in Figure 2.5. It also appeared that firms were outsourcing middle-office and back-office functions to third parties.

Numbers and size of firms in the UK asset management industry

Numbers of firms within the industry remained relatively high with the top five largest firms managing c39 per cent of funds and the top 10 managing 56 per cent of funds (Figure 2.6). The IA believe larger firms may be at an advantage with consumers as they can offer a larger array of services than smaller firms.

The IA's members account for over 80 per cent of UK AUM, but this is not to say that all firms which operate in the asset industry are members of the IA. Some detailed earlier such as hedge funds, private equity companies, commercial property management amongst others, are not members.

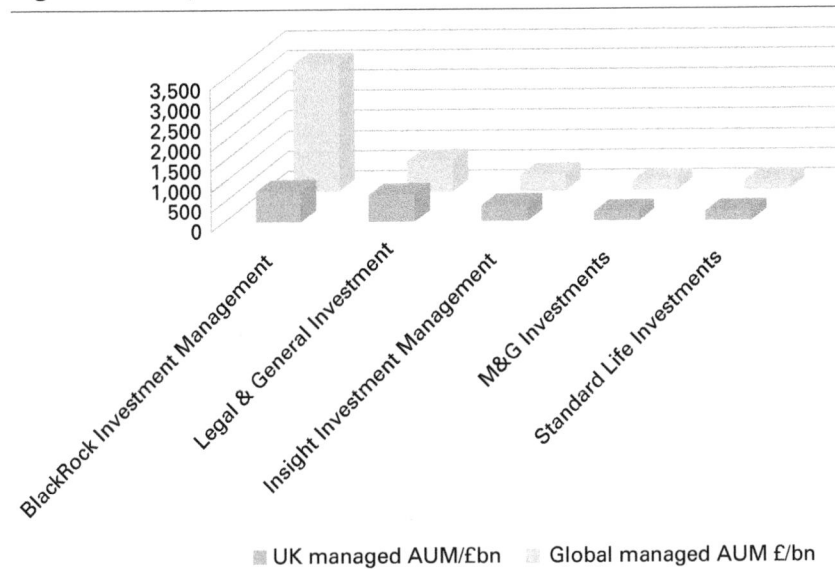

Figure 2.6 Top five firms managed by UK managed and global AUM

[Bar chart showing UK managed AUM/£bn and Global managed AUM £/bn for BlackRock Investment Management, Legal & General Investment, Insight Investment Management, M&G Investments, and Standard Life Investments; y-axis scale 0 to 3,500]

■ UK managed AUM/£bn   Global managed AUM £/bn

SOURCE The Investment Association, 2016 survey report

Management companies also appear to be growing more international with UK-owned asset managers accounting for 42 per cent of assets managed at end of 2015 compared to 60 per cent at end of 2005. This fall is partly due to the increase in US-owned organizations which now account for 47 per cent of total assets. Simultaneously, European organizations with a UK head office have reduced their asset management to 9 per cent of the market. This is felt likely to be due partly to the financial crisis and the subsequent restructuring of European banks.

Technology

This area is still seen as having huge potential for development in respect of communication with markets and clients; however, as in many areas, information security remains paramount and client data security looks set to grow in importance as companies try to protect themselves against attack and the negative reputational effects this could bring to the company through lost funds and misappropriated data.

Passive versus active investing

Pure passive funds, managed through an index, continue to rise in popularity and now account for about 23 per cent of total funds. However, hybrids, which fall between passive and active funds (eg smart Beta) were noted as staying static at approximately 3 per cent. It should be noted the IA does not include ETFs within their analysis. This movement towards passive investing is highlighted in Figure 2.7 which shows the flow of money into passive funds within the top five asset managers in Europe using fund levels received in 2016.

Who are the industry's clients?

The clear majority of clients (80 per cent) remain institutional investors, with pensions forming 40 per cent of this total. Insurance companies, at 18 per cent, were noted as having a stable presence in the market after decreasing in previous years.

More diversification by clients to assets outside the mainstream was also noted and it was suggested that this was partly due to the move from defined benefit pensions to defined contribution pensions as well as a move towards stability for pensioners. This trend would also suggest a further blurring between retail and institutional investment.

Approximately 38 per cent (£2.2 trillion) of assets were managed on behalf of overseas clients split between the US (£310 billion), Europe (£1.2 trillion) and the rest of the world (£660 billion).

Figure 2.7 Growth in passive flows compared to total net flows in 2016 for top five European asset managers

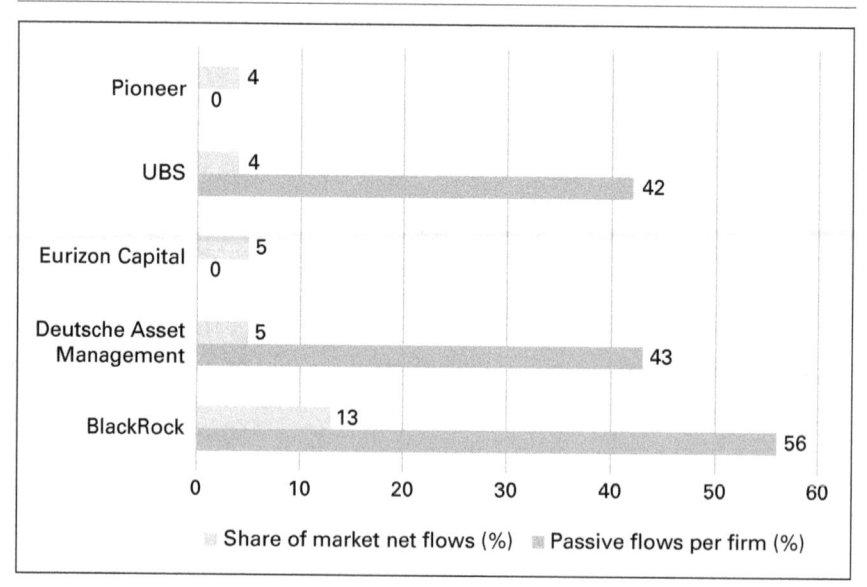

Firm	Share of market net flows (%)	Passive flows per firm (%)
Pioneer	0	4
UBS	42	4
Eurizon Capital	0	5
Deutsche Asset Management	43	5
BlackRock	56	13

SOURCE BCG Analysis Strategic Insight

The effect of Brexit

The UK is currently a member of the EU and is therefore entitled to establish a trading presence in any member state either within a country on an equal footing with domestic firms or via a cross-border service.

Brexit was noted as a serious source of uncertainty for the market as the UK industry was international but highly integrated into Europe. Future success it was felt would be measured by the industry's ability to adapt to the post-Brexit world.

Allocation of assets within the UK industry

Funds allocated to equity investment continued the trend of recent years by falling in 2016. However, with UK equities at 33 per cent of the total, it was suggested that previous years' reductions in UK investment had been halted. A small reduction of 1 per cent in the fixed-income sector was analysed as suggesting investors were looking for alternative sources of fixed-income return. It was also noted that investment in alternative assets had increased, though this was mostly in 'solutions-orientated' products rather than true alternatives.

Regulation

As part of the EU the UK is currently subject to all EU regulations resulting in financial instruments having the ability to be 'passported'. This means that, where certain criteria are met, such instruments can be sold in any EU member states without further regulation. At the time of writing the position following Brexit has yet to be determined, and commentators are concerned that operating outside the European Economic Area will diminish any influence the UK can have on future regulation. However, it was also considered that the value of the contribution made by the FCA in development of past and current EU legislation should not be underestimated and will potentially be missed within the EU. In addition, a movement towards global regulation, for example within the G20, has also been recognized and this may allow the UK to trade within the EU in the future and maintain its regulatory influence.

Asset management house structure

Figure 2.8 shows a very simplified structure for an asset management house, but it does identify the main roles within such a business. However, where organizations have multiple offices in multiple locations you will find some duplication of roles at office or country level with ultimate responsibility being held by head office.

The principal roles within this structure are as follows:

- Chief executive officer (CEO): overall responsibility for strategic direction and management of the organization through senior management team.
- Chief investment officer (CIO): overall responsibility for fund performance against set targets and in most companies promoting a culture which rewards team effort as opposed to 'star' managers, which can be difficult to achieve. The CIO has a team including:
    - strategy director: responsible for asset allocation, ie choosing between asset types and potentially market allocation. Manages teams of economists responsible for data analysts and trend forecasting.
    - head of equities: responsible for implementation of policy and management of trading desks.
    - head of bonds: responsible for implementation of policy and management of trading desks.
- Chief financial officer (CFO): essentially the finance director, but may also be responsible for overall administration of middle-office functions.

Figure 2.8 Example organizational structure of an asset management house

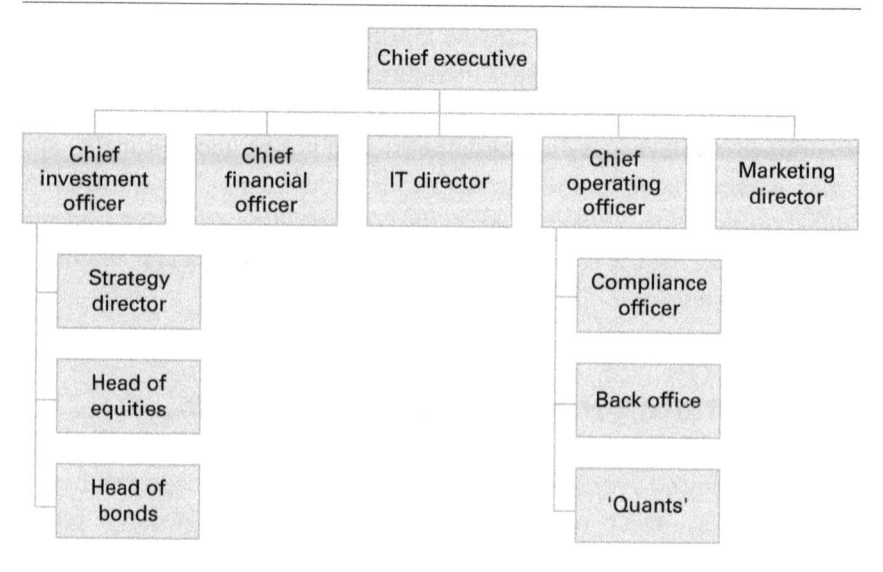

- IT director: overall responsibility for trading systems and back-office functioning of IT, including order management systems, dealing systems and investment accounting. This position is increasingly important due to malware and other cyber threats as well as client data protection. Data can include both trading data and real-time news from service providers such as Bloomberg as well as client account information.
- Chief operating officer (COO): overall responsibility for ensuring processes, regulation and compliance issues are followed in line with company procedures as well as liaising with trustees and regulators and some middle- and back-office functions. The following report to the COO:
  - compliance officer: overall responsibility for ensuring all regulations (eg FCA and laws) are adhered to in relevant trading jurisdictions.
  - back office: responsibility for ensuring transactions carried out (eg transaction settlement with brokers, reconciliation of client accounts, general record keeping, handling corporate actions on existing holdings) are in line with regulatory body requirements.
  - 'quants' or quantitative analysis: responsible for analysis of risk, performance and client reporting.
- Marketing director: overall responsibility for market profile and relationship with different market segments such as institutional investors eg pension funds and retail investors, usually through independent financial advisers (IFAs), ensuring existing clients' needs are met as well as selling to potential new clients.

Investment managers

Investment managers are required to have a high level of professional training to be able to undertake the analysis and maintain the strategic direction of investors' portfolios. To obtain employment, historically, a 2:1 undergraduate degree was a prerequisite, which could be in any subject although an element of business or economics within a degree was helpful. It is now possible to enter the financial industry following A-levels via an apprenticeship leading to professional qualifications.

Prized personal qualities in a fund manager include: self-motivation, analytical and problem-solving skills, resilience, the ability to work under pressure and as part of a team to a high standard. As a career, there are good prospects for promotion although hours are longer than for other careers.

Investment banks, asset management companies, stockbrokers and life assurance and insurance companies all employ fund managers and vacancies can be found in the media, for example the *Financial Times*, on job portals such as Targetjobs, and with specialist recruitment agencies acting for specific clients.

Investment manager positions will have different names depending not only on the type of company employing an individual but also between different companies. For example, Lloyds may use the prefix 'director' whereas Barclays would use the prefix 'president' in addition to describing the roles with different titles. There can also be differences in roles, for instance between an investment bank and an asset house, for example when you look at a dealer's roles. Therefore, it is important to look at the day-to-day responsibilities within the job specification to obtain a genuine understanding of the role being offered. That said, whilst the main roles are usually interchangeable between organizations there may be differences and specific responsibilities potential employees need to be aware of.

Fund managers

As investments are pooled, the fund manager will manage them on a discretionary basis, ie without the direct authority of the individual clients. He or she will set the portfolio's goals and budgets, and ensure the fund is run efficiently in line with the client's risk assessment, with the remit of producing stable returns which beat an appropriate benchmark for the client. The most senior managers will deal with the largest clients and it may be an investment manager has other roles, such as chief investment officer, overseeing the other managers, as well as managing their own funds. Fund managers are likely to attend a daily meeting each morning to share information in respect of economic and market conditions and details of any planned trading activity for the day.

Fund managers will be specifically responsible for ensuring:

- orders are executed accurately with the correct amount and type of stock purchased;
- the fund has sufficient cash to meet the liability stream or obligations of the fund such as paying pensions or funding insurance claims;
- confirming with the custodian for stock certificates that sold stock is available for delivery;
- all client purchases are made simultaneously in the market, ensuring they receive equal treatment.

Equity managers

As the equity market is usually divided into different areas it is usual to have a specific desk (group) responsible for each market. There may be a central European desk dealing in France and Germany and an Eastern European desk dealing in Hungary etc, or there may be a desk dealing with emerging markets.

The number of people within the desk and the resources will reflect the value of trading carried out with the domestic trading desk, ie the UK usually being the largest in an organization. In fact, the UK desk may be so large they have industry or sector specialists whilst other desks are likely to just have country specialists.

A large proportion of a manager's time will be spent collating data from broker research to formulate a plan, as well as preparing estimates of earnings and modelling the impact of economic changes on the prices, for example interest rate or oil price changes, as well as more specific news items.

Fixed interest managers

Managers will be measured against a benchmark and will be responsible for a strategy to ensure the benchmark is exceeded as well as ensuring clients have sufficient funds available to meet their liabilities when required. They will also be responsible for reinvesting cash on maturity of investments.

The market research managers will carry out to analyse the markets will concentrate on the following factors:

- directly affecting bond prices overall such as interest rates;
- which are one step back from the bond itself, eg factors affecting interest rate in general such as wage inflation and central bank policy;
- affecting specific bonds such as changes in government, company or bond credit ratings.

Property managers

The specialized nature of this type of investment may mean managers are hived off into a separate company within the organization. Firms will concentrate on commercial property investment assessing price, rental income levels and lease administration amongst other factors.

This area has several attributes which separate it from other markets:

- there is an inelastic product supply due to the nature of the investment and the scarcity of buildings and land to develop;

- it may have high overheads due to the requirement to use other professionals eg valuers, surveyors and legal professionals;
- property can be an illiquid asset which may also be difficult to value until sale;
- where the property has residential tenants, ie flats, a high level of regulatory compliance is required.

Cash managers (the treasury desk)

The objective of cash managers is to achieve the highest return levels available where a fund manager has allocated funds to cash securities. In addition, they are responsible for managing cash held for settlement in several days' time but which is currently available for investment. This is achieved by sweeping available cash into short-term stable and safe investments such as treasury bills and call deposits, balancing the requirement of having cash not invested overnight and ensuring the fund does not become overdrawn.

Dealer

There is a difference between the role of a dealer in an investment bank and an asset manager. In an investment bank, the dealer will trade his own 'book', ie his own account with the aim of making a profit. An asset management dealer is responsible for buying and selling securities on behalf of clients at the best available price as well as agreeing terms with brokers and any delivery arrangements.

Other investment/asset management positions

- Wealth managers: here clients are high net worth individuals and the wealth manager oversees some or all of their investments in capital markets as well as day-to-day banking transactions.
- Independent financial advisers: IFAs will offer recommendations and an suggestions regarding specific investments and manage the day-to-day transactions of clients to produce the highest possible returns available for the client's assessed risk profile. Advisers may work as individuals or as part of larger organizations.
- Portfolio or asset managers: this refers to mutual fund investments with decisions being made to maximize potential returns and based on research, profitability and predetermined targets set out in the fund's prospectus.

In practice

A day in the life of an investment manager

Overall, the investment manager is responsible for developing and implementing the investment strategy of an individual portfolio for their clients with a lot of the information on which they base their decisions coming from an investment analyst. A typical day for a fund manager may include some or all the following types of tasks:

- researching potential new portfolio investments including:
  - setting investment objectives;
  - formulating an investment plan;
  - establishing a portfolio strategy.

- reviewing financial briefings prepared by investment analysts;
- making informed recommendations and decisions to clients in face-to-face meetings or by written report;
- reviewing past investment decisions and ensuring they fulfil client requirements;
- ensuring they remain up-to-date in respect of current economic, political and legal news in the UK and abroad to consider any potential effects on their portfolios;
- researching new companies;
- meeting new and existing clients.

The physical tasks undertaken by individual managers will depend on the size of the firm, with smaller boutique firms, which lack large infrastructures, relying on managers to place orders to buy and sell investments as well as conducting marketing and administration functions which may include developing an ethical stance for their funds. Managers at larger funds will usually be supported by staff, including individuals who monitor the markets, make trades and support managers in operational roles. Whilst individuals run most funds, it is possible for funds to be run by a partnership of managers or a committee which votes to select the best investments. It is also possible that each manager may be given a proportion of a total fund to invest with a lead manager determining the amounts each subsidiary manager is given.

Managing active and passive funds

There are some differences between the management of an active fund and a passive index tracker fund.

For an active fund the manager is responsible for the purchase of assets using clients' money; therefore, managers pick investments based on their analysis and using a variety of predetermined measures, P/E ratio or dividend ratios for instance, in conjunction with their assessment of risk at both an individual stock level and at micro- and macroeconomic level to assess an investment. The criteria of the fund will determine the types of investments made, although managers do have some leeway in their choices, subject to the original aims of the fund.

For passive or index funds the manager's role is slightly different, as their aim is to replicate an index by purchasing stocks in the correct proportion for their fund. This may entail full replication, where all the stocks within an index, such as the FTSE 100, are purchased, or a partial replication where only some of the stocks are purchased. In this latter case, the manager must calculate which of the stocks will allow the fund to imitate or match the movement of the index most closely due to their patterns of movement. Such partial replication can be used where it is difficult to obtain every stock within an index, for example in an emerging market.

Assessing a fund manager's performance

Fund managers may work alone or in teams and are paid fees calculated as a percentage of the AUM. Thus, to increase their income, they need the value of their portfolio to increase through either: 1) new cash inflows; or 2) growth in value of the assets invested.

In addition to this, investors will be assessing fund managers on the consistency of their long-term performance within a fund in respect of how closely it matches their investment requirements and comparing it to other investment managers. For investors, the performance of the fund manager is critical as the fund manager's ability to read the market and make appropriate investment decisions will determine the returns earned. As management fees are paid to the fund managers their main benefit to the investor is to return more than could be achieved from tracking an index, ie making an 'abnormal return'.

Assessing individual fund managers returns requires measurement against a target benchmark which is identified when the fund is first launched, with the fund managers aiming to beat the movement of an index or benchmark in each period.

> **In practice**
>
> As an example, if the index has risen by 2 per cent, the manager will hope their return is greater than 2 per cent; if the index has fallen by 3 per cent they would hope their fund has only fallen by less than 3 per cent.
>
> This additional return or reduced loss is then used to justify the fund's management charges. The active manager potentially achieves this improved performance by changing the weighting of stocks and shares in their portfolio compared to the proportion of stocks and shares in the index which is known as 'style-drift'.

The level of flexibility the manager has in changing proportions of individual investments will be determined by the information contained in the prospectus. Investors can also be helped to make assessments of funds and their managers by using a rating service. For example, Morningstar will rate funds using a star system to help customers assess the specific funds (eg large cap funds or emerging market funds) of different providers. The best funds are those earning four or five stars out of a maximum of five.

Future developments in the fund management industry

Commentators suggest successful future asset management organizations will look primarily at two areas: 1) The number of products on offer, whether this will be narrow and reliant on specialization or broad to take advantage of passive investment in market-mimicking products; 2) The method of distribution, deciding whether it will be affiliated to other areas or open to all.

In the future, four main areas of development have been suggested by the IA, with several business models put forward that can be summarized as: Alpha or active investment houses; Beta factories; specialized outcome investment products; and high-volume distribution outlets.

The search for Alpha

Alpha is one of several technical risk ratios which may help investors determine the risk return profile of a mutual fund and its performance. It is often used as a surrogate for active management of investments as it compares the actual return on investment from a fund with the return on a comparative benchmark with the positive or negative difference between the two being attributed to the investment decisions of the fund manager. A number may be used to represent the Alpha score, for example, +2 or −7; however, these numbers are the percentage difference between the fund's return and the benchmark index, effectively therefore showing the return on investment which is not a result of a general market movement.

One assumption made when using Alpha as a performance measure is that the portfolio being measured is diversified and as such there is no unsystematic risk. Alpha initially came to prominence with the development of composite funds which mimic indices such as the S&P 500. This gave a benchmark against which managers could be measured to ascertain if their active decision making had produced a higher return than could be achieved with a passive fund.

Over recent years there has been a move from active management to passive management funds with online or 'robo' advisers which specialize in investment in index-tracking funds. Two main reasons for this have been suggested:

1 Index benchmarks are being seen to beat asset managers most of the time, which has led to a lack of faith in the capabilities of asset managers.

2 Fees are often still charged where a zero or close to zero Alpha is returned, and as such, investors may face a small loss.

For example, where an investor is charged a fee of 1.2 per cent of AUM per annum and the portfolio produces an Alpha of 1 (ie 1 per cent increase in value) the overall net effect will be a reduction in the value of the individual's portfolio.

Reasons put forward for the fall in Alpha generated over time include:

- a smaller number of investors prepared to include risk within their portfolios;
- an increased amount of money invested to achieve Alpha;
- technological advances making it easier for would-be investors to engage directly with the market through the internet.

Alpha, despite its potential as a metric, does need to be used with caution as it can be tempting to compare the Alphas of different types of funds or portfolios with each other. However, analysis will only be meaningful if assets which are in the same classes are compared. In addition, as Alpha uses a benchmark for comparison it is very important the benchmark is appropriate for the analysis being undertaken. In some cases, where no suitable benchmark is available it may be possible to synthesize a benchmark using algorithms.

Suggestions have been put forward that Alpha 'shops' will emerge in the future global fund market as, whilst the proportion of funds looking towards passive investment will increase, there will remain a sizeable value of funds where investors are looking for Alpha and they will be prepared to pay to achieve this, which in turn may lead to a proportional increase in revenues. Portfolios geared to Alpha, it is felt, will look to long-term investment strategy to allow growth, and will also benefit from the use of leverage.

Investors will include both institutions and high net worth, sophisticated individual investors who are willing to pay for individual products or products as part of a multi-asset investment solution.

Institutions specializing in Alpha will be using differentiation to produce a unique selling proposition (USP) for a limited number of clients. This will be achieved by using their specific asset or investment strategy expertise coupled with their size which will allow them to outperform other managers in the same area. There will however be a trade-off between the benefits which can be achieved from scale and the focus which may be lost as an organization grows. Technology will potentially both help and hinder firms, depending on their size. The development of data analytics and big data with their associated costs are making it more difficult to achieve Alpha, and as such it is more likely that the firms with the ability and money to utilize these analytical tools will be more successful.

Beta factories

Currently passive funds represent a small proportion of the total funds under management, but they are growing at a rapid rate and are the major source of new funds into the market. This has led to an increase in the number of asset classes and segments which have Beta funds available and an increase in the number of distribution channels. Passive managers rely on a low-cost high-volume model; however, even here there are developments in areas such as smart Beta which has the potential to drive the market to greater levels of innovation. As such there will be a reliance on operating scale to drive businesses, combined with high levels of liquidity and product development as well as requiring flexibility to adapt to price-point movements in the market.

Outcome-orientated investment products

Outcome-orientated products build portfolio strategy around overcoming a specific situation, for example mitigating a risk, achieving a specific goal or indeed multiple objectives. In real life, such objectives may be maximizing the Sharpe ratio or outperforming other manager funds in the same area or producing an absolute return. To be able to achieve success in such circumstances fund managers will need to have expertise in multi-asset portfolio construction as well as manager and market oversight. It is not expected that all such products will be complex: in fact it is anticipated end-user retail investing may be one of the most lucrative areas and access to retail users a competitive advantage.

The end-user market is segmented with importance placed on the following:

- High net worth investors who require more sophisticated solutions.
- Institutions looking to invest defined contribution pensions and endowments, for example. It is thought this segment may be one of the most competitive with the potential to add value by the outsourcing of CIO functions as part of the service.
- Independent IFAs looking to support mass market investors, and whose firms lack the potential scale to construct relevant portfolios and as such will seek asset managers with pre-packaged solutions to their requirements.

Distribution powerhouses

The distribution powerhouse is like the operating model currently seen in retail banking; the products on offer may not be the best in class, but due to the size and organization of the business involved, their ability to market products to a large audience and their access to a large segment of available retail funds they control a sizeable proportion of markets such as mortgages, savings etc. Such businesses, with similar market penetration have an ideal platform to launch products as consumers will ask advice of their current providers. In addition, it is felt their ability to collect and manipulate 'big data' will also provide a market advantage allowing 'sales' to maximize efficiency within the contact base.

As with all potential frameworks the competitive models above are unlikely in most cases to work independently of each other with most combinations being seen, except perhaps a combination of Alpha houses and Beta factories. Despite these combinations, it is expected individual organizations are expected to lean towards one speciality.

Summary

This chapter is an introductory snapshot of the size and complexity of the currency investment industry, the main organizations involved in the industry, and movements in fund levels and types in both the global and the UK asset management industry. This is such a complex area that there are whole books dedicated to the analysis of the industry both historically and in respect to anticipated future developments. However, we have identified a number of key developments which may impact the industry in the years to come: the rise of technology; an expectation by customers of flexible access to goods and services (not only in investing but in all aspects of life); changes in the policy direction in the UK following Brexit and in the US following the election of President Trump; an ageing population and movements towards passive investing. We are living in a fast-paced and volatile time which is likely to see fundamental changes in the asset management industry, as asset managers look to justify fees and investors look to maximize returns.

Check your understanding

1. What type of investment strategies have seen the largest growth in recent times, active or passive strategies?
2. Is the investment industry a significant export for the UK or a significant import?
3. What reasons do some commentators give for the reduction in Alpha return over recent years?
4. Which type of organization is most likely to be able to use 'big data' to help it attract new customers and funds?

Further reading

The following books may be useful:

Pinedo, M (2015) *Global Asset Management: An introduction to its processes and costs*, available at www.stern.nyu.edu/om/faculty/pinedo/processes_costs/chapterone.pdf

Walter, I (2015) *The Industrial Organization of the Global Asset Management Business*, CFA Institute Research Foundation

The following websites may be useful.

Employment information and details of professional qualifications

The Personal Investment Management and Financial Advice Association: www.pimfa.com.uk
Chartered Financial Analysts Institute: www.cfainstitute.org
Chartered Institute of Securities and Investment: www.cisi.org

Data and analysis of the global investment management

The Investment Association: www.theinvestmentassociation.org
The Association of International Wealth Management: www.theaiwm.org
Investment and Pensions Europe: www.ipe.com
Boston Consulting Group: www.bcg.com

Regulatory developments

The Financial Conduct Authority: www.fca.org.uk
The European system of financial supervision: https://ec.europa.eu/info/business-economy-euro/banking-and-finance/financial-supervision-and-risk-management/european-system-financial-supervision_en

Main market participants 03

By the end of this chapter you should have an understanding of the main market participants and their contribution, including:

- central bank;
- wholesale banking;
- retail banking;
- private banks;
- investment banks;
- private equity;
- sovereign wealth funds;
- hedge funds;
- pension funds and insurance companies;
- private investors.

Introduction

This chapter will not look to explore every possible market participant in microscopic detail, but will seek to identify and consider the importance of the main market participants who play a key role in the financial markets worldwide. The various participants fulfil different roles within the financial market, some complementary and some competitive; however, what is clear is that each participant has an important part to play in the financial markets, both domestic and global.

It is understood that the success of a secondary market within a country or region is dependent upon a robust and established primary market and the actions of the key market participants to be discussed in this chapter will have an influence upon the operation and success of both the primary and secondary markets in both mature and developing economies.

The emergence or continuation of domestic financial markets also depends upon the level of confidence in the financial market, which is underpinned by such factors as government policy, robust financial regulation and appropriate legislation to ensure fair trading and consumer protection.

It is also clear that the actions and influence of some of the market participants will have a greater impact upon the global markets than others due to the magnitude of funds at their disposal and their professional expertise, particularly in the case of the institutional investors. What is also apparent is that the market participants with greater influence have the ability to affect the financial markets both domestically and globally. The financial markets within any given country or region can only operate effectively if there exists a reasonable degree of liquidity across a range of tradeable assets; that is to say, there must be organizations or individuals who are buying and selling a range of assets within the financial market.

Central banks

> **Keyword**
>
> **Central banks** are not usually market-based institutions but are either owned by a specific country or region, or are afforded specific privileges and protection by the country's or region's laws. A country's central bank will normally have local control over the creation and distribution of money and credit, which gives the central bank the powers of issue for new bank notes and cash within the country. It is also common for the central bank to have the responsibility for implementing a country's monetary policy, together with regulating and supervising the country's banks. It is normal in most developed nations for central banks to be independent from political interference in order to engender confidence in their oversight.
>
> Examples of central banks include:
>
> the Federal Reserve in the United States of America;
>
> the Bank of England in the United Kingdom;
>
> the European Central Bank in the eurozone.

The recent global financial crisis, commonly referred to as the 'credit crunch' (see Chapter 1), fuelled the debate surrounding the need to carefully coordinate monetary, fiscal and regulatory policy within a country or zone, in order to maintain stability. Central banks are therefore in a position to play a key role in maintaining financial stability within a country which clearly affects public confidence in the financial institutions under its umbrella. Historically, it was the opinion of bankers and academics that maintaining low and stable inflation within a country would be sufficient to ensure macroeconomic stability; however, this is now deemed to be a simplistic view of the situation as it ignores such factors as market movements of asset prices. Central banks have also historically been established for other reasons; for example, the Bank of France was established by Napoleon Bonaparte in France, in order to raise finance to fund military operations at the time. Modern-day central banks will usually aim to fulfil three main functions:

1 financing central government planning in lieu of increasing taxation;
2 maintaining and promoting financial market infrastructure and liquidity (monetary aggregate);
3 operating as emergency lender to distressed banks and financial institutions.

Central banks will usually guide monetary policy by controlling and adjusting money supply and interest rates within the country in order to maintain the required financial stability. Central banks will also use tools such as guarantees, capital requirements and reserve requirements to regulate and provide supervision for the country's banks. Quite commonly, the key target for central banks is to maintain price stability by use of monetary policy.

In practice

Example of monetary policy

Price stability is normally described by an interest rate target specified by the government, which for many countries has typically been growth of around 2 per cent per year.

This is deemed to be modest and sustainable and helps to manage economic fluctuations.

A good example of a central bank for us to consider is the Bank of England in the United Kingdom. This is the exemplar that many central banks have based themselves upon and the Bank of England's Monetary Policy Committee adjusts the interest rates within the United Kingdom to levels that it expects will allow the government's inflation target to be met. The Bank of England issues an inflation report each quarter and the rate of inflation within the country may be identified to be either too high or too low, requiring central bank action to be taken. In times when very low levels of interest rates prevail, there may be little room for further interest rate reductions if required and so it may prove necessary to inject money directly into the economy in order to create the required economic stimulus. This technique has become known as quantitative easing and was considered to be a somewhat unconventional element of monetary policy, although this has become quite common in many countries in recent years.

Keyword

Quantitative easing requires the central bank to effectively create new money electronically, using these funds to purchase certain financial assets, for example government bonds, with the aim of encouraging increased private-sector spending in the economy, therefore putting inflation back on target.

Figure 3.1 Quantitative easing

Raising and lowering interest rates is a central bank's main tool for controlling growth; with lower interest rates people are encouraged to spend rather than save and borrowing is inexpensive especially for businesses. However, if interest rates are close to zero, quantitative easing is a tool that a central bank may use to provide stimulus to the economy if demand is weak.

⬇

Quantitative easing requires a central bank to create money and uses it to buy financial assets, such as government bonds and corporate bonds from businesses like pension funds. Quantitative easing does not involve printing more money; new central bank reserves are electronically created and used to purchase the assets in question.

The goal of quantitative easing is to encourage spending, whilst keeping inflation targets on track.

⬇

When the central bank buys assets, such as bonds, this increases their price, reducing the yield (the return) that investors make when they buy gilts. This encourages investors to buy alternative assets with higher yields, such as other corporate bonds and company shares. Demand will see their prices rise, which reduces borrowing costs for businesses which will encourage businesses to spend and invest more, creating jobs and increasing demand in the economy.

Conversely, in times of excessive inflation, interest rates would be increased in order to discourage borrowing and spending and to encourage saving, therefore reducing demand and reducing inflationary pressure.[1]

The Bank of England[2] has a clearly defined role in maintaining financial stability within the United Kingdom to maintain confidence, trust and promote a stable economy by:

- reinforcing trust and confidence in money itself;
- acting as lender and market maker of last resort at times of financial stress;
- promoting the safety and soundness of individual financial institutions (via the Prudential Regulation Authority);
- removing or reducing risks to the financial system as a whole via the Financial Policy Committee;
- supervising financial market infrastructure;
- safely resolving failing financial institutions;
- collaborating with other UK financial authorities to support UK financial sector business continuity and operational resilience.

Wholesale banking

Keyword

Wholesale banking is a broad term but in general it involves the provision of a variety of services between wholesale banks, sometimes referred to as 'merchant banks' and other financial institutions. It involves the practice of lending and borrowing between very large institutions and the provision of other services such as banking services, financing of plant and equipment, brokering deals, trust services and financial services. Wholesale banking is limited in its scope to much larger clients, for example other banks and large corporations or multinational businesses, whilst retail banking will concentrate on small businesses and individual clients.

Examples of wholesale banks include:

Barclays Capital in the United Kingdom;
Merrill Lynch in the United States;
Deutsche Bank in Europe.

Some banks will operate as both merchant banks offering wholesale banking services and as retail banks offering 'high-street' banking services. Wholesale banking will include provision of various services by these merchant banks to a broad range of other organizations such as;

- other banks and retail banks;
- financial institutions such as insurers;
- mortgage brokers;
- large corporate clients and medium-sized companies;
- property developers and property investors;
- international trade finance businesses;
- institutional customers such as pension funds and charities;
- government departments/entities/agencies;
- financial services companies;
- investment fund managers;
- stockbrokers.

Wholesale banking invariably involves corporate relationships or transactions between institutions on a much larger scale than retail banking and deals with the much larger financial needs and requirements of large businesses and institutions. These types of services will usually take place on the interbank market and frequently involve extremely large sums of money, the transactions frequently being offered at lower rates than are charged for retail services.

Borrowing and lending are only two of the services offered to organizations by wholesale banks; however, borrowing funds in sizeable amounts through wholesale financial institutions represents an opportunity for large institutions to obtain access to capital without the need to issue shares or bonds, which is a traditional method of capital raising for businesses. Another merit of this method of capital raising is quick access to funds, which may be crucial in enabling a business to take advantage of a business opportunity which requires rapid action. This type of wholesale funding is effectively a loan which requires structured repayments. This is a similar cashflow arrangement to the regular coupon payments required following the issue of a bond; however, the process requires less time and effort than the issue of a bond or indeed the offer of a new share issue to raise capital. Long-standing, creditworthy and financially secure companies will be able to arrange loans of this type on good terms which reflect a lower-than-average interest rate.

In addition to the lending and borrowing discussed, wholesale banks provide many other services to corporate clients, some of which are:

- fund management;
- currency conversion;
- working capital financing;
- consultancy services;
- underwriting;
- market making;
- mergers and acquisitions facilitation.

General advantages for a large organization utilizing wholesale banking may involve economies of scale: for example, a large corporation may require multiple account facilities for different business locations or multiple business accounts and credit cards for staff and executives. There may also be many hundreds or thousands of transactions each day, which is a scenario not best served by traditional retail banking services.

There are, of course, risks on both sides of the wholesale banking service and the providers of the service will price their services accordingly, whilst organizations using wholesale banking must satisfy themselves regarding the solvency of the bank that they do business with.

Retail banking

Keyword

Retail banking may also be referred to as consumer banking or mass-market banking and is distinct from other types of banking such as wholesale banking and investment banking, although it is not uncommon for a banking group to be active in all of these markets. Retail banking has its focus on individual consumers and small businesses and is usually branch-focused, offering services such as:

- debit and credit cards;
- current or chequing accounts;
- savings;

- mortgages;
- personal loans;
- other financial services such as insurance;
- advisory services (such as small business advisers).

Examples of retail banks include:

HSBC in the United Kingdom and Far East;

Santander in UK and Europe;

Bank of America in the United States of America.

Many consumers still prefer to make use of local branch banking services, where bank staff are available to provide immediate or appointment-based customer service to cater for the retail customer's banking requirements and needs, although many customers, particularly young people, prefer the flexibility of telephone or internet provision. Retail banks attempt to offer a broad spectrum of services and products to provide for the financial needs of retail clients. However, the ease with which clients may now 'shop around' and compare the prices of products and services with those of their competitors has created a difficult situation for retail banks. Factors such as demographics, growth and spread of technology, customer expectations and regulatory requirements have created the need for the retail banks to consider their offerings and their business model. Consumers expect that the full range of services will be available to them, but at their convenience, and the reality is that multiple local branches with many qualified staff, available throughout the week and the weekend, would represent an expensive overhead for a retail bank.

This has prompted the retail banks to explore both telephone and internet banking services whilst also expanding the services offered to retail banking customers. Branch networks are being reduced by most retail banks in favour of the 'remote' services, whilst equipping their teams of staff and advisers with a broad range of services and products, including wealth management, advisory services, private banking and retirement planning. Some retail banks also offer products and services through third-party links to other specialist providers. Improvements in convenience is increasingly being demanded by both small businesses and consumers and this has seen the appearance of 'challenger banks' such as Atom Bank and Metro Bank in the United Kingdom which are internet-based and have no network of branches to support.

Private banks

Keyword

Private banks provide a personal and bespoke banking and financial services provision which is usually targeted at a bank's wealthier clients, who are typically termed 'high net worth individuals'. The definition of high net worth individuals varies globally; for example, many banks in the United Kingdom would consider an individual to be of high net worth if they have £500,000 in liquid assets, whereas many private banks in the United States have a threshold of $1 million in liquid assets.

Private banks may be owned by an individual, a group of partners or be part of a larger group of companies and have had a long tradition in countries like Switzerland and the United Kingdom. To a lesser extent, private banks may also be sometimes refered to as 'non-government-owned banks' in some countries where nationalized banks were common, such as in some communist and socialist states.

Examples of private banks include:

Julius Baer in Zurich;

Brown Brothers Harriman & Co in New York;

C Hoare & Co in London.

Privacy is one of the key benefits of private banking, typically associated with Swiss banks and the dealings and services provided to and offered on behalf of private bank clients can usually be relied upon to remain anonymous. Private banks are in a position to provide their high net worth clients with bespoke services and advice and since these individuals have more wealth than typical individuals within the population, they will have the ability to access a much broader spectrum of products including both conventional and alternative investments.

It is common for clients of a private bank to be appointed a personal relationship manager or account manager and they will familiarize themselves with the client and their circumstances in some detail in order to tailor a bespoke service to the client. The client will liaise directly with their relationship manager, which maintains the privacy and exclusivity of the relationship and dealings are kept confidential in order to reduce the possibility of a competitor bank luring the client away.

The services provided go beyond the bespoke investment-related advice and incorporate all facets of the client's financial circumstances, for example, providing business finance solutions, future generation wealth planning, retirement planning and personal and family protection planning. One of the benefits offered in addition to the private, bespoke provision may include certain discounted services, for example, travel insurance and attractive foreign exchange rates for currency.

Private banking has faced some significant challenges in recent years, particularly following the global 'credit crunch', as the regulatory environment has become more challenging and there has been a requirement for greater transparency and accountability. There has been a requirement to demonstrate greater professionalism within the industry and a need to evidence that advice given to clients is appropriate and meets their needs and requirements. Additionally, high turnover of bank employees has not been helpful to the private banking industry, since the relationship between the client and the account manager is of fundamental importance to maintaining client satisfaction – and with this sort of offering, client satisfaction is paramount.

Investment banks

Keyword

Investment banks are financial intermediaries offering a wide spectrum of services to a variety of clients, many of them specializing in large and complicated financial transactions on behalf of their clients, although some do have retail divisions which provide services to individual high net worth customers. Not all investment banks are considered to be large institutions; however, large investment banks with global client bases make the full use of their size as an asset and are able to benefit from their huge client base to link sellers with buyers for mutual advantage. There are some investment banks which are more specialized than others, for example, specializing in specific sectors of industry.

Examples of large investment banks include:

Goldman Sachs in the United States;

Barclays Capital in the United Kingdom;

Credit Suisse in Switzerland.

Investment banking is considered to be a specialized division of banking, often thought of in relation to the creation of capital for clients, or raising capital on their behalf. Many of the investment banks are an integral part of a larger banking group and may also be sub-divided into separate 'private' and 'public' divisions. The demarcation between these divisions is important because the private departments of the investment bank may be handling matters involving privileged insider information that cannot be disclosed freely, whilst the public departments will be dealing with freely available information. The professional integrity of the company is at risk if this separation is not maintained.

We have mentioned that the services offered to their clients by investment banks are wide and varied and these services include:

- fulfilling a role as broker and/or financial adviser for institutional clients;
- assisting companies to list on an appropriate stock exchange;
- underwriting issues of securities;
- acting as an intermediary between a securities issuer and the investing public;
- facilitating and acting as intermediaries for mergers, acquisitions and corporate reorganizations;
- providing discretionary fund management services for private clients.

It is clear that investment banks assist companies to issue new shares as an initial public flotation or as a follow-on offering, whilst also facilitating debt financing by sourcing appropriate investors for corporate bond issues. The support offered to a client would include checking financial statements for accuracy and publishing of supporting documentation to explain the issue of securities to prospective investors prior to purchase. Investment banking is generally split into two main lines of business, which are referred to as 'sell-side' and 'buy-side'. The sell-side involves the trading of securities or the promotion of securities, whilst the buy-side centres on the advice process for clients requiring investment services. Not all investment banks will offer both buy- and sell-side services, some investment banks, particularly the smaller ones will specialize.

Typical clients of investment banks are varied and include:

- governments and government departments;
- banks;
- private equity funds;
- mutual funds;

- hedge funds;
- individual investors;
- corporations;
- life insurance companies;
- unit trusts;
- charities;
- local authorities.

Investment banks will make money in different ways either by generating profits through trading or by deriving fees as a result of advisory, facilitation and consultancy services. Jobs in investment banking are invariably well remunerated; however, as with many professions in the City, working hours can be long and unpredictable and it is also a highly stressed environment at times.

Private equity

Keyword

Private equity is also an asset class and consists of a combination of equity securities and debt in non-publicly traded operating companies and therefore private equity is not listed on a stock exchange. Private equity may also be identified as the broad category of private capital which refers to a situation where capital is supporting a long-term but usually illiquid investment strategy. Private equity investments are usually facilitated by a private equity firm with defined aims and investment strategies, which invests in the equity of companies making use of a variety of investment strategies, but typically leveraged buyout.

Private equity is therefore a rather broad spectrum which commonly refers to any 'investor' that is not listed on a recognized global stock market. Common investment strategies for private equity firms include leveraged buyouts, growth capital for more mature companies and venture capital for young or less mature companies aimed at launching or expanding fledgling companies.

A typical strategy for private equity firms is to acquire majority holding in underperforming mature companies which exhibit potential for good future growth. Growth in the underperforming company is created using a combination of strategies:

- utilizing the management team to improve performance;
- use of additional investment to create expansion;
- implementation of operational improvements;
- new product development;
- restructuring of the company's operations and/or management.

The model for a typical private equity firm will be a long-term multiyear investment into illiquid assets; for example, a mature company or property development which will allow the private equity firm to have control over management and assets to exert influence over the long-term returns. Individual private equity firms may specialize in specific industries or sectors utilizing their knowledge and expertise. This technique of leveraged buyout may also be successfully utilized to acquire a publicly held asset, bringing it under the control of the private equity firm. It is worth mentioning that short selling is not utilized in this asset class and therefore only long positions are appropriate.

Private equity firms would normally look to manage an acquired company for a number of years during which time the management and prospects of the company could be improved prior to relaunching the 'repaired' company on the stock market and, hopefully, crystallizing a significant profit. However, another strategy would include asset stripping the company and selling off appealing or desirable parts of the company or its assets, again at a profit.

The private equity fund is created as a limited partnership between the private equity firm and the partner investors who will provide additional investment capital to fund the company acquisitions. Investment capital is raised from a variety of sources and both institutional and retail investors provide the capital which may be employed for a variety of uses including new/upgraded technology, additional acquisitions, funding working capital and supporting the company's balance sheet. Partner investors may include:

- public pension funds;
- corporate pension funds;
- foundations;
- endowments;
- fund of funds;
- universities;
- insurance companies;
- high net worth individual investors.

Clearly, it is a requirement that the investors are in a position to tie up considerable tranches of money for a long timescale to allow sufficient time to successfully transform the fortunes of an underperforming or distressed company to allow a successful and profitable sale or listing. One of the most comprehensive studies of private equity performance was carried out in 2005 and although based upon private equity in the United States, still gives an interesting analysis.[3] The study suggests that some returns after fees are comparable with appropriate market returns; however, significant variation is observed across different funds, and a degree of persistency in performance is also noted. Availability of data has traditionally been a potential issue and particularly in the United Kingdom, which is recognized as the second largest private equity market globally, transparency has been considered and addressed. Such areas as management and performance fee structures together with the substantial salaries of the private equity firm employees are now more readily accessible, although this does not apply globally. Typical fee structures for private equity firms do vary quite significantly, but usually include both a performance fee and a management fee, together with retention of a share of the final profits generated. The risk that the potential investor must consider is that in the worst-case scenario, the intervention into the purchased company may be unsuccessful and may not result in a real improvement in the company's fortunes. This may ultimately result in the company being sold at a loss after a period of time, or an inability to sell or refloat the company on an exchange.

Sovereign wealth funds

Considering the maturity of the global financial markets, sovereign wealth funds are a comparatively new but nevertheless important institutional aspect of global finance, which represent the investment portfolios of individual countries.

Keyword

Sovereign wealth funds are comprised of money which a particular country may allocate from its reserves for investment purposes, with the ultimate aim of benefiting the country's economy. The reserves set aside for investment will usually be allocated by an individual country's central bank and may have been accumulated as a result of selling natural resources, such as oil or minerals, or alternatively derived as a result of either trading or budget surpluses.

The general trend has been that a country's sovereign wealth fund portfolio aims and allocations will be either driven by that country's strategic plans or as a part of the country's planned national development. Alexander Dyck and Adair Morse carried out some research on sovereign wealth funds in 2011 to examine the investment methods and goals.[4] It can be identified that the investment types and asset classes used by sovereign wealth funds will vary significantly between different countries, dependent upon their individual aims and priorities. Many sovereign wealth funds will prefer returns rather than liquidity and therefore have an elevated risk tolerance; however, a country which, for example, is concerned with the liquidity of their invested portfolio may restrict their investment strategy to very liquid assets. Although some funds may choose to invest indirectly in domestic industry, a recent article in the *Financial Times* commented that many sovereign wealth funds have chosen to avoid investing directly in private businesses due to issues surrounding valuations and the impact of other pressures.[5]

It is apparent that as the size and number of the world's sovereign wealth funds continue to increase, they will play an increasing role in the global financial markets and indeed in influencing corporate governance. It has been the aim for some countries to use these funds to augment national benefits; for example, Japan faces the demographic problems of an ageing population and diminishing labour market and therefore the sovereign wealth fund aims to assist with the provision of benefits to the retired population. Conversely, some countries such as the United Arab Emirates have a significant reliance upon natural resources for the country's wealth and therefore one of the aims of the sovereign wealth fund is to diversify revenue streams in the future. Commonly observed objectives of sovereign wealth funds include:

- increased returns in comparison to foreign exchange reserves;
- diversification of income from non-renewable commodity revenue;
- diversification of excess liquidity;
- building sustainable long-term capital growth;
- supporting political strategy;
- promotion of required social and economic development;
- protection of economy from excessive volatility in markets;
- augmentation and promotion of investment in future generations.

Table 3.1 Sovereign wealth fund rankings as at June 2016

Country	Sovereign wealth fund	Assets ($bn)	Inception date	Origin	Transparency Index*
Norway	Government Pension Fund - Global	850	1990	Oil	10
China	China Investment Corporation	814	2007	Non-commodity	8
UAE–Abu Dhabi	Abu Dhabi Investment Authority	792	1976	Oil	6
Saudi Arabia	SAMA Foreign Holdings	598	1952	Oil	4
Kuwait	Kuwait Investment Authority	592	1953	Oil	6
China	SAFE Investment Company	474	1997	Non-commodity	4
China–Hong Kong	Hong Kong Monetary Authority Investment Portfolio	442	1993	Non-commodity	8
Singapore	Government of Singapore Investment Corporation	350	1981	Non-commodity	6
Qatar	Qatar Investment Authority	335	2005	Oil & gas	5
China	National Social Security Fund	236	2000	Non-commodity	5
UAE–Dubai	Investment Corporation of Dubai	196	2006	Non-commodity	5
Singapore	Temasek Holdings	194	1974	Non-commodity	10
Saudi Arabia	Public Investment Fund	160	2008	Oil	4
UAE–Abu Dhabi	Abu Dhabi Investment Council	110	2007	Oil	n/a
Australia	Australian Future Fund	95	2006	Non-commodity	10

(continued)

Table 3.1 (Continued)

Country	Sovereign wealth fund	Assets ($bn)	Inception date	Origin	Transparency Index*
South Korea	Korea Investment Corporation	92	2005	Non-commodity	9
Kazakhstan	Kazakhstan National Fund	77	2000	Oil	2
Russia	National Welfare Fund	74	2008	Oil	5
Kazakhstan	Samruk-Kazyna JSC	69	2008	Non-commodity	n/a
UAE–Abu Dhabi	International Petroleum Investment Company	66	1984	Oil	9

SOURCE Sovereign Wealth Fund Institute[6]

* Linaburg-Maduell Transparency Index:[7] the Sovereign Wealth Fund Institute implemented this index in 2008. It is a 10-point scale based on 10 essential principles of transparency, each of which adds one point to the fund's index rating. This index is used by sovereign wealth funds within their published annual reports.

Sovereign wealth funds are rated in terms of their transparency by the Linaburg–Maduell Transparency Index, which was developed at the Sovereign Wealth Fund Institute by Carl Linaburg and Michael Maduell in 2008. This was a technique for measuring and indicating transparency to the public at a time when concerns were being voiced regarding the possibility of 'unethical agendas' being followed by certain sovereign wealth funds. The method is based around the application of 10 essential principles and a fund's rating on the index may change as additional information is released by the fund.[7]

In 2009, the International Forum of Sovereign Wealth Funds (IFSWF) was created, which is a global network of sovereign wealth funds. It was created to facilitate collaboration, dialogue regarding issues of common interest and to promote broader understanding of sovereign wealth funds' activities. There was also the aim to raise the standards for best practice and governance and voluntary acceptance of the Santiago Principles, the focus of which is transparency, accountability and prudent investment practices. The Santiago Principles, comprising 24 generally accepted principles and practices voluntarily adopted by IFSWF members, were identified by an International Working Group of Sovereign Wealth Funds and embraced by the International Monetary Fund's International Monetary Financial Committee in 2008. Objectives of the Principles are to:

- help maintain a stable global financial system and free flow of capital and investment;
- comply with all applicable regulatory and disclosure requirements in the countries in which sovereign wealth funds invest;
- ensure that sovereign wealth funds invest on the basis of economic and financial risk and return-related considerations;
- ensure that sovereign wealth funds have in place a transparent and sound governance structure that provides adequate operational controls, risk management and accountability.

Compliance with the Principles means that sovereign wealth funds will contribute to maintaining the stability of the global financial system, help to preserve an open and stable investment climate, and provide the opportunity for knowledge sharing which promotes continuous improvement and innovation.

Hedge funds

> **Keyword**
>
> **Hedge funds** originated in the 1940s and began as a way to reduce, or hedge, the risk in an investment fund, hence the name. Hedge funds are similar to mutual funds in that they are professionally managed and hold pools of capital to be invested on behalf of the investors; however, that is really where the similarity ends. Hedge funds are usually set up as limited liability partnerships or limited companies and are accessible mainly to a restricted number of accredited investors, institutional investors and experienced wealthy individuals; for example, corporate and public pension funds, insurance companies, charitable foundations, trusts and investment banks.

Hedge funds usually specify a substantial initial minimum investment amount and often also specify minimum investment periods which mean that from the investors' point of view they can be quite illiquid. Disinvestment may also be restricted to bi-annual or quarterly windows and this is referred to as being 'locked in'.

Hedge funds are viewed as alternative investments and use a variety of different strategies to pursue positive returns (alpha) on behalf of their investors. Hedge Funds are associated with aggressive management and may invest in a wide variety of assets; for example, equities, structured products, derivatives and commodities, often with complex portfolio construction and utilizing various risk management techniques. Use may be made of leverage and the fund may be active in both domestic and international markets with the usual aim being to generate absolute returns, regardless of the prevailing market conditions. The investment technique of leverage is essentially investing with borrowed money, which is a technique that could significantly increase potential return, but which also creates greater risk of loss. The nature of a hedge fund's asset mix will often mean that they may have low correlations with traditional portfolios comprised of company shares and bonds, which means that hedge funds may provide good diversification if the higher level of investment risk can be tolerated by the investor. Hedge funds would normally focus on a variety of short- or medium-term liquid securities and would not have direct control over a company or asset that they are investing in. Hedge funds will often be found to specialize in specific types of investments and transactions and because they are known to specialize in more speculative investments, they represent a higher level of investment risk than the overall market.

The strategy of different hedge funds is designed to make the most of certain market opportunities and therefore different hedge funds may be classified according to their investment style. This enables a degree of diversity in risk attributes and investment opportunities among hedge funds, affording appropriate investors flexibility and benefiting investors with a range of choices between differing funds. However, despite the general expectation that hedge funds signify risk and therefore volatility, there are times when this may not always be the case. According to research undertaken by the Hennessee Group, published in the *Hedge Fund Journal*, hedge funds were approximately one-third less volatile than the S&P 500 Index between 1993 and 2010.[8]

In terms of regulation, hedge funds (unlike mutual funds) were largely unregulated, mainly because they are not used by retail investors. However, in the aftermath of the global 'credit crunch', regulation has begun to include hedge funds, with the larger funds finding it much easier to absorb the associated costs of regulation. For example: previously in the USA the laws required that the majority of investors in a hedge fund be 'accredited'. This meant in practice that the investors must have substantial earnings, subject to a minimum amount of money annually and have a net worth of more than $1 million, together with a significant amount of investment knowledge and experience.

Hedge funds are run by a hedge fund manager or managers, who are responsible for the investment decisions and strategies pursued by the fund in order to achieve its stated aims and objectives. Managers of hedge funds are usually extremely well remunerated and therefore, despite the highly stressed nature of the job, it is often seen as an attractive career option. The most successful managers have clear investment strategies together with a strategy for risk management, good capitalization and a sound marketing and sales model. Hedge fund managers differ in their approach to transparency: some will only explain their strategies and performance record to clients whilst others take a much more open approach and publish periodic investment updates which are open to be publicly studied.

Hedge fund managers are usually remunerated by a combination of management fees and performance-related incentives. The management fees are usually based on a percentage of the assets under management, whilst the performance-related incentives are generally bonuses based upon a percentage of any profit generated by the fund. Typically, this may be a 2 per cent annual management fee plus an incentive bonus of up to 20 per cent of the profit accrued, although it is quite common to see fee caps in place to discourage excessive risk taking by managers. It is worth noting that hedge fund investors are usually quite happy to see the fund manager receive a huge annual bonus since this reflects an exceptional performance of the fund, from which they will benefit.

Pension funds and insurance companies

Many insurance companies operate and offer pension funds to their policyholders; however, the category of pension funds also includes occupational pension funds, provided by employers for the benefit of their employees. For this reason, pension funds deserve a separate heading although both pension funds and insurance companies are both major institutional investors in their own right.

> **Keyword**
>
> **Insurance companies** are usually classified as either mutual or proprietary; mutual insurance companies are owned by their policyholders and proprietary insurance companies are owned by shareholders. The model for insurance companies is to pool risk for specific types of loss by providing cover and charging premiums to large groups, in the knowledge that not all of the insured will incur the insured loss.

Insurance companies make use of statistical analysis to predict claim rates for specific types of losses and in this way will generate profit for the company. Insurance companies will therefore have capital to invest derived from policy premiums in addition to pooled funds being invested on behalf of clients. Examples of these types of pooled funds would be mutual funds, OEICs, unit trusts and exchange-traded funds. Individuals will invest in these types of professionally managed pooled funds which, in turn, will invest the capital in a variety of securities such as company shares, government bonds and corporate bonds.

> **Keyword**
>
> A **pension fund** is a fund or scheme which accumulates funds for the provision of retirement income, either for an individual or groups of individuals once they stop working.

Pension funds may be categorized in several different ways: they may be public or private, and may be either defined benefit or defined contribution. With defined benefit, the provider of the pension scheme guarantees the employee a specific benefit upon their retirement, whilst a defined contribution merely specifies the level of contribution into the pension plan; the benefits are then subject to market performance. Demand for defined contribution schemes has tended to be higher than defined benefit schemes in recent years for two reasons: firstly, because employers who sponsor the schemes have attempted to minimize the monetary risk and magnitude of their obligations; and secondly, because employees mindful of future employment mobility look to access funds that are easily and efficiently transferable between future employers.

Pension funds are also important shareholders of both listed and private companies together with holding a range of other assets which form a diverse and often risk-averse strategy.

In practice

Investment strategies in different countries are driven by a variety of factors, some of them country-specific or regulation-focused and the more mature pension markets, for example the US and UK markets, tend to have greater tolerance for equities within the funds. Pension funds will usually have a long investment horizon and this, combined with a diverse asset mix, a strategy of asset–liability matching and experienced professional management, allows a certain tolerance of investment risk.[9] The long-term investment horizon of pension funds is supported by the fact that an individual's access to their accumulating pension fund is usually severely restricted or even prohibited until their appropriate retirement date. This predominance of long-term liabilities allows pension funds the flexibility of investing into a wide and diverse spectrum of financial assets, including the holding of high-risk and high-return instruments.

Typically, domestic holdings may also include corporate equities, commercial property, government bonds, corporate bonds, securitized loans, with money market instruments and cash deposits to enhance liquidity. Additionally, foreign holdings of the assets and instruments previously mentioned may be used at the discretion of the pension fund manager. The growth of pension funds is also driven by the prevailing demographics of the mature economies, which feature ageing populations, but also the emerging markets and increasing earnings among the populations with the ability to save and invest for their future.

Growth of a country's insurance and pensions sector is broadly associated with the country's economic development and the strongest of these areas is currently the United States together with Northern European countries. The broad nature of the investments generated by these institutional tranches of capital are of great importance and influence within the financial markets globally and in both developed and developing countries, institutional investment supports government borrowing, corporate borrowing and expansion, as a result of purchasing securities such as bonds and company shares. The diverse nature of institutional investment ensures that a wide spectrum of assets (short-, medium- and long-term) have a willing market and are used to support strategies based upon risk management, diversification and liability matching techniques. Institutional investors such as insurance companies and pension funds are particularly important to the stock markets of individual countries which are usually dominated by big institutional investors. For instance, a recent report by the European Fund and Asset Management Association revealed that almost 75 per cent of the assets under management in Europe were derived from institutional sources, evidencing the key role played by institutional investors in financing the economies of European countries.[10]

The large and regular investment in the capital markets by the institutional investors also helps to maintain liquidity within the markets and in no small way helps the growth of developing countries since the maturity and development of a capital market improves the access for overseas investment into a country. The significant involvement of institutional investors in the equity and bond markets may also have a positive effect on topical issues such as corporate governance due to the positive pressures exerted by institutional investors supportive of the growing drive towards transparency, sustainability and good corporate governance.

Private investors

Keyword

Private investors are individuals, or in some cases groups of individuals, who are investing money, in contrast to companies or financial organizations investing money.

A private investor will invest their money with the expectation of a positive financial return, although the expectations of individual investors are often unrealistic and may sometimes be considered by investment professionals to be naïve. Private investors utilize a variety of different investments with the intention to achieve capital growth, provide an income stream or a combination of both. A very wide variety of investment vehicles appropriate for a private investor exist and these include:

- company shares (domestic and overseas);
- government, municipal and corporate bonds (domestic and overseas);
- commodities;
- cash and money deposits;
- collective investment funds (such as investment bonds, unit trusts, OEICS, investment trusts);
- exchange-traded funds;
- property (commercial and residential);
- options and futures
- endowment plans and pension plans.

Private investors may perform their own research involving basic or technical analysis to inform their decisions and help them to recognize investment opportunities, depending upon their level of knowledge and experience of the financial markets. Alternatively, they may seek the help and advice of an industry professional such as a stockbroker, financial adviser or an agent of one of the financial institutions, to assist with the investment decisions and process.

Some experienced and knowledgeable private investors have gained some level of understanding regarding the influencing factors related to investment finance; this financial awareness will help a private investor to understand the mechanism of the investment marketplace allowing them the opportunity to be more successful. Many private investors, however, will rely upon the advice and professionalism available from industry advisers and consultants, who will give advice to private investors to help them achieve their aims and objectives. In most mature economies there exists a robust and established system for investor protection through a combination of laws, financial regulations and enforcements by government agencies, set up to ensure that the financial market is fair, advice is appropriate and impartial and fraudulent activities are eliminated.

> **In practice**
>
> Examples of regulatory bodies and government agencies providing investor protection include:
>
> - Securities and Exchange Commission in the United States;
> - Financial Conduct Authority in the United Kingdom;
> - Securities and Futures Commission in Hong Kong.
>
> All of these exist to protect the interests of investors.

In general, the financial markets in countries with strong and robust systems to provide investor protection will usually grow and prosper more readily and quickly than the financial markets in countries with ineffective or poor levels of investor protection. Protection for investors will also include such measures as requirements for accurate financial reporting by public and private companies in order that investors can make informed decisions and have confidence in the data published by companies.

As a generalization, private investors will prefer to minimize the risk applicable to their investment whilst maximizing the returns that they achieve. In practice, private investors will encompass a wide variation of risk tolerances, investment styles, available capital, investment preferences and horizons. For example, cautious investors would have a preference for very low-risk investments and vehicles, such as cash deposits and government bonds, which would be expected to deliver modest returns in the financial market. Investors with a more balanced attitude to risk may be prepared to accept proportionately more risk if there is the possibility of realizing greater returns and may therefore be prepared to invest in more risky assets such as corporate bonds, property and even company shares. Aggressive investors are likely to be prepared to accept additional risk in an attempt to achieve greater investment returns and could consider more volatile assets to be attractive, such as commodities, overseas equities and structured products. In a small proportion of cases, aggressive private investors may be prepared to make use of derivative products, which usually involve significant acceptance of risk. However, this is likely to be restricted to wealthy, experienced investors seeking greater than market returns, possibly in difficult or challenging investment conditions and markets.

Private investors may also wish to pursue specific investment practices or consider certain restrictions in their investments in order to satisfy their own personal, ethical or religious beliefs and this has certainly been an area of growth within the financial markets over the last decade. Private investors who are prepared to use collective investments to access professional fund management may find it more convenient to generate long-term capital returns by utilizing the large range of exchange-traded funds, many of which are passively managed index-linked funds. These funds may also provide the private investor with the opportunity to gain access to markets which are difficult to access or markets where the private investor has little or no experience or knowledge.

In practice

It should be noted that whilst financial regulations are in place in many countries to protect private investors, these regulations and laws exist to protect against inappropriate or unqualified advice, financial impropriety and fraud. Regulation does not protect the private investor against the willing acceptance of risk and it is therefore most important that the private investor is realistic about the level of risk that they are prepared to accept and the possible downside to this acceptance of risk. It is a crucial and fundamental cornerstone of the financial advice process that private investors are fully aware of the risks that they are accepting when investing as part of an advised process and that they have been fully informed of those risks and their implications for the investor.

Each individual private investor would usually contribute comparatively small amounts to the overall magnitude of funds invested in the markets; however, there are a very large number of individual private investors so the total amount of funds invested in the markets by all private investors globally is appreciable. Private investors are also very often in need of advice and guidance in respect of their aims and objectives and therefore provide a steady stream of clients for the financial advice industry.

Summary

There is a clear interaction between market participants at different levels as well as the obvious competitive relationships and there are many different examples of this relationship. For instance, central banks will provide ongoing support for the domestic economy broadly, but also for the domestic banking industry specifically by 'wisely' implementing monetary policy. Investment banks may provide both advisory and discretionary services to pension funds and private investors, whilst retail banks, pension funds and insurance companies may also offer investment opportunities to private investors.

Check your understanding

1 Are you clear about the roles that the central, wholesale and retail banks play in the financial economy of each country?
2 What is the purpose of 'quantitative easing'?
3 Why do the aims of sovereign wealth funds differ between countries?
4 Consider the broad importance of pension funds within the economy; who benefits from pension funds?

Further reading

The following books may be useful:

Bodie, Z, Kane, A and Marcus, A (2014) *Essentials of Investments*, global edn, McGraw Hill/Irwin

Harrington, SE and Niehaus, GR (2004) *Risk Management and Insurance*, 2nd edn, McGraw Hill/Irwin

Mishkin, FS and Eakins, S (2005) *Financial Markets and Institutions*, Addison Wesley

The following websites may be useful:

https://www.investor.gov/introduction-investing/basics/how-market-works/market-participants
http://financemainpage.com/Market_Participants.html
http://www.investopedia.com/walkthrough/forex/beginner/level2/market-participants.aspx

Risk   04

By the end of this chapter you should have an understanding of:

- the main types of risk, including:
  - systematic and unsystematic risk;
  - interest rate risk;
  - inflation risk;
  - market risk;
  - credit risk;
  - liquidity risk;
  - political risk;
  - exchange rate risk;
  - capital risk;
  - income risk.
- the key indicators for measuring and monitoring risk.

Introduction

In the context of investing, risk is often loosely defined as the 'uncertainty of a future outcome', although Glyn Holton, writing in the *Financial Analysts Journal*, comments that there is no single accepted definition of 'risk' within the finance discipline.[1]

When looking at risk in the context of investment portfolios, it is reasonable to make the assumption that investors are generally 'risk-averse'; that is to say, if given the choice of two assets with the same rate of return, the risk-averse investor will select the asset with the lower level of risk.

This can be evidenced by looking at corporate bonds. The coupon available on a B-grade corporate bond will be found to be significantly higher than the coupon offered on an AAA-grade corporate bond. This reflects the need for the issuer to offer a higher return on the B-grade corporate bond to compensate for the higher level of risk that an investor must accept when they invest in a B-grade corporate bond relative to an AAA-grade corporate bond.

Equally, as investor we only experience risk when we are actually exposed to it. For example, equities are generally accepted to have a higher level of risk relative to bonds; however, if an investor chooses to invest only in a portfolio of bonds, they will not remove the risk of equities but will be unaffected by it.

Types of risk

To those investors inexperienced in the realities of the risk–reward balance, it may seem that the acceptance of additional risk will bring additional reward but this is most certainly not the case. In taking more risk we increase volatility and this brings with it the chance of greater reward, but also the chance of greater loss. Volatility, often described by standard deviation and beta coefficient, is not a welcome factor in an investment, since it gives an inherent uncertainty to the outcome which is not beneficial to the investor.

In this section we will look at many of the most common types of risk experienced by investors together with the characteristics and dangers of these risks. It is important to have a healthy respect for risk and accurately assessing the risk that an investor is prepared to accept is one of the fundamental foundations of the advice process in the financial services industry. There is invariably some element of risk in every type of *asset class*; however, the type of risk and the degree of risk varies significantly between different asset classes. For example, many inexperienced investors perceive that cash is a riskless asset although this is not the case. It is true to say that cash carries comparatively less risk than many other assets, such as equities, but is still subject to other forms of investment risk itself, such as inflation risk and therefore cannot be thought of as riskless.

Systematic and unsystematic risk

A good starting point from which to consider different types of risk is to look at systematic and unsystematic risk. Systematic risk is also referred to in various texts as market risk and also, helpfully, as non-diversifiable risk. Unsystematic risk is also known as unique risk, non-diversifiable risk, idiosyncratic risk and firm specific risk.

Figure 4.1 Pyramid of investment risk

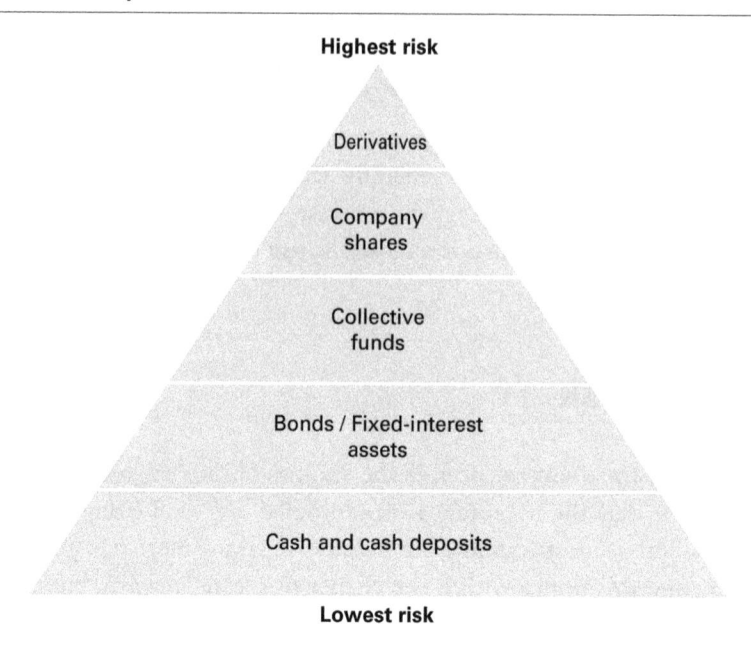

Highest risk

- Derivatives
- Company shares
- Collective funds
- Bonds / Fixed-interest assets
- Cash and cash deposits

Lowest risk

Keyword

Systematic risk is generally considered to be the variability of the returns of an asset which are attributed to the overall market movements and this can be measured by its Beta. An asset's Beta will inform us whether it is considered to be more or less volatile than the market and this is covered in another section (see p 124). This type of risk cannot be mitigated, or reduced, by diversification techniques. An example of a market risk would be a recessionary period, during which the whole market would be affected, not just a single asset class or company.

Unsystematic risk is the risk which is not shared by many different investments and for this reason is often considered to be specific to a particular company or asset. It is therefore possible to successfully use **diversification** techniques to mitigate, or reduce, the unsystematic element of risk within an investment portfolio. Indeed, in a well-diversified investment portfolio, it is reasonable to expect that unsystematic risk can be substantially eliminated. Examples of this type of risk include such things as protracted industrial action, failure of a key product line, and loss of key personnel.

Total risk is usually measured by standard deviation and is the variability of the return of an asset or portfolio. This is comprised of the two components, systematic and unsystematic risk, and therefore if the unsystematic element of risk can be partially or wholly mitigated by successful diversification, the total risk may be substantially reduced. This is discussed further in the section on diversification (see p 135).

Figure 4.2 Effect of diversification

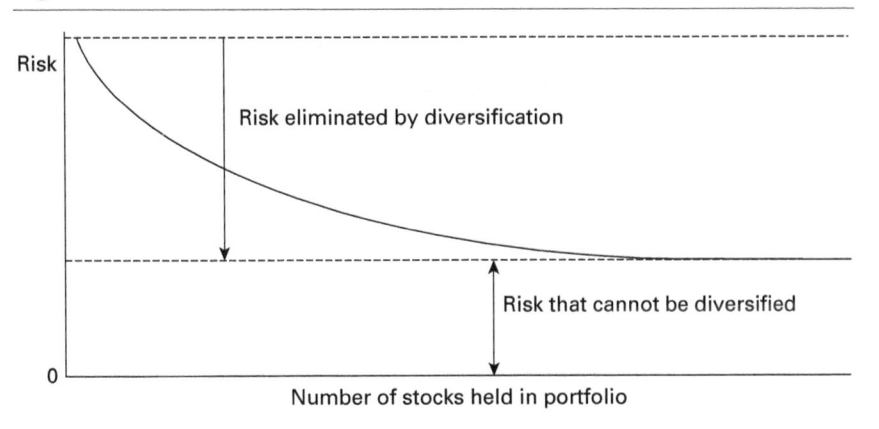

[Graph showing a downward-sloping curve with axes labelled "Risk" (vertical) and "Number of stocks held in portfolio" (horizontal). Annotations indicate "Risk eliminated by diversification" and "Risk that cannot be diversified".]

Systemic risk

Systemic risk should not be confused with systematic risk, which is discussed above. Systemic risk is considered to be the risk of the collapse or breakdown of the entire financial system within a country or region, rather than the risk of an individual asset or component of the financial system. This focuses on the interdependencies and links within financial systems or markets and represents the risk that failure of individual entities or clusters of entities may trigger a cascade effect which could catastrophically affect the entire financial system.

This effect can be effectively illustrated using the example of the problems experienced in the US economy in 2008 during the failure of Lehman Brothers. The company was considered 'too big to fail', was heavily integrated within the US economy and caused substantial market problems as a result of its bankruptcy at that time. During this same period in the late 2000s, the UK government offered substantial financial support to several UK banks in order to mitigate the market problems at that time. In its report, the UK National Audit Office commented that the government support for the banks was considered to be justified to guard against the potential damage to the markets and economy in general that would be caused by failure of one or more of the banks and maintaining confidence in the financial system.[2]

Interest rate risk

> **Keyword**
>
> **Interest rate risk** is the uncertainty regarding the change in market interest rates during the period of the investment.

Interest rate risk is not exclusive to fixed rate assets, for example government bonds, but it may be one of the most significant risks for investors holding fixed rate assets and this is because of the inverse relationship exhibited by bond prices and interest rates.

The duration is considered to be a direct measure of interest rate risk and may be used as an appropriate comparison of risk between fixed rate bonds. This is discussed in more detail in Chapter 5 on investment theory. Duration risk is the risk associated with the sensitivity of a bond's price to a 1 per cent change in interest rates.

Various factors impact upon bond prices, one of which is interest rates, although it is accepted that some bonds are more sensitive to interest rate changes than others. We know that usually, as interest rates rise, bond prices fall and as interest rates fall, so bond prices will rise. This occurs because, when interest rates increase, the opportunity cost of holding a bond effectively decreases as an investor may achieve a greater yield by switching to other investments which reflect the higher interest rate. For example, a bond with a 4 per cent coupon is worth more if interest rates decrease since the holder of the bond receives a fixed rate of return relative to the market, which will offer a lower rate of return as a result of the decrease in rates. We can quantify the likely change in price produced by a 1 per cent change in interest rates by performing a modified duration calculation, which is explained later in the chapter (see p 126).

It follows therefore, that the higher a bond's duration, the greater will be the sensitivity to changes in interest rates and this means that price fluctuations, either positive or negative, will be more pronounced. If a bond is held until maturity, the holder expects to receive the face value (par) when the capital is repaid; however, if the bond is sold on the secondary market prior to maturity, the price received will be influenced by prevailing interest rates and the bond's duration.

The interest rate risk of a particular bond is therefore related to the sensitivity of the bond's price to interest rate changes. This sensitivity depends upon two main factors: the coupon rate of the bond and the bond's remaining time to maturity. Interest rate risk actually has two components: the price risk and the reinvestment risk.

Price risk relates to the possibility that interest rates may change during the period of time between purchase of a particular bond and the expected investment horizon. If interest rates do change and the bond is sold before its maturity date, then the realized price of the bond will differ from its expected price if the interest rates had remained constant.

Reinvestment risk is created because there is an implicit assumption in the yield to maturity calculation that the cashflow generated by the bond's coupon payments will be reinvested at the prevailing interest rate at the time of purchase. Any changes in the market interest rates will therefore affect the ability of the investor to achieve this return.

It is worth commenting that a zero-coupon bond does not experience reinvestment risk since there is no cashflow from the coupon to reinvest. Also of note is that the duration of a zero-coupon bond is the same as its time to maturity due to the absence of a cashflow.

Inflation risk

Keyword

Also sometimes referred to as purchasing power risk, **inflation risk** represents the reduction in the purchasing power of any investment returns made during a given period.

Inflation affects different types of investment returns; for example, both cashflows from coupon payments on bonds and capital growth on equity investments. It is therefore important to have an accurate knowledge of the rate of inflation applicable to any specified period of investment performance being analysed.

When examining investment performance we can calculate nominal growth rate, which is the base growth of the investment. However, the real growth rate takes into account the effect of inflation on the purchasing power of the investment growth. The real growth rate may easily be calculated approximately by simply subtracting the rate of inflation from the growth rate achieved during the period of analysis, although a more accurate method of calculation is usually preferred and this is dealt with later in this chapter (see p 127).

It is rare, but not unheard of, for the rate of inflation in a country or zone to be zero although this situation does not usually exist for extended periods of time. For the duration of the zero-inflation period, the effect of inflation is nullified, but there is always the probability that this rate of inflation will change and therefore the risk still remains a factor to be considered and planned for.

There is the possibility of negative inflation, otherwise known as deflation, within a country or zone and the effect of this would be to enhance the purchasing power of the investment gains made during this deflationary period of time. This may sound an attractive proposition; however, deflationary periods are widely agreed to be bad for the general economy of a country and therefore not beneficial to sustainable, strong investment conditions.

In practice: Japan

The economy in Japan was considered to be stuck in a deflationary period throughout the 1990s. This deflation began in 1989, following an interest rate rise by the Bank of Japan which resulted in problems with the housing asset bubble. This, in turn, resulted in significant non-performing loans within the banking industry which further exacerbated the problems. During the following decade the Japanese economy grew at an average rate of just over 1 per cent, with businesses reducing debt, cutting back on spending and investment and reducing productivity. The Japanese public, fearing recession, stopped spending and saved their money to see them through the anticipated hard times.

According to a study by Daniel Okimoto at Stanford University, based on research by Ito and Mishkin,[3] several key factors contributing to the extended deflationary period were identified, including:

- banks retained non-performing loans on their books, effectively tying up capital needed for investment in the economy;
- tax rises were implemented in the late 1990s;
- the Japanese government did not take effective steps to kick-start the economy.

Market risk

> **Keyword**
>
> **Market risk** is systematic risk and reflects the chance that the value of assets will decrease due to prevailing market factors. It represents the possibility that an investor will incur losses in their investment due to the various factors which can influence the behaviour of the financial markets.

Whilst this type of risk cannot be successfully mitigated or eliminated by techniques such as diversification, it is possible to hedge against this type of risk. With regard to market risk it is fair to say that a single security has the same market risk as a diversified portfolio with the same Beta.

Linked to this market risk is the market timing risk. Market timing is a strategy which involves the buying or selling of assets on the market by attempting to accurately predict the price movements of the assets. This will often involve the use of techniques such as technical analysis or fundamental analysis to predict economic and market movements or trends. The risk reflects the potential for missing out on a positive price movement in a given asset due to errors in timing of either purchases or sales.

To illustrate the importance of timing and investment horizon, market timing risk may also be a factor if an investor must withdraw some or all of their invested funds at some particular time due to a specified event or commitment. This situation may not prove to be a positive outcome if markets are depressed and does not allow the investor to remain invested until market conditions are more favourable and may result in capital loss.

> **In practice**
>
> **Market timing risk: the wedding date**
>
> Mr and Mrs Fotheringham have invested a sum of cash into a portfolio of company shares, the aim of which is to accrue sufficient funds to pay for their daughter Penelope's wedding.
>
> Penelope has arranged her wedding for 1 July, but in late May the stock market suffers an unexpected and substantial fall of 20 per cent due to a global financial crisis. This reduces the value of the Fotheringham's share portfolio by around 20 per cent causing them unanticipated cashflow problems.

The reduced market price of the portfolio following the fall in value is now not sufficient to pay for their liability: the wedding. Since Penelope would be devastated at the prospect of the wedding being postponed, Mr and Mrs Fotheringham are therefore forced to liquidate their share portfolio at a time which is not advantageous and the shortfall in funds must be found from other sources.

If there was no fixed time frame for their liability, they would have been able to remain invested and await the market rising before liquidating their portfolio of shares.

Credit risk

Keyword

Credit risk is the risk to the investor of loss of capital or reward that may arise as a result of the failure of a counterparty to meet a contractual obligation of some sort. An example would be if a company, which is the issuer of a corporate bond, experiences financial difficulties and is unable to pay the coupon payments on the bond, or is unable to repay the capital to bondholders at the redemption date of the bond.

In general, the higher the perceived credit risk, the higher the reward will be required to compensate the investor for accepting the risk.

In practice

Credit risk

If Circle Plc has an AA credit rating, the coupon offered on their issued corporate bond will be lower than the corporate bond coupon payable by Square Plc with a credit rating of B. This reflects the lower risk accepted by the investor when investing in the Circle Plc corporate bonds compared to Square Plc corporate bonds.

This highlights the consequence to companies with lower credit ratings and their additional cost of capital raising and also the increased risk that bond investors must accept if they wish to access higher coupon returns.

This is linked to default risk, which considers the same type of risk but from the point of view of the debtor or issuer. Default risk is the possibility that either companies or individuals will be unable to meet the payments on or service their debt, in whatever form that takes.

Advisory companies such as Moody's and Standard & Poor's publish ratings of bonds which reflect the default risk of bonds, using a grading system which starts at AAA, for the highest grade, down to C, the lowest grade.[4,5] Bonds are rated as either investment grade or junk grade and it is worth mentioning that many individuals or companies responsible for investing on behalf of others, for example, trustees, corporate investors, pension schemes, are restricted to investing in the investment grade bonds.

Table 4.1 Typical Standard & Poor's bond ratings

Investment grade bonds	'Junk' bonds	Defaulted bonds
AAA	BB+	D
AA+	BB	
AA	B	
A	CCC	
BBB+	CC	
BBB	C	

Default risk is also sometimes referred to as counterparty risk and this may relate to different types of financial instruments or transactions, for example derivatives. In the case of derivative transactions, this reflects the possibility that one of the parties to the contract, buyer, seller or dealer, may not fulfil their obligations to the contract.

Liquidity risk

> **Keyword**
>
> In the context of investment assets, **liquidity risk** relates to the ease with which the investor can convert a particular asset into cash and this reflects the ability to trade the asset on the secondary market. This could be for a variety of reasons: to reduce or exit a particular asset; to rebalance a portfolio position; or to take profit and reinvest in another

asset. It is reasonable to say that the more difficult and time-consuming the process of conversion to cash and the greater the uncertainty regarding the realized price of disposal, the greater the liquidity risk.

Liquidity risk may relate to either buying or selling; therefore, liquidity risk is associated with the lack of marketability of an asset if it cannot be bought or sold in a required timescale to prevent/minimize loss or realize a gain. Generally, the smaller the market size of the asset, ie the typical level of daily trading in the asset, and the smaller the issuer, the larger the liquidity risk.

An example of a 'liquid' asset would include a high-grade government bond, for example US treasury bonds, UK government bonds and German government bonds, all of which may be acquired or disposed of very quickly with little price volatility. Shares of established and profitable companies, quoted on major global stock exchanges would also be considered to be quite 'liquid' under normal circumstances, although in times of crisis such as market crashes, even major stocks may be affected by liquidity issues.

Small-cap and micro-cap securities and assets with a small normal market size are examples where liquidity risk is a significant consideration for the investor. Foreign securities may also be considered a liquidity risk dependent upon various factors such as the size and the liquidity of the local market and indeed, upon the country in question. Developing countries, often considered to be emerging markets, may be considered to be an example of liquidity risk because much of the investment capital is likely to be foreign investment rather than from local investors. This has the potential to create liquidity risk if there is a widespread change in sentiment about the particular country, which may be compounded by other internal or external factors, such as political risk.

Political risk

Keyword

Political risk and **country risk** are often interchanged in discussions where investing overseas is under consideration. Country risk is generally considered to be an amalgamation of the various risks associated with investing in a different country which could reduce the expected return on an overseas investment. This will obviously vary significantly between different countries as this reflects the possibility of changes in the economic and/or political environment within a particular country. In extreme circumstances, the perceived level of risk is sufficient to completely discourage foreign investment in a country, which has implications for that country's economy.

Country risk involves consideration of factors such as the liquidity of secondary markets within a specific country and whether any of that country's securities are traded on other major global stock exchanges. Some countries are more obviously associated with country risk; for example, North Korea, Zimbabwe and Somalia, whilst countries such as Switzerland, Norway and Germany are considered to have low country risk. The effect of 'black swan' events should not be overlooked and may cause country risk to those areas affected, for a period of time.

Keyword

A **black swan event** is the term for a rare, high-impact and unpredictable occurrence. An example would be the 2011 earthquake and subsequent tsunami in Japan which caused major issues for many global corporations and markets.

Table 4.2 Global rankings of countries

Ranking 2015	Ranking 2014	Country	Institutional investor credit rating	One year change
1	1	Switzerland	95.1	−0.4
2	2	Norway	94.7	−1.1
3	4	Germany	94.4	0.4
4	8	Luxembourg	93.8	2.3
5	6	Canada	93.8	0.6
6	5	USA	93.5	0.5
7	7	Singapore	93.3	0.5
8	3	Sweden	93.3	−0.3

(continued)

Table 4.2 (Continued)

Ranking 2015	Ranking 2014	Country	Institutional investor credit rating	One year change
9	9	Denmark	91.3	0.5
10	10	Finland	91.0	-0.7
~	~	~	~	~
170	163	Chad	15.3	-0.7
171	166	Guinea-Bissau	14.9	1.7
172	173	Afghanistan	14.2	3.9
173	172	Syria	10.8	-1.6
174	175	Sudan	9.4	1.7
175	176	Central African Republic	8.8	1.5
176	164	South Sudan	7.9	1.5
177	177	North Korea	7.6	-1.9
178	178	Zimbabwe	7.5	2.4
179	179	Somalia	6.7	2.2
–	–	**Global average**	**44.1**	**-0.7**

SOURCE adapted from *Institutional Investor*, The 2015 Country Credit Survey

Political risk is the risk that investment returns may be less than anticipated as a result of political changes or instability and may also be seen to reflect a country's ability and willingness to honour its foreign obligations. The level of political risk in a country may change as a result of various factors; for example, legislative or regulation changes, changes in government or political posturing, taxation or currency restrictions and economic changes. It is often the case that politics and economics are inextricably connected as highlighted by the necessity for the eurozone support for Greece, and to a lesser extent Italy and Spain, and areas of the world experiencing civil wars and repeated terrorist incidents, all of which have resulted in elevated political risk. We should also consider that any factors which result in a change in a country's international competitiveness or global standing will also affect the domestic currency and therefore the exchange rates on the international currency markets.

Exchange rate risk

Keyword

Also referred to as **foreign exchange risk**, **exchange rate risk** is applicable because of the potential for currencies to fluctuate in value on the international markets relative to each other. An exchange rate is the rate at which an investor's domestic currency can be converted into a foreign currency and back to the domestic currency. There are many factors which can affect a country's currency, both economic and political. For example, the UK's decision to leave the European Union has resulted in the UK pound weakening against some other key currencies in the international markets.

For investment purposes, this is the risk an investor is subject to when purchasing or selling an asset in a currency other than their own domestic currency. This reflects the potential for movement in the two currencies relative to each other. Clearly this could work to the advantage of the investor but the risk is that the investor's domestic currency fluctuates relative to the currency of the asset they have purchased in a way that is not to the investor's advantage. This can clearly be seen to have an effect on both capital returns and also income.

In practice

If a French investor purchases shares in a Japanese company, these shares will be purchased in Japanese yen.

The investor will need to convert euros to yen to purchase the shares and this conversion will occur at the prevailing exchange rate between euro and yen on the day of purchase.

When the investor sells the shares at some point in the future, the sale proceeds will be in yen and the investor will then need to convert the yen back to euros at the appropriate exchange rate on the day of the sale.

Assume that the French investor has chosen wisely and the share price has increased significantly, so the investor has made a capital gain over the period of holding the shares. However, during this time period the value of the Japanese yen has weakened relative to the euro on the international market, so the effect is that more yen are required to purchase the same amount of euros.

The effect will be that upon converting yen back to euros, some of the capital growth achieved by holding the shares will be eroded by the weakening of yen relative to the euro.

We can consider a similar situation involving bonds. If a US investor has purchased UK government bonds, the purchase is made in UK pounds so conversion from US dollars to UK pounds is required initially. The coupon payments will be made in UK pounds and at redemption or sale of the bond, the proceeds will be in UK pounds. The UK pounds will then need to be converted back to US dollars for both the income and return of capital, at the prevailing exchange rate between the UK pound and US dollar. The return achieved by the investor is therefore subject to the fluctuation of the currencies relative to each other.

Clearly, the more volatile the exchange rate between an investor's domestic currency and the currency of their chosen investment, the more uncertain the outcome and therefore, the greater the potential risk.

Capital risk

Keyword

Capital risk may be considered to be the risk that an investor's initial capital falls in value; however, we may also consider that it is the risk that the investment does not succeed in attaining and maintaining an acceptable level of growth to achieve the investor's aims and objectives. The prospect of capital loss may be unacceptable for a very cautious investor, but a more aggressive investor would find underperformance of their invested capital equally disappointing.

It is clear that different assets will carry a different level of capital risk and therefore investors must be aware of and understand the magnitude of capital risk applicable to their chosen asset. For example, it is accepted that an equity-based investment will carry a significant capital risk, whilst investing in an instant access savings account with a reputable bank will involve comparatively little capital risk. This is why investors must consider the balance between risk and return, because it is true that an investment with a low risk will usually deliver a low rate of return; however, it does not necessarily follow that increasing the amount of risk taken is certain to generate a higher return. In general, risk and the potential for reward are positively correlated which means that investments which deliver higher returns will usually be considered to be of higher risk. This means that higher risk investments also have the potential for low or negative returns and therefore risk of capital loss.

Maintaining security of an investor's capital will therefore normally be associated with a comparatively low return which may also suffer the effects of *inflation risk*, unless the asset in question benefits from an index-linked option, for example, UK government index-linked gilts.

Income risk

> **Keyword**
>
> **Income risk** is applicable where an investment asset is generating a regular income return separate from the possibility of capital growth; for example, the interest payment on a cash deposit, or the dividend payment from a company share. This risk reflects the possibility that the income from the investment will not be maintained and this could be for a variety of reasons. For example, dividend payments to shareholders may be interrupted if the company fails to generate profit in a particular year and there are no profits, or fewer profits to distribute to shareholders in the form of dividends. There is also the possibility that the income may not be maintained due to the inability of a bond issuer to maintain coupon payments, which is linked to *default risk*.

The income may not actually stop but may reduce. So, for example, the interest paid on a cash deposit will reduce if the prevailing interest rate falls. Even if the income return on a particular asset continues unchanged, for example, the coupon payment on a corporate bond, this may still represent a risk if the level of inflation exceeds the asset's income return. This will negatively impact the anticipated return of the asset.

Black swan event

Stock markets and investment performance are affected by a variety of events, information and occurrences, some of which are predictable and some of which are certainly not. As referred to earlier, a black swan event is the term that is used to describe a rare, unpredictable and high-impact occurrence. It is therefore important for investors to give consideration to the possibility of a black swan event occurring together with the disproportionate effect this may have on economies and markets, both locally and indeed globally.

> **In practice**
>
> An example of this type of a black swan event is 'Black Monday', the day in October 1987 when the Dow Jones Industrial Average (DJIA) lost over 20 per cent of its value in one day and precipitated a global stock market decline. By the end of that month, most of the major global stock exchanges had also lost in excess of 20 per cent.[7]

Some commentators would say that this sort of event, together with events such as the 2008 global financial crisis have a degree of predictability; however, it is the magnitude of the effect on markets that is the main issue and reflects the risk to investors, both professional and private. It is therefore a prudent precaution for investors to be aware of the potential for the unexpected and to ensure that they have an appropriate emergency provision in place to allow them access to liquid funds in the event that one of these occurrences manifests itself.

We also see the use of the term 'grey swan event', which describes an event which it is thought may be anticipated, but is still considered to be unlikely to occur. Its impact on both securities and markets may also be considerable if it does occur.

All of these issues are, of course, outside the influence of the investor. This section has covered the majority of risks experienced in an investment scenario and leads to the ability and methods for measurement of risk.

Measuring risk

It is reasonable to make the assumption that investors wish to maximize the return on their investment, for a particular accepted level of risk. This also highlights the fundamental importance of accurately assessing an investor's tolerance of risk: that is, the amount of risk that a particular investor will be prepared to accept. It is crucial that an investor has a clear understanding of realistic expected returns and the level of risk involved in achieving those returns, prior to commencing a particular investment plan. This relationship between risk and return is an important concept which varies significantly for different asset classes and it is therefore an important part of the professional financial adviser's role to ensure that this important relationship is appreciated and understood by investors.

Some reasonable measurement of risk is therefore necessary in order to make an assessment of the risk involved when investing in a particular asset, whilst accepting that risk is not always as predictable as we would like. Inevitably, measurement of risk is based on historical data and whilst historical data cannot be guaranteed to reflect the future with any given asset, it still provides an indicator which we can make good use of. *Variance* and *standard deviation* are two of the most common measures used to quantify

Figure 4.3 Normal distribution of data

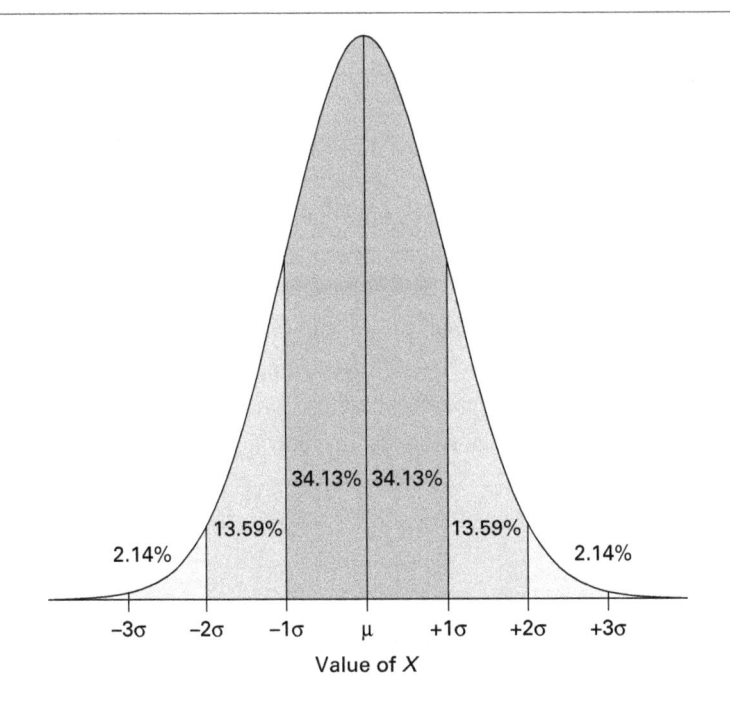

risk, although the use of these two statistics does assume that a normal distribution of data exists, which may not always be the case.

Standard deviation and variance

The measurement of risk of an asset or a portfolio may be seen as measuring the fluctuation in performance that the asset or portfolio has shown historically, which may be described as its volatility. So, for example, we may look at data for daily prices of a company share over a certain period of time and observe the dispersion of the daily share prices relative to the mean share price over the period of observation. Variance and standard deviation are both measures of how widely this dispersion of daily share prices presents, compared to the mean, and it is accepted that the more widely this dispersion is observed, the more volatile the share price may be considered to be.

Where we are looking to quantify the volatility and therefore the risk of an asset, it is possible to measure the variance and standard deviation using a given set of historic data for the asset in question. So, using the example of daily prices of a company share, the variance measures the spread between the prices in a particular data set for a specific company share. Statistically, the variance is measuring how far each price in the data set is from the mean price. The mean price in the data set is calculated by simply adding all the prices in the data set and dividing by the total number of prices in the data set.

Keyword

Variance is determined by calculating the difference between each price in the data set and the mean price, squaring the calculated difference and dividing the sum of the squares by the number of values in the set. The variance of the company share price calculated in this way is effectively measuring the variability from the mean, which represents the volatility of the share price. Since volatility is an accepted measure of risk, the calculated figure may assist in determining the risk being taken when purchasing this specific company share.

Variance can be calculated using the following equation:

$$\text{variance} = \sum \frac{(x_i - X_m)^2}{N}$$

where:
x_i = individual value; X_m = mean value; N = number in data set

Standard deviation and variance are two related statistics, the standard deviation being the square root of the variance.

> **Keyword**
>
> The **standard deviation** measures the dispersion of a set of data from its mean. So, using the example of an investment asset, the standard deviation would measure how widely dispersed is the value of the asset around its mean value, over a period of time. A larger standard deviation indicates a greater spread of value around the mean and therefore implies higher volatility. This is a useful tool in an investment scenario, particularly when comparisons are being made between prospective investment acquisitions. It would be expected that a rational investor would wish to invest in assets which have low volatility, but above average returns.
>
> The equation to find standard deviation is:
>
> $$\text{standard deviation } (\sigma) = \sqrt{\text{variance}}$$

It is quite common for investment companies and providers of investment funds (eg mutual funds and collective funds) to publish information regarding the standard deviation of their funds and other products. Within the finance and investment industry the standard deviation data is accepted as one of the most useful risk measures that wealth managers, financial advisers, financial analysts and fund managers may use. Standard deviation can also be explained quite easily to investors, clients, media and other finance professionals and therefore it is also often included in periodic reports and reviews.

One other point to consider with regard to the calculation of the variance and standard deviation for an asset is that we may, at times, be working with varied sample sizes. The smaller the sample size, the less this sample will be representative of the whole set of historic data for a given asset. So, for example, we are calculating the standard deviation of the share price of Company A and we have 12 months of daily share price data. If this Company A has been listed on the stock exchange for 20 years, then the data we are considering is only quite a small sample and may not accurately reflect the standard deviation of the stock over the whole period. It may, therefore, be prudent to make provision for this potential inaccuracy in our data and we can do this by using *Bessel's correction factor*.

Bessel's correction factor involves substituting $(n - 1)$ in place of (n) into the equation when we calculate the variance. This allows for the likelihood that we may be using what is effectively a small sample of data rather than the whole available data set for a particular asset calculation. The equation then becomes:

$$\text{variance} = \sum \frac{(x_i - X_m)^2}{N - 1}$$

It is also worth noting that when making comparisons between two investment assets, for example two different company shares, statistical techniques of this type may lead us to a false conclusion if looked at in isolation. For instance, if we are comparing two company shares where the share price is significantly different, then simply comparing the standard deviation of the two share prices is not sufficiently robust as this does not take into account the magnitude of the share price relative to each other. On the UK stock market for example, if a share in Company A is 567p and a share in Company B is 38p, if we use the straightforward standard deviation figure to compare the two shares, the difference in the magnitude of the share price will affect the result of the comparison and therefore we need to take an additional step and calculate the *coefficient of variation* to allow a more meaningful comparison.

Coefficient of variation

Keyword

The **coefficient of variation** is often used to measure volatility, for example, in the prices of company shares but also in other securities. It is particularly useful because it is a tool for fund managers, analysts and other finance professionals to use, when assessing the risks and when making comparisons between different potential investments.

It can be used as an alternative to the standard deviation, when seeking to compare data sets with significantly different magnitude or indeed different measures and is used to measure and therefore to manage investment risk. The coefficient of variation is said to be 'non-unitized' since it is independent of the units of measurement that are used in its calculation so it is expressed as a percentage. As with the standard deviation, a low figure for the calculated coefficient of variation is an indicator of lower volatility and therefore lower risk and a high coefficient of variation would indicate higher volatility and therefore higher risk. Coefficient of variation is calculated using the following formula:

$$\text{coefficient of variation} = \frac{\text{standard deviation}}{\text{mean return}}$$

Z-scores

Keyword

Used as part of a credit analysis strategy, **Z-scores** are one method for helping determine the default risk posed by a bond issuer, by attempting to predict the chance of financial distress in a company. Often used by investors active in the high-yield bond market, sometimes referred to as junk bonds, the aim is to assist investors and fund managers to select bonds which have a better chance of survival.

Reilly, Wright and Gentry were responsible for work which demonstrated that the credit quality of bonds may change over the business cycle, which evidenced the need for detailed analysis if the benefits of high-yield bonds are to be utilized to provide significant returns for the investor.[8] Junk bonds are those bonds which are rated as or below, by the rating advisory companies (see Table 4.1).

Z-score is often referred to as the Altman Z-score as it was created by Professor Edward Altman as a quicker and less complex method by which it is possible to estimate the overall financial health of a company and indeed to indicate if a company is close to bankruptcy.[9] The original calculation produces an output which would assist analysts, fund managers and investors to assess the possibility of bankruptcy for a publicly traded manufacturing company. The Z-score itself is derived from five key common financial ratios easily accessed within annual company reports. The Z-score calculation is shown on the next page:

$$\text{Z-score} = 1.2A + 1.4B + 3.3C + 0.6D + 1.0E$$

where:

$$A = \frac{\text{working capital}}{\text{total assets}}$$

$$B = \frac{\text{retained earnings}}{\text{total assets}}$$

$$C = \frac{\text{earnings before interest and taxes (EBIT)}}{\text{total assets}}$$

$$D = \frac{\text{market value of equity}}{\text{total liabilities}}$$

$$E = \frac{\text{sales}}{\text{total assets}}$$

Following the calculation, the fund manager, analyst or investor would have a number typically in the range −5.0 to +20.0. Generally, a score of less than 1.8 would indicate that the company under analysis is at increased risk of bankruptcy, whilst a score in excess of 3.0 would indicate that the company is unlikely to suffer bankruptcy in the next two years.

In 2012, Professor Altman developed the Altman Z-score Plus formula. The new method may be employed to assist investors, analysts and fund managers to evaluate both private and public companies, in the manufacturing and non-manufacturing sectors. It is also suitable for companies both inside and outside the United States.

Value at risk (VaR)

Volatility is probably the most common measure of risk; however, the issue with measuring risk by assessing volatility is that an asset may be considered to be volatile if it suddenly appreciates in value, since volatility applies in both appreciation and depreciation. It would be reasonable to suggest that neither fund managers nor investors are likely to be troubled by unexpected gains.

Keyword

The **value at risk** is effectively a statistical technique that may be utilized to measure and to quantify in monetary terms, the downside risk within an asset or an investment portfolio, over a particular period of time. This technique is used by fund managers and risk managers as it allows them to measure and control the level of risk taken. The reason for using this technique is to make sure that losses above and beyond an acceptable threshold are not incurred.

It is clear therefore, that there are three variables within the VaR method, which are:

- the timescale under analysis;
- the possible loss;
- the statistical probability of that loss.

In practice

As an example of the guidance that this technique may provide, let us consider that a fund manager has determined that her fund has a 5 per cent, one-month VaR of £750,000. This indicates that statistically, each month there is a 5 per cent chance that the fund may suffer losses in excess of £750,000. It is also worth noting that, based on this analysis, a loss of £750,000 should be anticipated every 20 months.

Financial institutions, fund managers and institutional investors make use of the VaR method to assist them with assessing portfolio risk and to estimate the liquid reserves needed to cover potential losses. The same method may also be used effectively to evaluate risk on individual company stocks or indeed stock indices such as NASDAQ, FTSE 100, or Hang Seng. Typically, high confidence limits of 95 per cent or even 99 per cent would be employed to maximize accuracy.

It is also important to think about the risk we are assessing in the appropriate context and to be aware of the magnitude of the downside risk relative to its importance for the institution or individual. So, for example, the 1 per cent possibility of a monthly loss in excess of $10,000 is unlikely to be a major concern for the manager of a $500 million fund.

Correlation coefficient

From an investment point of view, the correlation describes the relationship that different assets or investments exhibit relative to each other. It is important to determine and be aware of this relationship as it presents various uses within the financial industry. An example would be that this relationship may be used to describe the way an asset or fund behaves in relation to its peers, or in comparison to an appropriate benchmark. In a portfolio planning and management context, the addition of an appropriate negatively correlated asset to a portfolio may result in additional benefits of diversification.

Keyword

Correlation coefficient is a measurement which describes the way in which two funds or assets move in relation to each other. The correlation coefficient has a total spectrum ranging between –1.0 and +1.0. A correlation coefficient of +1.0 indicates a perfect positive correlation and a correlation coefficient of –1.0 indicates a perfect negative correlation.

In practice

To explain this correlation in terms of activity, we can consider shares in two listed companies, Company A and Company B, their share prices moving on the stock exchange in response to changes in market conditions.

If the two shares have a correlation coefficient of +1.0, this indicates that a perfect positive relationship is demonstrated between the two shares. In practical terms, this means that if there is a movement in the share price of Company A, either positive or negative, there will be a corresponding movement in the share price of Company B. This movement will be in the same direction and of the same magnitude, so if the share price of Company A increased by 5 per cent, the share price of Company B would also increase by 5 per cent.

Conversely, if the two shares in question have a correlation coefficient of -1.0, this means a perfect negative relationship exists between the two shares, which would suggest that the share prices will move in opposite directions. So, for example, if the price of shares in Company A increased by 10 per cent the share price of Company B would fall by 10 per cent.

The correlation coefficient applicable between two assets or funds may fall anywhere within the range +1.0 and –1.0. However, if the correlation coefficient between two assets or funds is zero, this indicates that no relationship exists between the two assets or funds. We can therefore say that if the shares in Company A and Company B have a correlation coefficient of zero, we would expect that they will react to market conditions totally independently of each other. The relative strength that exists in the relationship between the two assets or funds is dependent upon the magnitude of the correlation coefficient, so for example, a correlation coefficient of +0.1 reflects a weak positive relationship, whilst a value of –0.8 indicates a strong negative relationship.

The correlation between assets is an important factor for consideration when creating and managing an investment portfolio. High positive correlations between assets within the portfolio will be likely to generate significant positive returns when investment conditions are good, for example in a 'bull' market. However, in more challenging investment conditions, for example a 'bear' market, the high positive correlations will be likely to produce significant negative returns, which may have the effect of producing pronounced peaks and troughs in the performance of the investment portfolio.

Negative correlation between assets can be used as a tool to reduce the risk of an investment portfolio and so, for example, an investor holding company stocks in their investment portfolio may also choose to expose their portfolio to assets which are usually negatively correlated to the stock market, such as bonds or property. Negative correlation may therefore be helpful for an investor who is attempting to diversify and hedge their portfolio to reduce risk. This method of utilizing negatively correlated assets must be utilized carefully though. Consider a very simple portfolio which contains two assets, Asset X and Asset Y. If the two assets utilized are perfectly negatively correlated, that is to say they have a correlation of –1.0, then we would expect to see that any gains generated by Asset X are completely offset by the negative performance of Asset Y. In this situation, the investor would achieve little or no gains in their portfolio.

It is generally accepted, therefore, that it is preferable to utilize different assets which have small negative correlation relative to each other. It would be expected that if the correlation coefficient between the assets was low negative, for example –0.2 to –0.4, then it is possible the investor may reduce their losses in times when their primary assets are depreciating whilst still benefiting positively when their primary assets are appreciating in value.

Beta

Keyword

Beta is also known as the **beta coefficient** and is a useful measure of the volatility of an asset or a portfolio, compared to the market as a whole. Beta is usually calculated using regression analysis and is an historical indicator often used to describe the relative volatility of company shares in comparison to the stock market. The beta coefficient of an asset or portfolio is not fixed and will change over time. When Beta is being used as a comparison tool, or in some form of model, eg the capital asset pricing (CAPM) model, it is therefore important that the value of Beta for the time period under analysis is used.

The beta coefficient of the market is 1.0 so therefore a company share with a beta coefficient greater than 1.0 is considered to be more volatile than the market and therefore holding this share implies accepting a higher level of risk than the market risk. This will indicate that the share would be expected to rise or fall to a greater extent than the market. Conversely, a company share with a Beta of less than 1.0 would be expected to rise or fall to a lesser extent than the market and holding this share implies an acceptance of less than the market risk. This type of share would be considered to be a defensive stock. An asset or portfolio with a beta coefficient of 1.0 is considered to have the same level of risk and volatility as the market. This close link to the market means that beta coefficient is also considered to be a measure of the *systematic risk* of the asset or portfolio.

Using company shares as an example of an investment asset, investors may favour holding company shares with a higher beta coefficient when there is a steadily rising market as investors with a suitable appetite for risk are prepared to accept greater risks in return for the potential to enjoy greater rewards. Company shares with a lower beta coefficient are often termed defensive stocks because investors will frequently seek to hold them during periods of high volatility in the markets, or when the markets exhibit a downward trend.

In terms of magnitude, a company share with a beta coefficient of 2.0 would be expected to be twice as volatile as the market and company share with beta coefficient of 0.5 would be expected to be half as volatile as the market. To illustrate this, see the example in the following box:

In practice

Consider a share in Company X with a Beta of 1.5 and a share in Company Y with a Beta of 0.75.

If the market is expected to rise by 10 per cent, we would expect shares in Company X to rise by 15 per cent and shares in Company Y to rise by 7.5 per cent over the corresponding period of analysis.

The beta coefficient of assets or portfolios may also be used as a comparison with other assets or portfolios over the same time period of analysis. It should be remembered that since beta coefficient is a measure of volatility and therefore risk, the performance of assets relative to each other is not guaranteed by the magnitude of their beta coefficients. For example, consider Company A share, with a Beta of 1.2 and another Company B share, with a Beta of 0.9. We would normally expect that Company A shares would outperform both the market and the performance of Company B shares. We would also expect that Company B shares would underperform both Company A shares and the market in general. However, this is not guaranteed because volatility and risk bring uncertainty and it is quite possible for a company share with a lower Beta to outperform the market and for company shares with a higher Beta to underperform the market.

Duration

Keyword

Duration is a measure which characterizes the risk in a bond and allows a numeric representation of this risk. Duration is also sometimes referred to as the Macaulay duration after its creator Frederick Macaulay and describes the weighted average term to maturity of a bond's cashflows.

The Macaulay duration of a bond represents the period of time taken for the bond to effectively repay the initial investment in the bond, taking into account the weighted cashflow received from the bond in the form of coupon payments. A bond which pays a coupon, usually annually or semi-annually to an investor, will have an effective duration which is less than its term to maturity, because of the effect of the cashflow created by the coupon payments. This also means that a zero-coupon bond, which pays no coupon to the investor, will have a duration which is equal to the term to maturity of the bond, since that is when the original investment will be repaid, at maturity. The higher the duration of the bond, the more volatile the bond is considered to be as it is considered more likely to be at risk from interest rate fluctuations.

There are complex formulae which can be used to calculate the Macaulay duration although the duration data for most tradeable bonds is usually readily available through one of the respected data research systems such as Bloomberg. The Macaulay duration is effectively represented by:

$$\text{Macaulay duration} = \frac{\Sigma \,(\text{net present value of the bond's cashflow} \times \text{time period to receipt of cashflow})}{\Sigma \,(\text{net present value of the cashflows to be received})}$$

We know that bond prices usually exhibit an inverse relationship with interest rate changes, that is to say that if interest rates rise, we expect bond prices to fall and that if interest rates fall, we expect bond prices to rise. It is possible to calculate the expected change in bond prices given a 1 per cent movement in interest rates using a modified duration calculation. The modified duration formula allows us to measure the sensitivity of a security to interest rate changes and this concept is discussed further in Chapter 6 on fixed-interest investment:

$$\text{modified duration} = \frac{\text{Macaulay duration}}{\left(1 + \frac{\text{YTM}}{n}\right)}$$

where:
YTM = yield to maturity; n = number of time periods.

Inflation and investment returns

Inflation is a concept generally considered in relation to the performance of the overall economy and refers to a sustained trend of increasing prices from one year to the next. The rate of inflation is important in the context of investment performance as inflation will have the effect of eroding the performance of an asset or investment portfolio, affecting the real purchasing power over time. The current rate of inflation is also useful for investors because it informs investors of the very minimum return their investment is required to achieve in order to maintain the current purchasing power of their capital. Generally speaking, investors should aim for their investments to perform at a level greater than the current rate of inflation in order to achieve a positive real return and experience investment growth.

Any return on an investment that has not been adjusted to account for the effects of inflation is called the nominal return. However, the investment return after allowing for inflation is the real return.

The formula to calculate real return is as follows:

$$\text{real return} = \text{nominal return} - \text{inflation rate}$$

So if we have a savings account paying 6 per cent per annum then the nominal return is 6 per cent.

However, if the rate of inflation is currently 2 per cent then to find out the real return we say:

$$\text{real return} = 6 - 2 = 4\%$$

This method is a useful estimation; however, it is usually desirable to calculate an accurate measure of real return, in which case the following formula should be utilized:

$$(1 + \text{real rate of return}) = \frac{(1 + \text{nominal rate of return})}{(1 + \text{inflation rate})}$$

$$\text{real rate of return} = \frac{(1 + \text{nominal rate of return})}{(1 + \text{inflation rate})} - 1$$

In practice

For a nominal rate of return of 6 per cent and an annual rate of inflation of 2 per cent, the accurately measured real rate of return, taking inflation into account is:

$$\text{real rate of return} = \frac{(1 + \text{nominal rate of return})}{(1 + \text{inflation rate})} - 1$$

$$\text{real rate of return} = \frac{(1 + 0.06)}{(1 + 0.02)} - 1$$

$$\text{real rate of return} = 0.0392 = 3.92\%$$

The example above uses the same returns as the previous example; however, it can be seen that a more accurate result is obtained. It is clear that accounting for the effects of inflation is crucial to the investment process because inflation can significantly reduce the magnitude of 'real' investment returns. It is quite possible for the real return to be negative, in which case the buying power of the investment is decreasing each year, so therefore it is important for both investors and advisors to take into account the effects of inflation when planning financial matters. Investors may protect their investment returns and purchasing power over periods of time by making prudent use of 'inflation-protected securities', for example, inflation-linked bonds or treasury inflation-protected securities. These specific types of investments are designed to move along with the current rate of inflation and therefore are immune to inflation risk.

Summary

Risk is something that is often discussed, frequently misunderstood and ignored at the investor's peril. Most investment theory is based on the assumption that investors behave rationally; however, we know that in the real world this is not necessarily always true. A rational investor is expected to make choices that result in the optimal level of benefit for themselves and we therefore expect a rational investor to be prepared to accept a certain amount of additional risk, provided that there is the realistic opportunity for a proportionate increase in the available reward. There is much anecdotal evidence to suggest that investors do not always act in a rational way and *behavioural finance*, covered in Chapter 5 of this book, attempts to provide explanations for this phenomenon.

Check your understanding

1 Are you comfortable with the difference between systematic and unsystematic risk?

2 For which asset class would inflation risk and interest rate risk pose the greatest problems?

3 'Political risk would only be associated with developing countries.' True or false? Could you explain your opinions in depth?

4 Is standard deviation a good measure of volatility and does it have limitations in its use?

5 Why is the relative correlation of securities held within an investment fund important?

Further reading

The following books may be useful:

Chance, DM and Brooks, R (2016) *Introduction to Derivatives and Risk Management*, 10th edn, Cengage Learning

Pickford, J (2001) *Mastering Risk, Volume 1: Concepts*, Financial Times Prentice Hall

Strong, RA (2009) *Portfolio Construction, Management & Protection*, 5th edn, Cengage Learning

The following sites may be useful:

https://www.vanguard.co.uk/documents/portal/literature/investment-risk-guide.pdf
https://www.forbes.com/forbes/welcome/?toURL=https://www.forbes.com/sites/moneybuilder/2012/06/15/four-risks-of-investing
http://www.mandg.co.uk/investor/news/intelligence/myths-about-investment-risk/

Investment theory

05

This chapter will explore important areas of investment theory, by the end of which you should have an understanding of the following key areas:

- random walk theory;
- efficient market hypothesis;
- modern portfolio theory;
- measurement of performance under modern portfolio management;
- capital asset pricing model;
- arbitrage pricing theory;
- behavioural finance;
- investment return and useful calculations.

Introduction

There are a substantial number of theories and models in existence within the investment and asset management arena which seek to describe the behaviour of assets and securities and inform both the professional and private investor regarding their decisions. Many chapters have been written over the years to put forward and explain the various financial theories and models and many more have been written to prove, disprove or test the theories and models which underpin the investment management and analysis industries. Much discussion also surrounds the various uses, limitations and merits of these theories and models and some of them, for example arbitrage pricing theory, are still subject to ongoing research.

Much of the influential investment theory can be traced back to work completed decades ago, in the case of efficient market hypothesis the work of Fama, random walk theory was popularized when Malkiel published *A Random Walk Down Wall Street* in 1973 and modern portfolio theory introduced the capital asset pricing model (CAPM) when published by Markowitz in 1952.[1,2,3]

In this chapter we will not seek to justify, test, or affirm the various theories and models but simply to discuss them and explain their uses and limitations within the modern investment management arena. The reader who finds that their appetite for further knowledge has been awakened will no doubt wish to research the various topics in greater detail and this is certainly encouraged by the authors. Only by researching the various theories and models widely and in more depth can the reader make an informed decision regarding their personal opinions and preferred investment strategies.

Random walk theory

This theory traces its roots back to the early analysis of stock market price changes over periods of time. Maurice Kendall found to his surprise that he could not identify a predictable pattern in share price changes;[4] indeed, the prices appeared to behave in a random manner as they were as likely to rise as they were to fall on any given day. This was of concern to financial economists and analysts of that time, because it seemed to imply irrationality in the markets and cast doubts upon the skills of those involved in dealing in the markets. Closer study, however, indicated that the random nature of share price movements actually pointed to the market being efficient and this gave rise to the random walk theory and the efficient market hypothesis, with its lingering effects upon investment policy and methods. Much of the work initially carried out centred on large quantities of empirical analysis but little in the way of theoretical research.

> **Keyword**
>
> The **random walk theory** says that share prices take a random and unpredictable path and therefore the chance of the share price rising in the future is the same as the chance of the share price falling in the future. This suggests that the price of a share is independent of other factors, the implication of which is that past share price movements cannot be used to predict future share price movements.

Those who believe in this theory would say that it is not possible to predict future share prices because the share prices already reflect all the available information which would cause a movement in the share price and therefore it supports the belief that the markets are efficient. Furthermore, they argue that the momentum of a share price movement does not carry forward from one day to the next. Individuals who believe in the theory of random walk would say that it is only possible to outperform the market if you are prepared to take additional risk, above and beyond the market risk.

This theory was afforded further popularity when highlighted in Burton Malkiel's book, *A Random Walk Down Wall Street*, in 1973 (see above – still one of the bestselling finance texts). If this theory is indeed correct, then it would mean that both technical analysis and fundamental analysis techniques would be proven to be a waste of time and that they would be unsuccessful in outperforming the market. In this situation, the most successful investment strategy would be to use a buy-and-hold, long-term investment strategy, as techniques based on timing the markets, methods involving technical analysis or fundamental analysis, should fail to achieve success.

Investment professionals and analysts are divided on the merits of the random walk theory, with published studies available to support both sides in the debate surrounding its validity. It is possible to find evidence to support the theory, as records highlight that most mutual funds actually do fail to beat their benchmarks, which are normally appropriate indices such as the FTSE All-Share Index. On the other side, critics of the theory point to evidence of successful technical analysis techniques, where historic data has been used to predict future trends and therefore allow outperformance of the market by timing purchases and sales of shares.

From the point of view of limitations, we are clearly assuming that the markets are efficient and this means that they are rapidly reflecting 'new' information into the appropriate share price. We are also assuming that all 'new' information is costless and readily available to all investors.

Efficient market hypothesis

Keyword

Efficient market hypothesis (EMH) is a controversial theory which polarizes debate amongst academics, analysts and investment professionals. It is largely based on the key studies of the markets by

Eugene Fama and essentially states that, because information is freely available regarding listed companies, it is therefore known to investors and this will result in the shares being correctly priced on the markets. In the finance world, the description 'efficient market' is generally accepted to imply that the price of the share reflects fully all the available information pertaining to that company. This is both a bold and strong hypothesis and forms the basis of the controversy surrounding the theory.

To add further complexity, the theory is further divided into three separate versions, which reflect the different possibilities covered by the term 'all available information' and therefore correspond to how efficient the market actually is. The steps build on each other: ie semi-strong form includes the assumptions of weak form and strong form includes the assumptions of both semi-strong and weak form.

Weak form efficiency

Weak form efficient market hypothesis makes the assumption that current market share prices already incorporate all available historic market trading data. This includes past pricing and price movements, trading volumes, details of events and news relevant to the company in question. This version of the hypothesis implies that past data should have no relationship to future pricing since this historic data is already known by the market and has already been reflected in historic pricing of the share on the market. For this reason, it is implied that historic analysis techniques, such as technical analysis, should fail to provide any advantage in excess of the market return.

Semi-strong form efficiency

Semi-strong form efficient market hypothesis makes the assumption that current market share prices already incorporate all publicly available information. This includes all the historic data covered in weak form, together with published 'fundamental' information such as balance sheet data, key company ratios, product-based information, patents, management decisions and changes – indeed, any published news or information relevant to the company. For this reason, it is implied that fundamental analysis techniques should fail to provide any advantage in excess of the market return as the information studied and analysed during fundamental analysis is deemed to be already priced into the market share price.

Strong form efficiency

The strong form efficient market hypothesis includes both the weak form and the semi-strong-form data but goes further to take the most extreme position of the three options. The strong form makes the assumption that current market share prices reflect not only historic and publicly available data, but also reflect all available information which is relevant to the company including information which is privately held by those individuals inside the company.

> **In practice**
>
> The common factor across the three forms of efficient market hypothesis is the assumption that the market prices will rapidly reflect 'available' information, which acknowledges that investors and traders (and therefore the markets) cannot respond to information which is not available to them. It is proposed as a reasonable assumption that only 'new' information will result in changes within the market and that new information could reflect either good or bad news for the company in question and therefore result in a positive or negative movement of the market share price. If the markets are efficient then it should be difficult to outperform, or indeed underperform the market if the market level of risk is adopted. Advocates of market efficiency would propose a passive buy-and-hold policy involving a mix of shares representative of the market index.

Many studies have taken place to test the various forms of efficient market hypothesis; however, most of the trading rules tested have failed to outperform a simple buy-and-hold policy which is the type of passive strategy proposed by its proponents. This would tend to support the weak form of the hypothesis, although technical analysts would point to the success of some momentum based strategies. Evidence for the semi-strong form is certainly mixed and many 'event' studies appear to support the proposal of market efficiency; however, a range of time studies including studies into calendar effects highlight anomalies which are not consistent with the assertion of market efficiency. Strong form is the most difficult form to evidence and research of the studies again provides mixed support. Unsurprisingly, performance results for 'corporate individuals' did not support efficient markets; however, in many countries the use of privileged private information to obtain a financial advantage (insider dealing) is illegal and therefore the financial dealings of corporate officials and their close associates are carefully monitored. Examination of professional fund manager performance, however, reveals a broad inability to outperform a buy-and-hold passive strategy on a risk-adjusted basis.

The polarization of views regarding efficient market hypothesis will continue, fuelled by the assumptions which need to be made. We must assume that investors are rational and have equal access to the markets and the information which is available. It is also worth noting another interesting point that is raised by those who do not believe that the markets are efficient. The three forms of efficiency assume that information in the form of news will be rapidly assimilated into the share price by the market; however, this does not take into account that some investors may not discover news immediately or may choose to ignore it even though it is available. Additionally, institutional investors may have structured processes which form their decision making and this may also slow down the use of available information in practice.

Further insights will be considered in the section devoted to behavioural finance.

Modern portfolio theory

Keyword

Modern portfolio theory is a hypothesis by Harry Markowitz published in 1952. The principle is that a rational investor is risk-averse and recognizing that the acceptance of risk is an integral part of achieving a higher level of reward, the rational investor will require a greater return if he or she is prepared to accept a higher level of risk. Markowitz proposed that investors may therefore construct investment portfolios with the aim of optimizing expected return for a particular level of market risk.

Modern portfolio theory proposes that if the investor invests in more than one share and therefore creates a portfolio of shares, it is possible to benefit from the phenomenon-known as diversification, which will result in a reduction in the overall riskiness of the portfolio. This is based on the premise that the act of diversifying the investor's shareholding by including shares

Figure 5.1 Effect of diversification

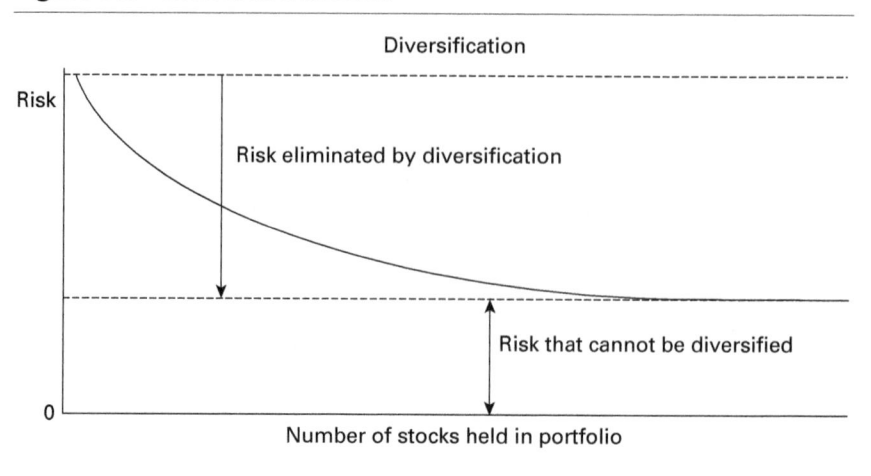

[Figure: A curve showing risk decreasing as the number of stocks held in portfolio increases. The y-axis is labelled "Risk" and the x-axis is labelled "Number of stocks held in portfolio". A horizontal dashed line at the top is labelled "Diversification". The area above the curve and below the top line represents "Risk eliminated by diversification". A lower horizontal dashed line separates the curve's asymptote; the area below this line represents "Risk that cannot be diversified".]

which are not strongly correlated will result in less risk being taken than by holding any one of the individual shares, even if individually the shares are considered to be higher risk.

The purpose of adding additional shares to the portfolio is to reduce the volatility, usually measured by the standard deviation. This is achieved in practice by continuing to add additional shares which do not have a high positive correlation to those already held; an example of this could be shares in a manufacturing company and shares in a supermarket chain. In this way it is possible to achieve substantial diversification benefits for the portfolio. The purpose is not simply to pick shares, but to select the correct mixture of shares to create an efficient portfolio. A point will be reached, as shown in Figure 5.1 (repeated from Figure 4.2), where the optimum level of diversification has been achieved and no further benefit of diversification will be gained by adding additional shares to the portfolio. The effect of diversification is to reduce the unsystematic element of risk within the portfolio of shares and at the point of optimum diversification; the unsystematic element of risk will be substantially removed. The remaining risk, the systematic or market risk, cannot be mitigated by diversification and will be unchanged.

We have concentrated on looking at a portfolio of different shares in the example above; however, it is also possible to create a well-diversified portfolio by using different asset classes which are not highly positively correlated. An example would be shares and bonds, or shares and property. A well-diversified portfolio may also be useful in protecting the overall value of the investment during challenging market conditions. It is quite

Figure 5.2 Efficient frontier diagram

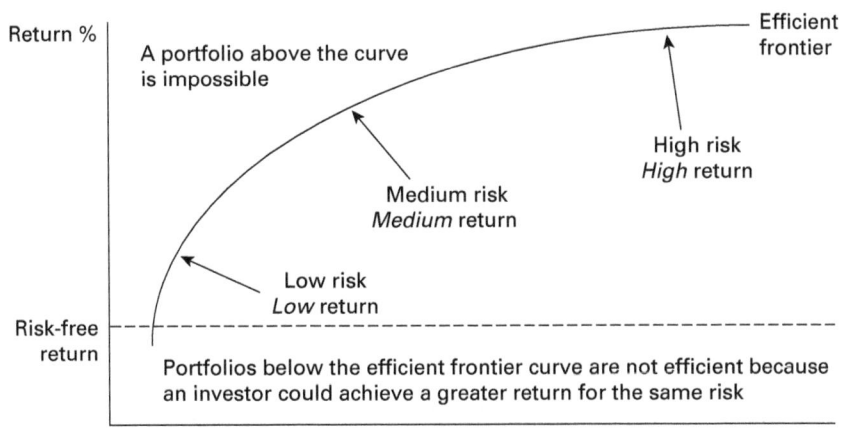

```
Return %                                              Efficient
         A portfolio above the curve                  frontier
         is impossible
                                            High risk
                                            High return
                        Medium risk
                        Medium return
                Low risk
                Low return
Risk-free
return
         Portfolios below the efficient frontier curve are not efficient because
         an investor could achieve a greater return for the same risk

                        Risk % (standard deviation)
```

feasible to construct portfolios with a range of risk and return characteristics to suit the needs and requirements of different investors and to satisfy the risk appetite of the individual. The balance between risk and return can be illustrated by the efficient frontier diagram (Figure 5.2) which shows the relationship between risk and return and may also incorporate an indication of the return expected from a risk-free asset. Portfolios are located along the curve described as the efficient frontier.

The shape and position of the efficient frontier curve will differ for different portfolio asset combinations. It can be seen from this example curve that an optimal risk portfolio will usually be found around the middle of the curve, as the higher we progress up the curve, an increase in return equates to a significantly higher increase in risk. A portfolio that is lower down on the curve would not be practical as the returns would be similar to the returns available using a risk-free asset. Portfolios below the curve are inefficient since greater return could be achieved along the curve for the same level of risk taken and portfolios above the curve are impossible.

In addition to diversification techniques, modern portfolio theory makes use of five different statistical measurements of risk which are considered to assist potential investors determine an investment's risk-reward profile. These risk measurements are:

- Beta;
- Alpha;

- standard deviation;
- R-squared;
- Sharpe ratio.

Beta

> **Keyword**
>
> **Beta** is a measure of volatility in comparison to the market or an appropriate benchmark and is discussed in detail in Chapter 4 on risk. It is considered to be a relative measurement of risk as Beta compares the volatility of a security against an appropriate benchmark; the Beta of a security is a historical indicator and is not a fixed value, but it does change over time.

Beta may be used in relation to individual securities, for example company shares, or it may also be used for funds and portfolios. The Beta of a fund or a portfolio may be calculated quite accurately by knowing the exact composition of the fund and knowing the Beta of the individual assets within the fund. Interpretation of Beta is quite simple; for example, a company share with a Beta of 1.0 is the same volatility as the market. If the share has a Beta which is greater than 1.0 it is more volatile than the market and if its Beta is less than 1.0, it is less volatile than the market.

Alpha

> **Keyword**
>
> **Alpha** is the measure of an asset's performance on a risk-adjusted basis. It measures the difference between the asset's actual return and its expected return, given the asset's level of risk, which is represented by its beta coefficient.

We can say that, if an asset's return is in excess of the return, then its Beta would indicate then it will have a positive Alpha; if its return is below the return, then its Beta would indicate then its Alpha will be negative.

Investment theory

In practice

Let's look at the following example.

A share in Green Plc has a Beta of 1.2 and the market return for the year we are analysing is 12 per cent.

This means that we would expect the Green Plc share to have an annual return of 14.4 per cent (12% × 1.2 = 14.4%).

If the Green Plc share has an annual performance greater than 14.4 per cent it has a positive Alpha.

Alpha may also be used as a measure of performance for funds and portfolios as well as individual securities and is sometimes used as an indicator to reflect the skill and judgement of the fund manager, or the 'added value' that the fund manager is deemed to have contributed to overall performance. With fund performance, the Alpha will represent the excess return achieved above the return of the fund's benchmark and will often be referred to as the excess return or the 'abnormal rate of return'. The abnormal rate of return is also the return that is generated in excess of the expected return indicated by an equilibrium model, such as the capital asset pricing model.

Whilst Alpha is certainly a useful measure, care should be exercised in its use. For example, since Alpha is measuring fund performance in excess of the benchmark it is crucial that the benchmark chosen is an appropriate one. This also means that comparison of funds or securities undertaken using Alpha should be limited to funds or securities within the same asset class(es).

It should also be noted that charges and fees will also affect overall performance and Alpha measurements cannot differentiate between underperformance as a result of high fees and charges and underperformance as a result of ineffective fund management.

Standard deviation

Standard deviation is defined as being the square root of the variance and measures the dispersion of a set of data from its mean; it is also discussed in detail in Chapter 4 on risk. A high standard deviation value indicates higher volatility in an asset or a fund and therefore may prove to be a useful tool in a situation where comparisons are being made between two or more prospective investment acquisitions. Care must be exercised however in such direct comparisons, particularly, for example, when comparing company shares with share prices which are significantly different from each other. Coefficient of variation may then prove to be a more appropriate comparison tool.

Financial companies globally will commonly publish information regarding the standard deviation of their funds and other products, as within the finance and investment industry standard deviation is considered to be one of the most useful risk measures for finance professionals and individual investors. Standard deviation is also quite easy to explain and for individuals to understand.

R-squared

Coefficient of determination is another way in which R-squared may be found to be expressed.

> **Keyword**
>
> **R-squared** is not a measurement of security or portfolio performance; it is actually a statistical tool which may be used to assess the ability or accuracy of a model to describe future outcomes. As a statistical tool, it measures the actual percentage of the movements attributable to a security or a fund which can be explained by the movements in the benchmark, which is often an appropriate index. R-squared is measured on a scale of 0 to 1, but is often quoted as a percentage, between the range 0–100 per cent.

Interpretation of R-squared is quite straightforward: a very low R-squared means that little of the movement of a security or fund may be attributed to the movement of the benchmark; a high R-squared means that the actions of the benchmark explain a large proportion of the movements of the security or fund. So, for example, an index tracker fund which invests only in the shares of companies listed on the FTSE 100 exchange will have a high R-squared, probably very close to 1 or 100 per cent. However, the reverse is true if we have an R-squared of 0.25, or 25 per cent. At this level we can say that only 25 per cent of the movement of the fund is explained by the movement of the benchmark.

Figure 5.3 Scatter plot: higher R-squared

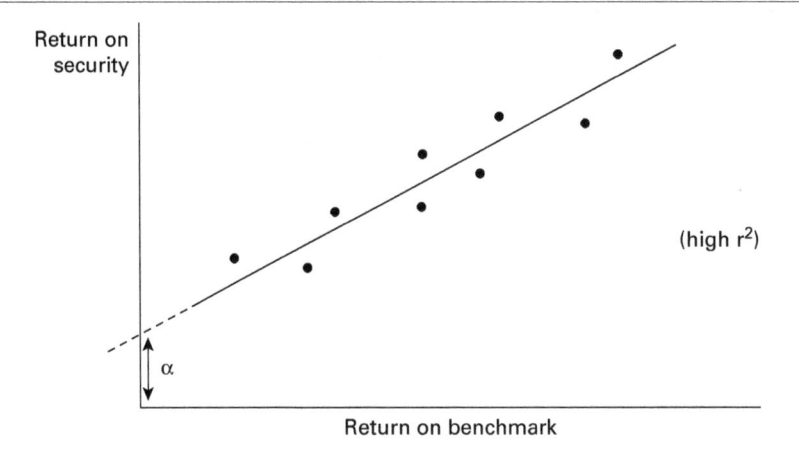

[Scatter plot showing Return on security vs Return on benchmark with points closely fitted to a line, labeled (high r²), with α marked on the y-axis intercept]

Figure 5.4 Scatter plot: lower R-squared

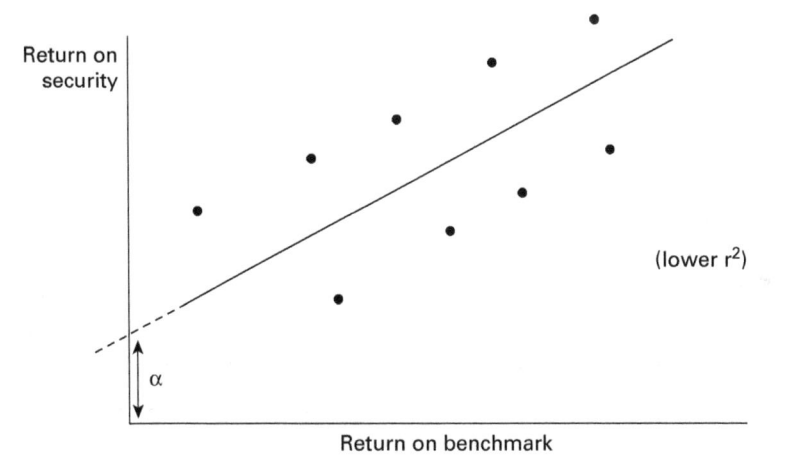

[Scatter plot showing Return on security vs Return on benchmark with points more dispersed around the line, labeled (lower r²), with α marked on the y-axis intercept]

The type of diagram shown in Figures 5.3 and Figure 5.4 shows the returns of a security or fund plotted against the returns of the appropriate benchmark. It is known as a 'scatter plot' and a straight line is drawn as a 'best fit' through the plotted points marked on the graph. We note that the point that the line intersects the security or fund return axis is an indication of the Alpha of the security or fund, whilst the gradient of the line represents the Beta of the security or fund.

As a generalization for the numerical representation of R-squared we can say that:

- 0.7 to 1 represents good correlation between returns of the security or fund and the returns of the benchmark;
- 0.3 to 0.7 represents an average correlation between returns of the security or fund and the returns of the benchmark;
- 0 to 0.3 represents low correlation between returns of the security or fund and the returns of the benchmark.

It is also worth noting that the R-squared value has a relevance to the Beta of a security or fund as it describes how accurately the Beta will reflect the volatility of the security or fund, with respect to the market. For example, if we are considering a fund with a low R-squared of 20 per cent then the Beta of that fund will be of less help to us in assessing the volatility of the fund with respect to the market.

Sharpe ratio

William F Sharpe developed the measure known as the Sharpe ratio in 1966 although it may also be found referred to in some texts as the Sharpe index and Sharpe measure.[5]

Keyword

Sharpe ratio has become an industry standard measure for the calculation of risk-adjusted returns and quantifies the return in excess of a risk-free return, relative to the standard deviation. Typical usage of the Sharpe ratio involves the quantification of the average return earned on a fund in excess of the risk-free rate per unit of total risk. This implies that the fund is not perfectly diversified, since the risk is measured by standard deviation in the case of the Sharpe ratio, standard deviation being representative of total risk. The formula for the calculation of Sharpe ratio is:

$$\text{Sharpe ratio} = \frac{(R_x - R_f)}{\sigma}$$

where:
R_x = return of Fund x
R_f = risk-free return
σ = standard deviation of Fund x

Investment theory

We know that modern portfolio theory indicates that if we add further uncorrelated assets to a diversified fund this allows us to reduce the risk inherent in the fund without compromising the returns. This type of action will increase the Sharpe ratio of the fund and therefore we can see that the higher the Sharpe ratio of a fund, the more suitable its returns have been relative to the risk that has been taken. In other words; the greater the Sharpe ratio, the more agreeable the risk-adjusted return to the investor.

In the context of its useful applications, Sharpe ratio may be utilized to evaluate whether the returns of a fund are attributable to astute and intelligent investment decisions or simply a result of the fund manager taking excessive risk. Comparing the Sharpe ratio of a fund with those of its peers will afford this useful illustration. It is worth noting that it is possible for a fund to exhibit a negative Sharpe ratio although this would indicate that the fund's performance has been inferior to that of a risk-free asset.

In practice

Let's look at an example:

Fund A has a three-year return of 14 per cent and a standard deviation of 5 per cent during the same period.

Fund B has a three-year return of 19 per cent and a standard deviation of 8 per cent over the same three-year period.

An appropriate risk-free rate of return over this three-year period is 2.9 per cent.

To decide which fund is the most suitable we would calculate the Sharpe ratio for both using the formula in the previous box:

$$\text{Fund A Sharpe ratio} = \frac{14 - 2.9}{5} = 2.22$$

$$\text{Fund B Sharpe ratio} = \frac{19 - 2.9}{8} = 2.01$$

We can therefore comment that despite its three-year return being lower than the return of Fund B, a rational investor would choose to invest in Fund A since it has a superior risk-adjusted return, as indicated by its higher Sharpe ratio. It follows that a fund with a high standard deviation must have a very high return in order to exhibit a high Sharpe ratio, so it is therefore worth bearing in mind that just because a fund has a high Sharpe ratio doesn't mean that it is not subject to volatility and therefore risk.

A Sharpe ratio may also be used to illustrate the potential changes in the risk–return characteristics of a fund, following the decision to add a new security or asset to the existing fund. Knowing the Sharpe ratio of the original fund, we can re-calculate the Sharpe ratio of the new fund composition following the proposed addition, and then compare the two. If the proposed addition of the new security or asset would increase the Sharpe ratio, then this would be a good decision, even if the new security or asset is a more risky one, because it can be seen to improve the risk–return characteristics of the fund. However, if the ratio would be reduced, the proposed changes would not be advisable. Limitations of using Sharpe ratio include the fact that it is based on analysis of historical data and that reliance upon using standard deviation to represent the risk assumes a normal distribution of the data.

Sharpe ratio is not the only performance measure which illustrates the risk–return relationship in a single value. There are three other measures which merit examination, which are Treynor ratio, Jensen's measure and information ratio.

Treynor ratio

Jack L Treynor was responsible for the development of the Treynor ratio, which he introduced in 1965.[6]

Keyword

The **Treynor ratio**, which may also be found to be referred to as the Treynor measure in some texts, seeks to identify how an investor is compensated by an investment fund given its level of risk, by illustrating the ratio of fund excess return to its Beta. Treynor ratio is quite similar to Sharpe ratio since it is a measurement which utilizes the established relationship between return and risk. There is a significant difference however, between Treynor ratio and Sharpe ratio: Treynor ratio makes use of market risk which is represented by Beta whilst Sharpe ratio uses the total risk, represented by the standard deviation.

The Treynor ratio is sometimes referred to as the ratio of reward to volatility and may be calculated using the following formula:

$$\text{Treynor ratio} = \frac{(R_x - R_f)}{\beta}$$

where:
R_x = return of Fund x
R_f = risk-free return
β = beta coefficient of Fund x

Treynor ratio is effectively a risk-adjusted measurement of an excess return relative to market, or systematic risk, since the Treynor ratio is utilizing Beta to gauge risk, which measures the sensitivity of an investment to market movements. It is worth remembering that the market, or systematic risk, represented by the beta coefficient, cannot be removed by diversification techniques.

In terms of its practical application, this was conceived as a performance measure which could apply to all investors regardless of their risk profile and it is reasonable to assume that all risk-averse investors will wish to maximize the excess return above the risk-free return for a given level of risk, indicated by the beta coefficient. With a higher Treynor ratio the implication is that the investor has generated a higher return relative to the market risk taken, so in a similar way to the Sharpe ratio, the greater the Treynor ratio, the more agreeable the risk-adjusted return to the investor. In the case of an investment fund, a higher Treynor ratio implies a higher degree of fund management skills.

The use of Treynor ratio is normally restricted to well-diversified funds as the use of Beta implies that the unsystematic element of risk in the fund has been mitigated by appropriate diversification. Also, the historic nature of the data being used must be acknowledged because the Beta of securities and assets held within investment funds will change over time and therefore the Beta of the fund itself will not be static.

Treynor ratio may be effectively utilized to compare the performance of investment funds with their peers and with an appropriate benchmark, taking care to analyse the comparison over the same time period to prevent errors.

In practice

Two investment funds, Fund X and Fund Y, are both comprised of shares which are listed on the FTSE 100 Index. Fund X has a one-year return of 9.5 per cent and a beta coefficient of 0.65 during the same period. Fund Y has a one-year return of 11.4 percent and a beta coefficient of 0.91 over the same one-year period.

During the period of analysis, a FTSE 100 Index tracker fund has achieved an annual return of 12.2 per cent and an appropriate risk-free rate of return over this period is 2.5 per cent. We can reasonably assume that the Beta of the FTSE Index tracker fund is 1.0.

To evaluate which fund is the most suitable we would calculate the Treynor ratio for both funds and for the benchmark index using the formula from the previous box:

$$\text{Fund X Treynor ratio} = \frac{9.5 - 2.5}{0.65} = 10.77$$

$$\text{Fund X Treynor ratio} = \frac{11.4 - 2.5}{0.91} = 9.78$$

$$\text{Index benchmark Treynor ratio} = \frac{12.2 - 2.5}{1.0} = 9.70$$

From the calculations above, it can be seen that, despite the annual return of Fund X being lower than the annual return of Fund Y, a rational investor would choose to invest in Fund X since it has a superior risk-adjusted return, as indicated by its higher Treynor ratio. In this case both funds have performed positively in comparison with the benchmark index.

Jensen's measure

Jensen's measure was proposed by the economist Michael C Jensen in 1968 and may also be seen referred to as Jensen's performance index, Jensen's alpha and sometimes simply Alpha, in various texts.[7] This measure was devised in order to attempt to evaluate the performance of fund managers and identify if fund managers were actually outperforming markets consistently.

Keyword

Jensen's measure may be used to determine the risk-adjusted performance of a fund or an asset relative to the expected market return. This is, of course, based on the **capital asset pricing model**.

We can see that if a particular fund or an asset exhibits a positive figure for Jensen's measure, or Alpha, this implies that a greater return has been achieved than the risk-adjusted return indicated by the capital asset pricing model. The higher the figure for Alpha, the more a fund or an asset has outperformed the expected return. For a rational investor, funds and assets with a positive Alpha are very inviting because this indicates a positive abnormal return.

The formula used to calculate Jensen's measure is:

$$\text{Jensen's measure} = R_x - \{R_f + \beta_x (R_m - R_f)\}$$

where:
R_x = expected return of the fund or asset in question
R_f = risk-free rate of return
β_x = Beta of the fund or asset in question
R_m = expected market return

For investors to assess the quality of a fund manager's performance it is necessary to consider the level of risk involved in achieving its investment return, as well as the overall performance of the fund. This allows the investor to judge whether the return provides adequate compensation for the risk taken. Rational investors wish to maximize the returns for a given level of risk and, ideally, will aim to achieve a high return on their investment whilst taking a minimum amount of risk. So, for example, if two investment funds achieved the same annual return but one of the funds was identified to be of lower risk, the lower-risk fund would be the appropriate option for a rational investor.

If the calculated Jensen's measure is positive, this indicates that the investment fund is achieving excess returns and this outperformance is an indicator that the fund manager has 'beaten the market'; however, a negative Jensen's measure is an indicator of underperformance relative to the risk taken. It is worth remembering that if the fund performance is determined to be in line with the capital asset pricing model, then the fund will lie in a position on the security market line. However, if the fund has outperformed or underperformed the return predicted by the capital asset pricing model, then the fund will lie above or below the security market line respectively.

In practice

An investment fund with a Beta of 1.12 achieves an annual return of 14.1 per cent and in the same annual period, the appropriate market index produced a return of 11.2 per cent.

During this period of analysis, the appropriate risk-free rate of return is 2.1 per cent. The Jensen's measure (Alpha) of the fund may be calculated using the formula shown in the key concept box above, ie:

> Jensen's measure (Alpha) = 14.1% − {2.1% + 1.12 × (11.2% − 2.1%)}
> = 14.1 − {2.1 + 10.2}
> = 1.8%
>
> Although it is not certain, we would expect the investment fund to achieve a higher return than the market index, as it has a beta coefficient of 1.12, which is greater than 1 and is therefore higher risk than the market. From the calculation above, it can be seen that the positive figure for Alpha indicates the fund manager in this example has achieved sufficient additional return to compensate for the additional risk taken by the fund, during the period of analysis.
>
> However, if the situation was slightly different and the fund's annual return was only 12.1 per cent then the figure for Alpha would be −0.2 per cent and this negative figure for Alpha would indicate that the fund manager had not been able to generate sufficient returns to justify the level of risk taken.

Information ratio

The information ratio is another example of a risk-adjusted performance measure and some commentators refer to it as a variation on the Sharpe ratio where the benchmark isn't specified to be a risk-free rate. Information ratio is considered to be a versatile and widely used measure of actively managed fund performance and was developed by Jack L Treynor and Fischer Black in 1973.[8] It was initially referred to as the 'appraisal ratio' and it aims to quantify the amount of value which is attributable to an active fund manager.

> **Keyword**
>
> **Information ratio** seeks to indicate the amount of additional excess return over a benchmark which may be obtained per additional unit of risk. The name information ratio is appropriate because it seeks to gauge how a fund manager uses skill, judgement, knowledge and information in the pursuit of enhancing investment returns. The information ratio is determined by subtracting the return of the fund's benchmark from the actual fund returns and dividing by the tracking error. The tracking error

is calculated as the standard deviation of the excess return over the benchmark and this tracking error represents a measure of the volatility of the excess returns. The formula for information ratio is:

$$\text{information ratio} = \frac{R_f - R_b}{\sigma_e}$$

where:
R_f = annual return of fund
R_b = annual return of appropriate benchmark for fund
σ_e = standard deviation of excess return (tracking error)
$(R_f - R_b)$ represents the excess return

This formula allows us to quantify the value, per unit of extra risk assumed, by which the manager's skills and judgement have augmented the market performance, represented by the fund's benchmark. The basic premise is this: take an example where a fund manager has made certain assumptions regarding the prospects of various assets within the markets. The manager will then take a position on those assets within the fund and by assuming an overweight or underweight position relative to the market portfolio, will take either more or less risk than the market. If an active fund manager takes no risk during the management of the fund then the performance of the fund would mirror the performance of the benchmark.

Therefore, by using the information ratio, an investor may determine how much additional return is attributable to the fund manager as a result of the additional risk involved in implementation of the fund manager's specific investment strategies and decisions. A higher value for the information ratio is preferable and as a broad guideline it is judged that an information ratio of 0.5 indicates good performance, 0.75 is very good performance and 1.00 reflects outstanding performance by the fund's manager. If the fund underperforms the benchmark there will be a negative figure generated for the information ratio and this reflects badly upon the fund manager's performance.

In practical terms, the information ratio proves useful when making a comparison between several similar funds with similar management styles and objectives. If an investor considers two comparable funds with similar Alphas the fund which exhibits the highest information ratio is run by the manager who has used more skill and judgement in the risks that have been taken which deviate from the benchmark. The fund with the lower information ratio indicates that the gains made reflect less active management skills and more to do with market movements.

In terms of the limitations of this metric, there is freedom for fund managers to choose the benchmark against which their performance is to be targeted and it is therefore important that an appropriate and accurate benchmark is selected. In practice, this will often be a market index, such as the S&P 500, Hang Seng or the DAX. Also, it must be noted that the R-squared correlation between the fund and its appropriate benchmark must be strong if an investor is to value the information ratio.

Measurement of performance under modern portfolio theory

We have already considered the implications of the theory, which says that it is possible to construct an 'efficient frontier' of optimal portfolios which will offer maximization of the expected return for a specific level of risk accepted. The further implications of the theory are that the risk and return characteristics of an individual asset should be considered in relation to the effect that the individual asset has on the whole portfolio's risk and return, rather than being considered in isolation.

Modern portfolio theory makes the assumption that investors are risk-averse, so investors will only accept more risk if they have the reasonable expectation of more reward. We can calculate the portfolio weighted return in order to use the returns of the individual assets and measure the return of the whole portfolio performance.

Portfolio weighted return

When analysing portfolios, it is necessary to consider the performance of each individual asset within the portfolio, relative to its proportion of the portfolio as a whole. It would be very unusual for a portfolio with multiple assets to have the assets split in equal proportions within the portfolio and therefore one method used, in order to see the impact of each asset on portfolio performance, is to undertake a weighted performance calculation. It is crucial that the weightings used are based on the market value at the start of the period to be examined. We can calculate the overall return for a portfolio which is comprised of several different assets, using the formula:

$$R_p = (w_a \times r_a) + (w_b \times r_b) + (w_c \times r_c) + (w_n \times r_n)$$

where:

R_p = overall total return on the portfolio comprising assets $a, b, c... n$
w_a = % weighting allocated in asset a (by market value)
r_a = % return attributable to asset a
w_n = % weighting allocated in asset n (by market value)
r_n = % return attributable to asset n

In practice

Let's consider this example.

We wish to calculate the expected return of a portfolio which has been built using five exactly equally-weighted assets: A, B, C, D and E.

The expected returns of each of the assets are as follows:

A - 7.5% B - 6.3% C - 7.2% D - 4.1% E - 5.6%

We can calculate the expected return of the portfolio using the formula above:

portfolio return = (A% × 20%) + (B% × 20%) + (C% × 20%) + (D% × 20%) + (E% × 20%)

= (7.5 × 20%) + (6.3 × 20%) + (7.2 × 20%) + (4.1 × 20%) + (5.6 × 20%)

= 6.14%

In the more likely event that the assets were not equally proportioned within the portfolio, it is necessary to determine the total market value of the portfolio as a whole, and then use the market value of each asset divided by the market value of the portfolio to determine the percentage of each asset and therefore the proportion of its performance, which will contribute to the performance of the portfolio.

Capital asset pricing model

Keyword

The **capital asset pricing model** relates the required rate of return for a security, for example a company share, to its Beta, which represents the systematic risk. The model, which is often seen abbreviated to CAPM, was developed by four economists, Jack Treynor, William Sharpe, John Lintner and Jan Mossin, in the 1960s.[9] The capital asset pricing model (CAPM) works on the expectation that investors will require that they are compensated both for the risk that they are prepared to take and for the **time value of money**.

What the CAPM model puts forward is that the expected return of a security or a fund is equal to the return on a **risk-free security** plus a **risk premium**. Investment in the security or fund should not occur if the expected return does not equal or exceed the required return, as this would not be a rational investment. This ensures that the investor is compensated for the additional risk they are prepared to take, in excess of the risk-free security, by indicating an appropriate required return.

This relationship between expected return and risk can be shown graphically by plotting security market line, which indicates the results of the CAPM model for a range of risk, denoted by Beta (Figure 5.5). The security market line illustrates that as the Beta and therefore the risk of a security increases, it follows that the expected return also increases. The difference between the expected return and the risk-free return is known as the market risk premium, or sometimes as the equity risk premium.

There is a formula which may be used to calculate the return that would be expected from a security in order for it to be considered to be a viable and rational investment and this is known as the CAPM formula, which is shown below. The risk-free rate of return is identified by the term Rf in the

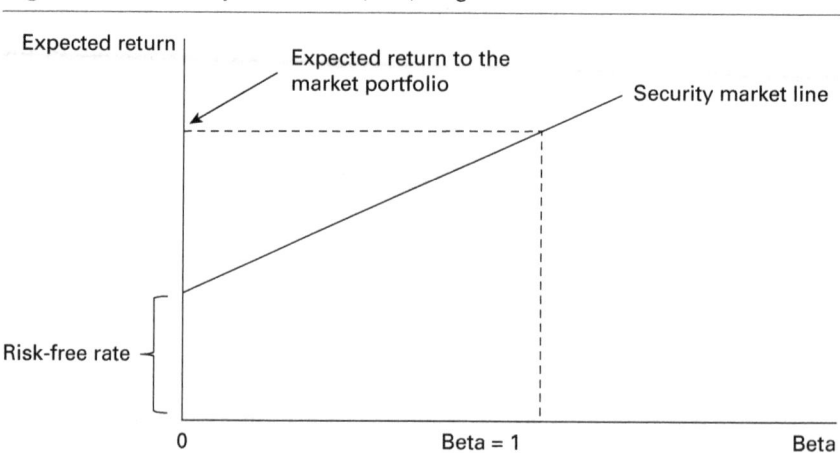

Figure 5.5 Security market line (SML) diagram

formula and this represents the time value of money. This element of the formula represents the return which compensates an investor for investing a sum of money over a given period of time.

The rest of the CAPM formula is representative of the risk and specifically the additional element of the return which is compensating the investor for accepting the excess risk above the risk-free return. This includes the volatility of the security in which funds are being invested, represented by the security's Beta and $(R_m - R_f)$, which is the element of the formula which identifies the market risk premium. The full CAPM formula is:

$$R_e = R_f + \beta (R_m - R_f)$$

where:
R_e = expected return of the security in question
R_f = risk-free rate of return
β = Beta of the security in question
R_m = expected market return

In practice

Where the investment security is a company share, the market return is usually represented by an appropriate index; so, for example, if the investor is considering investing in a Barclays Bank share, the market return could be the return of the FTSE 100 Index over the period of time in question.

Risk-free return

A risk-free return is a theoretical concept and is the return that is obtainable from an asset which bears no risk at all. This represents the return on invested funds that an investor could realize when investing in a risk-free asset over a specified period of time. In theory, this should represent the very minimum return that a rational investor would accept, since the rational investor would require a greater rate of return if any additional risk was accepted.

In reality, a 100 per cent risk-free rate does not actually exist because even investments which are technically extremely safe still bear a small element of risk. However, certain securities are considered so safe that in practice, they are considered to be effectively risk-free for the purposes of such financial models.

> **In practice**
>
> A risk-free rate will naturally vary depending upon the location of the investor; however, it is usually assumed to be the yield on government bonds such as UK gilts, US treasuries or bonds issued by other stable Western governments. It may reasonably be assumed that holding this type of security until redemption will involve minimal default risk and therefore may practically be assumed to generate risk-free rate of return. It is expected that rational investors will demand a higher return on equity or other higher-risk investments relative to low-risk alternatives because their invested capital is subjected to increased risk and this brings us to the market risk premium.

Market risk premium

The market risk premium is also sometimes referred to as the equity risk premium, particularly where investment in company shares or similar is involved. The market risk premium represents the part of the CAPM equation which illustrates the difference between returns from a market portfolio and the assumed risk-free rate of return. This is represented by the (Rm – Rf) element of the equation. The risk premium reflects required returns, historical returns and expected returns. The market risk premium will be the same for all investors in the same region during a given period of time since the value used is historic.

Time value of money

The time value of money represents the concept that an amount of an investor's money available at the present time is worth more than the same amount of the investor's money at some point in the future. This is because the money has the potential to earn additional returns between now and the point in the future in question. This principle is sound and provided the investor's money can earn some form of interest, any given amount of money is worth more now than the same amount in the future. The time value of money may sometimes be referred to as the present discounted value and is considered later in the chapter.

Security market line

The relationship between expected return and Beta is shown graphically by the security market line (see Figure 5.5). In order to create the security

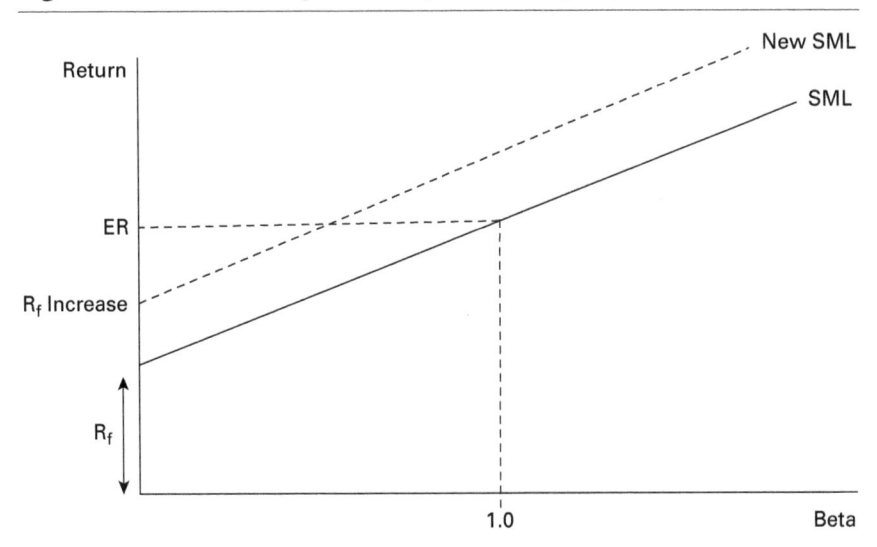

Figure 5.6 Parallel change in security market line (SML)

market line we need to plot two points. The first is the risk-free return, which corresponds to a Beta figure of zero and the second is the expected return of the market, which corresponds to a Beta equal to 1. If CAPM applies, then a straight line through these two points will illustrate the security market line as described by the CAPM formula. This illustrates the relationship between risk and return and is useful for both individual assets and for portfolios. If the CAPM relationship holds, that is to say that the security is priced 'fairly', the security will lie somewhere along the security market line, dependent upon its current beta coefficient. For a given Beta, the expected return of an asset may then be identified using the security market line.

It is possible for the security market line to change position; so, for example, changes in the market conditions which result in the risk-free return increasing or decreasing will result in a parallel movement up or down, for the security market line (see Figure 5.6).

Similarly, a change in the attitude of market participants to investment risk will result in the gradient of the security market line changing (see Figure 5.7). It is also worth noting that it is theoretically possible to have a security which exhibits a negative Beta, in which case it would plot along the security market line to the left side of the return axis, with both Beta and return values less than the risk-free rate of return.

If the market is not behaving efficiently then a security which is 'overpriced' would be expected to plot below the security market line and a security which is 'underpriced' would be expected to plot above the security market line.

Investment and Portfolio Management

Figure 5.7 Change in gradient of the security market line (SML)

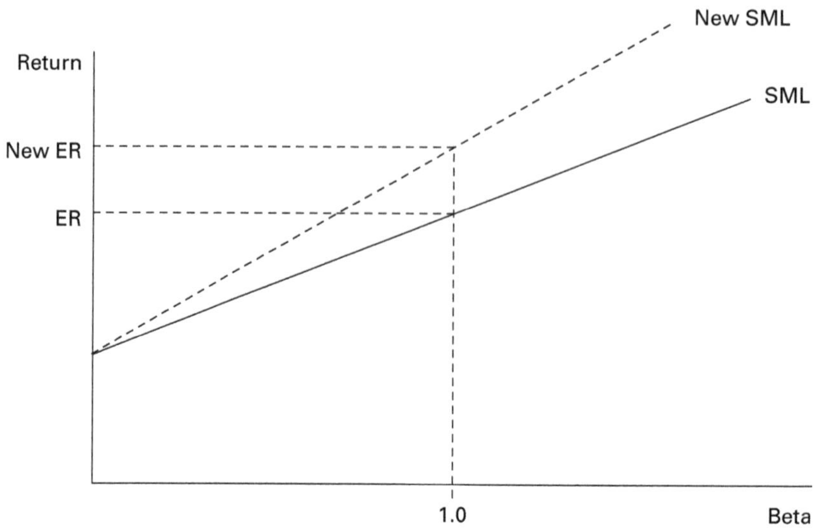

In practice

Consider a practical calculation of CAPM.

We are thinking about investing a sum of money in the shares of a company, Good Buy Plc.

Let us assume that the Beta of Good Buy Plc is 1.2, an appropriate risk-free rate of return is 2.0 per cent and the expected market return during the period in question is 9.0 per cent.

Using the CAPM formula shown earlier, we can calculate the expected return for the shares in Good Buy Plc. So using:

$$R_e = R_f + \beta (R_m - R_f)$$

$$R_e = 2.0 + 1.2(9.0 - 2.0)$$

$$R_e = 2.0 + (1.2 \times 7.0)$$

$$R_e = 10.4\%$$

we can say that the expected return of the shares in Good Buy Plc is 10.4 per cent and so if the actual return does not equal or exceed 10.4 per cent then it would not be appropriate for the investor to invest in Good Buy Plc shares at this time, based on the risk taken and the return achieved.

Assumptions for CAPM model

The CAPM model was proposed to predict the expected (or required) return of a security, given its beta coefficient which represents systematic risk. In order for this model to work, there are various conditions required and the assumptions we must make include the following:

- capital markets operate perfectly competitively;
- all information is available freely and at no cost, so that markets are able to evaluate risk;
- there is perfect diversification within the market portfolio;
- all market participants hold a diversified portfolio of equities representing the market risk;
- there is a single risk-free rate available to all market participants;
- there are no market imperfections such as taxes, regulation, transactions costs;
- all investors are rational.

It is quite clear that these assumptions are not realistic in the real financial world and simplify many complex issues. This is one of the reasons that have seen the relevance of the CAPM model questioned by some academics and finance professionals. However, it is still regarded as a key model in the financial arena and if the limitations of the model are carefully considered the CAPM model does have its uses, particularly in a comparison role.

There is always the need for caution to be exercised when using figures within the CAPM formula, particularly regarding the period of time for Rf and Rm. Clearly, since the markets are constantly changing, different time periods under examination will give different figures; furthermore, the value of Beta for individual companies will change over time. Also, due to the potential for volatility to have an element of unpredictability, sometimes high Beta stocks have low returns and low Beta stocks will perform surprisingly well.

With regard to the practical problems involved in the use of the CAPM model, clearly the choice of the market return and the risk-free rate of return will never be standardized throughout the universe of market participants and the availability of all assets cannot always be guaranteed. We cannot assume that all information is available to all market participants equally and freely and we certainly cannot assume that the available information will always be acted upon or indeed interpreted in the same way. Furthermore, whilst we know that the majority of investors will make use of appropriate diversification strategies, the ability of all market participants to diversify perfectly is absurd as they may not have the technical ability or knowledge to do so and it is not certain that appropriate diversification opportunities always exist.

On a positive note, the practical uses of the CAPM include the ease of ranking the riskiness of individual investments and the ability to measure the 'riskiness' of a portfolio, since the Beta of a portfolio may easily be calculated using the weighted average of the individual share Betas held within the portfolio.

Arbitrage pricing theory

Arbitrage pricing theory was developed by economist Stephen Ross in 1976 as an alternative to the CAPM, given the growing realization about the limitations of relying on Beta to represent all factors in a security's risk and the unrealistic assumptions that are made by the capital asset pricing model.[10]

Keyword

Arbitrage pricing theory considers the theory that a security's returns can be predicted by examining the relationship between the security and a series of common risk factors; a multifactor approach rather than relying on the relationship of a single Beta.

Arbitrage pricing theory looks at the influence of several different macroeconomic factors on the return of a security and it is considered that if the current price of the security differs from the projected price indicated by the model, there exists an opportunity for an investor to purchase and dispose of the security at a profit. In this situation, the theory suggests that the risk is low until the price of the security changes. It is recognized that within markets where security prices are identified to offer arbitrage opportunities, the markets would usually correct quite quickly and so the opportunity will disappear. However, if investors make use of arbitrage pricing theory and succeed in the identification of an 'incorrectly priced' security, then successful 'arbitrageurs' may create a profit if they are able to act quickly enough to take advantage of the opportunity prior to the market price correction.

Whilst CAPM makes use of the expected market return, arbitrage pricing theory uses the security's expected return and a risk premium figure for a number of common macroeconomic and industry-related factors. The macroeconomic and industry factors may vary and can include such variables as economic output, consumer confidence factors, unemployment, industrial output, inflation, interest rates and spread of yields between investment grade and non-investment grade bonds. As the considered factors vary, then so will the value of the security under consideration. One of the most challenging aspects of arbitrage pricing theory is the need for investors to identify which macroeconomic and industry factors may be deemed to influence a specific security.

The basic arbitrage pricing theory formula is:

$$ER_x = R_f + \lambda_1 b_1 + \lambda_2 b_2 + \cdots + \lambda_n b_n$$

where:
ER_x = expected return of asset x
R_f = risk-free rate of return
λ_1 = risk premium of the first factor (the sensitivity to the 1st factor)
b_1 = factor loadings for the first factor
λ_n = risk premium of the n'th factor (the sensitivity to the n'th factor)
b_n = factor loadings for the n'th factor

Arbitrage pricing theory identifies the price which a mispriced security should exhibit, so therefore a mispriced security will be priced differently to the theoretical price which is predicted by the model. In efficient markets it is expected that profitable opportunities will quickly disappear as a result of the activity of the market participants and therefore arbitrage opportunities are expected to exist for only a short period of time. On that basis, arbitrage pricing theory allows the feasibility of some securities not sitting on the security market line, which indicates that the security is mispriced. Arbitrage pricing theory is considered to be more general than CAPM because it considers an expected return and Beta relationship without the assumption of a 'market portfolio' and it also employs fewer, less restrictive assumptions, which include:

- capital markets are perfectly competitive;
- investors may create a portfolio where unsystematic risk is eliminated through diversification;
- no arbitrage opportunity exists amongst well-diversified portfolios and if arbitrage opportunities exist, they will be quickly exploited by market participants;
- investors seek to maximize their wealth.

Arbitrage pricing theory has the advantage that it is more general and uses fewer and more realistic assumptions than CAPM. It is also credited with a more accurate explanation of performance for a given security since it uses multifactors instead of simply using Beta to determine the risk of a security. It also enables the use of more realistic portfolios rather than the 'market portfolio' used by CAPM. There are, however, limitations to arbitrage pricing theory as it does rely on the multifactors that are used being uncorrelated with each other and there being an established relationship identified between the returns of the security and the multifactors employed.

Arbitrage is identified as being the ability to invest in an asset with a sure profit and this is a situation which may require investors to be both knowledgeable and opportunistic. There are also various types of opportunity for arbitrage; for example, in its simplest form an investor identifies a security which is trading on two different exchanges, at slightly different prices. It is therefore possible to purchase the stock on the exchange with the lower price and immediately sell on the exchange with the higher price, making use of this opportunity for sure profit.

Another example would be a 'triangular arbitrage' which may, for example, involve currencies. An astute investor may identify a situation where they can convert cash from one currency into a second currency, then into a third currency and finally back to the original currency. If the exchange rates have been favourable, it is possible to make a sure profit in this manner.

A different type of arbitrage would be to exploit the difference in demand and supply of a security or asset in different geographical markets. An example of this would be a precious metal such as silver, available in different locations globally.

In practice

Let us assume that the price of silver in Hong Kong is HK$158.98 per ounce and in London the price of silver is GBP14.04 per ounce. If the exchange rate between the British pound and the Hong Kong dollar is 1 GBP = 10.04 HK$, then this means that the Hong Kong dollar equivalent London silver price would be HK$140.96.

In this scenario, a trader would be able to benefit by buying silver in London and selling it in Hong Kong at the higher price. This type of trading is known as market location arbitrage and may provide a guaranteed profit although it is dependent upon various factors, the first of which is the cost of shipping. The time factor is also crucial, because the prices on the markets may fluctuate and the exchange rate between the two currencies may also change, to the benefit or the detriment of the trader.

Behavioural finance

Keywords

Behavioural finance is a complex topic in itself, but broadly seeks to provide explanations and offer insight into factors which influence decision-making processes in market participants. Many academics credit the authors and psychologists Daniel Kahneman and Amos Tversky with being the founders of the study regarding behavioural finance.[11] Beginning in the 1960s, their work focused on disciplines such as psychology to try to provide explanations for the irrational and illogical behaviour identified within the financial world.

The key financial theories assume that market participants behave in a rational and logical manner and wish to maximize wealth, and much evidence supported the job that theories such as EMH and CAPM did in predicting and illustrating market behaviour. Over a period of time, however, it was recognized that the theories may represent ideal and often unrealistic situations and that on occasion market participants behaved and acted in an unpredictable manner. This resulted in anomalies which could not be explained by the mainstream financial theories. Recurring anomalies such as the January effect and their continued existence, contradict modern financial and economic theories which of course make the assumption about rational, logical behaviour by market participants.

Behavioural finance therefore seeks to explain why the key financial theories may fail to explain market behaviour by offering insights from sociology, psychology, history and other heuristics. Behavioural finance puts forward the suggestion that market participants:

- are overconfident about their abilities;
- demonstrate a 'herd instinct', in other words 'follow the crowd';

- are 'myopic', so they will ignore information they consider inconvenient (confirmation bias);
- will often overreact to news (both good and bad news);
- often extrapolate perceived trends (for example, a willingness to believe in 'technical analysis').

Later work by Barberis, Schleifer and Vishny also reinforces this explanation and the concept of sentiment.[12] Clearly, emotionally driven decisions and errors of judgement may be seen to be behind some anomalies and irrational methods of analysis, such as using 'rules of thumb' will add to these issues. It is also observed that decisions may be affected by the concept of 'framing', which involves the context in which a decision is considered.[13] For example, individuals may be found to react differently when presented with a 50 per cent chance of a profit, than when considering a 50 per cent chance of a loss, even though the chance of both is the same.

Other findings involve the likelihood of allowing decisions to be influenced by various biases, examples of which are local bias, loss aversion and confirmation bias. Local bias involves the tendency to invest in 'local' companies due to the perception of having more information and knowledge about them. Loss aversion is based on the precept that many market participants will strongly prefer avoiding losses to making gains and may take a risk to avoid a loss in preference to taking the same risk to make gains. Confirmation bias refers to the practice of looking for information and evidence to support an existing idea, rather than looking for information which does not support it.

The section on theory has made reference on numerous occasions to the balance and the relationship between risk and return. Ideally, as an investor, we would like to take no risk but achieve substantial returns; however, in practice this is unlikely to be possible. It is realistic to assume that the majority of investors, either individual or institutional, will wish to maximize their returns relative to the level of risk they are prepared to take. Having given due consideration to various methods and theories for mitigation of investment risk, it is also important for the fund manager or the individual investor to accurately analyse returns in order to reflect upon the success of the chosen investment strategy.

There are many different techniques available to calculate investment returns and this is an appropriate section to consider some of the more common methods. It is also important to note that investment returns can be in the form of capital growth and income and that returns may be reinvested to boost capital growth or withdrawn, either as an income or profit-taking.

Investment returns

The achievement of investment return is generally considered in two different ways which are referred to as absolute return and relative return.

> **Keyword**
>
> An **absolute return** is a measure of the appreciation (or depreciation) that an asset achieves over a specific period of time. This is expressed as a percentage gain (or loss) and the asset could be any type of asset, for example an investment fund or a company share.
>
> The concept of absolute return is different to a relative return as it is simply focused upon the return generated by a particular asset and does not seek to compare the return to any form of benchmark. An absolute return will usually target a positive return in all market conditions including when the market is falling.
>
> Conversely, a **relative return** is where the return generated by an asset is compared with a benchmark. The choice of benchmark is flexible and may be, for example, a similar asset, an investment fund in the same investment universe, or an entire index. The choice of benchmark depends upon the fund manager or the investor; however, it is important that the benchmark chosen is appropriate and realistic in order to be an effective benchmark. For example, it would not be useful or appropriate to benchmark the performance of a global bond fund against the NASDAQ Composite Index. A relative return figure is useful as it provides a fund manager or an investor with an indication about the performance of one asset compared to that of another and generally, an asset is benchmarked against a particular asset or index and aims to outperform it. The aim is to make either more profits or fewer losses than if the asset simply tracked the index. This gives added value and the risk is that the asset underperforms the benchmark.

Evaluation of relative return is quite straightforward, so if we consider a simple investment scenario: an investor has a portfolio of assets which achieve positive growth of 10.6 per cent in the previous 12-month period and over the same 12-month period the investor's chosen benchmark index achieves a return of 12.9 per cent. In this situation we would determine that the investor's portfolio has achieved a relative return of –2.3 per cent for the 12-month period under analysis.

Various types of return may be calculated and we will now consider some of the more commonly used calculations.

Simple return

A simple return is a very easy way of calculating the basic investment return achieved when purchasing an asset, for example, a company share, holding for a period of time and then selling the asset. It also takes into account the cost of the transactions undertaken in the purchase and sale of the asset. This doesn't specify the holding period, but simply evaluates the return on the capital invested over the period of time that the asset is held. The formula for a simple return is:

$$\text{simple return} = \frac{(\text{net proceeds} + \text{dividends received})}{\text{cost basis}} - 1$$

In practice

Let us consider an example where an investor purchases a number of shares in Blakeney Plc for £1,400 and incurs a fee of £15 for this transaction. During the time that the investor holds the shares a total of £40 in dividends is received and the company shares are then sold for £1,850, incurring a fee of £15 for this transaction.

Using the formula above we can calculate the following:

$$\text{simple return} = \frac{(£1,835 + 40)}{£1,415} - 1 = 32.5\%$$

where:
Net proceeds are (£1,850 – £15) = £1,835
Cost basis is (£1,400 + £15) = £1,415

The simple return is a useful figure to calculate, but may be difficult to compare to the returns of other assets as there is no specified holding period and the holding period may be over a difficult period of time to easily compare with other assets returns, for example three years and three months. In this situation it may be useful to calculate an annualized growth rate to make fair comparison with other assets.

Annualized growth rate

An annualized return is where we calculate the average return achieved by the asset each year over a specified time period. This shows the average return that the investor would realize over a specified period of time if the asset's annual return was compounded. This, of course, shows just an indication of the asset's average investment performance and offers no indicator of the asset's volatility to the investor. The formula for the annualized growth rate is:

$$\text{annualized growth rate} = \text{simple return}^{1/n} - 1$$

where:
n = number of years asset is held

In practice

If we continue with the example considered in the simple return calculation above and assume that the Blakeney Plc shares purchased were held for three years and three months before disposal, using the formula above:

$$\begin{aligned}\text{annualized growth rate} &= 1.325^{1/3.25} - 1 \\ &= 1.325^{0.31} - 1 \\ &= 1.0912 - 1 \\ &= 9.12\%\end{aligned}$$

So, this indicates to us that the Blakeney Plc shares have been achieving on average 9.12 per cent growth per year during the holding period of 3.25 years.

Total return

Measuring the performance of an investment including both price change and any income accrued is often referred to as the total return. This is expressed as a percentage of the original purchase value of the asset. From an investment management point of view there are three methods used:

- holding period return/yield;
- money-weighted rate of return;
- time-weighted rate of return.

The holding period return is the simplest method and is often referred to as the total return. It is calculated using the formula below:

$$\text{total return or holding period return} = \frac{(V_e - V_s + I)}{V_s}$$

where:
V_s = value at the start of the holding period
V_e = value at the end of the holding period
I = total of all income received from the asset during the holding period

> **In practice**
>
> If we consider a simple situation in which an investor acquires a number of Holt Plc shares at a cost of £10,100 and disposes of the shares after one year, realizing proceeds of £13,250.
>
> During the year that the Holt Plc shares are held, dividends totalling £175 are received by the investor.
>
> Using the formula above, we can calculate:
>
> $$\text{Total return/Holding period return} = \frac{(£13{,}250 - £10{,}100 + £175)}{£10{,}100}$$
>
> $$= 0.329$$
> $$= 32.9\%$$

Money weighted rate of return may also be seen referred to as the internal rate of return in some texts and is a method which may be preferred when measuring more complex situations, such as evaluating investment performance during a period which includes both deposits and withdrawals. This calculation is complex and therefore determination of the growth rate not quite so precise. It may be calculated using the following formula:

$$V_e = \Sigma \, C_n \, (1 + r) \, W_n + V_b \, (1 + r)$$

where:
r = the rate to be determined (money-weighted rate of return)
V_e = end value of the fund
V_b = beginning value of the fund
C_n = cashflows made or received by the fund and n indicates the number of days since the initial investment (this may be in the form of cash injections, withdrawals or income)

Investment theory

$$W_n = \frac{(TD - D_n)}{TD}$$

TD = total number of days in the period of time analysed
D_n = number of days from the start of the period of analysis and n indicates each of the cashflows (1, 2, 3, 4, *n*)

This formula looks at the value at the start and the end of the period under analysis, together with the magnitude and timing of any cashflows. Without the use of a computer this method requires a 'trial-and-error' procedure to evaluate the figure for r, which represents the rate of return.

The time-weighted rate of return is a popular method of calculation used in the investment management industry and operates by effectively splitting down the total investment period into a series of subperiods of time. This subperiod could be weekly, monthly, quarterly or any other appropriate period.

A subperiod is created when there is movement of cashflow in or out of the fund and a fund valuation must be made immediately prior to the creation of each subperiod. The time-weighted rate of return is then calculated by compounding the return for each subperiod in turn, applying equal weighting to each subperiod. It may be calculated using the following formula:

$$Tt = \{(1 + r_{t1}) \times (1 + r_{t2}) \times (1 + r_{t3}) \times ... \times (1 + r_{tn})\} - 1$$

where:

$$r_{tn} = \frac{(V_e - V_b)}{V_b}$$

V_b = value of the portfolio including cash and income at the beginning of the period
V_e = value of the portfolio including cash and income at the end of the period

The time-weighted rate of return calculation is more widely used than the money-weighted rate of return in the fund management industry, although in some cases the differences between the two calculations may be quite small.

The impact of fees on returns

Due to the active management of some funds, investors must pay a fee to the fund manager. These fees could include an initial fee, ongoing management charges and performance-related fees (normally for hedge funds) and the fees for actively managed funds will be higher than those for passive funds. Any fees payable will be normally taken from income generated; however, this obviously impacts on the total return and compounding effect. For this reason, index trackers are normally much cheaper given that they can be run by computers and need very little oversight.

We have identified that investment returns include both capital growth and income and the calculations that we perform include both capital return and income to give the overall return for the asset. In particular, equity return will often include income in the form of dividends derived from company shares. There are various key ratios which are often considered when making decisions regarding the selection of assets for investment, although it is important not to look at this information in isolation and to treat each piece of information as 'one piece of the total picture' regarding an asset. Ratio analysis is a tool used to perform quantitative analysis with regard to published information about companies listed on financial exchanges. Ratio analysis is a useful process as it can provide an indication of potential improvements or deterioration of a company's financial situation or share performance. Certain key ratios may be found published or can be calculated and the results analysed and compared in various ways. Comparisons may be made with;

- previous year's figures for the company;
- other companies within the same industry/sector;
- the industry/sector in general.

The information generated is mainly used by proponents of fundamental analysis, as a method to judge the performance of the company. It is therefore useful to be able to calculate certain key ratios, some of which are covered below.

Dividend yield

Dividends are paid out in cash to shareholders over various timescales – annually, half-yearly or quarterly – and may be subject to taxation, depending upon the tax rules of the region in question. Dividend yield represents a financial ratio that indicates how much a company pays out in dividends each year relative to its share price. The aim of a dividend yield is to establish the net return to investors on dividends received so it is a method for measuring the cashflow an investor will receive from their equity position. The dividend yield may be calculated by using the following formula:

$$\text{dividend yield} = \frac{\text{annual dividend per share}}{\text{price per share}} \times 100$$

The resultant figure is expressed as a percentage and shows the dividend as a percentage of current share price. Care should be taken when sourcing this information from company reports and company accounts because these documents may simply report the total dividends paid to all shareholders and therefore a calculation must be done to establish what the dividend per share will be. Shareholders of companies in mature industries expect that dividends will be constant in real terms or will rise in real terms over time, whilst shareholders of companies in fast-growing areas will be looking for capital growth, which may involve rising share prices and either low dividends or no dividends.

In practice

For an example of a simple calculation, assume that Fastfood Plc pays a dividend per share of 38 pence per year and the current share price for Fastfood Plc is 768 pence per share. We can use the formula from above to calculate:

$$\text{dividend yield} = \frac{38}{768} \times 100 = 4.95\%$$

It has been mentioned earlier that the information provided by key ratio analysis should not be considered in isolation, but as part of a greater overall analysis and it should be noted that a company with a higher dividend yield is not always a better investment prospect than one with a lower dividend yield, and that there may be underlying reasons for a higher or lower yield figure. The higher dividend yield may have arisen because of various factors, for instance, because prospects are considered poor.

In practice

Apples Plc pays a 10p per share dividend and has a current share price of 100p. Therefore, the dividend yield for Apples Plc is 10 per cent.

One month later Apples Plc issues a profits warning, the markets react badly to the news and the share price falls to 50p.

The dividend yield is now 20 per cent which is a very attractive dividend yield, but not necessarily an attractive share to invest in at this time.

Earnings per share

The earnings per share is the portion of a company's profit which is allocated to each outstanding ordinary share (sometimes referred to as common stock). The ratio earnings per share is a useful indicator of a company's profitability. In essence, earnings per share are simply the total earnings divided by the number of ordinary shares in issue at that time. The phrase 'total earnings' means the profit after taxation and any preference dividend, but before any dividend on ordinary shares. The earnings per share may be calculated by using the following formula:

$$\text{earnings per share} = \frac{\text{total earnings}}{\text{number of ordinary shares in issue}}$$

$$= \frac{\text{profit after tax} - \text{preference dividend}}{\text{number of ordinary shares in issue}}$$

If we consider the significance of the earnings per share ratio, we find that earnings per share is generally believed to be one of the most important variables to consider when considering investment in a company's shares and it is also used to calculate the price-to-earnings ratio. Growth in earnings per share is also viewed as an important measure of management performance and steady growth of the earnings per share ratio over time is an attractive sign for a potential investor.

In practice

As an example calculation, Fish Plc has the following data:

Profit before tax	£225,000
Tax	£45,000
Number of preference shares in issue	0
Number of ordinary shares in issue	150,000

Using the formula from above, we can calculate the earnings per share for Fish Plc:

$$\text{earnings per share} = \frac{£180,000}{£150,000} = £1.20 \text{ per share}$$

Generally, if earnings are reinvested in the company this should result in an increase in the share price, but equally, if earnings are paid out in dividends this should result in increased dividend yield, which therefore makes shares more attractive to an investor. Earnings are said to 'have quality' when management is sound, the company shows steady increase in earnings and profits are in line with what has been forecast.

Price–earnings ratio

Price–earnings ratio is the ratio of a company's current price per ordinary share in comparison to its earnings per share and it is sometimes referred to as 'earnings multiple' in various texts. This ratio is considered to be one of the key pieces of information to consider when evaluating prospective investments. This measure is useful to make comparisons between company shares in the same sector because using share price as a comparison is not productive as all share prices differ. The price–earnings ratio shows the number of times the current share price exceeds the earnings per share:

$$\text{price earnings ratio} = \frac{\text{current share price}}{\text{earnings per share}}$$

The price–earnings ratio is a useful comparator and may be used to compare a company with other companies within the sector, or the sector average for a particular industry or sector. Under 'normal' circumstances, investors would favour a company with a high price–earnings ratio over a company with a lower price–earnings ratio.

Investment returns are clearly not limited to equity-based investments and will also be important for fixed-interest assets and cash, although these types of assets are usually associated with income returns. Flat yield and redemption yield are two factors often considered in respect of bonds as an asset class. The flat yield of a bond is simply the annual coupon payment divided by the current price. Flat yield is very easy to calculate and is often the first step to other calculations, although it is a rough approximation of the redemption yield for a bond with a long redemption date and of course is equal to the redemption yield of a perpetual bond. A perpetual bond has no maturity date and therefore the issuer will pay the coupon indefinitely as they are not obligated to redeem the principal.

$$\text{flat yield} = \frac{\text{annual coupon payment}}{\text{current market price}} \times 100$$

The redemption yield describes the total return expected from a bond if that bond is held until it is redeemed by the issuer of the bond. It is also referred to as the yield to maturity and whilst it is considered to be a 'long-term bond yield', it is expressed as an annual rate. Effectively, it represents the rate of return of a bond if the bond is held by the investor until maturity, assuming that all coupon payments are honoured and there is no default by the issuer. The redemption yield, or yield to maturity calculation generates a very useful piece of data because this gives an accurate measure of a bond's return, which may be used by the investor to compare bonds with different coupons and maturity dates. The full calculation for redemption yield, or yield to maturity, is very complex but we can approximately calculate the redemption yield using the formula below:

$$\text{redemption yield} = \text{flat yield} \pm \text{annual gain or loss}$$

where:

$$\text{annual gain or loss} = \frac{\text{price at maturity} - \text{price at time of purchase}}{\text{number of years until maturity}}$$

The redemption yield calculation clearly assumes that the bondholder will retain the bond until the bond is redeemed by the issuer and therefore this yield calculation includes two separate elements: the interest yield component and the capital appreciation or depreciation component. The capital appreciation/depreciation will depend upon at what price the holder purchased the bond on the market, since the bond will always be redeemed at par (issue) price. If the bond was purchased under-par then there will be an element of capital gain; however, if the bond was purchased over-par then this will result in a capital loss. Most bonds with coupons which are attractive to investors will be purchased over-par as they will be trading on the market at a price above their issue price due to their popularity.

In practice

Let us consider the example of a 9 per cent Treasury Bond 2020 with a current market price of 116.00.

Assume that today is 1 January 2015 and that the bond will be redeemed on 31 December 2020.

We can calculate the redemption yield of the bond using the formula above:

$$\text{flat yield} = \frac{9}{116} \times 100 = 7.76\%$$

$$\text{annual gain/loss} = \frac{100 - 116}{6} = -2.67 \text{ (loss)}$$

redemption yield = 7.76 − 2.67 = 5.09%

So the approximate redemption yield, or yield to maturity of this treasury bond to the investor will be 5.09 per cent before taxation.

The time value of money

We noted earlier in the chapter that the time value of money represents the concept that an amount of an investor's money available at the present time is worth more than the same amount of the investor's money at some point in the future. It is reasonable therefore, that if an investor has a choice between a lump sum now or the same size lump sum at some point in the future, it would be logical to choose the lump sum now. The lump sum will have more value than the same lump sum in the future and so it is reasonable that both investors and advisers must consider this issue of the time value of money. The effects of inflation will mean that a given sum of money loses its purchasing power, as we move forward in time.

This concept reflects the potential that a sum of money has to earn some form of return over a period of time; for example, generating interest in an interest-bearing account and also leads us to the compounding effect of leaving the money and the earned interest on deposit to increase the rate of growth. Compound interest enables an investment to grow faster when the investor leaves the interest invested rather than withdrawing it, so effectively the investor then earns interest on the initial investment and the interest, which increases growth. It is quite simple to make use of a 'present value' with a specific interest rate to determine a 'future value' following a specified period of time and conversely; if we know a future value we may discount in order to find the present value. This technique is quite useful with products such as fixed-interest savings accounts and perpetual bonds.

In practice

$1,000 invested at 10 per cent interest for two years if interest remains constant:

Original $1,000
Interest at end Year 1 (10%) $100

Investment at end Year 1 $1,100
Interest at end Year 2 (10%) $110
Investment at end Year 2 $1,210

So in this case, the present value of the original investment is $1,000 and the future value of the investment after two years is $1,210 after compounded interest of 10 per cent.

The future value may also be calculated by compounding the present value over the required period of time at a given interest rate, using the future value formula below:

$$FV = PV(1 + r)^n$$

where:
FV = future value
PV = present value
r = interest rate/return
n = number of compounding periods

We can also use a discounted cashflow to calculate the present value that will be required to achieve a desired future value, given a known rate of return and frequency, where the rate of interest is the discount rate; this is the reverse of the compounding procedure.

$$PV = \frac{FV}{(1 + r)^n}$$

In practice

We can calculate how much cash must be invested today, given an interest rate of 3 per cent per year, to generate a sum of £500 after a period of five years using the formula above:

$$PV = \frac{£500}{(1 + 0.03)^5}$$

$$= \frac{£500}{1.16} = £431.03$$

Summary

Some of the financial theories and models divide opinion, whilst others have limitations in their practical application. For example, it would be difficult to find a technical analyst, or a fundamental analyst who believes that the financial markets are efficient, as described by the efficient market hypothesis. The various theories and models we have examined in this chapter cover a diverse range of issues from risk versus return, risk mitigation and diversification, to the study of how markets react and behave. What we do know is that investors worldwide, both professional and private, use a diverse range of techniques and methods in the quest for both investment growth and risk mitigation, with an equally varied range of relative success. It is also certain that an investment technique which is always successful and consistent under all conditions has yet to be discovered, because if it currently existed then surely all investors would be using the same method.

Check your understanding

1 Do you accept efficient market hypothesis? Do you believe that the financial markets are efficient in this context?
2 What is the importance of diversification to an investor or a fund manager?
3 Consider the practical applications of measures such as Sharpe ratio and Treynor ratio.
4 Think about the possible uses of the CAPM model considering its limitations.
5 Consider the effect of fees and charges on investment returns.

Further reading

The following books may be useful:

Cuthbertson, K and Nitzsche, D (2008) *Investments*, 2nd edn, John Wiley & Sons
Elton, EJ, Gruber, MJ, Brown, SJ and Goetzmann, WN (2014) *Modern Portfolio Theory and Investment Analysis*, 9th edn, John Wiley & Sons
Jones, CP (2013) *Investments: Principles and Concepts,* 12th edn, John Wiley & Sons

The following websites may be useful:

http://viking.som.yale.edu/will/finman540/classnotes/notes.html
http://news.morningstar.com/classroom2/course.asp?docId=4494&page=1&CN=

Investment classes 06

Fixed-interest (debt)

By the end of this chapter you should have an understanding of:

- debt characteristics;
- bond types and issuers;
- coupon rate, nominal bond value and bond maturity;
- buying and selling bonds and the costs involved;
- pricing bonds and factors affecting price;
- measuring bond returns;
- risks of investing in bonds;
- taxation of bonds.

Introduction

Debt: a sum of money which is owed or due.

Oxford English Dictionary

On Tuesday Sam forgot her purse so she borrowed £5 for the day from George, her best friend. On Wednesday when she saw George she repaid the £5 she had borrowed.

This example shows the debt transaction in its simplest form. Sam owed George £5 overnight until she repaid him. This type of informal transaction occurs millions of times every day in the real world for various reasons.

In this chapter, we will show how this basic transaction can be formalized to produce a return for an investor; the potential risks an investor might face if they invest in debt; methods of measuring the return on a debt-based investment; and the levels of taxation the investment return may be subject to. Details of how bonds can be included in bond funds will be included in Chapter 8 on collectives.

Bonds and loans are both types of debt, ie one party wishes to borrow a sum of money from another party for a period. During the borrowing period the borrower usually pays the lender a fee (interest) for use of the money and either over the borrowing period or at its end the borrower will also repay the original sum borrowed (the capital). The money being lent can be used for any number of purposes by the borrower such as capital investment or the repayment of other financing. The use of the funds may influence the length of the lending period agreed between the two parties as well as other conditions of lending.

A loan tends to describe a situation where an agreement is made between two parties (they can be individuals or companies or a mixture of the two). So, whilst the general characteristics of lending remain the same, the implication is of a bespoke transaction between the two parties. Think of the simple example above with George and Sam or where an individual or company obtains a loan from a bank. Due to the bespoke nature of the agreement it will normally be more difficult for the lender to exit from the loan (investment) prior to the end of the agreed borrowing period, unless the borrower doesn't pay the interest or capital – at which point a whole new set of rules come into play.

A bond also provides the borrower with money for investment and the lender with a return (the interest paid) during the period of borrowing and ultimately repayment of the original amount. However, for an investor, a bond may potentially be an improvement on a loan as an investment product, as bonds have greater liquidity. This means there is the possibility, if the lender needs or wants to, to sell the bond to a third party before the end of the agreed lending period. This makes bonds more versatile and marketable – as they can be turned into cash more easily if required – which in turn makes them more valuable to an investor as the resale market allows investors to exit their investment more easily.

Keyword

Liquidity can be defined in finance in several ways depending on the context in which it is being used:

1 Asset: a liquid asset is one which can easily be converted into cash. Cash is the most liquid asset of all as it is the easiest to exchange for another asset.

2 Market: a liquid market is one where an asset can be bought or sold at a fair price in a short space of time. Liquid markets require sufficient buyers and sellers of an asset as well as sufficient trading volumes to ensure the market remains liquid. For instance, the London Stock Exchange is a liquid market for most financial instruments due to the volume of trade which is carried on there. In comparison, eg for some artworks, there may only be a very limited number of buyers and sellers and it may take some time for a piece to be sold for a fair value.

3 Financial accounting: liquidity may be measured using ratios, demonstrating a company's ability to pay its liabilities due in the short term using its most liquid assets (cash, trade receivables and inventory).

There are several reasons why a company may wish to issue bonds rather than borrow money from a bank:

1 Restrictions imposed by banks:

   a. End use: it is usual for a bank loan to specify what the funds raised can be used for. This is not the case for bonds which allows the company greater flexibility.

   b. Ongoing monitoring: banks will often include restrictions or covenants in the terms of the loan which may include, for example, producing management information regularly or not allowing the company to raise additional debt before the loan is repaid, both of which will affect a company's operating flexibility. Conditions for bonds may be much less onerous or even non-existent.

2 Interest rate:

   a. Rate may also be lower for bonds than for bank loans for several reasons; for companies looking to maximize shareholder wealth as their main objective minimizing costs is an important consideration.

   b. Interest on bank loans is often charged at a variable rate, being a margin above a reference rate such as LIBOR, which may mean uncertainty in interest charged over the life of a loan. Bond rates are usually fixed, which provides certainty to borrowers.

3 Flexible terms: bonds can incorporate many features in a combination determined by the lender, rather than the bank, when a bond is used. These may include:

   a. Long-term funding with repayment periods stretching up to 999 years, far longer than a bank would agree to.
   b. Bonds can include security or not (discussed later in this chapter).
   c. Bonds can be issued with options, eg callable bonds, where the issuer may buy them back at a date of the issuer's convenience rather than being told the repayment schedule by a bank, or potentially with the option to convert to equity later.

4 Increasing the number of potential lenders: bonds allow companies to aim their lending at far greater numbers of potential lenders rather than one bank or syndicate of banks.

5 Liquidity: as mentioned above, bonds are more liquid than bank loans.

For the purposes of this chapter we will only examine the bond market as this is the more common type of investment for individual investors.

Investors buy bonds for many reasons, but these normally include:

- providing a predictable income stream from the payment of interest at specific times over the bond's life;
- preserving capital due to the repayment of the nominal value of the bond if it is held to maturity;
- providing a portfolio approach to investing where bonds are used to offset more volatile investments.

Despite the above, investments have risks and as an adviser, you need to take on the position of risk assessor for your clients to decide if an investment is suitable because, effectively, your clients are lending their money to a third party when they invest in bonds and one of the main risks in bonds is default risk: the risk the money they invest will not be repaid. Therefore, you need to be confident the borrower will be able to repay the original sum and the interest agreed on the dates specified. To be able to assess all the risks of a specific debt investment you need to understand its characteristics as they will form the basis for your analysis, assessment and recommendation of a product's suitability for a client.

Bonds have four main characteristics and we will look at each in more detail:

- who issues the bond;
- the level of coupon or interest payable over the life of the bond;
- the nominal or par value of the bond;
- the maturity or repayment date of the bond.

Bond issuers and bond types

The party who wishes to borrow money issues the bond to a market where lenders (investors) decide if they wish to invest. Several different organizations issue bonds including supranational bodies, governments, public authorities, companies and building societies.

Supranational bodies

Supranational bodies include the European Investment Bank (EIB) and the International Bank for Reconstruction and Development (part of the World Trade Bank). Such organizations act as umbrella bodies for governments from different countries working together and are considered to be a high-quality investment.

Governments

It is usual for bond traders to deal simultaneously in debt from many different countries. We have organized the analysis below to give details of UK and overseas debt.

UK government

As with most governments the UK government currently has a shortfall between its income (for example, from taxes) and what it spends (for example, building roads, welfare etc): that is, it is spending more than it is receiving and as such has a deficit. This deficit is known as the central government net cash requirement (CGNCR). The CGNCR is part of the public-sector net cash requirement (PSNCR), the annual excess of spending over income for the whole public sector, ie central and local government and public corporations. To make up the shortfall and have sufficient funds available to carry out its spending plans the government issues bonds. These are issued by the UK Debt Management Office (DMO) on behalf of the Treasury. The two main types of UK government bonds are gilts and treasury bills and each have their own characteristics.

Gilts The gilt market has seen a huge rise in volume with the total nominal value of gilts in issue in the UK in 1980 being £71 billion compared to £1,462.2 billion in 2016. In addition, the characteristics of the gilt market have also changed from 100 per cent conventional gilts to a position where conventional gilts account for £1,075.6 billion and index-linked gilts account for £386.5 billion (see p 193 for an explanation of the difference between index-linked and conventional gilts).

Treasury bills Treasury bills are zero-coupon bonds issued at a discount to face value with potential maturity dates of up to 364 days in the future – although at present there are no 364-day bonds in issue and the normal timescale is 91 days. On redemption, investors will earn a return as the bills will be repaid at the nominal value.

In practice

A treasury bill with a £100 nominal value (an example value not real-life value) will be issued at a price of £86. Assuming a maturity of 91 days, if the buyer holds the bill for the whole period they will receive a repayment of £100, earning a return of £14 on their original investment of £86.

Treasury bills are issued by the DMO during weekly tender sessions which are normally held on Fridays. Members of the public can purchase treasury bills; however, they must do this through one of the market's primary participants. Primary participants are usually corporate or investment banks, such as JP Morgan Securities Plc and Lloyds Bank Plc. The minimum investment size is £500,000 nominal value.

The DMO website at www.DMO.gov.uk has further information available in respect of gilts and treasury bills issued by the government both currently and historically.

Overseas governments

Overseas governments run a similar system to the UK, supplementing receipts by borrowing as required so they can carry out their spending plans. Some governments issue more debt than others; for instance, the UK issues debt regularly to fund its deficit, whilst Saudi Arabia made its first application for a loan in April 2016 when it successfully borrowed $10 billion as a reported precursor to a bond issue later in 2016, used to bolster falling reserves and oil revenues.[1]

Each country has its own bond specifications; however, as noted above, these are variations of the general characteristics of bonds. This is a specialist area of investment due to the legal implications of holding foreign investments and the potential for increased risks as such portfolio managers should take the appropriate advice before recommending a client to invest in this area.

Local authorities

Since 2005 there have not been any direct bond issues from local authorities and borrowing has taken place instead through the Public Works Lending Board (PWLB), part of the DMO. As such it is not currently a large part of the debt market. This may change in future as from 2016 there is the potential for retail investors to finance local authority lending through the UK Municipal Bonds Agency Plc (UKMBA).

The UKMBA is a publicly quoted company owned by 56 local authorities and the Local Government Association. It aims to reduce local authority lending costs by offering an alternative to the PWLB, replicating similar schemes seen in countries such as Japan, Holland, France and Canada.

Investors will invest through usual market channels and local authorities included in a bond issue will cross-guarantee the loans of the other participating local authorities, providing comfort for investors in respect of potential default. Local authorities and their bonds will also be rated by a credit ratings agency.

Building societies

Building societies issue two types of debt to raise finance. The type issued depends on whether they are mutualized or demutualized:

- Permanent interest-bearing shares (PIBS) are, despite their name, subordinated debt issued by building societies to raise capital. PIBS rank behind

the deposits of building society customers and other more senior bonds in the event of insolvency.
- Perpetual bonds are debt raised by former building societies which have been demutualized or floated on the stock exchange.

It should also be remembered that whilst they are not often thought about in this way, customers' deposits are forms of debt for building societies as they represent a liability on the building society's balance sheet.

Companies

Any private limited (ie Ltd) or publicly limited (ie a Plc which is traded on a stock market) company can theoretically issue a bond, although due to their size it is far more unusual for a limited company to issue them. As mentioned earlier, bonds have the possibility of combining multiple features into different combinations. These combinations then provide the issuer with the characteristics of investment finance they require and the investor with the characteristics of investment which most suit them.

Only the bonds of public limited companies can be easily traded on a recognized market; bonds from limited companies cannot be traded in formal organized markets and must be sold in a transaction negotiated on a bespoke basis between two parties. This ability to easily resell bonds issued by Plcs makes them more valuable due to their increased liquidity.

At times, it appears there are as many types of corporate bond as there are fish in the sea and the following are some of the main types of bonds which a portfolio manager may be asked to assess:

Domestic bonds

Here the country of origin of the issuer, the currency in which the bond is issued and the market in which the bond is traded will all match. So, for instance a UK company issuing a sterling bond which trades on the UK bond market. Or a US company issuing a dollar bond to trade on the US stock exchange.

Bonds issued on foreign stock exchanges

International bonds These are issued by a foreign company in a foreign market in the domestic currency of the country where it is issued. For example, a UK company issues a bond in the US stock market in US dollars.

Eurobond Eurobonds are issued in a foreign market in a foreign currency from the market they are issued in. For example, a eurodollar bond will be issued by an American company in the UK stock market in US dollars. Eurobonds do not have to be issued in euros and do not have to be issued in Europe. It is possible for Eurobonds to be convertible to equity (see below.)

Other types of bonds

Convertible bond

Here the original bond will, at some point in the future, have the potential to change into equity. As with other bonds there will be fixed-interest payments for the period the bond exists. However, at an agreed date or between two dates the bondholder will have the option to exchange the bond for a predetermined number of shares. After a specified date the potential for conversion will expire and the bond will continue as before with its ongoing payments.

Debentures

These are bonds which are supported by additional security such as land or buildings which will be used to repay the investor in the event the issuer cannot make the payments of capital or interest owed.

High yield bonds

Also known as junk bonds, these have a credit rating of less than BBB-. This level of credit rating is known as below 'investment grade' and indicates an increased potential for default by the issuer. This makes the bond higher risk which in turn reduces the price investors are willing to pay for the bond. The effect of this is to increase the yield on the bond, assuming the coupon payments are made.

Contingent convertibles (CoCos)

Unlike convertible bonds, contingent convertibles do not change to equity over a specific period; rather they have the potential to change if a specific event occurs for example. Lloyds Bank Plc first issued CoCos in 2009. The conversion of CoCos to equity is usually based around a fall in equity prices, capital adequacy concerns or market regulation adjustments.

Green bonds

Investors are increasingly concerned about environmental issues and wish to invest in an environmentally aware way. Green bonds concentrate investments in areas of renewable energy, sustainable use of resources and clean transportation amongst others.

The London Stock Exchange has a dedicated green bond segment where issuers must provide the exchange with independent documentation certifying a bond's green credentials before it will be accepted. Further information can be found on the London Stock Exchange's website; however, clients can be reassured green bonds have the same regulatory status as non-green bonds and it is possible to purchase them on a wholesale or retail basis with quotes available on a continuous, end-of-day or trade-reporting basis as with other bonds.

Nominal or par value of a bond

Keyword

Nominal value or **par value** is the value of the bond when it is first issued and unless otherwise stated it will be the amount repaid to the bondholder at the end of the agreed borrowing period. It is also the amount which will be recorded in the borrower's financial statements and it will not change over the life of the bond.

In the UK, par value is usually £100; however, this is not always the case and the individual terms of the bond should be investigated to confirm the value. Other countries have different levels of par, so for instance, the USA has a 'usual' par value of $1,000 per bond.

The par value is not necessarily the price an investor will pay for a bond when it is first issued; for instance, a zero-coupon bond will be issued at a price below par value to allow investors to make a return from the difference between the issue price and the final redemption value.

Also, once the bond has been issued and started to trade on the market its value will change; as such it may be trading at a market price which is different to its par value.

Types of coupon or interest rates payable on a bond

Keyword

The interest or **coupon rate** as it is sometimes known, is the rate of return earned by the investor during the period of investment or borrowing. The rate or level of return required by the investor is based on the level of risk they perceive in lending money to this party (see Chapter 4).

When the bond is issued, the level of return is agreed, based on a predetermined level of risk, so it is imperative the lender (the client) assesses the risk position correctly, as over the period the bond is held, the investor will not wish the risk profile to change. This is because, as a rational investor, a higher level of risk will require a higher return level. The adjusted risk in the bond will not then fit with their portfolio requirements, and there is the potential for an increased risk of default. If the risk level of the bond changes so that it no longer justifies inclusion in a client's portfolio then the bond may be sold; however, the price of the bond will be affected as other investors adjust for their increased perception of the inherent risk by increasing the yield required from the bond, which may affect the level of capital returned.

That is not to say that the rate of interest itself cannot change; as we can see below, there are several different types of coupon which can be used in bonds. However, the terms of the bond should be analysed to ensure the coupon rate over the life of the bond is understood.

Fixed, floating and index-linked coupon bonds are found in all areas and as such have not been assigned to specific issuers in this section. The type of coupon may change for different bonds as we will discuss below; however, in each case the percentage coupon return will be based on the nominal value of the bond. As mentioned above, the nominal value of the bond will not change despite the market value being likely to change over time. A change in market value does not change the value of the coupon received.

Fixed-rate coupon

Here the coupon is a fixed percentage over the bond's life. For example, a 7 per cent fixed coupon bond with a nominal or par value of £100 will pay

7 per cent of £100 or £7 in interest payment per year until the bond matures. The 7 per cent in this example is the annual interest rate. As most bonds pay coupons twice a year an investor holding this bond will receive £3.50 each payment period.

Floating- and variable-rate coupons

Floating-rate coupons have a fixed and variable element. The variable element relates to a floating interest rate benchmark such as LIBOR (London Interbank Offer Rate) which is then combined with a margin (a fixed percentage); so, for example, a bond may pay a coupon of LIBOR plus 0.5 per cent, LIBOR being the variable element with the margin, 0.5 per cent, on top.

Variable-rate coupons are like floating-rate coupons; however, instead of the interest rate being fixed to a short-term interest benchmark such as LIBOR they are instead tied to rates which are usually reset annually.

Index-linked coupons

A major criticism of bonds is that returns may be eroded by inflation. This occurs as, unlike shares, returns are fixed and therefore do not increase as inflation increases, meaning the buying power of the coupon and the principal of the bond are eroded over time. One way of overcoming this is to index-link the coupon and the final redemption amount. This means that the value of the repayments is adjusted to account for inflation. Details of UK index-linked bonds can be seen on the DMO website. Other governments such as the US, France and Iceland also offer index-linked bonds, although the UK has the largest market.

As you may be aware, there is more than one way to measure inflation and each measure grows at its own rate due to the different methods of calculation. The two main inflation rates are the retail price index (RPI) and the consumer price index (CPI). Both measure inflation using a basket of goods and services although the content of each basket differs slightly, affecting the rate calculated.

It is important to be aware which inflation rate will be used to index a bond's coupon. The UK government currently uses RPI on their index-linked bonds (for other bonds this might not always be the case), whilst the headline inflation figure calculated by the Bank of England, and which is usually reported in the media, is CPI. This is used as it is most like the measures used in other European countries. CPI and RPI are currently not rising at the same speed, and are unlikely to do so in the future, so you need to make sure your client is aware of the rate in increase of their coupon they can expect, so they can manage their expectations.

Overall coupon levels on index-linked bonds (also known as linkers) are usually lower than bonds without indexation as each payment is adjusted to reflect price changes rather than having to build in a non-specific compensation for the loss of buying power. That is not to say the change will always be positive; in periods of deflation, it may be possible for payments to be reduced and this should always be highlighted to the client.

As each index bond payment is reliant on inflation statistics to be able to calculate payments the inflation rate used will be historic. In fact, up to 2004 there was an eight-month lag in the value of the RPI used to calculate the indexation value. For new bonds since then the lag has been reduced to three months; however, pre-2004 bonds remain on an eight-month adjustment period.

Zero-coupon bond

Here the bond pays no coupon to the investor during its lifetime; rather it is issued at a discount to par and is redeemed, usually at par, on maturity. Therefore, assuming the capital repayment is made, the investor knows their exact return on purchasing the debt.

When will the coupon or interest be paid?

Coupons may be paid monthly, quarterly, bi-annually or annually based on the agreement terms; however, normally payment is either once or twice a year. It may be important to a client requiring income from a bond portfolio that coupon payments are spread through the year or adequate cash budgeting is undertaken to ensure a steady income stream.

Government gilts

Government gilt coupons are paid twice a year, for example in March and September or July and December. The gilt should be researched to ensure payment days are known.

Local authority bonds

Payment terms for local authority bonds should be investigated on a bond-by-bond basis as these can vary between monthly, quarterly and bi-annual payments.

Corporate bonds

The payment dates on a corporate bond do not necessarily match to a calendar year. The payment cycle begins on what is known as the 'dated date' which is usually the issue date of the bond and ends on the date the bond matures when the final coupon is paid and the principal repaid.

Building society

Both PIBS and perpetual bonds have a fixed coupon rate which is paid twice a year based on the issue date of the bond.

Maturity or other repayment of a bond

Government gilts

Historically there were three main types of maturity dates for gilts: fixed, dual dated and undated.

Fixed

Fixed maturity dates (also known as bullet repayments) have one date given for repayment of the bond.

> **In practice**
>
> On the DMO gilt website there is an 8 per cent Treasury 2021 stock which can be seen to have a one repayment date of 7 June 2021 and that is the date it will mature.
>   The longest maturity on the website at June 2016 is a 3½ per cent Treasury Gilt 2068 which is due to mature on 22 July 2068. This gilt was issued by the government as a 55-year gilt in 2013 following consultation with the market.

Dual dated

Historically the Government has issued gilts which have the potential to be wholly or partly redeemed any time between two set dates if three months' notice was given in the *London Gazette*. The last of this type of gilt was 12 per cent Exchequer Stock 2013–17 which was repaid on 12 December 2013.

Undated

The last new undated UK gilt was issued in 1946; historically there were two types of undated gilts: those which had no date for redemption and those which had an 'earliest' date for redemption which had passed and where the gilt had not been redeemed by the government.

> **In practice**
>
> In 2014, the government undertook to repay the last eight outstanding undated gilts, some of the oldest UK government borrowing in existence. Repayment was achieved by 5 July 2015 when one of the last gilts repaid was £0.9 million of borrowing which had originally been issued on 13 June 1853 as a 0.5 per cent annuity. This 1853 annuity had itself originally been issued in exchange for stock and annuities which included a Bank of England 3 per cent annuity dated 1726 and one dated 1751.

Treasury bills

These bills are zero-coupon bonds issued at a discount to face value with potential maturity dates of up to 364 days in the future – although at present there are no 364-day bonds in issue and the normal timescale is 91 days. On redemption investors will earn a return as the bills will be redeemed at the nominal value.

> **In practice**
>
> If an investor buys a zero-coupon bond with a nominal value of £100, they will buy it at a discount on its nominal value, possibly paying £80 for it. They hold it for the agreed period and at the end of the period they will receive the £100 nominal value when the bond is redeemed. Their return coming from the difference between the price paid and the redemption value.

Corporate bonds

In addition to the possibility of having fixed or bullet repayments, dual dated and very long dated bonds as seen above in the gilt market, there are also other potential maturity characteristics which can be seen in corporate bonds.

Callable

It is possible, depending on the terms of the issue, for the issuer to redeem the bond before the maturity date on what is known as the call date. This may occur as the issuer feels there is a cost reduction or other benefit to refinancing. The bond is likely to be redeemed at par or a small premium.

Puttable

Here the investor, rather than the issuer, has the right to redeem a bond before maturity on specified dates at a specified price. It is likely that such terms will be exercised where the interest rate in the market has risen as this will allow the holder to make alternative arrangements for funds at a high interest rate and take advantage of pre-set redemption prices which may be above market prices.

Sinking fund

Whilst most bonds are repayable on maturity which may cause cashflow problems for the issuer due to the amounts involved, this may be offset slightly by the use of a sinking fund. Here the issue repays or 'retires' a set percentage of the bond issue each year thereby assisting with cashflow in respect of repayment.

Local authorities

The repayment schedule depends on the type of interest payable on the bond.

Fixed-rate bonds

These can have repayments using any one of three methods:

- annuity/equal repayments where fixed amounts are paid every six months and include capital and interest;
- equal instalments of principal (EIP) where equal payments of the capital are made every six months plus the accrued interest on the balance outstanding;
- maturity where interest is paid every six months and the capital is repaid at maturity.

Variable-rate bonds

These are repayable using either EIP or maturity capital repayments where interest is payable either monthly, quarterly or half-annually with interest payments starting at one, three or six months from the date of advance.

The authority chooses the period of the bond within the parameters set out in Table 6.1.

Table 6.1 Variable rate bonds: repayment schedule

Type of repayment	Minimum no. years	Maximum no. of years
Fixed rate bonds		
• Maturity	1 year	50 years
• Annuity	2 years	50 years
• EIP	2 years	50 years
Variable		
• Maturity	1 year	10 years
• EIP	2 years	20 years

Once chosen, the repayment schedule applies for the whole of the loan period, although, subject to a potential penalty, the borrower can request early repayments.

Building societies

PIBS do not have a maturity date as redeemable bonds do. Instead they have a 'callable' date on which the building society may buy back the bonds at the issue price or par as defined in the terms. For instance, Coventry Building Society issued the required notice on 5 May 2016 in the UK stock exchange to call its 6.092 per cent PIBS which were callable on 29 June 2016.

A building society is, however, under no obligation to do this. In addition, it is possible if the bond is not called, the interest rate on the bond will reduce to a pre-set lower rate which will result in a fall in the bond price to maintain yield levels.

Perpetual bonds, unlike PIBS or redeemable debt, have no callable date or redemption date; the only way to exit the bond is to sell them to another investor. As such, investors are at the mercy of stock market liquidity.

Identifying a bond

Issuers may have several bonds in issue at any one time so it is important to identify the correct bond to purchase for a client. Each bond, whoever issues it, is identified using a unique identifier based on the debt characteristics noted above.

Gilts

A list of all gilts in issue is available on the DMO website (www.dmo.gov.uk), split into conventional gilts and index-linked gilts.

> **In practice**
>
> At 22 June 2016, the first gilt in the list to be redeemable in 2019 is described as follows:
>
> **4½ per cent Treasury Gilt 2019**
>
> This shows us the Treasury has issued the gilt, it has a 4½ per cent coupon or interest rate and it will be redeemed in 2019. Looking at the additional information available on the DMO website we can see the actual date of redemption will be 7 March 2019 and the gilt issue has a total nominal value of £35.962 million. The coupon is paid biannually on 7 March and 7 September.

Corporate bonds

> **In practice**
>
> On 26 April 2016, the retail bond section of the London Stock Exchange website shows Burford Capital Plc made a second bond issue with a value of £100 million. Its unique identifier is:
>
> **BUR2 BURFORD CAPITAL PLC 6.125% GTD BDS 26/10/24**
>
> The fact that this is second issue for the company leads to the initials 'BUR2' at the beginning of the name. The name of the company and its

> legal status as a public limited company is also highlighted. The return of 6.125 per cent is an annual fixed-interest rate. You will also notice that the letters GTD are included in the identifier; this indicates the bond repayments are guaranteed by a third party (in this case the holding company of Burford Capital Plc). The letters BDS are an abbreviation of bonds. The bond is due to be redeemed on 26 October 2024 which will also be the last coupon date.

Where can investors buy bonds?

There are two types of market where bonds can be purchased: the primary and secondary markets. The primary market relates to the purchase of bonds when they are first issued whilst the secondary market relates to the purchase and resale of existing bonds.

Corporate bonds

Primary market (issuing a bond)

Once a company has decided to issue a bond they will engage a lead manager. Lead managers are often investment banks and will oversee the debt issue (or listing) process. Their role is to advise the issuer in respect of the size of the issue, its structure and timing. This information is known as the mandate. They will also appoint several investment banks, known as a syndicate, to market and sell the bonds. The syndicate may also underwrite (guarantee) the bond issue for a fee.

Legal advisers will then produce and verify all the information to be included in the listing documents, they will also prepare the prospectus and be part of the process of presenting the terms of the issue to the UKLA and the stock exchange.

Once the due diligence on the bond terms has been completed by the legal team an announcement will be made where the bank syndicate is invited to place the bonds with investors. Once all the legal documents are signed and executed the issuer will then receive the bond proceeds.

The bonds are now included on the London Stock Market and can be traded. The trustee of the issue represents the bondholders and ensures their rights are protected whilst the fiscal agent acts for the issuing company to ensure coupons and principal are paid on time whilst a paying agent ensures the bond interest payments are distributed to the bondholders.

Methods of issue

Private placing A private placing is a bond issue which is not offered to investors through an open market. Instead investors may be institutions such as insurance companies or high net worth individuals.

The main benefits of this method are its speed of issue and the fact there is no need for a detailed prospectus or for the involvement of brokers or underwriters. In addition, the company can retain flexibility (as they do not have to list) in the type of bond issued and the maturity date.

One drawback of this method is that there may only be a limited number of investors interested in such an issue and therefore it may not be possible to find enough investors willing to invest the amounts required. It may also be necessary to discount the bonds' selling price to compensate investors for the relatively illiquid nature of the debt and their greater potential risk.

Bought deal Here the bond issuer reduces the potential risk of not being able to sell the whole bond issue by obtaining an investment bank's agreement to buy the whole issue. This allows the issuer certainty but again, the price may be subject to a discount.

Fixed price reoffering Where an investment bank syndicate has underwritten a bond issue, they will agree not to sell the bonds on the secondary market at a price lower than the initial offer price until the issue is complete and the syndicate disbanded.

Secondary market

This is the market for bonds which have already been issued and are then for sale to investors who may or may not hold them to maturity. Unlike equities, most bonds are traded over-the-counter (OTC) rather than through exchanges, although the trading itself is part of the London Stock Exchange in the UK. This difference is due in part to the lower frequency of bond dealing, with only the top 3,000 bonds by volume trading at least once a day (www.icmagroup.org).

The difference between a wholesale bond and a retail bond

The EU Prospectus Directive distinguishes between retail and wholesale bonds when they are put up for sale on the bond market (Order book for Retail Bonds – ORB) which is part of the London Stock Exchange.

> **Keywords**
>
> **Retail bonds** are those traded in units of less than £50,000 which are usually purchased via intermediaries by individual investors. **Wholesale bonds** are those over the £50,000 cut-off and are usually sold directly to institutions. Whilst retail investors may not find wholesale bonds accessible as a direct investment they may invest in them through bond funds, which we will talk about in Chapter 8.

ORB was launched in 2010 to stimulate demand and provides access to gilts and supranational bonds as well as corporate bonds. The market is very like the equity market in its operation with daily set periods of trading with all trades being reported and published.

Gilts

Primary market

The DMO holds auctions where there are two ways for an investor to purchase;

- Participation in an auction:
  - gilt-edged market makers (GEMM) can bid on behalf of a client;
  - investors can participate directly in the auction if they are members of the DMO's approved group of investors.

The auctions can be competitive whereby potential investors tender on a blind basis with the bonds being issued to the highest priced bid. Such auctions have bid minimums of multiples of £1 million nominal value. Alternatively, there are non-competitive auctions with participants receiving the number of gilts applied for and paying a price which is a weighted average of all the accepted auction prices.

- Taps: this is where smaller issues of gilts are sold directly to GEMMs for onward sale to investors.

  On occasion the government may use this method to add to an existing gilt issue by issuing further stock under an existing title (name). This is known as a tranche, and is done to avoid having too many gilt issues in the market at any one time.

Secondary market

For existing gilts, the DMO also runs a purchase and sale service which can be accessed through its website. Direct participation in the sale and purchase process is possible through Computershare Investor Services Plc (Computershare) which facilitates the service on behalf of the DMO. Computershare also administers the gilt register. Alternatively, investors can access the secondary market using a stockbroker or bank.

Treasury bills

Primary market

These are issued by the DMO during weekly tender sessions normally held on Fridays. Members of the public can purchase treasury bills, but they must do this through one of the market's primary participants. Primary participants are usually corporate or investment banks, including JP Morgan Securities Plc and Lloyds Bank Plc, for example. The minimum investment size is £500,000 nominal value.

Secondary market

Treasury bills are traded by brokers in a secondary market which is based on a straight discounted price.

Building societies

PIBS and perpetual bonds are traded on the UK stock exchange and can be purchased through a broker on either a full-service or execution-only basis. Due to the number of mutualized building societies the PIBS market is perceived by commentators to be declining, which may impact on the liquidity of the debt in the future.

Bond ownership

Bonds come in two forms: registered and bearer.

> **Keywords**
>
> **Registered bonds**, as seen in the UK for both treasury debt and corporate debt, are registered. This means that the name of the holder of the bond is

held in electronic form (historically there would have been paper records) usually with Computershare. On maturity of the bond the redemption amount will be paid to the registered holder.

Bearer bonds are not held on a register and the owner of the bond is the person who currently physically holds the bond. We use bearer bonds in our daily lives – if you take out a £5 note you will see that it includes the words 'I promise to pay the bearer on demand the sum of £5'. This is a historical 'hangover' from the time when an individual could ask for their paper money to be exchanged for an equivalent amount of gold (www.bankofengland.co.uk).

Today bearer bonds have fallen out of favour as authorities feel that, whilst they have a high liquidity, they assist individuals in potentially evading taxes and laundering money. The USA stopped issuing such bonds in 1982 following legislation to outlaw them; however, other governments such as France, Germany and Japan still have such bonds in issue.

Costs of buying a bond

In addition to the purchase price, an investor will have to pay other additional fees for a bond purchase.

Purchase price

The price is the amount the lender pays to purchase the bond either when it is issued or when it is purchased on the secondary market. The market price of a bond, either at issue or when purchased on the secondary market, is not its nominal value, although in certain circumstances the nominal value and the market price may be the same amount. If this is the case the bond is said to be trading at par.

Unless otherwise instructed the broker will buy at the market price (as discussed below); however, there is also the potential for additional instructions in respect of the price to be paid to be given to the broker. These are for the broker to buy at the best possible price in the market (known as 'at best') or to only pay up to a maximum amount (known as a 'limit').

There are two potential market prices: clean price and dirty price. It is the dirty price which will be paid by the buyer.

Keywords

The price of a bond is made up of two elements: the capital value of the bond and the amount of interest which has accrued since the last coupon payment was made.

The **clean price** refers to the capital value of the bond.

The **dirty price** is the capital value (clean price) of the bond plus the amount of accrued interest.

In practice

Calculating the dirty price

To calculate the dirty price, you need to calculate the interest accruing on the bond as follows:

$$\text{accrued interest} = \text{period coupon} \times \frac{\text{number of days since last payment}}{\text{number of days in coupon period}}$$

For example:

Stan purchased a 3½ per cent treasury stock 2027 on 31 April 2016. The treasury stock pays interest on 7 March and 7 September each year.

The existing owner of the stock is due the accrued interest up to the point where Stan buys the treasury stock; as such Stan will pay the capital value for the stock plus an amount for the interest which has accrued between 7 March and 31 April 2016 when he makes his purchase.

The amount of accrued interest can be calculated as follows:

accrued interest per £100 of nominal
$$\text{value gilt} = (3.5\%/2) \times (54/184)$$
$$= 1.75\% \times 0.2934783$$
$$= £0.513589 \text{ per £100 nominal value}$$

Where does the accrued coupon go, to the buyer or the seller of the bond?

This depends on when the bond is bought or sold in relation to when the coupon is paid. If the bond is purchased cum-dividend (with the coupon payment attached) then the buyer will receive the payment. If the bond is purchased ex-dividend (without the coupon payment attached) then the seller will receive the payment.

The coupon will be paid to the registered holder of the bond on the ex-dividend date (even though a bond is not a share its return is conventionally called a dividend). The ex-dividend date is normally seven business days before the actual date of payment.

> **In practice**
>
> Sarah buys Beta Plc's bonds on Tuesday 7 March. The next coupon has an ex-dividend date of 13 March and is due to be paid on 22 March (remember: seven business days not seven days, so weekends do not count).
>
> In this case Sarah has purchased the bond cum-dividend and will be the registered holder at the ex-dividend date; as such she will receive the next coupon.
>
> If Sarah had purchased the bond on 14 March then she would have purchased it during the ex-dividend period and the coupon payment made on 22 March would go to the seller not to Sarah.

The elements of the above example have been summarized in Table 6.2.

Table 6.2 Example: accrued coupons – summary

	Investor buys	Investor sells
Cum-dividend	Costs INCLUDE interest from last payment date to settlement date	Proceeds INCLUDE interest from the last payment date to the settlement date
	Buyer physically receives next coupon paid	
Ex-dividend	Cost DOES NOT INCLUDE interest from the settlement date to the next payment date	Proceeds DO NOT INCLUDE interest from the settlement date to the next payment date
		Seller physically receives next coupon paid

Other fees payable

Where an investor uses a stockbroker to complete a purchase on their behalf a fee will be payable. The amount of the fee will vary between brokers but will also be based on the size of the deal and the level of advice a broker may provide, if any.

How quickly are you paid when you sell a bond?

From 6 October 2014, following a move by the EU to harmonize settlement terms for bonds, corporate bonds and gilts trading on ORB moved from T + 3 to T + 2, ie payment is made two business days after the date of the trade whilst gilts remained at T + 1.

Factors affecting bond prices

Most, but not all, bonds are negotiable or marketable and can therefore be traded on a recognized market or in some cases between two parties. Within any market, price will be determined by the supply and demand of the product, which in this case is the bonds. Therefore, factors which will alter the price of a bond are factors which will affect how much of one type of bond is for sale and how much of that bond is demanded by investors.

All the following factors should be considered in an assessment of the potential for reductions in future returns from income and capital gains/losses as they will determine the value and volume of bonds supplied by lenders and demanded by investors.

Liquidity

The ability to be able to sell assets as and when required in a short time period for their fair market price increases an asset's value by making it more desirable.

So, for investments where there is a large and/or guaranteed market, a triple A+ rated bond or a gilt, for instance, there will be little liquidity risk; however, for bond issues where there is smaller volume of daily trading or potentially issues with the credit rating of the issuer, this will potentially make liquidity more questionable.

General interest rates and a specific bond coupon rate

By buying a bond, the investor is in effect buying the right to a stream of future cashflow or income. The price of the right to the income will depend, as with all investments, on the level of risk perceived in the investment and the size of the coupon relative to other interest rates (income streams) investors can purchase in the market. Assuming the level of risk of a bond hasn't changed, then when the general level of interest rates changes this will affect the price of the bond.

> **In practice**
>
> Alpha Plc issues a 7 per cent bond at par value when the prevailing interest rate in the market is 7 per cent. Effectively therefore if an investor pays £100 for the bond he or she gets the right to obtain £7 income per year for the life of the bond. This gives them the same value as other methods of obtaining interest income in the market as the prevailing interest rate is also 7 per cent.
>
> Six months later general interest rates fall to 5 per cent. Suddenly Alpha Plc's bond looks like a good investment as the coupon is far higher than can be achieved by other investments in the market. There is an increase in demand for the bond in the secondary market which drives the price up from £100. The question is how high will the price go? Well the market certainly shouldn't pay more for Alpha Plc's cashflow stream than it can get anywhere else in the market.
>
> So, if for a £100 investment the market will give the investor an income stream of £5 then a £1 return is worth £20 of value (£100/£5). On this basis, to get a £7 income stream the investor should not pay more than 7 × £20 or £140.

The above example illustrates the idea of an inverse relationship between interest rates and bond prices. That is: as interest rates fall, bond prices rise and vice versa. Be aware, however, we are not talking about individual bond interest/coupon rates in this relationship; rather the relationship of the individual bond price to the general rate of interest prevailing in the market.

Economic environment

Changes in the economic environment can affect the price of bonds in several ways and this change, due to increasing globalization, can be affected by issues in both domestic and foreign markets.

For instance, the level of the PSNCR in the UK will affect the price of the gilt and domestic bond markets. This will also be the case for other foreign government and bonds. In addition, anything which is seen to identify changes in productivity levels and economic prosperity in a country will also affect prices. Such identifiers include:

- levels of gross domestic product (GDP) or gross national product (GNP);
- unemployment figures;
- business confidence index (BCI) or consumer confidence index (CCI) produced by the OECD and European Union amongst others.

Investor sentiment

Bonds are seen, in some cases, as being a potentially safe port in a storm and when the equity markets are volatile investors can be seen moving money to bonds until the volatility subsides. This is due to bond prices being less volatile overall and due to the relative certainty of the coupon return.

As with anything which involves human nature such moves can be difficult to predict and quantify.

Credit rating

One of the major risks of investing in debt is the possibility that the debt issuer will not have sufficient funds available to make coupon and redemption payments. Credit rating agencies provide an opinion on the potential for default. Whilst there are several credit rating agencies, the three main ones, Fitches, Moody's, and Standard & Poor's, control over 90 per cent of the total market. Since the financial crisis credit rating agencies have been criticized due to their analysis of some debt instruments available at that time which it was felt were rated too highly.

Credit ratings are given to countries and companies overall and to individual bond issues for companies. They provide useful information in investment assessments and as they use the same criteria for classification all over the world they can be used by investors to assess companies where the investor has limited knowledge.

Country or sovereign ratings provide investors with a general idea of the potential risk of investing in a country by looking at areas including economic conditions, the volume of public and private investment as well as political and economic stability to assess how credit-worthy the country is. It may be that investors will only consider specific companies within a country if the country achieves a certain level of credit rating. Credit ratings can then be given to individual companies or specific bonds issued by a company; however, these will only ever be equal to or lower than the country in which the company operates.

In each case agencies will consider the following broad areas:

- financial strength;
- management quality;
- industry competition;
- the economic and political context in which the firm operates.

The agencies operate a letter system with AAA+ being the highest possible grade and D being the lowest and representing debt which is in default. Bond issues which are graded BBB or above are known as investment grade and are a relatively good-quality issue. Those which are graded below this are known as high yield or junk bonds and are high-risk investments for sophisticated clients or clients who accept higher risk and the potential loss of capital.

Understanding risk in bonds and its effect on bond prices

As we discuss in more detail, bonds are not risk free and the risks faced fall into two main categories: those related to not being repaid coupons or principal owed; and those which relate to the bonds' relationships with general interest rates (as discussed above). What you need to be able to do as you assess a bond for suitability is to understand the relationship between risk and bond price to ensure a fair price is paid for the perceived level of risk.

Keyword

Risk for the investor can be distilled into two main factors:

1 How successful does the investor believe the issuer's business is now and will be in the future? The potential success of the business is a more subjective assessment which is made on a bond-by-bond basis, using techniques such as fundamental analysis of financial and market information, analysis of credit ratings and potentially, analysis of past price movements.

2 How likely are general interest rates to change and what effect would changes in rates have on a bond price?

Investment classes: Fixed-interest (debt)

The potential to quantify a bond's price sensitivity to changes in general interest rates can be calculated and is affected by seven factors, detailed below.

Length of time until maturity

The longer the time until maturity the greater the effect of any potential interest rate rises.

> **In practice**
>
> There are two bonds which both pay coupons twice a year and have interest rates of 4 per cent. Bond A will mature in one year whilst Bond B will mature in six years. If general interest rates fall by 1 per cent then this will only affect the remaining 2 coupon payments to be made by Bond A compared to the 12 coupon payments remaining for Bond B.
>
> In this instance as interest rates have fallen this will make the bonds more attractive in the market due to the inverse relationship between interest rates and prices and therefore both Bond A and Bond B would rise in price. However, we would expect Bond B to rise more as there is the potential for it to benefit over a longer period from the interest rate fall.

Coupon rate

A bond with a relatively low coupon is usually more volatile than one with a larger coupon as any change in general interest rates will proportionally affect the bond with the lower rate more. A bond with a higher coupon produces more income early in its life and therefore will have a shorter duration. A zero-coupon bond will have a duration equal to its maturity as it only has one cashflow at the end of its life.

> **In practice**
>
> If you have two bonds, Bond A and Bond B, Bond A has an interest rate of 3 per cent and Bond B has an interest rate of 6 per cent. In the market, general interest rates are 6 per cent. If general interest rates now rise by just 1 per cent, this represents a rise of 33.3 per cent for Bond A but only 16.7 per cent for Bond B, a much smaller proportional rise.

Credit rating

Junk or speculative bonds are more volatile due to having a greater potential for default, recognized in the fact that they are graded lower than BBB+, or investment grade, by credit rating agencies.

This factor mix produces a unique volatility signature for a bond which it is possible to quantify and use to compare one bond to another when modelling the effect on the bond of different economic circumstances. One of the simplest ways to quantify the potential for change in price is to calculate a bond's Macaulay duration which relates changes in general interest rates to the effect on a specific bond's price.

Bond price

In the calculation of the Macaulay duration below we can see that the present value of the weighted cashflows is divided by the market price. As such, if the market price either rises or falls then the duration of a bond will change.

A sinking fund

The presence of a sinking fund increases the cashflows in the earlier years therefore shortening the duration of a bond compared to one without a sinking fund.

Call provisions

A bond with a call provision (where the issuer has the right to repay and retire the bond) can potentially affect the duration of a bond if used.

Yield to maturity

A higher yield to maturity will produce a shorter duration as the present values of the cashflows furthest in the future, ie those with the heaviest weighting, are overshadowed by the earlier coupon payments.

The Macaulay duration

> **Keyword**
>
> **Macaulay duration** shows the value of coupon payments required to repay the original value of the principal.

The calculation is expressed in years ie three years of interest payments are required from Bond A to repay the principal, therefore the duration of Bond A is three years.

Whilst the duration is part of the normal suite of information calculated and reported for individual bonds by information systems such as Bloomberg, it is useful to understand how the number is calculated to be able to explain to clients. The formula can be summarized as:

$$\text{duration} = \frac{\Sigma \text{ (net present value of bonds cashflows} \times \text{time to cashflow being received)}}{\Sigma \text{ (net present value of the cashflows to be received)}}$$

In practice

George has invested in Alpha Plc's bond. The bond is three years from redemption and a coupon of 10 per cent paid is twice a year. George's investment has a nominal value of £10,000 and is trading at par (see Table 6.3).

We then need to divide the total PV of cashflow by the market value of £10,000, giving a duration of 5.33 years (53,278/10,000).

It should be noted this formula only approximates the relationship between bond prices and bond yields; as such it is more accurate where there is small change in yield.

Table 6.3 Macaulay duration: example

Period	Cashflow (£)	Weighted cashflow (£)	DF of £1 at 5%	PV of cashflow (£)
Column 1	Column 2	Column 3	Column 4	Column 5
1	500	500	0.952	476
2	500	1,000	0.907	907
3	500	1,500	0.863	1,295
4	500	2,000	0.822	1,644
5	500	2,500	0.783	1,958
6	10,500	63,000	0.746	46,998
			TOTAL	53,278

Notes

Column 1: This shows the periods where cashflow will be received. We have six periods as the coupon is paid twice a year so a period in this case is six months, but in other calculations it could be a year or a month depending on the terms.

Column 2: This is the actual cashflow received. Each six months the bond will pay the investor half the interest due. The total interest for a year is 10 per cent of £10,000 ie £1,000 so the investor will receive £500 every six months. In period 6 the investor will also receive the nominal value of the capital, as the bond is redeemed, as well as the interest payment.

Column 3: Here the amounts received are weighted by the period in which they are received, so column 1 is multiplied by column 2 to achieve the weighted value of the cashflow. This is because there is more uncertainty surrounding payments further in the future, so to calculate the potential risk of the payments being affected by interest rate changes means those which have the highest risk should have the highest value.

Column 4: This is the discount factor which is used to reduce the value of future cashflows back to an equivalent value on the day of the calculation.

Column 5: This is the weighted cashflow multiplied by the discount factor to provide the present value, at the date of the calculation of the future cashflow. The total value of column 5 is divided by the market value of the bond to calculate the Macaulay duration.

Duration provides a measure of risk as it links volatility to price with a higher duration relating to a higher price volatility. The bonds with the highest duration and therefore the highest sensitivity to interest rate change are ones which have a low coupon rate as:

- these will take a longer time to repay the principal amount;
- there is a longer period to maturity;
- they are liable to be more volatile.

In practice

Bond C's duration is five years. If general interest rates fall by 1 per cent the price of the bond will rise by 5 per cent and vice versa.

Investment classes: Fixed-interest (debt)

The ability to estimate how a change in the market may affect a bond's price can be a useful tool in deciding which investments may meet a client's future cash needs. For those investors requiring income and who want to minimize interest rate risk, as they believe interest rates might rise, this should help them understand why including bonds with high coupon payments and short maturities may be an appropriate strategy for them.

The modified duration

Keyword

The Macaulay duration can then be used to calculate the **modified duration** which enables us to estimate what effect a change in the yield will have on price.

$$\text{Modified duration} = \frac{\text{Macaulay duration}}{1 + \text{GRY}}$$

where:
GRY = gross redemption yield/yield to maturity
this can then be rearranged to:

$$\% \text{ change in price} = -(\text{modified duration} \times \% \text{ change in yield})$$

Note the minus sign on the right-hand side of the formula which highlights the inverse relationship between changes in price and changes in yield.

So, if Bond B has a Macaulay duration of 10 and a GRY of 5 per cent then we can calculate the modified duration as 10/(1.05) = 9.52. In this case, you can then suggest that for a 1 per cent increase in price you would expect to a see a 9.52 per cent drop in yield due to the inverse relationship.

Measuring the return on a bond

The return on any bond comes from two potential sources, depending on the type of bond held. These are: the income from the coupon; the repayment of the original amount borrowed.

The running yield

This yield is also known as the flat, interest or current yield and looks solely at the return generated from the coupon received by the investor as a percentage of the price paid:

running yield % = (annual coupon rate/market price) × 100/1

> **In practice**
>
> George has purchased £21,000 of Alpha Plc bonds. Alpha Plc issued the bonds in 2006 and they are due to be redeemed in 2026. The bonds have a coupon rate of 7 per cent and are currently trading in the market at £125 per £100 nominal. Assume we are currently in 2016.
>
> The running yield = (7/125) × 100/1 = 5.6%

This measurement is useful where cash returns generated by the investment are important to clients and for irredeemable bonds where there is no redemption.

It should be noted that this calculation does not take account of the timing of cashflows or the time value of money in any way.

The holding yield

This calculates the gain or loss from holding the bond. Such a capital gain or loss may occur as interest rates change which in turn will affect the price of bonds due to their inverse relationship.

$$\text{holding yield \%} = [(\text{price received at redemption} - \text{price paid})/\text{price paid}] \times 100/1$$

> **In practice**
>
> Using George's purchase of Alpha Plc bonds above as an example, we can work out the holding yield as follows:
>
> Holding yield % = [(100 − 125)/125] × 100/1 = − 20%
>
> As George paid more than nominal value for the bonds, if he holds them until redemption he will incur a capital loss of 20 per cent.

Annualized holding yield percentage

The holding return can then be averaged over the period remaining to maturity to show the potential annual level the capital value of the bond will fall.

$$\text{annual holding yield \%} = \left(\frac{\text{Holding yield \%}}{\text{Number of years to maturity}}\right) \times 100$$

> **In practice**
>
> In the example above, George has a –20 per cent holding yield which equates to an annualized value of –2 per cent. That is, –20 per cent divided by 10 years.

Gross redemption yield (GRY) or yield to redemption/maturity (YTM)

This takes account of both returns which may result from holding debt; that is, the income gain and the capital loss/gain (depending on the price paid for the debt). The GRY totals both the running yield for the bond and the annualized holding yield. This calculation can be made as an historic measure once the bond has been sold or can be used to estimate the return if the bond is held to maturity.

Returns in the real market

Government debt: UK and overseas

The relative yields on government bonds reflect the level of perceived risk associated with the country. Bloomberg's website (www.bloomberg.co.uk) on 23 June 2016 showed the following rates for 10-year bonds for some of the major economies of the world including the UK (see Table 6.4). These include a wide range of values, including a negative return for Swiss bonds.

The level of interest required to invest in Brazil is easily understood in relation to additional risk requiring additional return from a rational investor; however, the reasoning for investing in Switzerland with its negative return is more difficult to explain but does provide a good example of the negative yields now being seen in Europe. So why are investors

Table 6.4 Overseas government bond yields[2]

Country	10-year government bond yield %
USA	1.73
Brazil	12.35
UK	1.37
France	0.45
Switzerland	−0.43
Greece	7.54
Australia	2.25
South Korea	1.65

buying bonds which if they hold them to maturity will guarantee they lose money?

Commentators have suggested several reasons for this which include:

1 Capital preservation: using the base investing assumption that the global financial markets are heading towards a rerun of the meltdown in the 2008–09 financial crisis it becomes a lot easier to understand investors using strong government bonds as a haven to protect capital. The low and negative yields are seen as an acceptable cost of achieving this protection. However, this assumes the bonds being invested in are as safe as investors perceive.

2 Investors must purchase bonds: the underlying terms of some investors, such as pension funds or insurance companies, may require them to hold a percentage of funds in particular types of investments eg government bonds. As such they will be at the mercy of the returns in the market. In addition, for such companies there may also be cashflow demands from investors, leading to a requirement to hold such assets. Such portfolio allocation considerations may also force managers to purchase negative interest bonds based on a lack of acceptable alternatives.

3 Possible price increases in the future: A bond's price will move inversely with its yield, therefore as its yield goes down its price will rise. We may not be able to envisage a scenario which is worse from the point of view of yield than the current negative yields seen; however, it is possible one may occur. Currently the ECB is buying bonds to allow European financial institutions to boost lending and, as a result, boost European economies. The ECB has also reduced interest rates to negative rates on

centrally-held cash deposits to encourage banks to lend. If these policies become more aggressive over time and rates and yield become more negative then this will affect the price of existing bonds, as they may rise in price due to increased demand as their interest rate losses are lower than other newer bonds on the market. That said, if interest rates start to rise then the opposite will be true and prices for the bonds may fall leading to capital losses.

4 Exchange rates: for foreign investors, there is always the exchange rate perspective to be considered as, whilst the return on the bond may not be high or may be negative, they may be able to obtain a return due to exchange rate movements. For instance, in 2016 some US investors hoped the yen might rally against the dollar, so they moved to own yen bonds despite their negative returns, as they hoped to benefit from an exchange rate movement when bringing funds back to the US.

The risks of investing in bonds

Such risks are associated with two important factors: the potential for the coupon or redemption value not to be paid to an investor; and the potential for the coupon rate/return to be eroded and loose value.

Inflation

The headline rate of a coupon is known as the nominal rate of return, that is the rate of return before expenses or the potential cost of inflation is deducted. Inflation erodes the return on any fixed-income investment as it decreases the buying power of money over time. For instance, where there is inflation what you could buy with money received from fixed coupons will be lower in one year's time than it is now.

In practice

To be able to assess the effect of inflation on the nominal rate of return of a bond we need to deduct the inflation from the coupon.

For example, at its most basic, if we have a coupon with a nominal return of 6 per cent and inflation is currently 2 per cent, then the real return is approximately 4 per cent (6 per cent – 2 per cent).

Such erosion does not occur on index-linked bonds where both the coupon and the redemption amount are adjusted for inflation using the retail price index (RPI).

For further in-depth discussion, an article by Kang and Pflueger argues that corporate bond yields reflect fears of debt deflation using empirical data.[3]

Issuer or default risk

This is the risk that the bond issuer or borrower cannot generate sufficient cashflow to repay either or both the coupons and the redemption value. These payments are mandatory, unlike dividends for equity shares, and if not made it is likely the company will eventually enter an insolvency process. In such cases, as we discuss below in the section on security, there is a legal order in which investors in a company are repaid.

When assessing a bond issue, however, the area of issuer risk is one which must be seen in the context of the level of debt, the return generated and the relative risk between debt and equity.

As mentioned previously, the level of perceived risk in debt is less than that of equity and this reduced risk is reflected in the level of return which potentially can be generated from investing in bonds. Unlike equity holders who have accepted higher levels of risk, debt holders will not benefit from the upside of a very successful company generating profits higher than forecasts. This is because bondholder returns are fixed to the level of agreed coupon and the amount of the original debt.

That said, in times when cash generation is far less than expected, bondholders are more likely to have their coupon paid as this payment is mandatory unlike dividends for shareholders. For clients, this risk–return trade-off must be understood when deciding which product to invest in.

Governments are perceived to have the least risk of debt default as they have, in most cases via their central banks, the ability to print money which can be used to pay coupons. Corporate bonds are much riskier than government debt; however, the size and quality of a company will play a part in the level of risk of an investment. For instance, consider which of the following will be the riskiest investment:

- a bond held in a small Plc quoted on AIM with only two years' trading history;
- ordinary shares in a blue-chip multinational ranked 10th in the FTSE 100 which has traded for over 100 years and returned profits in line with forecasts.

I would say, in this instance, based on the information given, the equity holding would be less risky than the debt. Therefore, when looking at a single debt issue, whether debt is perceived as less risky than equity should be seen in the context of the potential for cash generation and issuer default.

Methods to reduce default risk

It is possible, as a lender, to mitigate the potential for default using, credit ratings, guarantees and other security measures.

Credit ratings

Credit ratings, as we previously discussed, show the potential for default by a bond issuer; however, it should be remembered that the ratings are only the opinions of those carrying out the review, which is paid for by corporate bond issuers. As seen in the financial crisis this is not a guarantee that payment will be made nor is the analysis infallible. It should also be noted that credit ratings do not change often over time, whereas the circumstances and economic context in which bonds exist can, and these disparities in timing as well as the other factors above should be noted when assessing a credit rating.

Guarantee

To reduce the perceived riskiness of a bond the issuer may attach a guarantee to a bond issue. The guarantee is not given by the issuer but by a third party such as another company in the same trading group or potentially a separate third party such as a bank or insurer who will guarantee the bond payments. In the event the issuer does not pay the interest or capital as required then the guarantor becomes liable for the payments.

The key when assessing an investment is to assess if the guarantor would be able to pay the monies due. If such guarantor monies have been ring-fenced then the potential for non-payment is reduced; however, assessments of the guarantor should be made over the life of the investment to ensure payment can be made if required.

Security

Loans and bonds can be either secured or unsecured. For unsecured loans, the lender is reliant on the borrower generating sufficient cashflow to pay the coupon over the life of the bond and the capital at redemption. If payment is not possible the company may enter an insolvency process where the company's assets will be sold to repay all those owed monies by the company.

Secured debt is most commonly seen in our personal lives when we buy a house using a mortgage. We borrow money from a bank or building society to pay for the house and we allow the bank to take security over the house using a legal charge. The legal charge allows the bank to repossess and sell our house if we do not make the agreed loan repayments to the bank.

Whilst this may appear quite a scary prospect, millions of people operate this system successfully every year. The benefit for the bank (the lender) and for us as borrowers is that by providing security to the bank we reduce the bank's perceived risk in lending to us. This is because unlike the unsecured debt example above, if we fail to make the agreed repayments the bank will still be able to recover the money lent and will not suffer a loss: unlike the assets noted in the unsecured example they do not have to share the proceeds with other creditors, but they can use all the proceeds to repay the debt. Because of this perceived reduction in risk the lender can charge a lower interest rate on the loan.

There are two different types of security on UK bonds or loans: 'fixed' or 'floating'.

Keywords

- **Fixed security** refers to a specific asset which will be named in the bond terms as security. The type of assets used for fixed security tend to have a long lifespan as they need to be available for the whole life of a bond, and they must be easily identifiable and potentially saleable. Examples of such assets may include office buildings or factories.

- **Floating security** refers to a legal charge over all the company's assets without defining any specific asset. Such assets are ones the company will always have, eg trade receivables or inventory. However, whilst they will always be available, individual items of stock or individual customers will change over time. For example, using trade receivables, the company will always have many customers who have traded with them on credit and are due to pay money to the company in the future. The exact total value of trade receivables may change over time as will the specific customers on the trade receivables list. For the investor/lender, using the trade receivables as security they will look not at the individuals but rather at the overall value of trade receivables and using a percentage of the total value as their security. For lenders, such assets are more difficult to manage and as such they perceive the value of floating security as less than fixed security.

In the event of a company entering liquidation or other insolvency process then the cash generated from the company's assets will be used to repay those who lent money to or invested money in the company in the following order:

1 secured debt – fixed;
2 secured debt – floating;
3 unsecured debt;
4 preference shares;
5 equity shares.

The money is not shared equally between each different class of investor; rather all the secured debt is paid first using money from secured assets, then all the unsecured debt and so on until there is no more money left. It is quite usual in such cases for equity shareholders and preference shareholders not to receive any repayment. In fact, it may be, if the company has a heavy debt burden, only the secured debt holders receive repayment. This highlights the importance of assessing the overall debt burden when assessing an investment as well as the terms of a bond issue.

Subordinated and unsubordinated debt

Two other terms, subordinated or unsubordinated, can also be used to describe debt and these should be borne in mind when assessing a fixed-income security:

- Unsubordinated debt, also known as senior debt, is debt which is paid before all other types of debt should a company cease to trade.
- Subordinated debt, also known as junior debt, is paid after other named amounts of debt. This can be particularly important within debt categories where there are insufficient funds available to repay all the holders in one category as it will determine who is paid first.

Building societies

A particular risk applies to building societies and investments in PIBS and perpetual bonds as they are not included in the Financial Services Compensation Scheme (FSCS). During the financial crisis, there were several instances where PIBS holders lost capital value.

In practice

The PIBS holders of Chelsea Building Society lost half of the value of their capital following its forced merger with Yorkshire Building Society. The merger was required because Chelsea lost about £41 million in a buy-to-let fraud and having £55 million of deposits frozen in Iceland. This may seem harsh, but it may well be that the PIBS holders, as subordinated debt holders, would have lost more of their capital if the merger had not taken place.

Bond taxation

Gilts/individual corporate bonds and bond funds

Bond income

Assuming an investment is not included in an ISA or a SIPP tax shelter then bond income will be taxable. That said, income from individual bonds and gilts and the income from bond funds are dealt with differently. All are subject to an investor's marginal rate of taxation in line with other income; however, individual gilts and bonds have their coupons paid gross whilst bond funds have 20 per cent deducted at source.

Capital gains

Again, if the investment is within an ISA or SIPP (self-invested pension plan) tax shelter then capital gains tax will not be payable on any increase in investment value.

For a bond fund capital gains tax is due at the marginal rates; however, both individual gilts and individual corporate bonds are exempt if the corporate bond is classed as a qualifying bond.

A qualifying bond is one which is issued in sterling with no rights of conversion or redemption in any other currency. It has no rights for conversion to shares or other securities and the rate of interest charged must be reasonable and not depend on the financial results of the issuer's business.

Building society

PIBS and perpetual bonds are taxed like other bonds and can also be included in a stocks and shares ISA and a SIPP. However, for the SIPP the callable date of the PIB must be at least five years in the future.

Table 6.5 Advantages and disadvantages of investing in bonds

Theme	Advantage	Disadvantage
Return	• Higher return than deposit accounts • Offers regular income	• Compounding not possible unless in bond fund • Long-term lower return than equities historically
Capital safety	• Relatively safe compared to equities	• Depends on position in credit ranking in insolvency
Price volatility	• Usually less volatile than stocks	• Can be volatile following an interest rate change • Long-term bonds more volatile than short-term bonds
Management	• Usually require less management time than equities	
Inflation	• Index-linked bonds provide inflation protection	• Most bonds are not index-linked
Diversification	• Possible in a bond fund	• Hard to achieve in a single bond

The advantages and disadvantages of investing in bonds

Summary

Debt, including both bonds and loans, permeate all sections of government, corporate and personal investment, allowing investment projects to be undertaken in an orderly fashion at a known cost. For investors, they provide a potentially lower risk investment, although risk is dependent on the quality of the borrower. Investing in debt is not without its risks, however, and whilst those risks are reduced in comparison to other investments such as equities and speculative derivatives, this perceived reduction in risk does penalize the investor by fixing the maximum level of return possible, unlike potential returns seen in in equity investments.

Check your understanding

1 Which type of government debt is issued as zero-coupon bonds?
2 What is the difference between an international bond and a Eurobond?
3 What is ORB?
4 What elements make up the price of a bond?
5 Why should an investor consider the size and 'quality' of a company when deciding where to invest?

Further reading

General

Financial Times, Microsoft issues the biggest bond of the year in debt market boom, Eric Platt and Thomas Hale, 30 January 2017, www.ft.com/content/7d0a5618-e70d-11e6-967b-c88452263daf

The Telegraph, What are bonds and how do they work? Charlotte Beugge, 26 June 2014, http://www.telegraph.co.uk/sponsored/finance/investment-library/low-risk-investments/10843733/how-bonds-work.html

Vaitilingam, R (2011) *FT Guide to Using the Financial Pages*, 6th edn, FT Prentice Hall

Sovereign bonds in emerging markets

FT.com, Upbeat mood drives record EM sovereign debt, James Kynge and Thomas Hale, 30 March 2017, www.ft.com/content/04eaacc8-155c-11e7-b0c1-37e417ee6c76

Global bond outlook

Financial Times, Global bond issuance highest in nearly a decade, Eric Platt, 18 September 2016, www.ft.com/content/a30ffee6-7c3f-11e6-ae24-f193b105145e

Schroders, *Outlook 2017: Global Corporate Bonds*, Rick Rezek, 29 December 2016, http://www.schroders.com/en/uk/private-investor/insights/markets/outlook-2017-global-corporate-bonds/

Investment classes 07

Equity

By the end of this chapter you should have an understanding of:

- the difference between a public limited company and a private limited company;
- the characteristics of ordinary and preference shares and the differences between them;
- the difference between the nominal and market value of a share;
- how and why companies may issue additional shares and the effect this may have on shareholders' wealth;
- the purpose of a stock exchange, how shares are traded and the costs involved;
- what returns equity investment provides and how they can be measured;
- advantages and disadvantages of investing in shares including risk factors and factors affecting price;
- the difference between equity and private equity.

Introduction

Investing in shares is potentially more risky than other investment types we have discussed so far in this book. That said, this type of investment also has the potential to produce some of the highest returns, which if your client is a rational investor who is not risk-averse, can be a very attractive proposition.

Investment classes: Equity

There are fundamental differences between investing in equities and other forms of assets such as bonds, cash and cash equivalents as we will discuss; however, the underlying premise for a portfolio manager remains the same: you are required to understand the investment to be able to assess its suitability for a specific client.

The essential basis for an equity investment is the limited liability company as investing in equity means buying a percentage of the business, although for modern multinational businesses such as Marks & Spencer Plc, buying a share buys a tiny fraction of a percent of total ownership. When we talk about limited liability companies we are talking about the legal structure and organization of a business. There are several legal structures which UK businesses can use: sole trader, partnership and company. Sole traders and partnerships do not have limited liability; if they become insolvent and owe amounts to creditors it is possible, if there is a shortfall in the amount owed, the business owners will have to pay those debts out of their own personal assets, for example by selling their family home or other personal assets. The owner's liability for the debts of the business is unlimited.

> **Keyword**
>
> **Limited liability** means that, if an investor buys shares worth £100 in a limited liability company, if that company becomes insolvent in the future the shareholder cannot be asked to contribute further money to pay any company debts which remain outstanding. This is important to an investor as they can know with certainty that their potential losses will be limited to the amount they have invested.

Companies on the other hand have limited liability.

There are two types of limited liability companies in the UK: private limited companies, usually known as 'Limited' companies, who use the abbreviation 'Ltd' after their name; and public limited companies who use the abbreviation 'Plc' after their name.

Only Plc shares are available for sale and resale to the public through a stock exchange – in the UK, the London Stock Exchange. Limited company shares are only sold through bespoke transactions between two parties. Plc shares are more liquid because of investors' ability to buy and sell them on a transparent exchange as required making them more flexible and valuable to the average investor. The sale of limited company shares is a more specialized area of investment and will not be covered in this chapter.

Types of shares

As discussed above shares (also known as equity) are the basis for a company's legal structure. They separate the owners of the company from the company itself. Individuals are natural people in law; however, companies also have a legal persona and are seen as a legal person in law, that is having a legal identity separate to its owners. At the simplest level, equity investors purchase part-ownership of a company by purchasing ordinary shares in it. That said, there are lots of different types of shares which companies may issue for different purposes and it is important to know which one you are advising a client to buy. This is because not all shares will provide you with a share of ownership and may have different characteristics which you need to make sure your client is aware of in order to make sure the investment suits their needs. There are two main types of shares: ordinary shares and preference shares. However, within those two types there are several share variations.

Ordinary shares

> **Keyword**
>
> Where any company is formed, the individuals who invest an amount of money into a company by buying **ordinary shares** will receive a specified number of shares in return for funds invested, giving them part-ownership of the company based on the number of shares purchased as a percentage of total ordinary shares in issue.

The rights and responsibilities of shareholders are included in a company's constitution which is known as the company's Articles of Association.

The investor's shareholding is recorded in a share register, (part of the official records of the company) for the period the investor owns the shares. In addition, the total value of shares issued will be recorded in the company's balance sheet/position statement.

When assessing an ordinary share purchase there are three main areas to be considered: voting rights, dividends and security. Each of these areas is treated differently for an ordinary share and a preference share.

Voting rights

Purchasing an ordinary share grants the owner the potential to vote on certain issues as detailed in the articles of association and any specific terms of the issue. Each share usually has one vote; however, this is not always the case as the special types of shares below show.

The right to vote entitles the owner to vote at a general meeting of the company. A general meeting is a pre-arranged meeting of shareholders, not the day-to-day meetings directors conduct to operate the business. When voting occurs at a general meeting the votes of individual shareholders must be totalled to decide if the vote has been passed or not. There is more than one method of vote counting. In some cases a show of hands will be used which will give each shareholder one vote irrespective of the number of shares that shareholder owns. This method is quick and can be useful where the resolution to be decided is widely agreed. In other circumstances a poll will be held where the number of shares held will be considered. A poll can be requested by two different mechanisms, either:

- through the articles of association which in the 'model form' allow a poll to be requested by two or more members or under company law (Companies Act 2006, sec 321);
- where any five or more members or the holders of at least 10 per cent of the voting rights can request a vote.

Dividends

> **Keyword**
>
> A **dividend** is a periodic payment made by a company, with the agreement of the directors, to their shareholders, with payment being made from cash generated by the organization. The level of dividend will be determined at points in the financial year based on current results and future forecasts

Ordinary shareholders (the most 'vanilla' form) are not entitled to receive a minimum level of dividend, unlike some ordinary share variants set out below and preference shareholders. Rather, the company considers whether it wishes or can afford to pay. The dividend may be split into an interim dividend received part-way through the year and/or a final dividend received after the end of the financial year.

Companies may issue dividend policies to try to give investors security about future dividends and the ability of their shares to generate income for the investor. However, there is no guarantee a dividend will be paid. The following practice box illustrates this.

> **In practice**
>
> 'Aviva usually pays dividends on its ordinary shares in May and November each year. Any dividend paid is declared by the directors at the interim and final results announcement and, in the case of a final dividend, approved by shareholders at the Annual General Meeting.
>
> 'Over the medium term, Aviva will look to pay out a dividend that is 50 per cent of its post-tax operating earnings per share (EPS).'
>
> www.aviva.com/investor-relations/shareholder-services/dividends

Security

Ordinary shares are the least secure of any type of company investment. In the event of company failure, they will be the last class of investors in the company to be repaid and in all likelihood shareholders will not receive any of their initial investment back from a failed company.

Other types of ordinary shares

Dual-class shares

Here more than one type of ordinary share is issued, often called by different letters, such as A and B to distinguish them. Each type will have different voting and dividend privileges. One set may have additional voting rights to those sold to the public; these will typically be given to company founders ensuring they retain control of the company. Such shares are controversial; some stock exchanges do not allow them (Hong Kong and Singapore); some exchanges discourage their use (London); whilst others live with them (USA).

Historically, dual-class shares were used to prevent hostile takeovers. Investments in companies' dual-class shares will potentially produce dividends and capital gains as other shares do; however, because of the reduced voting power of some shares this may make them higher risk, as the business may be controlled by one individual and run solely for their benefit with limited options for other shareholders to oppose this due to the voting structure.

> **In practice**
>
> **Alphabet Inc**
>
> Technology companies have been particularly proactive in using dual-class shares to protect their long-term, strategic vision. Google, recently renamed Alphabet Inc, has had a dual structure since its flotation in 2004 with founders Larry Page and Sergey Brin using 'super voting' shares to control the company and outweigh the votes of other share groups. Google's success with investors has undoubtedly been helped by its ability to generate cash; however, it has also remained in touch with the market, for example by increasing financial reporting transparency in 2005. So, despite the fact that shareholders can be outvoted by the original founders this system has worked for both parties.
>
> **Hollinger International**
>
> Not every instance of dual-class shares, however, is such a success. Hollinger International was run by its founder Conrad Black who owned 30 per cent of its equity value but was entitled to 73 per cent of the voting rights. Black filled the board with friends who did not provide any opposition to his plans allowing him to extract huge amounts of cash through management payments and dividends from the company, affecting financial and share performance with other shareholders powerless to stop him.

Academic research has also found that weak shareholder rights can affect shareholder returns. A US study by Paul Gompers and Andrew Metrick published in 2003 found that investors who sold US companies' shares with the weakest shareholder rights and replaced their investment with companies who had the strongest shareholder rights could potentially earn up to 8.5 per cent more overall.[1] An important decider when looking at which shares a client should invest in.

Redeemable shares

Redeemable shares are shares which include an agreement for the company to repurchase them from the holder at an agreed future date. The authorization for a company to issue this share type, as well as the terms of the repurchase, are often included in the company's articles of association.

Directors determine if the shares are redeemed using distributable profits or a new share issue; in either case the redeemed shares are retired. Depending on which route is chosen there may be a reduction in the nominal value of the company's overall share capital.

Deferred dividend shares

These ordinary shares hold full voting rights, but will only receive a dividend after an agreed date in the future. Despite the dividend being deferred the share will still benefit from any capital growth in value which may suit some investors who do not currently require income.

Founder shares

Also known as deferred ordinary shares, they are often issued to initial members of the company. Dividends are usually only paid once dividends to all other shareholders have been paid; however, as an incentive to hold them there may be differing voting rights and potentially a larger share of profits as dividend.

Preference shares

> **Keyword**
>
> **Preference shares** are a separate class of shares to ordinary shares and do not participate in the full risks of the business. They are also not described as equity funding, but rather as a hybrid, as they have several features which can make them appear to be a mixture of ordinary shares and debt.

Preference shares differ to ordinary shares in the following areas:

- Voting: unlike ordinary shareholders, normally preference shareholders have no voting rights within the company.

- Dividends: preference shareholders will be paid before ordinary shareholders can receive a dividend and the preference dividend itself is normally a fixed percentage of the nominal value of the share. For example, a 7 per cent preference share with a nominal value of £1 and a market price of £1.76 will pay a dividend of 7p per share. When a company is successful, preference shareholders do not have the same potential for dividend growth as ordinary shareholders do; however, they do have an increased certainty of being paid, as preference shareholders must be paid before ordinary shareholders. This is one of the factors which reduces the risk of investing in preference shares compared to equity and may lower investors' required rate of return in the investment.
- Security: this is particularly important should a company cease to trade. Preference shareholders are paid after all debt holders have been paid but before any payment is made to ordinary shareholders which improves their chances, if only marginally, of having their original investment repaid. Repayment in insolvency means the maximum repayment will be the nominal value of the share that is, the value at issue. This is not the market value of the share when the investor purchased it which may mean the investor still suffers a loss on their original investment. Whilst preference shares may be considered more secure as they are paid before ordinary shares, in insolvency situations the preference shareholders still rely on there being sufficient assets to pay them after all debt holders have been paid, which can often be unlikely.

Other types of preference share

Cumulative and non-cumulative

Most preference share dividends are cumulative, which means if a company makes insufficient profit to be able to pay the preference dividend in one year then the current year dividend is accrued until the following year. Outstanding dividends will continue to be accrued until all preference dividends outstanding have been paid. Such accruals will affect ordinary shareholders, especially where they are dependent on dividend income, as their dividend income may be delayed until all the preference share arrears have been paid.

Alternatively, preference shares can be non-cumulative which means if there is insufficient profit available to pay the preference dividend in one year that dividend is lost and does not carry forward to the next year. This puts ordinary shareholders in a much better position as they will not have to wait until all arrears are paid to receive a dividend themselves. The preference shareholders' position however is much worse as they have accepted a reduced return for increased security but lost all their expected return for a year.

Participating

Here the preference shareholder has a fixed dividend percentage as you would expect; however, they also have the potential to gain a further dividend return if the profits of the company exceed a pre-agreed level. The levels of additional dividend received and the levels of profits required before that additional dividend is received are determined on a share-by-share basis.

Redemption

As with debt it is possible for preference shares to be redeemed by a company. Here the redemption date is either fixed in the terms of the share or chosen by the company. On redemption, the shares are returned to the company by the shareholder in return for repayment of the nominal value. The company will then cancel the shares, effectively reducing the issued preference share capital of the company.

Conversion

It may also be included in the terms of the preference shares that under certain circumstances preference shares can be converted to a predetermined number of ordinary shares in a similar way to how debt can be converted to ordinary shares.

Nominal and market values of shares

When a company issues shares, the shares have a value which is recorded in the financial records of the company (in the balance sheet/position statement). This value may be made up of two elements depending on the price at which the shares are issued:

- nominal value: this is the underlying value of the share and can range from 10p to £1 per share;
- share premium: if the investor pays more than the nominal value for a share the difference between the price paid and the nominal value is included in a share premium account.

In practice

Alpha Plc issues 10,000 shares with a nominal value of £1 at a price of £1.50. George purchases 1,000 of the shares at issue.

Alpha Plc will record two amounts in its balance sheet in respect of the shares sold to George, a nominal value of £1,000 (1,000 shares at £1 each) and a share premium account value of £500 (1,000 shares at 50p). The total value of £1,500 will then equal the amount of cash physically received by the company for issuing the shares to George.

The value of George's investment is £1,500 (1,000 shares at £1.50) which equals the amount of cash he has paid.

As a share is bought and sold over time the market price of the share will change depending on the risk and return associated with the company amongst other factors, but the company itself does not alter the market value of a share directly.

The nominal value of a share however is fixed and can only be changed by the company in certain circumstances which we will discuss below.

Increases in the number of issued shares

It is possible that the numbers of shares might change and because of the change it is also possible the total nominal value of shares issued may change. The most common reasons for changes in numbers are known as corporate actions. Examples of corporate actions are explained below and it is important to understand the effect such changes will have on an investor's wealth.

For each of the following types of corporate action an 'ex-date' will be announced by the issuing company. This is the date at which the entitlement to purchase or receive the new shares will stay with the seller of the shares rather than being included in the buyer's purchase. So for shares sold on or after the ex-date the seller of the shares will retain the rights to the shares whilst for shares sold before the ex-date the buyer of the shares will receive the entitlement to the new shares.

In some cases, it may be possible to sell the right to receive new shares separately to the shares themselves (as is the case with a rights issue, see p 234) at which point a third party would receive the right to purchase the new share.

Capitalization issue

Keyword

Capitalization issue – also known as a bonus issue. A company will issue additional shares to existing shareholders, amending a company's capital structure but not receiving any new funds for the shares.

Where a company makes a capitalization issue, the number of shares will increase but the company will not receive any new funds from issuing the shares nor will the investor have to pay for the shares: they will receive them free of charge. The result of the issue is to simplify the company's balance sheet because the value of the share premium will be reduced by the value of the new shares issued.

In practice

Company A originally issued 1,000 shares with a nominal value of £1 each at an issue price of £2. An extract from the company's balance sheet recording the issue would look like this:

	£
Ordinary Shares	
Nominal value	1,000
Share premium	1,000
	2,000

Company A then decides to simplify its balance sheet by issuing 1,000 new £1 shares under a capitalization issue. The revised balance sheet would then look as follows:

	£
Ordinary Shares	
Nominal value	2,000

There is no change in the overall value of the company as there is no change in the value of the total assets and liabilities of the company and it is their value which determines the company's value in the financial statements.

Investment classes: Equity

The number of new shares issued does not have to be the same as the number already in issue. For instance, if a company had 1,000 shares in issue they could issue 250 new shares, or indeed any number.

The new shares are distributed on a pro rata basis between existing shareholders, so in the example above of Company A, existing shareholders will receive one new share for every share they hold, a 1 for 1.

This new issue of shares does not affect the value of the company in the financial statements or potentially its overall value in the marketplace; however, this type of corporate action is likely to affect the market price of the individual shares held.

> **In practice**
>
> Company A has 1,000 shares in issue with a nominal value of £1 each, the shares were issued at £2 and are currently trading in the market at £4 per share.
>
> The total market value of the company is £4,000 (1,000 shares at £4 each). With the issue of the 1,000 new shares the overall value of the company does not change, but we would expect to see the individual share price fall to £2 per share as the company's market value remains at £4,000 in total but the number of shares has doubled from 1,000 to 2,000, leading to an individual share price of approximately £2 per share (£4,000/2).

It is also possible that despite theory expecting the share price to fall to £2 per share in the example above (as there has been no change in the assets of the company or its expected cashflows) in reality this may not be the case and the shares may trade at a little more than £2 per share. This can happen sometimes as the fall in the individual share price makes them makes the shares liquid or marketable as more people are able to afford them, driving up demand and therefore price.

Share or stock split

> **Keyword**
>
> **Share (or stock) split** is a corporate action which increases the number of issued shares by dividing each share. This increases the number of shares in issue but not the overall value or market capitalization of the company – just as would happen if two £5 notes replace a £10 note.

Again, the company does not receive new funds with a share split and the investor does not have to pay for the new shares they receive. However, in contrast to the capitalization issue above which increased the overall nominal value of the issued share capital of the company, in a stock split, the overall nominal value of the issued share capital remains the same but the nominal value of each individual share reduces, allowing more shares to be issued.

> **In practice**
>
> Company A currently has a total nominal value of issued share capital of £1,000 made up of 1,000 shares at a nominal value of £1. If the company carried out a stock split and reduced the nominal value of each share to 50p the company would then have 2,000 shares of 50p each but the overall nominal value of the company's issued share capital would still be £1,000 (2,000 shares at 50p).

Again, the new shares are distributed on a pro rata basis so from the investors' point of view they would expect the market value of their individual shares to halve but their overall shareholding value should stay the same or may even increase slightly, due again to the potential for increased marketability due to lower prices.

Rights issue

> **Keyword**
>
> A **rights issue** is used when a company wishes to raise new funds by issuing new shares. Under UK company law any new shares issued must be offered to existing shareholders first to ensure their ownership and control is not diluted by new investors.

A rights issue is a different situation from the both the capitalization issue and share split, as in this case new funds are received by the company following the share issue and the investor, whilst they will receive a free right to obtain additional shares, will have to pay to receive the new shares, although the price is likely to be at a discount to the current market price.

The rights issue process issues all existing shareholders with a provisional letter of allotment detailing the investors 'right' to buy in terms of the price to be paid and the number of shares they are eligible to buy. The shareholder then has four potential courses of action:

- They decide to buy the new shares and invest further cash into the company.
- They decide they don't want to buy the new shares and therefore they sell the right to buy new shares to another investor. The existing shareholder receives cash in return for the sale of the rights.
- They sell some of the rights and use the proceeds to buy several new discounted shares without making further cash investment into the company.
- They do nothing and the rights lapse.

The choice made by an investor will affect their overall wealth and client managers should be aware of this.

For the investor, their decision to invest hinges on several different issues surrounding the alternative uses for the purchase money, the potential for the funds to generate additional cashflow and therefore increase the share price and what effect the rights issue may have on the existing share price.

A method of gauging the effect of the rights issue on a share price is to calculate the theoretical ex-rights share price.

The theoretical ex-rights share price (TERP)

The TERP is the price that the share should theoretically be valued at following the rights issue based on the cost of the shares to the investor. This is not necessarily the same as the actual market price the shares trade at following the rights issue as there are other factors to consider when determining a share price. However, it does give an investor an idea of a minimum value for their investment.

Keyword

The **TERP** is effectively the weighted average cost of both the shareholders' existing shares and the new shares from the rights issue and can be calculated on either a share-by-share basis or over the whole portfolio.

In practice

George owns 2,000 shares in Company A with a current total market price of £5,000. Company A has just issued George with notification of a 1 for 4 rights issue at a discount of 20 per cent on current market price.

George's existing shares are valued at £5,000 and as he owns 2,000 shares they have an individual value of £2.50.

The rights issue shares will cost George £2 per share (£2.50 × 80%) and he is entitled to 500 new shares as the rights issue is a 1 for 4. This means George can buy one new discounted share for every four he currently owns (2,000 shares/4). To buy all his entitlement would cost George £1,000 (500 shares at £2).

Following the rights issue George's total shareholding will theoretically be valued at:

Existing shares:	2,000 with a value of £5,000
Rights issue shares:	500 with a cost of £1,000
Total holding:	2,500 shares with a value of £6,000 (or £2.40 per share)

If George doesn't think his shares will trade at a value of £2.40 or more then he may decide not to buy the rights issue.

As we noted above there are several different options for an investor when they receive a rights issue notification and what they decide to do will affect their overall wealth. To explore this idea further, consider the following example.

In practice

Assume that George's total wealth is currently made up of the following:

- 2,000 shares in Company A with a current market value of £5,000;
- cash of £3,000.

Assuming the rights issue is offered in line with the terms in the TERP calculation we can calculate the effect on George's wealth for each potential action he could undertake.

In each case George starts with a total wealth made up of shares and cash of £8,000:

1 *Buy the shares allocated in the rights issue.* Buying the new shares would cost George £1,000 (500 shares at £2 per share). George would then hold 2,500 shares, which assuming the shares traded at the TERP price, would have a value of £6,000 (£2.40 per share).
Result: George's total wealth would be £2,000 cash (£3,000 less £1,000 to buy the shares) plus £6,000 in shares: a total of £8,000.

2 *George decides not to buy the rights issue shares but sells the rights separately.* The value of the rights is the difference between the TERP and the rights issue price, ie £2.40 and £2 = £0.40. George can then sell the rights for £200 (500 shares × 0.4).
Result: George will hold £3,200 of cash made up of his original cash holding of £3,000 plus £200 from the sale of the rights. His shares will be valued at £4,800 (2,000 shares at £2.40.): a total wealth of £8,000.

3 *George sells some of the rights and uses the proceeds to buy some additional shares.* In this case George could sell some of his rights to raise cash and then buy new shares. It is likely there won't be an exact match between the available number of rights and the shares he can buy. However, if he sells 420 rights he will gain £168 which will allow him to buy 80 shares, thereby using up his remaining rights. This will cost him £160 (£2/share for 80 shares) leaving him with £8 spare.
Result: His total wealth at the end of the transaction will be £3,008 of cash including the £8 from the sale of the rights. He will also hold 2,080 shares at £2.40 each £4,992: a total wealth of £8,000.

4 *George does nothing.* In this case, based on our calculations of the TERP, George's share value is likely to fall to £2.40 per share.
Result: George will retain his cash at a value of £3,000. However, he will face an overall reduction in the value of his shares which he will expect to trade at the TERP price, leading to an overall share value of £4,800 (2,000 shares at £2.40). This leads to a reduction in George's overall wealth of £200, which equates to the value of the rights which can be sold.

The conclusion from a client management point of view is that, whatever the client decides to do, an investment manager should ensure they understand the potential danger of doing nothing and the potential impact of this on their overall wealth.

Open offer

Keyword

An **open offer** is like a rights issue, in that the company will issue new shares at a discount to raise new funds and shares will be allocated to existing shareholders on a pro rata basis. The two main differences from a rights issue are: 1) the right to purchase the new shares is not tradeable and therefore cannot be sold; 2) whilst an individual shareholder is given an entitlement to new shares it may be possible for them to apply for additional shares over and above their initial entitlement.

Stock exchanges

Over the past 20 years there has been a move away from the traditional idea of a stock exchange which was historically a mutually owned not-for-profit organization with a monopoly in the physical trading of shares, mainly aimed at a domestic market of companies and investors. Stock exchanges today have been radically overhauled as a marketplace, with electronic trading of shares for national and international companies to domestic and international customers. There has also been a change in ownership structure with stock exchanges becoming listed companies themselves. The effect of these changes has been to increase the dynamism and speed of the stock trading environment as well as providing increasing amounts of capital for national, international and global business.

The London Stock Exchange (LSE) group

The LSE can trace its origins to 1698; however, it is now a multinational group headquartered in the UK with approximately 3,500 employees spread between its operations in the UK, USA, Italy and Sri Lanka. At the time of writing, the LSE may potentially merge with the German Stock Exchange, although this is currently under investigation by the EU.

The LSE group operates equity, bond and derivatives markets in London as well as, for example, the Borsa Italiana and Turquoise, a pan-European multilateral trading platform for equities and other investments. By providing access to capital markets for retail investors and institutions and for companies looking to fund growth, the markets provide an invaluable economic role in the UK and worldwide economy.

In addition to trading the group also provides benchmarking and analytical services, post-trade and risk management services and technology solutions including trading surveillance. The LSE has a very good website which gives far more details of its services and roles and this can be found at www.londonstockexchange.com.

As with all stock exchanges, a recognized investment exchange such as the LSE has several functions in addition to facilitating the trading of new and existing shares and bonds. These include ensuring all member firms are supervised and trading is regulated. Such regulation not only includes well-known areas such as policing insider trading but also ensuring all transactions are recorded and ensuring price-sensitive company information is disseminated through its regulatory news service.

London Stock Exchange markets

The LSE consists of the main market dealing in the capital raising and trading of the largest national and international companies which can be summarized in indices such as the FTSE 100 and FTSE 250.

In addition, there is the AIM (Alternative Investment Market) market for smaller domestic and international companies looking for start-up capital and also additional capital to expand. Since its inception in 1995, more than 3,000 companies have signed up to the AIM market raising nearly £100 billion in capital. Companies may be attracted to AIM by the less stringent rules and trading requirements compared to the main market. That said, many companies have started on AIM and transferred to the main market as they have grown and developed.

Identifying individual shares

The LSE website has an alphabetic search function which allows searches for individual company's shares with the listing providing several pieces of information in respect of the share.

> **In practice**
>
> A search on 30 September 2016 for Marks & Spencer Plc Ordinary Shares showed the following information:
>
> - Code: MKS
> - Name: Marks and Sp.
> - Currency: GBX
> - Price 316.50
> - Positive or negative change in price: –4.6
> - Positive or negative percentage change in price: 1.43 per cent
>
> Further to the headline information about the current market price, changes in price as well as their trading code for the market, there were options to order a free annual report and to view market news stories which are filed in date order. For instance, on 12 September 2016 an article has been registered in respect of a change in directors.

In addition to the above there are also management tools for registered users including the portfolio management tool and a watch-list tool to aid trading. Similar information is also provided for preference shares and includes the name, percentage dividend redemption date and currency.

Systems for trading shares on the London Stock Exchange

On the London Stock Exchange, there are several electronic and non-electronic methods of security trading.

SETS

This is the main electronic order book, trading FTSE 100, FTSE 250, FTSE SmallCap Index constituents, exchange-traded funds, exchange trading products as well as other liquid AIM, Irish and London Standard-listed securities and securitized derivatives (on a modified trading-cycle version of SETS).

Investment classes: Equity

It is one of the most liquid order books in Europe allowing multiple order types. This liquidity in conjunction with high levels of market supervision, wide stock coverage and the ability of market participants to trade anonymously due to the presence of two competing clearing houses makes the LSE a market leader.

SETSqx (Stock Exchange Electronic Trading Service – quotes and crosses)

SETSqx trades securities which are less liquid than those traded on SETS. It achieves this by mixing a periodic electronic auction with a non-electronic quote system. Electronic orders can be anonymous if required and auction uncrossings take place at set times during the day with the last trade at 4.35pm providing the closing price for the share for the day.

SEAQ

This is the LSE's non-electronic quotation service for AIM securities not traded electronically on SETS or SETSqx. The system also covers some fixed-interest securities as well.

Away from the LSE there are two other methods of trading financial instruments:

Alternative trading system (ATS)

An ATS matches the orders of buyers and sellers who subscribe to that specific ATS. This matching increases the liquidity of the market overall as well as individual shares. This is due to having more opportunity to buy and sell specific investments at a time which suits the investor. Higher liquidity for individual shares then creates a virtuous circle as it increases the popularity of those specific shares.

The UK hosts approximately 20 ATSs trading in bonds, equities, financial derivatives and commodities as well as hosting firms trading overseas ATSs. ATS examples include electronic communication networks and call markets and have allowed development of new trading strategies including posting limit orders and cross trades.

Over-the-counter (OTC)

Here a bilateral contract is used directly between two parties, often an investment bank and its client, to facilitate the buying and selling of stocks, bonds, derivatives or commodities. Trading is often conducted by phone or computer.

Trading shares

Who sells investors shares?

There are two sources investors can use to buy and sell shares: agents and principals.

Agent/broker

An agent doesn't own the shares they are selling; they merely facilitate the transaction between the principal/dealer (the person who owns the share) and the buyer (investor). The agents must provide the investor with a price which includes any 'mark-up' or profit the dealer expects. The agent is not allowed to add anything to the share price so their payment for arranging the deal is a transaction fee.

Principal

Principals on the other hand own the share they are selling and charge a mark-up or profit on the transaction. They do this by providing two prices to the market: a price at which they will buy stock from an investor (bid price) and a price at which they will sell stock to the investor (offer/ask price). The difference between the two prices is the 'spread' or margin and is how the dealer makes a profit.

> **In practice**
>
> A is a principal who deals in Zeta Plc's shares which are currently trading in the market at £2.50 per share. To make money A would be willing to sell shares in Zeta Plc for £2.55 and buy shares from investors for £2.45. Therefore, for every share purchased or sold A would make 10p; not a huge amount but if the volume of share sales is high this may turn into a large amount.

The example above is very simplified version of the real-life transaction and the level of margin is likely to be far smaller in a popular or low-risk share as investors can buy and sell from any dealer so will be looking for the best price and lowest margin.

Share purchase costs

The cost of purchasing a share may have four elements:

1 The cost of the share itself. If the share is being purchased from the issuing company (via a broker) then the price may be fixed through the process of an initial public offering. Alternatively, if the client is buying an existing share then the price will be determined by the market and this is discussed in more detail below.

2 Agents/brokers/buying platforms commission. The parties facilitating the sale and purchase of shares will expect a fee. The fee level depends on the platform used; for example, an online platform is cheaper than buying through an investment bank in most cases and potentially also through a broker.

   Brokers may decide to charge fees in several ways, eg flat fees, a rate per share or a percentage of the total trade value. They may even include a minimum fee level which can potentially make small share transactions disproportionately expensive for clients.

   Any fees charged reduce the overall return the client receives on a share; the most cost-effective route for a transaction should be identified in each case, subject to the individual circumstances of the sale.

3 Panel on Takeovers and Mergers levy. The Panel on Takeovers and Mergers (PTM) was set up in the 1960s to ensure all shareholders irrespective of size are treated equally in the event of a takeover and to administer the city code on takeovers and mergers. The levy is one of three main sources of income used to finance the panel's work.

   The PTM levy is a flat fee of £1 on sales and purchases of securities of companies in the UK, Channel Islands and Isle of Man where they are traded on the secondary market and the total transaction value is over £10,000. Where more than one security is traded in one transaction a levy is due for each security traded. The payment is only due on sales to retail investors and is collected by the broker.

4 Stamp duty reserve tax (SDRT) and stamp duty. SDRT is payable when you purchase shares through a paperless system, usually CREST (an electronic settlement and registration system administered by Euroclear). The CREST system automatically collects the SDRT on a transaction and sends it to HM Revenue and Customs (HMRC). The liability to pay CREST falls to the client and brokers will invoice their client for their commission and the CREST payment.

Shares covered by SDRT include shares in UK and foreign companies registered on the UK stock exchange. SDRT is charged at a flat rate of 0.5 per cent (rounded up or down to the nearest penny) based on the value paid for the shares not their physical worth. If a new issue of shares is made in accordance with EU Council Directive 2008/7/EC no SDRT is payable.

> **In practice**
>
> If George buys shares in Alpha Plc traded on the LSE for £10,000 through CREST, he will be liable for SDRT of £50.

A transaction may also be liable for SDRT where shares are transferred outside CREST but held by a nominee, such as a bank. In such cases a stockbroker will often complete the transaction and pay the SDRT directly to HMRC.

Stamp duty, in contrast to SDRT, is payable for transactions with a total value over £1,000 where the purchase is recorded on a stock transfer form. To complete the transaction, the form must be signed by HMRC and the stamp duty payment made to them.

Where the transaction is for £1,000 or less clients don't normally pay any stamp duty and HMRC don't need to be informed if the exemption certificate on the back of the stock transfer form is completed and the form is sent to the registrar of the company in which the client has purchased the shares. The registrar will then issue the client with a share certificate.

Off-market transactions

On occasions, transactions may be carried out which are off-market or completed outside a normal stock market system. In such cases stamp duty will be payable unless the shares have been received as a gift for no value.

> **In practice**
>
> If George swapped an 18th-century chest of drawers valued at £1,000 for 100 shares in Company A owned by his friend Beth, George would pay stamp duty on the value of the antique, which would make him liable for a payment of £5. He would have to inform HMRC of the transaction and make the payment.

The effect of corporate actions on the costs of buying and selling shares

As we discussed, a corporate action involves an existing shareholder receiving new shares. If a client in this position wishes to sell their existing shares before they have received the new shares this is possible; however, from a client management perspective you should be aware that if your client eventually wishes to sell both their existing and new shares they are likely to incur two sets of selling fees or minimum dealing costs. Whereas if the client waits until all the shares have been received they can sell them as one transaction and make a better return.

There is also the potential for a further delay in selling the shares in one transaction where the new shares are issued as 'registered' indicating a difference between the new and the existing shares. This difference is likely to be temporary – for example, if the new shares are not entitled to the next dividend – and eventually both sets of shares will merge. Following the merger, the new and existing shares can be sold as one transaction. Prior to merging, however, the shares will be charged two separate commissions by some sellers.

Possible returns from holding shares as an investment

An investor is hoping to receive a return from their equity holding in two ways: 1) income from dividends; 2) capital return through growth in the share price.

There are several measures investors use to assess the return, or success, of their investment. Such measures used are ratios and for the information calculated to be useful in measuring portfolio performance the most important aspect, other than accurate calculation of the ratios, is an understanding of what they tell us.

In the real world, there are several ways of obtaining a lot of the information required to calculate the ratios measured here. In fact, a number of websites will potentially calculate either the exact ratios set out below or a variation of the ratio for you. This highlights a potential data analysis point: different websites or analytical tools may calculate ratios differently. It is very important therefore that you understand how a ratio has been calculated or you may find you are comparing two items which have been calculated differently (ie comparing an apple and an orange) and that you have provided a recommendation based on misinterpreted analysis.

Some of the websites where analysis of share information can be found include:

- individual company websites;
- Yahoo! Finance;
- London Stock Exchange;
- Bloomberg – although a subscription may be required.

This type of analysis where a company's underlying performance is required is fundamental analysis and a comparison of this compared to technical analysis can be seen in Chapter 12. Whilst finding the information for an analysis and producing the ratios and analysing them can be time-consuming, it can also be very rewarding if it leads you to a greater understanding of a company and therefore a better recommendation which benefits your client.

Measuring returns from shares

Dividend measures

Dividend yield

$$\text{dividend yield (\%)} = \frac{\text{gross dividend paid}}{\text{market price (ex – dividend)}} \times \frac{100}{1}$$

Yield is calculated above on a gross basis allowing the investor's personal tax position to be assessed separately.

Once calculated the percentage yield can be used for two purposes:

1. To measure the yield on an investment, ie the return in relation to the price paid. This can then be compared to other investment types or other shares.

2. The formula can be rearranged so that the dividend paid from one company within an industry is compared to the dividend yield for another similar company in an industry, allowing the analyst to calculate an expected share price.

In practice

Sharon owns 100 shares in Alpha Plc which is currently trading at £4.50 cum-dividend. A dividend of 35p per share is to be paid in three weeks' time.

The current dividend yield for Sharon is the dividend payable of 35p divided by the ex-dividend market price, in this case £4.15 (£4.50 – £0.35). The calculation should be made in either pence or pounds for both the dividend and the share price. As such the dividend yield is (35/415) × (100/1) = 8.43%.

The yield calculation is based on the total dividend (interim and final) paid in the previous year to ordinary shareholders. The weakness in this approach is that you may be calculating a return on an investment which will not be repeated. As such, yield can also be calculated on a prospective rather than historic basis using a forecast dividend for the current year; however, again there is no certainty this payment will occur.

As we assume our clients are rational investors we expect that to take on increased risk they will require an increased return. Where a higher dividend yield is seen compared to previous years or other companies in the same industry then this may be due to the increased perception of the risk of the specific business or industry which is being priced in to the share by the market. As such the context of the result needs to be investigated to ensure the correct analysis of the situation.

The conundrum is that if a company is successful an investor would hope to see a 'real' increase in dividends over time, that is, an increase in the dividend above the level of inflation to ensure that the buying power of the dividend is maintained and hopefully increased. Of course, an increase in dividends should, if investors are happy with the company's performance, lead to an increasing share price. However, if there is a lag between these two factors, due for instance to new information about the company's improved potential results not being immediately included in the share price leading to the increase in dividends occurring before the increase in share price, this would affect the level of dividend yield seen and therefore how the company is perceived, at least for a short period of time.

Dividend cover

$$\text{dividend cover} = \frac{\text{EPS}}{\text{net dividend per share}}$$

As we can see in the price and earnings section below, earnings per share does not relate to the dividend paid; rather it relates to any income which is attributable to the ordinary shareholder of the company. Therefore, dividend cover is assessing how safe an investor's dividends are should there be a fall in the level of earnings of the company. Dividend cover is expressed as a 'number of times'. For example, if Company A has an EPS of 100p and a net dividend per share of 10p, then the dividend cover is 10 times.

A dividend cover level of 2 or below may be a relatively risky position for the investor. A higher level of dividend cover will be not only a safer current position for an investor but also potentially a safer future position as well. This is because the company is retaining cash which could be used in the future to ensure current dividend levels/projections are maintained even in years where the company has failed to accumulate sufficient cash to pay all dividends out of current earnings. Where a dividend is paid out of earnings from a previous year this is called an uncovered dividend.

Price and earnings

Earnings per share (EPS)

$$EPS = \frac{\text{earnings attributable to ordinary shareholders}}{\text{number of ordinary shares}}$$

Earnings attributable to ordinary shareholders are calculated as net profit after tax and preference dividends.

In this calculation, we are using earnings rather than dividends to reflect the potential return a shareholder may obtain from a company. It should be remembered though, that not all earnings will be distributed to shareholders. Some earnings may be retained and used to finance investment projects to generate increased future cashflow which in turn should be reflected in a higher share price for the company.

Earnings yield

$$\text{earnings yield (\%)} = \frac{\text{earnings per share gross}}{\text{market price per share}} \times \frac{100}{1}$$

If an investor is not reliant on income from their shareholding they may find the earnings a more useful measure than dividends. Earnings should generate strong future cashflow dividends if invested correctly as such earnings can be used to compare the relative strength of two companies.

Price–earnings (P/E) ratio

$$\text{P/E ratio} = \frac{\text{share price (ex div)}}{\text{EPS}}$$

The price–earnings ratio is a useful analysis tool for an investor in several ways, not just as measure of the price of a share as a multiple of its earnings. As an investment manager analysing a company you will have to ask yourself how the P/E ratio of a specific share compares to those of similar companies in the same industry and potentially other investments. Therefore, you will need to understand the relevance of the calculation you have made. As with all ratios, the P/E ratio can be interpreted in several ways and your final conclusions will depend on context. You will be analysing not only the company itself but also the industry in which it operates and comparing your results to other companies in the same industry.

Where a company has a P/E ratio which is lower than similar companies in the same industry there is always a temptation to think you may have come across a bargain which, if purchased, should produce a capital gain. This may be the case; however, you need to be sure of the company's circumstances before you come to this conclusion. The alternative explanation may be that the company is in financial difficulties and this has already been reflected in the P/E ratio by the market.

One of the major weaknesses of the P/E ratio, as with most ratios, is they often use historic information for the calculation, producing a result which is historic and which may not be repeated. Due to this the P/E ratio can also be calculated using forecast information, although this is prone to all the weaknesses associated with using projected figures.

Capital

Capital growth

The capital growth rate of a share over the period it is part of a portfolio can be calculated as:

$$\text{capital growth} = \frac{\text{closing share price} - \text{opening share price}}{\text{opening share price}}$$

The opening share price relates to the share price at the beginning of the period under review, whilst closing share price relates to the share price at the end of the period of review. The period under review can be a period within an overall period the share has been held or potentially it may be the date the share was purchased and sold.

The resulting answer is given as a percentage and allows an investor to compare the returns on individual shares held within a portfolio over a period, for instance where an annual client review of investments is being completed. It will also be used to calculate the return on a share over the total period an investor holds it, ie from the date it is purchased to the date it is sold.

Enterprise value

$$\text{enterprise value} = \text{market capitalization} + \text{preference share capital} + \text{debt value} - \text{cash and cash equivalents}$$

Market capitalization is the market value of an individual company's ordinary share multiplied by the number of shares in issue.

Enterprise value is not, however, a measure of a company's value, but rather the investor's estimate of the value of the organization's ongoing operations using the above elements as a proxy. As such it is sometimes used as a theoretical measure of the cost of taking over another business.

Risks of investing in shares

As we discussed in Chapter 6 on debt, it is important for a client manager to understand the risks of an investment to determine its suitability for a portfolio, and for retail investors in ordinary shares the risks faced are, excluding derivatives, some of the highest in the investment world.

Liquidity

This relates to how easy an investor finds it to sell a share for a fair value within a reasonable period. An above-average or below-average liquidity can affect the value of the share in conjunction with its performance.

In practice

Two companies, A and B, are identical in every way regarding their performance. The only difference between them was Company A's shares traded in large volumes daily compared to Company B's shares which traded in smaller quantities on average once a month. Potentially Company

> A shares may trade at a premium to Company B's. This is because investors would prefer Company A shares as they would find it easier to sell the shares at a fair price in a shorter timescale than they would the shares of Company B. The increased trading volumes and frequency allow investors to raise cash as and when they need it as well as providing up-to-date information on the value of the shares.

Low trading volumes are rarely an issue for blue-chip companies; however, some listed companies, especially those on AIM, may trade at low volumes making it difficult for a broker to find a buyer/seller combination, at any given time, at a good price. This idea of illiquidity is taken to its extremes when considering a limited company where transactions are bespoke between two parties. Where clients are considering investments in relatively illiquid shares the potential pitfalls in terms of time to sell and fair price should be highlighted.

Growth

In addition to the potential return of income from equity investing the investor will also be looking for capital growth through a rising share price. Such growth cannot be guaranteed and growth levels may be affected by many factors (discussed below).

Academic research has shown that small companies tend to return the best capital growth over time although this may be because only the successful ones are left in business to be measured. Blue-chip companies in established industries, overall, tend to grow at a lower rate than some new industries such as technology (known as speculative industries). Potential growth rates can be linked to the associated risk of investing. In all cases, however, time is a factor as growth is unlikely to be overnight and as such equities require capital to be tied up for potentially long periods to earn a satisfactory return.

Capital

Equity investors also need to remain aware that they are ranked last in an insolvency procedure. As such, the risk for them should the company fail is that they may lose 100 per cent of their capital investment.

Price volatility

Volatility describes the frequency and magnitude of share price movements. Investors ideally want a share whose value rises steadily over a period without any major falls in value. What can cause uncertainty is a share whose price rises and falls erratically even where the overall trend is upwards.

Investment managers measure volatility by looking at the price swings of individual securities and comparing them to the return gained over time. This information can then be compared to figures from similar companies and risk-free investments to determine if a share's historic return offsets the potential risk of holding the share.

One of the measures used to assess volatility is based on modern portfolio theory and uses standard deviation. Standard deviation measures how far a share's value moves from its average over a period. The smaller the standard deviation the lower the volatility of the share as there is a smaller chance of receiving a lower than expected return from the investment, thereby reducing the risk of holding it. Theoretically, 'risk' is the possibility of receiving a *different* return than expected, not just a *lower* one. But for clients it is the lower returns that cause problems.

An alternative measure of volatility, based on the capital asset pricing model, is Beta which is a measure of the systematic risk or volatility of a security which compares the expected return of the security to the expected market return adjusting for risk. The calculation of Beta is covered in Chapter 4.

The relationship between market performance and volatility is that in a bear market volatility increases as does risk, leading to a potential reduction in returns; in a bull market the opposite is true. Volatility is not always a bad thing; in fact some short-term or day traders can use share volatility to make a return. It may also be possible to use volatility as part of a predetermined investment strategy, known as pound cost averaging to purchase a share at a lower price as investors are driven to sell shares at a loss and thereby lowering the average cost of purchase.

> ### Keyword
>
> **Pound cost averaging** involves investing in a market on a regular basis over a period rather than in one lump sum. Investing regularly means more shares are purchased when prices are low and less when prices are high, which overall could improve the return on a portfolio, especially in a falling market.

Where a decision is made to invest in a potentially volatile stock there are several areas which should be considered and understood before the share becomes part of a client's portfolio:

- Understanding why a stock is volatile: this can be for several reasons in respect of both turnover and costs. For example, companies which are dependent on small numbers of high-value contracts will produce erratic results as contracts come onstream and go offstream. Alternatively, companies may have variable-rate funding, resulting in rising costs in a period of rising interest rates. Such questions covering the fundamental operations of the business need to be answered before an investment is undertaken.
- Understanding how long the shares will have to be held before they can be sold: whilst it may be possible to use pound cost averaging to reduce the overall price of investment in a company, this may not be sufficient to reduce the uncertainty completely. The investor may also have to hold the stock for a considerable period before there is a rise in the price above the value paid. This needs to be factored into the client's investment outlook.
- Value of investment required: if a client is to use pound cost averaging to reduce the overall cost of investment then potentially the value of stocks purchased in one company could grow and become substantial. This will need to be reviewed against the client's overall investment strategy.
- How inflation and the opportunity cost of capital may affect the level of return: inflation is usually said to be considered within share returns; however, where prices are volatile this may not always be the case. Taking inflation into account may lead an investor to surmise that the additional return they obtained for investing in a volatile stock was not sufficient for the additional risk they faced, even where they made a profit.

    The opportunity cost of investing in this type of risky share also needs to be considered in the light of where else the funds can be placed, ie the opportunity cost of investment, which again might suggest that alternatives may provide a higher level of return compared with the level of risk.
- How volatility will affect dividend income and corporate action benefits: holding shares for the long term leads to an expectation of some form of return from dividend income. However, shares with volatile prices may only pay dividends rarely owing to cashflow constraints and may not

pay a dividend at all. In addition, shares with volatile price movements are unlikely to undertake corporate actions such as stock splits etc, which is a potential source of value increase due to improved liquidity.

- How volatility will affect share liquidity: volatile share prices may drive investors from the market leading to illiquidity in shares which may adversely affect bid–ask spreads leading to long-term investors being disadvantaged by remaining in the market. However, the volatility of a market may provide opportunities for traders using algorithmic and high-frequency trading methods, as they are able to take advantage of the price movements in the market.

Industry and company-specific issues

A company's share price and its ability to pay dividends are linked to the industry they operate in and their structure; therefore, the following should be assessed when analysing the risks of a share purchase.

The nature of the industry.

Here we are differentiating between established blue-chip companies and those new companies potentially involved in areas of development. It is possible that the former would be considered a less and the latter a more risky investment, although such generalizations do not always follow – as we saw in the recent BHS insolvency, with BHS trading for over 100 years on the high street before its failure.[2]

Cyclicality of the industry

There are goods which are pro-cyclical, being demanded more in an upturn than a recession, for example luxury items, and those which are counter-cyclical, being demanded more in a downturn than a boom. There are also some goods and services which are demanded irrespective of the state of the economy, such as food. It is important to understand where the company being analysed fits into the economic cycle and where in the cycle the economy is at the time of investment.

Management quality

Management play a huge role in the success of a company. Again, BHS and its previous owners Dominic Chappell and Sir Phillip Green can be used as examples of how instrumental management can be and as such it is important that the experience and qualities of managers are judged in relation to the business in hand. More information about the BHS insolvency investigation is available.[3]

Company finances

The ability of the company to generate growth whilst paying dividends and meeting debt interest payments needs to be assessed. Companies which are highly geared but have volatile cashflows may suffer cashflow issues during periods of rising interest rates which in turn will affect share price and potentially dividend payments.

Market conditions

In addition to factors which directly affect the company, share values can be affected by the rise or fall of the market overall. Such market movements can affect a company specifically: as mentioned previously, the Beta of a company can be used as a measure to assess how a share is likely to move compared to the overall market in terms of magnitude and direction. However, in addition to this all shares will feel the effect of a moving market to a certain extent, so a relatively poorly performing share in a sector or industry is likely to rise in a rising market and conversely a solidly performing blue-chip company's share price is likely to see some decline in an overall falling market.

Factors which affect market conditions can include, amongst others: news in respect of inflation; interest rates; exchange rates and unemployment rates; the buying and selling patterns of institutional investors; as well as the overall level of available funds within the investing community.

Factors affecting the price of shares

The economy

Capitalism is ultimately about increasing profits which is achieved through growth. Since the financial crash growth levels have been low, uncertain and unevenly spread round the globe. In June 2016 the World Bank revised their annual global growth forecast down from 2.9 per cent to 2.4 per cent. That is not to say that all areas of the world are suffering however; whilst

Brazil has seen a 4 per cent contraction of its economy India has seen growth of 7.6 per cent overall. In most cases company profits will grow as an economy grows, and as such clients will be looking to invest in the next big growth area.

Company news

This can also be a major influence on prices. In line with stock market rules any major event, for example a profits warning, has to be announced to the market and this information may result in a share price movement. Explanations of the headlines on regulatory announcements are available.[4]

> **In practice**
>
> Information in respect of a profits warning must be given to the market and is likely to cause a share price fall.
>
> For instance, Universe Group Plc which trades on the AIM market issued a profits warning in September 2016 due to delays in rolling out new products to three major customers, leading to a 13 per cent drop in their share price.[5]

Alternatively, a story perceived as showing strong company projections, or if directors buy shares, may lead to a positive share price movement. Any new information does however require careful consideration and should not be taken blindly at face value. For instance, if two or three directors buy shares this can be a stronger indicator than just one director buying. Which directors are buying can also affect the potential strength of the information; for instance, if the CEO, sales director or financial director buys then this may signal an improving position which should be acted upon.

Interest rates

Whilst there is no direct relationship between interest rates and equity prices, if interest rates are low then investors may look to shares to improve their return which may raise prices due to increased demand. In addition, with low interest rates companies may be able to finance growth more cheaply leading to an increased potential future cashflow which would drive prices higher. The alternative tends to be true where interest rates are high.

Press and analysts reports

There is a plethora of share information on the web, in the media and in both free and 'pay to use' analysts' reports. The 'tips' provided can affect share prices, especially if a particularly negative or positive story is reported in the mainstream press.

Investor sentiment

This is linked to the behavioural analysis of share prices and can be difficult to explain with logical arguments. There may be times when shares grow without the underlying increase in potential cashflows or asset values which would be expected to drive prices, as was seen in the dot.com bubble. Alternatively, despite good performance share prices may refuse to rise. Behavioural finance attempts to explain how investors' emotions can affect decision making, using ideas such as herd mentality to explain why investors may make irrational decisions – for example, when investors sell at a low price as others in the market are selling, not because there is a flaw in their investment.

Behavioural finance also suggests investors can become emotionally involved in investing decisions rather than simply relying on facts to decide; for instance, where losses have been made due to share price falls but investors do not wish to realize them and continue to hold a stock when they would make more by selling and reinvesting the proceeds. Such behaviour can be seen despite the plethora of advice from experts such as Warren Buffet and many others, who believe that by watching the market, investors are more likely to be victims of their own irrationality and would be more successful if they concentrated on achieving a well-diversified portfolio capable of withstanding short periods of price movement.

Market consolidation

Where investors see they have made strong profits from a share price rise they may look to realize these and protect themselves by selling the shares, despite there being no negative signs in respect of future performance. If profit taking is carried out by enough investors at the same time it can mean prices will move and share prices are likely to reduce for a period.

Chartists

These investors analyse the stock market using previous share price trends to estimate when a share has reached a peak (to sell) or a dip (to buy).[6] If there are sufficient analysts using such techniques in a market it may be possible for this to affect prices.

Market makers

Market makers may also look to stimulate the market by reducing prices or even be required to buy or sell shares depending on what customers require from them. In sufficient amounts this may lead to a move in market prices.

Advantages and disadvantages of equity investment

Table 7.1 presents a summary of the advantages and disadvantages of investing in equities.

Table 7.1 Advantages and disadvantages of investing in equities

Advantages	Disadvantages
Historically have produced the highest returns of any asset class over the long term	Share prices can be volatile in the short term
Their return provides a hedge against inflation unlike returns from other fixed-income investments	It is possible the company may cease to trade at which point it is likely all investment will be lost
Way to increase diversification of investments due to potential to invest in different industries and geographical markets	
Holdings are liquid compared to some other asset classes eg property	Liquidity depends on trading volumes in the market, which for small listed companies and private companies may not be high

Are private equity and equity the same?

Private equity is different to equity. Equity refers to ordinary shares; private equity, whilst there is no one definition, relates to the purchase of ordinary shares to gain operational control of a company.

In practice

Alpha Private Equity Partnership (APEP) purchase all the issued ordinary shares (of which there are 1,000) of Gamma Plc through the London Stock Exchange where Gamma trades. To buy the whole company they pay a market value of £2,000. The ordinary shares have a nominal value of £1 each.

Here the private equity investor is APEP and they have purchased the equity of Gamma Plc, the equity being the 1,000 ordinary shares.

Private equity looks to provide medium- to long-term financial investment into companies in two ways which both include direct investment in the company and ownership of equity:

- Buying the existing share capital: in the above example APEP directly invested in Gamma Plc by purchasing the whole existing share capital of Gamma Plc. It would then own 100 per cent of Gamma Plc and as part of the transaction would take Gamma Plc from listed to unlisted status, removing it from the stock market, and making it a limited company. It would implement a reform programme which may include providing additional capital to the company.
- Purchasing new shares in Gamma Plc: another method APEP could have used to invest in Gamma would have been to purchase new shares issued by Gamma Plc. Again, delisting would have been part of the transaction.

In both cases the delisting of Gamma Plc allows the private equity company to reorganize the business, return it to profit or increase profits and then later to list the company again to provide the private equity company with an exit route to realize a return on their investment.

The two main types of investment strategy undertaken by private equity concerns are:

- Venture capital: this tends to be for early-stage businesses where funding cannot be obtained by conventional means to develop new ideas or products. Such funding may be seen in traditional industries; however, it is more often associated with technology companies.
- Growth capital: here we are looking at investment in more mature businesses, who are often looking to reorganize operational functions as well

as expand, but where the owners are unwilling to fund the whole transaction due to the risks involved. Private equity can provide a source of funds which allows the owner to sell a share of the business thereby realizing a return for themselves as well as having experienced partners to assist in developing the business.

Private equity will not always provide all the funding for a business. In fact, they may act in conjunction with debt providers, for example, in a leveraged buyout. Here a financial sponsor will raise debt to fund the buyout with only limited potential recourse to the sponsor if the investment fails, thereby minimizing the sponsors' risk and potentially maximizing their return.

If private equity funds invest directly into a company they are ideally looking to invest for between three and seven years in companies they believe will show high growth and therefore high returns, before refloating them to realize the gain in value.

Indirect investment

Here there is a fund of funds arrangement (see Chapter 8) where the fund does not invest directly in the company, but rather invests in a fund which in turn invests directly in the company.

Private equity funds can themselves be listed on a stock exchange such as LSE and shares in them may also be included in ISAs with capital investment often coming from institutional investors such as pension funds or insurance companies.

Summary

Whilst shareholders have the potential to gain the most from investing in equities there is also the potential for them to lose the most as well. Not only due to failure of the business in which they are investing leading to loss of capital but also due to the risks of volatility in the market.

That said, the potential for upside is great and over the past two centuries equities have produced some of the highest investment returns in the long term. It is this requirement of long-term investment which clients should be aware of when investing.

In addition to the potential for gains from capital and dividend due to increases in potential and actual cashflow there is also the potential for additional shares to be obtained through rights issues and other capital actions which will influence a client's shareholdings if not always their actual wealth.

Check your understanding

1 What type of companies are listed on the London Stock Exchange?
2 What is the difference between a cumulative and a non-cumulative preference share and how may this difference affect ordinary shareholders?
3 What are the four options open to an investor who receives notification of a rights issue?
4 What are the four costs involved in buying most shares?
5 What possible explanations are there for a company with a low P/E ratio?
6 What are the main risks in investing in shares?
7 Explain the difference between equity and private equity.

Further reading

There are a multitude of places where additional information can be obtained about equity investing including the 1949 book *The Intelligent Investor* by Benjamin Graham and cited by Warren Buffet as his investing bible, as well as websites such as the London Stock Exchange, Investopedia.com and Bloomberg.com amongst many others.

A useful discussion of equity finance and preference shares can be found in Watson, D and Head, A (2017) *Corporate Finance: Principles and practice*, 7th edn, Pearson Education.

The regulatory environment in respect of stock market listings can be studied on the UK Listing Authority website http://www.fac.org.uk/firms/markets/ukla.

Investment classes   08

Collective investments

By the end of this chapter you should have an understanding of the following key areas of collective investments:

- advantages for the investor in using collective investments;
- disadvantages for the investor in using collective investments;
- different types of collective.

Introduction

This chapter will explore the main types of collective investment funds including the characteristics, structure and the purpose of these investment vehicles. Investors may choose to select and manage their own investment assets; however, many investors will choose to delegate this responsibility to a third party, particularly if they do not have investment experience or are simply not confident in financial matters. This is known as an indirect investment strategy. (see Figure 8.1.)

Since the first collective investment funds appeared in the 19th century there has been a huge increase in the numbers and spread of this type of investment opportunity and there are now tens of thousands of collective investment funds available to investors worldwide, offering a remarkable range of investment opportunities to global investors across a wide variety of asset classes, geographical regions, sectors and risk factors. The manager of the collective investment fund will shepherd the fund and decide upon the asset allocation, select which assets should be held and when assets should be bought and sold. Collective investment funds do vary considerably and may be found across a wide range from a broad-spectrum fund to a tightly focussed fund. For example, an exchange-traded fund (ETF) tracker fund which aims to track the performance of the FTSE All-Share index is a broad-spectrum fund, whilst an example of a specifically focussed fund would be a Japanese smaller companies fund. Due to the large number and variety of collective investment funds in existence, it is likely that most investors will be able to identify a collective investment fund whose aims and objectives are compatible with their own, although it is important for the investor to also consider the level of risk that they are prepared to accept in the pursuit of their investment goals.

Collective investment funds offer the opportunity for large numbers of individual investors to benefit from the opportunities which would usually be available to investors with substantial funds to invest. Since collective investment funds are pooled in order to collectively purchase securities, this method of investment effectively enables a broader selection of investment opportunities, together with professional management expertise and lower overall investment fees than investors might be able to obtain individually. It is important therefore, to consider the positives and negatives of using

Figure 8.1 Indirect investment channels

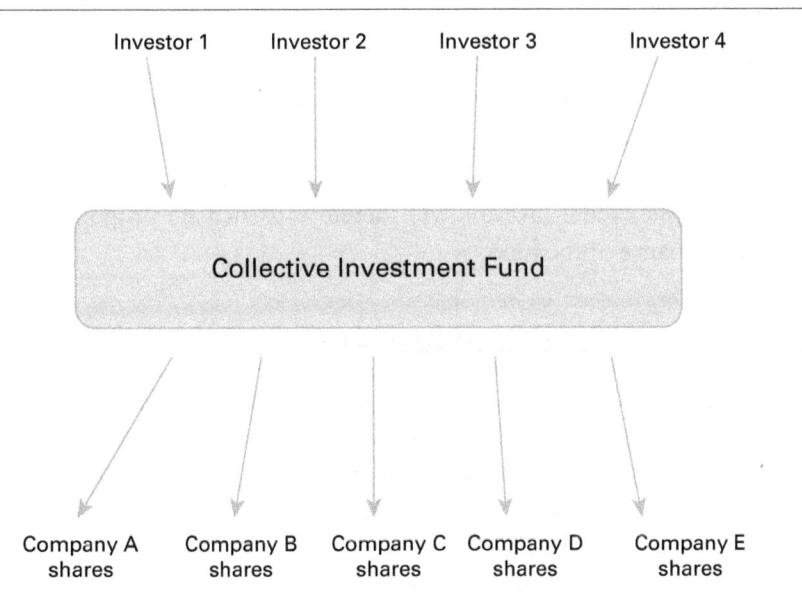

collective investment funds, from the point of view of the investor. The majority of these factors will be found to be common to most collective investment vehicles.

Advantages

The main advantages for investors in the use of collective investment funds are:

- ease of access;
- professional fund management;
- economies of scale;
- diversification of holdings;
- liquidity;
- regulation.

Ease of access

Investment into a collective investment vehicle is quite a simple process for an individual investor, even an investor with little experience in the financial market. Many insurance companies, banks and investment companies offer collective investment funds of various types. Investment in these vehicles may usually be in the form of a cash lump sum, a regular monthly payment, or a combination of both, and the minimum allowable investment is usually quite small, typically as low as around £50 per month or £500 as a lump sum. Each individual investor will therefore participate proportionally in the performance of the fund.

Professional fund management

A significant advantage in the use of collective investment vehicles is the ability to benefit from professional management of the money invested. Individual investors will invest in collective funds for several reasons; usually because they do not have the investment expertise, the knowledge and experience or the time to effectively manage their own assets. Collective investment funds provide an efficient and comparatively inexpensive way to allow individual investors access to industry professionals and to benefit from their management skills. These funds are managed by experienced industry professionals, who will invest the fund's capital with the aim to produce capital gains and/or income streams for the fund's investors. Collective investment funds are structured and managed in accordance with the stated investment aims and objectives published for the fund.

Economies of scale

Collective investment funds will acquire and dispose of a variety of different securities, for example, stocks, bonds, money market instruments and similar assets, as a result of the management of the fund's capital. Because these particular transactions will be of a much larger magnitude than an individual investor's trades, the overall effect of transaction costs will be significantly lower than an individual investor could achieve.

Diversification of holdings

Individual investors will benefit from diversification as a result of investing in a collective investment fund, because in comparison to holding assets such as individual company shares or bonds, the investment risk is spread by investing in a pooled fund. Diversification allows investment in a large number of securities, with the idea being that a loss in any one individual security is mitigated by gains in other securities held. Clearly, a collective investment fund has the ability to achieve much more effective diversification than an individual investor, even if the investor is a wealthy individual. For example, a large collective equity investment fund may conceivably hold hundreds of different stocks from across many different sectors, industries and even be geographically spread across different countries and continents. It would be prohibitive for an individual investor to acquire and hold this complex type of portfolio even with a substantial capital investment, but particularly so with modest investment funds.

Liquidity

Due to the relative ease of access, individual investors would usually be able to buy and sell units or shares in collective investment funds quite readily, affording a reasonable degree of liquidity to the investor's capital. Whilst this is usually the case, care must be taken by individual investors as in some cases, disinvestment from a collective fund may be restricted in certain circumstances. An example would be investment in a property fund, which may require a minimum notice period for individual investors to withdraw their capital, or may even prohibit withdrawals for certain periods to protect the interests of the other investors. In this case, liquidity may become an issue to certain investors.

Regulation

Another advantage for investors making use of collective investments is that they will benefit from the fact that the collective investment funds are regulated products and therefore the investor will benefit from the investor protection afforded by the appropriate domestic regulatory body when investing in this type of fund. This will not protect against poor investment performance; however, the benefits include such factors as transparency of charges, clear information and product data and fraud protection. This will also include regulated financial advice, if the investor chooses to seek professional financial advice regarding the decision to make use of a collective investment fund.

Disadvantages

In considering the features and characteristics of collective investment vehicles, we must also recognize that there are factors which may be considered a disadvantage for the individual investor investing their capital in this way. Individuals must weigh the advantages against the disadvantages that are applicable, in order to decide if it is advantageous and appropriate for them to invest in this sort of collective. Potential disadvantages include:

- costs;
- professional management;
- dilution;
- taxes;
- tracking error;
- loss of control.

Costs

The running and administration of a collective investment fund incurs significant ongoing costs such as the manager's salary, salaries of analysts, trading costs and administrative costs. All these expenses are paid for by the investors in that they are taken from the fund and therefore impact upon the long-term growth of the fund. Fees charged to investors will vary significantly between different funds, with the more 'well known' and successful managers being able to justify the levying of higher fees. Additionally, as a generalization, actively managed funds will have higher fee structures than more passively managed funds.

Higher fee levels may add to the pressure a fund manager is under as they must generate good performance to justify the higher fees that they are charging. The charges to investors may include an annual management fee levied as a percentage of the investment, an initial lump sum charged upon entry into the fund, or a combination of both dependent upon the individual fund.

Professional management

It is recognized that not all professional fund managers can be 'star performers' and that many fund managers do not have excellent records regarding their investment performance and fund management skills. For this reason, it is fair to be mindful that professional fund management may also sometimes be weighed to be a disadvantage. Sceptical investors may sometimes question if fund managers are actually adding value and if their stock-picking skills are warranting the charges that they levy. Fund managers will still be paid even if their performance is poor and although they may not achieve bonuses with their underperformance, fees and charges will still have been taken which will further accentuate the underperformance of a poorly performing fund.

Dilution

Whilst diversification is an advantage and a very useful tool in the mitigation of investment risk, it is also possible to have excessive diversification which may sometimes be seen to restrict growth potential. For example, if a fund has very small individual holdings in very many different companies, then substantial returns made by individual companies may have little effect upon the overall return of the fund.

Taxes

When the manager of the collective investment fund is trading securities on behalf of the fund, it is possible to trigger a taxable event as a result of the purchase or the sale of certain assets. This may be dependent not only upon the tax rules of the country in which the collective fund is based but also the domestic tax regulations of the investor, if they are not the same. Investors need to consider the impact of taxes when investing in collective investment funds and must also be mindful of their own individual tax position when disinvesting from these types of collective fund, since this may create a taxable event for them personally. Taxes can be mitigated by investing in tax efficient funds, by carefully planning the timing of disposals to make efficient use of personal allowances or by holding assets in a tax efficient manner; for example, in the UK an individual investor may make effective use of a new individual savings account (NISA).

Tracking error

This particular phenomenon does not apply to all collective investments, but is relevant to any collective investment fund which uses the tracking of a form of benchmark, such as the performance of an index, as part of its investment strategy. Because of the complexities of index-tracking it is virtually inevitable that the full performance of the index will not be replicated and this leads to tracking error.

Loss of control

When an investor chooses to invest their capital in a collective investment fund they pass on control of the investment decisions to the manager of their chosen fund. The individual investor therefore has no control over any investment decisions whilst their capital is invested within the collective fund. Whilst all investors have their own aims, objectives and tolerable risk levels, the manager of a collective investment fund will pursue the aims, objectives and risk strategy published in their fund documents and the responsibility rests with the individual investor to ensure that they have invested in a fund which is appropriate for them. Investment decisions are therefore taken on the basis of the fund's aims, not for the benefit of individual investors.

Additionally, investors must take care that if they are invested in more than one collective fund, or have other assets as well as investment in a collective, they consider the correlation of each individual holding with the others as high levels of positive correlation between investments will affect levels of overall risk and potentialy return.

> **In practice**
>
> **The unintended positive correlation of holdings by an investor**
>
> Take as an example an investor who holds individual company shares and these companies are in the FTSE 100 index.
>
> If the investor has also invested in a UK growth unit trust, then it is likely that this fund will also hold substantial numbers of company shares in FTSE 100-listed companies.
>
> This may result in significant duplication of holdings and therefore impact upon the diversification of the investor's overall investment holdings.

It is important for investors to understand that all collective investment funds have some level of risk because risk cannot be completely mitigated by diversification, although some funds would certainly be categorized as riskier than others. Individual collective investment funds will display different risk and reward characteristics; however, as a generalization we can say that the higher the potential return, the higher will be the potential risk of loss. Conversely, the more secure the fund the lower will be the potential returns. All collective investment funds will publish their own individual investment aims and objectives and this will dictate the manager's investment strategy, along with the choice and mix of assets. It is the responsibility of the investor, or the investor's adviser, to ensure that the aims and objectives of the fund are compatible with the investor's risk appetite and circumstances prior to investing in the fund. Collective investment funds will typically employ three main asset classes: company shares, bonds and money market instruments, or some combination of the three.

Different types of collective

Collective investment funds fall into two categories which are open-ended funds and closed-ended funds. Currently, the majority of collective investment funds worldwide are structured as open-ended funds and it is important to consider the difference between the two types of fund.

Keyword

Open-ended funds issue new shares or units in the fund to investors, which are created as new capital is invested into the fund. As investors withdraw capital from the fund their shares or units will be redeemed; both sale and redemption of the shares/units will take place at the quoted **net asset value per share**, calculated at the end of each trading day. Units are created and redeemed by the fund itself, not through a separate market as is the case with close-ended funds. Dependent on the fund in question, investors may be required to pay a fee for entry/exit of the fund. There is no limit to the number of shares or units that the fund may issue and these are created according to investor demand. If redemptions exceed sales within a short time period then the fund manager may need to liquidate fund assets in order to reimburse investors. The total size of an open-ended investment fund may therefore vary considerably and will depend initially upon the amount of capital invested at the time of the fund's creation. The fund size will subsequently vary dependent upon the magnitude of any further investment and redemptions that are made throughout the life of the fund.

Examples of these types of open-ended collective investment funds would include:

open-ended investment companies(OEICs);

exchange-traded funds (ETF);

unit trusts (UT);

mutual funds.

Keyword

Closed-ended funds are collective investments which raise a fixed amount of capital through an initial public offering issuing a fixed number of shares. These shares will be traded on the open market in the same way as a listed company share and are not redeemable through the fund manager. Purchase or sale of the shares would therefore usually be through a brokerage. Unlike open-ended funds, new capital is not brought into the fund from new investors and new shares are not created on demand by the fund manager, hence the term closed-ended funds. A closed-ended fund is effectively a publicly traded company and a legal entity in its own right so it has the power to issue debt against the security of its assets, although normally with limits upon the level of leverage.

Examples of these types of closed-ended collective investment funds would include investment trusts (ITs) and real estate investment trusts (REITs).

The net asset value of a closed-ended fund may be calculated for investor information; however, as the shares are traded on a recognized exchange, the share price is determined by the market, based upon supply and demand in the same way as a company share price, not based directly upon the net asset value. For this reason, a closed-ended fund may be said to trade at a premium or a discount to its net asset value and the share prices will fluctuate throughout the trading day. Because the shares are not created and redeemed on demand, there is no need for the fund manager to raise cash quickly to meet unanticipated redemptions and so the invested capital is considered to be more stable in closed-ended funds than in open-end funds. This longer-term stability allows the fund manager to take a longer-term view of the assets available and effectively reduces the risk of investing in more illiquid assets such as municipal bonds, lower grade corporate bonds, commercial property, emerging-market and smaller company shares.

The types of fund that we will consider in this section are the most common types of collective investment fund available globally and include the following:

- unit trusts (UT);
- open-ended investment companies (OEIC);
- exchange-traded funds (ETF);
- mutual funds;
- investment trusts (IT);
- real estate investment trusts (REIT);
- undertakings in collective investments in transferrable securities (UCITS).

Unit trusts (UT)

> **Keyword**
>
> **Unit trusts** are a form of open-ended investment fund in the UK and offer the opportunity for investors aged over 18 to have access to a wide range of funds managed by industry professionals.[1] Each unit trust will have individual published fund aims and objectives and will offer potential for either growth or income. It is usually advisable to view these types of funds as a medium- to long-term investment, which equates to 5 to 10 years or longer. Unit trusts have no minimum investment period, allowing the investor to disinvest some or all of their capital at any time, although unit trusts would not normally be considered suitable for short-term investment periods of less than five years due to the charging structure, risk profile and market volatility.

Unit trusts are collective investment funds which pool the capital from a large number of investors when they purchase units in the unit trust fund. This pooling of investment capital gives an advantage to the investors in that they may invest in a wider selection of assets than they could access individually. The effect of this is to diversify their investment and effectively reduces their overall exposure to risk. As this is an open-ended company the manager will create new units when new capital is invested and redeem the units when an investor withdraws funds. This means that the number of units in existence will vary, because as new investors join the fund more units are created and units are redeemed by the fund manager when investors withdraw money from the fund. New units are created to meet demand and there is no limit to how many units may be created in an individual unit trust fund.

It is worth considering what is meant by a unit in this context. When an individual investor invests their capital into a unit trust, they are buying units in the unit trust fund, together with many other investors. Each individual unit has a price which is based upon the net asset value of the fund and the net asset value of the unit trust fund is a reflection of the overall value of the various assets that the unit trust holds at that time. The net asset value reflects of the fund's total net assets, which equates to the fund's assets minus the fund's liabilities, divided by the number of shares in issue at that time.

Investment classes: Collective investments

The fund's liabilities include costs such as the manager's salary, taxes, fees to service providers and any other costs of running and managing the fund.

> **In practice**
>
> The method for calculation of the net asset value of a fund is quite straightforward. For example:
>
> A unit trust holds a mix of company shares, bonds and cash which totals £18,335,500.
>
> The current liabilities of the unit trust are a total of £920,000.
>
> There are 3,050,000 units already in issue.
>
> To calculate out the net asset value of the fund we use the following formula:
>
> $$\text{NAV} = \frac{\text{total assets} - \text{total liabilities}}{\text{total number of units in issue}}$$
>
> $$\text{NAV} = \frac{£18,335,500 - £920,000}{3,050,000}$$
>
> $$\text{NAV} = \frac{£17,415,500}{3,050,000} = 5.71 \text{ per unit}$$

The calculated value of the net asset value does not actually represent the exact price that an individual investor will pay for a unit in this unit trust, as the price of purchase or redemption will be affected by administration costs – for example, the bid–offer spread levied by the fund's manager. Unit trusts are known as 'dual-priced' funds and the fund's manager will value the fund twice to calculate the daily prices. The bid–offer spread is the difference between the price at which units are purchased by investors and the price at which the fund manager will redeem the units if the investor chooses to disinvest. The purchase price is known as the offer price and the price at which the fund manager buys back the units is known as the bid price. The fund manager has some flexibility in the price quoted each day, provided it is within the range of the bid and the offer price, although the financial regulator, the Financial Conduct Authority (FCA), lays down guidelines for fund managers to follow in the calculation of these prices. This flexibility allows fund managers to take into account factors such as initial charges, trading costs, liquidity of markets and the net inflow or outflow of investment into the fund on a daily basis.

> **In practice**
>
> This dual pricing of unit trust funds further serves to highlight the reason why these types of collective investment should not be considered a short-term investment vehicle, as it may take a period of time for the bid price of the units to exceed the offer price at which the investor originally purchased the units. Investors will increase their capital position by selling their units at a higher price than the price that they originally bought them for.

There are a wide variety of unit trust funds, although funds structured as OEICs are now a more popular format and more prevalent numerically. Unit trust funds are typically grouped by sectors and will be managed to address the areas, aims and level of risk that the fund has published as its targets. This may involve being actively or passively managed, investing in a specific geographical area, or having a tight focus on a specialist area such as property. The fund manager is responsible for pursuing the stated aims and objectives of the fund, the asset allocation and selection of the individual assets within the fund. The value of the units in the fund will rise and fall as a result of the fund's performance which will be linked to the assets held by the fund. Investors are always reminded that with all types of collective fund, the past performance of the fund is not a guarantee of future performance and that the value of their holding in the fund may fall as well as rise.

Investors wishing to invest in a unit trust as part of their investment strategy may purchase units in a particular unit trust directly from the fund management company, through the services of a tied agent, or an independent financial adviser. They may also be available through a fund platform service although individuals who are not experienced investors would usually be advised to seek independent financial advice before investing in a unit trust to ensure that the chosen fund is appropriate and meets the investor's aims, objectives and risk profile. The level of risk associated with a specific unit trust will depend on several factors such as which assets the fund is holding, the industry sector and/or geographical location and any prevailing market risk factors.

Unit trusts may offer a choice of units depending upon the type of return that investors are looking for. These are income units and accumulation units. Choosing income units will entitle investors to distribution of accrued income throughout the year from income-generating assets such as bonds and company shares. Selecting accumulation units, however, means that any income generated will be reinvested into the unit trust rather than being distributed as cash to the investors.

The charges included within the bid–offer spread will cover the typical charges incurred by the investor when investing in a unit trust and include the initial charge, which is typically between 2 and 5 per cent of the initial investment. Also included is the annual management charge, which ranges between 0.8 to 2 per cent, dependent upon the individual fund manager.

A unit trust is constituted under a trust deed and its trustees must ensure that the fund manager operates within the fund's published investment objectives. Unit trusts are also under the regulatory umbrella of the FCA in the UK and this offers the span of regulatory protection to investors. It should also be noted that investors benefiting from either income or capital growth from these products may have a tax liability depending upon their own individual personal circumstances and this will be explored in the chapter on taxation.

Open-ended investment companies (OEIC)

Keyword

At the time of writing, **open-ended investment companies** (OEICs) have taken over from unit trusts as the more popular form of open-ended investment fund in the UK[1] and offer the opportunity for investors aged over 18 to have access to a wide range of funds managed by industry professionals. OEICs are subject to company law, unlike unit trusts which are covered by trust law. Depending upon the individual fund's aims and objectives, OEIC funds will offer potential for either growth or income and just like unit trusts, it is usually prudent to view these types of funds as a medium- to long-term investment; that is to say for 5 to 10 years or longer. OEICs do not have a minimum investment period and therefore an investor may disinvest at any time; however, they would not normally be considered suitable for short-term investment periods of less than five years due to the charging structure, risk profile and market volatility.

Like unit trusts, OEICs are also collective investment funds which pool the capital from a large number of investors when they purchase shares in the fund. The advantage to the investors is that they may invest in a wider selection of assets than they could access individually, which spreads their investment and effectively reduces their exposure to risk. As this is an open-ended company the manager will create shares when new capital is invested and redeem the shares if required to by an investor withdrawing funds. As a result, the number of shares in existence will vary, because as new investors join the fund more shares are created and shares are redeemed by the fund manager when investors withdraw money from the fund.

There exists a wide variety of funds which are offered as OEICs, are grouped by sectors and cover the areas, aims and level of risk that the fund has been targeted for. This could involve being actively or passively managed, investing in a specific area geographically or focusing on a specialist area such as technology. The fund manager is responsible for pursuing the stated aims and objectives of the fund, the asset allocation and selection of the individual assets within the fund. The value of the shares in the fund will rise and fall as a result of the fund's performance which will be linked to the assets held by the fund. Investors are always reminded that with all types of collective fund, the past performance of the fund is not a guarantee of future performance and that the value of their holding in the fund may fall as well as rise.

In practice

Investors wishing to make use of an OEIC as part of their investment strategy may access shares in a particular OEIC directly from the fund management company, through the services of a tied agent, broker or an independent financial adviser. They may also be available through a **fund platform** service, a share-dealing service or a stockbroker. Individuals who are not experienced investors would usually be well advised to seek independent financial advice before investing in an OEIC in order to ensure that the fund is appropriate and meets the investor's requirements for aims, objectives and risk profile. The level of risk associated with a specific OEIC will depend on several factors such as which assets the fund is holding, the industry sector and/or geographical location and any prevailing market risk factors.

Unit trusts and OEICs are very similar; however, there is a significant difference in the pricing structure of OEICs. Unit trusts have two separate prices for their units, the offer price and the bid price, and the difference between these two prices is referred to as the bid–offer spread. OEICs, however, are a single-priced fund and have one price for both buying and selling shares in the fund. An OEIC share has a single price which is directly linked to the value of the assets held by the OEIC fund. Similar to the unit trust, the share price is calculated on a daily basis by calculating the value of all the assets held by the fund and dividing it by the number of shares currently in issue. The charges levied by the OEIC are taken separately. There are two main types of charges for OEICs, which are initial charges and annual management charges. Investors pay an initial charge of around 2 to 5 per cent which has the effect of reducing the amount of the initial investment going into the fund. An annual management charge may be typically 0.8 to 1.5 per cent based upon the value of the investor's shares and covers the fund managers' costs. It would be usual to find that OEICs which are not actively managed, for example index trackers, would have lower fees.

An investor will increase their capital position by selling their OEIC shares at a higher price than the price for which they originally bought them. The value of an investor's OEIC shares increases in line with the value of the underlying assets held within the OEIC and decreases when the overall value of the assets in the OEIC falls. Some OEICs may offer investors the option of choosing either income shares or accumulation shares, in a similar way to unit trusts. Income shares make a periodic distribution of any income that the OEIC fund earns. Conversely, accumulation shares will automatically reinvest accrued income back into the fund, which may have a positive effect upon long-term growth strategies.

An OEIC is structured as a company with a board referred to as a depository, which is charged with ensuring that the fund manager complies with current legislation and manages the OEIC in accordance with the published aims and objectives. Similar to unit trusts, OEICs are also under the regulatory umbrella of the FCA in the UK and this offers regulatory protection to investors. Investors benefiting from either income or capital growth from these products may have a tax liability depending upon their own individual personal circumstances and this will be explored in Chapter 13 on taxation.

Exchange-traded funds (ETF)

Keyword

Exchange-traded funds (ETF) trace their roots back to the USA in the 1990s and have grown in numbers and popularity since then in the global investment markets.[2] ETFs are now widely used by institutional and individual investors worldwide and many billions of pounds of capital are currently held in ETF investments. ETFs share many similarities with company shares because they can easily be bought and sold on an exchange and the price of the individual ETF may change through the course of a trading day. An institutional or individual investor is able to do anything with an ETF that can be done with a company share. Investors may also purchase an ETF regardless of where in the world it trades, which differs from collective investment funds like UTs and OEICs as they may only usually be purchased in the domestic market in which they are registered.

ETFs have the flexibility and attributes to be a useful asset in an investor's portfolio, regardless of whether the investor is an experienced industry professional or an inexperienced individual investor. They may be used in a range of roles either being used as the key asset within a portfolio or as an additional asset to complement an investor's existing portfolio. There are often significant differences in management style between ETFs and other collective investment funds, as many ETFs are passively managed, tracking a market index, whilst many collective investment funds would be actively managed.

In practice

Not all ETFs are trackers; however, many ETFs are designed to follow a particular market index and therefore their performance will reflect a similar, though not exactly the same, performance to the index that they are tracking.

This difference is known as the 'tracking error' and reflects the difference between the returns of the ETF fund and the returns of the index. This tracking error may be due to a variety of factors, eg differences in composition, the timing and application of dividends or the effect of fees and expenses.

For example, if an investor wishes to benefit from the performance of the S&P 500 index, but is unable to achieve this performance themselves, it is possible to purchase an ETF which will follow the movement of the S&P 500 index, subject to tracking error.

Tracker ETFs are not just limited in scope to tracking market indices; indeed, they are remarkably broad in scope. ETFs may also be used to track the prices of currencies, commodities and a variety of other assets. For example, if an investor wishes to invest in a commodity such as oil but has neither the facilities nor the wish to physically buy a quantity of oil, then the investor can buy an ETF oil tracker that will track the performance of oil on the markets. This may sometimes be referred to as an exchange-traded commodity, or ETC.

Consider the specific advantages for an investor when investing in an exchange-traded fund:

- ETFs provide investors with the opportunity to access an excellent tool for diversification without the need for individual stock-picking.
- ETFs also provide investors with the opportunity to experience a degree of market specialization or the opportunity to expose themselves to markets in which they have no experience themselves.
- Since ETFs trade like company shares, unlike many other collective investment funds, they can be bought and sold throughout the trading day.
- There are usually little or no minimum investment requirements, which give flexibility, particularly to small individual investors. Investors may be able to purchase a single ETF share or many, dependent upon their circumstances.
- Very low annual fees are a factor that ETFs are noted for and they have lower fees than even other types of traditional tracker funds. ETFs are significantly cheaper than unit trusts and OEICs as they do not need so much active involvement from a fund management team and have less frequent trading activity.
- Due to the very broad spectrum of market coverage afforded by ETFs, they offer the opportunity for investors to access a wide range of different investment markets.
- ETFs are considered to be tax efficient because buying and selling the ETF does not involve trading the underlying assets within the fund.

Having considered the advantages of ETFs, we should also look at the potential disadvantages of an ETF from the investor's point of view:

- ETFs do not usually afford investors the opportunity to outperform the market, particularly the trackers. Some other collective investment funds, for example OEICs, may be designed to outperform a particular market, although this is not guaranteed.

- Some of the many different types of ETF may not be suitable for individual investors due to the methods that they use to replicate the performance of a particular index and the additional risk inherent in these techniques. This may be beyond the limited experience and understanding of many individual investors.
- Due to the ease of trading ETFs, at times of market flux and volatility there may be a temptation to over-trade ETFs and effectively be buying and selling too frequently, particularly for inexperienced individual investors. This may incur higher costs and adversely impact upon investment returns.
- Tracking error is not usually of great magnitude, but must be considered and allowances made for this factor when utilizing tracker-type ETFs.

Transparency is an important factor with collective investment funds and is scrutinized carefully by regulatory bodies. ETFs are set up and managed to meet their stated aims and objectives; in many cases this will involve them tracking the performance of a specific market index or a particular commodity. They are quite transparent in the sense that prospective investors are aware of what they are buying into and may examine the specific holdings of the individual ETF. Many other types of collective investment funds may only report on their assets bi-annually and therefore there is not so much clarity regarding exactly what the investor is acquiring within their investment portfolio. Fees and charges are clearly published and one of the key advantages for investors, both institutional and individual, of investing in ETFs is their low fee structure in comparison to other collective investment funds. It must be noted, however, that investors will be required to pay fees/commission to a broker in order to buy and sell ETF shares and frequent buying and selling will result in costs of fees/commission rising and potentially impacting adversely upon the investors' returns.

In practice

Tracking error

Tracker ETFs will be holding cash for some periods throughout the investment year and this will contribute to the issue of tracking error because the benchmark index to be replicated will not have any cash in its composition. Dividend distributing ETFs will distribute dividends periodically and those which reinvest the dividends in the fund will do so in a similar manner, whereas the benchmark index performance assumes immediate reinvestment of dividends, which in practice are paid by companies throughout the course of the investment year. Investors who receive dividend distribution must then make additional purchases of ETF shares if they wish to reinvest their distribution.

ETFs are also considered to be more tax efficient than the other types of collective investment fund and even though this is a generalization it is widely accepted to be true, although in some cases, mutual tracker funds may have a similar level of efficiency. The tax efficiency may depend upon the domicile of the invested ETF in comparison to the domicile of the investor, since investors may purchase shares in ETFs globally. Broadly speaking, because tracker ETFs are passively managed it is fair to say that they offer more tax benefits than ordinary collective investment funds, such as actively managed mutual funds. This is because tracker ETFs engage in far less trading of assets which results in fewer taxable gains than collective investment funds that are actively managed. Additionally, distributed capital gains will be subject to capital gains tax rates, which are generally lower than income tax rates. This is, of course, dependent upon the individual circumstances of the investor and the tax rates of their country of domicile. In the UK, for example, there is no stamp duty payable on the purchase of shares in ETFs, although disposal of these shares at a profit may trigger a liability for capital gains tax.

Mutual funds

Keyword

A **mutual fund** is a collective investment fund which pools the capital invested by many individual investors and invests in a wide variety of different assets dependent upon the investment strategy of the fund. Mutual funds are managed by industry professionals who are empowered to invest the fund's capital in accordance with the published aims and objectives of the fund, in an attempt to generate income, capital growth or a combination of the two, on behalf of the fund's investors.[3] In larger mutual funds, the manager may be supported by analysts and researchers to assist in the effective running of the fund.

In practice

As of 2014, there were in excess of 79,000 mutual funds globally with a total value of assets under management of around US$31 trillion – more than half of these global assets were concentrated in the USA.[4]

The majority of mutual funds focus on three key asset classes, these being stocks, bonds and cash, although other assets may also be found particularly in more specialist funds. Investors in the mutual fund do not own the securities that the fund is holding; they simply own the shares in the mutual fund.

The price of each individual mutual fund is referred to as its net asset value and is based upon the total value of the assets held by the fund, divided by the number of the fund's shares in issue. This price will change daily as it is dependent upon the value of the assets held within the fund at close of business each day.

Individual investors, particularly smaller investors, may find that mutual funds represent a cost-effective way to invest. Minimum investment levels are modest with some mutual funds starting at around US$50 per month or US$500 lump sum. Mutual funds also represent a practical way to access a diversified investment since creating your own diversified portfolio of investments with small capital sums would be at best impractical and often impossible. Individual investors are able to buy shares in a mutual fund either through the services of a broker or from the fund itself and the price the investor will pay will be the net asset value per share plus fees. There are two different types of fees, these being transactional fees, sometimes referred to as sales loads, and annual management fees. Transactional fees are paid when an individual investor buys or sells shares in the fund and the annual management fees cover the expense of running the fund such as salaries for the fund manager and analysts and the fund's trading costs.

The shares in mutual funds are normally considered to be quite liquid, as an investor may redeem the shares to the mutual fund at any time for repayment, usually within seven days. Mutual funds give investors the advantage of having their investment professionally managed and offer the opportunity of generating income from dividend payments and bond coupons, and capital appreciation from the increase in the price of the mutual fund shares. There is the further opportunity of annual capital gain distributions from the fund as a result of internal fund trading gains. As each mutual fund will have its own asset allocation model and investment strategy, they will also differ across the risk spectrum and therefore it is important that individual investors ensure that the mutual fund that they propose to invest in is appropriate for their own risk appetite. It may be wise for investors to seek independent financial advice before investing in a mutual fund, particularly if they are inexperienced investors.

> **In practice**
>
> It should be noted that these types of funds are not suitable for short-term investment strategies due to the charges and the volatility of the fund's assets on the markets. They would therefore be more suited to a medium- or long-term savings or investment strategy. It would also generally be advisable to evaluate the performance of these funds over longer periods of time, although the usual caveat applies that past performance is not a guarantee of future performance. However, past performance may be an indicator of how volatile a particular mutual fund has been over a period of time and higher volatility would be an indicator of greater risk. Costs can also become a problem with mutual funds because the costs will have the effect of reducing any positive investment return and they are certainly one reason why mutual funds may experience disappointing investment performance. Transparency is also a significant issue and the fund industry is often criticized for being unclear regarding costs and for using unhelpful financial complexity and jargon, which mean that the investor often does not understand what they are paying for.

There are tax issues to be considered by the individual investor which will vary with each investor's personal circumstances. For example, income distributed by the mutual fund may create an income tax liability for the investor and annually distributed capital gains realized by the fund may be attributable to income tax or capital gains tax, which is more favourable. This is dependent upon how the securities were held by the fund.

As mentioned earlier, there is a wide variety of mutual funds available to investors and therefore it should be possible for the majority of investors to find a mutual fund which will meet their needs.[5] Types of fund available include:

- Money market funds – typically holding short-term debt instruments such as treasury bills. This would be considered to be a secure fund in which the investor is unlikely to have the worry of capital loss; however, returns are likely to be very modest – typically in the region of double the return of a basic savings account.

- Income/bond funds – these funds will look to provide a reliable income stream and typically invest in government and corporate debt. They may exhibit some capital increase; however, the main aim is to provide steady cashflow to typically low-risk investors or retired investors. Returns are likely to be higher than money market funds, but this comes with some degree of risk dependent upon the type of bond in which the fund invests. For example, a fund which invests in in high-yield 'junk' bonds will be riskier than a fund specializing in government-backed bonds.

- Balanced funds – generally, these funds offer a balanced mixture of income and modest capital growth through a mixture of fixed-income assets and equities, typically in a ratio somewhere around 50:50.

- Equity funds – usually, the objective would be to offer the prospect of long-term capital growth and potentially some income. This is the largest category of mutual funds and therefore there are many different types of equity funds representing many types of equities; for example, value, growth and large-cap. This type of fund offers significant risk of capital loss.

- International/global funds – international funds typically invest outside the domestic market, whilst global funds may invest anywhere in the world including the domestic market. These funds generally tend to be more volatile than domestic equity funds and may be subject to unique country and/or political risks; however, they may offer increased diversification.

- Specialty funds – broad and loose category consisting of funds that ignore broad diversification to concentrate on a specific sector of the economy, eg banking, technology and health. These funds are potentially extremely volatile and therefore offer the opportunity for greater gains, but also the possibility for significant capital losses.

- Socially-responsible funds (ethical funds) – invest only in companies meeting certain ethically sound guidelines and avoid certain categories of industry such as alcohol, gambling, tobacco and nuclear power.

- Index funds – typically aim to replicate the performance of a market index, for example the Dow Jones Industrial Average or the S&P 500 index. Investors in these funds do not expect to outperform the market; however, they will benefit from lower fees.

Investment trusts (IT)

Keyword

An **investment trust (IT)** is in fact a publicly listed company in its own right, whose shares are traded on its domestic stock exchange in the same way as any other public company. Most listed companies will either manufacture or sell products and services; however, ITs invest in various assets such as company shares, property and bonds and will manage the capital growth and revenue generated for the benefit of its shareholders. The shares of ITs are traded through the day and the market price of the shares is therefore subject to change through the day, unlike open-ended funds which are only priced once a day. ITs are referred to as closed-ended funds because each IT has a finite number of shares, so the share price is determined by the market forces of supply and demand as with other listed company shares. This means that unless an investor acquires IT shares at the initial public offering (IPO) where a fixed number of shares will be issued, shares in the IT will be acquired and disposed of through trading with other investors on the domestic stock exchange.

In practice

In the case of ITs, the share price may deviate significantly from the net asset value due to the market forces driving the share price. The net asset value represents the actual market value of the underlying assets held by the IT fund manager, whilst the share price is the price that investors are prepared to pay for the IT on the domestic stock exchange. The share price of an IT may deviate from the price of the underlying assets for various reasons; for example, if the fund management team loses the confidence of investors or the sector in which the IT specializes falls out of favour with investors. When the IT shares are trading on the market for more than the value of the assets held, this is referred to as being 'at a premium' and when the IT's shares are trading for less than the value of the assets owned it is known as being 'at a discount'.

Typically, many ITs will trade at a discount to their net asset value and whilst this is usually a sign of solid value it may also occasionally be interpreted as a loss of confidence in the individual IT, because if investor demand for a specific IT is poor, then shares may trade at a greater discount to their net asset value. Conversely, strong demand would inflate the price of the IT shares on the market meaning that they may trade at a premium. In general, the total expense ratios tend to be lower than with open-ended collective investment funds, resulting in potentially lower charging structures.

ITs may appear complicated in their management structure as they have a board which is independent of the fund management team and may ultimately choose to replace the fund manager if deemed necessary. The board has the responsibility of safeguarding the interests of investors and ensuring that the fund management team are fulfilling their obligations and operating within the aims and objectives of the fund. From the perspective of the IT fund manager, they have the opportunity to work with a stable pool of investment assets and have the freedom to buy and sell assets when they wish to and are not obligated to buy and sell when investors leave or join the IT. This is unlike open-ended funds and because investors are only trading the shares in the IT, the underlying assets held within the IT fund are unaffected by the trading of shares in the IT. This allows the fund manager of an IT to take a longer-term view of their invested assets and also allows for investment in assets which may be considered to be less liquid as the IT fund manager may choose their own timing of trades. We may consider whether this constitutes an advantage for an investor in holding a closed-ended fund over an open-ended fund. For example, if an investor in an open-ended fund wishes to exit the fund, this may be as a result of falling investment markets causing investors to lack confidence and this could be a bad time for the fund manager to be forced to sell assets to raise cash in order to redeem the units/shares of the investor. This could certainly have a negative effect on fund performance and is not an issue for the investors in closed-ended funds, although they may suffer a dip in share price during any volatile period.

In practice

When buying and selling the shares in ITs, investors would normally use the services of advisers or brokers and will usually pay brokerage commissions as in the case of trading shares of any publicly listed company. Investors may also be required to pay fees, particularly in the case where an element of investment advice has been sought and it would normally be advisable for investors to seek advice before investing in ITs to ensure that the specific IT in question meets the needs, objectives and the risk profile of the investor. ITs will also levy a management fee to cover the running of the fund, which will impact upon the returns of the fund. Additionally, investors may be liable to some form of taxation, dependent upon the domestic tax rules at the time of purchase or disposal. As with other collective investment funds, ITs are considered to be long-term investment vehicles and therefore prospective investors should be prepared to invest for at least 5 years, and preferably 10 years or more.

Investors will have the opportunity to benefit from returns either in the form of dividends paid to shareholders by the fund periodically, or as a result of the share price appreciating on the market to a higher price than the investor paid, or a combination of both. Unlike open-ended collective investment funds, ITs have the ability to 'hold back' a proportion of their income in certain years as a form of reserve. This action may allow ITs the ability to maintain or even increase their dividend distribution to shareholders even during more challenging investment conditions.[6]

As an IT is a limited company in its own right, one of the options open to the fund manager is to employ gearing as part of the investment strategy. Gearing is essentially borrowing and ITs may borrow money in order to augment their investment portfolio, in contrast for example to unit trusts, which have strict regulations limiting their borrowing potential. The procedure for employing gearing would be for the fund manager to negotiate borrowing, usually through a bank, and the borrowed money would then be invested in assets of the fund manager's choice. The borrowed money will effectively increase the available investment capital, although it is fair to say that the more highly geared the fund the more risky it is for the investor as the performance is magnified. Investors must be made aware that in the case of geared investment, if the value of the assets held appreciates significantly then the overall fund performance will be better than for an ungeared fund; however, if the assets held depreciate then the losses will also be magnified compared to those of an ungeared fund.

In practice

Let us consider an example showing the effects of 'gearing'.

An investment trust with £100 million in assets borrows an additional £20 million and then invests the entire sum of £120 million in the equity market.

> Assume a 25 per cent return on that £120 million investment, which would equate to a £30 million gain for the IT's fund.
>
> After the investment trust repays the £20 million loan, it is left with £130 million; this is the original £100 million, plus the £30 million it has earned on its investment dealings. That represents a 30 per cent return for the fund which is very desirable for the fund's investors.
>
> However, on the negative side, if we assume a 25 per cent loss on that same £120 million investment in the equity market, then this would equate to a £30 million loss for the fund. In this case 30 per cent of the fund's capital base would be lost, to the detriment of the investors. In addition repayment of the loan would be required.
>
> Clearly, gearing increases a fund's upside potential but also considerably magnifies its downside risk.

In summary, the factors which ensure that ITs differ from open-ended collective investment funds are:

- longer-term view – due to the closed-end nature of the IT the fund's manager may adopt a longer-term overview;
- gearing – ITs benefit from borrowing;
- smoothing income – ITs may retain a proportion of their income in any year to supplement income in future years;
- corporate governance – each IT has an independent board of directors to oversee shareholder interests;
- shareholder rights – investing in an IT gives investors the right to vote on various issues such as the appointment of directors and changes to investment policy;
- pricing – investment trusts may have lower overall operating costs than open-ended collective funds so their overall charges may be lower.

It is possible to acquire a unit trust and an investment trust with very similar portfolios of assets and managed by the same fund manager; however, the performance of the funds will differ. As a generalization, it is likely that a closed-ended fund will outperform a similar open-ended fund, particularly over longer time periods, mainly due to lower charging structures. ITs are clearly an effective opportunity for investors to access a diversified portfolio of assets and have many attractive features including dependable dividend streams.

Real estate investment trusts (REITs)

Keyword

Real estate investment trusts (REITs) have grown in numbers and geographical spread since they first appeared in the 1960s in the USA. They are now found worldwide in many countries including UK, Canada, Australia, Hong Kong and many of the EU countries.[7] REITs provide an opportunity for individual investors to access large-scale, income-producing property as a REIT is actually a company owning and managing income-producing property and property-related assets. The types of properties included in a portfolio may include hotels, office buildings, flats and apartments, retail outlets, hospitals and warehouses. REITs would usually purchase these types of property with the aim of developing and managing them as part of an investment portfolio. REITs may invest in both commercial and residential property and may also invest in mortgages and mortgage-backed securities.

REITs are similar to a mutual fund in the sense that they allow a range of investors, both small and large, the opportunity to access a variety of property-related assets but in a more liquid form since the REIT is traded on a stock exchange in a similar way to company shares. This offers a flexible opportunity for individual investors to diversify their investment portfolio with the inclusion of property as an uncorrelated asset, together with the potential for attractive dividend yields. The majority of ordinary investors would not be wealthy enough to purchase commercial property under normal circumstances and therefore this opportunity would not be open to them.

Often, the shares in ordinary property companies will be found to trade at a discount to the net asset value and will typically perform similarly to equities; however, this type of arrangement is not very tax efficient because investors are effectively suffering two sets of taxation. The company is liable for corporation tax on income and capital gains and investors will then be liable for taxation on the dividends received and the proceeds of sale when they dispose of their shares. For a property company, acquiring REIT status can carry substantial tax benefits. REITs are companies (or groups of companies) managing property and property-related assets in a portfolio for the benefit of their shareholders. They enjoy a special tax status which effectively results in no corporation tax payable on the profits of their rental business, subject to compliance with a number of conditions. The conditions may vary dependent upon the tax laws in the country of domicile; however, typically a REIT will be required to distribute a minimum percentage of its taxable income to shareholders annually. The shareholders of a REIT are then responsible for paying tax on the dividends and any capital gains they receive in respect of their REIT investment.

> **In practice**
>
> In the UK, for example, REITs must distribute 90 per cent of their property income to shareholders annually and the dividends paid to the investor are treated as property income and taxed accordingly. These dividends may be subject to a withholding tax although certain classes of investors, such as charities and pension funds, may apply to receive gross payments. Companies with REIT status must be engaged primarily in property investment, rather than simply property development or non-property-related activities.[8] Additionally, for UK investors, shares in REITs may be held in individual savings accounts (ISA) and in child trust funds (CTF) which results in these arrangements being very tax efficient. It is certainly appropriate for individual investors to seek professional advice before investing in these funds, both from an investment and indeed a taxation point of view.

Investors may invest in the shares of a publicly traded REIT by using the services of a financial adviser or broker, which will incur brokerage fees. There are also non-exchange-traded REITs available. However, because these do not trade on a recognized stock exchange, additional risks will be involved, for example, reduced liquidity and lack of transparency regarding both the share price and conflicts of interest. The benefits of REIT status, to both the company and the investor, can be summarized as follows:

- Benefits for companies:
    - tax efficient structure;
    - access to new investors/capital;
    - potentially closer performance to net asset value.

- Benefits for investors:
  - affordable access to property investment;
  - good portfolio diversification due to low correlation with other assets, such as equities and bonds;
  - good liquidity;
  - potentially strong corporate governance;
  - potentially tax efficient and tax transparent;
  - potential for high-yield returns;
  - usually low/controlled gearing.

Undertakings for collective investment in transferrable securities (UCITS)

Keyword

A **UCITS** is best described as a mutual-style fund covered by a harmonized regulatory regime based within the European Union and marketed to EU-based investors. UCITS funds are collective investment vehicles which take capital from investors and invest in a diversified pool of assets. Through this investment in collective funds, small investors can benefit from a professionally managed and diversified portfolio of assets. The overheads are spread across the pool of investors, reducing the average cost to each investor. At the heart of the UCITS fund is the concept of the **depository**. A UCITS depository is independent both from the fund and the fund manager. This independence is crucial as the depository is described as acting as the 'legal conscience' of the fund and as custodian of the fund's assets.[9]

Since UCITS are regulated investment funds available to investors throughout the EU it is clearly important that they should benefit from common standards of investor protection. The first UCITS Directive in the mid-1980s pursued the aim of allowing access to cross-border-enabled collective investment funds to retail investors. The regulatory framework of the European Commission exists to foster a harmonized regime within Europe for the management and sale of mutual-style collective investment funds.

> **In practice**
>
> Providers of UCITS funds who meet the prescribed standards are exempt from national regulation in individual European countries and therefore UCITS funds may now be registered in Europe and marketed to investors through the application of unified regulatory and investor protection requirements. Although UCITS funds are regulated in Europe, investors globally may now invest in them. UCITS funds, because of the associated directives, are perceived to be safe, soundly regulated investments and are therefore popular with investors who prefer collective investments to individual company shares.

A series of UCITS directives have been issued subsequently, covering various issues such as the overall investment spectrum, restrictions for index funds, the responsibilities and duties of depositories, enhanced investor protection and fund managers' remuneration. For example, one of the directives reflected a strict liability requirement holding the fund's depository liable for the avoidable loss of a financial instrument held in custody. New directives continue to be published as the funds and their scope evolve. There are a wide range of fund types available across a diverse risk spectrum, to suit the diverse needs and aims of global investors, which include:

- Money market funds – investing in money market instruments such as short-term debt instruments and time deposits. Generally lower risks than other types of investment fund and with returns that reflect short-term interest rates.
- Bond funds – invest mainly in fixed-interest securities such as bonds and other debt securities and with higher returns than money market funds and lower risks than equity funds. Usually considered to be low risk; however, not without risks particularly in respect of interest rate and inflation issues. Normally invested in a range of securities that vary in terms of risk and return.
- Equity funds – typically invest in publicly listed company shares but may invest in a wide spectrum of assets differentiated by company size, sector and geographic region. Aims to deliver long-term growth through capital gains, but may also generate income from dividends. Usually, the greater the expected growth, the greater the risk factor and these funds may be actively managed or passively track a specific stock market index or benchmark.

- Balanced funds – typically invest in a mix of equities, bonds and other fixed-income instruments and will attempt to provide a degree of growth and income at a reduced level of risk. Generally, as the equity component of the fund increases, the potential for higher returns increases; however, the risk increases.
- Exchange-traded funds – track the movements of a specific index or benchmark.
- Life-cycle funds – invest in a selection of securities in different asset classes and aim to meet the changing needs, aims and objectives of investors as they grow older. Normally attempt to deliver strong capital growth initially, followed by greater capital protection as the investor approaches retirement age.
- Guaranteed funds – sometimes referred to as 'capital protection funds'. Suitable for the very cautious investor and aim to ensure that all (or the majority) of the investor's capital is returned at the end of a specified investment period. These funds may rely on the use of complex financial mechanisms, and the cost of providing the guarantee (capital protection) restricts the returns of the fund in comparison to other funds.
- Funds of funds – offer access to a wide range of professional fund management skills and specialization, together with increased diversification. These funds invest in other investment funds rather than directly in assets such as shares and bonds.

Summary

It is possible for investors to enjoy a gain from collective investment funds in various ways, either in the form of positive capital returns, a periodic income, or a combination of both capital gains and the benefit of an income stream. The manager of a collective investment fund may generate an income stream derived from coupon payments by bonds, dividends paid from holdings of company shares, or a combination of both. Capital growth may be generated by the sale of assets which have appreciated in value during a period of time in which they have been held by the fund manager. Investors may have the choice to have income distributed to them by the fund periodically, or to be reinvested within the fund to increase the capital growth of the fund's assets. Investors may realize the benefits of the fund's capital performance by disposing of their holdings in the fund and liquidating to cash.

Check your understanding

1 Consider the advantages that an investor would benefit from when making use of a collective investment fund.

2 Do you have a clear understanding about what is meant by an open-ended or closed-ended investment fund? Give examples of each type of fund.

3 Think about the wide range of different mutual funds which are available. Why is it important to have such a wide range of choice?

4 Consider the particular challenges faced by managers of different collective investment funds.

Further reading

The following books may be useful:

Bodie, Z, Kane, A and Marcus, A (2014) *Essentials of Investments,* global edn, McGraw Hill/Irwin

Mayo, HB (2014) *Investments: An introduction,* 11th edn, Cengage Learning

Vaitilingam, R (2011) *FT Guide to Using the Financial Pages,* 6th edn, FT Prentice Hall

The following websites may be useful:

www.morningstar.com (Morningstar Mutual Fund Sourcebook)
http://www.investorschronicle.co.uk
http://citywire.co.uk/money

Investment classes

09

Derivatives

By the end of this chapter you should understand the following:

- the difference between risk and uncertainty;
- the uses of derivatives;
- the characteristics of the following derivatives including the advantages and disadvantages of each derivative type and valuation methods for:
  - forward contracts;
  - futures;
  - options;
  - equity warrants and covered warrants.
- methods of trading and closing out derivative contracts.

Introduction

A derivative contract obtains its value from the value of an asset which is separate from the contract but which underlies it. In this introductory chapter we will look at forward contracts, futures, options, credit swaps and warrants, although there are many more. Derivatives have two parties to each transaction, a buyer and a seller. The overall outcome of a derivative transaction is zero-sum, and as such there will be a 'winner' and a 'loser' as one party is effectively betting that an underlying asset value will rise and the other that it will fall. When we talk about assets in this context we are talking potentially about shares, bonds, interest rates, commodity prices, virtually anything in fact, and we will see that such assets may be physically held by the parties to the contract or the agreement may be made on the movement of an index or spot price without either party physically owning the asset.

By understanding the characteristics of each type of derivative we can assess how a client may use such instruments not only to hedge or protect the value of investments they currently hold, but also to speculate on asset price movements to obtain a return. For those parties looking to use derivatives to hedge their risk, then derivatives are a means by which this can be achieved, although the risk reduction may not be 100 per cent complete and be costly to the investor. For those wishing to use derivatives to speculate and make a return, such investments have been likened to weapons of mass destruction and have the potential for huge losses to be incurred. For this reason, derivatives are regarded as specialist investments to be used by the most sophisticated of investors who fully understand the implications of their investments in respect of risk and potential losses.

Uncertainty and risk

As Warren Buffet has said, the view from the front windscreen of a car is never as clear as the one from the back. The uncertain nature of future events compared to the certainty of past ones explains in part the development of derivatives. Organizations do not like uncertainty or risk; they wish to operate in a certain environment where they can plan for the outcomes of the decisions they make. Such conservative human nature helped in part to develop derivatives in the first instance, in order to reduce the potential for uncertainty and risk in business generally and latterly to extend their use to investment portfolio management. In addition, derivatives have been developed to provide a means of speculation as well hedging risk. In this chapter, we will look at some of the different types of derivatives, their characteristics as well as their relative advantages and disadvantages and their use in portfolio management. However, in the first instance it is important to consider the concept of uncertainty and how this differs from risk as the two are often used interchangeably in writing and conversations.

Uncertainty is commonly held to be the same as risk; however, this is not the case. Uncertainty explains the fact that a transaction may have an actual outcome which is different from the expected outcome. This difference may be positive (things may turn out better than expected) or negative (things turn out worse than expected). To change the amorphous concept of uncertainty into risk it must be given a measurable likelihood of occurrence, in effect attributing to it a probability of an outcome. Historically, this dislike of uncertainty and risk led to the development of derivative contracts, initially used to improve certainty between buyers and sellers in agriculture due to long lead times, providing certainty of price and quantity.

Price certainty is valued due to the potential for daily movements in asset prices which may be large on some occasions. In fact, each asset has a price today at which it can be purchased or sold, called a spot price. This spot price only applies to the current day and is quite likely to have changed by tomorrow. It may move during the day or even on a minute-by-minute basis. Over long periods of time prices can move a great deal, due to many factors (supply and demand for instance) creating uncertainty for both buyers and sellers in a transaction as changes can be difficult to forecast. Derivatives take some of the uncertainty out of future transactions by agreeing prices and amounts in advance of a delivery date.

Derivative uses for investors

Investors use derivatives for two reasons: to hedge against uncertainty in their portfolio or to speculate to generate profit.

Hedging

Investors looking to hedge want to bring certainty to their investing. For example, they may want to ensure:

- they don't have to pay above a certain price for an asset;
- they can sell an asset at or above a certain price;
- their overall portfolio value does not fall over a period.

Where investors are trying to secure the future purchase price of an investment they are said to be holding a 'long position in a derivative contract'. Where an investor is trying to secure the selling price of an investment they are said to be holding a 'short position' in a derivative contract. In both cases the investor is looking to reduce their risk by reducing the potential for price movements.

In practice

Sadie currently holds an investment portfolio of equities worth £1 million. In six months' time, she would like to sell the portfolio and use the funds

> generated from the sale as a deposit for a property, so she needs to ensure the value of the portfolio does not fall.
>
> To protect her investment position Sadie could purchase a derivative contract with Red Plc (Red) where Red agrees in the contract to buy Sadie's portfolio for £1 million in six months. The derivative agreement will ensure Sadie has £1 million in cash to use as a deposit in six months, irrespective of what happens to the market value of the individual shares within the portfolio over that period.

We have called the contract Sadie may take out a derivative contract; however, as we will see in this chapter there are many different types of derivative contract, each with its own characteristics, advantages and disadvantages and it is important that as portfolio managers we recommend the most appropriate type of agreement for each client.

An added advantage of derivatives for portfolio managers is that using derivatives may also allow them to carry out changes in strategy or asset allocations. For example, they can cover short-term market movements more efficiently and cost-effectively by achieving the same effect they would buying and selling the underlying assets without physically having to buy and sell them. This is an advantage, as it can be costly to put together a portfolio which includes all the components, for example, to mimic an index due to the transaction costs and management time involved. If the manager must physically buy and sell assets as prices move to maintain a strategic position or portfolio's value, this will increase the costs of running the portfolio therefore reducing the overall return to the client.

Speculation

Speculators are not aiming to minimize risk; rather they accept investment markets are inherently risky and volatile and attempt to use those characteristics to their advantage, hoping to profit from forecasting the very price changes clients who are hedging are attempting to protect themselves against.

Speculators have several strategies, which focus on entering the market to achieve a profit based on asset price movements, using the purchase and sale of derivatives rather than owning the underlying asset. They will try to: 1) buy the right to purchase a financial asset in the future at a relatively low price in a rising market and therefore benefit from the difference between the agreed buying price and the market price, selling the asset at a profit; 2) guarantee a future sales price in a falling market, using that to make a profit. This allows them to buy an asset at a lower price in the market and sell it at a previously agreed higher price, a strategy known as short selling.

Additional income may be earned for the client and the manager by lending assets, including bonds and shares, to third parties such as hedge funds who wish to profit from a short sell. Where assets are borrowed, the borrower will provide security to the lender by providing other suitable assets. In the UK, such borrowing entails a transfer of legal title (although the asset lenders still retain beneficial ownership) meaning the lender will lose out on income during the loan period. As such, the terms of an agreement will engineer an equivalent benefit for the lender during the loan period. Lenders tend to be institutions such as pension funds, insurance companies and mutual funds who have large amounts of stock which they trade passively. Fees earned are usually in the region of around 40 basis points for FTSE 100 equities and 5 basis points for a gilt although the amount depends on the terms of the transaction and the asset.

Keywords

Basis point: this is a most common measurement unit for interest rates. One basis point equals 1/100th of 1 per cent or 0.01 per cent.

Beneficial ownership is separate to **legal title** but both are included in total ownership of an asset. Beneficial ownership can be retained where legal title has been given to a third party. Beneficial ownership covers the use and title of an asset which may be retained by one person even where the legal title belongs to someone else.

Types of derivative

Forward contract (forwards)

Forward contracts developed historically in the agricultural sector where they were used to bring certainty to suppliers and buyers operating with long production lead times; however today they are commonly used for commodity and foreign exchange transactions. Forwards are OTC legal contracts where a buyer agrees to buy and a seller to sell a pre-agreed amount of an underlying asset at a pre-agreed price with the contract completing on a pre-agreed date.

Keyword

Over-the-counter (OTC): this describes a contract which is negotiated between two parties and as such is bespoke to them, not standardized in any way. Such contracts are not usually traded on exchanges due to their bespoke nature.

In practice

Tom, a farmer, wants to ensure he receives a certain price for his next wheat crop to allow him to plan. To achieve certainty, he negotiates a forward contract to supply Helena, the local brewer, with his wheat when it is ready in six months' time (the forward element of the contract). The contract between Tom and Helena specifies the amount (in this case 56.5 tonnes) and the price (£147/tonne) as well as the delivery date. The bespoke nature of the contract has advantages as it allows the two parties to negotiate an agreement which fits their individual circumstances exactly as well as reducing uncertainty for both parties in relation to delivery amounts and prices.

On the agreed date, Tom supplies the 56.5 tonnes of wheat to Helena who pays him £8,305.50 (56.5 tonnes × £147/tonne).

Based on the idea of a zero-sum game the spot rate on the day of delivery of the contract will determine which party benefits from this contract:

- The spot rate at delivery is £155 per tonne: here Helena benefits. If she had purchased the wheat at the spot price from the market she would have paid £155/tonne rather than the £147/tonne agreed in the forward contract. This is an additional £8/tonne, which on an order of 56.5 tonnes would have increased her costs by £452.

    On the other hand, if Tom had not signed the contract with Helena he would have been able to sell at spot in the market and would have gained an additional £452, something he is not able to do due to the legal obligation to sell his wheat to Helena.

- The spot price for wheat at delivery is £147 per tonne: here, neither party benefits as the market price at expiry of the contract and the forward contract price are the same.

- The spot price for wheat at delivery is £140 per tonne: in this instance, Tom will be the party who benefits. If he had not taken out the agreement with Helena and sold his wheat in the market he would have received £140/tonne. By taking out the agreement Tom has received an additional £395.50 (£7 × 56.5 tonnes). Helena on the other hand is obliged to pay more than she would otherwise have needed to (by £395.50) as she must fulfil the obligations of the contract rather than being able to buy in the market.

In this example, both parties have used the contract to gain both certainty of cost and certainty of supply, as the underlying product (wheat) forms the basis of their respective businesses (farmer and baker). This increased certainty was the main purpose of this transaction and as such it can be considered a success. However, when the two parties compare what they paid/received for the wheat to the market prices at the point of delivery and payment, one party is likely to have incurred a loss and the other a gain by using the derivative compared to selling into the market.

Whilst the above transaction illustrates the position where both parties are looking to use the underlying asset on expiry of the contract, this is not always the case. In fact, as opposed to a producer or user, a counterparty to the transaction may be a financial institution such as a bank or a specialist trader in the product. For instance, Glencore Grain offers forward contracts on grain. Whilst they may use some grain, they are also taking a speculative interest in contracts and attempting to benefit from price movements over time to make a return. Such speculators therefore may not hold the contract to maturity but rather for a period.

We have seen the potential benefits brought about by the bespoke nature of the forward; however, combined with the OTC nature of the transaction this raises risks for both parties.

One of the main risks is the potential for counterparty default. This is where one of the parties to the contract does not complete on the transaction. This risk is exacerbated by the fact that such contracts are in the main OTC rather than exchange-traded, although there are some traded-forward exchanges such as the London Metals Exchange which allows steel prices to be fixed in advance.

> **Keyword**
>
> **Exchange-traded derivatives**
>
> A **clearing house** is the part of an exchange or marketplace responsible for ensuring the market operates fairly and efficiently and remains liquid. This is achieved by guaranteeing the completion of each contract traded in the market. The guarantee is achieved by the clearing house becoming the formal counterparty for both the buyer and the seller – in effect sitting in the middle of the transaction – meaning parties trade anonymously and are only aware of the clearing house as the other party to the transaction. The result is the clearing house bears the counterparty risk for both the buyer and seller. As it wishes to minimize this risk the clearing house insists all trading parties deposit money on account (the **initial margin**) to cover any daily losses. The clearing house will total transactions made daily by each party to produce a profit or loss for each party on all the contracts it holds. It will then request additional funds from those suffering losses and credit money to those who have made profits. This daily movement is known as a **variation margin**. Should one of the parties default on the due date the clearing house uses the margin it holds as security to cover any potential loss.

Counterparty risk in conjunction with the flexibility of the contracts can make forwards slightly more expensive; they may also be less liquid due to their nature and the difficulty of finding a willing buyer as they are not exchange-traded.

Futures

> **Keyword**
>
> A **future** is an exchange-traded standardized contract between two parties which agrees a future delivery schedule for an asset.

The contract is still compulsory for both parties to complete; however, such contracts offer more flexibility as there will be equivalent contracts with different delivery periods and the contracts can be traded on an exchange due to their standardized terms. This overcomes one of the disadvantages with the forward contract which is its relative illiquidity. This illiquidity was due to the bespoke nature of the physical transaction as well as the contract's OTC arrangements. Should one party's circumstances change and the goods or services not be available or required, the obligation to complete the futures contract remains. This could potentially lead to monetary loss for either or both parties. However, if either party could sell on their obligation to a third party, such losses would be avoided. By trading through an exchange, futures have increased liquidity and increased contract transparency for all parties within the future trade.

In practice

Initially the first futures dealt in agricultural commodities with the Chicago Board of Trade (CBOT, which now operates as part of the CME group) trading different commodities such as grains, oil and 'softs' (eg coffee). Taking wheat as an example, the CBOT will trade wheat options. Each contract will specify:

- The quality: for example milling or feed wheat, the former being used for flour, the latter for animal feed.
- The quantity: this is pre-set on each exchange – for the CBOT exchange the standard quantity is 5,000 bushels per contract. A bushel is a standard wheat measurement which differs slightly between countries but is between 35–36 litres of dry wheat.
- The delivery address of the product, including naming acceptable warehouses.
- The delivery date: this is fixed by the exchange, with CBOT wheat futures being traded on specific days in March, May, July, September and December.

Both parties agree the price of the individual futures contracts; however, the exchange sets minimum price movements. For wheat on the CBOT the minimum movement is ¼ of a cent ($0.0025) per bushel. As each contract has a standard quantity of 5,000 bushels the minimum price movement, also known as the **tick** size, is $12.50 per contract (5,000 bushels × $0.0025).

In the examples used above we have concentrated on the trading of physical commodities; however, in 1975 the CBOT developed the first financial future based on intangible underlying assets which now include interest rates, exchange rates and stock market indices.

Investment and Portfolio Management

Futures contracts in real life

As with a forward contract a future imposes an obligation on both parties holding the future. If the future is held to expiry the buyer/holder at that time will have to meet the delivery obligations of the contract. These delivery obligations may require physical delivery of the commodity or it may be possible to negotiate the settlement of the contract by the exchange of cash, discussed below. Within each contract there are two positions taken, with one party agreeing to buy an underlying asset at a set price and the other agreeing to sell at a set price. These are known as opening a long and opening a short respectively.

During a contract term, there is a relationship between the daily spot price and the futures price of the underlying asset with the two moving broadly in line with each other. Where the futures price is above the spot price this is known as Contango whereas where the futures price is below the spot price it is known as backwardation. At expiry, the spot price and the futures price will be the same.

Opening a long Here the investor agrees to buy an underlying asset at a pre-agreed price in the future with the intention of profiting from a future rise in the market price.

In practice

During June, having considered the world's ongoing economic volatility, Joyce believes the gold price will rise in future months. Speculating on this, Joyce purchases a future from Beta Bank which obliges her to physically buy 2,000 oz of gold in September for $1,200/oz.

By September gold's spot price is $1,300/oz. As Joyce has purchased a physical future she will take delivery of the gold (not personally but to an approved secure warehouse) paying the seller $2,400,000 (2,000 oz × $1,200). She then has two potential options; her choice will depend on her analysis of future price movements:

- selling the gold on the market at spot for a total of $2,600,000 (2,000 oz × $1,300), realizing a profit of $200,000;
- or holding the gold for a further period.

The potential profits and losses of this long position can be represented graphically (see Figure 9.1) and analysed as follows:

- Maximum loss: for Joyce's transaction, her potential loss is maximized when the value of the underlying gold falls to zero as she would have to buy at an asset which had no value, at a price of $1,200/oz (however unlikely that is for gold!).

- Profit: looking at Joyce's transaction line which runs upwards from left to right on the graph we can see she will make a profit if the spot price of the gold rises above $1,200/oz as she will be able to buy at $1,200/oz from her counterparty and sell into the market at a higher price.

- Maximum profit: her maximum profits are theoretically unlimited, as the selling price of gold could rise to infinity and she has fixed a pre-agreed buying price of $1,200/oz. Again, this is unrealistic, but for Joyce the higher the price the greater the return she will earn.

- The counterparty Beta Bank will make a profit if the price falls below $1,200/oz as they are taking the short position. Beta Bank will be able to sell gold to Joyce at $1,200/oz having bought in the market at a price below $1,200/oz.

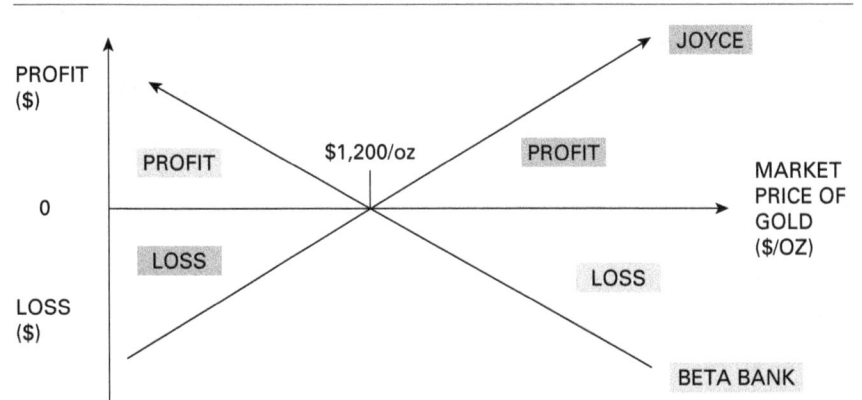

Figure 9.1 Profit and loss of long position in gold

Opening a short Here the investor (buyer) agrees to sell an underlying asset with the intention of profiting from a future price fall. This will be done by agreeing a selling price using a futures contract with the hope that the market value of the product will fall in the future. This will then allow the buyer to purchase the asset on the open market at the agreed date at a lower price, allowing them to then sell to the counterparty at the pre-agreed higher price, thus realizing a profit.

In practice

During September, John watches the economic movements in the UK and believes that, due to increased economic certainty, the market price of gold is likely to fall in the coming months from its current price of $1,300/oz. Based on his analysis John purchases a future from Alpha Bank (Alpha) where he agrees to sell and physically deliver 1,500 oz of gold at a price of $1,250/oz to Alpha in March the following year. By March John's forecast of the price of gold has been proved correct and the spot price has fallen to £1,150/oz.

To fulfil his futures contract John buys 1,500 oz of gold in the market for $1,725,000 (1,500 × $1,150/oz). He then sells the gold to his counterparty, Alpha, under the terms of the future for $1,875,000 (1,500 oz at $1,250/oz), making a profit of $150,000.

John's transaction can be represented graphically (see Figure 9.2) showing the potential profits and losses for both Alpha Bank and for John, as follows:

- John's profit: looking at John's line which runs from right to left on the graph we can see that he will make a profit if the price of the gold falls below $1,250 as he will be able to sell at $1,250 but buy below that figure. John has taken the short position.

- Alpha's profit: alternatively, Alpha Bank will make a profit if the price rises above $1,250 as they are taking the long position. Alpha Bank will be able to buy gold from John at $1,250/oz and sell into a market at a price above that.

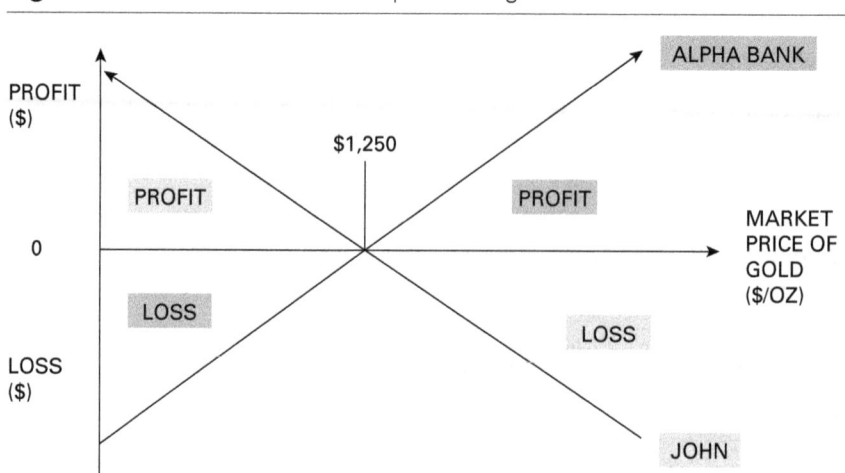

Figure 9.2 Profit and loss of short position in gold

In both the above examples Joyce and John are reliant on the price of the underlying asset moving as they forecast to make a profit. If this does not happen they will make a loss. Going back to John's example, if the price of gold had moved to $1,300/oz in March rather than $1,150/oz used in the example John would still have to buy 1,500 oz of gold which would have cost him $1,950,000 (1,500 oz × $1,300/oz) and he would then have had to sell it at the pre-agreed futures price of $1,250/oz, making a loss of $75,000 ($50/oz on 1,500 oz).

Advantages of using futures rather than buying the underlying investment directly

There are several advantages of buying a gilt or equity future rather than directly purchasing the gilt or equity:

- lower transaction costs;
- increased levels of liquidity compared to the underlying asset;
- increased transaction speed compared to the relevant direct investment market;
- possibility of taking a short position which may not be possible in the direct market;
- the margin system increases leverage by allowing exposure to the asset without requiring 100 per cent of cash outlay.

Risks associated with futures

There are three main risks associated with futures, related to market, counterparty and liquidity.

Market risk

> **Keyword**
>
> **CAPM** describes the relationship between the risk and return of a share. This relationship is between risk, specifically systematic risk and the expected theoretical return required by an investor to take the investment risk of buying a particular share. CAPM can be used by investors to calculate a required rate of return and by companies to calculate an expected cost of capital (the other side of the same coin, as investors provide the capital companies use).

CAPM theory splits market risk into two separate types: systematic risk and unsystematic risk:

- Systematic risk is a risk which affects the performance of the financial market overall rather than one company or industry. Systematic risk cannot be eliminated by diversification, only by hedging. Examples of systematic risks include recessions, interest rate change and natural disasters.

- Unsystematic risk directly affects the results of one area of the market or one specific security. Investors can protect against unsystematic risk by diversifying their portfolio to ensure it includes assets which:

    - do not correlate with one another;
    - in some cases, do not correlate with the market;
    - are spread over many types of investment, industry, maturity dates and geographical locations.

Counterparty risk This is the risk of default by the other party to the transaction. This risk is reduced in a futures transaction as the future is exchange-traded which means the exchange becomes the counterparty to both the buyer and the seller through the exchange's clearing house which processes all exchange transactions. Whilst default risk is reduced by the clearing house, it should be remembered such risk may also occur in the relationship between the client and their broker and between the broker and the clearing house.

Liquidity risk This is the risk that it is not possible to trade an asset at its fair value in a reasonable period and without incurring high trading costs in a market due to a lack of counterparties willing to provide the other side of the trade. This is particularly important for clients who are currently holding derivatives which they wish to close out.

Spread betting (spreads)

The futures described above involve buying (going long) or selling (going short) a contract allowing the two parties to speculate on the price movement of goods or financial services over a period. Spreads take this one stage further as investors attempt to make a gain between two different contracts based on the same commodity or financial instrument. Such derivatives are considered far safer than the trading of naked futures; however, investors should only use capital which they are happy and can afford to lose as all trading in derivatives is high risk.

Swaps

A swap, also known as a contract for difference, is an OTC agreement between two parties to exchange a series of future cashflows, essentially a series of forward contracts.

Options

As we have discussed, despite the increased flexibility of futures contracts, both futures and forward contracts require the original contract to be completed, either physically or by agreed monetary compensation. In some circumstances buyers may prefer to abandon an agreement rather than complete it or sell it on. From this requirement for an added level of flexibility the idea of options was developed.

Whilst the idea of an option was around for some time they were not used commercially until the 1970s when two American economists, Black and Scholes, developed a pricing model. Standardized option exchanges were quickly developed with the Chicago Board Options Exchange (CBOE) opening in 1973 the same year as the Black and Scholes research paper was published. Options markets continued to develop and expand and today options can be traded through both exchanges and OTC.

Options overcome the disadvantage of compulsory completion of the agreement by giving the option buyer (who may also be known as the holder or long position) the right but not the obligation to purchase from or sell to the writer of the option, a pre-agreed asset at a pre-agreed price in a pre-agreed timescale. This allows the buyer to make the decision on expiry as to whether the transaction goes ahead so the buyer can speculate or protect themselves against a price movement of an underlying asset without being forced to complete the transaction at expiry, either by a contract for difference or being asked to sell the underlying asset.

The option writer, who can also be described as having the short position, on the other hand retains an obligation and must abide by the decision of the buyer and carry out the buyer's wishes in relation to the transaction. As compensation for their obligations when the option agreement is signed the writer will charge the buyer a non-refundable premium. The premium is a fraction of the value of the notional amount of the option, but separates the transaction from others such as futures as the purchaser gains a right to a transaction in exchange for a specific payment rather than entering the transaction itself.

There are many variations of option terms but two different options types, each of which have a buyer and a writer:

Put option

- the buyer purchases the right, but not the obligation to sell an underlying asset to the writer of the option at a pre-agreed price on a pre-agreed date following payment of a premium;
- the writer must buy the asset from the seller at the previously agreed price if the buyer wishes to exercise the option; the writer receives a premium at the date of the agreement as compensation.

Call option

- the buyer purchases the right but not the obligation to buy an underlying asset from the writer of the option at a pre-agreed price on a pre-agreed date following payment of a premium;
- the writer must sell the asset to the buyer at the previously agreed price if the buyer wishes to exercise the option; the writer receives a premium at the date of the agreement as compensation.

One major variation in the terms commonly seen is in respect of the expiry date of the option, with two possible expiry characteristics: European, where an option can only be exercised on the last day of the option's life; American, where the option can be exercised over a period agreed by the two parties which can be any date between inception and expiry.

In practice

A European put option

Assume today is 1 January. Gill manages a portfolio of UK blue-chip equities, for a client, valued at £10 million. The portfolio is due to be valued in 90 days' time and Gill's client is eager to protect the value of their portfolio so it doesn't fall before the valuation.

Gill arranges to buy a European put option from Demma Options. The option covers assets valued up to £10 million and the writer of the put, Demma

Options, charges Gill a premium of £50,000 for the option. The premium is paid on 1 January, the date the option is agreed and is non-refundable.

A put option allows Gill to protect her client's position as she is buying the right to sell the portfolio for £10 million in 90 days, the date of the valuation, ensuring the value of the portfolio is maintained. At the expiry date in 90 days there are three possible outcomes and Gill will have to decide what to do depending on the circumstances.

At expiry of the option the portfolio has a market value of £9 million

Where the portfolio value is less than the option value at expiry the option is described as 'in the money'.

Gill's aim was to protect her client's portfolio value at £10 million. Therefore, Gill could use the option to sell the portfolio for £10 million to Demma. Demma is obliged to buy the portfolio for £10 million even though they could buy the same portfolio in the market on that day for £9 million.

There are two ways of completing this transaction bearing in mind Gill's objective is not to sell the portfolio but rather to maintain its value:

1 The underlying portfolio assets could be sold to Demma, the option writer, for £10 million.

2 There could be a cash settlement, meaning Gill and Demma agree the difference in value between the market value of the portfolio (£9 million) and the put option value of the portfolio (£10 million) and in this case, the writer, Demma, will pay the difference in value of £1 million to Gill, the buyer.

For Gill the cash settlement better fits her objective as at the portfolio valuation date the client will have total wealth of £10 million, a portfolio worth £9 million and £1 million cash, which fulfils their original requirement of maintaining the value of the portfolio. In addition, by settling the transaction via a cash payment there is the added benefit of the underlying portfolio remaining intact. Maintaining an intact portfolio may be a longer-term requirement of the client as well as avoiding transaction costs incurred when selling and then replacing the portfolio. It should be remembered however that the client has incurred the £50,000 premium at the date of the original option transaction which will affect their overall return.

At expiry of the option the market value and the option value of the portfolio are both £10 million

Where the portfolio value is equal to the option value at expiry the option is described as 'at the money'.

As Gill's client's portfolio has maintained its value up to the valuation date, which was the client's aim, they will not require the option and it will be abandoned. The client's only cost in this scenario will be the non-refundable premium of £50,000 which was paid when the option was taken out.

Demma Options as the writer will retain the £50,000 premium. For them this is a best possible outcome and the highest profit possible.

At expiry of the option the market value of the portfolio is £11 million, £1 million more than the option value of £10 million

Where the portfolio value is more than the option value at expiry the option is described as 'out of the money'.

Again, Gill will abandon the put option as her aim was to protect the portfolio's value which as the market value is now £11 million does not require the option to achieve. The cost to the investor is the £50,000 cost of the premium.

The writer will retain the £50,000 premium and take no further action which is the best outcome for them.

The possible returns for each party in the scenario described above are shown on the graphs in Figures 9.3 and 9.4, and it is important to understand how to read this type of information.

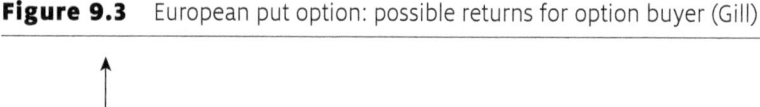

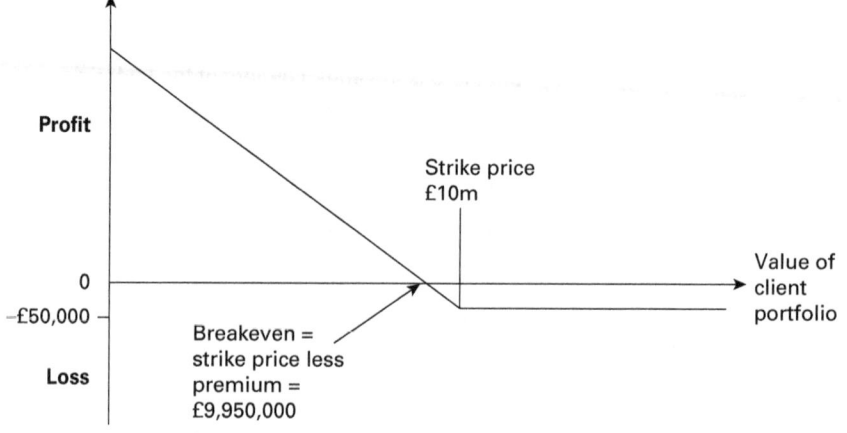

Figure 9.3 European put option: possible returns for option buyer (Gill)

Investment Classes: Derivatives

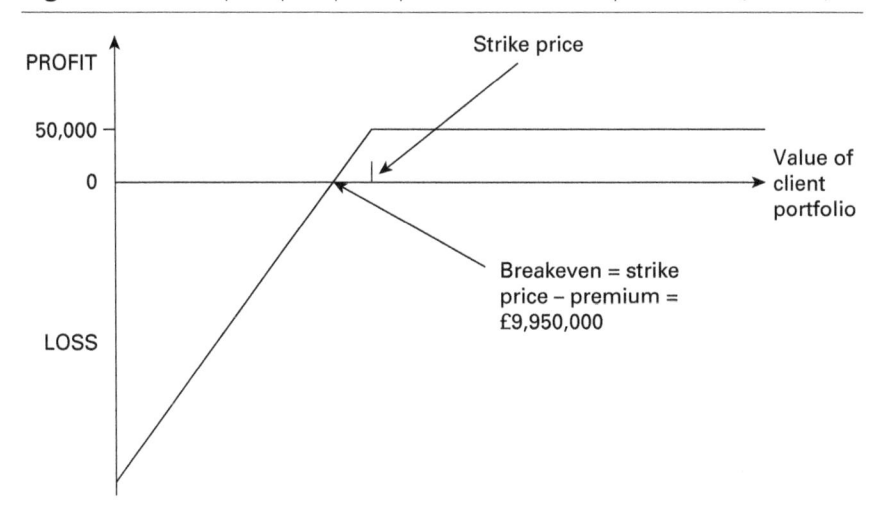

Figure 9.4 European put option: possible returns for option writer (Demma)

[Graph showing: PROFIT/LOSS axis vs Value of client portfolio. Strike price marked. Breakeven = strike price − premium = £9,950,000. Profit level at 50,000.]

In practice

Gill, the option buyer

Gill's possible outcomes can be represented graphically in Figure 9.3 with the graph showing:

- Gill's maximum profit: this would theoretically be generated where the portfolio value was zero (although such an event is unlikely in real life). This is because Gill has purchased the right to sell her assets at a fixed price, so even when the portfolio has a zero-asset value, the option writer, Demma, would have to pay £10 million to buy it at the option's expiry date. At this point, Gill's profit would be the £10 million she would receive from Demma less the cost of the premium of £50,000, ie a profit of £9.95 million.

- Gill's breakeven point: the breakeven point is the point where no loss and no profit is made on the transaction. In Gill's case the breakeven point is where the portfolio's underlying value equals the option price plus the cost of the premium, in this case £9,950,000 (£10,000,000 − £50,000). Here the profit on completing the transaction of £50,000 is offset by the cost of the premium of £50,000.

- Gill's maximum loss: the maximum loss will always be the premium as the buyer can abandon the option at their choice. The graph shows Gill's maximum loss which is the value of £50,000.

Demma, the option writer

The maximum profit for the writer is the £50,000 premium whilst the maximum loss they can incur is £9,950,000 in the unlikely event that the varying assets leave no value.

In the last example, we considered a European put option ie the right to sell an asset on a specific day. Here we will look at an example of an American call option ie the right to buy an asset over a prespecified period.

In practice

An American call option

Jason is convinced XYZ Plc's shares, which are currently trading in the market at 75p per share, will rise over the next six months. He buys an American call option on the shares from Halle Options with an exercise price of 90p, paying a premium of 5p per share.

If the shares of XYZ Plc rise above 90p per share on a day prior to the option expiring Jason can use the call option to buy the shares from Halle Options at a price of 90p per share. He can then sell the shares in the open market for a higher price. For an American option, Jason doesn't have to wait until the agreed expiry date to use the option as he would with a European option, with the option available to be used any day up to expiry.

XYZ Plc market share price remains below 90p for the duration of the option

Here the option is known as being 'out of the money' as the underlying asset market price is below the strike price of the asset.

Jason will abandon the option, losing the 5p premium per share in the process. He may then buy the shares in the open market if he still wishes to.

Halle Options will retain the 5p per share premium and take no further action.

XYZ Plc's market share price equals 90p during the options exercise period

In this case, the share price is equal to the strike price which is known as being 'at the money'.

It is likely Jason will abandon the option, losing the 5p per share premium.

Halle Options will retain the 5p per share premium and take no further action.

XYZ Plc's market share price goes above 90p during the option's exercise period

In this case, the option is known as being 'in the money' as the underlying asset price is above the option strike price.

Jason needs to judge the best time to use the option as it can only be used once. This will depend on his forecasts of the potential market share price over the option period. Once he has decided to use the option he will then arrange to buy the shares which he will then be able to hold or resell or, depending on the terms of the agreement, he could arrange for a cash settlement with the writer.

Halle Options will have to sell the shares to Jason at 90p irrespective of the share price in the market. Up to a share price of 95p Halle will not make a loss as they can offset the premium they have received of 5p per share. Above that they will start to incur a loss on the transaction.

The possible returns in this scenario are shown on the graph in Figures 9.5 and 9.6. Again, it is important to understand how to read such information.

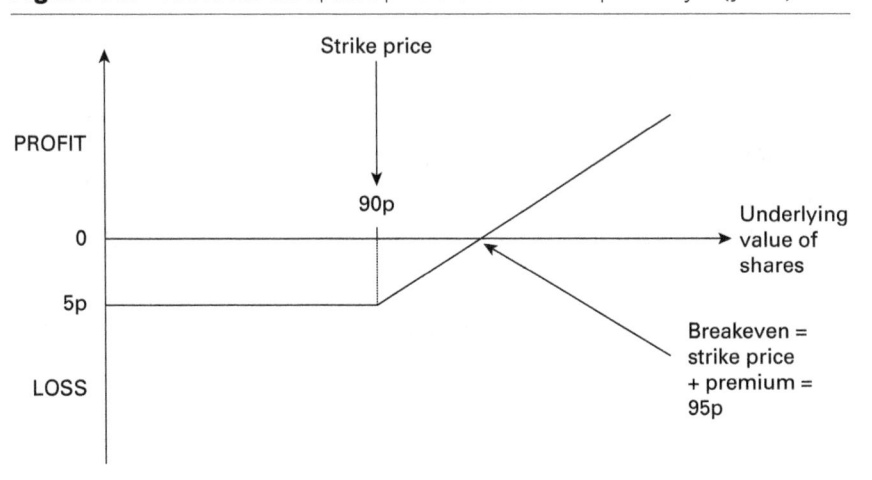

Figure 9.5 American call option: possible returns for option buyer (Jason)

Figure 9.6 American call option: possible returns for option writer (Halle)

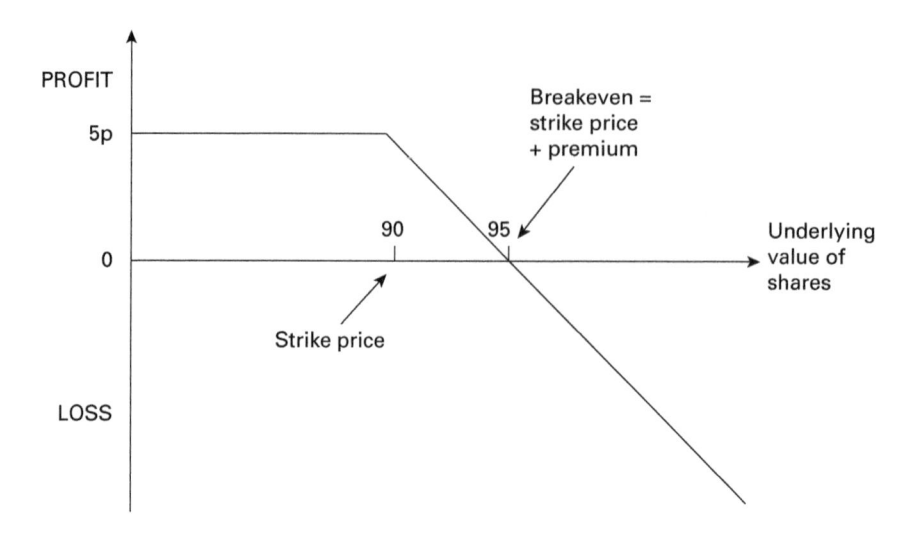

[Graph showing profit/loss for option writer: horizontal line at 5p profit from 0 to strike price of 90, then sloping downward through breakeven at 95 (strike price + premium), continuing into loss territory as underlying value of shares increases.]

In practice

Jason, the call option buyer

The possible outcomes for Jason are:

- Jason's maximum profit: this is potentially unlimited, as he has purchased the right to buy the asset which he can then sell in the market. Therefore, theoretically, the higher the price of the asset the higher the profit.
- Jason's breakeven point: the point at which his transaction does not make a profit or a loss is where the market price of the share equals the strike price plus the premium ie 95p (90p share price plus 5p premium).
- Jason's maximum loss: this is limited to the cost of the premium as Jason will abandon the option if the share price does not rise above the 90p.

Halle Options, writers of the call option

The possible outcomes for Halle Options are:

- Halle's maximum profit: this is earned where Jason takes out the option and pays the 5p premium but the price of XYZ Plc's shares does not

rise above the strike price so the buyer abandons it. Therefore, the maximum profit the writer can make is the 5p price of the premium.
- Halle's breakeven point: this will come where they buy the shares (to be able to sell them to Jason) at 95p as at that point they have paid the price of 95p but they have received 5p premium and will receive 90p from Jason
- Halle's maximum loss: this is unlimited, as the writer will have to sell the asset to the buyer at the agreed price, however high the market price of the asset is when the Jason decides to use the option.

Determining the option premium

Complex mathematical models form the basis of option pricing and we will not be discussing those. However, by using an example we can identify certain factors which affect the option premium amount.

Table 9.1 shows data for American-style put and call options available on a single ABC Plc share at 15 September. ABC shares are trading at 937.8p today.

Table 9.1 American-style put and call options

Exercise price (p)	Call options (p)			Put options (p)		
	September	October	November	September	October	November
920	19.5	31	37.5	1.5	13	19
940	5.5	19.5	26	8	21	27.5

From the information given we can deduce:

- The table shows the premiums for a call or a put option for one share in ABC. This is a simplified version of real life as contracts are usually for blocks of 1,000 shares.
- The current market price of ABC shares is 937.8p and there are two potential exercise prices for both call and put options, 920p and 940p. The exercise price is the agreed price the share can be bought or sold at.
- The options are American-style and therefore potentially exercisable on several dates over a set period, depending on the market price of ABC shares.

Option prices have two elements, intrinsic value and time value, and we can see them in practice using the example data:

The intrinsic value = share price − exercise price
The time value = option premium − intrinsic value

Consider the following example of a call option.

A call option gives the buyer the right to buy a share at a fixed price. As such if an investor buys a September 920p call option for ABC shares today then the buyer has the right to buy one ABC share at 920p and can immediately sell it in the market for 937.5p. Therefore the option must be worth at least 17.5p (937.5p − 920p). However, the actual option is trading at 19.5p and the additional 2p is the time value of the option.

Time to expiry

The longer the time to expiry of the option the higher the premium, as the greater the chance the option will expire in the money. In Table 9.1, we can see that, for both puts and calls, the October premiums are more expensive than the September ones, which in turn are more expensive than the August premiums.

Share price volatility

The greater the volatility of the share price, measured using standard deviation, the more likely an option will expire in the money and potentially very much in the money. Therefore, the greater the potential of earning a profit from buying an option on a volatile share than on a less volatile share. The higher the potential profit, the higher the cost to buy the asset and therefore the higher the premium.

Discount rate

Keyword

Risk-free interest rate: this is the interest rate return on investments considered to be risk free in theory and in real life as risk free as is available, ie UK government gilts where there is little chance of default due to government's ability to print its own currency to cover any repayments.

As investments are valued at the present value of their future cashflows and the required rate of return an investor will request on a cashflow is made up of the risk-free rate plus a premium for risk, the higher the risk-free rate is the lower the present value of the cashflows will be and the lower the option premium.

The Greeks

Whilst we are not going to delve deeply into this area readers should be aware of these symbols and the fact they denote the sensitivity of option prices with respect to several pricing factors which overall suggests the option premium effectively equates to:

PV (probability an option expires in the money × expected payoff if option does expire in the money)

where PV = present value.

We mentioned the Black–Scholes pricing model earlier in this chapter and this ties into their assumptions about premium levels and the distribution of future outcomes. Theirs is not the only model, however; others include the binomial model, which is more generalized but does intersect with the Black–Scholes model on occasions.

The factors to which option premiums are sensitive are:

- Option Delta (Δ): an option premium's sensitivity to changes in the underlying asset price. Delta is used in pricing options and when managing portfolios including both shares and options, as it is important to understand the relationship between the two assets' prices to assess volatility.

- Option Theta (Θ): an option premium's sensitivity in relation to the passage of time.

- Option Vega (N): an option premium's sensitivity to changes in the underlying assets' volatility. Vega is not a Greek letter; however, the letter N (identical to the Greek letter nu) is used as a representative symbol.

- Option Rho (P): an option premium's sensitivity in relation to interest rate changes.

Equity warrants and covered warrants

Equity warrants

These are effectively call options issued by a company in respect of its own shares giving the holders the right to buy the company's own shares at a pre-agreed exercise price. Warrants can be European or American and generally have a longer life of up to five years.

There are some specific differences however:

- Companies issue their own warrants either as equity warrants or attached to bonds, rather than being issued by third parties.
- Warrants are usually traded over-the-counter (OTC) rather than through exchanges, although the LSE has a small market.
- Small numbers of exchanges can make trading warrants difficult and costly, as there is limited information in the market regarding price and limited ability to operate a margin call system. The size of the markets, despite using the same pricing principles as options, can lead to a lack of liquidity.
- Warrants tend to have a longer life, with expiry often being years rather than months in advance as seen with pure options.
- Warrants lead to new share issues and therefore dilute control and ownership of the company when they are exercised.

Pricing a warrant

As with a call option premium a warrant's price has two elements: formula value and premium value.

Formula value (the equivalent of the intrinsic value of an option) The formula value will be zero where the warrant is out of the money and between the spot price and the exercise price where the warrant is in the money. The formula value can be calculated as

$$FV = (S - X) \times N$$

where:
FV = formula value
S = current share price
X = exercise price
N = number of new shares created by the warrant

In practice

The current share price of A Plc's shares is £3.60, the exercise price of a warrant issued by the company is £3.00. Each warrant will create three new shares.

The formula value of the warrant can be calculated as (£3.60 − £3.00) × 3 = £1.80.

Premium value (the equivalent of the time value of an option) The premium value will fall as the warrant moves closer to its expiry date.

The percentage premium of an in-the-money warrant is calculated using the formula

$$PP = \frac{\text{(warrant price} - \text{formula value)}}{\text{(number of shares issued if warrant exercised} \times \text{stock price)}} \times 100$$

In practice

Using the information from the formula value calculation above but adding the fact that the warrant is trading at £1.90 in the market we can calculate the premium percentage:

$$PP = \frac{(£1.90 - £1.80)}{(3 \times £3.60)} \times 100 = \frac{£0.10}{£10.80} \times 100 = 0.093 \times 100 = 0.93\%$$

Covered warrants

Covered warrants are issued by third-party financial institutions such as investment banks, in respect of different underlying assets such as currencies, commodities shares, indices and other financial instruments from both the UK market and foreign markets. They also represent the potential to buy the underlying asset; however in this case, no new assets are being created (eg new shares) therefore the transaction has no diluting effect. The holder of the warrant has the right to buy or sell the asset, but as they have no obligation their maximum loss is the amount of the premium paid. Timescales are potentially much longer for covered warrants, with expiry up to six years, although most have a life of between 6 and 12 months. There are also European- and American-style covered warrants available.

The issuing institution will also buy or sell the asset in the market so they have them available if they need to deliver them at the end of the period. Covered warrants are exchange-traded on the LSE with settlement through CREST which increases their liquidity with most being cash settled to avoid stamp duty reserve tax. As the market is regulated by the FCA, covered warrants can be traded by retail investors and can provide the basis for a defensive strategy, to guard against an overall asset price fall or a speculative strategy.

Retail contracts for difference

> **Keyword**
>
> A **contract for difference (CFD)** is an agreement between two parties to exchange the difference between the opening price and the closing price of an asset multiplied by the underlying contract size.

CFDs can be traded in many assets including stocks, interest rates and commodities, with a swap being an OTC CFD. The aim of a CFD is to allow an investor to experience the benefits of owning a commodity, allowing them to go short or go long more easily, without incurring the transaction costs associated with stock borrowing.

Some CFDs have been developed directly for sale to retail investors. This has caused some concern, with the FCA proposing tighter trading rules in December 2016 as their initial investigations suggest approximately 82 per cent of investors undertaking such trades lose money, not least due to the high levels of leverage possible.

As such contracts are normally arranged using a broker authorized under the Financial Services and Markets Act 2000 the FCA is also concerned that insufficient analysis of the client's investment capabilities and risk appetite is being undertaken.

Methods of ending a derivative contract

As we have discussed it is possible to hold a contract to expiry. However, investors may not wish to do this and may trade the contract. If it is held to expiry there are three possible outcomes depending on the circumstances:

- Physical delivery: investors may take physical delivery of the assets.
- Contract (or cash) for difference (CFD): in the previous examples, we have assumed physical delivery of the underlying asset at expiry of the contract. However, in the real world over 95 per cent of contracts are not physically delivered and for some assets, such as financial instruments, this would not even be possible as such products may include interest or exchange rate movements which are intangible. Instead the contract is

closed out, meaning instead of physical delivery the profit or loss on the contract is worked out for each party and cash is transferred between the two parties to reflect the overall position.

> **In practice**
>
> George believes the FTSE 250 will rise over the next six months so he buys a future at a price of 6,789 points. The terms include a payment from the seller of £5 for every point over the agreed amount of 6,789. In six months' time, at the date of expiry, the index stands at 7,103. George has seen his prediction come true, the market has risen and therefore in line with the terms of the futures contract, he has made a gain. Due to the nature of the underlying asset, no physical delivery is possible; instead the party making the loss will pay a cash amount to George, who has made the gain, with George receiving a payment of £1,570 (314 points × £5) from the counterparty.

- Close out using an offsetting position in the market: here, prior to delivery, a decision will be made to end the trade and this will be done by the investor taking out an opposite trade effectively neutralizing the first trade.

> **In practice**
>
> An investor may buy 10 wheat contracts for delivery in September. In August, they decide to close out the position and purchase the right to sell 10 wheat contracts for delivery in September. At expiry, the buy contract position will be offset by the sell contract position with zero gain or loss.

Trading derivatives

Self-managed

Individual investors can trade with their own account; however, this means the investors will be making all the decisions themselves without the expertise of a broker or manager. This will include generating, analysing and monitoring information on the assets being traded as well as undertaking the trades themselves. This can be time-consuming, difficult and expensive if the investor has insufficient expertise.

Managed accounts

Here a broker will trade on an investor's behalf based on conditions set when the account was opened. This may reduce the investor's risk as the professional is likely to have access to information and will be making informed decisions on the investor's behalf. However, they will not always make a profit and the individual investor remains liable for any losses incurred as well as management charges.

Community pool

As with a mutual fund, investors pool their investments to be able to trade in specific investments. As such they do not own the derivatives directly: rather they own a proportion of the asset pool based on the value of their investment. The derivatives are then traded in the normal way and gains and losses are received by the investor in proportion to the size of their investment. As with a mutual fund such arrangements can increase diversification, thereby reducing portfolio risk due to the increased ability of the pool to invest in a wider selection of investments. However, as with all trading the underlying risks associated with the asset type, in this case derivatives, remain and the investor is reliant on the skills of the trading manager to generate positive returns.

Summary

Derivatives rely on the underlying value of separate assets for their own value. Such assets can be physical assets of a single type such as commodities, intangible assets of a single type such as exchange rates or a combination of assets in an index, for instance.

Derivatives overall allow investors to hedge risks or speculate. However, the method of achieving investors' aims can be varied due to the number of different derivatives available, each with their own characteristics, advantages and disadvantages. Whilst there is a myriad of derivatives, we have only covered the most common types, with options being probably the most flexible for the buyer, although this flexibility comes at a cost as a non-refundable premium is payable at the outset of the agreement. The value of the premium is determined by several factors which need to be understood as does a premium's sensitivity to changes in economic and financial indicators, with calculations for different factors represented by Greek letters and known collectively as 'the Greeks'.

The potential outcomes from a derivative can be represented graphically and it is important to be able to understand the information represented in the graphs for both the writers and the buyers of a derivative as this will allow analysis and understanding of potential losses for each party, as well as breakeven points and profits, as well as when a derivative is likely to be used as it is 'in the money'.

Such derivatives are not without risk for the investor though and this has been seen most recently in the contracts for difference market which is being investigated by the FCA due to the level of losses being sustained by retail investors. This highlights that whilst derivates may be useful for hedging and have the potential for high levels of speculative gains they remain a high-risk investment with the potential to produce high losses for unwary and unsophisticated investors.

Check your understanding

1   What are the similarities and differences between a forward contract and a future?
2   What is the tick size on the Chicago Board of Trade exchange and how does this relate to a bushel of wheat?
3   What is the maximum loss an investor can incur where they open a long future?
4   Does a put option give the right to sell an asset or the right to buy an asset?
5   In an option, which party has an obligation in the agreement?
6   What is the maximum loss a writer can incur on a put option?
7   What are the two components which make up the option premium?
8   What are the Greeks?
9   What are the two elements of a warrant's price?
10 What methods can an investor use to trade derivatives?

Further reading

For more in-depth analysis of option strategies, *Investopedia* has an article 'Ten Option Strategies to Know' at http://www.investopedia.com/slide-show/options-strategies/.

Details of trading and up-to-date news on covered warrants can be found on the LSE website at http://www.londonstockexchange.com/exchange/prices-and-markets/covered-warrants/covered-warrants-home.html.

Additional information on CFDs can be found at the Financial Conduct Authority's website at https://www.fca.org.uk/firms/contracts-for-difference.

Further reading on financial futures can be found in Romesh Vaitilingam's book *Using the Financial Pages,* 6th edn, FT Prentice Hall.

Investment classes

10

Alternative investments

By the end of this chapter you should have an understanding of the following key areas of alternative investments:

- the general risks associated with investing in alternative assets;
- characteristics of the following types of alternative assets:
  - chattels and collectibles;
  - commodities including direct and indirect investment in gold;
  - direct and indirect property investments;
  - the characteristics of REITs, unit trusts and PAIFs as well as the advantages and disadvantages of investing in each;
  - structured products.

Introduction

As returns from so called 'traditional investment classes' such as shares and bonds have reduced, investors have sought out alternatives to maintain income and growth levels leading to an increase in the level of investment in alternative assets.

Alternative assets can be difficult to define. Even saying an alternative asset is 'something which is not traditional' has weaknesses as a definition as some investors will describe an asset as mainstream, whilst others will describe it as alternative – property is one of those assets which may be defined as either – making a standard definition very difficult to achieve. People may use the term 'alternative' but mean different things by it, which can also lead to confusion. As such, it is important to know what clients understand by terms as they are discussed to avoid any miscommunication.

For this chapter, we will be looking at the following specific alternative investments:

- collectibles and chattels;
- commodities;
- direct and indirect investment in gold;
- direct and indirect investment in property;
- structured products.

General risks of investing in alternative assets

There are several risks of investing in alternative assets and whilst each is presented individually here you will recognize in the examples given that the risks can be interdependent due to the nature of the assets.

Liquidity

Here we are looking at how easy it is to sell a type of asset for its fair value within a reasonable time. Liquidity will be dependent on the numbers of buyers and sellers for a market and the trading volumes within a market. Where an asset is very valuable or rare, access to the market will often be through specialist auctioneers with limited numbers of buyers available. This may lead to a reduced liquidity and as a result a reduced price, especially where an investor needs to sell quickly to realize cash. Where assets suffer from liquidity issues, they are unlikely to be suitable for investors who require ready access to cash.

Valuation

Due to the specialist nature of some assets, where there have been no recent sales of a similar asset, a valuation may be based solely on a valuer's opinion. This may result in an inaccurate opinion of the product's value which may only become accurately known when the item is put to the market.

In practice

In September 2015 three items were auctioned in New York: an Apple 1 motherboard, a 79-year-old TV and the last surviving supercomputer designed by Seymour Cray. Neither the Apple 1 nor the television sold, despite the Apple 1 being one of only 50 in the world. The reserve price for the Apple 1 had been set at $300,000 lower than previous sales prices seen in 2014 ($365,000) and 2013 ($905,000).

At the other extreme a collection of 100 pieces of Chinese porcelain purchased in the 1950s and 60s was expected to sell for approximately £20 million when it was auctioned in Hong Kong in early 2016; they fetched more than £45 million in the sale.

These examples illustrate the difficulty of obtaining accurate valuations for some assets and also that valuations may change over time without the investor being aware of it, particularly if similar assets have not been traded on the market for some time.

Trends and fashions

A change in trends or fashion or even just a lack of interest can also reduce or increase the value of the asset dramatically. As we saw above, the value of Asian antiques has risen rapidly in recent years due to a surge in interest from Chinese dealers and investors looking to repatriate antiques sold abroad during the 19th century.

Lack of income

Unless the items can be hired out, such as a classic car hired for a photo shoot or for use in a period film, the items are unlikely to produce income for an investor, which may limit their usefulness within a portfolio depending on the client's personal requirements.

Transaction costs

Transaction costs may be high due to the specialized nature of the markets involved. For instance, where art is being sold at auction, both the buyer and the seller pay an auction fee. For the seller this can vary from 8 per cent to 20 per cent plus VAT, whilst the buyer's fee is usually around 10 per cent plus VAT. In both cases this will reduce the funds received from the asset sale.

That said, whilst such assets may have high initial upfront investment and selling costs, overall transaction costs may be lower due to the lower turnover levels for such assets compared to turnover levels for conventional assets.

Cost of storage and insurance

In the case of some assets, specialized storage will be required to ensure the assets' value is maintained.

> **In practice**
>
> Fine wine is well known for requiring specific specialist storage conditions such as humidity and temperature as well as other microclimatic factors to maintain quality and therefore value. Such specialized storage costs vary but can be between £10 and £20 per case per year.
>
> This type of professional storage often includes insurance cover for assets; however, it is important to understand the level of cover offered to ensure that your asset is insured for its full replacement value in all eventualities, as well as ensuring insurance premiums are paid and cover is valid.

Regulation

Unlike bank deposits which are covered by the Financial Services Compensation Scheme or investments designed for retail investors such as UCITS regulated by the EU, there is no regulation of alternative assets in the main, unless they are in a form, such as exchange-traded funds, where the investment method itself is regulated.

Even where there is some form of regulation in the investment method and it is considered suitable for the retail market, as an investment manager you need to be aware of any potential mismatch between the asset in the fund and the structure of the fund. Following the Brexit vote in 2016 the

UK saw several property funds with investments in commercial offices etc close their doors to investors wishing to cash in funds. This is because it was not possible for them to liquidate their assets at the speed required without leading to a fall in value.

Fraud and forgery

> **Keyword**
>
> **Provenance** is the ability to provide the buyer with information about the origins of an asset and therefore prove it is genuine.

In addition to providing specific storage conditions to maintain the quality of your asset, it is essential to establish the provenance of your asset and a third-party storage provider can be useful in achieving this.

> **In practice**
>
> For wine, the best way to secure provenance is for it to be purchased in unmixed sealed cases using original wooden cases and for the wine to be stored in bonded warehouses. These warehouses, such as London City Bond, not only control the wine physically to ensure it is not contaminated or altered but also ensure investors are not liable for taxes such as VAT or excise duty whilst the wine is held. This is done by regular inspections by HM Customs and Revenue, restricted access and a guarantee being given that the wine will not leave the warehouse.

Some markets are notorious for forgery and fakes and the art market is one of those. There are a number of stories about fakes which have been sold for large sums of money as genuine.

One prolific recent faker was Wolfgang Beltracchi who served half of a six-year prison sentence for pleading guilty to faking 14 works of art by a number of modern artists such as Max Ernst, Fernand Léger and Kees van Dongen, which sold in total for approximately $45 million.

Without provenance, it is unlikely an investor will be able to sell their investments for an amount near to their fair value or even potentially sell them at all.

Collectibles and chattels

> **Keyword**
>
> Collectibles or **chattels** are legally defined as tangible, moveable things:
>
> - tangible means it has a physical existence – ie you can physically kick it as opposed to some investments which are intangible, ie they don't have a physical presence (eg a financial derivative);
> - moveable means they are not fixed to the land they occupy and can be moved.

In addition to the better-known items such as antiques, art and fine wines, there are other less well-known areas for investment including commodities, gold, crowdfunding, property, collective funds and structured products, which we will examine in the following sections.

Collectibles and chattels can include jewellery, books, art, classic cars, posters, coins, racehorses, toys, memorabilia, fine wines, antiques and precious metals, to name a few. Due to the nature of some of the above assets, for example books, they are known as wasting assets, where their value reduces over time due to deterioration in the condition of the asset. Where an asset qualifies as a wasting asset it will have no capital gains tax liability.

Such assets can provide a means of portfolio diversification and for some types of investor have the additional benefit of providing the pleasure of collecting or displaying the asset, for example where art or antiques are displayed in the investor's home. Even institutional investors are starting to allocate small amounts (up to 10 per cent of portfolios) to alternative investments due to their low correlation to standard investments which can be useful where investors are facing volatile markets.

Collectibles are available at all price entry points and as such can be used by all levels of investors. It is possible that there may be a high increase in the level of value in a collection over time but this is never certain and indeed there may be a decrease in value due to differing tastes. In addition, there are also potentially higher risks attributable to this type of investing, not least due to the lack of regulation in some areas.

Commodities

> **Keyword**
>
> **Commodities** are resources or products which have a connection to the earth either by being extracted or mined (hard commodities) or grown (soft commodities). There are three main types of commodity:
>
> - energy – eg shale gas;
> - metals – which fall into two categories: base metals (eg copper) and precious metals (eg platinum and gold);
> - agriculture – which has three main categories grains (eg barley), 'softs' (eg sugar) and livestock (eg pigs).

Commodity indices

The Commodity Futures Trading Commission estimated the total commodities market at a value of over $230 billion in 2015. As such, the performance of this market is important and there are several commodity indices, with different characteristics available to measure returns.

Bloomberg Commodity Index (BCOM)

This index relies on a commodity's relative trading volumes which in conjunction with dollar-adjusted worldwide production data is averaged over a year to determine the weights attributable to each component. There is a minimum weight of 2 per cent and a maximum of 33 per cent. The index is rebalanced annually.

The Rogers International Commodity Index (RICI)

This is a composite index made up of the total return of 38 commodities from 18 international exchanges. Calculations are made in real time and settlement values are published daily. Where commodities are traded on more than one exchange, the most liquid contract is included in calculations.

Commodities are split into three categories, agriculture, energy and metals with individual commodities included if they play a significant role in global consumption as measured by imports and exports.

Thomson Reuters/Jeffries CRB Index

This is an equally weighted arithmetic average of 19 commodity categories including orange juice and oil.

S&P GSCI

This index weights the commodities in its index based on a five-year moving average of world production values which are rebalanced annually.

Commodities as a hedge against inflation and risk events

> **Keyword**
>
> **Hedging** is method of minimizing or offsetting the risk of losses from volatility in investment prices. Hedging transfers risk from the investor without using insurance. It is possible to use several different methods to achieve a hedge; however, overall it amounts to making an investment in one market and taking an opposite investment position in another market, ie believing one market will rise and the other fall. Hedging can also protect capital against inflation by using assets such as property and financial instruments.

Commodities are priced in US dollars and have an inverse correlation with the value of the dollar. This may also be the case in the relationship between equities and commodities, where commodities can potentially react differently to unexpected economic events; for example, war can lead to a shortage of oil which in turn can lead to price inflation. This is contrary to the potential effects on the stock market which can show falls due to increased levels of uncertainty. As such, commodities can protect again unexpected inflation. Due to this negative correlation, they may also be useful as a diversification method for equity investors.

There is also a positive correlation between some commodities and inflation; for example, a fall in oil prices leads to higher disposable income for consumers which in turn fuels consumer spending due to the deflationary pressure on prices, whilst a rise in commodity prices will lead to a corresponding rise in transport, industrial and energy costs and inflation.

For clients with lower risk appetites a UK-listed collective with interests in natural resources or commodities may give the widest diversification and exposure to the sector with the least risk.

How are commodities traded?

Commodities can be traded in both physical and synthetic form, with the latter based on commodities indices. For synthetic investments, the fund does not own physical commodities; rather they are looking to 'bet' on price movements over time. There are several types of synthetic commodity investments and we will look to analyse these below using gold as an example investment.

In addition to trading in commodities directly there is also the potential to trade in companies who extract commodities; for example, mining companies or agricultural producers. This is, however, equity investing and should be assessed as such, rather than being assessed as commodity investing.

Gold

This can be a volatile investment with prices at 14 April 2017 of £1,285.90/oz compared to a low over the last 10 years of $640.25/oz and a high of $1,889.70/oz. This price change has included some dramatic falls such as the 25 per cent fall in 2013, although as Adrian Ash comments below, volatility in the other markets and the world in general has led to a price resurgence since its low of 2000:

> It is up 465 per cent in that time, against a 164 per cent rise in house prices, 96 per cent total return from the FTSE, and 55 per cent on cash. It has also performed over the past 12 months, rising 45 per cent against just 0.4 per cent on cash.
>
> **SOURCE** Adrian Ash, Head of Research at gold broker BullionVault.com

As we mentioned above, there are several different direct and indirect investment methods for commodities, which we will examine using gold as an example investment.

Direct investment

Bullion

Bullion is the term for investment-grade gold coins and ingots. These can be purchased in a range of weights from 1/10th oz to 1 kg, although the most common weight is 1 oz. The value of bullion follows the gold spot price plus a small premium. Investors value the divisibility of holding smaller coins or ingots which can aid liquidity. Some 1 oz coins are so well known they have their own names, including krugerrands from South Africa, Britannias from the UK and Eagles from the USA. Such coins are popular with investors who keep them amongst personal possessions or may store them at a third-party depository for safe keeping.

Depositories, as opposed to bank safety deposit boxes, which may also be used, are often offered by bullion brokers. As well as providing depository services, these brokers can also act as buyers and sellers for individual investors. Due to the value of the investment it is imperative that the history of the depository provider is known including details of their net worth and credit rating, ensuring legal title to the gold remains with the investor following deposit, and appropriate and regular independent audits are carried out. That said, there are always potential security issues as the depositors at the Hatton Garden Depository found out when it was robbed and over £25 million of gold and other jewels stolen in London in 2015.

While bullion is rated as investment grade it also has the advantage for investors of not having a liability to stamp duty as equities do and currently being VAT exempt due to the EU gold Directive of 2000, both of which will reduce transaction costs.

Jewellery and coins

As well as modern coins there is also the potential to hold numismatic or older and rare coins. Such coins have both the precious metal content as well as an aesthetic appeal. The UK Gold Sovereign is one of the most widely traded and owned semi-numismatic gold coins which also has the added advantage of being exempt from capital gains tax. As mentioned previously, the USA has the Eagle (a $10 gold coin) and the Double Eagle ($20), both of which can vary in price not only due to the gold content but also due to the design included on the coin.

On the whole, such coins will usually rise in value more quickly than the spot gold price in a bull market but decrease more rapidly in value in a bear market.

Gold certificates

The Perth Mint Certificate, which is backed by the Australian government, allows investors to buy investment-grade gold which is held in the vaults of the Australian mint in Perth and insured by Lloyds of London.

The certificate is evidence of ownership of an unallocated account: an investor is the legal owner of gold although not of any specific physical gold. Rather, the investor owns a promise from the certificate provider (the custodian) to give them gold on request. The security of such schemes is dependent on the quality of the custodian, which in the case of the Perth scheme is relatively safe as the backers are the Australian government. Holding gold in this way over a long period can be cost efficient as an investor will not incur shipping, investment or holding fees and there is the flexibility of transferring to an allocated account (physical gold holding) for a small fee should the investor wish to do this.

Exchange-traded fund

> **Keyword**
>
> **Exchange-traded funds** usually track the price of a single commodity or a group of commodities measured as an index. Price tracking is achieved by tracking futures contracts or the physical asset itself.

There are two types of ETF: funds that hold physical gold; and funds which track the price of gold. Two popular funds which can be purchased through stockbrokers are SPDR Gold Trust (NYSEARCA:GLD) and London ETF Securities' Gold Bullion Securities (LSE GBS).

Funds which hold physical gold are inherently safer than those which track the price of gold as there is always a capital value to fall back on in times of falling prices. The funds also provide a way for a relatively small investment to be made in gold in a cost-effective manner with administration fees of between 0.4 and 0.5 per cent annually.

Indirect investment

Secondary equity investing

Instead of investing in gold directly investors could consider investment in companies who mine gold and other precious metals or companies who supply into the mining industry. It is important to remember that whilst price movements in investments in such companies may not be as volatile as the commodity itself, they may not represent the commodity accurately as their operations may be more diversified. This can be a good or a bad thing and as with all equity investment it is prudent to diversify holdings through several metals, geographical locations and companies, as such investment is far riskier than investing in the final product. It should also be remembered that share prices can be affected by factors other than the price of the underlying asset; however, due to the liquidity of shares this may be a suitable method for some retail investors.

Derivative investments

It is also possible to use derivatives to invest in gold including options, futures and spread betting. Whilst such methods of investment can increase your potential returns through leverage, such investment policies are inherently risky and can lead to a total loss of capital and potentially unlimited losses in some cases, and as such should only be used by the most experienced of investors.

Crowdfunding

This is a relatively new phenomenon which some commentators believe was first seen in 1997 with the band Marillion, funding a USA tour by raising $60,000 indirectly on social media. Social media has made this direct relationship between investors and entrepreneurs possible leading to growth and diversification in the finance market. The ease of fund transmission via funding platforms and low production costs for information whilst reaching large numbers of potential investors has moved investment from large sums being invested by a small number of people to small sums being invested by large numbers of people. Certain industries are using crowdfunding regularly including music bands, films and computer game makers who may reward investors with non-financial incentives such as advance copies of computer games as well as a financial return. The funding platform obtains its income as a percentage of the funds raised.

In practice

Over $20 million was raised by a company using the crowdfunding site Kickstarter to finance an alternative to the Apple Watch. The finance was raised by approximately 80,000 people giving an average investment of $250.

Within the general heading of crowdfunding there are three main types of investment: donor, debt and equity.

Donor/reward crowdfunding

Here funders have a personal or social motive for investing in a cause. Returns may not be directly financial or potentially even tangible but encourage a feeling of 'giving back' or helping. Physical rewards may include free gifts, regular news updates or acknowledgement on an album for example.

Examples of sites in the UK include www.crowdfunder.co.uk and www.pleasefundushubbub.net.

Debt crowdfunding/peer-to-peer (P2P) lending

This is a more traditional method of financing, using new technology to reach a new investor base. Here investors receive an interest return as well as their original capital at the end of the lending period. The main difference relates to the use of a social media platform to bring borrowers and investors together, bypassing traditional banks. There is also the potential for a social element to investment through microfinance. Microfinance is the lending of small sums of money, often in developing countries to the poorest people allowing micro-businesses to be started. This type of lending charges no interest to the borrower, so for clients it will not be a source of income generation but will provide a charitable or ethical element to a portfolio. Sites include www.buzzbnk.org and www.trillionfund.com.

Equity crowdfunding

As with traditional equity funding, investment in a business using equity crowdfunding leads to ownership of a small part of an organization. If successful, the investment will grow in value. From the entrepreneur's point of view this can be a way to raise capital without giving up control to private equity or venture capitalists.

Example sites include www.seedrs.com and www.crowdcube.com.

Regulation of crowdfunding

The FCA controls regulation of this in the UK; however, as a developing investment area not all countries have the same level of investor protection. This, coupled with the ease of access to foreign markets, makes such investments potentially high risk. Information is available in respect of the regulatory regimes for specific countries via the International Organization of Securities Commissions which, in 2014, published a paper looking at comparative regulatory provisions in different countries. Research and other initiatives are also being carried out by the European Banking Authority and the European Securities and Markets Authority and it is likely that additional regulation will be put in place as the market develops.

Property

There are many types of property investments which can be undertaken. These can include direct and indirect investment in both residential and commercial property and it is important to understand what is being purchased as well as the returns and responsibilities of owning such assets and the tax implications.

Types of property

Property assets in the UK fall into two main categories: 1) residential including buy-to-let houses, second homes and holiday homes; 2) commercial including retail (shopping centres, department stores), offices and industrial (factories, warehouses).

Each category has its own characteristics (see Table 10.1).

Ownership

Historically in England and Wales there have been two main types of interest in land:

Table 10.1 Characteristics of property assets

Characteristic	Residential	Commercial
Direct investment	Yes	Size usually means limited to property company and institutional investors
Length of tenancy	Typically short and renewable	Long-term, often over 10 years
Responsibility for repairs	Landlord	Usually tenant
Return generated by	Largely house price increases	Largely income from rental

- Freehold: this is the ultimate form of ownership and lasts indefinitely. Freeholders have the right to create a lease out of their freehold. This means that for a fee a third party (the lessee) has the right to use the land for a set period of time. At the end of the lease the lessee (the person granted the lease) is no longer entitled to use the land. The freeholder retains the ownership of the land whoever is using it.

- Leasehold: here a lessee or tenant can use the property for a set period in return for payment of a fee (ground rent). There is currently controversy as some house developers are selling new homes under the leasehold system. Buyers are not fully aware that such an arrangement makes them liable for ground rents in coming years, with some ground rents doubling and trebling over a period and affecting the value of the house when owners come to sell, due to the additional costs of owning such a home.

It may be possible, if the terms of the lease agreement allow, for the lessee to create their own lease, called a sublease. This will be granted to a third party for a fee over a specified period of time which does not exceed the period of the original lease. Such arrangements are more commonly associated with commercial properties rather than retail properties.

In practice

Helen owns a factory freehold. She leases the factory for a period of 20 years to George for a sum of £40,000 per year. George realizes he does not need to use all the factory so, after reviewing the terms of his lease agreement with Helen, he leases 20 per cent of it to Sarah for a period of 15 years at a rent of £10,000 per year.

In this case Helen is the freeholder and is also the lessor; that is, she grants George a lease. George is a lessee or the person taking the lease. George however is also a lessor as he has granted a sublease to Sarah. The terms of the sublease should be carefully drafted, so that Sarah ceases to be a tenant before George finishes the original lease as this may lead to problems for George when he comes to vacate the property.

Commonhold

Prior to the Commonhold and Leasehold Reform Act 2002 the only two types of property ownership were freehold and leasehold. However, problems had been noted in multioccupancy buildings for instance where there were flats and/or shops as well as common areas in one building. The new commonhold arrangement brought into force splits the ownership of the whole building into two different types depending which part of the building it relates to: individual flats/shops are held as freehold properties with the owners called unit holders; common areas, such as stairs and foyers, are owned and managed by a Commonhold Association.

The membership of the Commonhold Association is limited to the unit holders, who therefore have two types of interest in the building, as freeholders over their individual unit and as commonhold members over the common areas. The Commonhold Association is a limited company which manages the common parts of the building. Their rights and obligations are set out in a commonhold community statement, including dispute resolution procedures, which is registered at Companies House along with the company memorandum and articles.

The most important benefits of commonhold are:

- there is no depreciation in ownership value unlike a lease which decreases rapidly in value over the final few years of its existence;
- the Commonhold Association and unit holders manage the building, negating the need for a landlord;
- standardized paperwork allows easier recognition of rights and obligations reducing the potential for disputes.

Returns from property

Rent

Both commercial and residential property produce rental income from the tenant. However, the cycles of commercial property and residential property tend to move independently as the latter is affected by interest rates and disposable income whilst the former is affected by the economic cycle.

Rental income will depend on several factors such as:

- the quality of the property;
- general levels of supply and demand in the market;
- the agreed terms of the tenancy, especially in the case of commercial agreements which usually cover far longer periods than residential tenancies.

Because of the length of tenure for commercial property is it usual for rent reviews and break clauses to be included in commercial leases:

Investment classes: Alternative investments

- A rent review is a set period of time after which rents are renegotiated between the lessee and the lessor. The terms of negotiation should be included in the lease itself including when the rent review will take place and if, for instance, it is an upward-only review, that is, the rent can only stay the same or rise following negotiations rather than being able to reduce.

- A 'break clause' allows either one or both parties at set times to terminate the lease with an appropriate notice period. Again, the terms of such a clause will be included in the lease itself. This allows certainty for both parties as breaks can only be implemented at certain times during the lease but will allow some flexibility as both parties may leave the lease, depending on the terms, before the end of the lease period, which may be up to 20 years.

The return from rent is measured using the yield calculation:

$$\text{rental yield \%} = \frac{\text{gross rent} - \text{expenses}}{\text{cost or property, including purchase costs}}$$

Expenses can potentially include management fees, buildings and contents insurance and renewal of furnishings.

Purchase costs can potentially include costs of surveys and valuation, legal fees, and Stamp Duty Land Tax. In most cases the seller of a building will pay the estate agent's fees, although if a search agent is used by the purchaser then this cost can be included.

In practice

Sonia purchased a house which she has rented out to Colin over the last year for a rent of £10,000. Sonia pays the following expenses:

- Middleman Ltd estate agents: 10 per cent of gross rental income to manage the property;
- buildings insurance of £450.

Colin pays £200 for contents insurance as Sarah lets the property unfurnished.

Sonia paid £325,000 for the house financed by a deposit of £125,000 and a mortgage of £200,000 at 3 per cent over 25 years. When she purchased the house she paid £3,000 for surveys and valuations and £700 for legal fees.

> To work out Sonia's yield:
>
> $$\text{rental yield \%} = \frac{10{,}000 - (1{,}000 + 450)}{(325{,}000 + 3{,}000 + 700)} = \frac{8{,}550}{328{,}700} = 2.60\%$$
>
> Notice that the rental yield does not include the cost of finance; rather the yield is a way to compare the return being generated by the capital asset with the cost of financing the asset. In this case the asset is returning 2.6 per cent based on rent compared to the 3 per cent it is costing Sonia for finance. However, this does not take account of any capital growth in the property value.

Two major factors affecting the level of rental return generated are:

- *Tenant quality*: this relates to rent defaults (as processes to obtain payment of arrears or evict tenants are both costly and time-consuming), as well as tenants not leaving the property in good order or damaging the property. Such matters can eat into rental yield due to the costs of replacement fittings and repairs at the end of a tenancy, where it is not possible to recover the costs from the tenant.

- *Occupancy levels*: where the property is without a tenant, this is called a void period and will affect rental yield. Whilst 100 per cent occupancy is desirable it may not always be possible and as such investors should consider including a percentage of void periods into their assessment of any potential property purchase.

Rental yield will fluctuate depending on the current circumstances of the lease. Therefore, for investment assessment it can be helpful to calculate rental yield for specific periods of time and for the whole period of ownership to allow more valid comparison to other investments.

Capital

Movements in capital values of property depend on their type and their reaction to different factors. For instance, commercial property may be more affected by exchange rate movements as these can influence the number of overseas institutional investors coming into the property market which disproportionately affects the commercial sector due to the large capital values required to purchase office blocks and warehouses etc.

Investment classes: Alternative investments

Domestic and international institutional investors will also be assessing property returns compared to other asset classes such as bonds and therefore movements in these markets can affect capital values.

Interest rate movements will affect all property types with the value being affected because of servicing costs, with higher interest rates usually leading to a reduction in value and lower rates to an increase in value.

In addition, to maintain a property's value and stop it depreciating, property repairs will be required. If repairs are not carried out the worst-case scenario will be that the land will be the only value realizable as the property will be beyond repair.

There are a number of ways to estimate the capital value of a property, outlined below.

Gross rent multiplier Here the income and market price of similar recently sold properties are used to calculate a gross rent multiplier figure. This multiplier can then be used in conjunction with the rental value of a client property to estimate a potential market price.

In practice

George owns a buy-to-let house, 12 Acacia Gardens, which generates rent of £12,000 a year. He is looking to sell the house but is unsure what the potential selling price should be. No 22 Acacia Gardens was recently sold for £188,000 having previously been rented for a gross rent of £11,000 per year.

The gross rent multiplier for 22 Acacia Gardens can be calculated as 188,000/11,000 = 17.09.

George can now use this multiplier to calculate an estimated market price for his house of £205,090 (£12,000 gross rent × 17.09 multiplier).

This is a very crude measure, however, as it takes no account of the relative size of the properties, the level of rents comparatively between the properties or the maintenance of the properties, all of which would also affect the sales value.

Capitalization rate

$$\text{capitalization rate \%} = \frac{\text{net operating income}}{\text{salesprice/valueof property}}$$

The capitalization rate should provide a more realistic valuation as its calculation includes not only the selling price but also takes account of expenses and voids. As the seller is trying to obtain the highest price for a property he or she will look to minimize the capitalization rate whilst a buyer will look to try to maximize it. Overall if net operating incomes and capitalization rates are decreasing then the value of properties will be increasing and vice versa.

Capitalization rates will also be affected by the risks associated with the property including how desirable the location is, levels of crime and general condition of an area.

Revisionary value of leases

Keyword

Revisionary value is the value of a building based on its expected value at the end of the lease.

In general, leases decrease in value over time. A long-term lease, say with more than 50 years left to run, is worth more proportionally on the open market than a short-term one.

In some cases, the leaseholder may have the right to negotiate an extension to the length of the lease and this may increase the value of the lease; however, a payment for extension would be due to the freeholder with the amount depending on the location and type of property. Any increase in value from a lease extension can be assessed by an independent surveyor based on other properties in the area.

Buying and selling a property

Buyers and sellers of properties have different responsibilities and will incur different costs; however, whether buying or selling, both parties will incur costs and will also rely on professionals such as estate agents or solicitors during the process.

Transaction costs: sellers

Property sellers will pay for:

- Their own legal fees payable to the solicitor or conveyancer who draws up their legal documentation. Fees can vary, and there has been a move to online platforms to reduce costs.
- Estate agent fees for the marketing of a property. These are usually between 1 per cent and 2 per cent of the selling price but often include a guaranteed minimum amount. Again, sellers are looking to the internet to reduce costs.

Transaction costs: buyers

Property buyers will pay for:

- The cost of the house. This may be the total cost of the house or a deposit provided by the buyer to qualify for a mortgage.
- Survey or valuation fees. A survey or valuation will usually be requested by a mortgage lender where they are financing a purchase. This is usually the most basic form of survey which does not look closely at the condition of a house. Other more in-depth surveys can be carried out at an additional cost. Costs of surveys carried out by a finance provider may be included within the overall mortgage costs.
- Legal fees.
- Mortgage arrangement fees where finance is used for part of the purchase. Such fees will vary between lenders.
- Stamp Duty Land Tax which is only payable by the buyers of a house.

Stamp Duty Land Tax (SDLT)

Sellers in England will usually be liable for Stamp Duty Land Tax (SDLT) which is payable on the purchase of properties over a specified value. Sellers in Scotland pay a land and buildings transaction tax instead.

SDLT rates depend on: the property type being purchased, whether it is residential or non-residential; if the property is purchased as leasehold or freehold or even potentially exempt.

For the year to 5 April 2018 the freehold rates of SDLT are currently:

Table 10.2 SDLT rates for year to April 2018

Freehold	SDLT Rate
Up to £125,000	Nil
£125,001 to 250,000	2%
£250,001 to £925,000	5%
£925,001 to £1.5m	10%
Amounts above £1.5m	12%
Over £500,000 purchased by corporate bodies	15%

Leasehold premiums

New residential leasehold property uses the same scale of SDLT as freehold property, calculating SDLT on the lease premium, or purchase price of the lease. If the total rent over the lease's life, which is known as the net present value, is over £125,000, 1 per cent SDLT will be payable on the amount over £125,000 unless the lease is an existing lease which is being assigned (sold) to the new buyer.

Second-home owners

Since 1 April 2016 individuals have also had to pay an additional 3 per cent on top of normal SDLT rates if they buy a new residential property when they already own one. This additional amount will not be payable if they are replacing their existing main residence which has already been sold and may be reclaimable if they sell the original property within 36 months.

In practice

Alistair has agreed the sale of his current home, Monk Farm, for £2 million to Mr and Mrs Smith. Alistair is purchasing Simble House for £2.5 million. The Smiths are due to complete the purchase of Alistair's house on 25 May, the same day Alistair is due to complete the purchase on Simble House.

Due to problems discovered during the survey of Monk Farm it is not possible for Mr and Mrs Smith to buy Alistair's house on 25 May. Alistair obtains a bridging loan from the bank to allow him to purchase Simble House and Mr and Mrs Smith eventually buy Monk Farm on 30 September.

Table 10.3 sets out Alistair's SDLT payments:

Table 10.3 Example: SDLT payable

Purchase price	SDLT Rate	Amount/£	£
Up to £125,000	Nil	£125,000	Nil
£125,001 to 250,000	2%	£125,000	2,500
£250,001 to £925,000	5%	£725,000	36,250
£925,001 to £1.5m	10%	£575,000	57,500
Amounts above £1.5m	12%	£950,000	114,000
Premium for two houses	3%	£2,500,000	75,000
Total payable			**£285,250**

Whilst it may not have been possible to do this, had Alistair been able to delay purchasing Simble House until Monk Farm had been sold this would have saved him £75,000 as he would only have owned one house. Alistair may be able to reclaim the 3 per cent premium amount as the Smiths have purchased his house within 36 months of buying Simble House.

Conveyancing

Keyword

Conveyancing is the process of legally transferring land ownership from one party to another. The buyer and the seller will each have their own conveyancer or solicitor who will act on their behalf during the buying/selling process. A conveyancer's actions will depend on whether they are working for the buyer or the seller of the property.

The seller's conveyancer/solicitor will:

- Request a copy of the Land Registry entry for the property. Historically a review of title deeds would have been carried out; however, most properties are now registered with the Land Registry and have been allotted a title number and plan, making deeds of title irrelevant. However, where a house has not been sold for a long time (over approximately 25 years depending on area) then it is possible it may not have been registered with the Land Registry. Where this is the case the seller's solicitor will have to register the property prior to the sale.

- Prepare the contract. Once the title plan has been received the solicitors will prepare the sales contract including details of the sale price and any information on the property the buyer needs to be aware of. Such information can cover many aspects but may include, for instance, the maintenance of boundaries or a requirement that no caravans can be left on a driveway.

The buyer's solicitor will:

- Apply for searches: this entails requesting written confirmation from specific bodies to assess any potential problems with the property. For instance, the conveyance may request searches from UK Coal to assess if the property may be liable to mining subsidence. Other searches may include those with the local authority, for details of any future building in the area, drainage and flooding etc.
- Assess the contract for sale: this is to ensure all the details within the contract are correct and as expected and there is nothing which will adversely affect their client's legal position.
- Raise queries: if the conveyancer does find areas in the contract they are unhappy with they will raise a query with the seller's conveyancer who will then have to resolve them.

Once the contract has been agreed between the solicitors and all searches have been returned contracts will be exchanged. It is at this point that the buyer and seller become legally obligated to complete the sale. Prior to this point either party can pull out and the only costs they will incur are their own legal and estate agent's costs already due. Following exchange if one party withdraws the other may sue for breach of contract and damages.

Exchange of contracts normally includes agreement on a date for completion. It is at completion that the purchase price is paid for the property in exchange for the keys and the legal transfer of ownership is finalized.

Taxation of property income

Residential property

In most cases, owners will be considered to be running a business where a whole residential building is let and as such will be required to inform HMRC of the income received which will be taxed under income tax rules.

Tax will be due on the total rental income less allowable expenses. Further details of tax calculations and changes to allowable financial expenses can be found in Chapter 13. Holiday lettings are taxed on a separate basis.

Where individuals rent out rooms in their homes they can earn up to £7,500 per year, tax free.

Commercial property

Commercial property rental is taxed in the same way as other rental income and in addition to allowable deductions for general repairs the investor will also be allowed to claim capital allowances based on the value of the building. Capital allowances are the HMRC equivalent of depreciation (which is not tax deductible) and are used to reflect the decreasing value of a building over time. Presently capital allowances are calculated on a straight-line basis over a 25-year life.

> **Keyword**
>
> **Straight-line capital allowances**: the cost of the building is divided by 25 and an equal amount is allowed against profits over the life of the building. If a building is sold then the value of the building for tax is compared to the sale value and a balancing allowance or charge is made in the tax computation for the year. This is a specialized area of taxation and such calculations should be made by a qualified, experienced practitioner.

Capital gains tax

Capital gains tax is chargeable on disposal of land and buildings for both companies and individuals unless the building is a UK-domiciled individual's nominated main or principal private residence. Disposal for individuals can include both selling and gifting of the asset unless the disposal is between spouses made on death at which point the disposal is exempt.

Individuals pay capital gains based on their individual income after an annual exemption of £11,500 (2017/18) at a rate of 10 or 20 per cent.

Indirect property investment

For some investors, the time required to manage a property directly on a day-to-day basis may not suit them. Alternatively, they may have insufficient funds available to buy a whole property or invest directly in property in a way which allows sufficient diversification and risk reduction. There are several methods of indirect property investment which may overcome these two concerns. Table 10.4 sets out the advantages and disadvantages of the principal methods.

Property company shares

There are several different types of property companies:

- new house/commercial property builders;
- property developers looking to renovate existing undervalued properties;
- letting companies who manage let properties.

Limited liability partnerships

As opposed to using a company or trust vehicle as the legal basis for property investment a limited partnership may be used instead. Such a structure is mostly used for direct property investment and its use is usually restricted to sophisticated high net worth investors. Such schemes are reviewed carefully by HMRC.

> **Keyword**
>
> **Limited liability partnership**: this is a partnership which is incorporated and where all the partners, unlike a traditional partnership, have limited liabilities. Limited liability means individual partners are not responsible for another partner's misconduct, negligence or partnership debts, which is the case in a traditional partnership.

Collective funds

Unit trusts

Historically unit trusts have not been able to invest directly into commercial property or property company shares, but this is not the case now. Today unit trusts can be specialized and deal with areas such as urban regeneration or may be more general in their investments.

Investment classes: Alternative investments

In respect of direct commercial property investment certain rules in respect of property quality must be adhered to:

- no more than 15 per cent of the value of fund assets can be invested in one property;
- limits are placed on the level of gearing the trust can undertake;
- limits are placed on the number of properties allowed within the unit trust with leases of less than 60 years or which are unoccupied.

As with all types of property investment there are advantages and disadvantages (Table 10.4).

Property authorised investment fund (PAIF)

Keyword

A **PAIF** is a regulated open-ended investment fund which provides an alternative means to UK REITs of investing in professionally managed property portfolios.

Prior to the introduction of PAIFs other regulated property funds were taxed within the fund itself, meaning tax-exempt investors (including charities, ISA investors and pension funds as well as individuals) found such funds inefficient as they were unable to reclaim tax paid. PAIFs overcame this by transferring the tax liability, mostly, to the individual investor.

For a fund to qualify as a PAIF it must fulfil the following conditions:

- no corporate investor can hold more than 10 per cent of the NAV of the fund and shares should be widely held;
- at least 60 per cent of the total value of PAIF assets must be in property investment;
- at least 60 per cent of net income must be from the property investment business.

The advantages and disadvantages of using PAIFs are presented in Table 10.4.

Real estate investment trust (REIT)

> **Keyword**
>
> **REITs** are indirect methods of property investment which emphasize tax-efficient investing and diversification. They are relatively new, originating in the USA and being introduced to the UK in 2007.

Benchmarks are available for REITs. The most common UK one is the FTSE EPRA/NAREIT UK index whilst worldwide indices include the FTSE Russell. It is also possible to invest based on the movements of these indices via ETFs and active funds.

A fund must meet the following conditions to qualify as a REIT:

- The REIT must:
  - be an individual company;
  - have a minimum of 100 shares;
  - have shares which are fully transferable;
  - have shares listed on a recognized stock exchange;
  - be a UK-resident company for taxation;
  - be owned by at least five shareholders (so it is not defined as a closed company) with no single shareholder owning more than 10 per cent of share capital or voting rights.
- At least 90 per cent of taxable income must be paid as dividends.
- In respect of the company's investments:
  - at least 75 per cent of investments must be in property which can be residential or commercial and situated in the UK or abroad;
  - at least 75 per cent of the REIT's income must come from rents with the remaining income from other sources in line with the business of a REIT;
  - no individual property can represent more than 40 per cent of the total value of invested properties;
  - the REIT must have at least three properties representing 75 per cent of the company's asset value.
- The ratio of interest paid on borrowing to rental income should be less than 1.25:1.00

Offshore property funds

Property funds can be established in several offshore jurisdictions; for example, Isle of Man, Jersey, Cayman Islands.

Investment trusts

These are closed-ended vehicles which trade their shares on the LSE and invest in the shares and securities of property companies but not directly in property.

Fund of funds

Investment in a fund of funds is made up of investments in several different funds related to the property market. As such the fund never owns any shares directly; rather it owns units in other funds.

Life assurance property bonds

> **Keyword**
>
> **Life assurance property bonds** are life insurance policies where the monies paid in are invested in several different types of fund including funds which have an element of property investment. The return on such bonds is dependent on the performance of the underlying investments over the period of the investment.

Most such investments are 'whole of life' meaning there is no minimum term of investment, although investors should be looking to invest for at least five years to produce a good return. Repayment of the bond comes as a lump sum payment either on the death of the investor or if the bond is surrendered.

Some funds may guarantee an investor's capital or return; however, if this is not the case then the value of the fund may reduce as well as increase. The bond includes an amount of life insurance and therefore if an investor dies during the bond's term the payment received may be slightly more than the value of the fund.

Table 10.4 Advantages and disadvantages of alternative property investments

Type of investment	Advantages	Disadvantages
Indirect investment	Liquidity: where such properties are listed this may increase the investments' liquidity as shares can be easily traded on an exchange	Share prices may deviate from the underlying asset value due to movements in supply and demand
	Some property companies may pay dividend income where properties are let	Increasing or high levels of gearing within the company may increase share price volatility
		No dividend income may be payable in some cases where development is the primary company objective with shareholder wealth increasing through capital gains
Unit trusts	Due to the different types of unit trust and underlying assets, individual investors' needs may be better suited and diversification can be ensured by using eg authorized unit trusts and REITs	Despite the increase in available secondary markets where a unit trust holds a large proportion of investments directly in commercial property, as opposed to company property shares, the unit trusts may find themselves in a position where they cannot liquidate sufficient assets to ensure all investors can sell their positions at a time. In such cases unit trust managers may impose a moratorium on sales for a period which may adversely affect investors cashflow
	The fund has no capital gains tax (CGT) liability although individual investors may be liable for CGT when they sell their units	
	Funds are regulated by the FCA	
	A developing secondary market means increasing liquidity for this investment type	
PAIFs	100% of property taxable income must be distributed, 10% more than a REIT	Dividends are paid net of 10% tax credit which is not reclaimable by non-taxpayers
	No tax is paid within the fund on rental profits and other property-related income; all other income is charged 20% CGT	

	Investors receive property income net of basic rate income tax which can be reclaimed by non-taxpayers as can interest	
	No CGT is payable within the fund, with gains being charged to individual investors when they dispose of their investments	
	Trading does not produce a stamp duty liability and there is no VAT element to management charges	
	An open-ended structure allows steady growth of the fund and removes any correlation with equity investments	
REITs	Can be included in an ISA or Child Trust Fund	In the short term share prices can be volatile and exhibit a correlation with equity
	Tax transparency	Stamp Duty Land Tax is payable at 0.5% when investing in REITs
	Portfolio diversification due to low long-term correlation to other asset classes such as equities	Can be exposed to currency risk depending on where investment properties are located
	Strong corporate governance and low levels of gearing	
	Good liquidity	
	Transaction costs are much lower than direct property investment	

(continued)

Table 10.4 (Continued)

Type of investment	Advantages	Disadvantages
Offshore property funds	Can provide income for investors due to high levels of dividend payments	
	May be tax efficient for specific investors	
	Many jurisdictions have reduced level of regulations which may reduce operating costs or allow greater flexibility in operations, eg such jurisdictions may not require diversification levels to be as high or for assets to be held in certain legal formats	
Investment trusts	High levels of liquidity	The share price will fluctuate based on levels of supply and demand and may trade at a premium or discount to NAV
	Gearing is possible within the investment trust which can increase the risk for the investor	
Fund of funds	Greater levels of diversification possible	Higher management fees due to an extra layer of management
	Access to areas of specialist expertise in the funds	If solely investing in property there is only a limited amount of diversification possible

If an investor requires cash, a withdrawal of up to 5 per cent of the investment value can be made without triggering a tax liability at the withdrawal point. Tax is still payable on the withdrawal but the payment is deferred until the bond is finally cashed in. It should be noted there may be penalties and charges for withdrawing cash and the terms and conditions of the bond should be reviewed carefully to ensure these are understood.

Structured products

Structured products are a means of saving and investment with several general characteristics:

- funds are invested for a fixed period, although the time to maturity depends on the product type;
- returns will be generated from income or capital growth but not both together;
- potential returns and risk levels will be known when monies are first invested;
- returns are linked to an external index eg gold or oil prices, stock prices or equity indices.

There are two main types of structured product:

- Structured deposits: here investments are made within deposit-taking banks and are protected by the FSCS guarantee. At maturity, the product aims to repay the original capital plus a return. The original investment will be deposited in cash; however, the return will be calculated based on the performance of a separate asset (eg the price of gold) between the original investment date and maturity.
- Structured investments: here the investment is in assets, rather than UK deposits, which may include derivatives, commodities, debt issues and foreign currency. Due to the nature of the investments these structured products are not protected by the FSCS guarantee. Such investments, explained in more detail below, can be used for diversification through asset allocation or to 'ride' the market as an alternative to direct investment.

Structured investment can be subdivided into those investments which potentially protect the original capital and those which do not. This protection relies on the counterparty not defaulting and repaying the original investment at maturity, as it is the issuer which retains the legal liability to repay. The financial crisis showed how counterparties can default, with Lehman Brothers for example being unable to meet their obligations following their cessation of trade, leaving supposedly principal protected structured product holders on a par with other bondholders. In some cases, it is possible to have higher credit ratings on the underlying investments than the issuer itself has and clients should bear this in mind when considering risk levels.

This counterparty risk coupled with the potential lack of price transparency due to a wide variety of characteristics making comparison difficult and the complex nature of the products themselves means clients need to be fully informed and understand the risks of any investment undertaken in this area.

Types of structured investment products

Principal protected investments

Here investors' original capital is protected and will be returned. Products generally have a maturity of five to seven years and investors should look to hold the investment until maturity. It possible to link the product to a diverse range of assets such as a broad equity index or group of mixed stocks. The 'trade-off' for having capital protection is forgoing part of the return generated to compensate the issuer for the extra risk inherent in the product.

In practice

Henry invests £10,000 in a principal protected structured product. The product is equity-based and linked to the FTSE 250, has a maturity of five years and an 85 per cent participation in the index appreciation. We will now look at the returns Henry will make, assuming he holds the product to maturity.

If the index rises by 40 per cent over the life of the product

On maturity Henry will receive both his original capital of £10,000 and a return from the rise in the index value. The index has risen by 40 per cent. However, Henry doesn't receive a £4,000 return as he has sacrificed part of his potential gain to protect his principal. As stated above Henry will have an 85 per cent participation in the rise, so he will receive £3,400 (10,000 × 40% × 0.85). The remainder of the rise will be taken as a fee by the issuer.

If the index falls by 40 per cent over the period of the product

As Henry has protected his principal he will not lose any capital and will receive £10,000 on maturity with the issuer bearing the loss.

Buffer zone investments

Buffer zone products tend to have a slightly shorter maturity period than principal protected products, usually between two and four years, and they also provide a potentially higher rate of return. The trade-off for the higher returns is that the investor's original capital is not 100 per cent protected. Instead a lower percentage is protected, but there is a possibility some capital loss may occur.

> ### In practice
>
> Our client, Henry is so pleased with his principal protected product he decides that he would like to invest an additional £5,000 in structured products. However, he now feels more confident and able to bear slightly more risk. Therefore, he invests his £5,000 in a buffered product linked to the NASDAQ 100. The product has a 4-year life and to receive a return of 90 per cent Henry accepts a buffer zone of 25 per cent. Assuming Henry holds the product to maturity we will now calculate his returns in three different scenarios.
>
> **If the index rises by 45 per cent over the product's 4-year life**
>
> Henry will receive back his original capital plus 90 per cent of the rise which is £2,025 (ie the original investment of £5,000 × the 45 per cent rise in value = £2,250 of which Henry receives 90 per cent or £2,025).
>
> **If the index falls by 20 per cent over the product's 4-year life**
>
> Henry's investment is within the 25 per cent buffer zone, and therefore he will receive his original capital on maturity.
>
> **If the index falls by 35 per cent over the product's 4-year life**
>
> This fall is higher than the buffer zone allowance; as such, not all of Henry's capital will be protected. In this case the value of Henry's investment has fallen by £1,750 to £3,250. However, 25 per cent of the fall is protected, so Henry will only suffer a 10 per cent fall ie £500 and will receive £4,500 at maturity of the product.

Return enhanced investments

Here the investor is looking to take advantage of what they believe will be a flat or rising market over a short timescale of one to three years. For accepting 100 per cent of any downside loss they can earn a return which may be double or triple the market rise in an index to a pre-specified maximum amount.

In practice

Henry is confident the equity market in the UK is set to grow and as such decides to invest £10,000 in a return enhanced structured product. The product he chooses has the following characteristics:

- the investment term is two years;
- the investor will receive 1.5 times the increase in the FTSE 100 over the period subject to a maximum return of 25 per cent of the capital invested;
- there is no principal protection so every 1 per cent reduction in the index will lead to a loss of 1 per cent of Henry's original capital.

Assuming Henry holds the products to maturity we will now look at Henry's return in three scenarios.

Where the index has risen by 14 per cent

Henry will receive his original investment of £10,000 plus 1.5 times the rise in the index which will be 21 per cent (14 per cent plus 7 per cent) of his original investment or £2,100. Henry will receive the total rise as it is below the cap of 25 per cent so in total he will receive £12,100 at maturity.

If the FTSE 100 rises by 18 per cent

Potentially Henry could have received his original investment at maturity plus a return of 27 per cent (ie 1.5 times 18 per cent). However as there is a cap in place the maximum Henry can receive is 25 per cent or £2,500. As such, at maturity Henry will receive his original investment and £2,500 ie £12,500 in total.

Where the FTSE 100 falls by 10 per cent

Henry will suffer a reduction in his original investment as there is no capital protection available to him. If the FTSE falls by 10 per cent Henry will lose 10 per cent of his original investment ie £1,000 and will therefore receive £9,000 at maturity.

Summary

There is a myriad of potential alternative investments available to clients. However, they all have their own unique set of risks which need to be fully understood and appreciated. Investment may be done directly or indirectly through a series of funds which are regulated and aimed at retail investors; that said, the underlying investments, despite regulation, may take time to sell and there may be circumstance where investors are unable to liquidate their holdings within what they consider an acceptable timescale. Tax remains an important consideration within these investments as it affects return levels and for some alternative investments it may be difficult to find benchmarks or even assess the returns earned due to the nature of the assets. That said, this is a fascinating area which appears to be becoming more mainstream due to volatility in other markets and investors looking for diversification.

Check your understanding

1. Name three risks associated with holding collectibles.
2. What is the name of a well-known gold bullion coin from the USA?
3. What are the three main categories of commodities?
4. How many commodities make up the Rogers International Commodity Index?
5. Define hedging.
6. What organization insures the Perth Mint Certificate?
7. What can the gross rent multiplier be used to estimate?
8. Which party's solicitor requests searches from organizations such as UK Coal and local authorities in a conveyance?
9. What is the minimum number of shareholders a REIT can have?
10. Which two types of structured product protect an investor's capital to some extent?

Further reading

Other books and articles which provide additional information about alternative assets include:

Lustig, Y (2016) *Saving and Investing for Retirement: The definitive handbook to securing your financial future*, Pearson Education

PWC, *Alternative Asset Management 2020: Fast forward to centre stage*, www.pwc.com/jg/en/publications/alternative-asset-management-2020.pdf

Walker, ST (2014) *Understanding Alternative Investments,* Palgrave Macmillan

Portfolio management

11

The adviser and the client

By the end of this chapter you should have an understanding of the following key areas of the adviser and client relationship including:

- the client relationship;
- the advisory and planning process;
- investment strategies;
- the client review process.

Introduction

For those individuals already active in the financial services industry and for new entrants to the industry, one of the challenges to overcome in order to be successful is the bad reputation that has blighted the industry in a similar way to the banking industry. There have been many well-publicized mis-selling scandals over the last two decades including pension transfers, endowments and now more recently payment protection insurance. With each issue comes an associated fall in the level of public trust afforded to individuals working in the profession and the perception of the financial services industry as a haven for commission-driven salesmen with little conscience may often be a difficult perception to overcome. Those of us who have been active in the financial services industry are painfully aware that historically there have been some individuals in the industry whose professionalism may be called into question; however, this can be said to be the same for all professions. In reality, the majority of people within financial services are hard-working professionals, with good moral character and who are doing their best to provide a reliable and professional service to their valued clients.[1]

Many people within the financial services industry believe that trust is the foundation upon which the relationship with clients is built. Trust is a two-way concept; it must be earned not demanded and may take a long time and much hard work to achieve. In 2013, the Chartered Financial Analyst Institute (CFA), a global association of investment professionals, carried out a survey of investors to assess the importance of trust within the industry. Interestingly, one of the key findings was that trust was the single most important attribute indicated by investors, when asked to consider what factors would influence their decision to engage the services of an industry professional.[2]

Client relationship

There is much about the client relationship which is subject to regulatory requirements, put in place by domestic regulatory bodies for the protection of the client. It is partly this regulatory framework which gives the client the confidence to trust the industry professional to advise them on their aims and objectives, to safeguard their personal information and indeed, their money. It is incumbent upon the industry professional to promote a sound client relationship and to demonstrate to the investor their honesty, integrity, industry experience and to prove themselves worthy of trust. The relationship between the client and the industry professional will focus around three key factors:

- the skills of the adviser;
- the status of the adviser; and
- the information about the client.

Adviser skills

In order to be a successful adviser, an individual must have a broad range of skills and may also be required to run a business if they are not employed by somebody else. The list of skills is not exhaustive but will certainly include:

- professional competence;
- integrity;
- organization;
- interpersonal skills.

An individual in a financial advisory capacity will be required to demonstrate appropriate technical competence, in other words they must have sound knowledge and skills in order to show themselves to be worthy of the client's confidence and trust and provide a professional service. They must also be prepared to call upon the services of other industry professionals if it is sound practice to do so and in the best interests of the client; for example, a tax specialist or a lawyer.

Advisers must demonstrate integrity by acting in the best interests of the client at all times and are also required to safeguard the personal and confidential information that has been entrusted to them by the client. Equally, industry professionals have a requirement to operate within the regulatory guidelines; so, for example, must not advise upon products or services in which they are not qualified.

The financial services industry is a fast-paced and complex industry and to be successful, an individual will need to have good organizational skills to balance the demands of multiple clients, meetings and activities. Records must be meticulously and accurately maintained; paperwork and other important tasks must be dealt with promptly and efficiently. For example, certain transactions may be time-sensitive, such as applications for investment products or disposal of assets.

Interpersonal skills may be honed with experience; however, the adviser must foster an open and trusting relationship with his or her client. This will require appropriate rapport building and the skills to be friendly and approachable whilst remaining professional. It must be recognized that the client will be revealing deeply personal information, which may sometimes be embarrassing and the adviser will need to be understanding and sensitive with their questioning techniques. The adviser must always be truthful and should not be afraid to give bad news as well as good news as it is crucial to be transparent in dealings with clients.

Status of the adviser

The client–agent relationship may be entered into by willing and legally able parties to complete any legal transaction. This may be formally described in a contract; however, whether through a written contract or an implied contract, this creates a fiduciary relationship between the parties involved. Agents have the responsibility for carrying out the client's reasonable instructions and are obligated to display reasonable skill and care in their actions. Agents may not put themselves in a position where that will create a conflict of interest.

It is very important that clients are in no doubt of the legal relationship between them and the adviser. This relationship, the status of the adviser, must be disclosed clearly to the client at the earliest possible opportunity, upon first contact. The importance of this is highlighted by the different legal responsibility to a client, dependent upon adviser status.

> **In practice**
>
> If the adviser is an employee of a product provider or is either tied or multi-tied to one or more product providers, then they are acting as the agent of the provider(s) and not as the agent of the client.
>
> However, if the adviser is not employed by, or tied to any particular product provider – for example, an independent financial adviser (IFA) – then they are acting as the agent of the client for any transactions that they arrange.
>
> In this situation, the adviser is responsible for giving the client the best advice based on a variety of suitable options.

In some cases, the client will be an individual requiring advice or a service from an industry professional and the agent is the professional doing the work or providing the advice. However, it may also be that the client is another body, for example, a charity or a company. It is also possible that the agent may be a company or an institution, such as an insurance company or a bank.

> **In practice**
>
> **An example of a client–agent relationship**
>
> A private investor invests a sum of capital into an exchange-traded fund (ETF). To do this the investor buys shares in the ETF.
>
> The investor is the client and the ETF fund manager becomes the client's agent.
>
> The fund's manager must manage the fund in accordance with the published aims and objectives of the fund. However, the fund will contain the invested capital of many clients and as an agent, the fund manager must manage the fund to the best of his or her ability in order to maximize the returns for the given level of risk.

It is worth noting that institutions may also pursue and forge relationships with clients, for example, retail banks and their customers. This type of institution will look to exploit the positives from their customer relationship and this is often termed 'relationship banking'. With relationship banking, institutions look to cross-sell financial products and services with the aim of improving and cementing their relationship with individual customers and therefore increasing customer loyalty and, ultimately, profitability for the institution. This process will involve making a wide range of financial products and services available to customers, in addition to the basic offerings of current accounts and savings accounts, for example, insurance, credit cards, investments and loans.

Client information

We have identified that an adviser is obligated to act in the best interests of the client and it is therefore logical that the adviser must have a detailed knowledge of the client's circumstances. In fact, in order to perform their duties effectively and to offer appropriate advice, the adviser will be required to formulate a clear, accurate and up-to-date assessment of both the client's current and proposed financial position. Financial advisers will need to obtain a substantial amount of detailed information about their clients encompassing their current financial situation, their aims, objectives and financial aspirations. This will usually include both personal and sensitive information about the client and their family and is the sort of information that a client will only disclose fully and openly if they have trust in the confidentiality and integrity of the adviser.

Keyword

In order to acquire this knowledge, a great deal of information must be gathered from the client in an organized and structured manner and to facilitate this collection of information it is common for advisers to make use of a **standardized data questionnaire**. This will allow the collection and recording of the required, important data and may be done either electronically or as a paper form. The questionnaire acts as a prompt for the adviser to ask the appropriate questions; however, experienced advisers will be able to acquire the information conversationally rather than by rigidly asking questions as they are laid out on the form and this may be less stressful and appear less intrusive to clients.

The process of collecting this crucial information may be done in several ways; for example, in a personal meeting, by telephone or electronically over the internet. The method preferred will depend upon the nature of the relationship and the adviser's model for supplying their services; however, a personal meeting would usually be the preferred approach as this will facilitate the development of a much closer working relationship and therefore develop greater trust between the two parties, which is the ultimate aim.

The information collected will be securely and confidentially retained for an indefinite period and it is good practice to update this information on a regular basis to ensure currency and accuracy of the data. The information will be retained in a client data document, sometimes referred to as a 'fact-find' document and forms the foundation of the client file.

In practice

The type of information will vary between different clients but would typically include the following information as a minimum:

- personal information;
- current income and expenditure;
- anticipated changes to income and expenditure;
- financial products;
- attitude to risk;
- aims and objectives.

Personal information will vary widely dependent upon client circumstances; however, it commonly includes full name and correspondence address, date of birth, nationality and domicile, marital status, details of dependants, occupation and employment status and a certain amount of detail regarding health status. Verification of this data may also be obtained at an early stage for anti-money-laundering purposes.

Current income from all sources will also need to be accurately acquired; for example, income from employment, self-employment, savings, investments and rental income. This will also serve to identify the client's tax status. Expenditure will include all financial liabilities such as rent, mortgages, loan or credit card repayments, local taxes, utility bills and insurance premiums. Expenditure would also include other commitments such as maintenance payments, regular savings and regular household outgoings such as food bills. This process will enable the adviser and client to accurately assess the client's disposable income, which is crucial in the determination of affordability and forms part of the foundation that is the suitability of the advice given.

> ### In practice
>
> It is also important to ask the client to give careful consideration to any anticipated or known future changes in circumstances, which may affect either their income, expenditure or both. This may include such things as changes in employment, house moves, planned events such as holidays, new commitments such as school fees, or anticipated inheritances. Any or all of these events could significantly affect the advice offered to a client and is also particularly relevant to both continued affordability and suitability of the advice.

Financial products would include any existing assets, insurances, accounts, loans or financial instruments that the client currently owns or benefits from; for example, mortgages, loans, credit cards, company shares, bonds or insurance policies. Complete and accurate and up-to-date information regarding all of these existing products is very important and should include specific details such as the terms, expiry dates, cancellation penalties and rates applicable, so that an accurate assessment of their continued suitability may be made.

The accurate assessment of a client's attitude to risk is fundamental to the advice process and its importance cannot be over-emphasized. This is an area in which financial regulators are particularly keen, because incorrectly identifying a client's risk appetite has the potential to cause significant problems for both the client and indeed for the adviser.

Techniques for attitude to risk assessment have varied significantly over the years and are now subject to intense scrutiny by domestic regulators, given the importance of this early step in the advice process. Early methods focused on one-dimensional measures, typically involving simple questions such as 'how risk tolerant are you on a scale of 1 to 10'. However, it is widely accepted that such simple approaches are invariably misleading both for the adviser and the client.[3] Methods involving more sophisticated risk-profiling tools acquired popularity in the early 2000s and these methods often made use of a series of targeted questions for the client to answer, recorded by a scoring system which indicated a typical attitude to risk for the client.[4] More recently, it has been accepted that risk-profiling tools have merit but should only form a part of the assessment process and this process should include not only the client's willingness to accept risk, but also the need and the ability to accept risk. This will allow for a more in-depth and accurate assessment of a client's risk appetite.[5,6]

In practice

These are examples of typical questions which may be included in a risk-profiling tool. The client would be required to give one of the following responses:

Strongly disagree / Disagree / Neither agree or disagree / Agree / Strongly agree

- Compared to the average person, I would say I take more risks.
- I would be willing to risk a percentage of my income in order to get a good return on an investment.
- To achieve high returns, it is necessary to choose high-risk investments.
- I have been extremely cautious in my past financial investments.
- Even if I experienced a substantial loss on an investment, I would not be put off making risky investments.
- I believe that it is reckless to take financial risks.
- When I'm faced with a financial decision I am generally more concerned about the possible losses than the probable gains.
- I would rather know that I was getting a guaranteed rate of return than be uncertain about my investments.
- Compared to the average person, I take lower financial risks.
- I would rather put my money in a bank account than invest in shares.
- I do not feel comfortable with financial uncertainty.
- If my investment portfolio dropped significantly in value during the first three months, it would not bother me.

It is the function of the adviser to help the client to achieve their aims and objectives, if feasible and it is therefore important to ascertain from the client what their aims and objectives are and to assist in prioritizing them. It is necessary to encourage the clients to be realistic, but not to tell the clients what their objectives should be. For example, the client may wish to move to a larger property or to retire at age 50 and it will be the role of the adviser to help the client to achieve this aim, or explain why it is not realistic.

It is clear that trust will be a significant factor for a client when divulging the information we have identified as being crucial to the advisory process and a successful adviser must have the interpersonal skills to engender trust. It may be the case that clients will 'test' the adviser by engaging their services for a small task, before committing their full trust. This is where a well-developed referral process may benefit both adviser and client.

Keyword

Client referral: if an existing client introduces or refers a friend, relative or colleague to their adviser, then there will be an element of trust promoted by the referral process which may serve to speed up the process of trusting.

In this way, close professional relationships may be built effectively and more quickly.

When the adviser has succeeded in building an accurate and detailed picture of the client's current circumstances and has identified and prioritized the client's aims and objectives, the next step in the relationship is to determine appropriate solutions to help the client achieve their requirements. This is where the adviser begins to add value and demonstrates their worth and professionalism, as it is rare that a client will have the resources to address all of their needs immediately. A logical prioritization together with a structured and carefully planned financial strategy is needed, to match resources to requirements. All of this must be explained to the client in a detailed, clear and transparent manner. Detailed and meticulous record keeping are important for the adviser to be able to demonstrate that client affordability has been evidenced and that the suitability of the advice given is proven.

> **In practice**
>
> Domestic regulators will have guidelines for how advisers should conduct themselves in this aspect of the relationship. For example, in the UK the Financial Conduct Authority (FCA) have a handbook called the *Conduct of Business Sourcebook* (COBS), which details the regulatory requirements for financial advisers.[7]

Remuneration of the adviser

Another part of the relationship which is of significance is the level of remuneration for the adviser and the method of remuneration. The issue of remuneration is clearly an important part of the adviser–client relationship because clients must be comfortable with the payments they are making in respect of the advice and services they receive, whilst the adviser requires appropriate remuneration for the time-consuming work they are undertaking.

It is common for the domestic regulator to lay down guidelines to ensure transparency of remuneration so that the client is aware exactly how much the adviser is paid and how this payment is taken. The specifics may vary across different countries. For example, in the UK, as a result of the Retail Distribution Review in 2013, advisers may no longer be paid by commissions from investment providers.[8] Instead, fees must be agreed with clients in advance either in the form of an hourly rate or a one-off fee and paid by the client to the adviser. Regular servicing agreements may also be negotiated but no additional fees may be charged without the prior agreement of the client. This movement away from commission payment was intended to increase transparency and to position advisers on a more professional level. However, an unfortunate consequence of the rule changes is that clients who are unwilling or unable to pay fees to advisers are denied access to independent financial advice.

The advisory and planning process

The advice process is a structured one and each step in the process builds upon the previous step. The adviser, upon meeting the client for the first time, will clearly disclose their status and present the client with their credentials.

The adviser must then build rapport with the client to earn their trust and the process of collecting the crucial client data will follow.

Once the client's current circumstances have been firmly established by the collection of detailed information, it is necessary to accurately establish the client's risk profile, aims and objectives and time horizon. Prioritizing aims and objectives may be necessary since clients may have multiple objectives over a particular timescale and resources may not be sufficient to immediately address all of these at once. It must be noted that it is also prudent to ensure that the client maintains an adequate level of liquidity throughout this process, sometimes known as a 'rainy-day fund', as unforeseen events may necessitate the use of some of their resources in an emergency; for example, if their car breaks down and requires expensive repairs. It may not be convenient or advisable to disinvest from a long-term asset in order to fund an emergency and therefore an emergency cash reserve is almost always advised.

The next step is for the adviser to carry out appropriate research and create a strategy which will offer the best opportunity to fulfil the client's aims and objectives, within the available budget and in accordance with the required time horizon. This may include the utilization of some or all of the client's existing assets, but must take account of any penalties incurred if existing assets or contracts are disposed of. This financial strategy will then be presented to the client together with recommendations for the disposal of any inappropriate assets or contracts and the acquisition of additional assets or products which will be of future use to the client in attaining their objectives. The recommendations will also be given to the client in writing, including details of all costs, charges, fees and anticipated penalties incurred. Any risks and important facts for the client to consider must also be included in these written recommendations, together with any areas where action has been deferred or it has not been possible to address them at all. It must be clearly explained to the client in plain terminology why the recommended actions are appropriate and suitable for the client's needs. This written report detailing the adviser's recommendations is often referred to as a 'suitability report'. It is also worth noting that it is the responsibility of the adviser to assess the level of professionalism and understanding that the client has for financial matters, in order to word the report in a way that can be easily understood by the client and is not confusing or misleading.

This report is presented to the client prior to the client making any decision to proceed, or not to proceed, with the recommendations. If the client is not happy to proceed then there may be amendments made to the recommendations, or the client may choose not to proceed at all.

Figure 11.1 Advisory and planning process

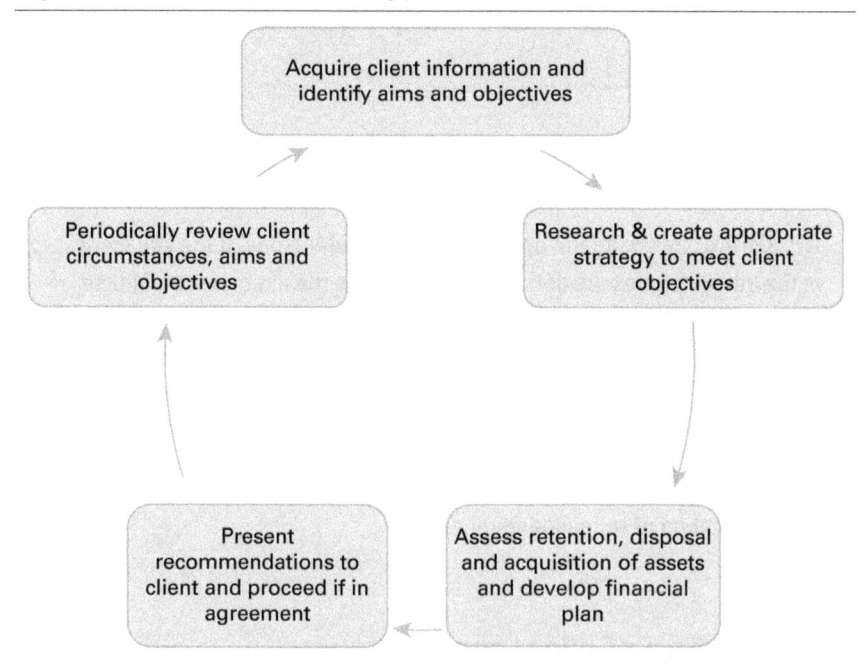

```
        ┌─────────────────────────────┐
        │ Acquire client information  │
        │  and identify aims and      │
        │        objectives           │
        └─────────────────────────────┘
          ↗                        ↘
┌──────────────────────┐    ┌──────────────────────┐
│ Periodically review  │    │ Research & create    │
│ client circumstances,│    │ appropriate strategy │
│    aims and          │    │   to meet client     │
│    objectives        │    │      objectives      │
└──────────────────────┘    └──────────────────────┘
          ↑                          ↓
┌──────────────────────┐    ┌──────────────────────┐
│      Present         │    │ Assess retention,    │
│ recommendations to   │ ←  │ disposal and         │
│ client and proceed   │    │ acquisition of assets│
│   if in agreement    │    │ and develop financial│
│                      │    │         plan         │
└──────────────────────┘    └──────────────────────┘
```

It is not only good business practice, but also positively encouraged by domestic regulators that an adviser should agree the level of frequency with which reviews will take place.

Whether this review takes place will depend upon a variety of factors and will depend on whether the advice was part of a one-off instruction or part of an ongoing relationship. It is good practice to discuss with the client the advantages of regular reviews, for example monitoring the ongoing performance of financial assets and strategies, updating client's changing needs, aims and objectives, and ensuring that planned strategies are still relevant and meeting the client's requirements. Additionally, there are often several issues which are identified as part of the financial planning exercise and it would be unusual to be in a position to adequately address all of them immediately. This may be as a result of practical affordability, as the client may have insufficient disposable income to address all the identified issues immediately, or the client may prefer to defer certain issues for their own reasons.

It represents sound practice to review the performance of any recommended investment products on a regular basis to ensure that performance is acceptable and to consider that changes in the economy may warrant amendments to keep the chosen investment strategy on track. It is also quite likely that over a period of time the client's circumstances may change and therefore their aims and objectives may also change. For example, an unmarried client may marry and have children which would be very likely to result in changes to their attitude to risk and their needs, aims and objectives.

> **In practice**
>
> It is worthwhile taking the opportunity to consider some of the key steps in the advice process in detail, to acknowledge the importance of these individual parts of the process:
>
> - identification of client requirement;
> - assess risk, suitability and the ability to bear losses;
> - establish affordability;
> - presentation of recommendations.

Identification of client requirements

Following the initial process of collecting the detailed client information, the adviser will have the required data to build a concise picture of the client's needs and requirements. We have established that careful and accurate appraisal of client circumstances is crucial, including an accurate analysis of the client's availability of liquid cash reserves, or emergency funds, in the event of unforeseen circumstances arising.

Advisers and wealth managers are expected to evaluate the main financial needs of clients which involves the evaluation of client attitudes towards key areas such as investment, savings, debt management, budgeting, borrowing and also protection of family and assets. Since each investor is an individual and therefore will display varying objectives and expectations, prior to advising, the adviser must be aware of the needs, preferences, expectations and precise financial circumstances of the client. The next step is to classify and to prioritize these needs, some of which may include:

- maximizing future capital growth;
- protecting real value of capital;
- generating a required income (now or in the future);
- protecting against future events (known and unknown);
- saving for a future liability, for example children's education;
- tax planning.

Whilst it may be tempting to try to identify a typical financial life-cycle it must be acknowledged that every individual client is different and will have many variations in individual circumstances. This means that it is inadvisable to try to standardize financial advice and the professional approach is to have a bespoke solution which will address the client's specific situation. It is also apparent that individual investors will reach the stages of the life-cycle at different ages dependent upon their individual financial circumstances and some investors may never complete the full investor's life-cycle.

Figure 11.2 Typical investor life-cycle

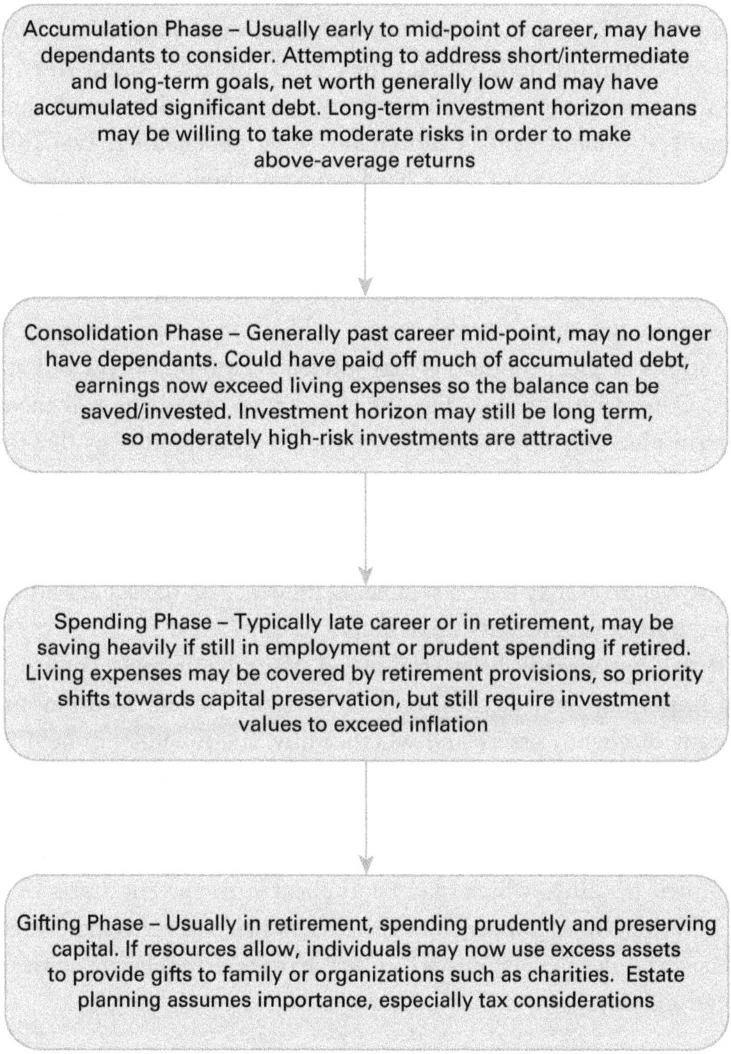

Accumulation Phase – Usually early to mid-point of career, may have dependants to consider. Attempting to address short/intermediate and long-term goals, net worth generally low and may have accumulated significant debt. Long-term investment horizon means may be willing to take moderate risks in order to make above-average returns

Consolidation Phase – Generally past career mid-point, may no longer have dependants. Could have paid off much of accumulated debt, earnings now exceed living expenses so the balance can be saved/invested. Investment horizon may still be long term, so moderately high-risk investments are attractive

Spending Phase – Typically late career or in retirement, may be saving heavily if still in employment or prudent spending if retired. Living expenses may be covered by retirement provisions, so priority shifts towards capital preservation, but still require investment values to exceed inflation

Gifting Phase – Usually in retirement, spending prudently and preserving capital. If resources allow, individuals may now use excess assets to provide gifts to family or organizations such as charities. Estate planning assumes importance, especially tax considerations

When considering an investor's aims and objectives their relative wealth is an important consideration because if they have significant investment capital available, it is prudent for them to make the best use of that capital. Conversely, it is also possible for clients with limited capital to gain exposure to investment markets; however, the inherent risks must be carefully weighed against the possible gains and the impact of capital loss may be deemed to be too disadvantageous under these circumstances. In this regulated financial environment, the practice of borrowing money to invest would normally be viewed as inappropriate and may result in significant liabilities. As a generalization, it would be reasonable to say that an individual should only be prepared to invest what they can afford to lose. In particular, an investor's age, their stage in the life-cycle and their commitments all affect their aims, objectives and risk profile. Excessive risk-taking is usually not advisable for clients with substantial financial commitments, children and other dependants. Availability of time may also be a factor for a hard-working client with a young family which may make them more amenable to use the services of a professional financial adviser.

Various other factors will be drivers for the client's aims and objectives; for example, the client's health status is likely to be an important factor since serious medical conditions may influence both objectives and attitude to risk. Considerations regarding the expectancy of old age will encourage long-term planning and may influence the investment strategy due to need for growth and/or income for many years. However, impaired health may drive a strategy for more immediate income and a shorter-term approach to needs and requirements. Also, the addition of dependants such as children or elderly relatives may have a significant influence on the client's attitude to risk and impact significantly upon aims and objectives.

If it has not already been established, the adviser must confirm additional important data at this point such as the current location and tax treatment of client's assets and whether any investments are held in any form of tax wrapper, for example an individual savings account (ISA). It is also important to establish if any investment gains or losses have been incurred for purposes of capital gains tax and the details of any early encashment penalties which may be applicable to current assets or products. Additionally, factors such as the client's place of birth may determine residency and domicile status which are particularly relevant with regard to taxation issues.

In practice

It is also worth noting that during the course of this process, the adviser has a responsibility to ensure that normal anti-money-laundering checks are undertaken and the source of any client funds must be positively established. It is always possible that the adviser could discover unusual activity during the course of their advice and planning process; for example, the client may be deliberately avoiding paying tax, which is classed as financial crime. The adviser is obligated to report any such suspicions to the appropriate authorities as part of their professional responsibilities and may face personal sanctions if they do not do so.

Risk and the ability to bear losses

We have already identified that a client's risk tolerance will be one of the key factors which will inform the financial planning strategy recommended by an adviser and will certainly be a major factor in the selection of appropriate investment products. Appropriate identification of attitude to risk is under constant scrutiny by domestic regulators as discussed earlier in this chapter and it is important that the process for determining a client's attitude to risk is a robust one. The problem with the definition of risk is that definitions of risk profiles are both imprecise and varied and therefore this is not an easy process for the adviser to undertake. It is important that the adviser demonstrates detailed knowledge of their client in the application of this risk assessment process and applies their experience, skill and knowledge to match appropriate solutions to the client's aims and objectives. Examples of appropriate risk-profiling tools are varied; however, many in the UK particularly are based upon the work of Alistair Byrne and David Blake at the Pensions Institute.[9]

Following the identification, prioritization and agreement of the client's objectives the adviser will need to identify the client's risk tolerance, time horizons, liquidity requirements and any investment preferences to enable them to develop an appropriate investment strategy to achieve the client's objectives. Table 11.1 provides a broad but effective overview of the spectrum of risk.

A series of objective factors may be identified which will assist in the analysis of a client's risk profile, the most important being:

- age of client;
- relative wealth;
- investment timescale (horizon);

- commitments;
- stage of life-cycle.

The client's age, together with some or all of the other factors above will have relevance in influencing the level of risk that the client is prepared to accept. The relative wealth will affect the available capital and the

Table 11.1 Typical investor risk spectrum

Risk Level	Characteristic
No risk	Client not prepared to accept fall in value of investments. Appropriate assets may be cash-type assets/short-dated government bonds.
	May consider capital guaranteed products.
	Low-risk investors must understand that their caution may mean their investments may not keep pace with inflation and may fall short of their objective.
Low risk	Client is cautious but will be prepared to accept some value fluctuation in return for long-term growth but will invest mainly in secure investments.
	Investors with longer-term time horizons may have portfolios with a majority of bonds and cash, but with some exposure to equities or similar.
	Usually, would prefer not to take risk with their investments, but they may be persuaded to do so to a limited extent.
Medium risk	Client will have some cash or bond holding but also a fair proportion in direct or indirect equity assets (possibly even some in high-risk funds).
	Client will be prepared to accept some additional risk with at least a proportion of their available assets if there is a proportionate chance of improved returns.
High risk	Client keeps cash reserves minimal.
	Holds mainstream and secondary equities and may even accept derivatives or other high-risk investments in an attempt to achieve high returns.
	In general, high-risk investors seek the best possible return on their capital and are willing to take significant risk to achieve this.
	They are usually willing to take risks with a large proportion, or even all of their available assets.
	There is a strong chance that the client could lose a substantial amount (or all) of their investment.

disposable income available to the client and therefore significantly affects the ability to invest and to accept higher levels of risk. For example, a client with minimal assets is likely to be reluctant to accept significant risk. An acceptable level of risk is likely to vary dependent upon the timescale available to an investor. For example, a long investment horizon may make a higher level of risk seem more justified and palatable, whilst short periods of time are not usually considered to be suitable for investments which involve the potential for higher volatility. In this way, it is likely that certain assets and products may be discounted depending upon the investment horizon available.

The issue of commitments applies equally to both current and future planned commitments. Any commitments, particularly of a family nature, will influence a client's risk profile because it is reasonable to expect that individuals will wish to fulfil their obligations and therefore this may require a more cautious and considered approach rather than a more risky and aggressive stance.

In practice

Example 1

Mr & Mrs Horton are in their mid-forties and have three children, one of which has secured a place at university to study medicine. The other two children are currently in secondary education and would also like to secure places at university. Mr & Mrs Horton both work full-time and would like to help their children with the financial burdens associated with undergraduate education. They have recently won a modest sum of money on the national lottery and require advice regarding the most appropriate way to make their windfall work for them.

Example 2

Mrs Schmidt is 63 years old, divorced and has minimal retirement provision. Her two children are independent and live overseas in the United States and Australia and she has little contact with them. She recently inherited a sum of money when her father died which is on deposit in an interest-bearing account, the returns on which are very poor. She is very close to her mother who is quite elderly and infirm and is considering if she should move house so that her mother may live with her.

> **Example 3**
>
> Andrew is a young professional graduate working in the fast-paced IT industry and is living in his own flat in the city centre. He is currently single, enjoys challenging outdoor physical exercise and his salary allows him a comfortable and exciting lifestyle. He has recently received his annual bonus and is looking to take advice on how to invest this to maximize its growth potential.
>
> Looking at these three clients; who do you think will be prepared to take a greater degree of risk in order to achieve their aims?

The stage that a client has reached in life is a significant influencing factor on risk appetite. As a generalization, younger individuals and more mature individuals with no dependants are likely to be prepared to accept greater risk in order to have the opportunity of greater returns, whilst those close to retirement will be less likely to be prepared to accept higher levels of risk. Individuals at the stage of life where they have dependants and associated commitments are also less likely to be prepared to accept higher levels of risk because of the potential consequences.

It is also important to consider any existing assets held by the client and that it may not be possible or prudent to dispose of or discontinue these for various reasons, such as severe exit penalties. All assets held by the client should be supportive of the investor's aims, objectives and attitude to investment risk and this should be carefully considered as part of the overall planning process. The adviser also has the obligation to assess both their client's knowledge and experience and the way in which this affects their ability to understand risks. It is also considered to be good practice that regardless of their attitude to risk, no investor should be totally invested in equities or more volatile assets and consideration should be given to a 'rainy-day fund'.

> **Keyword**
>
> A **rainy-day fund** is funds held, usually on deposit and available at short notice.
>
> This will ensure provision is made for unforeseen circumstances and emergencies, in the form of liquid funds, eg cash.
>
> There are times when it may not be convenient or prudent to disinvest from certain asset classes so the holding of some liquid assets is a sensible precaution.

The use of these types of objective factors provides an accurate and easily evidenced way to help assess a client's risk profile. However, it is clear that subjective factors may also have a significant effect upon a client's attitude to risk and these may be more challenging for an adviser to understand and to document. For example, a client's background, experiences and personality will also be influential factors and will contribute to their decision-making processes. A client may have the available capital, an appropriate investment horizon and higher-risk assets may be appropriate for their aims and objectives, but if the client is not comfortable with the potential uncertainty that these types of assets exhibit, then they must be avoided.[10] It also merits consideration that it is quite common for clients to have an attitude to risk which differs between different objectives. For example, a client may have a balanced attitude to risk for long-term investments but a cautious approach to retirement planning. This adds a degree of complexity to the task of designing an appropriate strategy and to the adviser's justification and documentation of the process.

Another important issue for the adviser to address is the client's capacity to bear loss, which is linked to, but separate from, the attitude to risk. This is another area which is carefully scrutinized by domestic regulators and advisers must demonstrate that they have given this issue due consideration as part of their detailed assessment of the client's financial position.

In practice

In the UK the regulatory body is the FCA which addresses the issue of client capacity to bear losses in the following way:

> by 'capacity for loss' we refer to the customer's ability to absorb falls in the value of their investment. If any loss of capital would have a materially detrimental effect on their standard of living, this should be taken into account in assessing the risk that they are able to take.[11]

Part of the risk-profiling process undertaken by the adviser should assess accurately both the client's attitude to risk and their associated capacity for bearing financial loss.

Affordability and suitability

Once the adviser has identified the client's aims and objectives it is then possible to consider the client's specific needs and if necessary prioritize them in a logical and professional manner. To address each of the client's needs, available products and strategies may be considered and various factors may be applied to identify an appropriate and suitable proposal. Consideration of key factors including liquidity, risk, cost, flexibility, tax issues and compatibility with aims and objectives will allow unsuitable products and strategies to be effectively eliminated and appropriate options to be given due consideration.

When producing the recommendations to propose for a particular investor, advisers must take into account the current overall investment and economic environment both in the present and going forwards, to the best of their ability. Additionally, client-specific issues should also be given consideration, such as risk tolerance, return requirements, investment time horizon, availability of financial resources, together with prioritized aims and objectives. All of these factors will combine to influence which investment assets or products will be assessed to be suitable for them, based upon their current circumstances. This suitability will also be balanced by the constraints of regulations, liquidity, taxation issues and any specific needs or preferences imposed by the client; for example, the wish to invest in an ethical manner.

Keyword

Any products or assets recommended to the client must be demonstrated to be suitable and appropriate to meet the client's aims and objectives and this will be a test of the regulatory requirement to **'know your client'** The detailed, accurate information collected and documented during the earlier stages of the advisory process will be fundamental to this requirement and will form the basis of the evidence that the recommendations are indeed suitable for the client's requirements. Meticulous documentation of the client's existing financial circumstances, together with identification of their aims and objectives, will serve to clearly highlight any shortfall or deficiency in their existing financial strategy and plans and permit a logical assessment, together with the recommendations to address this situation.

The selection of appropriate assets and products which merit inclusion in the recommendations will involve consideration of many specific factors including tax treatment, charges, product or asset features, price, availability, and use of trusts. In addition, further research will be carried out with regard to individual product providers, since many investment products are available from a wide variety of providers. Once again, there are various factors which would merit consideration before recommending a specific product provider and these would include financial strength, quality of service, choice and performance.

> **In practice**
>
> The ultimate aim, for the adviser, is to deliver a series of recommendations which will comprehensively address the identified aims and objectives of the client and provide the means for them to effectively achieve all of their identified needs.
>
> However, it must be recognized that it may not always be possible to achieve this for every client due to the complex combination of factors such as client circumstances, economic conditions, legal and regulatory constraints and availability of suitable products.

Financial advisers must assess not only the suitability of the investment opportunities available to the client, but also the affordability both now and in the future. It is paramount that recommendations to the client are made with care to evidence that affordability has been considered on an ongoing basis. For example, recommending a regular payment into an investment product to address an agreed savings shortfall would not be justifiable if the investor is likely to experience difficulties in maintaining the regular payments due to affordability issues in the future. The detailed and accurate information regarding the client's financial circumstances previously obtained proves crucial to this part of the advice process, because clear evidence of available budget and client affordability both now and into the future may be established and will serve to inform the suitability and affordability of the recommendations.

The experience and knowledge possessed by professional financial advisers allows them to recognize that a client's willingness to accept a certain amount of risk may not always be supported by their current or predicted future financial circumstances. For example, it would not be prudent to recommend that a client with an appetite for significant risk who is currently experiencing difficult financial circumstances should adopt an aggressive investment strategy. To do this may prejudice their financial situation and it is part of the role of the financial adviser to discuss this conflict with the client and explain the potential consequences of taking unnecessary or ill-advised risk.

> **In practice**
>
> It is quite possible that clients may have more than one identified objective or need and it is quite a common scenario to see multiple needs, all of which require addressing. It may not therefore be the case that only one solution exists; indeed there may be several possible solutions for discussion with the client. It may be that the adviser was originally engaged to address a particular client need and that additional issues were identified as part of the ongoing advice process. However, the adviser should take a comprehensive approach in offering advice and prioritizing identified needs. Clearly the adviser should give appropriate consideration to the client's original aims and objectives when recommending suitable solutions and any additional identified needs may form the basis for further discussion.

We have also identified the possibility that a client with more than one objective may have a different attitude to investment risk for the different objectives and this must also be carefully considered by the adviser and appropriate explanations offered as part of the solution recommended, to evidence suitability. The situation may be further complicated if the adviser is providing advice to more than one client; for example, a husband and wife. It is often the case that each client may have differing attitudes to investment risk for the same objective and may require more than one solution to be recommended. This will add a further layer of complexity and require additional and careful discussion to ensure a suitable and appropriate outcome is recommended for both clients.

The status of the adviser, which was identified earlier in the chapter, may also have bearing upon the service and advice offered to the client. Depending upon the adviser's status, which could be independent, tied or multi-tied, they may be able to advise clients based on the whole of the market, just a single provider or a limited number of providers. It is important that the investor is clear on this issue of adviser status as it may significantly affect the advice that may be offered.

Keyword

A **tied adviser** may be able to offer recommendations to a client in respect of specific needs, but may not be able to offer advice on some of the existing products which the client holds if they are not products offered by the provider to which they are tied. This situation may create potential problems for the client in the future in respect of their overall financial situation.

Presentation of recommendations

Once the adviser has completed the research and has formulated a strategy to address the client's aims and objectives, the next step is to arrange a meeting with the client and to present and discuss the recommendations in detail. The meeting could be in person, whether face-to-face, over the telephone or a video conference. However, most advisers would prefer to meet the client face-to-face to ensure the best possible rapport and to offer the best possible explanation of the recommendations. The recommendations will also be given to the client in the form of a written report, which is an important part of the financial advice process. The written report provides a way of effectively evidencing the adviser's recommendations that have been discussed with the client and a copy of this report will be held on the client file together with all the client information and evidence of research carried out.

In practice

In fact, the provision of a written copy of the recommendations report to the client serves several purposes which include:

- provides a permanent formal record of the recommendations both for the adviser and the client;
- sets out the details of the key client information on which the recommendations are based;
- helps to avoid any misunderstandings about the advice that has been given;

- allows the client to re-visit the recommendations at their leisure and therefore may make complex issues easier to understand;
- puts recommendations into context with client's agreed aims, objectives and circumstances.

The written report, signed and dated by the adviser will be given to the client and supplied in conjunction with appropriate quotations, illustrations and product literature which is appropriate to the recommendations made. This report is often referred to in the financial services industry as a suitability report, as it details the recommendations and explains the reasons for the suitability of these recommendations for addressing the client's needs. Much of the content of the report is mandatory in order to satisfy the guidelines and requirements laid down by domestic regulators, as the written recommendations report is a key document in the financial advice process, which is heavily regulated for the protection of investors. It is required that the report presents appropriate information in a clear and understandable manner, should be as concise and clear as possible and the language used should not include complex or confusing wording and jargon, except when absolutely necessary to explain points being made. As a minimum, the financial planning report to a client must offer:

- brief introduction to explain the purpose of the report;
- summary of the client's current financial and personal circumstances;
- statement of the aims and objectives agreed with the client;
- explanation of any prioritization together with any objectives which have been deferred and the reasoning behind this deferral;
- full details of recommendations proposed and links with aims, objectives and prioritization;
- if applicable, robust justification of specific product providers recommended;
- if applicable, robust justification of recommendations to cancel, suspend or discontinue any existing arrangements;
- identification and explanation of any charges, fees, penalties or tax implications of the recommendations;
- specific risk warnings relevant to each recommendation;

- explanation of any actions needed to action the recommendations, together with timescale;
- explanation of the consequences of not acting upon the recommendations;
- details of cancellation rights and the right of the client to change their mind.

It is regrettable that these suitability reports are very likely to be quite long and complex in nature due to the scope and amount of information to be covered in necessary detail. Despite this, advisers are reminded by the regulator that information must be presented in a clear and understandable manner which will ensure that clients understand the advice being offered to them and the recommendations being made.

> **In practice**
>
> Advisers have an obligation to assess a client's level of knowledge and financial experience.
>
> The adviser must then tailor their explanations to maximize the client's ability to understand the recommendations and the risks.
>
> For example: a financial adviser is meeting with two clients today following comprehensive research into their objectives, the purpose of which is to present recommendations and confirm the client's agreement to proceed.
>
> The first client is Charlotte: an educated and financially astute chartered accountant, with over 20 years' experience in the finance industry.
>
> The second client is Christine: she has been working for six months as a trainee hairdresser, having left school at 18 with disappointing grades.
>
> Consider how the adviser may tailor the discussions and explanations for these two clients and the types of terminology they may reasonably use.

As a result of the long and complex nature of this type of report, it is prudent for the adviser to have a face-to-face meeting with the client, to answer any further questions the client may have following the recommendations and to take the opportunity to address any potential misunderstandings which may arise following this process. It is also a valuable opportunity for the adviser to confirm that the client has read and understood the recommendations and to obtain a final agreement to proceed.

In the event that the client does not agree with some or all of the recommendations it may be that a revised strategy will need to be devised and presented to the client for approval, again following the process previously detailed. It may be that a client insists on a specific investment strategy that differs in some way from the adviser's recommendations and the adviser may need to accept this. However, if the adviser does not believe that this course of action is in the client's best interests, or may be inappropriate, they always have the option to withdraw their services and decline to help the client to proceed. Whatever the outcome of the planning process, any decisions made and actions taken will be following a rigorous and thorough review of the client's personal and financial circumstances, attitude to risk, aims and objectives.

Investment strategies

We have identified that investment strategies will be client-driven, based upon the client's aims and objectives and tailored to the client's accurately assessed attitude to investment risk. The investment process has begun with the establishment of a sound adviser/client relationship which may build into an enduring long-term relationship between them. This should suit both parties because the client's trust of an adviser is certainly built up over a period of time and it is far more effective for advisers to build long-term relationships with clients than spend valuable time and money constantly seeking new clients.

One of the pivotal factors in the chosen investment strategy will be the decision regarding the asset allocation mix. The key to this will be to create a portfolio with an appropriate balance of assets; for example, equities, bonds, collectives and property, chosen to deliver an outcome which is based upon the client's identified aims and objectives. This investment portfolio may be chosen to achieve either short-term outcomes, long-term outcomes or a combination of both. Short-term allocations may often require regular or continuous adjustment and are referred to as tactical asset allocations, whilst long-term asset allocation decisions are often likely to be 'buy-and-hold' decisions and are referred to as strategic asset allocations. The composition and type of assets included within the portfolio will be influenced by various factors including:

- client's identified attitude to investment risk;
- anticipated timescale of the investment;
- the requirement for growth or income or a combination of both.

Attitude to risk

We have already identified that an accurate and rigorous assessment of the client's attitude to investment risk is crucial to the investment process. This information will be fundamental to the asset allocation decision process and the risk classification; for example, cautious, balanced or aggressive, together with other information such as the client's expectations of returns, will be used to inform the choice of an appropriate asset allocation mix. A portfolio may be created which will reflect a balance between the different risk characteristics of different investment asset classes; for example, bonds, cash, equities and property.

Alternatively, in specific cases, some asset classes may not be considered appropriate and the portfolio may be restricted to fewer asset classes or even a single asset class. For example, a very cautious investor may be recommended to invest in 100 per cent cash.

Other relevant factors may also influence the asset allocation process, such as investors requiring their ethical and socially responsible beliefs to be taken into consideration within investment and portfolio management strategy. Factors of this nature must be rigorously identified within the client information collection process and specifically featured within the detailed justification of recommendations.

> **In practice**
>
> It is vital that the client be fully informed regarding recommendations and decisions of this nature.
>
> For example, ethical and socially responsible investments may expose the client to specific risks such as reduced diversification of assets, less liquidity and potential unexpected price volatility. So whilst clients may like the idea of investing in an 'ethical' manner, they may not be aware of the practical restrictions and potential risk issues that this type of investment strategy may expose them to.

> It is therefore important that clients wishing to invest in a specific manner, for whatever reason, are fully aware of the implications of their preferred investment style so that they may make an informed decision.

Timescale of investment

As a generalization in the investment world, a period of less than five years would be considered to be short term, whilst long term would be considered to be a period of 10 years or more. The client's identified investment time horizon is an important factor and will also serve to inform the asset allocation decision-making process. Careful thought must be given to how the liquidity and volatility characteristics of available assets are considered with regard to the client's investment timescale and which assets are therefore appropriate under the circumstances.

> **In practice**
>
> Property is generally considered to be an illiquid asset and would therefore only usually be recommended as part of a long-term investment strategy, which is normally recognized as a period of 10 years or more.
>
> Company shares traded on a major global stock exchange are considered to be more liquid, but will have potential volatility issues which make short-term investment particularly risky.
>
> Certain collective investments, such as ETFs may be highly liquid due to their popularity with the institutional investors; however, they may suffer volatility in the same way as equities.
>
> Bonds are usually considered to be liquid, particularly major government-issued bonds and investment-grade corporate bonds, although in certain circumstances bonds may also suffer volatility issues.
>
> Cash is the most liquid of the asset classes although not immune from risk.
>
> Given these characteristics, how would you consider that the different asset classes fit in with client's potential short-, medium- and long-term investment time horizons?

Equity-based investments such as company shares or collectives are unlikely to be considered appropriate if the client will require access to their capital within a period of five years. This is due to potential volatility issues and the possibility that the capital value may have fallen, with the risk to the client of capital loss. If the client may require access to the capital within a few months, it may be that the only appropriate asset for the client is cash, despite the restrictions that this creates. If the investment horizon is greater than 6 to 12 months then fixed-interest assets may be appropriate to be considered.

Growth or income

An assessment of the client's current and future requirements for income, capital growth or a combination of both will have been identified during the process of assessing the client's aims and objectives. This requirement will be one of the significant factors that will have an impact upon the decisions taken regarding the mix of assets chosen to achieve the aims and objectives specified by the client. With the anticipation of producing income, growth or a combination of the two, an appropriate mix of assets and funds may be chosen to reflect the desired outcome, as different assets will be preferable for each output in addition to being relevant to the risk appetite of the client.

In practice

Thinking about the characteristics of different asset classes, when making a recommendation to a client looking to achieve capital growth, would you recommend that they should invest in bonds or equities?

Feedback

Bonds would not usually be selected with the aim of producing a capital growth return, although it is not unknown for astute investors to purchase certain bonds 'under-par' and hold them until redemption if the timescale is not too long, therefore generating capital growth.

However, equities, whilst normally used to facilitate capital growth over the long term, may also generate regular income as a result of dividend distribution. This dividend income may be reinvested to increase investment growth if an income stream is not required by the investor.

It is worth noting that the income generated by equities may not be as reliable as the income generated by bonds because although bonds are subject to default risk, the dividends provided by equities are not guaranteed and may fluctuate over periods of time.

There is an overlap here with regard to timescale of investments because clients requiring an objective of capital growth may need access to some or all of their capital at some point in the future, which means that the liquidity of the recommended asset or fund must be considered carefully. Clients who require an income stream may need this to commence immediately or at some specified time in the future and for it to be fixed or increasing in nature, to offset the effects of inflation. It is not uncommon with client requirements for there to be the dual aim to generate a reliable income stream together with long-term capital growth. This requires careful consideration of the asset mix. However, it is possible to accommodate these dual aims, for example, by using a mixture of assets such as equities, bonds and property. This is of course subject to the client having an appropriate risk appetite and a long-term investment strategy being appropriate.

Following the above considerations, a decision will be taken regarding an appropriate asset allocation, bearing in mind the current economic conditions and the prospects for those sectors within favoured asset markets under consideration. Final selection of assets will be made using the various research tools available to professional advisers and techniques such as fundamental or technical analysis or a combination of the two. Decisions must also be made regarding the most appropriate style of investment management for the client's circumstances and budget. Other factors to be considered include the client's tax position in the present and in the future, as this may have an impact upon on how the client's funds are invested and indeed disinvested at an appropriate time.

In practice

The client's current tax position may influence the use of specific investment products; for example, individual savings accounts (ISAs) in the UK and investment bonds may have advantageous features with regard to tax efficiency and may therefore merit consideration within the overall investment strategy.

The client's tax position may also influence the way that the client is advised to access funds when necessary; for example, under certain circumstances an income requirement may be satisfied in a more tax efficient manner by utilizing a withdrawal of a capital sum and depositing it in a savings account to withdraw as needed, rather than by taking a regular income stream from an investment product.

Tax efficiency characteristics of various products are covered in other chapters.

Many effective investment portfolios may typically be constructed using three of the main asset classes: money market assets such as cash; fixed-interest assets such as bonds; and equities or collectives.

Money market assets offer the liquidity and the flexibility to provide for emergencies and short-term needs as they will usually provide penalty-free instant access to cash. Fixed-interest assets such as bonds may usually be relied upon to provide secure, reliable income streams which may also be inflation-proofed if index-linked bonds are utilized. This may usually be achieved by careful consideration of a selection of government-backed and corporate bonds, although default risk must be remembered. Capital growth, particularly long-term capital growth, would normally be provided by the use of equities or collectives and may be achieved through a combination of asset price appreciation and reinvestment of generated income.

There are of course other key asset classes such as property and derivatives, which may feature within a properly constructed portfolio and which would be included because of a combination of their asset characteristics, risk factors, applicable investment time horizon and their correlation to other asset classes.

In practice

It is worth mentioning that it would be unusual to see the use of derivatives within the investment portfolio unless the client in question was a sophisticated, experienced investor with an aggressive attitude to investment risk.

The additional risks posed by the use of derivative products would not normally be justifiable and appropriate for use with the majority of ordinary private clients.

Property may be a useful asset class in the right circumstances, usually accessed through a collective such as an ETF or a unit trust fund.

> Property is usually negatively correlated with equities and when used as a long-term investment, may be a useful source of both income and capital growth, although care must be taken as it is generally considered to be comparatively illiquid in nature.

The adviser will also need to give appropriate consideration to the way that the client's investment portfolio is to be managed because it is unlikely, under normal circumstances, that a single fund or asset will be sufficient to meet the client's requirements. The adviser must professionally approach the selection of suitable assets for the creation of the client's portfolio, considering the need to diversify and to meet the client's aims and objectives. An appropriate investment strategy is tailored to meet a client's specified objectives and various options are available for the type of investment service which may be appropriate to the client and their circumstances. The range of services which may be made available to meet the client's needs includes:

- periodic management;
- active management;
- discretionary fund management.

Periodic management service

The adviser will construct an appropriate portfolio of investment assets and will meet periodically with the client to review the performance of the portfolio in relation to the aims and objectives. This type of periodic approach will result in a minimal number of changes and adjustments over the course of the agreed investment horizon and costs to the client will therefore be minimized, although the longer the period between reviews, the more likely that the investment portfolio may stray from the objective being pursued. It is common that a benchmark may be designated against which the investment portfolio's performance is monitored and this benchmark may vary significantly dependent upon the client's aims and objectives. For example, the benchmark may be a specified index such as the FTSE 100 index, the S&P 500 index or the Hang Seng index. At the periodic meetings, changes or adjustments would be recommended by the adviser if there appeared to be significant differences between the client's portfolio and the benchmark performances. Or if no benchmark was set, changes would be recommended if the performance of the client's portfolio did not appear to be 'on track' to meet the client's aims and objectives. With this type of service, any recommended changes would be carried out with the client's agreement.

> **In practice**
>
> Advisers offering passive management approaches may offer a limited range of pre-prepared portfolios with 'generic' investment objectives; for example, cautious objective or income objective.
>
> These may often be index-tracking portfolios and may be recommended to clients, depending how closely they match with the client's attitude to risk, investment horizon, aims and objectives.

Active management service

With an active managed fund service the adviser will construct an appropriate portfolio of investment assets and will monitor this regularly on behalf of the client. The adviser will contact and meet with the client on a regular basis as necessary to review the performance of the portfolio in relation to the aims and objectives. The adviser or their company will undertake active management of the client's portfolio and make regular recommendations to the client if adjustments or changes are required to improve the performance of the portfolio, or to correct deviation from the agreed objectives. These recommended changes will also be carried out only with the client's agreement. An active management approach may also utilize an appropriate benchmark in the same way as a passive approach in order to measure the performance of the client's investment portfolio. Where a benchmark is utilized, the returns are assessed as a 'relative return'; that is to say, the return is relative to that of the chosen benchmark.

> **Keyword**
>
> To outperform the benchmark on a relative return basis, it is necessary to make either more profit or less loss than the benchmark.
>
> However, if there is no benchmark comparison, the return of the client's portfolio is expressed as an **'absolute return'**.

Typically, absolute return strategies are more common with aggressive investing approaches as they would normally seek to make positive returns in all market conditions, including falling markets. To do this they would need to employ a wide range of higher-risk techniques, for example, short selling, arbitrage and the use of derivatives and other unconventional assets. It would be unusual to recommend these types of techniques to clients other than very experienced, sophisticated and aggressive investors, due to the high levels of risk involved and the complex justification of this type of investment approach.

> **In practice**
>
> Advisers offering active management approaches may also offer a limited range of pre-prepared portfolios with 'generic' investment objectives. Examples would be cautious, growth, income and aggressive.
>
> These may be recommended to clients, depending upon how closely they match with the client's attitude to risk, investment horizon, aims and objectives.

Discretionary fund management

The discretionary portfolio management services are more likely to be utilized with clients who are wealthy, typically high net worth clients and have larger and more complex investment portfolios, although this is not always exclusively the case. This will still involve the adviser recommending and constructing an appropriate portfolio of assets, bespoke to the agreed aims and objectives of the client.

However, this management style differs from the previous two methods because with a discretionary fund management service, the changes and adjustments to the portfolio content and asset mix are at the discretion of the investment manager, not the client. This means that any buy and sell decisions will be made by the adviser or portfolio manager, on behalf of the client and do not require prior approval of the client. With this method, there would usually be an agreed benchmark that the fund manager would seek to outperform and this would be appropriate to the identified and agreed aims and objectives of the client. The cost to the client for this type and level of service is likely to be significantly higher than the previous types of service. It is likely that this level of bespoke service will also involve a minimum level of investment capital which may be quite significant and may therefore put this service out of the reach of many investors. A minimum investment of £100,000 or more would not be uncommon in order to make this level of service worthwhile for the adviser or the adviser's company.

Client review process

We have identified that individual investors will exhibit a wide variety of aims, objectives and expectations and this spectrum of investors dictates the importance of the adviser or wealth manager having a detailed awareness of the needs, financial circumstances, individual preferences and specific expectations of their client. With any individual, these factors are obviously subject to change over a period of time and this may be due to various factors, some unexpected and sometimes anticipated. If we consider that both the adviser and client have spent an appreciable amount of valuable time identifying and documenting financial circumstances, aims, objectives and expectations then it is logical that this information should be appropriately monitored and reviewed periodically to ensure both currency and relevance, and that any recommendations put in place are still appropriate and meeting their objectives. Of course, this will depend upon whether the advice offered initially was seen as a one-off exercise or an ongoing service to the client as part of a strategy to build a long-term relationship with the client. For the majority of advisers, this long-term relationship is the preferred option as this offers future opportunities for doing business with the client and a long-term relationship will help to cement the trust between parties. Clients may be readily educated to understand the advantages of regular financial reviews and it is sound practice for financial advisers to offer to meet regularly with their clients. Practically, from the adviser's point of view, it is usually more profitable to efficiently service their existing clients than spend valuable time and resources seeking new business. Not only will this servicing process result in repeat business from their clients, but it is also likely to lead to high-quality business referrals to the client's friends, family and work colleagues.

It is therefore good practice early in the adviser/client relationship to have a discussion to confirm if ongoing monitoring and review will be agreeable to the client and will be part of the adviser's remit. If agreement is reached then the adviser should lay out a proposal detailing the proposed frequency of updates, further meetings and additional communications. The proposals would typically include periodic communications to provide the client with up-to-date information on the value and performance of their investments and may include some form of internet monitoring facility which allows client access to company web-based portals. Discussions will identify the most appropriate method of communication with clients to maintain their awareness because, for example, not all clients may be comfortable with internet-based contact. Clients may also be offered periodic face-to-face meetings, together with documentation of investment performance, and any other appropriate information relevant to the client's circumstances.

As a generalization, the advisory and financial planning process should not be viewed as a one-off process, particularly because of the potential for change. Client aims and objectives are subject to change for a variety of reasons and could be because:

- the client's circumstances change;
- the financial environment changes;
- a combination of both events arises.

Changes in client circumstances

Over an extended period of time it would be quite surprising if a client's personal circumstances did not change and with changes in circumstances we may anticipate that there will be changes in the client's aims and objectives.

> ### In practice
>
> Typical changes in client circumstances over time may include, but not be limited to:
>
> - personal and financial circumstances;
> - tolerance to risk;
> - investment time horizon;
> - liquidity requirements;
> - tax position;
> - overall investment preferences.

Many different changes may occur to a client's personal and financial circumstances over a period of time; for example, promotion, redundancy, getting married or divorced, having a child and inheriting money or property.

These types of changes may result in significant changes in the client's aims and objectives, including key factors such as their risk tolerance, investment horizon and liquidity requirements. Alternatively, the client may simply have undergone a period of reflection and decided to modify their expectations or refine their investment preferences to a more ethical requirement. Any changes which affect affordability either positively or negatively are also notable events. It is common that during the advice and planning process there may be more factors or issues identified than can be addressed immediately. It may be that affordability proves to be a limiting factor, or simply that the client is only prepared to address a certain number of factors at one time. Changes in client circumstances may also impact upon the client's priorities and a change in priorities may influence the client's overall aims and objectives.

Changes in the financial environment

Keyword

The financial environment both domestically and globally is in a constant state of flux and many of the changes may be anticipated to impact upon an individual client's personal or financial situation. For example, economies enter and exit recessionary periods which affect employment prospects, taxation regimes change constantly, legal and regulatory changes are constant ongoing issues and investment markets fluctuate on a regular basis. Any and all of these types of changes may warrant action being taken on behalf of the client to adjust their investment position or address changes in their circumstances.

Changes in both the domestic and global financial markets may prompt an adjustment to the client's current asset allocation position, but equally a period of sustained growth or contraction may require a rebalancing of the client's portfolio as certain asset classes appreciate relative to others and therefore create an imbalance. Changes in the overall financial environment may also influence the client's priorities, in addition to aims and objectives and this may result in the need for adjustment of the overall financial strategy. For example. product changes or the availability of new products on the market may create opportunities whilst legislative or regulatory changes may either restrict or change potential financial planning strategies. Or, the client may have previously invested in various company shares or collective investment products and as a result of economic or market circumstances, a situation may arise where it is prudent to take profit or to modify the client's position.

Overall, it is easy to demonstrate how important it is for clients to be afforded a regular review of their financial arrangements and for advisers to closely monitor progress towards planned aims and objectives. In the absence of such reviews, it is quite likely that progress may falter, focus may be lost and as a result of the long-term nature of many investments quite minor deficiencies in the short term may eventually result in a substantial cumulative effect on a client's overall financial plans. Regular periodic reviews, together with the disciplined implementation of an agreed financial planning process should ensure:

- continued suitability of investment strategy;
- appropriate management of risk;
- progress towards aims and objectives;
- effective minimization of costs, charges and taxation issues;
- maximization of investment performance;
- compliance with regulatory and legislative changes.

Over extended periods of time it is quite important that the overall balance of a client's investment portfolio is monitored because even if conditions have not substantially changed in the financial environment and the client's circumstances have not prompted amendments, the portfolio will naturally 'drift' away from the intended asset mix. This drift may be minimal over short periods of time; however, if uncorrected over longer periods a significant change in asset mix may develop leading to the portfolio becoming inappropriate for the client's risk appetite.

Consider a portfolio with an initial asset allocation of 50 per cent equities, 25 per cent bonds and 25 per cent property.

Assume equities, bonds and property appreciate in value by 12 per cent, 1 per cent and 3 per cent respectively, in Year 1 and again in Year 2.

The example in Table 11.2 shows that after a period of only two years, a significant change in the asset allocation has occurred which then changes the overall risk level of the portfolio. Rebalancing the client portfolio involves adjustments to the various asset classes within the portfolio to return the asset mix to the appropriate levels and it is prudent to consider this on an annual basis. If the use of an appropriate benchmark has been utilized in order to assist with measurement of the client's portfolio performance, it would also

Table 11.2 Change in asset allocation mix over time

Asset class	Value at inception (£)	Holding at inception (%)	Value after Year 1 growth (£)	Holding after Year 1 growth (%)	Value after Year 2 growth (£)	Holding after Year 2 growth (%)
Equity	60,000	50	67,200	52.3	75,264	54.7
Bond	30,000	25	31,100	23.6	30,603	22.2
Property	30,000	25	30,900	24.1	31,827	23.1

be reasonable to review the benchmark periodically in order to ensure that it is still representative of the portfolio's objectives. Significant changes to the client's portfolio may require that the benchmark is changed or modified to ensure that it remains an appropriate measure. Following periodic reviews, if changes in circumstances have been identified and amendments to the financial strategy are required, the adviser should prepare new recommendations to present to the client and the advice process described earlier should be followed as with the initial recommendations.

Summary

Trust, honesty and integrity are considered to be of great importance by the financial regulatory bodies globally and not surprisingly financial professionals must demonstrate these qualities in all their dealings with clients. It is important to remember that trust may also be lost as a result of one transgression and once lost may be very difficult, if not impossible, to recover.

Check your understanding

1 How important do you think the interpersonal relationship is between a professional financial adviser and their client?
2 Consider the importance of information in the advisory process.
3 What factors may influence the development of an investment strategy?

4 Can you explain the difference between periodic fund management and discretionary fund management?

5 How would a financial adviser monitor changes in their client's circumstances and is this important?

Further reading

The following books may be useful:

Bodie, Z, Kane, A and Marcus, A (2013) *Essentials of Investments,* 9th global edn, McGraw Hill

Jones, CP (2013) *Investments: Principles and Concepts*, 12th edn, John Wiley & Sons

The following sites may be useful:

www.fca.org.uk
www.cfapubs.org/doi/pdf

Portfolio management   12

Utilization of retail fund management products

By the end of this chapter you should have an understanding of the issues involved in the management of retail fund management products, including:

- identification and setting of portfolio objectives;
- implementation of appropriate investment strategy and covering:
  - asset allocation;
  - selection of securities;
  - management style;
  - specific client requirements;
  - costs and charges;
  - performance measurement and review.

Introduction

For those readers working through this book in a linear fashion, it will be apparent that this chapter directly follows on from and builds upon Chapter 11 concerning the adviser/client relationship.

As a generalization, most investors do not have the knowledge, experience or confidence to effectively manage their own investments and will therefore often seek the advice and assistance of financial professionals. These may be wealth managers, financial advisers or investment fund managers, all of which are well placed to play an important role in the managing of capital on behalf of individuals. This process may involve the creation of bespoke investment portfolios for an individual investor or simply deciding to place the capital into an appropriate collective investment product, where the investor's capital will be pooled together with other investors' capital and professionally managed. In either case the individual's invested capital will benefit from the experience and professionalism of the industry professional in question and will almost certainly enjoy a better outcome than if the individual investor chose to manage the investment of their capital themselves.

Portfolio management has assumed a greater degree of importance in recent years where the art of successful stock picking was previously considered to be the answer to investment performance. Much informed opinion supports a degree of market efficiency in recent years which implies that the opportunities for easy gains by simple stock-picking techniques are likely to be brief and not easily identified. A well-constructed investment portfolio, however, may be reasonably expected to deliver the targeted level of return whilst minimizing the level of risk taken to do so. In this respect, the finance professional may help fulfil the investor's aims and objectives whilst managing the risk by utilizing a portfolio of appropriate assets. Many investment portfolios are still constructed in accordance with the broad principles of modern portfolio theory despite the understanding in the 'real investment world' that many of the assumptions made by modern portfolio theory are not sound.[1,2] For example, the assumption that investment returns follow a normal distribution is unsound and we know from first-hand experience the assumption that investors behave rationally is certainly not correct.

Key steps in portfolio management

Finance professionals and portfolio managers employ a variety of techniques and methods in the management of investment portfolios and there is no single method which guarantees success all the time; if there were such a method then surely everybody would be utilizing it. There are, however, key steps in the process which many finance professionals use which form an efficient process to follow for effective portfolio management, as shown in Figure 12.1.

Figure 12.1 Steps for portfolio management

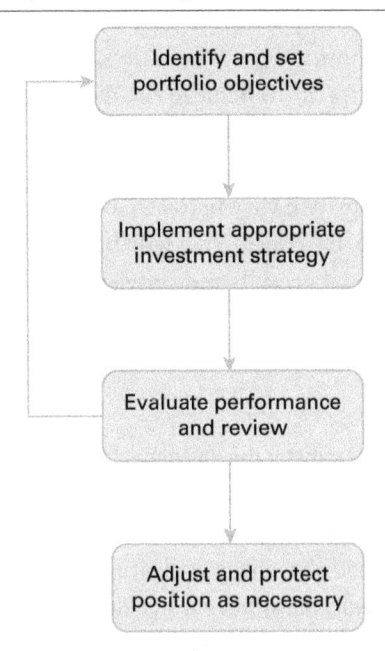

```
Identify and set
portfolio objectives
        ↓
Implement appropriate
investment strategy
        ↓
Evaluate performance
and review
        ↓
Adjust and protect
position as necessary
```

Identification and setting of portfolio objectives

The driver for this part of the process will be the detailed discussions with the investor where the aims and objectives to be pursued are established and confirmed. The adviser will identify and confirm these details in writing and this information will inform the required objectives for the investment portfolio. The objectives could be quite simple and based upon a definite agreed timescale; for example, investing a specified lump-sum of capital for a stated period of time with the aim of growing the value of this capital to a specified amount to meet an identified liability. However, the objectives could also be quite complex and involve a series of separate objectives to be met, perhaps over a staggered time frame. The objectives to be achieved may involve meeting a growth target, producing a specified level of income, or a combination of income and capital growth. These types of targets are not usually mutually exclusive.

As we discussed in Chapter 11, each investor is an individual with their own defined aims and objectives to pursue. However, it is not at all uncommon for investors to have multiple aims and objectives over a varied timescale.

The more complex the aims and objectives are, the more likely it will be that multiple asset classes will need to be employed as part of the investment strategy and careful monitoring will be necessary to ensure that the strategy employed remains 'on track' to achieve the desired aims. It is important to identify and set the portfolio objectives because it is against these targeted objectives that the success or failure of the portfolio's performance will be decided. The terminology will vary between industry professionals; however, the main objectives to be considered will be the security of the original investment capital, capital growth and provision of income.

> **In practice**
>
> The desired level of security for the investment capital will be informed by the investor's attitude to investment risk and may vary between a requirement for total capital security, to being prepared to take substantial risk which may result in the loss of some of or all the original investment capital.
>
> This requirement will clearly have a significant impact upon the asset classes which may be employed within the portfolio. It is also possible that the investor may be prepared to take some degree of investment risk with a proportion of the original investment capital, if they can be satisfied that the remainder is quite secure and not likely to be lost.
>
> Part of the role of the investment professional in these circumstances is to manage the expectations of the investor and ensure that the investor's objectives are realistic, bearing in mind their appetite for investment risk.

The requirement for capital growth may be unspecified in that an investor may simply seek 'reasonable' capital growth for an unspecified or indefinite period of time, within the confines of their appetite for investment risk. Clearly, it is important that the expectation of 'reasonable' capital growth is quantified in advance to ensure that the expectation is realistic and to enable appropriate performance monitoring. Alternatively, the investor may seek a specified level of capital appreciation over a defined or undefined time period. It would usually be considered mutually exclusive to generate appreciable capital growth whilst seeking substantial capital security, although with careful consideration of asset mix and possible use of specialist investment products, modest levels of capital appreciation may be enjoyed whilst preserving the original investment capital. Consideration must also be given to the client's tax position, because capital gains would not usually be subject to taxation until the gains are actually realized, in contrast to income which is potentially taxable immediately.

The investor may have no requirement for income at all; indeed, generating income may be punitive dependent upon the investor's individual tax position. If the investor does require an income provision then it may be that a specified level of income is required immediately or to commence at some time in the future; for example, to coincide with the retirement of the investor or another future liability which requires the provision of income, such as a child going to university. The income provision may be required for a finite period of time or to continue indefinitely and it would be likely that a long-term requirement for income may also include the preference for the income stream to increase over time, in order to protect the buying power of the income from the effects of inflation. It is clear that the specifics of the required income provision will dictate the type of asset used to generate the income stream.

In practice

Richard, a UK-based individual who is a higher-rate taxpayer, wishes to invest some capital in order to achieve a better return than is available to him with a deposit-based arrangement.

A liability emerges at some point in the future; for example, funding university fees for a child and assuming that Richard remains a higher-rate taxpayer, it would be preferable for Richard to withdraw lump sums from his investment to service the liability rather than generating income.

At the time of writing, the current higher-rate tax band applicable in the UK is 40 per cent, whilst the capital gains (CGT) tax band for higher-rate taxpayers is 20 per cent and the first £11,300 of annual capital gains are exempt from CGT.

This is because the rate of capital gains tax payable would be significantly lower than the higher rate of income tax which would be incurred by generating income. The individual would also be able to make efficient use of their nil rate annual capital gains tax allowance to mitigate the tax liability.

It is worth noting that it is quite common for investors to have multiple objectives, over various timescales, and therefore the capital security and capital growth requirements may be addressed separately from any income needs, by careful use of a mixed-asset investment portfolio. This is clearly dependent upon the client's attitude to investment risk as the asset mix must take into account the investor's risk appetite, but if appropriate, certain asset classes may be utilized to generate both income and capital growth; for example, equities. An investor with complex aims and objectives may find that they have short-, medium- and long-term requirements; for example, savings and investment plus retirement goals to be achieved. In this type of situation, it would be common to find that the investor has insufficient resources to make provision for all their aims and objectives initially and that the investment strategy must be adjusted over a period of time, possibly over several years, in order to address all of the investor's aims.

Keyword

Whilst pursuing the aims and objectives identified by the client, appropriate to the client's risk profile, it is important not to forget any liquidity requirements identified during the detailed discussions. The amount of flexibility available in the selection of appropriate investment assets will depend partly upon the nature of the liquidity requirements that have been identified. So, for example, if there is a need for the majority of the investment capital to be highly liquid, this will significantly restrict the use of certain asset classes in the portfolio, such as equities and property.

Implementation of appropriate investment strategy

The next step, knowing the constraints of risk appetite and armed with the targeted aims and objectives, is to devise and implement an investment strategy which aims to fulfil the client's identified requirements.

In practice

The creation of an appropriate investment strategy will involve consideration of many factors, which will include:

- asset allocation;
- selection of securities;

- management style;
- specific client requirements;
- costs and charges;
- performance measurement and review.

In practice, these factors cannot be dealt with individually in isolation as the various factors will have a degree of impact on each other; for example, the selection of individual securities will depend upon the asset allocation strategy adopted and upon specific client requirements, whilst the management style may be dictated by the asset allocation which has been adopted and the type of securities selected.

Asset allocation

The asset allocation strategy is the start of the construction stage of the portfolio management process, and one of the first factors to be considered when creating an appropriate investment portfolio is to identify the optimal asset allocation mix which satisfies the desired risk profile and addresses the required aims and objectives. Effective portfolio design will reflect a balance between investment assets with different levels of risk; for example, cash, fixed-interest, equities and derivatives. It is clear that the ideal mix depends on the client's expectations regarding returns and their tolerance of risk. A very cautious investor may wish to be invested totally in cash, whilst an aggressive investor will wish to take risks in the pursuit of greater rewards. Many portfolios are still created with the modern portfolio theory in mind and seek to combine different asset classes, whose returns are not adversely correlated, in order to reduce the total variance and therefore the risk of the portfolio. This technique prevails despite the challenges raised by disciplines such as behavioural finance, regarding many of the assumptions made in modern portfolio theory. When selecting different asset classes to create an appropriate asset allocation mix, consideration must be given to the relative correlation between the different asset classes employed. An analysis of this correlation will show how the performance of one asset class has fluctuated historically in relation to another. It is worth noting that high correlations are generally associated with elevated portfolio volatility and that the correlation relationship between two different assets is not fixed, that is to say, it may change over a period of time and may be unpredictable in nature.

Keyword

Asset class correlation: two asset classes may be said to have positive correlation if their returns are observed to move in the same direction at the same time. Conversely, they have negative correlation if their returns are observed to move in opposite directions at the same time.

Correlation is measured on a scale which ranges from +1 to –1 and both high negative and high positive correlations are not usually considered to be advantageous when creating an efficient investment portfolio. Assets with a correlation of zero would be expected to have returns which would move independently of each other and as a generalization, assets with a low or negative correlation are considered to be advantageous in the creation of an effective investment portfolio.

An example of maximum positive correlation (+1) would be the shares of two companies in the same sector whose business models and products/services are very similar, such as two major banks.

An example of maximum negative correlation (–1) would be the shares of two companies in different sectors, with very different business models and products/services that would be expected to benefit very differently from prevailing conditions, such as an ice-cream manufacturer and a company manufacturing thermal hats and gloves.

It can be seen that diversification may be effectively achieved by using an appropriate combination of asset classes, geographical regions, sectors and timescales. We have identified that correlations between two different investment asset classes may show significant variations over a period of time and certain circumstances have been found to show an increase in correlation between asset classes; for example, periods of market volatility and financial crisis like recessions. Research conducted over the last 25 years has also indicated that relative correlations between certain asset classes have shown an overall increase, which makes efficient asset class diversification more challenging.[3,4,5,6,7]

When considering an appropriate asset allocation mix it is clear that different securities holding similar characteristics are classified into broad asset classes.

Keyword

Asset class: an asset class is a group of securities that exhibit similar characteristics, behave similarly in the marketplace and are subject to the same laws and regulations.

The three main asset classes are: equities; fixed-income or bonds; and cash. For example, company shares will be classified as equities, whilst government debt will be classified as bonds. Each asset class will have its own typical risk and return characteristics and these will differ from other asset classes based upon the historic performance, risk and correlation relative to other asset classes, over the same period.

This type of asset allocation mix may be effectively employed to even out investment performance over a period of time by spreading investment capital across a range of asset classes, whilst matching the portfolio to the desired risk profile. It is important, however, to consider carefully the use of historic data and be mindful of both the advantages and limitations of this type of data. When beginning the process of constructing an investment portfolio, historic data may prove very useful in various ways such as assessing the performance of individual asset classes and identifying trends, as well as analysing key statistical measures of returns, standard deviations, beta coefficients and correlations. These types of statistics may then be used to compare against appropriate benchmarks; for example, to assess fund manager performance or to perform individual security performance analysis.

In practice

It must also be remembered that regardless of the asset class in question, past performance is not a guarantee of future performance and with global markets exhibiting periods of enhanced volatility, eg the global 'credit crunch' and sovereign debt problems, the investment professional's job has been made more difficult due to non-normal distributions. As we have referred to earlier, in recent years correlations between different asset classes have increased and, together with global market volatility, have restricted the opportunities available for investment professionals and investors alike to achieve satisfactory risk diversification.

The process of asset allocation divides the available investment capital among different asset classes, subject to the investor's risk profile and the investor's aims and objectives, to create an appropriate investment portfolio. The challenge for the investment professional is to employ an appropriate mixture of asset classes within the investment portfolio to give the investor a high probability of achieving their agreed aims and objectives over the stated investment horizon. The initial asset allocation will be based upon the required types and levels of investment return needed to achieve the investor's aims and objectives, together with the risk appetite and liquidity requirements of the investor. Successful asset allocation will provide sufficient diversification within the investment portfolio to minimize volatility and therefore risk, whilst enabling the investor to realize their financial aims and objectives.

As we can see, it is possible to achieve effective diversification within the portfolio by spreading the investment capital across various available and appropriate asset classes and whilst the most commonly used asset classes are equities, cash and bonds, it is also possible to make use of other asset classes, such as property, commodities and derivatives, subject to restrictions imposed by risk appetite and liquidity constraints. Even in a simple asset allocation mix involving just two separate assets, equities and bonds, it is possible to vary the percentage holding of each asset to significantly alter the characteristics, risk and investment performance of the portfolio. For example, a portfolio which contains 10 per cent equities and 90 per cent bonds will be substantially less risky than a portfolio containing 60 per cent equities and 40 per cent bonds, but under normal circumstances and over a reasonable period of time would exhibit much less capital growth. This portfolio asset allocation mix may be used regardless of the objective, whether it is capital growth or income (see Table 12.1).

Table 12.1 Risk tolerance and investment mix for growth and income

Investment objective	Risk tolerance	Attitude to risk/possible investments
Capital Growth	Cautious	Seeking maximum growth consistent with modest degree of risk
		Equities will form a significant percentage of the portfolio along with other asset class(es)
	Moderate	Seeking to balance potential risk with growth of capital
		Equities will form the principal part of the portfolio along with other asset class(es)

(continued)

Table 12.1 *(Continued)*

Investment objective	Risk tolerance	Attitude to risk/possible investments
	Aggressive	Typically able to adopt a longer-term view that allows pursuit of a more aggressive investment strategy
		Equities may form the whole of the portfolio
Income	Cautious	Willing to accept a lower level of income in return for lower risk
		Bonds will be likely to form the principal part of the portfolio; however, exposure to high-yield bonds and equities will be low
	Moderate	Seeking to balance potential risk with potential for higher level of income
		Significant percentage bond holdings; however, exposure to high-yield bonds and equities will be higher
	Aggressive	Willing to adopt more aggressive strategies that offer potential for higher levels of income
		Exposure to high-yield bonds and equities may be substantial

Diversification is not restricted to simply mixing asset classes. Indeed it may be effectively achieved in many different ways, if not restricted, including exposure to different:

- asset classes (equities, bonds, property);
- geographical regions (UK, Far East, USA, Europe);
- industrial sectors (banking, manufacturing, retail, mining);
- maturities (bonds) (short-, medium- and long-term);
- currencies (and major global currency or asset priced in other currencies).

The decision-making process to select the initial asset allocation profile may be made from one of two different perspectives; strategic asset allocation or tactical asset allocation. Strategic asset allocation would normally be the method of choice initially, unless there were significant reasons to take a short-term view, such as the client having substantial liquidity requirements.

Keyword

With **strategic asset allocation** the decisions regarding the investment portfolio construction would be made with a long-term perspective in mind. Capital market predictions and expectations, together with the client's risk profile, liquidity requirements, aims and objectives would all be considered as part of the investment portfolio construction process. The long-term behaviour of the various assets under consideration would be considered, long term in the investment arena being usually assumed to be 10 years or more. The investment professional will determine the appropriate weighting of each asset class under consideration, relative to the whole portfolio, and this weighting is identified by market value as a proportion of the market value of the whole portfolio.

Once the portfolio is created with 'live traded' assets, it is clear that the actual proportions of the various assets will not remain fixed over a period of time as the assets fluctuate in value relative to each other. This is due to the market values of the various assets changing, potentially on a daily basis. Since certain asset classes are likely to grow in value more quickly than others, this can become a potential problem over extended periods of time and the investment portfolio may become 'unbalanced'. For example, a portfolio which begins as 50 per cent equity/50 per cent bond will potentially become 60 per cent equity/40 per cent bond quite quickly in normal market conditions, as the value of the equity element of the portfolio increases more quickly than the value of the bond element and this has the effect of creating a more 'risky' portfolio due to the greater volatility of the equity element.

In practice

Examine what occurs to a theoretical portfolio of assets over a period of time following an initial asset allocation of 40 per cent equities, 50 per cent bonds and 10 per cent cash.

If we assume that equities, bonds and cash appreciate in value by 14 per cent, 3 per cent and 0.5 per cent respectively, in Year 1 and then again in Year 2, we find the following result:

Table 12.A

Asset class	Value at inception (£)	Holding at inception (%)	Value after Year 1 growth (£)	Holding Value after Year 1 growth (%)	Value after Year 2 growth (£)	Holding after Year 2 growth (%)
Equities	40,000	40	45,600	42.6	51,984	45.2
Bonds	50,000	50	51,500	48.1	53,045	46.1
Cash	10,000	10	10,050	9.4	10,100	8.8

So, we can see that even over a short period of two years, the asset balance has changed significantly, resulting in an elevated level of portfolio risk.

For this reason asset allocation reviews must be carried out by the investment professional on a regular basis as a part of the management of the portfolio, in order to avoid potential problems with mismatching of the portfolio relative to the aims and objectives. The approaches taken to create appropriate asset allocation for specific client circumstances will obviously differ between investment professionals, although a mixture of qualitative and quantitative evaluation is likely to be employed. The adviser will be required by the domestic regulatory body to retain evidence of appropriate research on the client file, in order to justify and support the chosen portfolio structure.

Whilst strategic asset allocation is viewed as a long-term approach the opposite can be said for tactical asset allocation.

Keyword

Tactical asset allocation is a shorter-term strategy and often considered to be an 'active' strategy. Tactical asset allocation may often be employed in order to take advantage of specific or unusual investment opportunities, followed by reversion to the strategic asset allocation strategy when a desired short-term aim is achieved or is no longer viable. Adopting a tactical asset allocation strategy may be appropriate if the client has restrictions, such as liquidity requirements, which mean that a long-term investment strategy is not appropriate. Tactical asset allocation may also be employed at times when it becomes necessary to rebalance the portfolio in order to return to the desired long-term asset position, following a review process.

Selection of securities

When the decision has been made regarding the overall asset allocation mix to be employed for a specific client, based upon the identified risk profile, liquidity requirements, aims and objectives, the next step is to select the individual securities within each asset class that will constitute the investment portfolio.

The decision regarding the selection of an appropriate asset allocation will have required consideration of the current and future prospects for each of the main asset classes within major investment regions and also required thought to global economic, political and social environments. Following a final decision on asset allocation, consideration must be given to current and future prospects for the bond, equity and other appropriate security markets within these sectors and a combination of fundamental and technical analysis techniques may be used to cement a final decision regarding the individual securities which will be selected for the investment portfolio.[8,9] Once again, a variety of methods may be employed to facilitate the selection of individual securities; however, we can categorize them into two types of approach: a top-down approach and a bottom-up approach.

Keyword

A **top-down investment management system** will generally follow a three-stage process beginning with the overall asset allocation, followed by the identification of appropriate sectors and finally the selection of individual securities within the identified sectors. Investment professionals have their own 'tried and tested' selection methods and will also employ a variety of research tools to inform their decision making; for example, the Bloomberg research system. Quantitative models may also be used together with variations on fundamental and technical analysis techniques, to assist the process of deciding which geographical areas, sectors and ultimately individual securities, have a high possibility of delivering consistent investment returns, within the parameters that reflect the client's aims, objectives and risk appetite.

The top-down process will take into consideration various key factors influencing investment conditions within geographical regions and industrial sectors which are under consideration. These will include, for example, economic, political and social factors. It is clear that there exists a strong relationship between economic factors and investment performance and so geographic and sector selection will be heavily influenced by both economic performance and the current and anticipated future position within the economic cycle (see Table 12.2).

The changing economic factors comprise a full economic business cycle which is generally accepted to comprise four phases: growth, peak, contraction and recovery. The growth cycle usually finds lower interest rates, falling

Table 12.2 Typical performance of asset classes in varying economic conditions

Asset type	Economic contraction or recession	Economic growth or booming economy
Bonds and fixed interest	Bonds, fixed-interest investments and cash are often seen as a 'safe haven' during slowing economic conditions and recessionary periods	Investment performance of bonds and fixed-interest investments will usually be outstripped by equities during these periods and demand is therefore reduced
	Recessionary periods will usually signal a fall in interest rates which benefits bond performance although results in poor returns on cash	Extended periods of economic growth will usually result in rising inflation which will eventually result in increasing interest rates. This will impact adversely on bond prices, making them less attractive. Returns on cash will increase as interest rates increase
	Gold is also seen by many investors to be a safe investment during recessionary periods	
Equities	During these periods many investors will lose confidence in equities	During these periods investors are likely to be much more confident with equity-based investments
	Unemployment may be rising and consumer spending falling, affecting demand	Employment is likely to be more secure and unemployment falling
	Certain sectors will still provide reasonable returns: eg utilities, energy, healthcare and consumer staples like food, beverage and household personal products – often referred to as defensive sectors	Typically, interest rates will have fallen previously, allowing consumers to spend more freely, which fuels demand
		Sectors which will be likely to perform well include various industrials, financials, IT, mining and basic materials

unemployment, increasing consumer confidence, spending and therefore demand. Businesses experience higher sales and profits along with the potential for expansion. The peak will follow and may persist for a significant period of time, although the momentum of economic growth usually begins to slow and eventually inflationary pressures will result in a rise in interest rates. Contraction of the economy follows as the higher prices affect demand and increasing interest rates make borrowing less attractive. Unemployment may begin to rise, further affecting demand and influencing consumer confidence. Contraction of the economy does not necessarily result in a recessionary period, but may simply lead to a recovery period, which represents a low point in consumer confidence and in business and consumer spending.

Top-down investment strategy is often viewed as a more opportunistic approach, focused on macroeconomic factors, but also allowing the opportunity for investors to take advantage of and close out investment positions quickly, to make short-term investment gains if appropriate. Bond markets and investments generally tend to be macro focused and therefore suited to a top-down investment approach, as do commodity investments. Equity-based investments, however, are equally suited to top-down or bottom-up investment approaches. Top-down equity investors consider the overall performance of the economy and then identify sectors with sound performance, followed by selecting the best securities within that sector.

Keywords

A **bottom-up equity investing strategy** involves identification of companies with sound performance following in-depth research prior to investing. The bottom-up investing strategy, therefore, focuses on the analysis of individual securities; for example, a specific company share and therefore identifies a specific company rather than the broad sector in which that company operates. With a bottom-up investment strategy, consideration is primarily given to microeconomic issues, including factors such as a company's key financial statements, products or services, general financial status, supply and demand issues, together with any other specific individual factors unique to that particular company.

For example, a company's niche/innovative product or unique marketing strategy may be a significant identifier in enticing a bottom-up investment strategy.

> Although a bottom-up approach to investment selection focuses primarily upon the merits of individual securities, circumstances and prospects for markets and the global economy will still be given due consideration, but will be seen as secondary to factors specific to the security under consideration.

This type of investment approach makes the assumption that well-run individual companies can be successful even if the sector as a whole is not performing particularly well, but confidence of this nature is only possible following thorough and detailed research into the company in question. It is often considered that a robustly researched bottom-up investing approach is capable of delivering superior investment returns over long-term investment periods for investors who have a long-term investment strategy, despite the fact that periodically, this technique may exhibit variations in comparison to sector or market returns. Consequently, less importance may be attributed to the overall sector and economic conditions when making investment decisions. Bottom-up strategies are therefore usually only employed in situations when at least part of the client's investment capital may be suited for investing as a long-term, buy-and-hold strategy.

Selection of individual securities will clearly be influenced by the aims and objectives being pursued by the investment portfolio on behalf of the client; for example, are we seeking to achieve capital growth, provision of income or indeed a combination of both? The traditional asset classes which are most likely to be given consideration in the construction of a client portfolio include the following:

- Money market securities: cash deposits or securities with a maturity of less than one year. This asset class has the advantage of meeting the short-term liquidity requirements of an investment portfolio, either to meet liabilities or unforeseen eventualities, or to take advantage of short-term investment opportunities without the need to disinvest other assets. It also has the advantage of a high level of security and a low chance of capital loss, and may be utilized as a simple, low-risk method of achieving a savings target.

- Bonds or fixed-income (domestic): an investment portfolio may utilize a mixture of short-, medium- and long-term maturity securities for diversification. The portfolio may also feature the addition of index-linked securities, in order to make some provision for inflation protection. Bond and fixed-interest instruments would normally be utilized in the provision of a low-risk, reliable income stream with a return of the invested capital and not for capital growth, although it is possible to generate capital growth using this type of asset. This is also a useful asset class in the matching of assets to liabilities, sometimes referred to as an immunization strategy.

- Bonds or fixed-income (international): the investment portfolio may also use overseas securities, again with a mix of short-, medium- and long-term maturity to provide additional diversification. Additional risk factors must be considered including foreign exchange risk.
- Company shares (domestic) – equities: individual company shares can be used to pursue both value or growth opportunities and may also deliver a regular income stream if shares with a reliable dividend history are included. These securities are usually distinguished by their market capitalization; eg large-cap, intermediate and small-cap shares. These provide the opportunity for diversification within the asset class.
- Collectives (domestic): these are also treated as equities and have the useful attribute of built-in diversification, although the correlation with any other securities held within the portfolio must be carefully monitored. There is a huge range of opportunities available and they may also be used to gain exposure to specialist markets. They include ETFs, unit trusts, OEICs and investment trusts.
- Equities (international): the investment portfolio may also consider individual overseas company shares for value or growth opportunities and to deliver a regular income stream. These securities are also distinguished by their market capitalization and provide the opportunity for diversification; however, the additional risks of investing in overseas equities must be taken into consideration. This area will also include emerging markets and overseas collectives.
- Alternative investments: this asset class covers a variety of additional securities including property, commodities and derivative products. This asset class offers sound diversification opportunities due to lower correlation with the main asset classes; however, there may be enhanced or unique risks involved in the use of this category of assets and these risks must be carefully weighed against the potential positives of using the asset. For example, use of derivatives is usually only considered with experienced, sophisticated investors who have an appropriate risk appetite and investment in property may often include significant liquidity restrictions which may pose their own additional risk. Collective vehicles may also be used to access this asset class, for example, REITs and ETFs.

> **In practice**
>
> Overall, we see that a portfolio system of investing is generally considered to be an effective method by which to pursue a well-diversified investment strategy and we have identified that diversification within asset classes may be effectively achieved by using a combination of issuers, geographical regions, sectors and timescales. The right kind of diversification – where the assets' returns show a degree of negative co-variance – will reduce, but not eliminate, the risk in an investment portfolio.

Money market securities held within the portfolio will provide liquidity, but may also be used to reduce downside from market risk, to control volatility and to facilitate appropriate tactical asset allocation. However, care must be taken because in a low-interest-rate and low-return environment, cash will generally act as a drag upon the overall portfolio returns.

Bonds and fixed-income securities offer predictable interest payments and repayment of capital, and therefore have a key role in constructing a portfolio to meet investor needs by offering security, dependable income and in some cases inflation protection. There is a diverse range of bonds available enabling investments to be tailored to an individual's objectives, income needs and tolerance to risk. Diversification within the bond element of a portfolio is needed to manage associated risks and utilizing bonds of different types, different issuers and different maturities helps to reduce risk. If the risk profile permits, then ideally an appropriate balance is sought between investment grade, high-yielding, government and corporate issuers.

There may be valid reasons for fixed-interest securities within a balanced portfolio as well as equities. Usually, equities afford a real rate of return above inflation over long periods; however, there are times in an economic cycle when a client could achieve a better short-term return from a fixed-interest security. Equity exposure in the investment portfolio can be effected either by direct investment in company shares or indirectly through the use of mutual funds, collectives or a combination of both. Company shares are considered to be relatively high risk, but they do have the potential for higher returns compared to bonds, particularly over longer periods of investment. We must consider time horizons when investing in equities and this type of investment would usually be considered to be a longer-term investment of at least 5 and preferably

10 years. Consideration must be given to the volatility in equity prices as markets react to both economic and company news. In addition to considering geographical regions and market sectors, the selection of individual company shares may take account of the market capitalization of the shares. So, for example, the investment strategy may consider exposure to large, mid and small capitalization shares, varying sectors and a range of global markets in order to pursue a balance of risk and reward to meet the investor's aims and objectives.

Alternative asset classes have become more popular in use during the last decade as investment professionals seek to find negative correlation within their investment portfolios. A derivative is a financial instrument whose price is based on the price of an underlying asset, which could be a financial asset or commodity; for example, bonds, company shares, indices, interest rates, oil, gold and wheat. Most derivatives utilized in investment scenarios are in the form of forwards, futures or options contracts. Derivatives may be used in investment situations for either hedging or speculation purposes, often to obtain exposure more cheaply to assets, or to illiquid markets. Care must be taken by the investment professional in the use of derivative products due to the complex nature and risks involved and they are usually only considered suitable in the case of very experienced, sophisticated investors, with an aggressive attitude to risk. Property is another common type of alternative asset and would usually be accessed either through the use of a collective investment vehicle, such as a REIT or an ETF, but a significant range of property unit trusts, OEICS and investment trusts are also available.

The statistical measures highlighted by modern portfolio theory may prove to be useful for investment professionals when constructing client portfolios; however, it is important to consider the famous warning that 'past performance is not a guarantee of future performance', when making investment decisions. Many statistics on individual assets and funds are readily available and may be considered as part of the overall picture but it must be acknowledged that they are based on past performance data. So, for example, utilization of assets or funds with attractive Alpha and Beta history does not mean that they will perform similarly in the future. Market conditions may change to the detriment of a specific asset or the manager of a fund under consideration may change strategy or even leave. It would therefore be inadvisable to try to construct an investment portfolio by, for example, simply aiming for a specific beta coefficient, or indeed by relying on any single piece of historic data. Note the example in the following box.

In practice

Diversification is successful in reducing the total risk of an investment portfolio but cannot eliminate all the risk, as the systematic or market risk will always remain, even in a well-diversified portfolio. We know that the beta coefficient of an asset or fund is a measure of its volatility relative to the market risk; however, it would be wrong to think that a portfolio with a very low beta coefficient is therefore an ideal portfolio, since different investors will be prepared to accept different levels of risk. It is quite possible to create a well-diversified portfolio with a high beta coefficient as it is also possible to have a well-diversified portfolio with a low beta coefficient if the risk profile of the client dictates this.

Similarly, we know that Alpha is a measure of the difference between actual performance and expected performance for a given level of risk, measured by Beta. A positive figure for Alpha indicates that the asset or fund has 'overperformed'; that is to say its performance is in excess of the performance that its Beta would predict. Conversely, a negative figure for Alpha denotes an underperformance compared to what its Beta would predict.

So: can we use Beta and Alpha data to help select appropriate securities and funds to use in a client's investment portfolio?

It must be remembered that when we make use of Beta or Alpha statistics for an asset or a fund it is crucial to be aware of the market or the index that is being used for comparison. It is also very important to know the data for the R-squared for the movement of the asset or fund relative to the market or index. If the R-squared is low, this indicates that Beta and Alpha are not good estimates of the actual behaviour of the asset or fund. It is therefore quite possible to be misled by the Beta and Alpha data for an asset or a fund if the R-squared data is not known and a complete picture has not been established.

Management style

As a part of the investment strategy adopted the investment professional will need to decide how the client's investment portfolio is to be managed on an ongoing basis. It is not sufficient to simply set up a portfolio and then walk away as this does not constitute effective advice, financial management or customer service. The management style which is appropriate in each individual case will depend upon several factors which will include the client's agreed aims and objectives, the investment horizon, client liquidity requirements, client's risk profile and, crucially, the willingness of the client to pay for a management service.

Depending upon the complexity of the client's aims and objectives there may be few or many factors to be considered and addressed.

> **In practice**
>
> If the client is very low risk and requires a simple secure provision for savings and rapid levels of access to funds at all times then a simple series of money market accounts requiring little management or monitoring may actually suffice.
>
> Conversely, a client with multiple objectives over differing timescales with different risk profiles and a long-term investment horizon will be more suited to an actively managed approach requiring regular monitoring and input from an investment professional.

Following discussions with and subject to the agreement of the client, the investment professional will recommend utilizing either a passive or an active investment management strategy.

With a passive investment strategy the investment portfolio, once created, remains largely unchanged and is often referred to as a buy-and-hold strategy. This may appear rather simplistic; however, if robust research has taken place to inform the original security selection, then unless specific securities no longer warrant inclusion in the portfolio there is a body of opinion which favours the maxim 'if it isn't broken then don't fix it'. Furthermore, recent research has shown that many active fund managers have failed to outperform their sector benchmarks net of fees in recent years, so an active management approach does not necessarily translate into successful investment returns.[10] Clearly there will be a need for some trading over a period of time, possibly to reflect changes in the markets or the economic cycle, or to rebalance the portfolio asset mix which will change over a period of time. It is also worth noting that the greater the amount of trading activity then the greater the accumulated costs to be borne by the investment portfolio, which will have a negative impact upon the overall investment performance.

Passive investment management is also seen in index-tracker-type collective investment funds and this is a style of management which characterizes many ETF funds. In the case of these types of collective funds, an investment portfolio is constructed to track or replicate the performance of an index, subject to tracking error. This strategy of indexation assumes that securities on the market are efficiently priced and the performance cannot therefore be exceeded consistently without assuming higher risk. Collectives of this type may be included within a passively managed portfolio to add further specialist expertise and diversification.

> **In practice**
>
> Disadvantages of an indexation strategy include:
>
> - investment performance may be adversely affected by the need to rebalance the portfolio to replicate changes in the index;
> - index fund performances usually assume reinvestment of income on the declared date; in reality the portfolio cannot reinvest distributed income until it has been physically received which may be several weeks later;
> - indexed funds are not tailored to specific investor objectives;
> - indexed funds will track an index down as well as up.

As a contrast to passive management, active management of an investment portfolio is a more dynamic process and would normally try to outperform an identified, appropriate benchmark over a specified period of time. Fundamental and technical analysis techniques may be employed to identify individual securities for sale or purchase and to indicate the optimum timing of these transactions. This may be pursued on either a top-down or a bottom-up basis, or a combination of the two techniques. With active portfolio management, we would expect that asset allocation, geographic, sector and specific security selection would be fluxed to reflect the current market circumstances and enable the investment portfolio to pursue the client's aims and objectives more effectively. If a more active investment management strategy is chosen then techniques such as sector rotation may be effectively employed. With this method, investment is directed into securities representing the sectors of the economy that are expected to perform strongly in the current phase of the business cycle. Active management also allows the investment professional to take both a short-term and a long-term view, dependent upon the aims and objectives being pursued.

Performance of individual securities will be driven by a variety of factors, some of which will be short term, for example, general news and company announcements, but also long-term factors such as expectations of earnings, dividends and growth prospects. Generally, active management approaches aim to outperform the market by using the knowledge, experience and judgement of the investment professional to analyse the market and invest in securities with the potential to deliver superior investment returns over the available time horizon. Active management techniques may also be used in a timely manner to adjust the portfolio's assets to minimize potential losses; for example, to avoid specific securities, sectors or geographical regions which may underperform over a certain period.

It is worth mentioning that the two methods of portfolio management discussed, active and passive, should not be considered to be mutually exclusive and it is neither unreasonable nor unusual to manage an investment portfolio with a combination of the two techniques. A popular technique for combining these two different management styles would be the core–satellite portfolio management approach.[11,12] Core-satellite style portfolios can be fine-tuned to be as cautious or as aggressive as any other type of investment portfolio and the specific mix of securities selected for inclusion within the portfolio will depend on the agreed investment objectives. The core–satellite approach is not a new strategy but a proven investment strategy which applies a foundation of rigorous academic research in a real-world application.

In practice

The most traditional core–satellite portfolio includes a core of assets which typically tend to include long-term and low-cost securities; for example, a selection of index-tracker funds such as ETFs. Satellites may be comprised of securities which may be considered to be more specialist, possibly shorter term or of a higher risk and are not highly correlated with core investments.

When employing this method of investment management, a decision must be made regarding the proportion of each asset class which should be allocated to the core portfolio and what proportion of each asset class is to be allocated to the satellites. The balance between asset classes will clearly be governed by the degree of risk that the overall investment portfolio is prepared to reflect.

Figure 12.2 Core–satellite investment approach

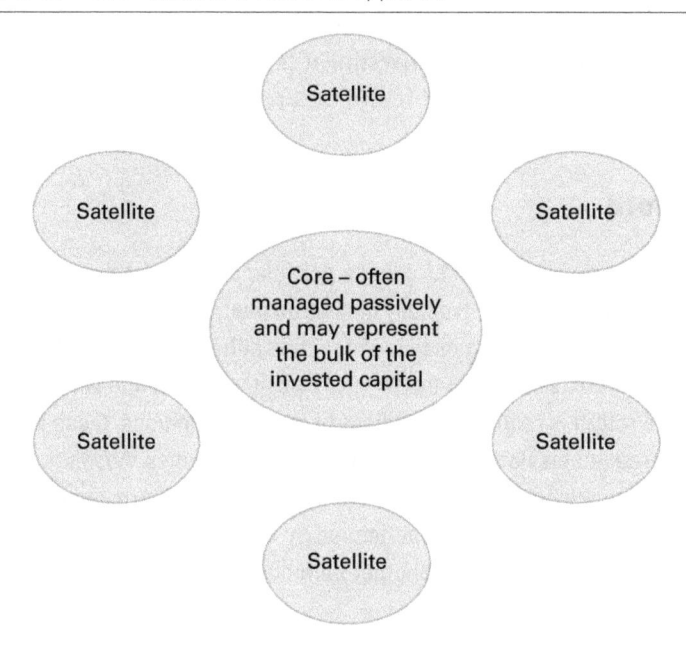

```
                    Satellite

      Satellite                  Satellite

                Core – often
                managed passively
                and may represent
                the bulk of the
                invested capital

      Satellite                  Satellite

                    Satellite
```

NOTE the satellites are likely to each represent only a small percentage of the invested capital and may be actively managed

For the portfolio construction we will first consider the core part of the portfolio. Typically, assets used in construction of the core may be those which are intended to be managed passively. This may include mutual funds, lower-risk collectives of various types, bonds and any other combination of index-tracking investments; for example, ETFs tracking indices such as the FTSE 100 or the S&P 500.

For the satellites, which may be an actively managed portion of the portfolio, the aim is to choose assets which offer the opportunity to earn greater returns than the core of the portfolio; these would sometimes be referred to as Alpha-seeking investments. So, for example, this may comprise securities such as high-yield bonds, individual company shares, equity-based collectives such as unit trusts, OEICs and investment trusts, specialist funds and commodity ETFs.[13,14] It is clear that the investment professional may effectively employ a variety of portfolio construction options in order to create a well-balanced and diversified investment portfolio, the purpose of which is to achieve the aims and objectives agreed with the client. A competent wealth manager/adviser will seek to maximize returns for investors without taking more risk than is necessary and within the scope of the client's identified risk appetite. Another key aspect of the management style is the way in which the performance of the investment portfolio will be assessed and this is usually as either an absolute return or a relative return.

> **Keyword**
>
> An **absolute return** is the return that a portfolio or an asset achieves over a specific period of time, typically measured over a 12-month period. Absolute returns may be positive or negative although the pursuit of an absolute return is usually in the form of a positive return and since an absolute return is required regardless of market conditions, these are considered uncorrelated with regard to market activities. Absolute return may also sometimes be found referred to as the total return and effectively measures the gain (or loss) experienced by an investment portfolio or an asset without comparison to another benchmark.

An absolute return strategy would seek to deliver a positive return even during volatile, flat or falling market periods and the investment methods used to pursue this type of strategy are likely to involve higher levels of risk and assets which would be considered to be more volatile, for example, futures, options, unconventional assets and using short selling, arbitrage and leverage. As a generalization, it is unlikely that this type of strategy would be suitable for most retail investors, but may be appropriate for the needs of wealthier, more sophisticated, knowledgeable and experienced investors who are willing to accept higher investment risks.

> **Keyword**
>
> A **relative return** describes the return that a portfolio or an asset has achieved over a specific period of time in comparison to the return of an appropriate benchmark over the same period. We can also say that the relative return is effectively the difference between the absolute return achieved by the portfolio or the asset and the return achieved by the chosen benchmark.

In practice

When selecting a benchmark against which to measure the relative return of a portfolio or an asset, it is important that the chosen benchmark is an appropriate comparison.

For example; we have assembled an investment portfolio which is holding a selection of company shares, all of which are listed on the FTSE 100 Index. The obvious choice for an appropriate benchmark would therefore be the FTSE 100 Index itself, as this represents the market in which the company shares are based. It would therefore be a fair comparison to compare the performance of the investment portfolio against the performance of the FTSE 100 Index, over the same time period.

It would not be appropriate to compare the performance of the investment portfolio against an overseas index, such as the Hang Seng or the S&P 500, as this would not be representative of the market in which the individual company shares are based.

The benchmark chosen must also be appropriate for the asset class held within the investment portfolio. So, it would not be appropriate to measure the performance of our portfolio of company shares against a bond index, as this represents a different asset class.

Relative returns are more commonly used when reviewing the performance of an individual investment portfolio, the performance of an investment fund or that of a collective fund. Generally, the investment portfolio or the funds are expected to achieve higher returns than the chosen benchmark, in order to justify the fees or charges levied to the client or investor. The benchmark may be selected from a variety of options, provided that the comparison can be justified to be a fair one. It is quite common to use a market index as a benchmark, for example, the FTSE All-Share Index, the S&P 500 Index or the Shanghai Composite Index. However, other options may also be considered. Individual assets or funds may be effectively compared to sector average performances or peer performances and it is also possible to create bespoke benchmarks for more complex situations. For example, with an investment portfolio which contains multiple asset types and same type assets but from different markets, a bespoke benchmark may be created which reflects a fair comparison with the assets held in the portfolio, and performance may then be measured against this benchmark.

Keyword

It is worth noting that when considering a relative investment return, the aim is to 'outperform' the appropriate benchmark and this means making more gains or fewer losses than the benchmark. Therefore, it is possible to have a successful outcome even if a negative return is experienced in a particular investment period, provided that the benchmark has suffered a greater negative return.

In practice

Example 1

Your investment portfolio achieves a positive return of 14 per cent over the previous 12-month period.

Over the same 12-month period, the appropriate benchmark index achieves a return of 17 per cent.

We can therefore say that the investment portfolio has achieved a relative return of –3 per cent for the investment period in question.

Example 2

Your investment portfolio achieves a return of –3 per cent over the previous 12-month period.

Over the same 12-month period, the appropriate benchmark index achieves a return of –7 per cent.

We can therefore say that the investment portfolio has achieved a relative return of 4 per cent for the investment period in question.

Specific client requirements

This section is intended to address issues other than affordability and attitude to investment risk, which will have been identified and discussed at an earlier stage in the process. Investors may often have certain preferences and beliefs which they will want incorporating into their investment strategy and these may include factors such as accessibility, personal dislikes of certain institutions and ethical beliefs. Whilst the investment professional may not share the opinions or beliefs of the investor, their wishes and instructions must still be taken into consideration, discussed and incorporated into the investment strategy if the client insists on their inclusion. It is certainly an issue which merits careful discussion with the client, particularly if, in the opinion of the investment professional, the restrictions placed upon the investment strategy may have a material effect upon performance and outcomes. One of the most common and topical issues which may be the subject of careful discussion is when investors have definite ethical and socially responsible beliefs, which they insist on being incorporated into the investment strategy. Some investors may feel so strongly about these issues that they wish to avoid their capital being invested in companies of which they do not approve. It is important that this sort of issue is discussed in a thorough but sensitive way because investors must be made aware that the greater the restrictions they place on the portfolio construction process, the more limits there are for suitable performance as there will be fewer investment options from which to select.

In practice

Placing significant investment restrictions may have the unintended consequences of increasing the risk within the investment portfolio due to restricting the availability of diversification opportunities and the possibility of over-concentrating in sectors which may be strongly correlated.

Many larger companies may inadvertently be screened out of ethical funds due to the broad spread of their activities either directly, or by association with subsidiaries within the broader group, and this may also effectively restrict the available investment choices to a greater number of smaller and therefore higher-risk companies.

Prior to commencing the assembly of an ethically sensitive portfolio, the investment professional will encourage the client to carefully consider their specific concerns and identify what types of issues or corporate activities are of particular concern. Some of the more common issues which are of concern to ethically minded investors include avoiding investing in companies which are associated with certain negative criteria including:

- nuclear power;
- pornography;
- gambling;

- animal testing;
- intensive farming and genetic modification of food;
- arms dealing or military manufacturing;
- poor records on human rights/child labour.

Some investors go a step further than negative screening and wish to direct their investment capital towards companies in which they positively approve, which may mean companies which display some degree of social responsibility and/or support socially desirable activities.

> **In practice**
>
> **A step beyond negative screening**
>
> This is termed 'socially responsible investment' and the type of positive factors in question will include:
>
> - sound supply chain practices, for example ensuring that a fair price is paid to raw material suppliers;
> - ecologically friendly products and services;
> - sound corporate governance;
> - equal opportunities employer;
> - good record of contribution to the community.

This ethical and socially responsible investment process is possible as there are now sufficient collective investment funds and individual company shares which fulfil these criteria. The Ethical Investment Research Service (EIRIS) is the leading independent provider of research into ethical performance of companies and provides valuable specialist assistance and information to help finance professionals and investors in making investment decisions.[15] It offers comprehensive research into around 3,000 companies in Europe, North America and the Asia-Pacific region and covers over 60 different social, environmental and ethical areas. Research is undertaken in areas such as environment, human rights, supply chain issues, corporate governance, international conventions and stakeholder issues. There are also a number of indices which measure the performance of companies which meet appropriate ethical standards, including the FTSE4Good index, Domini 400 Social Index and the Dow Jones EURO STOXX Sustainability Index.[16,17,18]

Costs and charges

It is not possible to address the process of creating an effective investment strategy without giving careful consideration to the effects of costs and charges upon the investment. The importance is unchallenged because fees, costs, penalties and charges will reduce the overall investment return achieved and clearly, the higher the magnitude of the overall costs of investing, the greater will be the effect upon the net return to the investor. We can assess the impact of costs and charges on investment performance funds simply by recognizing that the greater the magnitude of costs and charges, the greater the detrimental effect upon net investment returns. A range of charges may be applicable to an investment portfolio dependent upon the assets which are held and some of the charges will be applied at different times in the investment cycle.

In practice

Example 1

In the case of initial charges, these reduce the amount of capital that is actually invested in the product at the beginning of the investment period. So, if we invest £100,000 into an investment product where a 5 per cent initial charge is levied, then £5,000 in charges are taken and only £95,000 is actually invested initially. This means that the capital growth in the early period of investment is actually replacing the loss made by the effect of the charges.

Example 2

In the case of ongoing charges, such as annual management charges, higher charges would have a greater cumulative effect on the total charges paid over a long period of time. So, if we have an annual management charge of say, 1.5 per cent per year, this charge will be taken every year that the investment capital is under management and is charged at 1.5 per cent of the value of the investment fund. If the value of the fund is increasing year-on-year, then this charge will also be increasing as it is 1.5 per cent of the value of the fund. Over a period of years, this may amount to quite a substantial cumulative charge.

It is clear that when comparing investment products various characteristics are important; however, when comparing two similar products, such as collective funds, if performance is comparable then the investor may be best served by a fund with a lower charging structure as this is likely to result in greater net returns compared with a more expensive fund. The investment horizon may also have a significant bearing upon investment outcomes, depending upon the different types of charges, as this will affect the period of time that the capital will remain invested. Investment products with high initial charges are not ideal for short-term investing as the high initial charge spread over a short period of time may effectively prove to be costly and affect net returns disproportionately. Equally, investment products with low initial charges but high ongoing charges, such as annual management charges, may prove to be expensive in terms of cumulative costs over a long investment period.

Domestic regulatory bodies are keen to ensure that prospective investors are made aware of the charging structure of retail investment products and require the publication of detailed data to ensure that costs and charges are transparent, to allow informed choice. Investment professionals are required to disclose this information clearly to prospective investors prior to investment decisions being finalized. The industry-standard measure of the impact of total charges is termed the 'reduction in yield' and this takes account of both initial charges and ongoing charges applied to an investment product. The published data would usually show the effect of the charges on an example investment lump-sum, over a standard investment period which is typically 10 years. The aim of the published data is to permit industry professionals and investors to conduct an informed comparison of different retail investment products under consideration. The data is published in table form showing the charges in cash terms and the reduction in yield as a percentage. A standard worded sentence will accompany the table of data to clearly disclose the effect of the charges by saying; for example, 'Putting it another way, this will have the same effect as bringing investment growth down from 8 per cent per year to 6.3 per cent per year.' (See Figure 12.3.)

In practice

This information, whilst useful, is not always a perfect fit for the needs of every situation because the data is disclosed over a standard 10-year period and the investor's time horizon may be quite different to that. Furthermore, the growth rate assumptions made should not lead investors to have unrealistic expectations of investment growth, as these will simply be used for disclosure purposes rather than to encourage expectations of the magnitude of investment returns.

Figure 12.3 Example: transparent publishing of the effect of charges

Examples of the effect of charges (for illustrative purposes only)

Growth fund:

		Standard growth rates applied:	
Lump sum invested:	£10,000	ISA	5%
Ongoing charge:	0.86%	Investment Account	4.50%
Service fee:	0.35%		

£10,000 invested in a growth fund in an ISA

At end of year	Effect of charges to date	What you might get back at 5%
1	£126	£10,300
3	£413	£11,100
5	£749	£12,000
10	£1,850	£14,400

In this example, charges would reduce the amount your investment grows each year by 1.3%. Putting it another way, this would have the effect of bringing the illustrated investment growth down from 5.0% to 3.7%.

£10,000 invested in a growth fund in an Investment Fund Account

Effect of charges to date	What you might get back at 4.5%
£126	£10,300
£407	£11,000
£732	£11,700
£1,770	£13,700

In this example, charges would reduce the amount your investment grows each year by 1.3%. Putting it another way, this would have the effect of bringing the illustrated investment growth down from 4.5% to 3.2%.

Income fund:

		Standard growth rates applied:	
Lump sum invested:	£10,000	ISA	5%
Ongoing charge:	0.86%	Investment Account	4.50%
Service fee:	0.35%		

(continued)

Figure 12.3 (Continued)

	£10,000 invested in an income fund in an ISA			£10,000 invested in an income fund in an Investment Fund Account		
At end of year	Effect of charges to date	Income paid out	What you might get back at 5%	Effect of charges to date	Income paid out	What you might get back at 4.5%
1	£123	£302	£10,000	£122	£301	£10,000
3	£277	£912	£10,200	£372	£905	£10,000
5	£645	£1,520	£10,300	£630	£1,510	£10,100
10	£1,370	£3,110	£10,700	£1,310	£3,030	£10,200

In this example, charges would reduce the amount your investment grows each year by 1.3%. Putting it another way, this would have the effect of bringing the illustrated investment growth down from 5% to 3.7%.

In this example, charges would reduce the amount your investment grows each year by 1.3%. Putting it another way, this would have the effect of bringing the illustrated investment growth down from 4.5% to 3.2%.

There are a variety of types of fees and charges which may be levied by retail investment products and these include:

- Initial charges: may be referred to as a front-end loading and applied upon initial investment when investors acquire shares or units in an investment product.
- Annual charges: may be referred to as an annual management charge or annual management fee and will be periodically charged, based upon the value of the investment fund. For collective investment funds the magnitude of this charge will be around 1.0-1.5 per cent per year although some collectives such as ETFs are likely to be rather lower at around 0.5 per cent per year or less.
- Exit charges: the exit charge may sometimes be referred to as a back-end loading and may be levied when investors disinvest from the fund and sell their shares/units in the fund. Usually, this type of charge would be taken in lieu of a front-end loading or initial charge and may be seen as an incentive for investors to remain invested in the fund for a minimum period of time, as the exit charges are usually staggered over a period of time, reducing in magnitude. For example, exit charges typically may be for the first five years of investment and may be structured as 5/4/3/2/1 per cent so they are falling over the 5-year period.
- Performance-related charges: certain types of fund may carry additional performance fees which aim to reward the fund manager with an additional fee, typically percentage based, if a specified benchmark is outperformed. This type of fee structure may be quite complex and is usually subject to meeting certain criteria in addition to performance.

In addition to product-based charges, investors who seek the advice and assistance of a finance professional in arranging and managing their investments will also be required to pay fees for this service; the professionals in question may be financial advisers, wealth managers or investment managers. Financial advice can be paid for in various ways depending upon the domestic regulations in force. Historically in the UK, for example, advice provided by a finance professional could be paid for by a fees structure and/or a commission-based system involving a payment of initial commission and/or commission paid from the investment product over its lifetime, known as a repeat or trail commission. The repeat commission was a payment usually based upon a percentage of the value of the fund. The previous UK regulatory body, the FSA, conducted the 'Retail Regulatory Review' (RDR), which came into effect on 31 December 2012 and its intention was to address the long-standing perception of bias in the advice given by financial advisers to their retail investment clients. Prior to the RDR, initial and/or trail commission was a popular form of remuneration for finance professionals and permitted advisers to be remunerated by a commission basis, for giving their clients new and ongoing investment advice. The commission payments were made by the financial institution or fund manager and taken from the initial or annual management fee. Initial commissions varied between, typically 3 to 5 per cent and the trail commissions were typically 0.5 per cent of the value of the investment fund, paid annually.

As a result of the reforms introduced in the UK by the RDR, the payment of advisers by commission has been banned and therefore product providers may no longer pay commissions to advisors for distributing their financial products and therefore the commission-based system has been replaced by a completely fee-based charges system, known as adviser charging. All authorized retail finance professionals now have in place a charging structure that must be explained and agreed by a prospective investor and retail client. Payment for advisory services must be paid directly by clients and charging structures may take a number of forms which range from a fixed fee, an hourly rate to a proportional fee based on a percentage of the amount initially invested. These types of fees may also be augmented by agreed ongoing charges paid monthly or annually, if an ongoing service is being provided.

In practice

The cost of the advice process is deemed to be completely transparent and the types and magnitude of fees that may be charged are provided to the investor and agreed at the outset, with no further fees charged, without prior agreement with the client. Where ongoing management is offered as a service, additional fees may be charged to the investor based upon the value of any investments under management; however, these must also be disclosed and agreed prior to commencement of the management process.

The unfortunate consequence of this commission ban has been that many ordinary investors are now unable to afford independent financial advice as they cannot afford to pay the fees charged by advisers and do not have the option of a commission-based remuneration to access professional financial advice.

The type of service offered and the level of fees charged for advisory and wealth management services provided will clearly differ with different finance professionals and it is therefore important that investors are satisfied that the range of services and fee structures offered by their chosen investment professional meet with their approval and match their requirements and needs. With the fee-charging model it would be common for there to be some form of service level agreement agreed, which will include bespoke financial advice and/or investment management as part of a structured service along with periodic reviews carried out at an agreed frequency. In addition to the fees payable for the advice and management services, it is possible that there may also be fees payable for additional specialist services which may be required. These may include:

- Accountancy/tax specialist: whilst finance professionals are aware and competent in dealing with tax issues, it may be prudent in the case of complex situations, or very large investments, to engage the services of a tax specialist in order to avoid potential adverse taxation implications at some future time.
- Stockbroker: it may also be necessary to make use of the services of a stockbroker, particularly when considering direct investment in company shares or other market-traded assets.
- Legal: some parts of financial planning may involve the use of complex legal documents such as trusts and it may be prudent in this situation to engage the services of a solicitor, experienced in these matters, in order to avoid incorrect use of complex legal devices.

Performance measurement and review

It is important that the outcome of the investment process and the decisions that have been made are readily quantifiable and this is achieved by a thorough analysis of the investment performance. This process of measuring and analysing investment outcomes is generally referred to as 'investment performance evaluation'. To carry out an effective performance evaluation on an investment portfolio or an investment fund, we must first decide how best to measure the performance in a fair way. It is most common to measure this type of investment performance by comparison with an appropriate benchmark. We considered the concept of absolute returns and relative returns earlier in this chapter and this form of investment performance measurement corresponds to a relative return. Some form of a performance benchmark is an important part of the investment process as it provides both investors and the investment professional with a useful reference point against which to gauge or monitor the performance of an investment portfolio or fund.

Following the creation of an investment portfolio the investment professional and the client should agree upon a realistic benchmark to adopt; the choice of the benchmark will be dictated by the asset mix utilized within the investment portfolio and compatibility with the risk and expected return profile. Portfolio performance will rarely be measured as an absolute return, but usually relative to appropriate benchmark. It is also important that the investment professional and the client agree on an appropriate frequency of review in order to monitor performance and to ensure continued adherence to the client's objectives. It would be usual to utilize a time-weighted measure of return, which is most suitable to determine returns achieved and then determine the adequacy of the return either by absolute or relative performance return measures.

Keyword

The **time-weighted rate of return (TWRR)** is generally viewed as the preferred method to calculate the rate of return in the investment management industry, as it removes the impact of cashflows on the rate of return calculation. With this method, returns are averaged over time and the time-weighted rate of return is obtained by splitting the total investment period in question into 'subperiods', which may be monthly, annually or another appropriate period of time. A subperiod is created at any point when there is a movement of capital either into or out of the portfolio. A new valuation of the portfolio must be obtained just prior to the capital movement, so that the rate of return is not distorted by the magnitude and the timing of the capital movement. The process then involves calculation of the holding period return for each subperiod and then linking all the subperiod returns together. The time-weighted rate of return is calculated by compounding the rate of return for each individual subperiod, whilst applying an equal weight to each subperiod in the process.

The formula used for TWRR is:

$$R_{TWRR} = [(1 + r_{t,1}) \times (1 + r_{t,2}) \times \cdots \times (1 + r_{t,n})] - 1$$

where:

$$r_{t,n} = \frac{V_1 - V_0}{V_0}$$

and

V_1 = value of the portfolio including accrued income at the period end
V_0 = value of the portfolio including accrued income at the period start

In practice

Given the following scenario:

- an initial investment of £250,000 is made on 31 December 2015 and on 31 August 2016 the investment portfolio is valued at £270,500;
- at this point an additional capital investment of £30,000 is added to the investment portfolio, increasing the value to £300,500;
- following challenging market conditions, by 31 December 2016 the investment portfolio had decreased in value to £290,200.

Calculate the time-weighted rate of return for the year:

$$R_{TWRR} = (1 + r_{t,1}) \times (1 + r_{t,2}) - 1$$

where:

$$r_{t,1} = \frac{(270{,}500 - 250{,}000)}{250{,}000} = 0.082$$

$$r_{t,2} = \frac{(290{,}200 - 300{,}500)}{300{,}500} = -0.034$$

So:

$$R_{TWRR} = (1 + 0.082) \times (1 - 0.034) - 1$$
$$= (1.082) \times (0.966) - 1$$
$$= 0.045$$
$$= 4.5\%$$

Benchmarks may vary depending upon circumstances and the ease with which an appropriate benchmark may be identified. The use of an inappropriate benchmark will render the performance comparison process invalid and of little use. One of three common options will usually be selected to form an appropriate benchmark:

- Funds within the same investment universe – comparison against the performance of same sector or similar funds, with similar aims and objectives.
- Relevant bond or stock market index – comparison against the performance of an appropriate market index.
- Composite benchmark – sometimes known as a synthetic benchmark, comparison with a custom or bespoke benchmark may be required for funds with very specific investment objectives or constraints, or in the case where the portfolio contains multiple asset classes. A composite index construction involves identification of several relevant indices, taking their individual return and multiplying by the appropriate asset class weighting relative to the investment portfolio composition. This will identify a composite return against which to benchmark.

Broader guidelines are also in place for large fund managers and the performance management industry benefited from the introduction of Global Investment Performance Standards (GIPS) which was established in 1999 by the CFA Institute.[19] This voluntary standard has been adopted in over 20 countries globally and lays down global standards for calculating and presenting performance figures, therefore promoting best standards for investment management firms when calculating and presenting results to clients. This type of analysis of investment outcomes is applicable to overall investment performance; however, certain types of performance may also be measured specifically against the investor's identified aims and objectives which need to be to be fulfilled; for example, the provision of a certain level of income stream at a specified date in the future and for a specified or indefinite period of time.

We must also consider that the investment performance of the portfolio should not be considered in isolation, as consideration must be given to the risk that has been taken in achieving the investment returns. A rational investor will take no more risk than is necessary to achieve the required level of returns and it is the responsibility of the investment professional to ensure that the risk within the investment portfolio is commensurate with the investor's identified risk appetite and that no more risk is taken than is absolutely necessary to achieve the investor's identified investment aims and objectives. It would be over-simplistic for investors to judge the performance of their investment portfolios, or prospective investment choices, entirely based upon the investment returns achieved, as consideration must be given to the risk taken to achieve those returns. Investment professionals have at their disposal, a range of performance measurement tools to assist with portfolio evaluations and consider the issue of risk and return; for example, the Sharpe and Treynor ratios. These are commonly utilized in investment performance evaluation and both Sharpe and Treynor ratios combine risk and return performance into a single value, allowing a measure of performance that includes risk, applicable across a range of investment risk preference. We know from Chapter 4 on risk that the two ratios are similar but consider risk in a slightly different way; however, they can prove to be useful in assessing risk-adjusted performance for both prospective investment decisions and also in assessing the suitability of the investor's portfolio performance.

Sharpe ratio uses standard deviation of the asset or portfolio as the risk measure, rather than considering only systematic risk represented by the beta coefficient. This effectively evaluates the portfolio for both return and diversification so it is generally considered to be most appropriate for use with well-diversified portfolios.

In practice

Example of Sharpe ratio

An adviser is researching two suitable investment funds and will choose one to recommend to a client.

The fund data is shown in the table below and an appropriate risk-free rate has been assumed for the period of this analysis, which is 1.5 per cent.

Table 12.B

	Fund A	Fund B
Return (%)	12.4	14.1
Standard deviation (%)	4.0	5.5

Using the formula:

$$\text{Sharpe ratio} = \frac{\text{fund return} - \text{risk-free return}}{\text{standard deviation}}$$

$$\text{Sharpe ratio (A)} = \frac{12.4 - 1.5}{4} = 2.72$$

$$\text{Sharpe ratio (B)} = \frac{14.1 - 1.5}{5.5} = 2.29$$

The adviser would recommend Fund A, despite Fund B having better performance, because the Sharpe ratio of Fund A is higher and therefore this indicates more skill and judgement is being exhibited by the manager of Fund A.

It is notable that the most suitable asset or portfolio is not identified to be one with the highest investment performance, but one with the most superior risk-adjusted return.

Sometimes referred to as the reward to volatility ratio, Treynor ratio takes into consideration risk from fluctuations in the market and the risk from fluctuations of individual assets. Unlike the Sharpe ratio, Treynor ratio utilizes beta coefficient, which is a measure of systematic risk. It makes the assumption that the investor has a well-diversified portfolio and therefore, unsystematic risk is not considered. For this reason, Treynor ratio is more suitable for use with adequately diversified portfolios.

In practice

Example of Treynor ratio

An advisor has researched the data provided below in order to select a preferred choice of fund on behalf of a client.

During the period in question, an appropriate risk-free rate of return is 1.6 per cent.

Table 12.C

	Fund X	Fund Y	Fund Z
Fund return (%)	11.2	13.1	14.6
Fund Beta	0.84	0.95	1.12

Using the formula:

$$\text{Treynor ratio} = \frac{\text{fund return} - \text{risk-free return}}{\text{Beta coefficient}}$$

$$\text{Treynor ratio (X)} = \frac{11.2 - 1.6}{0.84} = 11.43$$

$$\text{Treynor ratio (Y)} = \frac{13.1 - 1.6}{0.95} = 12.11$$

$$\text{Treynor ratio (Z)} = \frac{14.6 - 1.6}{1.12} = 11.61$$

So the preferred fund would be Fund Y, as the higher Treynor ratio implies a greater level of management skill being employed in order to generate the return.

In the case of both Sharpe and Treynor ratios, the greater the magnitude of the ratio observed, the more suitable is the risk-adjusted performance and therefore, the better the asset or the portfolio. The effective measurement and evaluation of portfolio performance can therefore be seen to be a key aspect of the investment process and will serve to reliably inform investors with regard to how effectively their capital has been invested.

It is therefore clear that a key requirement for an investment professional, whether an adviser or a wealth manager, is the provision of current, reliable and accurate reports regarding the content and performance of an investor's investment portfolio. This must also ensure that any other relevant contextual information is provided to assist their client to understand and therefore make meaningful use of information provided. This may for example include an assessment of the current economic situation and market outlook. Investment professionals may provide continuous monitoring facilities such as web-based portals which allow clients to inspect portfolio performance at their leisure. Effective execution of a portfolio management strategy therefore requires that the investment portfolio is monitored and reviewed regularly to ensure it maintains positive progress against the key factors including objectives, suitability, costs, charges and performance criteria. The periodic review period will also be the opportunity to ensure that the measures to manage risks continue to be appropriate and effective and that there have been no changes in either legislation or domestic regulation which would require there to be changes in the investment portfolio. It is therefore also important to maintain an appropriate method of communication with clients in addition to a scheduled periodic review and this may include web-based portals and the provision of hard-copy documents.

The length and frequency of periodic review meetings would usually be discussed and agreed in advance in order to support the portfolio management strategy that has been implemented. However, there should also ideally be the flexibility to contact and discuss interim issues as they arise; for example, changes in taxation allowances, legislative issues and the opportunity of new investment products or features. Investment professionals also recognize that the implementation of an investment portfolio is not a one-off exercise because of various factors, including changes in investor's circumstances, changes in the markets and the constant fluctuation of asset prices relative to each other. The last factor is a particularly important issue because, as asset prices fluctuate on the markets, this will result in a change in the relative weight of each asset held within in the investment portfolio. Equity-based assets usually outperform fixed-interest assets, particularly over extended time periods and therefore this has the consequence that over time, a mixed-asset investment portfolio will stray towards a riskier weighting than intended.

The review process serves to 'close the loop' seen in Figure 12.1 (p. 407) and allows the investment professional to keep in touch with changes in the investor's personal circumstances which may require amendments to the aims and objectives to be pursued and therefore prompt changes to the investment portfolio. Maintaining the ability to be flexible in the event of changing circumstances is one of the reasons for retaining an 'emergency fund' and also for ensuring a certain amount of liquidity within the investment portfolio. It is also quite common for periodic changes in the economic cycle or financial markets to impact the investment portfolio to the point where the investment portfolio will require a review to assess the impact of these changes and to determine any appropriate changes for minimizing the impact. This review process may require changes ranging from a relatively simple re-balancing of the investment portfolio through to a fundamental re-assessment of the whole portfolio content and strategy.

A consequence of this review process may also be that a review of the 'appropriate' benchmark may be required if this is no longer deemed to be representative of the portfolio objective or the assets held within the new portfolio. Investment professionals may encourage investors to contact them when changes in personal circumstances occur or are anticipated, in order to maintain accurate records which reflect the client's circumstances. Alternatively, it may be that the investment professional will use the periodic review meeting to refresh their records and update any material changes.

Summary

The process of investment management involves various factors; however, the overall process should result in the maximization of agreed outcomes for the investor whilst minimizing the risk taken in order to achieve the outcomes. It would not be rational, reasonable or professional to expose the investor's capital to any more risk than was necessary to achieve the investor's objectives. We have examined the client/adviser relationship in Chapter 11, which describes the process that the finance professional must follow to accurately identify factors such as the investor's aims, objectives, investment horizon and attitude to investment risk. It is of paramount importance that a robust process has been followed to determine this crucial information prior to commencement of the investment management process. The investment management process is often referred to as a portfolio management process because it would be unusual, but not impossible, for an investor's interests to be best served by restricting their invested capital to a single asset or security. This is, of course, very much dependent upon a plethora of factors including the individual's personal circumstances, available capital, liquidity requirements and appetite for investment risk.

Check your understanding

1 What is the relevance of asset allocation in the context of investment portfolios?
2 How will changes in the financial economy and changes in the domestic business cycle affect security selection in an investment portfolio?
3 Consider the different management styles and their implications within investment funds.

4 What factors would be of concern to an ethically minded investor?

5 What is the importance of the following with regard to investment performance: a) charges; b) benchmarks?

Further reading

The following books may be useful:

Bodie, Z, Kane, A and Marcus, A (2013) *Essentials of Investments,* 9th global edn, McGraw Hill

Reilly, F and Brown, K (2011) *Analysis of Investments and Management of Portfolios*, international edn, South-Western College

Strong, RA (2008) *Portfolio Construction, Management and Protection*, 5th edn, South-Western College

The following sites may be useful:

www.cfainstitute.org/
www.ft.com
www.bloomberg.com

Taxation 13

By the end of this chapter you should have an understanding of the following key areas of taxation:

- the difference between domicile and residency and its effect on the type and amount of taxation paid by an individual;
- the liability to pay income tax on earned and unearned income, including calculating amounts due and payment methods;
- the liability to pay national insurance (NI), rates and the relationship between employment status and the types and amount of NI;
- the liability for capital gains tax including calculating amounts due and methods to minimize payments;
- the liability to pay inheritance tax including lifetime transfers, transfers on death, intestacy and the interaction of income tax and inheritance tax and tax minimizing strategies;
- the liability to pay stamp duty on sales of shares and property and calculation of amount due;
- the liability to pay VAT and calculation of amounts due;
- the liability to pay corporation tax including calculation of amounts due.

Introduction

Legal entities, such as people, companies and trusts are taxed throughout their existence depending on their circumstances, others such as charities and investment vehicles may not be. Taxation levels vary and we will see that taxation can be due on the following: gains in value of some assets realized on sale; when goods and services are purchased and sold; on earned and unearned income for companies and individuals; and potentially on the value of assets held when individuals die. As investment managers, whilst taxation may not seem to be a primary area of concern, not only does it affect the level of clients' returns and their cashflow but also potentially our own businesses. Therefore, we need to be aware of the possible effects of taxation to ensure clients factor its effects into their investment decisions both in the amount and date it is due to be paid.

Financial advisers are often privy to a client's most private financial information which may, if released in error, have a negative impact on an individual or their business. As such, managers have a general duty to maintain confidentiality in respect of a client's income. In addition, as finance managers are holding information in respect of individual clients they are obligated to safeguard retained data under the Data Protection Act to ensure it is only released to third parties with the proper authorization. There may be occasions where a financial adviser becomes aware of information which may constitute a breach of the law and this may result in an obligation to disclose information to the relevant authorities, for example under the Proceeds of Crime Act (2002). In such circumstances and to avoid criminal charges themselves, managers should report their suspicions to the appropriate person within an organization. In the case of the Proceeds of Crime Act, for instance, this would be the Money Laundering Reporting Officer (MLRO) who in turn will report to the National Crime Agency if appropriate.

In this chapter we will cover each of the following taxes in detail looking at when a tax liability may arise, the amount of taxation which may be due, who may be liable for payment, when payment may be required and consider if there are any potential tax-planning strategies available:

- Income tax: liability based on earned and unearned income for individuals, charities and trustees.
- National insurance: liability based on employees and self-employed earned income and used to build entitlement to state benefits.
- Capital gains tax: liability based on the increases in value of certain assets when they are disposed of.
- Inheritance tax: liability based on value of assets given away during life and following death.
- Stamp duty, Stamp Duty Reserve Tax and Stamp Duty Land Tax: liability based on transfer of stocks and property.
- Corporation tax: liability based on earned and unearned income for companies.
- Value added tax: liability based on the value added to goods and services through processing

Tax avoidance and tax evasion

> **Keyword**
>
> **Tax avoidance** is a legal method of minimizing a client's tax payments; **tax evasion** is an illegal method of minimizing a client's tax payments.

Finance managers can legally assist clients to minimize or delay their tax liabilities. Such policies are known as tax avoidance or tax mitigation and are legal. In fact, one aspect of tax planning can be to defer taxation payments with the aim of improving a client's cashflow by retaining cash for a longer period before payment and, by the time the tax liability occurs, to potentially have reduced tax rates due to changes in income levels over time, for example, due to retirement. Tax avoidance is different from tax evasion, which is illegal and involves not paying all taxation legally due by withholding information from the tax authorities or other methods of reducing payments. Such actions may result in a criminal conviction with punishments including severe fines and penalties for both the client and the manager involved as well as potential prison sentences.

Tax evasion has been highlighted in the media over recent years and there is an ongoing global initiative to eradicate it initiated in the United States in 2014 (Foreign Account Tax Compliance Act (FATCA)). FATCA has now been superseded by the Common Reporting Standard (CRS) developed by the OECD (Organization for Economic Co-operation and Development) and incorporated into EU and UK law by the European Directive on Administrative Co-operation (DAC) and the International Tax Compliance Regulations 2015, respectively. The CRS rules are like FATCA but are wider ranging and include a framework for the approximately 90 signatories to obtain information from domestic financial institutions provision for an annual automatic sharing of information between the member jurisdictions.

In the UK, the first financial statements covered by CRS were those in existence on 1 January 2016, which will be reported to HMRC by 31 May 2017 with HMRC sharing the information with participating jurisdictions by 30 September 2017.

> **In practice**
>
> New UK tax evasion penalties came into force on 1 January 2017. For more information, see Kate Allen's article in the *Financial Times* from January 2017.[1]
>
> On 11 August 2016 HMRC website published details of two tax avoidance cases where it has won more than £820 million of tax and interest owed.[2] This was from a tax avoidance scheme where artificial losses from investments in films such as *Avatar* and *Die Hard 4* were used to offset other income.

Payment of taxation can reduce the return from specific assets, and as such the client and the manager should be aware of the impact of their actions on taxation due when investing. On occasions, however, both clients and advisers can become obsessed with minimizing taxation paid leading to complex tax avoidance schemes being used where the cost of the scheme does not equate to the levels of tax saved. Such avoidance should not be the primary reasoning behind investing; instead investments should be based on an individual's requirements for income and capital gains in conjunction with their personal circumstances and risk profile. In fact, as we have seen in the media during 2016, historic tax-planning strategies may be attacked by HMRC through the courts leading to them being ineffective. Therefore, finance managers should consider the following ideas, for example, when considering the taxation implications of investing for a specific client:

- the use of a taxation or legal specialist to assess a client's individual complex tax requirements;
- details of ongoing consultations or proposed alterations to tax law;
- ensuring all relevant allowances and tax wrappers are utilized;
- ensuring all the relevant requirements to obtain tax relief are fulfilled;
- ensure all reporting requirements to the relevant authorities are fulfilled.

Tax years

Tax years separate income and gains into distinct periods allowing them to be assessed, with different income and gains being assessed often by different taxes. On some occasions tax is paid monthly and deducted from salary, for other tax liabilities an annual tax return will be completed including calculations of taxation due. This will be sent to HMRC to agree and following agreement the liability will fall due on a specific date.

> **Keyword**
>
> The tax year is different from a calendar year, which can make everything slightly more confusing, with tax years running from 6 April one year to 5 April the following year. So, for instance the 2017–18 tax year runs from 6 April 2017 to 5 April 2018.

Residency and domicile

The total amount of UK taxation individuals pay in the UK will be determined initially by two factors: 1) whether they were considered a UK resident for tax purposes in a tax year; 2) whether they were domiciled or non-domiciled in the UK, ie is the UK their legal permanent home?

For most clients, it will be easy to tell where they are resident and/or domiciled. However, for some, especially those who work or live abroad for part of the year it can be more difficult and due to the implications for the payment and rates of tax suffered it is important to be sure of an individual's residency and domicile status.

> **In practice**
>
> Financial institutions in the UK and in Crown Dependencies (Jersey, Guernsey and Isle of Man) and Overseas Territories (Anguilla, Bermuda, British Virgin Islands, Cayman Islands, Gibraltar, Montserrat and the Turks & Caicos) are required to obtain information, using a self-certification form, potentially in conjunction with other information, to verify a client's residency when they open a new account. The information received will be validated with money-laundering information and know your customer (KYC) information. This residency information will then be shared between tax jurisdictions to ensure transparency regarding residents of one country opening accounts in other jurisdictions.

Domicile

Keyword

Domicile is the easier of the two concepts to confirm. Unless an individual changes domicile when they become an adult, domicile is assumed to be the same as their father's. So, if you are born and live in the UK, your father is British and you have no strong connections with another country you will be domiciled in the UK.

Residency can be a little more difficult to identify, relying on the answers to three separate tests:

- the automatic overseas test, which if an individual meets the criteria means they are deemed non-resident for taxation;
- the automatic residence test, where if individuals meet any of the criteria they are deemed to be resident for taxation in the UK;
- the sufficient ties test which is used as a last test, if either the automatic overseas or automatic residence test cannot provide a clear conclusion.

In practice

The automatic overseas test

If individuals meet any of the test criteria they are deemed to be non-UK resident for tax purposes:

1. They work overseas full-time AND only work in the UK for a maximum of 30 days per year (work includes incidental duties such as training, travel and reporting duties and a working day occurs when more than three hours in the day is spent at work) AND they spend 90 days or fewer per year in the UK.
2. They were deemed resident for tax purposes in one or more of the preceding three tax years and were in the UK for fewer than 16 days in the current tax year.
3. They were not present in the UK for any of the three preceding tax years and present for fewer than 46 days in the current tax year.

The automatic residency test

If an individual does not meet the criteria to be considered non-UK resident using the automatic overseas test then they will be assessed using the automatic residency test to determine if they are UK residents. The criteria used are:

1. The individual spends at least 183 days in the UK in a tax year.
2. Their only or main home is in the UK. This home must be available to be used for at least 91 days and they must physically reside there for at least 30 days – this does not have to be on consecutive nights; they can be individual nights or short stays.
3. They work full-time in the UK for 365 days a year.

The sufficient ties test

If neither of the above tests proves conclusive the sufficient ties test is used. This is not a binary yes or no, rather there is a sliding scale which assesses a combination of the amount of time spent in the UK and the number of ties required, to prove UK residency.

Table 13.A

Days spent in the UK in the tax year under consideration	No. of UK ties needed if UK resident for at least one of the three tax years preceding the tax year being considered	No. of ties needed if NOT a UK resident in any of the three tax years preceding the tax year under consideration
16–45	At least 4 ties required	N/A
46–90	At least 3 ties required	All 4
91–120	At least 2 ties required	At least 3 ties required
Over 120	At least 1 tie required	At least 2 ties required

The four ties are:

1. Family:
   a. individual's spouse; civil partner; common law partner or minor children live in the UK;
   b. for minor children, this does not include time spent in the UK for education or if the individual is visiting minors for fewer than 61 days per tax year.

> 2 Accommodation:
>
>   a. individuals have accessible UK accommodation deemed available for use for at least 91 days continuously in a tax year AND they spend at least one night there;
>
>   b. work:
>
>   individuals work for at least three hours a day for 40 days or more either self-employed or as an employee.
>
> 3 90 day:
>
>   a. the individual has spent at least 90 days in the UK in either of the last two tax years.
>
> In addition, for individuals leaving the country there is an additional potential tie, which determines if they have spent more days in the UK in one tax year than in any other single country.

In most cases, individuals are deemed to be resident or non-resident for the whole of a tax year. However, on occasion, for instance due to work commitments, an individual may leave or arrive in the UK part-way through a tax year. In such circumstances, they may be eligible for a split tax year, which assesses them partially as a UK resident and partially as a non-UK resident.

The effect of residency and domicile on the amount of tax paid

Individuals will potentially be one of four combinations of residency and domicile in each tax year and that combination will determine what income and gains are taxed, the rates of taxation and their eligibility to certain personal allowances, for example, annual allowance for income tax or capital gains tax. Table 13.1 summarizes the possible combinations for individuals.

The two possible methods of paying taxation noted above are:

- Arising basis: pay UK taxes on worldwide income as it arises and worldwide gains as they accrue.
- Remittance basis:

Table 13.1 Residency/domicile combinations for tax purposes

	UK-domiciled	**Non-UK-domiciled**
UK resident for tax	Normally use arising basis of taxation for worldwide income	Can use remittance basis or arising basis of taxation for worldwide income
Non-UK resident for tax	Can use remittance basis or arising basis for taxation of worldwide income but capital gains will be assessed on the arising basis	No taxation liability as no connection to the UK

- Pay UK taxes on UK income and UK gains as they arise and accrue respectively.
- Income and gains from the rest of the world are only taxed in the UK as they are remitted to the UK.
- Foreign income/gains may already have been taxed in the country of origin. In that case, they should still be declared in the UK via a self-assessment tax return. It may be possible to claim double taxation relief, where tax already paid in a foreign company partly or totally offsets any UK tax liability.
- The remittance basis is only allowable in a tax year where an individual has foreign income or gains.
- The remittance basis does not have to be used and will result in the loss of personal allowances.

Choosing to use the remittance basis

Individuals will need to assess their personal circumstances to decide whether to use the arising basis and keep their personal allowance, or use the remittance basis and lose their personal allowance; whether the remittance basis will have to be returned via a separate form and if they will be liable for the remittance-based charge (RBC). This decision will be made based on:

- the amount of foreign income and or gains which arise in a tax year in which the individual lives outside the UK;
- if the individual is under or over 18;
- how long an individual has been resident in the UK.

In practice

Table 13.B

Amount of unremitted foreign income and/or gains which arise or accrue in the relevant tax year	
Less than £2,000	£2,000 or more*
Remittance basis can be used without making a formal claim or losing entitlement to personal allowances and the CGT exemption	If individuals wish to use the remittance method, a formal claim must be made via the relevant section of the self-assessment tax return, resulting in personal allowances and capital gains exemptions being lost

* In addition, if the amount is above £2,000 then the RBC charge may be payable if the individual is aged 18 or over and has been resident in the UK for at least seven of the nine previous years. The charge is annual and made through the self-assessed taxation system.

Paying the RBC does not exclude an individual from paying UK tax on UK income and gains (if you are domiciled in the UK but not tax resident) and any foreign income and gains you remit to the UK. The current level of remittance charge is:

- £30,000 for individuals resident for 7 of the last 9 years.
- £60,000 for individuals resident for 12 of the last 14 years.
- Individuals resident for at least 15 of the last 20 years will be deemed UK-domiciled for tax purposes and will not be able to use the remittance basis or any other rules applicable to non-domiciles and assets will be subject to inheritance tax.

The definition of UK income and gains does not include overseas income and gains remitted to the UK for investment in a qualifying purpose, for example, investing in a business.

Withholding tax

Withholding tax is deducted by the government of one country when paying income to a person overseas; for example, withholding tax may be deducted by the French government where savings interest from an investment in France is paid to a person living in the UK. The amounts deducted can range between 10 and 30 per cent, with rates being affected by a person's residency status and the type of income received. It may be possible to reduce the tax liability from withholding tax if a double tax treaty is in place.

> **Keyword**
>
> A **double taxation treaty (DTT)** is an agreement between two jurisdictions where tax will only be charged in the country where the income originates.

Where a double taxation treaty exists, a reduction in taxation may be achieved by the withholding tax being: 1) credited against any domestic tax due; 2) relieved at source when the residency of the individual is identified to the appropriate authorities.

Income taxation

Individuals

Each person can earn up to a set amount (their personal allowance) before any tax is charged and this can apply to both earned (eg from employment or self-employment) and unearned (eg savings, dividends, and other investments) income. Above the personal allowance all income in a tax year is liable for tax with the rate charged depending on the amount of income received and its source. The amount of personal allowance allocated to an individual can be affected by several factors, including their marital status, any physical disability they may have and the level of income earned.

Personal allowances

The basic personal allowance for the tax year 2017/18 is £11,500 and this allowance is received in full by every adult earning a total income of up to £100,000. Once the £100,000 income limit is reached every additional £2 earned reduces the personal allowance by £1. If sufficient amounts are earned the personal allowance will be reduced to zero.

> **In practice**
>
> Jeremy's total income is £123,000 whilst his brother Colm's total income is £109,500. Jeremy's personal allowance will be reduced by £1 for every £2 earned above £100,000; therefore, his personal allowance will be reduced to zero, as he earns more than £22,000 over the £100,000 threshold. Colm meanwhile will have his personal allowance reduced by £4,750 (9,500/2) to £6,250.

Minors and the personal allowance

A minor, aged under 18, has a full personal allowance and if they work they can earn up to the personal allowance before any tax is due. Health and safety legislation restricts the hours children can work; however, work could be done within a parent's business.

Parents may consider transferring income to their children to take advantage of their child's personal allowance or basic rate tax band, especially if they are higher or additional rate income tax-payers themselves. However, HMRC does not allow this and where the amount transferred is more than £100 the income is assessed for taxation as though it had been paid to the parent; so a parent cannot benefit. This legislation only applies to the transfer of income from a parent; income transferred from other relatives, for example grandparents, is not assessed in the same way and may be used to reduce the grandparent's income tax liability, although, as we will see later in the chapter, this may influence other possible tax liabilities such as inheritance tax which needs to be considered before any action is taken.

Blind persons allowance

Individuals registered as blind are allowed an additional personal allowance which is £2,320 in the 2017/18 tax year.

Married couples/civil partners

There are two potential allowances which may allow couples who are married or in civil partnerships to reduce their overall income tax liability where one is a low earner.

Marriage allowance

There is the potential to reduce a couple's taxation by up to £230 in the 2017/18 tax year by transferring up to £1,150 of personal allowance from one person to the other, subject to certain eligibility rules.

To qualify to transfer part of your personal allowance to your spouse/partner you must be married or in a civil partnership, earn an income under £11,500 and have a partner earning between £11,501 and £45,000.

Married couples allowance

Marriage allowance replaced married couples allowance, which was a similar idea. However, to be eligible for married couples allowance: 1) a couple must be married/in a civil partnership and living together; and 2) and one of the couple must be born before 6 April 1935.

In such cases, it is possible to reduce a couple's tax bill by between £326 and £844.50 per year depending on income levels. For couples married before 5 December 2005 the husband's income is used to calculate the allowance; for marriages and civil partnerships after that date the income of the highest earner is used.

Tax-planning strategy for married/civil partnerships couples

Where a couple jointly owns an income-generating asset which is subject to income tax, HMRC automatically assumes the asset is owned 50:50 by the couple which may not be the case. In fact, it may be that, due to one party having a lower income, they receive more of the income than the other. In such cases a joint declaration can be made to HMRC so income is assessed in lines with the percentage of ownership/receipt of income. This may lead to an overall lower tax burden than previously if more of the income is attributed to the lower earning spouse.

Income tax bands

Once an individual's income exceeds their personal allowance, income above that amount will be taxed, with the tax rate charged depending on the type of income and the amount. Income is taxed depending on which band it falls into as we can see in Table 13.2 for the 2016/17 tax year.

Where a person earns over £100,000, for every £2 of income received over £100,000 they will lose £1 of personal allowance, so by the time their income reaches £123,000 they will have a personal allowance reduced to zero.

Table 13.2 Tax bands 2017/18

Tax band	Tax rate	Income
Personal allowance	0%	£0–£11,500
Basic rate	20%	£11,501–£45,000
Higher rate	40%	£45,001–£150,000
Additional rate	45%	Over £150,000

> **In practice**
>
> James works as a financial analyst for Alpha Bank and earns £135,000 per year. He is not married or in a civil partnership. Therefore, James will initially have a standard personal allowance of £11,500. However, as he earns over £100,000 his personal allowance will reduce by £1 for every £2 earned over £100,000. On this basis, he will receive no personal allowance as the maximum which can be earned over £100,000 before the personal allowance is lost is £23,000 and James earns more than that.
>
> **Table 13.C**
>
> | Tax band | Tax rate | Cumulative income/£ | Tax liability/£ |
> |---|---|---|---|
> | Personal allowance | 0% | 0 | 0 |
> | Basic rate | 20% | 45,000 | 9,000 |
> | Higher rate | 40% | 90,000 | 36,000 |
> | Total /£ | | 135,000 | 45,000 |
>
> As an employee, James' income tax liability will be deducted monthly from his salary based on a tax code calculated by HMRC and disclosed to his employer's payroll department. This tax code will consider the amount of James' salary and the fact he has no personal allowance. James will also be due to pay employees national insurance and this will also be deducted from his salary.

Charities

Most charities' income may be exempt from taxation if the charity is registered with HMRC and generated income is used for charitable purposes. It is also possible for charities to claim gift aid on donations allowing an uplift of 25p for every £1 received by the charity.

Trusts

Trusts can be set up for many different reasons, for example, to protect family assets, to pass on assets whilst the holder is still alive, where an individual has died without making a will or where individuals are too young or are unable to make their own financial decisions or manage assets and investments. Trusts are legal arrangements which allow money, chattels, land and buildings to be managed by creating a relationship between three parties:

- The settlor, who originally owns the assets, creates a trust by having a trust deed drawn up. This will determine the type of trust to be used and the rules by which the trust will operate. Because of setting up the trust the settlor gives up all legal rights to the assets placed in the trust.
- The beneficiary benefits from the trust. There can be one or more beneficiaries and beneficiaries may be related to the settlor or an unrelated group. They may receive income from the trust, such as rental income from renting a house held in trust; or capital, for example receiving full ownership of shares after a certain age; or potentially both.
- The trustee becomes the legal owner of the asset and manages the assets, using the rules contained in the trust deed, for the benefit of the beneficiary. Trustees' duties will include day-to-day asset management, including paying any tax liabilities, investing or distributing assets in line with the wishes of the settlor as detailed in the trust deed. Trustees can change, for example, they may resign, but there must always be at least one trustee.

Types of trust

Table 13.3 outlines the various types of trust. On some occasions, a settlor may also be a beneficiary to the trust they set up. Such trusts can be interest in possession, accumulation or discretionary trusts. By setting up such a trust the settlor ensures funds are available in the future and allows payments to be received from trusts where required, for example, where illness affects the beneficiary's ability to manage their own affairs.

Table 13.3 Types of trust

Type of trust	Example
Bare trust: Where the beneficiary has an immediate and total right to the assets in the trust once they reach 18 in England and Wales and 16 in Scotland. Used to protect assets for the young until they are old enough to control them.	Two sisters, Sarah and Amy, live in Oxford. Sarah leaves her sister, Amy, who is 12, £50,000 in trust in her will. Once Amy reaches 18, as they live in England, she will have complete control over the £50,000 and the trust will end.
Interest in possession trust: The beneficiary has the right to the use the asset or the income from an asset held in trust for their lifetime but the ultimate ownership of the asset will pass to a different beneficiary	Gerald creates an interest in possession trust in respect of his house which he shared with his partner Peter. The trust says Peter may live in the house for the rest of his life, but on his death ownership reverts to Gerald's children. Peter has an interest in possession but not the legal right to own the house.
Discretionary trust: Here the trustees can arrange to pay income and capital to beneficiaries at their discretion, with trustees deciding how much is paid out, when, to whom and if the payments have conditions attached.	Joyce settled £500,000 in a trust to cover the day to day running costs for her aunt Isabelle who has been diagnosed with advanced Alzheimer's. The trustees use their discretion to ensure all Aunt Isabelle's needs are met as and when required as her condition develops.
Accumulation trust: One or more beneficiaries who must become entitled to the income or capital by an agreed age which cannot be older than 25. Up to that point the income generated by the trust assets must be retained within the trust and used to maintain, educate or for the general benefit of the beneficiary.	John settled £1m within an accumulation trust for Peter his nephew. Until the age of 25 the trust arranged for payments to be made to cover Peter's school fees and household costs. At the age of 25 Peter became entitled to all the income generated by the remaining investment.

Liability to pay and rates of income tax payable by trusts

Accumulation trusts and discretionary trusts

The trustees are responsible for declaring and paying tax on all trust income. This will include tax on all dividends received as trustees do not qualify for the new dividend income allowance. The trustees do not usually pay the tax out of their own assets, rather it is paid out of trust assets.

Table 13.4 Trust tax rates: accumulation and discretionary trusts

Income type	Tax rate where trust income is up to £1,000 per year	Tax rate where trust income is more than £1,000 per year
All other income	20%	45%
Dividend-type income	7.5%	38.1%

There is no dividend allowance for trusts.

The first £1,000 of income received by these trusts is known as the standard band (see Table 13.4). If a settlor has more than one trust in operation this standard band is split between the existing trusts.

> **In practice**
>
> George, a settlor, has four trusts in operation. The standard band for each trust would be £250, which is the total standard band of £1,000 divided by the four trusts.

Interest in possession trusts

As with the previous trusts the trustees are responsible for paying income tax on funds generated within the trust. However, where the beneficiary is entitled to the income in a trust, the beneficiary is liable for the income tax due on the income, whether they leave the income in the fund or have it paid to them. In such circumstances, the beneficiary will receive a tax credit for any tax paid by the trustees which they can include in their tax return.

It is also possible that some income can be mandated and paid directly to the beneficiary; in such circumstances the liability for payment rests entirely with the beneficiary who will include the income on their personal tax return and pay the tax due. Table 13.5 summarizes the rates of taxation due on dividend and other income received by the trust.

Table 13.5 Interest in possession trusts: tax rates by type of income

Type of income	Tax rate on income
All other income	20%
Dividend-type income	7.5%

Bare trusts

Here the law looks at the substantive legal position, ie who controls the income, which in the case of a bare trust is the beneficiary. Therefore, beneficiaries of bare trusts are responsible for paying income tax on income at their own personal rate after allowing for their personal allowances. The only exception to this is where assets are put in trust for minors. Whilst minors have their own personal tax allowances, income from bare trust settlements, whilst the child is a minor and unmarried, is amalgamated with the parent's income and taxed at the parent's rate of income tax.

Settlor-interested trusts

The rate of income tax paid by a settlor-interested trust will depend on the type of trust used; however, in all cases the settlor is responsible for the income tax on income generated by such trusts irrespective of whether income is paid or retained in the trust. The trustees are responsible for paying the income tax from trust assets using a trust and estate tax return, the trustees then provide the settlor with a statement of income amounts, types and tax paid. The settlor then informs HMRC about the tax paid on their behalf.

Collective investments

The rate of tax payable on income from collectives will depend on the underlying assets within the collective and the tax position of the individual investor (Table 13.6).

Table 13.6 Tax rates on collective investments income

Funds mainly invested in	Main types of distributions made	Rate of tax applicable
Cash deposits and interest-bearing securities	Mostly interest	Rates for savings income
Companies	Dividends	Rates for dividends

Open-ended investment companies (OEICs), unit trusts and exchange-traded funds (ETFs)

Table 13.7 Tax rates on OEICs, unit trusts and EFTs

Investing mainly in shares	Investing mainly in fixed-interest securities	Equalization payments
Collective pays dividend gross to individual investor whose income tax liability is based on their circumstances	Collective pays dividend gross to investor whose income tax liability is based on their circumstances	No income tax is due and amount can be deducted from any capital gain on sale

HMRC is not concerned whether the income has been physically paid to investors or 'rolled' up (accumulated). In either scenario HMRC assumes income has been earned by the investor and as such it should be included on their tax return for the period.

Equalization payments

When investors purchase units in a collective the unit price paid is based on the net asset value per unit. The net asset value of a unit equates to the value of the assets held in the fund plus any income which the fund has received but not yet paid to unit holders divided by the number of units in existence. At the next dividend paid by the collective the holder will receive a distribution which is made up partly of income which was held by the collective when they bought their units. This is effectively returning part of their initial investment as the income would be included in the net asset value of the fund; as such it is not income, but rather it is a return of capital and therefore no income tax liability is due. The investor should receive a certificate splitting the distribution between the amount of the dividend and the amount of the equalization payment.

REITs

To retain their tax status REITs are required to pay investors a dividend equivalent to at least 90 per cent of the property rental income they receive in a year. Such dividends are known as property income distribution (PID). Where a REIT makes a dividend payment from other activities these are known as a non-property income distribution (non-PID).

The tax treatment of PID dividends and non-PID dividends is different. PIDs are treated as property-letting income for the investor (although they are kept separate from other property-letting income) rather than as ordinary dividends. PID dividends are normally received net of a 20 per cent withholding tax which is deducted by the collective and paid by them to HMRC on behalf of the investor. It is possible for some classes of investors to receive PID income gross if an application is made to HMRC. PID income is then included on an individual's tax return under other income and income tax is payable based on their personal circumstances.

Non-PID dividends are treated as dividends from a UK company and as such will be eligible for the tax-free dividend allowance in line with other dividends and the investor's personal circumstances.

Overall, an investor should suffer less taxation through a REIT compared to distributions from a property-owning company. This is because the REITs do not pay corporation tax if they distribute their income as dividends whereas property companies will pay corporation tax and capital gains tax on their activities prior to making any distributions to investors, reducing the overall funds available for distribution.

Investment trusts

Investment trusts will receive income from the underlying assets invested in, and they will also distribute dividends to investors. Income from underlying assets will be taxed as shown in Table 13.8.

UK company dividends are paid out of after-tax profit, ie the company has already paid corporation tax on its profits before making the dividend distribution. To avoid corporate income being 'double taxed' franked income was introduced which ensures that where a dividend is paid from one company to another it is received as a tax-free distribution.

Investors in investment trusts will be taxed on the dividends received from the investment trust at the same levels as for other dividends.

Table 13.8 Investment trust: tax on income

UK dividend income	Overseas dividend income	Other income
UK company dividends are received as **franked income**	The trust is liable for corporation tax on the gross amount of income received. However, physically the income may be received net of foreign **withholding tax** which may offset some of the liability	Liable for tax at the relevant corporation tax rate

National insurance (NI)

NI is a form of taxation on earned income which is paid to qualify individuals for specific state benefits including the state pension.

National insurance classes

We can see from Table 13.9 that there are several different NI types or classes. The rate of NI to be paid will be determined by:

- an individual's employment status;
- how much they earn;
- any gaps in their NI record.

An individual must pay national insurance if they are 16 or over and either: a) employed and earning more than £157 per week; or b) self-employed and producing a profit of at least £6,025 per year.

The tax is collected using a unique NI number which is allocated to a person at 16 and stays with them for life. Individuals stop paying class 1 and class 2 national insurance payments when they reach state pension age and class 4 national insurance from the start of the tax year following reaching state pension age. For the current tax year (2017/18) the classes and rates in force are set out in Table 13.10.

An individual may wish to make voluntary contributions for several reasons, which ensures they retain entitlement to benefits and state pensions. For example:

Table 13.9 National insurance classes

NI Class	Class 1	Class 2	Class 3
Who pays	Employees	Self-employed	*Voluntary contributions*
Basic state pension	Yes	Yes	Yes
Additional state pension	Yes	No	No
New state pension	Yes	Yes	Yes
Contribution-based job seekers allowance	Yes	No	No
Contribution-based employment and support allowance	Yes	Yes	No
Maternity allowance	Yes	Yes	No
Bereavement benefit	Yes	Yes	Yes

Table 13.10 National insurance rates for the year 2017/18

National Insurance class	Paid by
Class 1	Employees under state pension age have NI deducted from their salary by employers at the appropriate rate: £0 –£157* pay nil; £158–£866 per week 12%**; over £866 per week 2%**
Class 1A/1B	Paid directly by employers in respect of employee's expenses
Class 2	Paid by self-employed through self-assessment. Profit of £0–£6,025 only pay on voluntary basis (£2.85 per week). Class 2 paid on profits above £6,025 at a flat rate of £2.85 per week
Class 3	Voluntary contributions at a rate of £14.25 per week (see below)
Class 4***	Self-employed with profits over £8,164 a year. The rates are 9% on profits between £8,164 and £45,000 and a further 2% on profits over £45,000

NOTES

* £157 is known as the 'primary threshold'. It is possible to generate an entitlement to a state pension and other benefits above a salary of £112 per week (known as the lower earnings limit)
** A lower rate will be paid if the employer is part of the employer's contracted-out pension scheme
*** Class 4 national insurance does not contribute to benefit entitlement

- an individual is currently living abroad and therefore not earning in the UK;
- an individual is unemployed but not claiming benefits and thereby will not be having their NI entitlement topped up;
- an individual may be self-employed but have profits under the minimum level to make class 2 contributions;
- an individual may be employed but earn an amount below the minimum threshold for class 1 NI contributions.

Voluntary contributions can be used to fill in past or anticipated gaps in a person's NI record. Usually they are made under the class 3 heading; however, for self-employed individuals it may be possible to make them under class 2 as well, and this can be advantageous as the cost is lower and the benefit entitlement wider.

Payment of NI

Employers are responsible for calculating and physically paying both employees' and employers' contributions to HMRC. This includes maintaining adequate records to show the NIC liability for each employee and payments made.

For employees, NI is deducted at source by employers at the same time as income tax, and is shown on an individual's payslip. This may also be the case if you are a director of a company and classed as an employee.

If an individual is self-employed the levels of class 2 and class 4 NI paid will depend on profits for the year so are usually paid through the self-assessment process.

Where individuals are both employed and self-employed, employers will deduct class 1 NI from salaries in the normal way and the individual is responsible for paying class 2 and class 4 via self-assessment.

Investment income or unearned income tax

Unearned income covers all forms of income which are not generated from employment, including:

- savings income;
- dividend income;

- rental income;
- collective investment income.

Savings income

Income from savings includes:

- interest from banks and building societies, credit unions and National Savings and Investments (NS&I);
- interest payments from authorized investment trusts (AUTs), investment trusts and open-ended investment companies (OEICs);
- income from corporate and government bonds;
- most purchased life annuity payments.

It does not include:

- interest from individual savings accounts which are not included in the personal savings allowance and are tax-free;
- interest on Eurobonds which is taxed via the individual's tax return.

Taxing saving income

2016 saw several material changes to the taxation of savings and investment income. From the 2016/17 tax year all banks and building societies pay interest to deposit account holders gross, ie without deducting any taxation.

Individuals will be able to earn an amount of savings free of income tax. The tax-free amount will depend on three factors:

- Personal allowance: an individual may earn up to the personal allowance level of income tax unless this allowance has been used up with other income such as wages or pension payments.
- Starting rates for savings: this is determined by income levels. It is possible to earn up to £5,000 of savings income tax-free in addition to your personal allowance; however, an individual is only eligible for this starting rate if their other income, for example from wages or pension, is less than £16,500 in the 2017/18 tax year. If other income is over £16,500 they are not eligible for the starting tax rate on savings. In addition, for every £1 earned in other income in excess of the personal allowance earned, the tax-free savings band will be reduced by £1.
- Personal savings allowance: this is determined by income tax band. An individual may also be eligible for an additional £1,000 of interest

tax-free depending on their tax band. Individuals in the basic rate tax band will be able to earn £1,000 of interest tax-free, whilst those in the higher rate band will be able to earn £500 tax-free.

Amounts over the tax-free level incur a tax liability at an individual's usual rate of income tax. Where a person is employed this will be calculated using their tax code and for the self-employed using the self-assessment system.

In practice

Sally earns £16,000 per year from her job and receives gross interest on her building society account of £600.

Given the following scenario, calculate the total amount of income tax payable:

- Sally will deduct her personal allowance of £11,500 from her wages leaving her with taxable earned income from employment of £4,500.
- This £4,500 is also set against her starting rate allowance for savings of £5,000, leaving her just £500 of starting rate allowance for savings income.
- As Sally has £600 of interest she does not have sufficient starting rate to cover all her savings interest. However, as she is a basic rate taxpayer she can earn up to £1,000 in interest tax-free under her personal savings allowance. Therefore, she will not pay tax on any savings income.

Sally's tax calculation will be as follows:

Table 13.D

Tax band	Tax rate	Cumulative income/£	Tax liability/£
Personal allowance	0%	11,500	0
Basic rate			
Earned income	20%	4,500	900
Total /£		16,000	900

In addition, Sally has £500 of tax-free savings income bringing her total income to £16,600.

Dividend income

The taxation of dividends also materially changed in April 2016 with the first £5,000 of any dividend income in a tax year now being free of any tax liability. When dividend vouchers are received, they should include details of the gross and net amounts of dividend paid.

For dividend payments above the tax-free amount and the individual's personal allowance and any blind person allowance, income tax is payable at the rates set out in Table 13.11.

Table 13.11 Dividend income: tax rates

Tax band	Tax rate
Basic rate	7.5%
Higher rate	32.5%
Additional rate	38.1%

Dividends are not taxable where the investment is held in an ISA tax wrapper.

Dividends falling within your personal allowance amount do not form part of your £5,000 dividend allowance, and as such up to £16,500 can be earned in dividends before any income tax is due.

Rental income

The two main types of rental income from property are from residential and commercial property. In most areas taxation of the two is the same, although there are some differences.

Residential property

There two main types of rental:

- A homeowner rents out a room in a house they occupy. For the 'Rent a room' scheme householders, the rules are very simple: they can earn up to £7,500 per tax year tax-free from renting a room.

- An investor holds a buy-to-let property which is rented. For buy-to-let properties investors are deemed to be running a business, meaning they will have to submit details of their net rental profit (rent received – allowable expenses) to HMRC using a self-assessment tax return. Allowable expenses include the costs of running the property as well as the actual cost of replacing any furnishings which have become unusable. In addition, there is also tax relief for interest payments made on mortgage loans.

Interest tax relief Prior to the 2017/18 tax year it was possible for landlords to receive income tax relief on interest payments of up to 40 per cent and 45 per cent for higher and additional taxpayers. However, between April 2017 and April 2020 this higher rate relief is being reduced on a phased basis, so by April 2020 only basic tax relief on mortgage interest will be available. The phased reductions are set out in Table 13.12.

Table 13.12 Tax relief reduction on property 2017–2021

Tax year	% of finance costs deductible from rental income (A)	% of basic rate tax reduction
2017/18	75%	25%
2018/19	50%	50%
2019/20	25%	75%
2020/21	0%	100%

During this phased period, the tax reduction will be calculated as the lower of 20 per cent (that is the basic rate value) of:

- finance costs, defined as:
  - costs not deducted from rental income in the tax year, ie a proportion of finance costs for the transitional period (column A in Table 13.12);
  - any finance costs brought forward.
- property business profits:
  - in the current tax year, less any losses brought forward.

> **In practice**
>
> Simon is employed as an estate agent with a salary of £28,000 per year. In addition, he rents a residential property for £12,000 a year. He pays £9,000 in mortgage interest for the rental property and has £1,000 in other allowable expenses.

During the 2017/18 transitional year 25 per cent of the mortgage payments tax relief will be withdrawn and will be given as a reduction in the basic rate of tax paid:

Table 13.E

Detail	£	£
Salary		28,000
Rental income	12,000	
Less finance costs (9,000 × 75%)	(6,750)	
Less other allowable expenses	(1,000)	4,250
Total income		32,250

Simon's income tax calculation will be as follows:

Table 13.F

Tax band	Simons Income	Tax rate	Tax payable/£
£0–£11,500	11,500	0%	0
£11,501–£45,000	20,750	20%	4,150
Less 20% tax reduction for remaining 25% of finance costs (9,000 × 0.25% = 2,250)		20%	(450)
Final income tax			3,700

The reason the finance costs are used as opposed to the property profits is because the finance cost figure is the lower of the two:
    Finance cost not deducted = £2,000
    Property profits = £4,250

Commercial property

As with residential letting, commercial property owners are taxed on their gross rental income less allowable expenses. Such expenses can include the cost of running the property and unlike residential property may include capital allowances. Capital allowances are payments which reflect the reduction in value of the asset as it ages with allowable rates published by HMRC, dependent on the type of asset.

Capital gains tax (CGT)

When an asset is disposed of, which may include sale or gifting, it is likely to have either increased or decreased in value from the point at which it was purchased. Any increase in value may lead to a payment of CGT whilst a loss in value may produce an allowable loss which can be used to reduce CGT payments from gains generated on the disposal of other assets.

Calculating chargeable capital gain/allowable loss on a disposal

To calculate if a chargeable gain or an allowable loss has been generated on the disposal of an asset two questions need to be asked:

Question 1: Has there been a disposal of an asset and is the disposal chargeable to capital gains tax?

Disposal of an asset means any transfer of ownership including:

- sale of an asset;
- gifting an asset;
- receiving a capital sum from an asset, eg equity release from a buy-to-let property;
- destruction of an asset.

However, not all disposals are chargeable to CGT; in fact the following disposals will not generate a capital gains liability:

- where it is between spouses;
- where it is made following a death;
- where it is of an exempt asset.

If the answer to Question 1 is yes, there has been an asset disposal, and yes, the disposal is chargeable to capital gains, then you need to move to Question 2. If the answer to Question 1 is no, no further work is required.

Question 2: Has a capital gain or an allowable loss been generated because of the asset's disposal?

A capital gain or allowable loss reflects the potential increase or decrease in the value of the asset after considering certain expenses which occur because of both the original transfer of the asset to the current holder (ie when they purchased it/were gifted it) and disposal of the asset by the current holder (when they sell it/gift it to someone else). The calculation is summarized in Table 13.13.

Table 13.13 Calculation of capital gain/allowable loss

Detail	£	£
Sales proceeds (consideration)		X
Less incidental cost of disposal:		
• Valuation fees	X	
• Estate agency and legal fees	X	
• Advertising costs	X	(X)
Net proceeds		X
Less allowable costs:		
• The original cost of acquiring an asset	X	
• Any incidental costs of acquiring an asset	X	
• Capital expenditure incurred in enhancing the asset	X	(X)
Chargeable gain/allowable loss		X

NOTE (X) in brackets denotes the amount is deducted from the figure above it

The table covers all potential incidental disposal costs; however, not all types of costs will apply to each transaction as the appropriate costs will depend very much on the characteristics of the asset being disposed.

In Table 13.13 (X) denotes the amount is deducted from the figure above it.

In practice

Elise owns a buy-to-let property, 14 Newburt Road, which she has advertised for sale. She has accepted an offer from Keith for the asking price of £250,000. Elise bought the property in 2004 for £175,000. On purchasing the property she paid legal fees of £1,000 and a survey fee of £1,500. Since buying the property Elise has repainted it twice at a cost of £2,000 each time. She has also installed double glazing (cost £10,000) and an extension (cost £30,000). Elise has used a local estate agent, Tower Estate Agents, to sell the property. Tower Estates have charged her 2 per cent of the gross sale price as well as £300 in advertising fees. Her solicitors, Brown & Sons, will produce the legal documentation for the sale for a fee of £700.

What is the value of chargeable gain or allowable loss Elise has made on her buy-to-let property?

The first thing to determine is if the sale will generate a capital gain or loss on disposal. Looking at the two questions above we can see the sale of an asset will be liable for CGT and her sale does not fall in an exempt category.

To calculate any capital gains tax payable in respect of this asset we will need to calculate if Elise has made a capital gain or loss on the sale:

Table 13.G

Detail	£	£
Sale proceeds of 14 Newburt Road		250,000
Less incidental costs of disposal:		
• Estate agent (2% of £250,000)	5,000	
• Legal fees	700	
• Advertising costs	300	(6,000)
		244,000
Less allowable costs:		
• Original cost of the asset	175,000	
• Incidental costs of acquiring the asset (1,000 + 1,500)	2,500	
• Capital expenditure enhancing the asset (10,000 + 30,000)	40,000	(217,500)
Capital gain		**26,500**

As we can see, the sale of the property generates a gain which will be liable to CGT. The amount of capital gains Elise will be due to pay will depend on other asset disposals in the year as well as previous years' CGT losses which may be carried forward and her rate of income.

The above example demonstrates an asset disposal through a sale; this is not always the case and could just as easily have involved Elise gifting the asset, although not to a spouse. The value of painting the property has not been included as it does not fulfil the criteria of enhancing the asset. Rather this is an expense of maintaining the property and may well have been an allowable expense against rental income.

Assets which generate a chargeable gain or allowable loss on disposal

As we noted above, whilst most assets will generate a capital gain/allowable loss on transfer there are some assets which are exempt. In fact, there can be occasions where the same type of asset can be both chargeable and exempt (see Table 13.14) due to specific circumstances such as value in the case of jewellery:

Table 13.14 Chargeable and exempt assets

Chargeable asset	Exempt asset
Land and buildings	Except: UK domiciled individuals nominated main or principal private residence (PPR)
Units in a unit trust	
Jewellery, paintings and antiques	Except: Jewellery, paintings, antiques and personal effects individually valued at £6,000 or less
Shares in a company	Except: Gilts and qualifying corporate bonds and enterprise investment scheme (EIS) and venture capital trust (VCT) if held for qualifying period
Assets used in a business	
	Savings certificates and premium bonds
	Assets held in an individual savings account (ISA)
	Betting, lottery or football pool winnings
	Personal injury compensation
	Assets held in approved pension arrangements

Amount and liability for capital gains tax

Individuals

Individuals pay capital gains tax on net chargeable assets. Net chargeable assets are calculated using net gains for each separate tax year, less allowable losses which can be losses brought forward from earlier tax years or losses calculated in the current tax year (Table 13.15). Any allowable losses not used in a tax year can be carried forward. Carry forward may be allowed for several years or indefinitely and you should ensure you know which applies to your particular asset to ensure losses are used most efficiently for your client.

Table 13.15 Calculation of CGT on chargeable assets

	£	£
Chargeable gains for the current tax year		X
Less:		
Chargeable losses brought forward from previous tax years	X	
Chargeable losses generated in the current year	X	(X)
Net chargeable gain for the current tax year		X

CGT may be due on assets located anywhere in the world; they do not have to be in the UK. The individual's residency status generates the liability. If they are resident or ordinarily resident (ie if residency is normally the UK) then they will be liable for CGT in the UK on their worldwide assets subject to any double taxation agreements the UK may have with the countries in which their assets are located.

As with income tax, each person can earn a set amount in net gains before CGT is charged. For the tax year 2017/18 this amount is £11,300; however, it is possible this amount may change over time and portfolio managers should ensure they are aware of current limits. For gains above the exempt amount, individuals will pay CGT based on their individual level of income, with the basic rate being 10 per cent and the higher rate being 20 per cent.

There are some exceptions to the standard rates which managers need to be aware of:

- Since April 2016, to reduce the speed of house price growth generally and in areas where there are high levels of second homes, residential property other than an individual's main residence is now charged on sale at a CGT rate of 18 per cent for basic rate taxpayers and 28 per cent for higher rate taxpayers.

- Also in 2016, to stimulate creation of new companies, entrepreneur's tax relief was extended. Here qualifying investments are charged at a CGT rate of 10 per cent as well as having a separate lifetime limit of £10 million of gains. Investments which qualify, subject to some conditions, include disposing of any of the following:

  – all or part of your business as a sole trader or business partner – including the business's assets after it closed;
  – shares or securities in a company where you have at least 5 per cent of shares and voting rights (known as a 'personal company');
  – shares you got through an Enterprise Management Incentive (EMI) scheme after 5 April 2013.

Charities

Where asset disposal proceeds are applied, or are to be applied, for charitable purposes, charities are exempt from CGT.

Trusts

The liability for CGT within trusts falls on the trustee, although as with income tax, the tax itself is usually paid out of trust funds with current rates of 20 per cent from April 2017. Trustees have an individual annual CGT exemption which is usually £5,650 except for personal representatives of the deceased and trustees of some settlements for the disabled where the amount is £11,300.

There is also the potential for the settlor to be liable for CGT, if they or their spouse or civil partner and minor child or step-child benefit from the trust or the trust is held offshore.

The tax rates paid depend on the level of gains and other income generated during the tax period.

Collective investments

Real estate investment trusts (REITs) If the REIT adheres to the REIT rule to distribute at least 90 per cent of profits as dividends to shareholders the REIT will not pay capital gains tax.

For individual investors:

- Capital gains tax may be payable when they dispose of the REIT investment. However, this will depend on the disposal generating a chargeable gain and their own personal circumstances in the tax year of the disposal.
- For capital losses, it may be possible to offset generated losses against other gains or carry them forward to future tax years if there are no gains in the current year against which to offset them.

Investment trusts If the investment trust adheres to the relevant rules it will not be liable for CGT.

For individual investors:

- They may pay CGT when they dispose of the investment trust; however, the same rules apply as for REITs above.
- Individuals can also offset any losses against gains made elsewhere or carry them forward if there are no gains available in the current year against which to offset them.

Open-ended investment companies (OEICs) The OEIC is exempt from CGT for any capital gains within the collective.

Individual investors:

- May pay CGT on disposal depending on their personal circumstances for the tax year.
- Can offset allowable losses against realized gains made from other assets and can carry forward losses to future tax years if there are no gains available in the current tax year against which to offset them.

Tax planning for CGT

Timing of disposals

As the tax year and therefore annual exemptions run from 6 April to 5 April the following year it may be possible to delay disposal of assets where the current CGT exemption has been used in a particular financial year.

For some types of asset it may also be possible to dispose of it in 'chunks' depending on the disposal timescale required, allowing a client to take advantage of two or more CGT exemptions over a period as well as potentially having a lower CGT rate dependent on levels of other income at the time, for example if they move from being a higher rate taxpayer to a basic rate taxpayer over a period of time.

It may also be possible for assets to be revalued on occasions which would allow for uplift in value in a tax year thereby reducing the tax payable on the eventual disposal.

Tax wrappers

These vehicles allow income or gains to be shielded from the effects of tax for their whole life. Whilst there are others such as pensions, SIPPs and investment bonds, the most widely used is the Individual Savings Account (ISA) which shields capital gains from taxation. The current ISA investment amount is £20,000 from April 2017.

In the 2016 budget an extension of the ISA was announced with the new Lifetime ISA promoted as a means of encouraging saving for retirement or buying a property. Here the government will boost savings by 20 per cent, paying in £1 for every £4 saved by an individual up to the age of 50. The proceeds from the account can be used to purchase a first house or must be retained in the account till the individual is 60.

Inheritance tax (IHT)

Inheritance tax is a tax on the transfer of wealth from an individual's (the donor's) estate leading to the individual having a reduced total wealth. Where such transfers are made as lifetime gifts the value of the transfer may include both the value of the asset and also any tax payable. An inheritance tax liability is not generated by the sale of an item at market price although this may generate a CGT liability. Gifts, which may attract inheritance tax, are known as chargeable transfers and are any transfers of value not covered by an exemption. Such gifts/transfers may be made: 1) as a lifetime transfer (ie whilst the donor is alive), known as a potentially exempt transfer (PET); 2) on death (ie following the death of a donor) via a will or intestacy rules if no valid will is available.

The potential liability to IHT for an individual depends on their domicile:

- for individuals domiciled in the UK, IHT is charged on the transfers of assets worldwide;
- for individuals not domiciled in the UK, IHT is charged on transfers of UK assets.

Trusts may also be liable to IHT in certain circumstances, such as where assets are transferred into or out of a trust, and where assets are held in a trust for 10 years or more. Different trusts have different rules about liability and they should be investigated as necessary.

Potentially exempt transfer (PET)

These are transfers of assets between individuals whilst the donor is still alive. As the name suggests they are treated as being exempt from IHT at the time they are given and will remain exempt if the donor lives for seven years after the gift. If the donor dies at some point within the following seven years then IHT will become payable; however, the rate of tax payable reduces over time with the potential for rates to be tapered by up to 100 per cent if the donor lives for at least seven years (Table 13.16). Any tax due following a donor's death will be payable by the beneficiary.

PETs can be used as part of a strategic tax plan to minimize inheritance tax; however, there is always the possibility that tax will become payable in the future. In addition, as we will see when we look at transfers following death, PETs will form part of the value of the estate and will be considered when deciding if the nil rate band has been exceeded.

Table 13.16 Inheritance tax rates

Time between date of gift and date of death	Inheritance tax rate
Less than 3 years	40%
3–4 years	32%
4–5 years	24%
5–6 years	16%
6–7 years	8%
More than 7 years	0%

Transfers on death

When a person dies, the following steps are taken to determine how much, if any, inheritance tax will be payable:

1 Review the gifts made by the deceased over the last seven years to determine if any chargeable lifetime transfers (CLT) have been made. If they have, the value of these will be deducted from the individual's nil rate band.
2 Calculate the net value of the estate at death which is value of the assets held at death less any outstanding liabilities such as loans, funeral expenses, mortgages, etc.
3 Deduct the deceased's remaining nil rate band value (following the CLTs deducted in step 1) and the RNNB where appropriate (see below) from the net value of the estate. Multiply the remaining amount by the relevant rate of IHT, the standard rate will be 40 per cent but may drop to 36 per cent where a percentage of the estate has been left to charity.
4 Tax is usually paid on the estate assets from estate funds, unless otherwise stated.

Residential nil rate band (RNNB) from 1 April 2017

From the start of the 2017/18 tax year, in addition to an individual's nil rate band, there will be an additional nil rate allowance of £100,000 for estates valued up to £2 million where the family home is passed to a direct descendant, such as a child, following death. By 2020/21 this allowance will have risen to £175,000 and will continue to rise by CPI from that date on. The rate will be tapered where estates have a net value of more than £2 million with a £1 deduction for every £2 over the £2 million value.

Where an individual has downsized from a larger house since 8 July 2015 and ceased to own a house, if assets are passed to direct descendants the RNNB allowance will apply to those assets even though they are not in the form of a house.

IHT exemptions

IHT will not be payable on some transfers and these fall under three categories:

- exemptions applying only to lifetime transfers including PETs;
- exemptions applying to lifetime transfers and transfers on death;
- exemptions only applying to transfers on death.

Exemptions applying to lifetime transfers including PETs

There are some lifetime gifts which are exempt from IHT irrespective of the period the donor lives after the gift. This exemption applies to all lifetime transfers including PETs and whilst the gifts individually are often small in value they can be a useful way of distributing wealth if carried out regularly. Transfers which are exempt include:

- Normal expenditure out of income: as IHT relates to gifts of capital if a donor can prove gifts are made from income they will not be liable to IHT. The gift must fulfil certain conditions to qualify:
  - the gift must be part of the normal day-to-day expenditure of the donor;
  - on average the gift has to be made from income, allowing capital to be used if there are short-term cashflow issues;
  - the gift does not require the donor to make any alterations to their normal living standards.

Examples of such items include regular presents, payments of income under a deed of covenant, payment of life assurance policy premiums for a third party and potentially payment of items such as school fees.

- Small gifts exemption: this exemption applies to individuals (not to trusts) with exemption for amounts of up to £250 to as many individuals as the donor wishes over a tax year in one or more payments. If the amount to one individual exceeds £250 the whole amount becomes chargeable for IHT.

- Annual exemption: there is a £3,000 annual exemption from IHT, although this cannot be used in conjunction with the small gifts exemption to give an individual £3,250. This exemption will be the last to be utilized, after other exemptions such as charitable and spousal transfers, with the exemption being applied to the earliest gifts where several are made in one year.
- Gifts on marriage or civil partnership: there is an exemption on gifts from a single donor in respect of a specific marriage or civil partnership. A parent can make a gift of up to £5,000, whilst grandparents and other remoter ancestors can make gifts of up to £2,500 and any individuals can make gifts of up to £1,000.

Exemptions applying to both lifetime transfers and transfers on death

In addition to the above exemptions there are some exemptions which apply to both lifetime transfers and transfers on death:

- Transfers between spouses or civil partners: transfers between spouses/civil partners are exempt if the recipient is domiciled in the UK and the couple are not divorced, although they do not have to be physically living together.
- Transfers to charity: transfers to charity, directly or via a trust are exempt from IHT. Also, to boost charitable donations, individuals may be able to pay a lower amount of inheritance tax (36 per cent rather than 40 per cent) on amounts over the nil rate band if they leave 10 per cent of their net estate (after deducting liabilities, reliefs, exemptions and the nil rate band) to charity.
- Gifts to a qualifying political party: such gifts are exempt where at the last general election either the party returned two MPs to parliament or they returned one MP to parliament and polled more than 150,000 votes.
- Gifts for national purposes: such gifts are exempt when made to eligible recipients including museums, art galleries and the National Trust.
- Gifts to housing associations: these are exempt.
- Maintenance settlement trusts: these may be exempt if put in place to provide for an historic property's maintenance.

Gifts with reservation

The key to exemption from IHT is that the gift must be made in full; there can be no holding back any benefits from the asset gifted or any element of control of the asset. Where gifts are made which do not fulfil those criteria, they are known as 'gifts with reservation of title' and do not qualify as PETs or reduce the value of an individual's estate on their death. Assets are deemed to be given, subject to a reservation of title where:

- Property is not enjoyed virtually entirely to the exclusion of the donor, that is, the donor may enjoy some benefit from the property but it will be very minimal. For instance, if a donor gave away a house, they would be allowed to visit to see family or friends but not stay for any great length of time or on a regular basis, as this would create a reservation.

- Possession and enjoyment of the property is not properly assumed by the person receiving the gift. So, for instance, using the above property example, the person receiving the gift of the house cannot decide when they wish to stay there or take control of the asset, eg making alterations etc without the donor's agreement.

There are two ways for a donor to gift an asset without creating a reservation whilst retaining the use of the asset:

1. Where the property is land or chattels it is possible for the donor to give the asset away but retain the right to occupy or enjoy it by paying full market rent to the recipient.
2. Where there is an interest in land, if the circumstances of the donor change substantially in a way which was not foreseen at the time of the gift and the use of the asset represents a reasonable provision to care for and maintain the donor as an elderly or infirm relative, no reservation will be created.

Where a reservation is created then the gift is deemed to be PET or chargeable transfer depending on the asset. In such cases the rules following the death of the donor are slightly different from normal depending on whether the reservation still exists at the time of the donor's death:

- Where the reservation still exists: the value of the asset included in the deceased's estate will be the value at the date of death not the date of the gift, thereby ensuring assets are not undervalued.

- Where the reservation ceases up to seven years before death: the asset is treated as a PET from the date the reservation ceases with the charge to the estate being based on the value of the asset at the date it became a PET. The annual exemption is not available to this asset when calculating its value as a PET.

The interaction of income tax and IHT

As a belt-and-braces approach to the problem of gifts with reservation, HMRC introduced a rule in 2005 to prevent donors from circumventing the market value rule, where income tax became due on any asset which had been gifted but where the donor still obtained benefit at a reduced or nil cost. The rule applied to several different types of assets, assuming the value of the benefit is more than £5,000 per year:

- land, including buildings: income tax based on rental value;
- chattels: income tax based on the statutory rate of interest to the value of the asset minus any payments made for use of the asset;
- gifts into settlements (trusts) of intangible assets: income tax based on the statutory rate of interest to the value of the asset less any CGT payable.

It is possible to use transition procedures to opt out of the above income tax charges; however in such cases, the assets then form part of an individual's estate.

IHT on transfers into and out of trusts and on trust assets

Most transfers of assets (other than transfers into a discretionary trust where a donor's IHT allowance is exceeded at the transfer date) are regarded as PETs. Therefore, assuming the donor lives for seven years following the gift, no IHT liability will arise following the donor's death.

For the beneficiary, any IHT liability will depend on the amount received from the trust and the period between the gift and the death of the donor. Any cash or assets received, if they are still held at the beneficiary's death, will form part of the beneficiary's estate and IHT may be payable where their personal IHT allowance is exceeded.

Asset valuation following death

Market values are required to be able to calculate the total value of an individual's estate; however, in some cases, the nature of the asset may mean values are not easily calculated.

Property

This is the price the property may be expected to fetch in the open market following a reasonable period of marketing. Such valuations will be required to be completed by a third party, for example estate agents or surveyors for residential and commercial properties.

Unit trusts

These are valued at the lower of the two quoted prices (the bid price).

Shares and securities

- Quoted shares: for traded shares valuations are easily obtained. The bid and offer price allow inheritance tax valuations to be completed based on the 'quarter up' rule where the lower price is taken and a quarter of the difference between the bid and the ask price is added to produce the share value. So, for example, if share A has a bid–ask spread of 265p–269p, then the value for inheritance tax would be 266p (265p + ¼ of the difference between 265 and 269 ie 1p). Valuations on death must include the value of the next dividend payment ie a cum-dividend valuation.
- Quoted securities: they are valued as the lower of the 'quarter up' value or the average of the highest and lowest marked bargains for the day ignoring any special bargains. The quarter up price is calculated in the same way as for quoted shares. Valuations on death must include the value of the next interest payment.
- Unquoted shares: shares in limited companies can be particularly difficult to value and also require the agreement of the valuation division of HMRC. Where no agreement can be reached, there is the possibility of appeal to HMRC special commissioners and ultimately to the courts.

Life policies

Where a person takes out a life policy on their own life which matures on their death: the proceeds, payable to the deceased's personal representatives, must be included in the valuation of their estate for IHT.

Where a person takes out a life policy and assigns the policy/places it in trust for someone else, they are deemed to make a PET, as follows:

- The value of the PET is the larger of:
  - the value of the premiums;
  - other consideration paid before the transfer of the policy;
  - the open market value of the policy at the transfer date.

- The proceeds are not paid to the estate; rather they are paid directly to the beneficiary and are not part of the deceased's estate or subject to IHT. This is common practice with the premiums being deemed to come out of normal income so also being IHT exempt.

Where a person's estate includes a life policy which matures on a third party's death then the market value of the policy will be included in their estate.

What happens to assets within an estate on death?

In most cases the distribution of the estate follows the same basic processes in England and Wales, depending on the existence or non-existence of a valid will.

Valid will exists

If there is a valid will:

- The legal right to access and distribute the deceased's property, money and assets by executors or administrators identified in the will is obtained by applying for a grant of representation (also known as probate or letters of administration). Executors or administrators do not have to complete tasks themselves; they can appoint representatives such as solicitors to do the day-to-day tasks for them.
- Once probate/letters of administration are agreed the executors, administrator or their representative will:
  - collect the estate's assets which unless otherwise directed in the will, will be liquidated;
  - pay all outstanding liabilities including bills and inheritance tax as appropriate;
  - distribute the estate to the beneficiaries in line with the instructions in the will.

A grant of representation may not be needed where an estate is very simple, for example:

- it only includes money rather than land property or shares; or
- where all the estate passes to the surviving spouse or civil partner as assets were in joint names.

In respect of savings accounts the depositing organization will need to be contacted to identify what information may be required to access funds or transfer them to a sole name. This may include copies of the death certificate.

Invalid will

Several conditions need to be met for a will to be valid and it is important that clients understand the need for wills to be drawn up correctly and accurately and realize the consequences where a will is invalid.

For a will to be valid:

- It must be made in writing by a person over 18 and who is not under wilful pressure by anyone else to complete the will. The individual must be of sound mind.
- The will must be signed (and should be dated) by the individual making it and by two witnesses, the witnesses being unable to benefit from the will.

If the will is not valid the assets of the estate will be shared out in line with the rules on intestacy below.

No will

Where there is no will the individual is said to have died intestate and any assets will be distributed in line with the intestacy rules. In such cases, instead of having an executor as detailed in a will, an application will have to be made for an individual to be the administrator of the estate; this is often done by the next of kin or their legal representative. The next of kin can be the spouse or civil partner of the deceased (but not their partner where there was no marriage or civil partnership), or their child. The distribution of the estate and the order of inheritance is fixed by law and dependent on whether the deceased has children and/or a civil partner or spouse and the value of their estate, as follows:

- Where the deceased has children (issue) and a spouse or civil partner:
  - The spouse/civil partner is entitled to a legacy of £250,000, the personal chattels of the deceased and half of the remaining estate absolutely.
  - The children are entitled to the other half of the remainder when they reach 18.
- Where the deceased has a spouse or civil partner but no children, the spouse or civil partner inherits the whole estate.
- Where there are children but no surviving spouse or civil partner:

- To be eligible to inherit, a spouse or civil partner must be married/registered at the time of the death; anyone who is divorced or has legally ended their partnership will not inherit. Those who have separated informally will inherit. Anyone who lives with a person but is not their spouse or registered civil partner will not inherit under intestacy rules.
- In such cases the child/children will inherit equally. If any children have died prior to their parents their share will pass to their children if they have had any. Children are recognized from all previous relationships including those where the parents are not married or in a civil partnership.
- Where there are no children or surviving spouse or civil partner: other relatives inherit under set rules, starting with those closest by blood to the deceased and becoming more remote:
  - The parents of the deceased – equally if both still living.
  - Brothers and sisters of the whole blood (full brothers/sisters) – equally or to their children if they have died.
  - Brothers and sisters of the half-blood (half-brothers/sisters) equally or to their children if they have died.
  - Grandparents – equally if more than one is still alive.
  - Uncles and aunts of the whole blood – equally if there is more than one and to their children if they have died.
  - Uncles and aunts of the half-blood – equally if there is more than one and to their children if they have died.
- Where there are no living relatives: the estate passes to the Crown, the Duchy of Cornwall or the Duchy of Lancaster under a process known as Bon Vacantia.

Tax-planning strategies

It is possible to use several IHT tax minimizing strategies; however as with all tax planning, IHT reduction should not become an end in itself and the donor needs to consider the fact that they should plan for their own financial and social needs in future years, as once gifted they will lose control of the assets as well as understanding the potential risks from IHT strategies.

Lifetime gifts

In line with the available exemptions noted above for lifetime gifts it may be possible to materially reduce an estate's value by such gifts if completed regularly over several years. In addition, it may also be possible to make a series of PETs which may also reduce the amount of IHT due, depending on the number of years which pass between the PET and subsequent death of the donor.

Transferability of nil rate IHT band

Married couples and those in civil partnerships can now use their personal IHT nil band allowance to pass assets between each other on death. Where all the assets pass between spouses or civil partners on the death of an individual and the individual's IHT allowance, currently £325,000, is not used it will also pass to the surviving spouse. It is possible for the last surviving spouse to have an IHT nil rate band of up to £650,000 on their death.

Jointly owned property

Major assets for individuals are often their family residence and cash savings and it may be possible to pass these on death without them forming part of the IHT estate. This is based on the method of ownership. There are two ways of owning property jointly:

- Beneficial joint tenancies: under this method, the house is viewed as being completely equally owned, to the extent it is not possible to separate the two owners' shares. On death, the surviving partner will inherit the deceased's share of the property and it will not form part of the deceased's estate.

- Tenancy in common: the alternative method of owning property, which may also be used where joint buyers are not related or are buying for business purposes, is tenancy in common. In such cases, each owner is allotted a percentage share of the property and where used between spouses the surviving partner does not automatically inherit on death, rather the value of the deceased's share becomes part of their estate to be distributed in accordance with their will.

Where a couple have a joint bank account and one dies, the remaining partner will inherit the money within the account. This is not the case for cash, which will be valued as part of the estate.

Borrowing to release cash

Borrowing may be used as a method of releasing cash which can then be gifted; however, there are a number of issues which need to be highlighted. Such arrangements are often advertised in the media by equity release firms where the firm lends money to the house owner so they receive a lump sum. The interest charge then rolls up and increases the total amount owed on death. Such equity release firms can charge high interest rates which can reduce the value of the asset remaining.

An alternative method of achieving the same effect would be to use an interest-only mortgage with a mainstream lender. However, this may not be possible due to the age of the clients, although there are a few financial firms which offer this service. The client should also consider the long-term effect of this choice. Where a loan is made against an asset and capital repayments are not made and interest rolls up over a period, there can be very little equity available when the asset is sold, which can be a surprise to some clients. This problem can be made worse by using a variable interest rate which may rise over time.

The use of trusts

It is possible to use trusts tax efficiently to distribute wealth and reduce the value of an estate; however, such schemes are complex and clients should be referred to tax and legal experts as appropriate.

It should be noted that in certain circumstances there may be an exit charge on assets taken out of a trust based on the value of the assets in the trust. There may also be a 10-year anniversary charge to be paid where assets are held in trusts over long periods. Both charges are complex to calculate and depend on the individual circumstances of the trust, thereby requiring specialist taxation support for the client to avoid additional liabilities.

Non-financial issues

Other aspects which need to be considered, as with all investment decisions, are the potential for change in a client's circumstances, the degree of flexibility required from investments and the potential for the client to retain control of specific assets. This can be a general requirement but may also arise from blended family units and the wish for certain assets to be distributed in certain ways in the event of an individual's death. In conjunction with this, it is also important for clients to update and amend their wills on a regular basis especially where major events such as weddings take place as this can affect the validity of an existing will.

Stamp duty

You will often hear the expression 'stamp duty' in relation to financial transactions; however, there is not one type of stamp duty, but three, two variations of which apply to share transactions and one to the purchase of land. Stamp duty first arose in the 17th century as a way for the state to raise funds by taxing land transactions. The stamp referred to was literally a stamp on a document making it an official legal document.

Stamp duty and Stamp Duty Reserve Tax (SDRT)

Stamp duty and SDRT are the taxes paid on share purchases of UK incorporated companies or foreign companies who maintain a share register in the UK. The former is used for paper-based transfers made by stock transfer form whilst the latter is paid when the transaction is made electronically using CREST (Certificateless Registry for Electronic Share Transfer). SDRT is 0.5 per cent of the value of the transaction rounded to the nearest penny, whilst stamp duty is 0.5 per cent of the transaction's value where the transaction is not settled through CREST and is valued at over £1,000, with the amount payable rounded up to the nearest £5. Whilst stamp duty/SDRT is payable on the purchase of shares, if the shares are received as a gift no stamp duty/SDRT is payable. In addition to the purchase of shares there are other investments (Table 13.17) where stamp duty/SDRT is payable.

Table 13.17 Stamp duty/SDRT

Stamp duty/SDRT is payable on	Stamp duty/SDRT is not payable on
Share options purchased from UK companies and foreign companies with a UK share register	Government bonds/gilts
Convertible loan stocks, irrespective of whether the right to convert has been taken up at that point or will be later	Corporate bonds
OEICs/unit trusts will pay stamp duty when they purchase individual shares	Units in an OEIC/investment trust
	Exchange-traded funds

Stamp Duty Land Tax (SDLT)

Where land or property is purchased, stamp duty land tax is paid by the purchaser; however, this is different from the stamp duty/SDRT discussed above. The amount of SDLT paid depends on who is purchasing the property, ie an individual or a company, and the purchase price of the land/property. Table 13.18 details the rates for individuals who only own one property as their main residence. From April 2016 if an individual purchases a new residential property in addition to their main residence they will pay an additional 3 per cent; so, for example, if a company buys a property which is valued at £500,000 or above they will pay a total rate of 15 per cent.

Table 13.18 Tax band for SDLT

Tax band/ £ value	Tax rate %
£0–£125,000	0%
£125,001–£250,000	2%
£250,001–£925,000	5%
£925,001–£1,500,000	10%
Above £1,500,001	12%

In practice

Sarah is buying a new property for £1,050,000 and has sold her existing house for £925,000. She will have to pay SDLT on the property she is purchasing, not the one she is selling. She will also not be liable for the 3 per cent charge as she is replacing her main residence rather than buying a second house. On this basis, she will be liable for the following amount of SDLT:

Table 13.H

Tax band	Tax rate	Cumulative value of house	Tax due to nearest £
£0–£125,000	0%	£125,000	£0
£125,001–£250,000	2%	£124,999	£2,500
£250,001–£925,000	5%	£674,999	£33,750
£925,001–£1,500,000	10%	£125,002	£12,500
Total		£1,050,000	£48,750

Value added tax (VAT)

Value added tax is a consumer tax. This means that, whilst products liable to VAT are taxed during the production process when they are turned from raw materials to finished products, the burden of paying the tax falls on the consumer when they buy the finished product or service. VAT is charged throughout the EU and is charged on both domestic goods and imports but not necessarily exports where they are sold outside the EU. The standard rate of VAT is 20 per cent, although there are exceptions to this.

Businesses providing goods and services, which are also known as taxable supplies, must register for VAT if their turnover for the previous 12 months exceeded £85,000 or they expect their turnover to exceed £85,000 soon. It is possible for a business to register for VAT voluntarily if they wish and some businesses may find this financially useful where their customers are businesses who can reclaim input VAT and where they themselves are subject to input VAT.

What is VAT charged on and what rates of VAT are payable?

VAT is charged on all goods and services except those which are exempt either by law, including:

- insurance and providing credit;
- if certain conditions are met – education and training, fundraising by charities and membership subscriptions;
- most doctor and dentist services;
- financial and land transactions.

or because they are outside the scope of VAT:

- non-business activities such as hobbies;
- statutory fees which are fixed by law including MOT test fees.

For those items where VAT is chargeable there are three possible rates:

- standard – currently at a rate of 20 per cent: applies to most goods and services;

Taxation

- reduced – currently at a rate of 5 per cent: examples include energy;
- zero – currently at a rate of 0 per cent: examples include food and children's clothes.

Calculation of VAT

This is probably easiest to understand using an example (see Table 13.19).

In this example, Product X is mined and must be processed by three different companies before it can be sold to the public.

Table 13.19 Calculation of VAT: example

Stage of production	Selling/purchase price	Detailed calculations
Raw material mined	**Input VAT:** VAT on inputs £x **Output VAT:** Selling price £100 + VAT	Company 1 extracts the product and sells it to Company 2 for a net sale price of £100/tonne plus 20 per cent VAT ie £20 to get a selling price of £120
		Company 1 will produce a VAT return and following that will pay the net difference between the input and output VAT to HMRC ie £20 less any input VAT applicable
Process 1	**Input VAT:** Purchase price £120/tonne **Output VAT:** Sales price £150/tonne + VAT	Company 2 sells the product to Company 3 for £150/tonne plus 20 per cent VAT ie £30, a total of £180/tonne
		Company 2 will be allowed to offset £20 of input VAT against the output VAT they collect and pay to HMRC
		The net payment made by Company 2 to HMRC will be £10 (£30–£20)
Process 2	**Input VAT:** Purchase price of £180/tonne **Output VAT:** Selling price of £200/tonne + VAT	Company 3 sells the product to Company 4, the retailer, for £200/tonne plus 20 per cent (£40) of VAT
		Company 3 will be allowed to offset £30 of input VAT against the output VAT paid to HMRC paying £10 (£40–£30) to HMRC

(continued)

Table 13.19 (Continued)

Stage of production	Selling/purchase price	Detailed calculations
Retailer	**Input VAT:** Purchase price of £240/tonne	Company 4 as a retailer selling to the public will sell the products at a price including VAT
	Output VAT: Selling price £360/tonne	The selling price is £360/tonne and the VAT on this can be calculated as £360/120 × 20 = £60
		The company will be allowed to offset £40 of input VAT against output VAT paid to HMRC paying a net £20 to HMRC

The above is a very simplified version of the real-life process but it does show the interaction between input VAT (ie VAT suffered by a business through its costs) and output VAT (which a business charges on its sales). At each stage of the production process the relevant company pays the difference between the input and output VAT to HMRC; however, ultimately consumers bear the tax as they have no way of reclaiming VAT.

Zero-rated or exempt supplies and sales

The above example also illustrates why it can be important for a firm to determine whether their input and outputs are exempt or zero-rated:

- If a company's purchases and sales are rated as taxable supplies but have a rate of 0 per cent then no VAT is added to the selling price but VAT on purchases can be reclaimed.
- Where a company's supplies are only partially rated, ie some are exempt, then it is usually possible to reclaim a proportion of input tax based on the proportion of rated sales. It may not be financially beneficial, however, for zero-rated output tax business to register for VAT if they pay little or no input tax, in which case they can apply for exemption from registration.
- Unlike 0 per cent-rated supplies, exempt supplies do not allow a firm to reclaim any input tax, which can significantly increase the company's cost of production.

Corporation tax

Corporation tax is paid by UK private limited (Ltd) and public limited (Plc) companies, foreign companies with a UK branch or office and clubs, cooperatives and other unincorporated associations. Self-employed individuals and partnerships pay income tax rather than corporation tax. For UK organizations where corporation tax is due, this is based on profits from trading in the UK and worldwide, whilst for foreign companies they will only pay corporation tax on profits made in the UK. Taxable profits include profits made from trading, investments and chargeable gains from selling assets.

Every organization liable to corporation tax produces a set of annual financial statements which includes details of the income made during the period including the gains from the sale of any assets. Where dividend income is received from other companies, such dividend income is known as franked income and no further tax will be payable on it by the receiving company as it has already been taxed. This is because dividends are paid out of after-tax profits.

From this income, allowable expenses will be deducted (these are legally defined as 'wholly, necessarily and exclusively' for the use of the business) to produce a profit figure. The financial statements form the basis of the company's taxable profits. These profits may be reduced by tax-allowable expenses such as capital allowances which may be available on the cost of assets used in the business, for example cars, machinery, property, etc. These capital allowances replace depreciation which is not tax-allowable. The rate of capital allowances given will depend on the type of asset and the tax year in question.

The tax-allowable profit is calculated and included on the corporation tax return also detailing the amount of tax to be paid. This is submitted to HMRC and if agreed the tax payment is due 9 months and 1 day after the end of the accounting period. The current rate of corporation tax for all standard companies in the tax year 2017/18 is 19 per cent, although different rates apply to ring-fenced companies which are those companies obtaining income and gains from oil extraction or oil rights in the UK and on the UK Continental Shelf. For ring-fenced companies the small companies profit rate (for profits of up to £300,000) is 19 per cent and the ring-fence fraction is 11/400. The main rate is 30 per cent for profits over £300,000.

Summary

- Taxes are paid on earned (income tax, NI) and unearned income and gains (capital gains tax and income tax); on the purchase of assets (stamp duty and Stamp Duty Land Tax) in life and in death (inheritance tax).
- Earned income can occur when employed or self-employed with income tax being payable above a personal allowance level. Employment status and amounts earned will affect the type and level of NI paid.
- Corporation tax is paid by companies on profits in a financial year except for franked income.
- A chargeable person pays capital gains tax on asset disposals where a gain is made above an annual exempted level.
- Inheritance tax covers any transfer of value from an individual's estate in life or in death which is not covered by capital gains tax. The IHT payable depends on the circumstances of the gift and whether the donor is living or deceased.
- Due to the potential for taxation to affect the level of return not only through the amount of tax payable on an investment but also due to the timing of the payment it is important a portfolio manager stays abreast of taxation rates and rules.
- That said, taxation should not be the primary reason for investment decisions, rather they should be a consideration in line with the investor's requirements and characteristics.
- Tax avoidance is legal, although aggressive avoidance schemes are being questioned in the media. Tax evasion is not legal and all taxes due should be paid.

Check your understanding

1. What was the name of the tax evasion legislation incorporated into UK legislation as part of the Common Reporting Standard?
2. What is the name of the final test to prove residency, used when both the automatic overseas and automatic residency tests have proved inconclusive?
3. How much is the personal allowance for income tax in the tax year?

4 What type of trust allows a beneficiary the right to use income from an asset during their lifetime but on their death the ultimate ownership of the asset will transfer to a different beneficiary?
5 What factors determine which type and rate of national insurance is paid?
6 What two question needs to be answered to determine if a chargeable gain or loss has been generated on an asset disposal?
7 What three categories of exemptions from inheritance tax are there?
8 What is Bon Vacantia?
9 What two reasons may make a good or service exempt from VAT?
10 In the tax year 2016/2017 what is the current rate of corporation tax for standard companies?

Further reading

One of the easiest places to gain an understanding of current tax rules is the HMRC website which includes information on all taxation and includes examples. This can be found at www.gov.uk/government/organisations/hm-revenue-customs.

Financial regulation and supervision

14

By the end of this chapter you should have an understanding of the key issues involved in global financial regulation and supervision, including:

- the reasons for regulating the financial industry and the importance of financial stability;
- the regulatory landscape in the main global financial centres of the UK, European Union, United States, Hong Kong, China and Singapore;
- regulation and supervision styles;
- anti-money-laundering and prevention of financial crime;
- complaints and dispute resolution.

Introduction

Financial regulations encompass a collection of regulations, laws, guidelines and policies to which financial institutions must adhere and in accordance with which they must conduct themselves. The regulations provide specific restrictions, requirements and guidelines, the aim being to maintain financial integrity and discipline within a country or a region. It is usually the government and the state bank in a particular country which are responsible for the domestic financial regulations, although in some countries there are non-governmental organizations tasked with their implementation; for example, the Financial Services and Markets Act 2000 in the UK.

It is common for there to be numerous laws relating to financial institutions in existence within any country with a developed domestic financial system and all domestic and overseas financial institutions operating within the country's domestic financial markets must adhere to these laws. The domestic financial regulators are there to enforce these laws and regulations and will have powers to sanction any individual or financial institution that fails to abide by them. The implementation and maintenance of this type of robust regulatory regime promotes financial stability within the country or region and allows problems to be addressed effectively. The detail and specifics of the regulations applied by the domestic regulatory bodies to financial institutions will differ from one country to another; however, the common factor is that the principal objective of these regulatory bodies is to supervise and regulate the financial institutions and activities within each country.

It has been suggested that we currently have over-regulation and this is often the consequence of a financial crisis; however, it is without question that the financial consequences of the last global financial crisis are still being experienced by many millions of people worldwide. Increased and vigorous action from domestic regulatory bodies globally was a certain consequence of the last financial crisis and the acid test of the success of these measures will no doubt be when the next financial crisis manifests itself and the effects are measured and assessed. If the regulatory reforms that have been implemented prove to be measured and proportionate then the capital markets will continue to grow and flourish, competition and innovation will thrive and a stable and sound global economy will be the benefit.

The reasons for regulation: the importance of financial stability

A key reason for regulation and supervision of the financial system is the information asymmetry between financial intermediaries, markets and investors.[1] One of the main objectives of a domestic financial regulator is to promote the effective function of the domestic financial system through regulation and supervision, to maintain financial stability in domestic markets and to enhance the ability to absorb shocks within the financial markets. Financial instability may occur when large and often unexpected shocks to the financial system have an adverse impact on the ability of business and trade to carry on as normal.

A disruption of this nature in the domestic financial system may result in severe and long-term economic effects. It may for example be caused by the collapse of an important financial institution, such as a bank or insurance company.

> **In practice**
>
> **The collapse of Lehman Brothers**
>
> US investment bank Lehman Brothers filed for bankruptcy on 15 September 2008 with assets of around $640 billion and debts of around $620 billion. At the time, Lehman's bankruptcy filing was the largest in history and it was the fourth-largest US investment bank, having around 25,000 employees globally.
>
> Lehman's collapse was labelled the biggest casualty of the financial crisis that blighted the global financial markets in 2008 and contributed to the attrition of around $10 trillion from global equity markets in October that year. This represented the biggest ever monthly decline on record at the time.

Statutory objectives of domestic regulatory bodies would usually include the following:

- market confidence: to promote and maintain confidence in the domestic financial markets is one of the most important objectives;
- financial stability: to promote and enhance the stability of the domestic financial system;
- consumer protection: to ensure a suitable and robust level of consumer protection within the financial markets;
- public awareness: to promote and encourage public awareness and understanding of the financial markets and processes through transparency, information and education;
- fighting financial crime: to reduce frequency and scope of financial crime and fraud.

Governments and domestic regulatory bodies seek to create a robust financial system where investors are less likely to be abused by unscrupulous companies and individuals whose practices come close to committing financial fraud. Rigorous laws, standards and regulations are required in order to guarantee the effective viability of equity markets, and the absence, or ineffective maintenance, of these regulatory and legal standards provides a significant impediment in many developing countries, for example, Vietnam.

Financial regulation and supervision

In the modern global markets, the presence of international financial companies is now common and cross-border financial business, products and transactions are assuming greater importance. It is therefore prudent and necessary that financial regulation must evolve in order to effectively police this growing internationalization within the financial industry. This raises important issues of regulation, supervision and control which must be addressed by domestic and regional regulatory bodies. These prudential and conduct of business issues are common to those across domestic financial services and span the insurance, banking and investment sectors.

The issues in question involve both prudential risk issues[2,3,4] and conduct of business issues.[5,6]

Keywords

Prudential scrutiny primarily focusses upon making sure that financial institutions and companies maintain adequate financial resources and are properly controlled, whilst conduct of business scrutiny focuses upon the aspects of investor protection, maintaining professional integrity and ethics and maintaining appropriate standards in the operation of financial markets. Prudential regulation will also encompass the operation of international financial services companies and includes the concept of **lead supervision.**

With financial services groups operating across borders and regional boundaries, the principal regulatory responsibility will lie with the domestic regulator in the home country in which the financial services group or company is based. There will also be subordinate regulatory responsibilities attached to the regulatory supervisor in any other country in which the financial services group or company operates. It is considered to be equally important that 'over-regulation' does not stifle the innovation and flexibility of the financial services industry and impose unnecessary burdens and complexity upon the financial markets.

Broad regulatory principles followed by the domestic regulators of financial institutions include the following:

- competition: supervision should ensure healthy market competition but minimize any harmful consequences and effects;
- management: senior management of financial institutions are monitored and bear responsibility for their decision making;

- innovation: should not be stifled, but financial products and services must be compliant with established rules, regulations and guidelines;
- proportionality: it is expected that regulatory intervention should be proportional to the advantages anticipated from the regulations;
- global markets: regulatory supervision should ensure that internationally agreed standards are maintained.

In this chapter we will focus primarily upon the UK financial regulatory regime, although reference will also be made to other key regulatory regimes in major financial regions as appropriate. It is generally accepted that the principles and importance of financial regulation, if not the minute detail, are applicable globally. However, financial regulation is a substantial and growing cost within the global financial world.

> **In practice**
>
> A report published by think tank New City Agenda in 2016 identifies that the cost of financial services regulation in the UK is around £1.2 billion per year currently. It comments further that there has been a substantial increase in cost in recent years with financial regulatory costs rising from around £200 million per year in 2000.

It is reasonable to say that financial regulation will involve the domestic regulatory body monitoring the behaviour and conduct of regulated companies and individuals to confirm their compliance with the financial regulations which are in place. It will also require the domestic regulatory body to monitor and support financial markets and financial institutions to promote stability and fair practice and, ultimately, to be prepared to undertake enforcement action to ensure compliance with current laws and regulations.

Extensive financial regulation exists globally and has continued to grow in recent years including developing economies. It is reasonable to suggest that the scope and influence of global financial regulation is unlikely to reduce in the future and despite mixed evidence, there is broad consumer support for robust and effective financial regulation. Informed debate continues to flow regarding the best ways to make financial regulation and supervision more effective and efficient although most financial, economic and political commentators agree that financial regulation and supervision remains fundamental to maintaining financial stability both in domestic and global financial markets. The ability and willingness to be proactive in combatting deplorable business practices, financial scandals and unfair actions are important in order to promote and maintain public and investor confidence in the financial system. It remains important, however, to resist imposing on the financial sector the burdens of over-regulation and to stop short of allowing financial regulation to become too prescriptive. This may lead to problems within the industry, including:

- a confrontational relationship may develop between the regulator and regulated companies and individuals resulting in over-reactions to new or existing regulatory requirements;
- over-zealous balance sheet rules may prove restrictive or inappropriate in a fast-moving financial environment;
- financial innovation may be disincentivized or stifled;
- rules escalation may occur where new rules are introduced to reflect the changing financial environment without deletion of existing rules which may be superseded;
- highly detailed and complex rules may be widely perceived as being over-prescriptive or unnecessary and may serve to undermine support for the regulatory regime;
- even detailed rules may not always be sufficient to address highly complex or unexpected risks;
- financial institutions, companies and individuals may be encouraged to adhere to the letter of the regulation rather than to the spirit of the regulatory process, especially if the focus is on processes rather than outcomes;
- moral hazard may arise if financial institutions, companies and individuals consider they have freedom in respect of any activities not specifically covered by regulations.

Regulatory landscape in the United Kingdom

The financial services sector is of immense importance to the economy of the UK and contributes significantly to the country's economic output, employment and tax income.

Investment and Portfolio Management

> **In practice**
>
> Figures published in 2014 show that the financial services industry and related professional services employed around 2.2 million people, representing in excess of 7 per cent of the workforce and contributing around £66 billion in taxes. The sector produces almost 12 per cent of total economic output for the UK, generating a trade surplus of around £72 billion. Overseas companies have invested in excess of £100 billion into the UK financial services sector since 2007 and UK fund managers are responsible for around £4.3 trillion in financial assets.[8]

Post-financial crisis considerations resulted in the Financial Services Act 2012, which established a new regulatory landscape within the UK comprised of the Bank of England, the Prudential Regulation Authority (PRA) and the Financial Conduct Authority (FCA).[9] The changes introduced by the Financial Services Act 2012 focused mainly upon creating the new structure of the dual-regulatory bodies, together with a new scope of operation and new powers. Additionally, a new Financial Policy Committee (FPC) was established at the Bank of England made up of 13 members, who meet on a quarterly basis. The remit of the FPC is to monitor, identify and take appropriate action to mitigate or remove systemic risks. This is intended to protect and enhance the resilience of the financial system. The FPC will also act to support the UK government's economic policies (See Figure 14.1).

Bank of England

The key bodies in the UK financial regulatory system became the Bank of England, the Prudential Regulation Authority and the Financial Conduct Authority. Following the creation of the PRA the current governor of the Bank of England, Mark Carney, announced the 'One Bank' initiative.[10] This initiative, known as the One Bank Strategy, identifies the values which underpin the culture of the Bank of England and which should act as the benchmark against which to measure future performance. There were five core values specified by Mark Carney:

- Collaborative: we are committed to working together to ensure our best possible contribution to the public good. We share information, skills and expertise freely.

Financial regulation and supervision

- Inclusive: we actively encourage challenge and divergent views, and create an environment where all staff can speak up, share their views and influence outcomes.
- Empowering: we expect initiative-taking, creative thinking and rigorous analysis in all areas. To achieve this, we will clearly delegate suitable responsibility and accountability for analysis, recommendations and decisions.
- Decisive: we support decisive action grounded in policy. We will create an environment that is agile, where all staff can respond swiftly to changing priorities, with a focus on delivery.
- Open: we encourage open debate as the most constructive way to resolve conflicts. And we ensure that communication is open and transparent in discharging our duties in pursuit of our mission.

In practice

The current regulatory structure in place in the UK, the joint Prudential Regulation Authority and Financial Conduct Authority model, is a 'twin peaks' model for financial regulation which was considered to be pioneered by Australia back in 1998. This model separates the prudential regulator from the conduct regulator. The prudential regulator is charged with overseeing larger, more systemic firms, whilst the conduct regulator oversees larger numbers of smaller companies and individuals.

Prudential Regulation Authority (PRA)

The Prudential Regulation Authority (PRA) was initially created as a subsidiary of the Bank of England by the Financial Services Act (2012) but is now a part of the Bank of England. The PRA is responsible for the prudential regulation and supervision of major financial institutions, including around 1,700 banks, building societies, credit unions, insurers and major investment firms. The overall objectives of the PRA are laid down within the Financial Services and Markets Act 2000.[11] The PRA has three main statutory objectives:

- to promote the safety and soundness of the firms it regulates;
- to contribute to the securing of an appropriate degree of protection for those who are or may become insurance policyholders (specific to insurance firms);
- to facilitate effective competition.

The PRA maintains close working relationships with other areas of the Bank of England, such as the Financial Policy Committee and most key decisions are made by the PRA board which include the CEO of the PRA, governor of the Bank of England, deputy governor for financial stability and appointed independent non-executive members. The approach taken to regulation and supervision has three facets: judgement-based, forward-looking and focused approaches:

- judgement-based: using judgement to determine if financial businesses are sound, if insurers provide appropriate policyholder protection and if companies continue to meet appropriate threshold conditions;
- forward-looking: assessing financial companies against risks which may arise in the future and not just for current risks, with any necessary intervention usually effected at an early stage;
- focused: targeting companies and issues which are deemed to pose the greatest risk to the stability of the UK financial system and policyholders.

This approach to supervision does not guarantee a 'zero-failure' within the financial system; however, the aim is to achieve a situation where the failure of a financial company will not result in significant disruption to the supply of critical financial services within the UK financial market.

Financial Conduct Authority (FCA)

The Financial Conduct Authority (FCA) is the current UK conduct regulator and has a responsibility for around 56,000 financial services companies and financial markets in the UK whilst also being the prudential regulator for over 24,000 of those companies. The FCA was established on 1 April 2013, and took over the responsibility for conduct and in the case of some companies, relevant prudential regulation, from the Financial Services Authority (FSA). As in the case of the PRA, the scope and objectives of the FCA is laid down by the Financial Services and Markets Act 2000. In addition to acting as financial regulator for over 56,000 companies, the FCA is also the regulatory body for over 125,000 approved persons in the financial services industry.[12]

The strategic objectives of the FCA, as laid down in their business plan, are to ensure that the relevant financial markets function efficiently, with further operational objectives including:

- protect consumers: to secure an appropriate degree of protection for consumers;

- protect financial markets: to protect and enhance the integrity of the UK financial system;
- promote competition: to promote effective competition in the interests of consumers.

> **In practice**
>
> The FCA is an independent public body which derives its funding entirely from the companies and individuals that it regulates; this is achieved by the charging of fees which are based upon the size, nature and scope of the financial services business conducted. The FCA is accountable to the UK Treasury, which is responsible for the UK's financial system and to the UK government. Following its creation, the FCA disseminated a series of important core characteristics and values to be embraced by the financial services industry within the UK and also affirmed the implementation of a new culture within the organization based on a 'forward-thinking' and more 'judgement-based' approach. The FCA works with a wide range of stakeholders including consumer groups, trade associations, professional bodies, EU legislators and other domestic regulators and pursues a proportionate approach to regulation, with priority given to the areas and companies which are deemed to pose a higher risk to their objectives.

Regulatory landscape in the European Union

The European Union (EU) seeks single European markets in a variety of sectors and the financial sector represents one of the most important. The aim of the single market is to remove barriers to cross-border trade and this can be helped by adopting common regulatory rules across the EU. In practice, for an investor or a consumer of financial services this should mean that they would be free to invest in or purchase a financial product either from a provider in their home country, or from a provider in another EU member country, without compromising their investor protection. With a single EU-wide financial market, a financial institution which is authorized to provide financial services in one EU member country is able to provide the same services throughout the member countries of the EU, covered by one consistent regulatory umbrella. In theory, the advantages of this include:

Figure 14.1 Financial regulatory landscape in the UK

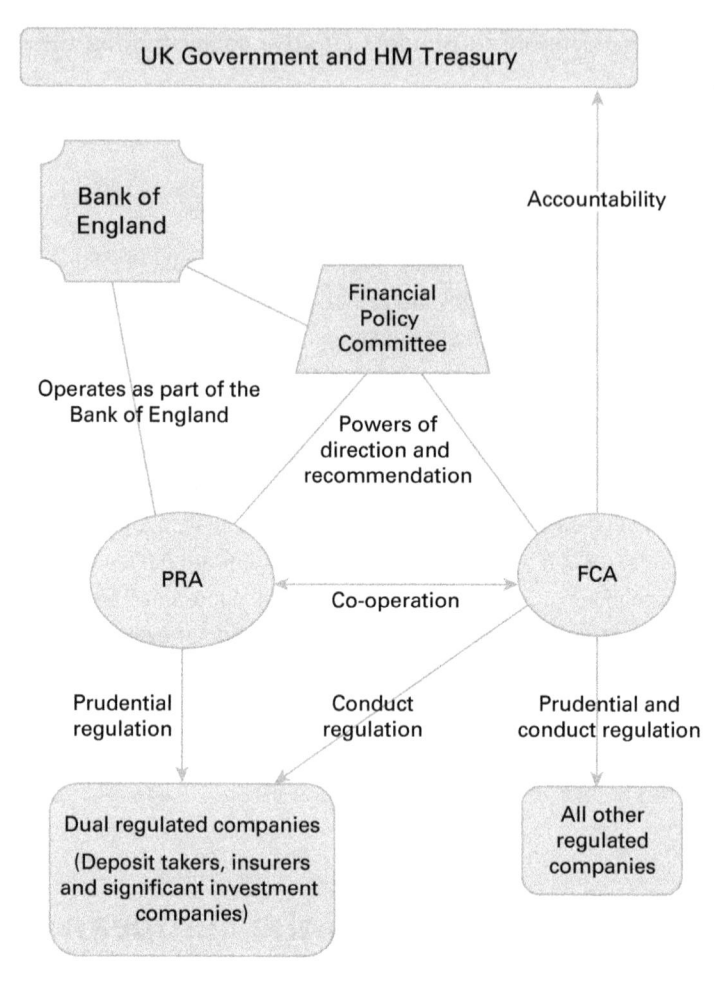

SOURCE FCA Business Plan 2013/14[13]

- a single market in financial services should act as a catalyst for economic growth across all sectors of the economy;
- the single financial market should provide lower-cost and better-quality financial products for both consumers and business.

In practice, though, integration of financial markets through the EU has been much slower in retail financial products and services than between financial institutions due to various factors, amongst them product segregation and domestic preferences.[14, 15]

European System of Financial Supervision (ESFS)

The European System of Financial Supervision represents the current landscape for financial regulation and supervision within the European Union and has been in place since 2011, following proposals made by the European Commission in the aftermath of the global financial crisis in 2008. The European System of Financial Supervision is composed of the European Supervisory Authorities, the European Systemic Risk Board, the Joint Committee of the European Supervisory Authorities, together with the national supervisory authorities of EU member states:

- the European Banking Authority (EBA) in London;
- the European Securities and Markets Authority (ESMA) in Paris;
- the European Insurance and Occupational Pensions Authority (EIOPA) in Frankfurt; and
- the European Systemic Risk Board (ESRB).

The European Banking Authority (EBA) is made up of senior representatives of the EU member banking supervisory authorities and central banks. They advise the European Commission periodically or by request regarding banking activities and help to implement broad EU directives and supervisory practices, whilst promoting regulatory and supervisory cooperation and sharing of information.

The European Securities and Markets Authority (ESMA) has a remit to help safeguard the financial stability of the financial system in the EU. It works to improve investor protection within the EU and to ensure the transparency, integrity and efficiency of the securities markets. It works in conjunction with the other European Supervisory Authorities to encourage regulatory and supervisory collaboration and to target any impediments to EU financial stability. In situations of financial crisis the ESMA will act as a coordinator of responses throughout the EU. On a positive note, the ESMA is considered to be equipped with stronger powers than its predecessor and despite being independent it retains full accountability to the European Parliament. This authority reports periodically and in the medium of an annual report.

The European Insurance and Occupational Pensions Authority (EIOPA) is another independent body which acts in an advisory capacity both to the European Parliament and the EU Council. Its remit is to support and to facilitate protection for a broad spectrum of consumers including insurance policyholders, pension scheme members and beneficiaries. It is also tasked with ensuring the transparency of financial markets and financial products, together with providing support for the overall stability of the financial system within the EU.

The three European Supervisory Authorities (ESAs) noted above are considered to bear the responsibility for the micro-prudential oversight within the EU region and in addition to these bodies, the European Systemic Risk Board (ESRB) has responsibility for the macro-prudential oversight across the European Union and therefore complements the role of the EBA, ESMA and EIOPA. The ESRB is based at the European Central Bank in Frankfurt and includes representatives from each of the European Central Bank, EU members' individual central banks, together with representatives of the regulatory and supervisory authorities of EU member states, and the European Commission.

European Central Bank (ECB)

The European Central Bank (ECB), established in 1998, holds the exclusive right for the issue of euro banknotes and the capital stock of the bank is owned by the central banks of all 28 EU member states as shareholders.[16] The European Central Bank is tasked with supporting and maintaining price stability in the EU and maintaining the stability and the purchasing power of the 'euro', Europe's single currency, for which the ECB is the central bank, and with administering the chosen monetary policy of the eurozone, the 17 countries who have chosen to adopt the European single currency since 1999. The ECB strives for optimum integrity, competence, efficiency and transparency within the euro-system in order to maintain financial stability. The euro-system is made up of the ECB together with the central banks of the 28 EU member countries, although at the time of writing there is the imminent likelihood of the UK leaving the European Union which will certainly have a future impact on both UK and EU regulatory issues.

In practice

Talking points from the current financial world (1)

In June 2016, a referendum was held in the United Kingdom (UK) to allow the British public to decide whether the UK should leave or remain in the European Union (EU). The result of the vote was that the UK should leave the EU. The UK commenced the process of leaving at the end of March

2017 and there is a timescale of around two years for the process to take place, dependent upon the timetable agreed during the negotiations. The UK government will also enact legislation which will end the primacy of EU law in the UK and return primary legislative powers to the UK government.

At the same time, regulators in the EU blocked the proposed merger between the London Stock Exchange and the German stock exchange Deutsche Börse, due to concerns that the deal would not have been in the best interests of competition. The merger would have combined the two largest stock exchange operators in Europe.

What do you think that the impact of these two events may be from an economic and regulatory point of view, in the near and long-term future?

Regulatory landscape in the United States of America

In the United States, financial regulation and supervision is intended to reduce financial instability and to protect both borrowers and investors in the financial markets. Banking regulation within the USA traditionally tends to focus on prudence and the business decisions made by the banks are supervised and regulated with respect to safety, soundness and capital adequacy. Banks are also allowed access to the Federal Reserve (covered in more detail later in the chapter) as a lender of last resort.[17] Traditionally in the USA, federal securities regulation and supervision has focused on the areas of disclosure, eliminating conflicts of interest, fraud and manipulation of the markets, rather than specifically upon prudence.

In practice

Regulation and supervision of securities has its focus on ensuring that market participants have sufficient access to information to allow them to make informed decisions, rather than restricting the business models of companies in the financial sector. At the time of writing there are many rumours of regulatory changes within the USA; however, the following describes the current financial regulatory and supervisory position.

The regulatory agencies

In the USA there are five separate federal regulators of depository institutions in addition to at least one regulator in each state. State regulators also have a responsibility to regulate mortgage lenders within their region. A separate federal agency has the responsibility for regulating the Federal Home Loan Mortgage Corporation and Federal National Mortgage Association (known as Freddie Mae and Fannie Mac respectively) and additionally the Federal Home Loan Bank System. The Federal Home Loan Mortgage Corporation (Freddie Mac) and Federal National Mortgage Association (Fannie Mae) are both government-sponsored entities which purchase mortgages from the lenders who issued them and retain some whilst selling others in the form of securities; thereby creating a secondary market in home mortgages within the USA.

In addition to these regulatory bodies, there are also two federal regulators and 50 separate state regulators with the responsibility of regulating and supervising the markets for securities and financial instruments. Another two federal agencies and 50 state regulators are also responsible for the supervision and regulation of pension funds, whilst insurance companies are supervised and regulated by each of 50 state systems. Consumer fraud is the responsibility of a separate federal regulator and 50 individual state bodies. This complex and convoluted system is responsible for significant overlap of responsibility between the regulatory agencies.

The Office of the Comptroller of the Currency (OCC)

In 2011 the Office of the Comptroller of the Currency assumed responsibility for the regulation and supervision of federal savings associations and the rule-making for all state and federal savings associations. The OCC has its head office in Washington, DC, as well as four district offices and a London office which is intended to supervise international dealings of the national banks. Additionally, the OCC has responsibility for chartering, regulating and supervising all national banks and for the supervision of both agencies and federal branches of foreign banks. The agency issues rules and legal interpretations regarding banking, bank investments and other aspects of bank operations such as community development activities.

The Securities and Exchange Commission (SEC)

The Securities and Exchange Commission in the USA is tasked with maintaining fair, organized and efficient financial markets, facilitation of capital formation and investor protection. The laws and rules applicable to the regulation and supervision of the securities industry in the USA focus on ensuring that all investors, whether institutions or private investors, should have access to certain basic facts about a particular investment to allow them to make informed decisions. This should apply prior to the investment and for the period the investment is held. The SEC therefore requires the continuous availability of current, comprehensive and accurate information from public companies, financial and non-financial, so that investors may make sound and informed investment decisions. The SEC regulates and supervises all of the securities brokers and dealers, investment advisers, mutual funds and key securities exchanges and its primary role is to maintain fair practice in dealing, prevent fraud and promote the disclosure of important market-related information. The responsibilities of the SEC include:

- interpretation of federal securities laws;
- issuance of new rules and/or amendment of existing rules;
- overseeing the inspection and supervision of brokers, investment advisers, securities companies and ratings agencies;
- overseeing private regulatory organizations involved in auditing, securities and accounting;
- the coordination of US securities regulation with foreign authorities and US federal and state authorities.

In practice

Some of the important pieces of US legislation relevant to this area include:

- Investment Company Act 1940;
- Investment Advisers Act of 1940;
- Sarbanes–Oxley Act of 2002;
- Dodd–Frank Act.

The Investment Company Act 1940 was created to regulate the organization of companies that engage primarily in investing, reinvesting or trading in securities, whose own securities are offered to the investors, for example, mutual funds. The aim of this regulation is to minimize conflicts of interest.

The Investment Advisers Act of 1940 was created to regulate investment advisers and states that firms or individuals who are paid for advising on securities and investments must register with the SEC and conform to regulations which are designed to protect investors.

The Sarbanes–Oxley Act of 2002 put forward reforms enhancing corporate responsibility and financial disclosures together with reducing both corporate and accounting fraud. The Public Company Accounting Oversight Board (PCAOB) was created in order to monitor the activities of the auditing profession.

The Dodd–Frank Wall Street Reform and Consumer Protection Act is the full name of this act, which is comprised of federal regulations relating to financial institutions and their customers. The purpose was to lower risk in the US financial system and to prevent any recurrence of events which led to the 2008 financial crisis.

The Financial Industry Regulatory Authority (FINRA)

The largest independent regulator of all securities firms conducting financial business in the USA is the Financial Industry Regulatory Authority (FINRA), which regulates and supervises around 4,500 brokerage companies and around 632,000 registered securities representatives.

It is contracted to perform market regulation for the National Association of Securities Dealers Automated Quotation (NASDAQ) stock market, the New York Stock Exchange (NYSE) and the International Securities Exchange (ISE). FINRA's responsibilities include:

- protection for investors against fraud and bad practice;
- enforcement of industry rules and federal securities law;
- educating and informing investors;
- promotion and maintenance of fairness within the industry;
- monitoring of financial markets;
- registration, testing and education of brokers;
- ensuring that investors are not misled or misinformed;
- administration of the provision of dispute resolution.

Commodity Futures Trading Commission (CFTC)

The Commodity Futures Trading Commission (CFTC) is an independent agency of the US government with responsibility for the regulation and supervision of the derivatives markets. The CFTC monitors the derivatives markets for a variety of abuses and bad practices and to date has implemented the majority of the requirements of the Dodd–Frank Act. The CFTC has the responsibility for:

- protecting both market participants and the public from fraudulent practice and manipulation related to derivatives, eg futures and swaps markets;
- protecting market participants and the public from derivative-related systemic risk;
- promoting and monitoring market stability, integrity and investor protection;
- fostering transparent, open, competitive and financially sound markets;
- protecting investor funds.

In order to accomplish this, the CFTC monitors and oversees the derivatives market participants including derivatives clearing organizations, swap data repositories, swap dealers, intermediaries, contract markets, swap execution facilities, futures commission merchants and commodity pool operators.

The Federal Reserve

The Federal Reserve, often referred to as 'the Fed', is regarded as the most powerful financial institution in the world and is the central bank of the United States of America.[18] It has a board of governors based in Washington, DC together with 12 regional federal reserve banks, each of which is responsible for a specific geographic area of the USA.

It was founded in 1913, its purpose being to provide a secure, flexible and stable monetary and financial system. The Federal Reserve works towards the US government's economic and financial policy objectives and is subject to oversight by the US Congress. However, it is considered to be politically independent since its decisions are not ratified by any government official. The responsibilities and duties of the Federal Reserve include:

- carrying out US monetary policy by influencing monetary and credit conditions in the economy to ensure maximum employment, stable prices and moderate long-term interest rates;
- supervision and regulation of US banking institutions to ensure the safety of the banking and financial system and to protect consumer credit rights;

- overseeing and maintaining the security and stability of the US financial system and minimizing systemic risk;
- provision of financial services to US depository institutions, the US government and foreign official institutions.

> **In practice**
>
> The federal reserve banks were established by Congress with the purpose of being the operational arm of the US central banking system and they issue and redeem government securities, hold cash reserves for depository institutions and extend loan facilities to them. They are responsible for the currency circulation and the daily processing of cheques. They also supervise and examine member banks for safety and soundness.

The US Treasury

The Treasury Department in the USA is an executive agency with the responsibility for promoting both the economic prosperity and ensuring the financial security of the United States.[19] The Treasury advises the US president on both economic and financial issues, encouraging sustainable economic growth, and fosters improved governance in financial institutions. The Treasury operates and maintains systems critical to the US financial infrastructure; for example, production of currency, the disbursement of payments to the public, revenue collection and appropriate borrowing of funds, as necessary to run the US federal government. The Treasury works with other federal agencies, foreign governments and international financial institutions for the common good on a variety of projects; for example, to encourage global economic growth, raise standards of living and to try to predict and prevent economic and financial crises. The Treasury is also responsible for fulfilling roles which enhance national security; for example, implementing economic sanctions against foreign threats, identifying and targeting the financial support networks of national security threats, and improving the safeguards of US financial systems.

The Treasury is organized into two major components: the departmental offices and the operating bureaux. The departmental offices are primarily responsible for the formulation of policy and management of the Treasury, whilst the operating bureaux carry out the specific operations assigned to the Treasury. The main functions of the Treasury include:

- management of federal finances;
- collection of taxes, duties and monies paid to the US;
- paying all bills of the US;
- production of currency and coinage;
- management of US government accounts and public debt;
- supervision of national banks and thrift institutions;
- advising US government officials on various issues, eg domestic and international financial, monetary, economic, trade and tax policy;
- enforcing federal finance and tax laws;
- investigating and prosecuting tax evaders and forgers.

In practice

Talking points from the current financial world (2)

Do you see any similarities between the UK and the US regulatory structures?

January 2017 saw the inauguration of Donald Trump as president of the USA and brought with it the campaign promise to reform financial regulation in the US; in particular the Dodd–Frank Act.

Spend a little time researching the proposals being discussed and consider the following:

- How do you think that this may affect the financial regulation in the US and will this have a positive or negative effect on the US economy?
- Will changes of the type proposed weaken financial regulation and the protections against new financial crises?

Regulatory landscape in Hong Kong

Background to the Hong Kong financial industry

In addition to the major global financial hubs located in the Western hemisphere, there are also several key globally influential financial regions located in the East, which include Singapore, Hong Kong and China. Hong Kong occupies a strategic location quite centrally within Asia and close to many of the region's business markets. Hong Kong is often referred to as the gateway to mainland China due to its convenience for foreign firms seeking access to mainland China and conversely for mainland enterprises seeking global access. It is also helpful for business that major business centres such as Beijing, Shanghai, Singapore, Kuala Lumpur and Perth are in the same time zone as Hong Kong.

In practice

Hong Kong is noted for its sound financial infrastructure, effective regulatory regime and free flow of information and capital resulting in a great resource of both professional and financial expertise. It is therefore respected globally as a major asset management, banking and insurance hub with a trusted legal system, business-friendly environment and the additional advantage of low taxation. The World Bank and International Finance Corporation commissioned the study *Paying Taxes* in 2016 which addresses the cost of taxes and the administrative burden of tax compliance, and measures the ease of paying taxes across 189 economies globally. Hong Kong was found by the study to be one of the most tax-friendly economies in the world partly because there are only three direct taxes together with the availability of various allowances and deductions which reduce the overall tax burden. The three are:

- profits tax (capped at 16.5 per cent);
- salaries tax (maximum of 15 per cent);
- property tax 15 per cent.

Additionally, Hong Kong does not impose:

- sales tax or VAT;
- withholding tax;
- capital gains tax;
- tax on dividends;
- estate tax.

Hong Kong returned to Chinese sovereignty in 1997. However, it has a separate political and legal system which is based upon its 'One Country,

Two Systems' concept and has succeeded in retaining the strengths that make Hong Kong a vibrant global business city. Key factors include:

- autonomous executive and legislative powers;
- government and rule of law upheld by an independent judiciary;
- fully convertible Hong Kong dollar separate from the Chinese renminbi (RMB);
- independent participation in international forums;
- free movement of capital, goods and information;
- both English and Chinese as official languages–English is the usual language for business and contracts.

Hong Kong has also become the most comprehensive and competitive platform for offshore Chinese RMB-denominated business for local banks, overseas banks and companies, with settlements in excess of RMB 6.8 trillion handled by Hong Kong banks in 2015. In addition to the provision of the full range of RMB-denominated banking services, including trade settlements and financing, Hong Kong also has the largest pool of offshore RMB liquidity with RMB deposits and outstanding certificates of deposits exceeding RMB 1,060 billion in 2015. The financial services industry in Hong Kong is one of four 'pillar industries' employing almost a quarter of a million people and accounted for more than 15 per cent of Hong Kong GDP. Hong Kong can claim to be one of the key global banking centres with 71 of the world's top 100 banks being established there.[20]

Regulatory landscape in Hong Kong

Regulation of the financial services sector in Hong Kong is quite complex and is the responsibility of several key bodies, which include:

- Hong Kong Monetary Authority (HKMA);
- Securities and Futures Commission (SFC);
- Stock Exchange of Hong Kong (SEHK);
- Hong Kong Futures Exchange (HKFE);
- Independent Insurance Authority (IIA).

Hong Kong Monetary Authority (HKMA)

The Hong Kong Monetary Authority (HKMA) was established in 1993 as a result of the merger of the Office of the Exchange Fund with the Office of the

Commissioner of Banking. The HKMA may be seen to regulate the banking industry in Hong Kong and also assumes the obligations of a central bank. The HKMA is the government authority in Hong Kong with the responsibility for maintaining both monetary and banking stability.[21] The HKMA reports to the financial secretary and its key functions and responsibilities are governed by the Exchange Fund Ordinance and the Banking Ordinance. The main functions of the HKMA include:

- promoting and helping to maintain Hong Kong's status as an international financial centre;
- maintenance and development of the financial infrastructure in Hong Kong;
- maintaining currency stability within the framework of the Linked Exchange Rate system;
- promoting both the stability and the integrity of the financial system, including the banking system;
- managing the Exchange Fund.

Securities and Futures Commission (SFC)

The Securities and Futures Commission (SFC) is an independent statutory body set up in 1989 and has responsibility for the regulation and supervision of the securities and futures markets in Hong Kong.[22] The SFC has wide-ranging powers: investigative, remedial and disciplinary, which are set out in the Securities and Futures Ordinance (SFO) and the subsidiary legislation. The Securities and Futures Commission benefits from operational independence with respect to the government of the Hong Kong Special Administrative Region and its funding is primarily through the use of transaction levies and licensing fees. The roles, responsibilities and powers of the SFC, defined by the Securities and Futures Ordinance, provide clear regulatory objectives which include:

- developing and maintaining competitive, efficient, fair and transparent securities and futures markets;
- providing protection for the investing public;
- minimization of crime and misconduct in the markets;
- reduction of systemic risks within the industry;
- promoting and assisting the HK government in the task of maintaining Hong Kong's overall financial stability;

- promoting and assisting public understanding of the workings of the securities and futures industry.

> **In practice**
>
> With regard to the objective of promoting public understanding of the workings of the securities and futures industry, it is worth noting that the SFC is the only Hong Kong financial regulator which is given the mandate to educate the investing public. The Investor Education Centre (IEC) was created as a subsidiary of the SFC after the enactment of the Securities and Futures (Amendment) Ordinance in 2012, with the aim being to facilitate the education of the public regarding a broad range of retail financial products and services and it is also the intention that the IEC will play a key role in improving the overall 'financial literacy' of the general public in Hong Kong. The SFC has overall responsibility for the regulation and supervision of the securities and futures market, which includes the responsibility for issuing licences to all individuals and companies who wish to carry out a range of activities which includes areas such as asset management, advising on securities, futures contracts and corporate finance, dealing in securities and futures contracts, foreign exchange trading and providing automated trading services.

Stock Exchange of Hong Kong (SEHK)

The Securities and Futures Commission has the additional responsibility of overseeing the Hong Kong Exchanges and Clearing (HKEX), which is one of the largest financial market operators in the world and is the holding company of both the Stock Exchange of Hong Kong and the Hong Kong Futures Exchange. The Stock Exchange of Hong Kong is the main body responsible for the regulation and supervision of both stock exchange participants and companies listed on the stock exchange; the listing included over 1,900 companies in 2016. It is no surprise that HKEX hosts the trading of a wide range of products which include equities, ETFs, REITs, bonds, structured products, equity-index and single-stock derivatives, currency futures and commodity derivatives. HKEX also acts as the clearing house and settlement system for both exchange-traded and selected over-the-counter transactions, together with the provision of a comprehensive range of real-time, delayed and historic market data feeds.

Hong Kong Futures Exchange (HKFE)

The Hong Kong Futures Exchange merged with the Stock Exchange of Hong Kong in March 2000, and together with Hong Kong Securities Clearing Company formed Hong Kong Exchanges and Clearing Limited. Hong Kong Futures Exchange Limited therefore operates as a subsidiary of Hong Kong Exchanges and Clearing Limited. Whilst the Hong Kong Futures Exchange has the primary responsibility for the regulation and supervision of the futures exchange participants there is also a role for the SFC, which is responsible for the discipline of both sponsors and compliance advisers. The SFC also retains a role in the regulation of individuals who participate in securities and futures trading, as the SFC monitors both market misconduct and other breaches of securities and futures law and will conduct investigations into these circumstances and take appropriate punitive action in the case of wrong-doing.

Independent Insurance Authority (IIA)

As a result of the Insurance Companies (Amendment) Ordinance 2015, the Independent Insurance Authority has been established and has taken over the functions and responsibilities of the current regulator, the Office of the Commissioner for Insurance (OCI). The objectives of creating the IIA are to modernize the overall regulatory infrastructure and to promote the stability and development of the insurance industry, provide better protection for policyholders, and align with the growing international standard that financial regulators should be both financially and operationally independent of the government.

Under the modernized regulatory regime, companies or individuals who wish to undertake 'regulated activities' will be required to obtain a licence from the IIA. Regulated activities will include activities related to both advising upon insurance and the sale and post-sale administration of insurance policies. Lloyd's underwriters will continue to operate under their existing Hong Kong licence. The IIA will be self-financing in order to maintain its independence from government. It will derive income streams from the insurance industry and additionally from a policyholder levy on premiums for all insurance policies written by a Hong Kong intermediary or service company. The long-term target is for the IIA to maintain its financial independence from the Hong Kong government, with up to 70 per cent of its expenditure being met by the policyholder levy and the balance being met by the various authorization, licence and user fees.

Regulatory landscape in China

The People's Bank of China (PBOC) is the central bank of the People's Republic of China and, as a central bank, is expected to play a crucial role in China's macroeconomic management. Key roles attributed to the PBOC are the responsibility to formulate and to implement monetary policy and additionally to supervise and regulate the financial industry. In addition to its role in relation to monetary policy, the PBOC is the lead agency for anti-money-laundering activities and has the responsibility for Chinese interbank lending, bond and foreign exchange markets.[23]

In practice

In 2016 the PBOC published a financial stability report which highlighted various factors regarding the financial and regulatory landscape in China at that time. It asserted that the performance of the Chinese economy was stable despite some slow-down in growth and the reform of the financial sector had progressed in a positive way with improved competitiveness between financial institutions. The building of sound financial market infrastructure had made further progress and the development of financial markets was progressing along with both enhanced innovation and regulation. The Chinese financial system was therefore considered to be stable and sound and the development of the financial sector was well regulated. The assets of the banking sector and of the insurance sector continued to expand and in particular, income from insurance premiums continued to grow rapidly and the investment yield of insurance funds increased substantially.

The financial stability report by PBOC said that generally, financial infrastructure improvement continued, performance of financial markets was stable and both products and market participants were considered diversified. The system governing accounting standards had been further improved, along with the payment, clearing and settlement systems and financial laws, regulations and rules had been subject to appropriate enhancement. The mechanism of Joint Ministerial Conference on Financial Regulatory Coordination was improved, further studies on major financial topics undertaken and coordination between macroeconomic management and financial regulation was enhanced. It was also reported that there had been enhancement of systemic risk monitoring and assessment, as well as regulation of systemically important financial institutions and that macro-prudential regulation had been strengthened.[24]

Looking forward, the report commented that the implementation of the deposit insurance scheme will continue to improve the financial safety net. It is also proposed that key reforms will be continued, financial regulation enhanced and the macro-prudential policy framework improved. Additionally, the financial risk monitoring, assessment, early warning and resolution system will be improved. All this re-affirmed the Chinese government's commitment to this continued reform and improvement of the financial regulatory process, reported earlier in the same year.[25]

The key roles of the People's Bank of China therefore include:

- participating in international financial activities in the capacity of Chinese central bank;
- drafting and enforcing relevant laws, rules and regulations related to fulfilling the bank's functions;
- formulating and implementing monetary policy in accordance with Chinese law;
- issuing the currency, renminbi (RMB), and administering its circulation;
- regulation of the financial markets, eg the interbank lending market, the interbank bond market, foreign exchange market and gold market;
- monitoring, preventing and mitigating systemic financial risks to safeguard overall financial stability;
- maintaining and supporting the RMB exchange rate;
- holding and managing the state foreign exchange and gold reserves;
- supervising anti-money-laundering work in the financial sector and monitoring suspicious fund movement.

In practice

In addition to the People's Bank of China, the other main bodies responsible for the regulation and supervision of financial services in China are:

- the China Banking Regulatory Commission (CBRC);
- the China Insurance Regulatory Commission (CIRC);
- the China Securities Regulatory Commission (CSRC).

The China Banking Regulatory Commission (CBRC)

The China Banking Regulatory Commission (CBRC) is an agency of the People's Republic of China (PRC) empowered by the State Council to regulate and supervise the banking sector in China. Hong Kong and Macau are not regulated by the CBRC as they are designated 'special administrative regions' and are therefore outside the scope of the CBRC. The Chinese government established the CBRC as the country's independent banking regulator in 2003 as a way to counter lack of transparency, increasing debt and undercapitalization within the banking sector.

The CBRC has broad supervisory and disciplinary functions in relation to banking activities in mainland China, which include overseeing the regulation, licensing, market entry and operations of banking institutions, together with investigation of any behaviour or practice deemed to contravene the regulations and laws. The CBRC is also empowered to take enforcement action against institutions when required. The regulatory objectives of the CBRC include the following:

- to enhance the public knowledge of finance through both education and by promoting information disclosure;
- to protect the interests of depositors and consumers by prudential and effective supervision;
- to maintain market confidence through prudential and effective supervision;
- to monitor and combat financial crime.

The China Insurance Regulatory Commission (CIRC)

The China Insurance Regulatory Commission (CIRC) is another agency of the People's Republic of China, also empowered by the State Council to regulate the insurance products and services market in China and to maintain the stable operations of the insurance industry. Initially founded in 1998 but upgraded to a ministerial institution in 2003, CIRC has over 30 local offices distributed across the Chinese provinces.

The CIRC regulates and supervises the insurance market in mainland China but not Hong Kong and it is responsible for overseeing the establishment and operation of both insurance companies and their subsidiaries, the setting of regulations and the monitoring of compliance with appropriate standards for both insurance agents and the senior management of insurance companies. The CIRC is also responsible for the regulation of insurance brokers and insurance loss adjusters and oversees the system for policyholder protection, which is funded by industry levies. The main duties of the CIRC include the following:

- create guidelines and policies to develop insurance business and to draw up development strategies and plans for the industry;
- formulate laws, rules and regulations for insurance supervision and introduce the rules and regulations within the insurance industry;
- examine and approve the establishment of insurance companies (and subsidiaries), insurance group companies and insurance holding companies;
- work together with related departments to examine and approve the establishment of insurance assets management companies;
- approve the establishment of representative offices of overseas insurance institutions in China;
- examine and approve insurance intermediary institutions, eg insurance agencies and broker companies;
- examine and approve insurance agencies to be established overseas by Chinese insurance and non-insurance institutions;
- oversee and approve any mergers, splits and dissolution of insurance institutions including bankruptcy of insurance companies;
- examine and approve the qualifications of senior managers of insurance institutions and create basic standards for the qualifications of staff engaged in insurance.

The China Securities Regulatory Commission (CSRC)

Another ministerial public institution directly under the State Council, the China Securities Regulatory Commission (CSRC) was created in 1992 and is the main regulator of the securities industry in China. The CSRC performs the key regulatory function, in accordance with the appropriate laws and regulations, over the securities and futures market of the People's Republic of China. The CSRC also has the responsibility to maintain an orderly securities and futures market and to ensure the legal operations of the capital market. The CSRC has the ultimate responsibility for the regulation of the stock markets in both Shanghai and Shenzhen, the futures exchange in Shanghai, and the commodities exchanges in Zhengzhou and Dalian, although the local exchanges retain some front-line regulatory functions under the supervision of the CSRC.

In its role of supervision and administration of the securities and futures markets, the CSRC is empowered to perform functions including:

- formulate policies and development plans for the securities and futures markets;
- draft, implement, modify and revise relevant laws and regulations on the securities and futures markets;
- supervise the communication of the securities and futures markets information: monitor and manage improved information disclosure for the securities and futures markets;
- investigate and penalize the activities of individuals and companies in violation of the relevant securities and futures laws and regulations;
- monitor and make preparations to prevent or contain financial crises;
- supervise the issuance, listing, trading, custody and settlement of securities including futures, stocks, securities funds and bonds;
- supervise the securities and futures exchanges as well as their senior managerial personnel in accordance with the relevant regulations.

In practice

Talking points from the current financial world (3)

Total economic unification: a future likelihood?

Hong Kong is officially considered to be a Special Administrative Region of the People's Republic of China; that is to say, Hong Kong is in effect a territory of China which enjoys a high degree of autonomy.

Mainland China and Hong Kong complement each other economically although there are clearly many political and economic differences which remain. The Chinese economy is much more dependent on manufacturing, although the services sector has begun to grow in the last few years. Conversely, Hong Kong has an economy which is built upon low tax rates, free trade and low levels of government intervention. It is fair to say that the relationship between Hong Kong and China works well because they maintain good economic relations and provide a stimulus to each other's economies. Mainland China currently represents Hong Kong's largest trading partner and a reliable source of foreign direct investment.

> Hong Kong represents a gateway to mainland China for other countries interested in doing business on the mainland or indeed as a method of accessing Chinese stocks or investments, whilst Hong Kong is the preferred market for mainland Chinese companies seeking a listing, as the Chinese stock markets are considered to be more conservative. Hong Kong is also the main hub for the global offshore renminbi (RMB) business and is the largest and most liquid RMB market outside of mainland China.
>
> Think about the possibility of full integration of Hong Kong with mainland China... do you think that this is likely to occur?

Regulatory landscape in Singapore

Singapore is an established and influential international financial centre and, given its reasonably central location in the Asia-Pacific region, it has become home to many and varied financial institutions. The financial services industry in Singapore covers a variety of business including:

- banks, merchant banks and finance companies;
- insurance;
- securities, futures and fund management;
- financial advisers, money brokers;
- business trusts and trust companies;
- payment and settlement systems.

In practice

Some of these financial institutions have also chosen Singapore to be either their global or regional headquarters. Singapore is also recognized as a growing wealth management hub and is widely accepted as one of the most competitive financial centres in the world, behind only London and New York. In recent years, Singapore has also overtaken Japan to become the largest foreign exchange centre in the Asia region. The key bodies responsible for regulating and supervising financial services in Singapore are:

- Monetary Authority of Singapore (MAS);
- Singapore Exchange Securities Trading (SGX);
- Securities Industry Council (SIC);
- Accounting and Corporate Regulatory Authority (ACRA).

Monetary Authority of Singapore (MAS)

The Monetary Authority of Singapore (MAS) is Singapore's central bank and it is also the sole regulator in Singapore, having regulatory and supervisory oversight of the financial services industry across the various financial sectors.[26]

In the past, monetary functions associated with a central bank were performed by a variety of government departments and agencies; however, as Singapore grew in importance within the region the increasing demands of the complex finance, banking and monetary environment required that changes be facilitated to develop a more sound and coherent policy on monetary matters. The Singapore Parliament passed the Monetary Authority of Singapore Act in 1970 and the Monetary Authority of Singapore was created in 1971, with the authority to regulate the financial services sector in Singapore. The powers of the MAS include the remit to act as central bank and financial agent of the Singapore government, with the aims being to promote monetary stability and to pursue credit and exchange policies designed to promote the sustainable growth of the economy. The Singapore government also decided to bring the regulation of the insurance industry under the power of the MAS in 1977 and additionally, the regulatory responsibilities of the Securities Industry Act (1973) in 1984.

In its capacity as sole regulator over the financial services sector in Singapore, the MAS has six separate oversight responsibilities, which include:

- regulation: this involves the creation of risk-based capital and prudential requirements;
- authorization: the responsibility for authorizing individuals and companies offering financial services in Singapore;
- supervision: supervising the conduct of financial business by individuals and companies including areas such as prudential, anti-money-laundering efforts and the countering the financing of terrorism;

- financial monitoring and surveillance;
- enforcement: taking enforcement and punitive action against individuals and companies in breach of prudential, and conduct rules and regulations.

> ### In practice
>
> As the central bank of Singapore, the Monetary Authority of Singapore (MAS) is empowered to monitor macroeconomic factors, emerging trends and potential vulnerabilities within the financial system in Singapore, whilst promoting sustainable, non-inflationary economic growth through appropriate monetary policy. MAS is also responsible for the administration of foreign reserves, liquidity within the banking sector and the maintenance of Singapore's exchange rate. MAS has the responsibility to supervise all of the various financial institutions in Singapore, including the stock exchange, banks, insurers, market intermediaries and financial advisers. To emphasize the scope of the responsibilities, MAS also has a mandate to promote a sound corporate governance framework within the financial services sector and to oversee compliance with international accounting standards. The MAS works closely with both financial institutions and other government agencies to promote overall financial stability, confidence, and to continue the development of Singapore as a globally recognized financial centre.

The MAS also has the responsibility to promote and support the financial education of retail investors, to administer various statutes in relation to the broad financial sector, banking, insurance and securities. Since 2002, the MAS also has the role of overseeing and issuing currency. Overall designated functions of the MAS include:

- to act as the central bank of Singapore, including the conduct of monetary policy, oversight of payment systems, serving as banker financial agent to the government of Singapore and the issue of currency;
- to develop and promote Singapore as a global financial centre;
- to supervise financial services and promote/maintain financial stability;
- to manage the Singapore foreign reserves.

Singapore Exchange Securities Trading (SGX)

The Singapore Exchange (SGX) is the stock exchange in Singapore and it also performs regulatory functions in relation to listings, issuer regulation, member supervision and the monitoring of securities markets. The Singapore Exchange is the Asia-Pacific region's first demutualized and integrated securities and derivatives exchange and includes organizations trading in both securities and derivatives. The SGX facilitates all functions within the trading process, including order routing, trading, matching, clearing, settlement, depository and data services. The regulatory functions fulfilled by SGX include acting as front-line regulator for the markets and clearing houses in Singapore, and SGX works closely with the relevant regulatory authorities, including MAS and the Commercial Affairs Department (CAD), in the development and the enforcement of rules and regulations to ensure a robust and secure financial marketplace. SGX also monitors the securities and derivatives markets in order to detect irregular or illegal trading activities and to take appropriate enforcement action if necessary.

Singapore Exchange (SGX) is a multi-asset exchange which includes equity, fixed-income and derivatives markets operated to the highest regulatory standards, including listed companies and bonds originating outside Singapore together with sound links across the Asian region and in Europe. SGX offers access to derivatives products across Asian equity indices, commodities and currencies, and is widely considered to represent the most liquid offshore market for the benchmark equity indices of China, India, Japan and the ASEAN member states (Figure 14.2).

Figure 14.2 ASEAN member states

ASEAN is the Association of Southeast Asian Nations and is a regional organization of 10 Southeast Asian states which was created in order to promote cooperation and to facilitate economic integration for the mutual benefits of its members.[27] The ASEAN member states include:

| Indonesia | Thailand | Singapore | Malaysia | Brunei |
| Myanmar | Philippines | Vietnam | Cambodia | Laos |

SOURCE Association of Southeast Asian Nations[27]

Securities Industry Council (SIC)

The Securities Industry Council is a non-statutory advisory body, the purpose of which is to help and advise the minister of finance on issues relevant to the securities industry and consists of representatives of the private sector, public sector, Monetary Authority of Singapore and any other individuals who are deemed appropriate for appointment by the finance minister. The Securities Industry Council was originally created in 1973 under the Securities Industry Act but then continued under the later Securities and Futures Act (SFA).

In Singapore, all takeovers and mergers are subject to non-statutory rules which are laid down in the Singapore Code on Takeovers and Mergers and the Securities Industry Council is responsible for the monitoring, enforcement and administration of this code. The SIC produces guidance notes on the application of specific principles and rules and also retains legal power to investigate any trading or dealing in securities that has connection to either mergers or takeover situations. The rules and practices within the Singapore Code on Takeovers and Mergers are also subject to periodic review by the SIC, who will recommend amendments and changes to be confirmed by the Monetary Authority of Singapore.

Accounting and Corporate Regulatory Authority (ACRA)

The Accounting and Corporate Regulatory Authority regulates business entities, public accountants and corporate service providers in Singapore and is therefore also a relevant body with regard to the general conduct of business in Singapore. The main role of the ACRA is to work with the main regulator and to support the monitoring of corporate compliance, adherence to disclosure requirements and the regulation of public accountants performing statutory audit. The objective is to achieve and maintain sound corporate governance, high-quality corporate financial reporting and also high-quality auditing standards within the Singapore financial and corporate sectors. This supports the long-term aim of making Singapore globally respected and trusted as a business environment, which is fostered by a trusted regulatory environment for businesses, public accountants and corporate service providers.

Regulation and supervision style

Regulation

We have considered the issue of regulation and supervision in the major financial centres around the world and the importance of robust regulation and supervision to promote and maintain confidence in financial markets has been established. The option of rules- or principles-based regulation is much debated and it is useful to consider the difference between rules- and principles-based regulation and the positives and negatives for the choice between these two options, to achieve regulatory objectives. It is perfectly acceptable for regulation to take the form of either rules or principles and the distinction between the two models is equivocal, which is why rules may be preferred to principles in certain situations and viceversa.

It is interesting to note that during very positive market conditions, when there is a preference for flexibility within the markets, principles-based regulation is usually very popular as it allows for dynamic new product development, innovation with regard to conducting business and the application of judgement in changing market conditions. Difficult market conditions and financial crisis periods bring with them a call for stricter rules and prescribed punishments for transgressors. On the negative side, it is considered that principles may be seen to be missing an element of predictability and certainty; however, on the positive side principles are valued for the promotion of both flexibility and adaptability. The opposite is considered to be the case for rules, which are seen to be fixed and certain with little or no flexibility. It is accepted that principles will require appropriate judgement to be exercised in order to be applied successfully; however, rules are more prescriptive and will impose specific conduct which requires no flexibility of judgement.

As a broad generalization, it is accepted that the decision to adopt either rules or principles should be signposted by which model will be able to achieve the regulatory objective efficiently, at the least cost in resources, under the prevailing circumstances and with minimal regulatory intervention in the operation of the market. This decision-making process may regrettably be affected by government bias and political viewpoints which can impair the regulator's effectiveness and many of the major regulatory bodies around the world have therefore evolved to be independent of government.

A rules-based system will lay down a series of rules, known to companies and individuals in advance, which prescribe certain standards of practice, prohibit certain actions, specify methods of conduct and offer little or no flexibility. However, 'interpretation' of rules is often problematic and attempts to provide clarity may result in very complex wording and greater detail within a specific rule, but 'loop-holes' and gaps may remain if the rule-writer does not contemplate a particular activity or does not encompass all possible circumstances. It is also an unintended consequence of rules-based systems that regulatory compliance may turn into observing the letter of the rules: a box-ticking exercise, without consideration for the purpose and aims of the rules.

> **In practice**
>
> **An example of a regulatory rule[28]**
>
> SEC Rule 17a-4 is a regulation in the United States of America, issued by the US Securities and Exchange Commission. It outlines the regulatory requirements for data retention, indexing and accessibility for companies involved in the trading or brokering of financial securities; for example, company shares, bonds and futures.
>
> The rule states that the records of various types of transaction must be retained, stored and indexed on indelible media with immediate accessibility for a period of two years. It further states that the transaction records must then be retained for a period of at least six years with delayed access. The rule goes on to specify that it is required that duplicate records must also be kept within the same time frame at an off-site location.

Principles-based systems do appear to have the advantage that they will allow an element of flexibility which may be seen to be needed to allow innovation and the ability to adapt to changing markets, although some applications of principles may therefore be seen to be very broad and lacking in control. It is possible for regulators using principles-based systems to give some direction and guidance through the use of illustrations of good and bad practice. However, regulators could be reluctant to offer too much guidance and risk being prescriptive and evolving the principles into rules. In essence, principles may be seen as either a guide to action or a series of preferred objectives and therefore the application of principles will require a company or individuals to exercise judgement.

> **In practice**
>
> **Example of regulatory principles**[29]
>
> The following are examples of some of the principles for business laid down in the UK's FCA handbook:
>
> Principle 2 A firm must conduct its business with due skill, care and diligence.
>
> Principle 3 A firm must take reasonable care to organize and control its affairs responsibly and effectively, with adequate risk management systems.
>
> Principle 9 A firm must take reasonable care to ensure the suitability of its advice and discretionary decisions for any customer who is entitled to rely upon its judgement.
>
> Principle 11 A firm must deal with its regulators in an open and cooperative way and must disclose to the appropriate regulator appropriately anything relating to the firm of which that regulator would reasonably expect notice.

The positive attributes of the principles-based systems may also be perceived as a weakness in this type of regulatory system because the inherent flexibility of the principles-based system could result in a lack of certainty and predictability, particularly if the regulator is reluctant to provide regulated companies and individuals with illustrations or guidelines for application of the principles. Furthermore, if regulated companies and individuals lack understanding with regard to how principles will be applied by the regulator, they may adopt an overly cautious approach, which may have the unintended consequence of stifling innovation.

It follows, therefore, that there exists no simple model of what a rules-based or a principles-based regulatory system should look like as the systems used around the world are tailored to the landscape that they regulate and it is quite likely that a hybrid of the two systems will often be encountered. This may take the form, for example, of a rules-based regulatory system which employs a principles-based enforcement policy, since it remains rare to encounter mandatory penalties.

Supervision

The process of supervision is multifaceted and may include a variety of responsibilities for the body or agency in question, including:

- authorization;
- monitoring compliance;
- enforcement action;
- punitive action.

Authorization of companies or individuals will involve an element of thorough research into the background and history and may be dependent upon reaching a minimum level of qualifications or prescribed standards of conduct. The precise method and intensity of monitoring will depend upon the level of risk posed by the company or individual, the perceived likelihood of breaching the rules/regulations, the potential consequences of a breach in the rules/regulations and the supervising agency's resources. Any enforcement procedures may occur for a variety of reasons including the supervisor's monitoring activities, or a complaint by a customer or another market participant. Enforcement procedures would usually involve some form of investigation to determine exactly what has occurred, the root cause and if further action or sanction is required. The supervising agency may employ the use of enforcement officers with powers to investigate and to gather information. It may be that there is an agency which is appointed with the responsibility for monitoring compliance and the identification of suspected rule breaking, but a separate agency has the responsibility to determine if the suspicion is proven and if so, to apply an appropriate penalty, sanction or impose compensation.

Regulation in financial markets

It is generally accepted that the operations of the financial markets are pivotal in the development of any economy and the financial sector is the mechanism which facilitates the exchange of goods and services in the economy and to transfer the savings of an economy into investments. A sound, efficient and well-managed financial sector will accomplish this process, encouraging more savings and therefore more investment in the process. This should result in faster economic growth, improved levels of income and therefore the end result should be the improvement of well-being domestically, within the economy. Strong and efficient domestic financial markets may also be of significant benefit to global growth in the form of investment capital movement from wealthier, more developed economies, to emerging and developing economies.

It has been mentioned earlier in the chapter that one of the reasons for robust regulatory regimes being so important is the issue that information asymmetry exists, within the finance sector, between the sellers of financial products and the buyers. Generally, most markets work well when there is a high frequency of repeat purchases of a given product, because in these market circumstances, it is quite straightforward for an individual to determine the inherent quality of the product. It is also easy for the individual to switch away from a poor quality product to a product of better quality and not to make the same error in the future.

> **In practice**
>
> **High-frequency repeat purchase**
>
> Henrietta is a young trainee professional who lives in a rented one-bedroom flat with three well-known supermarkets (A, B and C) nearby. Being financially astute, she usually shops around and prefers 'own brand' products, in order to get 'value for money' and has purchased a can of beans for her lunch from supermarket A.
>
> She is not satisfied with the beans from supermarket A, because she feels that the sauce is too watery and therefore she buys a can of beans from supermarket B the next day. Having tried this can of beans she is still not happy because the taste of the sauce is not to her liking and so the next day she purchases a can of beans from supermarket C.
>
> She likes the can of beans from supermarket C and is now happy to purchase cans of beans from supermarket C in the future.
>
> If Henrietta had been looking for a personal pension product, it may have been many years before she discovered that it was not suitable for her needs and requirements.

It is often the case with financial products that individuals will only purchase relatively few such products and any one of these products may have a substantial financial impact upon the individual either now or in the future; for example, a pension, mortgage, investment bond or a life assurance policy. Furthermore, with certain long-term products it may only become apparent to the individual that the financial product is not satisfactory many years into the future. At this point, it may be difficult or even impossible to put in place an effective remedy. It is therefore crucial to have reliable and robust financial regulation to safeguard the well-being of inexperienced consumers of financial products, whose knowledge is limited in comparison to the finance professionals advising upon and selling these products. In particular, the process of prudential regulation with respect to major financial institutions such as banks, insurance companies and pension providers must be seen to be rigorous. This is because insolvency, or even the prospect of insolvencies amongst these types of key institutions, would be deeply unsettling to consumers and would therefore seriously undermine the confidence of consumers and investors and therefore be harmful to the economy as a whole.

It could reasonably be argued that the most important objective of any prudential regulator would be to ensure that financial companies have an appropriate level of capital. This is to ensure that sufficient capital exists to absorb financial losses that may occur in the event of adverse economic conditions resulting in pronounced financial stress. Furthermore, following the circumstances of financial stress, sufficient capital should remain to allow the company to be safely wound up, or to continue its market function whilst retaining the confidence of its customers and market counterparties.

In practice

Prior to the financial crisis of 2008, many financial firms had appeared to hold sufficient capital to meet their regulatory requirements, but this proved to be unfounded. In a number of cases capital reserves were insufficient, in part due to the fact that the rules specifying what could be considered as capital had been weakened over time. This did focus attention upon the 'quality' of capital and indeed the expediency of having a capital buffer above the minimum acceptable level and/or to have some reliable method of creating extra capital in a financial crisis. The latter solution could be partly effected by restricting distributions such as dividend payments or staff bonuses.

What was noticeable during the 2008 financial crisis is that the point at which a financial institution loses the trust of customers may arise significantly before it runs out of capital. It is also worth noting that this may be compounded by the observation that once a firm is deemed to be experiencing financial trouble, the actual marketable value of the assets that it holds may, in practice, be found to be less than valued in the company's accounts. This phenomenon would result in much greater losses than originally expected following the occurrence of a financial stress event.

Stress-testing

It is not easy to specify capital requirements for financial companies without some point of reference regarding the magnitude of future stress. The process of stress-testing addresses this by modelling potential losses as a result of various hypothetical macroeconomic scenarios.

Keyword

Stress-testing is a computer-generated simulation technique used in various financial scenarios including the banking industry and asset-holding portfolios, the purpose of which is to examine reaction to different financial situations.

Under the guidance of the Prudential Regulation Authority, the Financial Policy Committee performed stress tests for the major UK banks for the first time in 2014, in order to determine if they were appropriately capitalized to support the real economy in a severe, broad and synchronized financial stress scenario.

In practice

Stress-testing

Consider a financial institution with a portfolio of mortgage loans. An appropriate example of a stress test would be to assume a recessionary period, which included an associated fall in the housing market, rise in unemployment and increase in the number of households experiencing difficulties in meeting their financial commitments to mortgage repayments.

This scenario would effectively stress the portfolio of mortgage loans. However, for the institution in question, the ability to simply meet the minimum prudential requirements after this stress may not be sufficient to ensure financial stability. If this represented an economy-wide financial stress and banks with portfolios of mortgage loans responded to depleted capital reserves by reducing their lending, this would have an adverse effect upon the housing market and the economy as a whole. The stress tests would be calibrated to ensure that the financial institution would preserve sufficient capital to at least maintain their levels of lending to the economy at the level required by the assumption of reduced demand.

Simultaneous stress-testing for the major banks within the UK is now installed as an established part of the UK supervisory process, and is scheduled to be a regular annual exercise. This regular stress-testing is also the process in the US, and the European Banking Authority has also undertaken similar testing for the major European banks. At the time of writing, BASEL III is also affecting banks worldwide.[30] Basel III was developed by the Basel Committee on Banking Supervision and represents reform measures in banking prudential regulation. Its aim is to strengthen the regulation, supervision and risk management of the banking sector in order to improve the resilience of the EU banking sector. This should ensure that the banking sector is sufficiently robust to absorb economic shocks whilst also being able to continue to finance economic activity and growth.

Anti-money-laundering and prevention of financial crime

Invariably it is the responsibility of the domestic financial regulator to take responsibility for the monitoring, detection and prevention of financial crime and money-laundering within each country or economic region. In recent years there has been substantial global police action and focus into this issue and much effort and resources have been aimed at making it much more difficult to hide or launder assets derived from criminal or fraudulent activities and to more effectively monitor the global movement of money.

Keyword

The phrase **money-laundering** is broadly used to describe the process of concealing or disguising the origin and ownership of assets which are the proceeds of criminal activity. The process, if successful, will result in these assets having the appearance of being derived from a legitimate and legal source. Assets which have been acquired as a result of criminal activities may be successfully laundered through methods other than the financial sector; for example, by making use of a cash business such as restaurants, fast-food establishments and taxi companies. However, the broad nature of the products and services within the financial services industry results in the industry being vulnerable to the actions of potential money-launderers.

Financial regulation and supervision

It is thought that globally hundreds of billions of dollars of funds derived from illegal activities is 'laundered' through the financial services industries each year, often by transferring funds through foreign banks, purchase and surrender or sale of financial products, or by clandestine use of legitimate businesses (Figure 14.3). Most serious crimes which derive a financial gain for the criminals involved will lead to the potential for money-laundering activities; for example, terrorism, drug dealing, illegal gambling, theft, prostitution, fraud and corruption. The initial proceeds of these types of practices are considered evidence of the criminal activity and are therefore difficult and dangerous to spend; however, once the proceeds have passed through an effective laundering process this will conceal their origins and legitimize the funds. For this reason, the authorities globally have viewed the coordinated anti-money-laundering actions as being the first line of defence against such activities as terrorism, organized crime and drug dealing.

Regulators globally each have their own rules and regulations in place to combat the problems created by money-laundering activities, which have developed sophisticated and complex techniques over the years in order to make it more difficult for the police and financial authorities to uncover these activities. Much cooperation exists globally between regulatory bodies to track and minimize the effectiveness of these illegal activities.

In practice

The current rules and regulations within the United Kingdom in relation to money-laundering emanate from various sources including:

- Proceeds of Crime Act (POCA) 2002;
- Serious Organised Crime and Police Act (SOCPA) 2005;
- Money Laundering (ML) Regulations 2007;
- Joint Money Laundering Steering Group (JMLSG): guidance for the financial services industry;
- FCA Senior Management Arrangements, Systems and Controls (SYSC) Sourcebook.

Figure 14.3 The money-laundering process

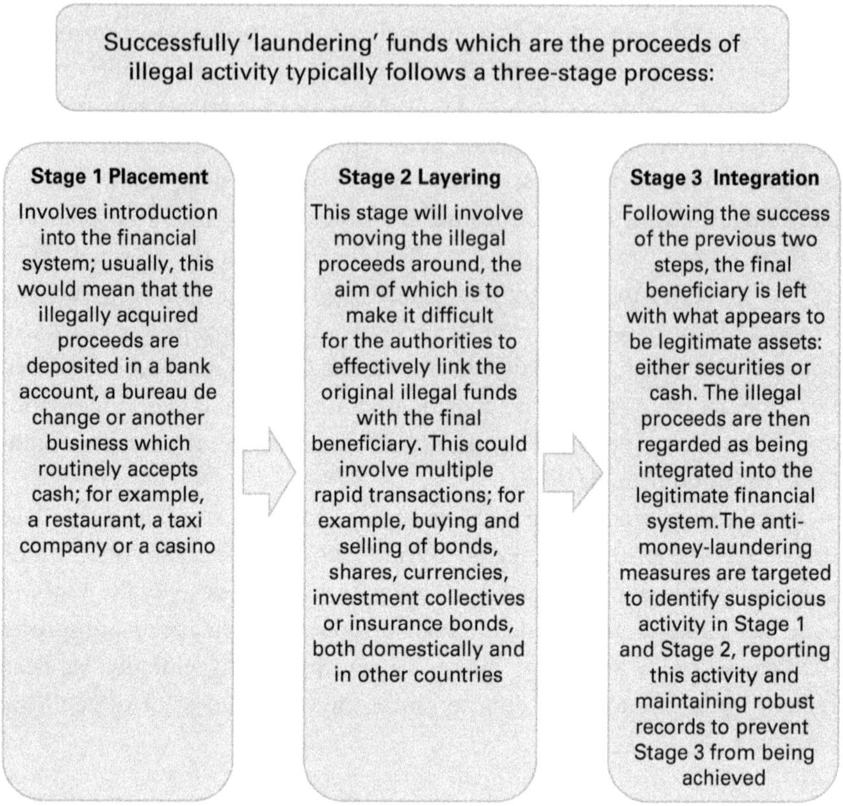

> Successfully 'laundering' funds which are the proceeds of illegal activity typically follows a three-stage process:

Stage 1 Placement
Involves introduction into the financial system; usually, this would mean that the illegally acquired proceeds are deposited in a bank account, a bureau de change or another business which routinely accepts cash; for example, a restaurant, a taxi company or a casino

Stage 2 Layering
This stage will involve moving the illegal proceeds around, the aim of which is to make it difficult for the authorities to effectively link the original illegal funds with the final beneficiary. This could involve multiple rapid transactions; for example, buying and selling of bonds, shares, currencies, investment collectives or insurance bonds, both domestically and in other countries

Stage 3 Integration
Following the success of the previous two steps, the final beneficiary is left with what appears to be legitimate assets: either securities or cash. The illegal proceeds are then regarded as being integrated into the legitimate financial system. The anti-money-laundering measures are targeted to identify suspicious activity in Stage 1 and Stage 2, reporting this activity and maintaining robust records to prevent Stage 3 from being achieved

The Proceeds of Crime Act (2002) specifies that money-laundering relates to any asset that has its origin from illegal activity. Property is criminal property if an individual either knows or suspects that it is criminal property and the requirement is for companies or individuals to report their suspicions of money-laundering activities to the appropriate authorities.

To support this requirement, the Proceeds of Crime Act (2002) has established five separate offences, which are:

- concealing;
- arrangements;
- acquisition, use and possession;
- failure to disclose;
- tipping off.

Concealing means it is an offence for a person to conceal or disguise criminal property. Arrangements means being involved in an arrangement which the individual knows or suspects, facilitates the acquisition, retention, use or control of criminal property for another person. Acquisition, use and possession involves acquiring, using or having possession of criminal property. Under failure to disclose, three conditions need to be satisfied for this offence:

- the person knows or suspects (or has reasonable grounds to know or suspect) that another person is laundering money;
- the information giving rise to the knowledge or suspicion came to him or her during the course of business in a regulated sector;
- the person does not make the required disclosure as soon as is practicable.

Tipping off means giving another person information, knowing or suspecting that a money-laundering report has been made to the authorities, when that information is likely to prejudice the investigation.

In practice

An individual has a defence against the first three offences if they make the required disclosure to the Money Laundering Reporting Officer or the National Crime Agency in accordance with protocol.

The Serious Organised Crime and Police Act (2005) amended certain sections of the Proceeds of Crime Act (2002). One key feature involves addressing issues carried out legally in another country, which would have been considered to be illegal in the UK.

The Money Laundering Regulations (2007) represent detailed regulations which were implemented in accordance with broad EU directives. They address the administrative provisions that companies and individuals must put in place in order to effectively combat money-laundering, including systems, training and identity checking of new customers. Three main requirements were imposed upon companies and individuals:

- administrative: carry out identification procedures, implement reporting procedures for suspicions and maintain adequate records in relation to anti-money-laundering;

- training: provide appropriate training for staff with respect to the money-laundering regulations and how to recognize and deal with suspicious transactions;
- preventative: establish internal controls to identify and prevent money-laundering activities. It is an offence (liable to a jail term and fine) for companies or individuals who fail to comply with the money-laundering regulations.

The Joint Money Laundering Steering Group issued guidance to the UK financial services industry in 2007, which detailed how authorized companies and individuals should manage their risk with regard to money-laundering issues. This guidance has influenced how all authorized companies and individuals deal with their customers. This guidance requires that companies and individuals:

- take a risk-based and proportionate approach to the prevention of money-laundering;
- simplify the identity verification requirements for some customers;
- allow for greater reliance on identification verification carried out by other companies, since the guidance specifies the identification requirement for all types of customers.

Additionally, the latest guidance notes:

- introduced some new/revised definitions which includes beneficial owners and politically exposed persons; primarily because they may be more vulnerable or susceptible to corruption;
- set out the customer due diligence measures to be applied in various circumstances and that customer due diligence required a risk-based approach;
- identified how much to rely on the customer due diligence work of other regulated firms;
- identified situations when simplified customer due diligence measures may be applied;
- identified when enhanced due diligence must be applied in higher-risk situations; for example, in connection with correspondent banking and when clients have not been seen in person.

In practice

The customer due diligence requirements will assist regulated companies and individuals to satisfy themselves that they have rigorously confirmed the customer's identity, there is no legal reason preventing the business relationship and to assist law enforcement agencies. In this context, the customer due diligence must be pursued by individuals and companies whilst being mindful of the risk posed by various types of business and at the outset of the relationship, regulated individuals and companies must:

- identify the customer;
- obtain verification of the customer's identity;
- confirm the nature of the proposed business relationship.

This represents the standard level of customer due diligence required for personal clients and is quite simply satisfied by examination of common forms of identification; for example, passport or photo-card driving licence. In accordance with the risk-based approach, enhanced due diligence may be conducted if the circumstances warrant, but is specifically required in certain higher-risk situations including:

- when the client is a politically exposed person;
- circumstances when a face-to-face meeting has not occurred;
- distance banking relationships (online).

Additionally, the Financial Conduct Authority's Senior Management Arrangements, Systems and Controls Sourcebook lays down specific rules, but also gives guidelines regarding the implementation and application of the anti-money-laundering steps within the United Kingdom.

In practice

The FCA principles-based approach to prevention of money-laundering

The Financial Conduct Authority's sourcebook of Senior Management Arrangements, Systems and Controls stipulates specific requirements for regulated individuals and companies.

One such requirement is that senior management are obliged to ensure appropriate systems and controls are in place to ensure prevention of both money-laundering and terrorist-funding activities.

Guidance notes issued by the Joint Money Laundering Steering Group in the UK are intended to assist regulated companies and individuals to interpret and apply these requirements and obligations for their specific business.

To determine the necessary procedures and controls for each particular regulated business, senior management must employ a risk assessment in the context of their own business's practice and model, including factors such as:

- the specific scope and nature of the firm's products and services;
- the nature of its client base and geographical location;
- how these factors may result in the business being vulnerable to abuse by criminals.

Complaints and dispute resolution

Regulatory bodies globally are acutely aware that in the financial services industry there will be cause for complaints against a regulated company or individual. It is inevitable that a proportion of the complaints will be valid, whilst some will be without foundation or vexatious; however, domestic regulators will have in place rules and procedures to be followed in the event that a complaint is received regarding a product, service or the conduct of an individual.

In practice

Example: in the UK the FCA requires that authorized companies and individuals deal with complaints from eligible complainants both promptly and fairly.

All regulated companies and individuals must be able to demonstrate that they have appropriate complaints procedures in place and that they are adhered to for all types of complaint, whether expressed written or orally.

This forms a part of the FCA's 'treating customers fairly' initiative.

Financial regulation and supervision

In the UK the FCA's regulatory stance is that it is the responsibility of the company to ensure that all regulated individuals conform to required professional and ethical standards when dealing with customer complaints. The company's senior management bear the responsibility for ensuring that adequate systems and controls are put in place for this purpose and that these controls are reviewed on an ongoing basis. It is also an FCA requirement that appropriate records must be kept regarding complaints for FCA monitoring purposes and regulated companies and individuals are required to provide the regulator with bi-annual reports on complaints.

The provisions of the Financial Services and Markets Act 2000 empowered the UK regulator to make rules in relation to the appropriate handling of complaints and established an independent body, the Financial Ombudsman Service, to operate and administer a dispute resolution scheme. The Financial Ombudsman Service aims to resolve complaints about financial services companies and individual firms quickly and fairly and is available at no charge to complainants, effectively removing the impediment and deterrent of legal costs.

Keyword

The **Financial Ombudsman Service (FOS)** is empowered to make a regulated company or individual pay fair compensation as a result of an upheld complaint, currently to a maximum amount of £150,000; although if a monetary award is made, the FOS may agree compensation for factors including financial loss, reputational damage and inconvenience and including a proportion, or all of the costs, reasonably incurred by the complainant. Additionally, there is provision within the regulations for specified consumer organizations to raise 'super-complaints' in the event of large-scale damage or loss to consumers.

There is a further provision in the UK which provides an element of protection for consumers in the event of default by a regulated company or individual and this is provided by the Financial Services Compensation Scheme. The scheme was set up under the Financial Services and Markets Act 2000, is free to consumers and is independent of government and the financial industry.

The role of the Financial Services Compensation Scheme (FSCS) is to pay compensation to eligible claimants where an authorized company or individual is in default; for example, has ceased trading or is unable to pay the agreed compensation. There are, however, prescribed limits to the amount of compensation which the FSCS will pay to eligible claimants. The FSCS is funded by the financial services industry as each firm authorized by UK regulators is required to pay an annual levy, which goes towards the FSCS running costs and compensation awards made. It therefore represents a form of insurance, funded by all authorized companies and individuals, providing protection to clients in the event of default. Some similar provision may be found globally; for example, with deposit insurance which is available in many countries and regions around the world.

Summary

There have been many and various reforms in the area of financial regulation and supervision since the global financial crisis of 2008 and we must ask the question: will these reforms prevent a future financial crisis? The answer is of course, probably not.

Financial crises may be caused by a variety of unexpected and unpredictable events; for example, earthquakes, tsunamis and recessions – typically black swan events. It is therefore quite likely that there will be further financial crises in the future. However, the reforms that have taken place over the last few years will hopefully mean that the financial systems around the world will be more able to withstand the shocks of a financial crisis. The measures which have been put in place by the regulatory authorities in the major financial centres around the world should result in a smaller incidence of financial instability and therefore the financial sector as a whole should be more resilient. This should, in turn, be of benefit to the wider economy.

The future events in the area of regulation are likely to be interesting in various areas of the world, not the least being the UK, Europe and the USA. At the time of writing, the UK have just given notice to leave the European Union and the implications for financial regulations are yet to be observed; however, it is likely that the authorities responsible for two of the most influential global financial markets will seek to work closely together to maintain standards, consumer protection measures and of course, anti-money-laundering safeguards that are effective. Speculation continues regarding the future of the European Union, the strength of some of the member states and if the EU will exist in its present form in 10 years' time.

Equally, the US under the new Trump administration shows signs of an appetite to make changes to financial regulations with notable focus in the election campaign aimed at reducing regulation, particularly in the banking sector. The UK, EU and USA are not regions which would have been readily associated with significant political risk until quite recently; however, these regions of the world seem certain to be the source of much discussion in the near future and are unlikely to be boring over the next five years.

Check your understanding

1 It is clear that the financial cost of regulation is significant; so why is it necessary?
2 Who is responsible for domestic regulation within a country?
3 Why is Singapore important as a financial hub?
4 What are the different types of regulation and how do they differ?
5 Explain the importance of rigorous identification procedures for new clients.

Further reading

The following books may be useful:

Davies, H and Green, D (2013) *Global Financial Regulation: The essential guide,* John Wiley & Sons

Mishkin, FS and Eakins, S (2006) *Financial Markets and Institutions,* 5th edn, Pearson

Kotz, HD (2015) *Financial Regulation and Compliance: How to manage competing and overlapping regulatory oversight,* John Wiley & Sons

International Investment Law and the Global Financial Architecture (2017) eds CJ Tams, SW Schill and R Hofmann, Elgar

The following sites may be useful:

www.fca.org.uk
www.ecb.europa.eu
www.federalreserve.gov

GLOSSARY

abnormal return   a return generated by a security or a portfolio over a defined period of time, that differs from the expected rate of return

absolute return   a measure of the gain or loss on an investment portfolio expressed as a percentage of invested capital. Absolute return investing is where a fund manager is targeted to achieve a positive return regardless of how well or badly markets are performing

accumulation units   targeted to enhance growth in the fund rather than to generate and distribute income; any income generated will be reinvested within the fund

active management   a type of investment approach usually employed to aim to generate returns in excess of an investment benchmark index. Active management is employed to take advantage of pricing anomalies in the securities markets by utilising techniques such as fundamental analysis and/or technical analysis

agency   the theoretical relationship between a principal or owners of a company and their agent, the directors of a company, who run it on a day-to-day basis

agency costs   costs arising from the agency relationship

alpha   the return from a security or a portfolio in excess of a risk-adjusted benchmark return

Alternative Investment Market (AIM)   the London Stock Exchange's market for smaller UK public limited companies. AIM has less demanding admission requirements and places less onerous continuing obligation requirements upon those companies admitted to the market than those applying for a full list on the LSE

American option   an option which can be exercised on any date up and to and including its expiry date

annual equivalent rate (AER)   a notional rate that is quoted on the interest paid on savings and investments

annuity   a regular payment of a fixed amount over a fixed period

arbitrage   the process of deriving a risk-free profit from simultaneously buying and selling the same asset in two different markets, where a price difference exists

arbitrage pricing theory (APT)   an asset pricing model based on the idea that an asset's returns can be predicted using the relationship between it and common risk factors. The theory describes the price where a mispriced asset is expected to be

asset allocation the process of deciding on the division of a portfolio's assets between asset classes and geographically before deciding upon which securities to buy

asset class a group of securities that exhibit similar characteristics, behave similarly in the marketplace and are subject to the same laws and regulations

asymmetry of information different amounts of information available to different parites, for instance shareholders often have less information than directors and as such suffer from asymmetry of information

authorization the Financial Services and Markets Act (FSMA2000) requires firms to obtain authorisation prior to conducting investment business. Authorization is gained from the FCA and/or the PRA

Bank of England the UK's central bank which acts as the government's banker and determines interest rates via its Monetary Policy Committee

base rate the minimum rate at which banks will lend money to individuals. In the UK, this is set each month by the Monetary Policy Committee at the Bank of England

bear market a persistent downward trend in securities prices. In a bear market securities prices fall and widespread pessimism causes the stock market's downward spiral to be self-sustaining

behavioural finance seeks to use a combination of behavioural and cognitive psychological theory to offer explanations as to why individuals make financial decisions which are not rational and the consequences for the financial markets

benchmark effectively a standard against which the performance of a security, fund or portfolio may be measured. Generally a market index or a sector index may be chosen for this purpose

beneficiaries the specified beneficial owners of trust property

Beta coefficient the relationship between the returns on a stock and returns on the market and is often referred to simply as beta. Beta is a measure of the volatility, or systematic risk, of a security or a portfolio in comparison to the market as a whole. Beta is used in the capital asset pricing model (CAPM)

bid-ask spread also referred to as the bid-offer spread, the amount by which the ask price exceeds the bid price for an asset in the market. It represents the difference between the highest price that a buyer may pay for an asset and the lowest price that a seller may receive when selling it

bid-offer spread *See* bid-ask spread

black swan event an event or occurrence that deviates beyond what is normally expected of a situation and is extremely difficult to predict - itis an unpredictable, rare, but nevertheless high-impact event

bond medium- or long-term debt, repayable to lender over a set period and may be liable for interest payments

bonus issue a corporate action also known as a scrip issue where new shares are issued free to shareholders but no new funds are generated

bottom-up approach   focuses on selecting a security based on the individual attributes of a specific company. Advocates of this approach will look for strong companies with positive prospects, regardless of industry or macroeconomic factors

bottom-up equity investing strategy   *See* bottom-up approach

brokerage   a financial business which assists with the buying and selling of financial securities or financial products, eg securities, collectives, retail financial products

bull market   a situation of persistently rising share prices is often called a bull market. A bull market is a financial market in which prices are rising or are expected to rise – it is most often used to refer to the stock market but may refer to anything that is traded, such as bonds, currencies and commodities

CAC 40   the most commonly used indicator of the French stock market, it reflects the performance of the 40 largest listed equities in France as measured by market-capitalization and liquidity

call option   an agreement which gives the holder the right, but not the obligation, to buy an asset (which includes shares, bonds, commodities and other instruments) at a specified price within a specific period

capital adequacy directive   a European directive which aims to establish uniform capital requirements for both banking and non-bank securities companies. (See also capital requirements directive)

capital asset pricing model (CAPM)   a financial model which expresses a relationship between risk and return. It is a formula for calculating the expected return of an asset given its risk and based upon a risk-free rate of return plus a risk premium

capital gain   the difference between the original price of an investment and its higher sale price which may be liable to capital gains tax

capital gains tax (CGT)   tax paid on profits realised by selling assets. In the UK there is an annual exemption limit which may change annually as a result of the government's budget. CGT is paid at the investor's highest marginal tax rate, adjusted for any capital losses

capital growth (or loss)   the difference between the current value of an asset compared to the amount originally invested in it

capital market line   the linear risk and return trade-off for investors spreading their money between risk free assets and the market portfolio

capital markets   financial markets where long term securities are traded

capital requirements directive   previously the Capital Adequacy Directive, this sets out the financial rules for financial companies, applies to banks, building societies and most investment companies and has been successfully implemented in the UK. Its aim is to ensure that companies hold adequate financial resources and have adequate systems and controls to prudently manage both business and the associated risks

capital risk   the risk facing an investor that they may lose some or all of the initial amount invested

central bank usually, central banks have responsibility for setting a country's or a region's short-term interest rate, controlling the money supply, acting as banker and lender of last resort to the banking system and managing the national debt

chartist analysts attempting to make gains through share trading, by forecasting future share prices using historical shares prices

client individuals or companies which use the services of finance professionals to conduct business. Every client is classified as either a customer (retail or professional) or an eligible counterparty

client assets securities or other assets held by the client directly or by a company on behalf of its clients. In the latter case, the assets must be kept separate from the firm's own assets

closed-ended funds or companies which are a fixed size as determined by their share capital. Often used to distinguish investment trusts (closed-ended funds) from unit trusts and OEICs (open-ended funds)

coefficient of variation (CV) the ratio of the standard deviation to the mean; that is, standard deviation divided by mean

collective investment funds (or pooled investment funds) groups of assets from individuals and organizations to be managed together in a larger, diversified portfolio

collective investment scheme (CIS) open-ended funds such as unit trusts and open-ended investment companies (OEICS), also known as investment companies with variable capital (ICVCS)

commodity any legally traded items, such as coffee, wheat, oil and gold. Derivatives of commodities are also traded on exchanges (eg copper futures)

compound interest interest earned on the principal deposit left on deposit with the principal. Future interest is then calculated on the initial principal plus the accumulated interest of previous periods of a deposit

conduct of business conduct of business rules govern the way a business is conducted with regard to the consumer and the fair treatment of the consumer

Conduct of Business Sourcebook rules rules made by the FCA under the Financial Services and Markets Act 2000 relating mainly to the relationship between an authorised firm and its clients

consumer prices index (CPI) a measure of inflation used in the UK economy. It measures changes in the price of a basket of consumer goods and services typically purchased by households and is a statistical estimate constructed using periodic sampling of prices

convertible bond bond which is convertible from the bond into a certain number of the issuing company's shares

corporate bonds bonds issued by a corporation in order to raise finance for various reasons such as ongoing operations, mergers and acquisitions, or to expand. Corporate bond is usually applied to longer-term debt instruments, with a period to maturity of at least one year. When an investor buys a corporate bond they are effectively lending a company money and in return will receive interest and the issuer promises to pay back the loan on a specified date. In terms of risk, bonds generally sit between cash and shares

corporate governance   statutory and non-statutory regulation of companies by their stakeholders

correlation   in investment terms, correlation is the extent to which the values of different types of investments move in tandem with one another in response to changing economic and market conditions

cost of capital   cost of finance incurred by a company, will be equal to required rate of return for investors looking to invest in the company

cost of debt   the rate of return required by investors providing debt finance to a company

cost of equity   the rate of return required by investors providing equity finance to a company

coupon   the regular periodic interest payment made by the issuer to the holder of a bond

counterparty risk   counterparty risk (also referred to as credit risk or default risk) is the risk that your counterparty in a transaction cannot honour its obligation to you

country risk   a collection of risks associated with investing in a foreign country. These risks include political risk, exchange rate risk, economic risk, sovereign risk and transfer risk (the risk of capital being locked up or frozen by government action)

credit agency   a third-party agency, eg S&P or Fitch, which analyses governments, countries and companies to assess their ability to repay outstanding debt finance. Grades are based on a combination of letters and numbers ranging from AAA to D (default)

credit rating   an assessment of the likelihood of repayment of debt securities by an independent credit agency

credit risk   most simply defined as the potential that a borrower or counterparty will fail to meet their obligations in accordance with agreed terms. A credit risk is the risk of default on a debt that may arise from a borrower failing to make required payments – the lender may lose the principal of the loan and/or the interest associated with it

CREST   CREST was the recognized clearing house in the UK that facilitated the clearing and settlement of trades in UK and Irish company shares. From 2007 CREST changed its name to Euroclear UK & Ireland, although the term CREST is still used for the clearing and settlement system itself

cum dividend price   the market price of equity including the right to be paid the next dividend due

currency risk   also referred to as exchange rate risk. The possibility that currency depreciation will negatively affect the value of assets, investments and their related income streams, especially those securities denominated in a foreign currency

Data Protection Act 1998 legislation governing how personal data should be held and processed, including guidelines regarding the rights of access to this information

DAX a blue chip stock market index which consists of the 30 major German companies trading on the Frankfurt Stock Exchange

debentures fixed interest irredeemable bonds normally secured on non current company assets

debt securities securities where the issuer acknowledges a loan made to them. The term includes instruments such as bonds, gilts, Treasury bills, certificates of deposit and commercial paper

deep discount bonds bonds issued at a significant discount to their nominal value where part of the return is made up of a capital gain. Coupon rates are lower than bonds issued at par

default risk default risk is the chance that either companies or individuals will be unable to complete the required payments on their debt obligations. Lenders and investors are exposed to default risk in most forms of credit extensions

defensive shares shares with a Beta of less than 1

deflation deflation describes a general fall in the level of prices of goods and services. Deflation occurs when the inflation rate falls below 0% (a negative inflation rate)

depository a depository acts as a custodian and monitor of a fund. The depository ensures that the fund's assets are held independently of the investment manager, accounting records are reconciled with third-party records and that entitlements of investors are correctly calculated. The depository acts as a safeguard against fraud, accounting errors and conflicts of interest between the fund's manager and the fund

derivatives instruments where the price or value is derived from an underlying asset. Examples include options, futures and swaps

directives legislation issued by the European Union (EU) to its member states requiring them to enact and implement local legislation

disinflation a reduction in the rate of inflation, which means a slowing of price growth rather than a fall in prices

diversifiable risk risk which can be reduced by diversifying a portfolio

diversification a risk management technique that mixes a wide variety of investments within a portfolio with the purpose of spreading (or mitigating) risk

dividend companies may distribute some of their profits to their shareholders by paying them a cash dividend payment

dividend yield most recent dividend as a percentage of current market share price

domicile general legal concept referring to the country which is the permanent home of an individual

Dow Jones Industrial Average one of the key stock market indices in the USA

duration risk *See* Macaulay duration

earnings per share distributable profit divided by the number of shares in issue

economies of scale a decrease in average cost per unit due to an increase in level of goods produced by a given economic resource

efficient frontier represents the optimal portfolios offering the highest expected return for a defined level of risk or the lowest risk for a given level of expected return. Portfolios that lie below the efficient frontier are deemed below optimal as they do not provide sufficient return for the level of risk taken

efficient market hypothesis EMH is one of the key theories used in the study of market psychology. It states that because information about companies is generally freely available and known to markets, investors and potential investors, it will lead to their shares (or other securities) being correctly priced on the market

equalization payment when an investor first buys units or shares in a fund, they may receive an equalisation payment as part of the next distribution that the fund pays

equities a broad category of assets including company shares

euro the currency issued by the European Central Bank (ECB). Currently, 17 EU member states have adopted the euro within the Eurozone. It is a daily traded currency on the Forex market

Eurobond long-term debt securities denominated in a currency different from the domestic currency of their country of origin

Euroclear UK & Ireland a recognized clearing house (see CREST)

European Economic Area currently the 28 member states of the European Union plus Norway, Iceland and Liechtenstein

exchange a marketplace for trading various securities and assets

exchange rate the rate at which one currency can be exchanged for another currency

exchange rate risk (also foreign exchange risk, FX risk, currency risk) the financial risk of an investment's value changing due to the changes in currency exchange rates

exchange traded funds (ETFs) a type of open-ended investment fund listed and traded on a stock exchange in a similar way to a company share. Many are known as 'trackers' and typically track the performance of an index and trade very close to their NAV

ex-dividend (XD) the period during which the purchase of shares or bonds (on which a dividend or coupon payment has already been declared) does not entitle the new holder to this next dividend or interest payment

exempt persons firms exempt from the need to be authorised to carry on regulated activities. The term includes bodies such as recognised investment exchanges and recognised clearing houses

exercise price the price at which an option holder can exercise their options

Financial Conduct Authority (FCA) one of the two regulators of the financial services sector in the UK. The Financial Conduct Authority replaced the Financial Services Authority as the body responsible for regulating conduct in retail and wholesale markets; supervising the trading infrastructure that supports those markets and for the prudential regulation of firms not prudentially regulated by the Prudential Regulation Authority (PRA)

Financial Ombudsman Service (FOS)   the FOS is responsible for receiving and investigating complaints against authorised persons, if they cannot be satisfactorily resolved between the two parties directly

Financial Policy Committee (FPC)   sets policy to meet the Bank of England's statutory objective for financial stability

Financial Services Compensation Scheme   a compensation fund of last resort and is the statutory compensation scheme for customers of authorised financial services in the UK. (coverage includes banks, building societies, credit unions and insurance)

Financial Services and Markets Act 2000   the legislation that established the new financial regulator (the FSA) and empowered it to regulate the financial services industry. The FSA was split in April 2013, into the FCA and the PRA. Broadly; the FCA looks after conduct issues and the PRA looks after prudential issues

firm specific risk   *See* unsystematic risk

foreign bond   a bond issued in a domestic market by a foreign company in the domestic markets currency

FTSE 100   main UK share index of the 100 largest listed company shares measured by market capitalization

FTSE All Share Index   UK share index comprising more than 90% of UK listed shares by value

fundamental analysis   the in-depth process of analysis and research, calculation and interpretation of yields, ratios and discounted cash flows performed in an attempt to establish the intrinsic value of a security or the correct valuation of the broader market

fund manager   firm or individual that makes investment decisions on behalf of either investment funds or clients

fund platform   services which allow investors to purchase investments easily online and normally at a discounted price. In many cases the investments purchased may be held in some form of tax efficient wrapper

future   a futures contract is a legally binding arrangement with which parties commit to buy or sell a standard quantity of an asset from another party, at an agreed price, on a specified date in the future. Because the price is agreed at the outset, the seller is protected from a change in the price of the underlying asset in the intervening time period

gearing   gearing is also referred to as financial leverage and is the financial ratio of a company's long-term debt to its equity capital

gilt-edged security (gilt)   a UK government bond. They may be for fixed terms, long, medium or short term, or undated (eg, War Loan)

gross domestic product (GDP)   a measure of a country's output; measures the amount of goods and services produced each year

gross redemption yield (GRY) the annual compound return from holding a bond to maturity taking into account both interest payments and any capital gain or loss at maturity. This may also be referred to as the yield to maturity; it is the internal rate of return on the bond based on its trading price

Hang Seng the main stock market index in Hong Kong

hedge fund an investment vehicle used by corporate institutions, high net worth individuals and private partnerships permitted by regulators to undertake a wider range of trading including derivatives and short selling whilst using high levels of borrowing

hedging a technique employed to reduce the impact of adverse price movements on financial assets held

Her Majesty's Revenue & Customs (HMRC) the government department responsible for the administration and collection of tax in the UK

home state the term used for the european union country where a financial services firm conducting cross-border business is based

hybrid security a security showing characteristics of both debt and equity eg preference shares

idiosyncratic risk *See* unsystematic risk

illiquid assets describes a security or other asset which cannot easily be sold or exchanged for cash without a substantial loss in value. Illiquid assets may prove difficult to sell quickly because of the lack of investors or speculators who are willing to purchase the asset

immunization often used in the management of bond assets, a strategy that matches the durations of assets and liabilities, thereby minimizing the impact of interest rates on the fund/portfolio value. Immunization can be accomplished by techniques such as cash flow matching, duration matching and trading forwards, futures and options on bonds

income risk the risk that the income stream from an investment portfolio or a fund will decrease in response to a change in market conditions (eg a fall in interest rates). This risk is most prevalent in money market and other short-term income fund strategies but may also apply to reduction in income stream from dividends due to market circumstances

income tax a tax based on individuals earned and unearned income in a tax year

inflation return (or inflation-adjusted return) the measure of return taking into account the inflation rate during the period in question

inflation risk the risk that inflation will undermine the performance of the investment during the period under measurement

inside information any information relating to a specific asset, or an issuer, which is not publicly known and which would affect the price of the security if it was made public

insider dealing an offence which may be committed by an insider in possession of unpublished price-sensitive information. This applies if they make any attempt to deal in affected securities, or encourage others to do so, or pass the sensitive information on

institutional investors large financial institutions such as pension funds investing large amounts in company shares and other financial investments

insurance company a business that provides cover in the form of compensation for events resulting in loss, damage, injury or hardship in exchange for the payment of premiums

integration the third stage of money laundering; integration represents the point at which the laundered funds have the appearance of being legitimate

international bond issued by a borrower in a foreign country, in a foreign currency, including foreign bonds and Eurobonds

intestacy where somene dies without making a valid will

investment bank specialized banks that help both individuals and organizations to raise capital and that will also provide financial consultancy services, often acting as intermediaries between issuers of securities and investors, therefore helping new firms to go public

investment company with variable capital (ICVC) See open-ended investment company (OEIC)

investment trust a company (not a trust) which invests in a diversified range of investments. It is a form of collective investment (a closed-ended fund) whose shares are traded on the secondary market

investment universe normally considered to be a group of securities which share a common feature such as the same market capitalization, sector, industry or index

irredeemable bond a bond with no agreed redemption date and pay interest in perpetuity

January effect a seasonal effect which results in an increase in stock prices during January. Often attributed to an increase in buying, following a fall in prices often experienced in December when investors may generate a tax loss to offset realized capital gains. Other possible explanations include investors using end-of-year bonuses to purchase investments in January and investors/fund managers who have 'taken profits' at the end of year, purchasing shares in January resulting in an increase in the markets

Jensen's measure (Jensen's Alpha) a risk-adjusted performance measure representing the average return on an investment or a portfolio, above or below that predicted by the capital asset pricing model (CAPM), for a given beta and average market return

junk bond unsecured corporate bond rated by credit agencies as below BBB–, paying high interest rate to compensate for high levels of risk

know your customer (KYC) the Money Laundering Regulations 2007 and the Financial Conduct Authority (FCA) Rules requiring companies and individuals to take sufficient steps, before taking on a customer, to satisfy themselves of the identity of that customer

Glossary

layering the second stage of the 'money laundering' process; in which money or assets are typically passed through a series of financial transactions in order to make it difficult or impossible to confirm their original source

lead supervisor has the responsibility to coordinate the supervision programme where more than one point of supervisory contact exists

lessee a company or individual who leases a property from its freehold owner

lessor a company or individual who owns the freehold of a property from which they grant a lease to the lessor

leverage in the context of investment; leverage involves the use of borrowed funds to purchase assets. The aim is that the net income/return will exceed the cost of borrowing

liquidity is the ease and speed with which a holding in an asset may be turned into cash at the prevailing market price

listing companies whose securities are 'listed' are available to be traded on a stock exchange

London Interbank Offered Rate (LIBOR) the average interbank interest rate at which a selection of banks on the London money market are prepared to extend short-term lending to each other

London Metal Exchange (LME) a recognized investment exchange which is the market for trading contracts in base metals and some plastics

London Stock Exchange (LSE) the main UK market for trading in a variety of securities, especially shares and bonds. The LSE is a recognised investment exchange

long position position taken when an investor purchases a security

Macaulay Duration the weighted average number of years an investor must maintain a position in the bond until the present value of the bond's cash flows equals the amount that the investor originally paid for the bond. It represents the number of years taken for the investor to recoup their original investment

market abuse potential offences introduced under the Financial Services and Markets Act 2000 which are judged against what would be deemed to be a failure to observe required market standards. Offences include abuse of information, misleading the market, and distortion of the market

market capitalization market price per share multiplied by the number of company shares in issue

market maker a firm which quotes bid and offer prices for a named list of securities in the market. Such a firm is normally under an obligation to make a price in any security for which it is market maker at all times

market risk See Systematic risk

Markets in Financial Instruments Directive (MIFID) a European Union directive which allows firms authorised in one member state to provide/offer financial services to customers in another member state, subject to some restrictions

market timing risk the risk an investor takes when trying to buy or sell a stock based on future price predictions. For example buying when the price is low and selling when the price is high

maturity with bonds, the date when the principal on a bond is repaid

merchant bank a bank specializing in wholesale rather than retail transactions to the general public

micro-cap securities the shares of public companies with a market capitalization of less than £100m (UK) or $50 to $300m (USA)

modern portfolio theory an investment theory suggesting that risk-averse investors may construct portfolios to maximize expected return based on a given level of market risk

modified duration modified duration is the price sensitivity of a bond in response to a change in interest rates

monetary policy committee (MPC) committee of the Bank of England that meets to set UK interest rates

money laundering the process whereby criminals take steps to conceal the origin of proceeds of criminal or illegal activities. The aim is to create false legitimacy by introducing these illegal proceeds into the mainstream financial system

Money Laundering Regulations 2007 authorised companies are required to comply with certain obligations to prevent their services from being used for the purpose of money laundering. The obligations include record-keeping, identification of clients, appointment of a nominated officer to receive suspicion reports and specific staff training. Failure to comply may result in a fine and/or imprisonment

money laundering reporting officer a senior employee who is responsible for assessing reports regarding suspicious transactions and behaviour and reporting those suspicions to the National Crime Agency if justified

money markets markets for borrowing and lending short term funds

mutual fund an investment fund which pools money from many investors to purchase securities to be held within the fund. It is managed by a professional fund manager

NASDAQ the second largest stock exchange in the USA. The NASDAQ lists many US and international stocks and provides a secondary market that links buyers and sellers worldwide. NASDAQ tends to specialize in the shares of technology companies

National Crime Agency the law enforcement agency to which suspicions of money laundering must be reported by a company's money laundering reporting officer

net asset value per share for a company or a fund; the value of a single share. It is calculated by subtracting the fund's total liabilities from its total assets and dividing by the total number of issued shares

Nikkei 225 the main Japanese share index

Glossary

nominal return an investment return which has not been adjusted to account for the effects of inflation

nominal value the amount that will be repaid on maturity of a bond. This is also known as the face or par value

non-current assets assets with a long life including buildings, land, plant and machinery, which are not traded by the company

non-diversifiable risk *see* Systematic risk

normal yield curve a normal yield curve has a positive (upward) slope, which reflects the fact that securities with more time remaining to maturity have a slightly higher yield than shorter-dated securities

NYSE Euronext LIFFE a recognized investment exchange for traded futures and traded options

offer price some asset prices such as bond and share prices are quoted as bid and offer. The offer is the higher of the two prices and is what would be paid by a buyer

official list the list of companies registered on the London Stock Exchange

open-ended fund type of investment, such as OEICs or unit trusts, which may expand without limit

open-ended investment company (OEIC) a collective investment vehicle which is similar to a unit trust, but is constituted as an open-ended company. This means that its share capital can expand or contract to meet investor supply and demand

option a derivative instrument giving the buyer the right, but not the obligation, to buy or sell an asset in the future at a pre-agreed price. There are two basic types of option; put and call options. The holder of a call option has the right to buy and the holder of a put option has the right to sell the underlying asset

OTC (over the counter) derivatives which are bespoke and traded directly between two parties rather than through an exchange

passive investment management passive management is often referred to as index-tracking. Index-tracking or indexation, requires the construction of a portfolio to track or replicate the performance of a recognized index

passporting the method by which firms authorised under the Markets in Financial Instruments Directive (MIFID) in one European Union member state, are permitted to carry out regulated financial services activities in another state without the need to become fully authorised in that state

pension fund a retirement provision that requires an employee and/or employer to make contributions into a pool of funds set aside for an individual's benefit in retirement

perpetual bonds perpetual bonds are bonds which have no maturity date. They may be treated as equity rather than debt. Issuers pay coupons on perpetual bonds forever as they do not have to redeem the principal

perpetuity equal cash payments made at regular intervals indefinitely

placement   represents the first stage of money laundering where dirty money is introduced into the financial system

political risk   the risk that an investment's returns may suffer as a result of political changes or instability in a specific country. Instability affecting investment returns could result from factors such as a change in government, legislative changes, regulation or military control

preference share   preference shares have preference over ordinary shares in relation to the payment of dividends and in default situations. They usually pay fixed dividends but do not have voting rights

primary market   markets where shares are issued

private banks   non-incorporated banking institutions owned by an individual or a small number of shareholders. Usually providing exclusive banking services to high net-worth individuals

private equity   composed of funds and investors that directly invest in private companies

private investor   a company or an individual who may choose to invest their own money into securities and assets

Prudential Regulation Authority   part of the Bank of England, is one of two regulators of the financial services sector in the UK and is responsible for the prudential regulation of financial firms, including banks, investment banks, building societies and insurance companies

prudential risk   in the context of the regulatory responsibility; this involves the responsibility to monitor a company's management of its financial risks and to minimize detrimental 'domino' effects on customers, counterparties and overall market stability

put option   an option that gives the buyer the right, but not the obligation to sell an underlying asset at a pre-agreed price, on or before a specified date

quantitative easing   a form of monetary policy where a Central Bank creates new money electronically to buy certain financial assets, for example government bonds

rainy-day fund   an emergency fund set aside by individuals or organizations to assist in the event of unexpected financial problems, for example disruption in income stream

random walk theory   the idea that stocks take a random and unpredictable path, meaning that historic performance and trends cannot be used to predict future movements

real estate investment trust (REIT)   an investment trust which specialises in investing in commercial property

real return   an investment return which has been adjusted to account for the effects of inflation

recognized clearing house   a term used to denote those clearing houses recognized by the Financial Conduct Authority as providing appropriate standards of

Glossary

protection in the provision of clearing and settlement facilities to certain markets

recognized investment exchange a term used to denote those UK exchanges which operate markets in investments, meeting certain standards set by the Financial Conduct Authority

recognized overseas investment exchange an overseas exchange which provides facilities within the UK, and is recognized by the Financial Conduct Authority (FCA) as meeting appropriate standards of investor protection

redemption the repayment of initial investment (principal) to the holder of a redeemable security

reduction in yield an industry standard measure of the impact of total charges. It takes into account both initial charges and ongoing charges applied to an asset or a policy

regulated activities activities for which authorization from the domestic regulator (Financial Conduct Authority in the UK) or exemption from the need for that authorisation is required. Regulated activities are defined in relation both to the activities themselves, and to the investments to which they relate

reinvestment risk the risk that the proceeds from the payment of coupons and repayment of principal will have to be reinvested at a lower rate than the original investment. Particularly applicable to bonds

relative return relative return is a measure of the return of an investment portfolio relative to a benchmark. In this type of portfolio management the aim is to outperform the benchmark; which means achieving greater profits or fewer losses than the benchmark

retail banking (or consumer banking) typical mass-market banking in which banks provide a variety of services to individual customers, often through a local branch network

retail prices index (RPI) index that measures the movement of prices experienced by retail consumers in the uk and a measure of inflation in the uk

rights issue the issue of new ordinary shares to a company's shareholders in proportion to each shareholder's existing share -holding. The issue is made in accordance with the shareholder's rights and the new shares are usually offered at a discounted price to that prevailing in the market

risk-free asset an asset whose future return is known with certainty. Commonly defined as a short-term UK/US government bond

risk-free return risk-free return is the theoretical rate of return attributed to an investment with zero risk

risk-free security the risk-free rate of return is theoretical and represents the rate of return of an investment with zero risk. This means that the risk-free rate represents the return that an investor would expect from an absolutely risk-free investment over a specified period of time. In practice a risk-free rate does not exist because even the safest investments carry a very small amount of risk and therefore appropriate 'risk-free' rates are assumed to be returns on investments whose risk is so low as to be negligible. So therefore; return on a three-month US Treasury Bill is often used as the risk-free rate for US-based investors

risk premium return required by investors in excess of risk free return to accept a riskier asset

R-squared a statistical measure representing the percentage of a fund or security's movements that can be explained by movements in a benchmark index

running yield also called the Interest or flat yield. Interest rate of security divided by market price as a percentage

running yield the running yield (also known as the interest yield) on a gilt expresses the income received on it, as a percentage of the investor's outlay

secondary markets where existing shares are traded

security-market line the security-market line is a line drawn on a graph which serves as a representation of the capital asset pricing model (CAPM). This displays levels of systematic risk of various marketable securities plotted against the expected return of the whole market, at a given point in time

settlor with regard to trust law; is the person who was the original owner of the asset / property that is to be transferred to and held by the Trust

Shanghai Stock Exchange Composite Index (SSE Composite Index) one of the key indices in mainland China, a stock market index of all stocks traded at the Shanghai Stock Exchange

Sharpe ratio the Sharpe ratio measures the return over and above the risk-free interest rate from an undiversified equity portfolio for each unit of risk assumed by the portfolio, where risk is measured by the standard deviation of the portfolio's returns. A high Sharpe ratio is preferable to investors and indicates a more suitable risk-adjusted return

small-cap securities the shares of public companies with a market capitalization of around £150 to £500m (UK) or $300m to $2bn (USA)

sociably responsible investment (SRI) businesses that exhibit a degree of social responsibility or are deemed to be proactive in certain desirable activities

sovereign wealth fund state-owned investment funds that invest in financial assets such as stocks, bonds, property and commodities, or in alternative investments such as hedge funds

specific risk *See* unsystematic risk

spot market market for immediate transactions eg currency

spot rate rate at which investments can be traded on a specific day eg currency

Stamp Duty Land Tax payable by the purchaser on purchases of land and property in the UK for most residential property

standard deviation a measure of the dispersion of a set of data from its mean. The standard deviation of a share price measures the average price over a period of time by showing the degree to which its price fluctuates in relation to its mean

stochastic modelling stochastic modelling is the use of historical data to model thousands of possible investment return outcomes, for almost all asset allocation combinations

Stock Exchange Electronic Trading System (SETS) the single platform trading various assets from the FTSE All Share Index, ETFs and exchange-traded commodities, along with over 180 of the most traded AIM and Irish securities

strategic asset allocation this is a long-term portfolio strategy which involves setting optimum allocations for various asset classes and the requirement to periodically rebalance the portfolio back to the original allocations following differing returns from various assets

stress-testing a simulation technique (usually computer-generated) particularly useful in the banking industry. Often used on asset and liability portfolios to determine their reactions to different financial situations

strike price price at which an option holder can exercise an option

suitability report a written report given to a client by an adviser detailing their recommendations

swaps an agreement by two parties to exchange interest payments based on an agreed principal amount

systematic risks these are market risks that cannot be diversified away

systemic risk systemic risk implies the risk of breakdown of an entire system rather than individual parts. For the financial context systemic risk is the risk of a 'cascading failure' in the financial sector caused by links within the financial system and resulting in an economic downturn

T bonds bonds with a maturity of over ten years, issued by the US and Canadian governments

tactical asset allocation a short-term active management strategy which aims to adjust the allocation of various assets to take advantage of market pricing anomalies, strong market sectors or other opportunities

technical analysis using past share prices to forecast future share price. See also chartists

tick the smallest possible movement in the price of futures contracts standardised as 0.01% of the contract size

time value of money a core finance principle which suggests that money available at the present time is worth more than the same amount in the future, because of its potential earning capacity

time-weighted rate of return this is a measure of the compound rate of growth in a fund or portfolio. The method eliminates the effects created by inflows and outflows of new money and is therefore a useful measure to compare the returns of investment managers

tipping off this is a specific offence established under UK anti-money laundering and terrorist financing legislation. It is where there is disclosure that an investigation is, or may soon be under way, if that disclosure may prejudice that investigation

top-down approach top-down investing is an investment approach that involves looking at the overall picture of the economy. It is a strategy that first considers macroeconomic factors when making an investment decision followed by examining sectors and finally individual securities

top-down investment management system   *See* top-down approach

total risk   the systematic risk plus the unsystematic risk on an investment. The overall potential for financial loss

tracking error   the difference between the performance of a fund or a portfolio and the performance of the appropriate benchmark which is being tracked

Treasury   the government department that is responsible for formulating and implementing the government's financial and economic policies. Also responsible for financial services regulation in the UK

Treasury bills   short-term government borrowings, often three months. Issued at a discount to the nominal value at which they will mature and actively traded in the money market

Treynor ratio   (sometimes referred to as the reward-to-volatility ratio) a risk-adjusted measurement of a return based on systematic risk and is similar to the Sharpe ratio. The difference between the two ratios is that Treynor ratio uses market risk (beta) as a measure of volatility whilst Sharpe ratio uses total risk (standard deviation) to measure volatility

trust   a means of holding assets on behalf of beneficial owners; these assets are legally owned by the trustees. Investment portfolios within a trust may be professionally managed, and are governed by the Trustee Act 2000

trustee   a person or organization who is the legal owner of assets held in trust on behalf of the nominated beneficiary. The trustee is responsible for safeguarding the assets, complying with the trust deed and overseeing the activities of any appointed finance professional

uncertainty   where there is more than one possible outcome and the probability of a specific outcome is not known

underlying   an asset from which the value of a derivative is derived

undertakings for collective investment in transferable securities (UCITS)   a type of collective investment scheme (CIS) established under the UCITS Directives. These directives are intended to harmonize European Union (EU) member states' laws so as to allow for the marketing of UCITS schemes across EU borders

unique risk   *See* unsystematic risk

unit trust   a form of collective investment constituted under a trust deed. Money from many investors is pooled together and invested collectively on their behalf. Unit trusts are open-ended investments; the underlying value of the assets is always directly represented by the total number of units issued, multiplied by the unit price, less the transaction or management fee charged and any other associated costs. Each fund has a specified investment objective prescribing management aims and limitations

unsystematic risk these are the risks associated with a specific security and can be diversified away by increasing the number of securities in a portfolio

value-added tax (VAT) a tax charged on many goods and services that VAT-registered businesses provide in the UK. VAT is placed on a product whenever value is added at a stage of production and at final sale

value at risk (VaR) a statistical technique used to measure and quantify the level of financial risk within an asset or investment portfolio over a specific time frame. Most commonly used by investment managers to determine the extent of potential losses in their portfolios

variance measures the variability (volatility) from an average or mean and can therefore help determine the risk an investor might take when purchasing a specific security

venture capital capital supplied by specialist organisations to smaller companies who may struggle to raise finance

venture capital trusts companies listed on the London Stock Exchange, similar to investment trusts. They are designed to enable individuals to invest indirectly in a range of small higher-risk trading companies, whose shares and securities are not listed on a recognized stock exchange, by investing through VCTs

volatility associated with the tendency of an asset to change rapidly and unpredictably, especially for the worse. Historic volatility is usually indicated by standard deviation or beta coefficient

warrants tradeable share options issued by company's which may be attached to bonds

wholesale banking banking services offered to government agencies, other banks, institutional customers (such as pension funds), large businesses and corporations, often involving very large sums (in contrast to retail banking)

withholding tax a tax levied be a foreign country on profits remitted to the home country

yield income from an investment expressed as a percentage of the current price

yield curve shows the relationship between the yields and the maturity of bonds of the same type

zero-coupon bonds bonds that do not pay a coupon – usually issued at a discount to their nominal value but redeemed at par on a specified future date

zero-sum game a situation where for one party to gain the other part to the transaction must lose

Z-scores a numerical measurement of a value's relationship to the mean in a group of values. If a Z-score is 0, it means that the score is identical to the mean score

REFERENCES

Chapter 1

1. www.bbc.co.uk/news/business-37751599
2. www.forbes.com/sites/stevedenning/2011/11/22/5086/#21be5607f92f
3. www.ft.com/cms/s/0/5c052cfc-4e6e-11df-b48d-00144feab49a.html?ft_site=falcon&desktop=true
4. www.theguardian.com/business/2017/jan/14/moodys-864m-penalty-for-ratings-in-run-up-to-2008-financial-crisis

Chapter 3

1. www.bankofengland.co.uk/monetarypolicy/Pages/how.aspx
2. www.bankofengland.co.uk/financialstability/Pages/default.aspx
3. Kaplan, S and Schoar, A (2005) Private equity performance: Returns, persistence, and capital flows, *The Journal of Finance*, 60 (4), pp1791–1823
4. Dyck, IJ and Morse, A (2011) Sovereign wealth fund portfolios, Chicago Booth Research Paper, No. 11–15
5. www.ft.com/content/42c80bee-4447-11e6-9b66-0712b3873ae1
6. www.swfinstitute.org/sovereign-wealth-fund-rankings/
7. www.swfinstitute.org/statistics-research/linaburg-maduell-transparency-index/
8. Hennessee Group (2010) Protecting capital during market downturns, *Hedge Fund Journal*, 22 July
9. www.cityoflondon.gov.uk/business/support-promotion-and-advice/promoting-the-city-internationally/china/Documents/Insurance%20companies%20and%20pension%20funds%20report.pdf
10. www.efama.org/Publications/Statistics/Asset_Management_Report/Asset_Management_Report_2015.pdf

Chapter 4

1. Holton, G (2004) Defining risk, *Financial Analysts Journal*, 60 (6), pp 19–25
2. National Audit Office, www.nao.org.uk/highlights/taxpayer-support-for-uk-banks

3. Ito, T and Mishkin, FS (2004) Two decades of Japanese Monetary Policy and the Deflation Problem, National Bureau of Economic Research, October, Working Paper 10878, available at www0.gsb.columbia.edu/faculty/fmishkin/PDFpapers/2536-w10878.pdf
4. www.moodys.com
5. www.standardandpoors.com
6. *Institutional Investor* (2015) The 2015 Country Credit Survey, September
7. http://news.bbc.co.uk/onthisday/hi/dates/stories/october/19/newsid_3959000/3959713.stm
8. Reilly, FK, Wright, DJ and Gentry, JA (2009) Historic changes in the high yield bond market, *Journal of Applied Corporate Finance*, **21** (3), pp 65–79
9. Altman, EI (2013) Predicting financial distress of companies: revisiting the Z-Score and ZETA models, in *Handbook of Research Methods and Applications in Empirical Finance,* eds AR Bell, C Brooks and M Prokopczuk, Edward Elgar Publishing, Cheltenham

Chapter 5

1. Malkiel, BG and Fama, EF (1970) Efficient capital markets: A review of theory and empirical work, *The Journal of Finance*, **25** (2), pp 383–417
2. Malkiel, BG (1973) *A Random Walk Down Wall Street,* 6th edn, WW Norton & Company, London
3. Markowitz, HM (1952) Portfolio Selection, *The Journal of Finance*, **7** (1), pp 77–91
4. Kendall, MG and Hill, AB (1953) The analysis of economic time-series (Part I: Prices), *Journal of the Royal Statistical Society,* Series A (General), **116** (1), pp 11–34
5. Sharpe, WF (1994) The Sharpe ratio, *The Journal of Portfolio Management*, 21, pp 49–58
6. Treynor, JL (1965) How to rate management of investment funds, *Harvard Business Review,* **43** (1) pp 63–75
7. Jensen, MC (1968) The performance of mutual funds in the period 1945–1964, *The Journal of Finance*, **23** (2), pp 389–416
8. Treynor, JL and Black, F (1973) How to use security analysis to improve portfolio selection, *The Journal of Business*, 46(1), pp 66–86
9. Perold, AF (2004) *The capital pricing model, Journal of Economic Perspectives*, 18(3), Summer 2004, pp 3–24
10. Ross, SA (1976) The arbitrage theory of capital asset pricing, *Journal of Economic Theory*, **13**, pp 341–60
11. Kahneman, D, and Tversky, A (1979) Prospect theory: an analysis of decision under risk, *Econometrica*. 47 (2), p 263

12 Barberis, N, Shleifer A and Vishny. R (1998) A model of investor sentiment, *Journal of Financial Economics*, **49** (3), pp 307–43
13 Tversky, A and Kahneman, D (1985) The framing of decisions and the psychology of choice, in *Environmental Impact Assessment, Technology Assessment, and Risk Analysis*, ed VT Covello, JL Mumpower, PJM Stallen and VRR Uppuluri, pp 107–29, Springer, Berlin

Chapter 6

1 Kerr, S and Moore, E (2016) *Financial Times*, Saudi Arabia takes out $10bn in bank loans, 19 April
2 www.bloomberg.com/markets/rates-bonds
3 Kang, J and Pflueger, CE (2015), Inflation Risk in Corporate Bonds, *The Journal of Finance*, 70, pp 115–62, doi:10.1111/jofi.12195

Chapter 7

1 Gompers, PA, Ishii, JL and Metrick, A (2003) Corporate governance and equity prices, *Quarterly Journal of Economics*, **118** (1), pp 107–55
2 http://news.sky.com/story/retailer-bhs-goes-into-administration-10257668g
3 www.retailgazette.co.uk/blog/2017/02/bhs-investigation-wont-be-over-until-at-least-april-2019-insolvency-watchdog
4 www.londonstockexchange.com/products-and-services/rns/regulatory/headline/explained.htm
5 www.londonstockexchange.com/exchange/news/alliance-news/detail/1474962972393325800.html
6 www.investopedia.com/university/technical/techanalysis8.asp

Chapter 8

1 www.morningstar.co.uk/uk/funds/default.aspx
2 www.bloomberg.com/features/2016-etf-files/
3 www.nasdaq.com/investing/glossary/m/mutual-fund
4 www.statista.com/topics/1441/mutual-funds/
5 https://investor.gov/additional-resources/general-resources/publications-research/mutual-funds-etfs-%E2%80%93-guide
6 www.schroders.co.uk/its
7 www.epra.com/regulation-and-reporting/taxation/reit-survey/
8 www.londonstockexchange.com/specialist-issuers/reits/reits.htm
9 http://europa.eu/rapid/press-release_MEMO-12-515_en.htm

Chapter 11

1. www.cii.co.uk/media/4269487/journal_febmar_dps.pdf
2. www.cfapubs.org/doi/pdf/10.2469/ccb.v2013.n14.1
3. Grable, JE and Lytton, RH (2003) The development of a risk assessment instrument: A follow-up study, *Financial Services Review*, **12** (3), pp 257–74
4. www.lv.com/lifeassets/assets/documents/20-questions-paper-based-risk-profiler-client-and-partner.pdf
5. *IIMB Management Review*, **27** (3), September 2015, pp 175–84
6. *International Journal of Applied Business and Economic Research*, **14** (10) 2016, pp 6,863–78
7. www.handbook.fca.org.uk/handbook/COBS.pdf
8. www.morningstar.co.uk/uk/news/96826/what-is-rdr.aspx
9. Byrne, A and Blake, D (2014) *Investment Risk and Financial Advice*, Vanguard, London
10. www.pensions-institute.org/reports/SaversRisk.pdf
11. www.fca.org.uk/publication/finalised-guidance/fsa-fg11-05.pdf

Chapter 12

1. Markowitz, H (1952) Portfolio selection, *The Journal of Finance*, **7** (1), pp 77–91
2. Low, RKY, Faff, R and Aas, K (2013) Enhancing mean–variance portfolio selection by modeling distributional asymmetries, *Journal of Economics and Business*, **85**, May–June 2016, pp 49–72, 1 January 2013
3. www.cboe.com/institutional/jpmcrossassetcorrelations.pdf
4. www.investing.com/analysis/are-correlations-between-asset-classes-rising-200132584
5. www.bloomberg.com/news/articles/2016-09-08/asset-contagion-worse-than-2008-as-markets-held-hostage-to-rates
6. www.morganstanley.com/ideas/portfolio-construction-bonds-stocks-correlation
7. Baele, L, Bekaert, G and Inghelbrecht K (2010) The determinants of stock and bond comovements, *Review of Financial Studies*, **23** (6), pp 2,374–428
8. Evans, JL and Archer, SH (1968) Diversification and the reduction of dispersion: an empirical analysis, *Journal of Finance*, **23** (5), pp 761–67
9. Benjelloun, H (2010) Evans and Archer – forty years later, *Investment Management and Financial Innovations*, **7** (1), pp 98–104
10. www.ft.com/content/96184a9a-b231-11e6-9c37-5787335499a0
11. Welch, S (2008) The Hitchhiker's Guide to Core/Satellite Investing, *The Journal of Wealth Management*, **11** (3), p 97

12 Amenc, N, Goltz, F and Grigoriu, A (2010) Risk control through dynamic core-satellite portfolios of ETFs: Applications to absolute return funds and tactical asset allocation, *The Journal of Alternative Investments*, **13** (2), p 47
13 www2.deloitte.com/content/dam/Deloitte/lu/Documents/financial-services/IM/lu-combining-active-passive-management-portfolio-11052015.pdf
14 Sorensen, EH, Miller, KL and Samak, V (1998) Allocating between active and passive management, *Financial Analysts Journal*, **54** (5), pp 18–31
15 www.eiris.org/advisers/ethical-funds/
16 www.ftse.com/products/downloads/F4G-Index-Inclusion-Rules.pdf
17 www.domini.com/
18 www.djindexes.com/sustainability/
19 www.cfainstitute.org/ethics/codes/gipsstandards/pages/index.aspx

Chapter 13

1 www.ft.com/content/e84ce490-cf5c-11e6-9341-7393bb2e1b51
2 www.gov.uk/government/news/hmrc-wins-blockbuster-tax-avoidance-cases

Chapter 14

1 Heremans, D (1999) Regulation of banking and financial markets, in *Encyclopaedia of Law and Economics*, ed B Bouckaert and G De Geest, Edward Elgar Publishing, Cheltenham
2 www.bankofengland.co.uk/publications/Documents/speeches/2013/speech663.pdf
3 White, WR (2014) The prudential regulation of financial institutions, OECD Economics Department working paper
4 Tarullo, DK (2014) 'Rethinking the Aims of Prudential Regulation', speech delivered at the Federal Reserve Bank of Chicago Bank Structure Conference, Chicago, 8 May
5 Tuch, AF (2014) 'Conduct of Business Regulation' Washington University, St Louis, School of Law, 30 June
6 Pacces, AM (2000) Financial intermediation in the securities markets law and economics of conduct of business regulation, *International Review of Law and Economics*, **20** (4), pp 479–510
7 https://newcityagenda.co.uk/wp-content/uploads/2016/10/NCA-Cultural-change-in-regulators report_embargoed.pdf
8 www.thecityuk.com/assets/2016/Reports-PDF/Key-facts-about-UK-financial-and-related-professional-services-2016.pdf
9 www.legislation.gov.uk/ukpga/2012/21/contents/enacted

References

10 Speech by Mark Carney, Governor of the Bank of England, 'One Mission. One Bank', Promoting the good of the people of the United Kingdom, 8 March 2014
11 www.bankofengland.co.uk/pra/Pages/default.aspx
12 Financial Conduct Authority, Business Plan 2016/17, p 10
13 Financial Conduct Authority Diagram, FCA Business Plan 2013/14, p 58
14 www.fca.org.uk/publication/archive/european-union-legislative-process.pdf
15 Schaub, A (2005) *Journal of Financial Regulation and Compliance*, 13 (2), pp 110–20
16 www.ecb.europa.eu/home/html/index.en.html
17 https://fas.org/sgp/crs/misc/R43087.pdf
18 www.federalreserve.gov/aboutthefed/default.htm
19 www.treasury.gov/Pages/default.aspx
20 www.investhk.gov.hk/business-opportunities/financial-services.html
21 www.hkma.gov.hk/eng/about-the-hkma/hkma/about-hkma.shtml
22 www.sfc.hk/web/EN/index.html
23 www.pbc.gov.cn/english/130712/index.html
24 The Peoples Bank of China (2016) China Financial Stability Report 2016, 30 August
25 www.chinadaily.com.cn/business/2016-03/16/content_23892170.htm
26 www.mas.gov.sg/About-MAS.aspx
27 http://asean.org/asean/asean-member-states/
28 www.sec.gov
29 www.handbook.fca.org.uk/handbook/PRIN/2
30 www.eba.europa.eu/regulation-and-policy/implementing-basel-iii-europe

INDEX

Alpha – technical risk ratio 65–67, 138–39, 141, 146, 147–48 *see also* keywords
   houses 68
   used as performance measure 66
Alpha-seeking investments 429
Alternative Investment Market (AIM) 214, 239–41, 251, 256
Altman, E (and) 119–20 *see also* risk, measuring
   Altman Z-score 119
   Altman Z-score Plus 120
arbitrage pricing theory 130, 158–61 *see also* Ross, S
articles/papers (on)
   2008 financial crisis in *Financial Times* and *The Guardian* (Kirchgaessner, S *and* Sieff, K) 36
   commenting on sovereign wealth fund investments (*Financial Times*) 85
   crowdfunding: comparative regulatory provisions of different countries (International Organization of Securities Commissions, 2014) 340
   'How Big Bang changed the city of London for ever' (Robertson, J) 4
   'Lest we forget why we had a financial crisis': *Forbes* magazine (Denning, S) 36
   research paper (Black and Scholes) 309
   tax evasion: *Financial Times* (Allen, K) 454
ASEAN member states 539, *539*
Ash, A (head of research, Bullion Vault.com) 335
Asia 6, 7
   markets 9
asset management firms: the top five 43–44
   BlackRock 43
   BNY Mellon 44
   Fidelity International 44
   history of 43
   State Street Global Advisors (SSGA) 44
   Vanguard Asset Management 44
Australia
   financial regulation in (1998) 513
   Perth Mint Certificate 337 *see also* gold

Bank of England 512–14
   Financial Policy Committee (FPC) 512, 514
   five core values of 512–13 *see also* Carney, M
   Monetary Policy Committee 73–74
   'One Bank' initiative/One Bank Strategy 512
   quarterly inflation reports 73–74 *see also* quantitative easing
banks/banking *see also* Bank of England *and* main market participants
   Atom Bank 78
   Bank of Japan 47
   Bank of Scotland 32
   central banks 72–75, *74*
   'challenger' internet-based banks 78
   Deutsche Bank: 'four eyes' policy 29
   European Banking Authority and stress-testing 548
   European Central (ECB) 47, 518–19
   investment 80–82
   Metro Bank 78
   Monetary Authority of Singapore (MAS) 537–38
   People's Bank of China (PBOC) 531, 532
   private 79–86
   restructuring of European 55
   retail 78
   Royal Bank of Scotland 32
   and stress-testing for major UK banks 547
Barbaris, N 162
BASEL III and Basel Committee on Banking Supervision 548
behavioural finance *see* investment theory
Beltracchi, W (faker of art works) 331
benchmarks 60, 61, 64, 66–67, 122, 132, 138, 139–42, 145–46, 148–50, 163, 187, 239, 268, 280–81, 292–93, 363, 396–98, 402–03, 413, 426–27, 430–32, 439, 441–42, 444, 449, 539
   REITs (for FTSE EPRA/NAREIT UK index *and* FTS Russell) 354
Beta 105, 199, 124–25, 138–39, 141–42, 144–45, 147, 151–60, 200, 252, 255, 424–25

Beta *(Continued)*
    Bank 304–05
    factories 65, 67, 68
'Big Bang' (1986) 4, 7 *see also* articles
Black, F 148, 309
black swan events 109
    'Black Monday' (1987) 114
    and grey swan events 114
Blake, D 379
Bloomberg 59, 207
    Commodity Index 333
    research system 126, 418
    website 211, 246
Bogle, J (founder of Vanguard) 44
bonds 7, 12, 17, 25, 76, 89, 103, 107, *107*,
    119, 123, 126, 128, 136, 172–73,
    197–204, 209–13 *see also*
    investment classes: fixed-interest
    (debt)
    corporate 91, 92, 94, 95, 98–99, 106
    government 74, 91, 92, 95, 102, 108,
        112, 154, 284
    investing in 219, *219*
    issuers and types of 180–85
    ownership of 197–98
    taxation of 218–19
Brexit 2, 69, 111, 518–19, 556
    effect of 57
    vote 27, 330–31
Buffet, W 296
Byrne, A 379

capital pricing model (CAPM) 124, 130,
    131, 151–57, 252, 307–08
    assumptions for 157–61
Carney, M (governor, Bank of England)
    512–13
    and One Bank Strategy: five core values
        512–13
case study: assets under management
    (AUM) 50–52
Chappell, D 254
chapter summaries (for)
    financial markets 37
    financial regulation and supervision
        556–57
    global fund management industry 69
    investment classes
        alternative investments 362–63
        derivatives 324–25
        equity 260
        fixed-interest (debt) 220
        mutual funds 293
    investment theory 175
    main market participants 96

portfolio management: adviser and
    client 403
portfolio management: utilization of
    retail fund management products
    449
risk, types of 128
taxation 504
Chartered Financial Analyst Institute (CFA)
    365
check your understanding for
    financial markets 37
    financial regulation and supervision 557
    global fund management industry 69
    investment classes
        alternative investments 363
        derivatives 325
        equity 261
        fixed-interest (debt) 220
        mutual funds 294
    investment theory 175
    main market participants 97
    portfolio management: adviser and
        client 403–04
    portfolio management: utilization of
        retail fund management products
        449–50
    risk, types of 128–29
    taxation 504–05
China, regulatory landscape in (and)
    531–36 *see also* banks
    China Banking Regulatory Commission
        (CBRC) 533
    China Insurance Regulatory
        Commission (CIRC) 533–34
    China Securities Regulatory Commission
        (CSRC) 534–35
    Joint Ministerial Conference on financial
        Regulatory Coordination 531
    key roles of People's Bank of China 532
    in practice 531, 532
    in practice: talking points from current
        financial world (3) 535–36 *see
        also* Hong Kong, regulatory
        landscape in
China 6, 526, 539
    and National Congress (2017) 47
commodity indices 333–34
    Bloomberg Commodity Index (BCOM)
        333
    and Commodity Futures Trading
        Commission 333
    Rogers International Commodity Index
        (RICI) 333–34
    S&P GSCI 334
    Thomson Reuters/Jeffries CRB Index 334

Index

CREST (Certificateless Registry for Electronic Share Transfer) 498
crowdfunding 338–40 *see also* investment classes: alternative investments
  debt crowdfunding/peer-to-peer (P2P) lending 339
  donor/reward 339
  equity 339
  in practice 338–39
  regulation of 339–40

definition of debt (OED) 176
developing countries 93, 108, 339, 508
Dyck, A 85

Economic Co-operation and Development, Organization for 203, 453
efficient market hypothesis (EMH) 13 *see also* Fama, E F
EMEA countries (Europe, Middle East, Africa) 6, 43
ETF exchange-traded funds 3, 11, 40, 43–44, 56, 263, 270, 271, 277–81, 354, 367, 392, 395, 422, 424, 427, 428, 429, 439, 469, 529, 469
  London ETF Securities' Gold Bullion Securities (LSE GBS) 337
  SPDR Gold Trust 337
Ethical Investment Research Service (EIRIS) 434
Euromarket 14
European Banking Authority (EBA) 340, 517, 548
European Economic Area 57
European Fund and Asset Management Association 93
European Parliament 517
European Securities and Markets Authority (ESMA) 340, 517
  database of European MTFs 25
European Systemic Risk Board 517, 518
European Union, regulatory landscape in (and) 515–19, 516
  European Central Bank (ECB) 518–19 *see also* banks
  European Insurance and Occupational Pensions Authority (EIOPA) 517–18
  European Supervisory Authorities (ESAs) 517–18
  European System of Financial Supervision (ESFS) 517–18
  in practice: talking point from current financial world (1): Brexit 518–19
European Union (EU) 556 *see also* Brexit
  Council 517
  directive: Markets in Financial Instruments (MiFID) 25–26
  focus on single unified market 7
  MTFs grouped in 25
  regulation: Undertakings for the Collective Investment of Transferable Securities (UCITS) 5, 330
  regulations 5, 57
  and UK regulation levels 47

Fama, E F 131, 133
figures
  advisory and planning process 375
  American call option: possible returns for option buyer (Jason) 315
  American call option: possible returns for option writer (Halle) 316
  ASEAN member states 539
  change in gradient of the security market line (SML) 156
  core-satellite investment approach 429
  effect of diversification 101, 136
  efficient frontier diagram 137
  European put option: possible returns for option buyer (Gill) 312
  European put option: possible returns for option writer (Demma) 313
  financial regulatory landscape in the UK 516
  growth in passive flows compared to total net flows in 2016 for top five European asset managers 56
  indirect investment channels 263
  investment management relationships 40
  the money-laundering process 550
  normal distribution of data 115
  organizational structure of an asset management house (example) 58
  parallel change in security market line (SML) 155
  percentage of staff directly employed by asset managers in UK by function 54
  portfolio management, steps for 407
  profit and loss of long position in gold 305
  profit and loss of short position in gold 306
  pyramid of investment risk 100
  quantitative easing 74
  relative size of the world's stock markets at end 2015 7
  scatter plot: higher R-squared 141
  scatter plot: lower R-squared 141
  security market line (SML) diagram 152

figures *(Continued)*
  single most important independent business concerns (%) (November 2016) *48*
  size of investment management industry by assets under management (AUM) *42*
  top five asset managers 2015 (€m) *42*
  top five firms managed by UK managed and global AUM *55*
  transaction outcomes *23*
  transparent publishing of the effect of charges (example) *437–38*
  typical investor life-cycle *377*
Financial Analysis Journal 98
Financial Conduct Authority (FCA) 5, 95, 322, 325, 512, 513
  and *The Conduct of Business Sourcebook* (COBS) 373
  and crowdfunding 339
  guidelines for fund managers 273
  handbook 543
  and money-laundering 553–54
  in practice 515
  strategic objectives of 514–15
financial crises 31–32, 33–36, 55, 359–60, 556 *see also* articles/papers
  Great Depression (1920s, 1930s) 32
  Great Recession (2008) 32, 114, 546 *see also* banks
  OPEC (1970s) 32
  over-regulation as consequence of 507
  speculative cashflows invested into 'Asian Tigers' (1990s) 32
financial markets, categorization of 10–18
  capital markets 10–13
    debt or bond 12–13
    equity 10
    in practice: stock exchanges 11–12 *see also* stock exchanges (in)
  commodities markets and examples 15–17
    in practice: key commodities markets around the world 16–17
  derivatives markets 17–18
  money markets 13–14
financial markets 1–37
  categorization of *see* financial markets, categorization of
  cross-border and global transactions, issues affecting 22–24
    accommodation trades: the effect of foreign exchange 23–24, *23*
    latency 24
  defining 2–3

  and financial crises 31–32, *33–36 see also* financial crises
  history and development of 3–4
  key participants in 18–22
    buyers, sellers, support services *and* trading venues 18–19
    and organizing buyers and sellers 21–22
    traders vs investors 19–20
  recent developments in 25–31
    alternative trading systems (ATSs) and electronic communication networks (ECNs) 30
    auction exchanges, electronic exchanges and over the counter (OTC) 31
    dark pools 26
    day trading 29–30
    fat finger trades 28–29
    flash crashes 27
    high-frequency trading 26–27
    Markets in Financial Instruments Directive (MiFID) 25–26
    multilateral trading facilities (MTFs) 25 *see also* key concepts
financial markets today 5–10
  bases for/size of 5–10, *7*
  most important 9–10
  reasons for importance of 8
  tasks undertaken by 8–9
  and types of financial instruments traded 7
Financial Ombudsman Service (FOS) 52, 555
financial regulation and supervision (and) 506–57 *see also* money-laundering
  anti-money-laundering/prevention of financial crime 548–54, *550 see also* keywords
  complaints and dispute resolution 554–56 *see also* keywords
  current UK rules/regulations re money-laundering 549–54, *550 see also* legislation (UK)
  customer due diligence requirements 553
  FCA principles-based approach to prevention of money-laundering 553–54
  Joint Money Laundering Steering Group guidance (2007) 552
  reasons for regulation: importance of financial stability (and) 507–11 *see also* keywords *and* Lehman Brothers

issues: prudential risk *and* conduct of business 509
regulatory principles 509–10 *see also* reports
statutory objectives of domestic regulatory bodies 508
regulatory landscapes in 511–40 *see also* banks *and countries listed*
  China 531–36
  European Union 515–19, *516*
  Hong Kong 525–30
  Singapore 536–40, *539*
  United Kingdom 511–15
  United States of America 519–25
regulation and supervision style 541–48
  regulation in financial markets 544–46
  regulation: rules- and principles-based systems 541–43
  regulatory principles example 543
  regulatory rule example: SEC Rule 17a-4 (USA) 542
  stress-testing 547–48 *see also* keywords
  supervision 543–44
Financial Services Authority (FSA) 514
  and Retail Regulatory Review (RDR) 439–40
Financial Services Compensation Scheme 330, 555
The Financial Times 60
France 46, 53, 61
FTSE indices *see also* indices
  FTSE 100 index 17, 28, 64, 121, 140, 145, 153, 214, 239, 269, 299, 362, 396, 429, 431
  FTSE All-Share Index 132, 263, 431
  FTSE SmallCap Index 240
  FTSE4Good 434
further reading for
  financial markets 37
  financial regulation and supervision 557
  global fund management industry 69–70
  investment classes
    alternative investments 363
    derivatives 325–26
    equity 261
    fixed-interest (debt) 220–21
    mutual funds 294
  investment theory 175
  main market participants 97
  portfolio management: adviser and client 404
  portfolio management: utilization of retail fund management products 450

risk, types of 129
taxation 505
futures 302–08 *see also* keywords
  advantages of using 307
  and associated risks: market, counterparty and liquidity 307–08
  contracts in real life 304–07
    opening a long 304–05, *305*
    opening a short 305–06, *306*

Gentry, J A 119
Germany 25, 46, 53, 61, 109 *see also* stock exchanges
global fund management industry (and) 38–70
  asset management house structure 57–59, *58*
    principal roles within 58–59
  fund valuation and AUM (assets under management) 49
  pooled vehicles and segregated mandates 49
  future developments in the fund management industry 65–68
    Alpha – technical risk ratio, the search for 65–67
    Beta factories 67
    distribution powerhouses 68
    outcome-orientated investment products 68
  global issues shaping investing in 2017 (and rising) 45–47
    deregulation rather than new regulation 47, *48*
    inflation following period of stagflation 46–47
    interest in fiscal rather than monetary policies 47
    populism and anti-global sentiment 46
  investment manager(s) 59–65
    assessing a fund manager's performance, and in practice 64–65
    cash managers (the treasury desk) 62
    a day in the life of an 63
    dealers 62
    equity managers 61
    fixed interest managers 61
    fund managers 60
    managing active and passive funds 64
    and other investment/asset management positions 62
    property managers 61–62
  major players in 39–45, *40*
    and barriers to entry in the market 45

global fund management industry (and) *(Continued)*
  fund management organizations 41
  in practice *see* asset management firms – the top five
  and size of the industry 41, 42
  measurement of AUM in the UK (and) 50–57
    the Financial Conduct Authority (FCA) Return 52–53
    Investment Association 50–52
    in practice *see* case study: assets under management (AUM)
    UK fund management industry (2016) 53–57, 54, 55, 56 *see also* subject entry
  size of 41
  size of UK investment management industry 48
Global Investment Performance Standards (GIPS) 444
  and CFA Institute 444
gold 337–38 *see also* Australia
Goldman Sachs (GS)
  to assess potential for deregulation based on President Trump's appointments as US Regulators 47
  monitors first 100 days of US (Trump) presidency 46
Greece 35–36, 110
Green, Sir P (BHS) 254

Hamilton, A (founder of BNY Mellon) 44
Hassell, G (CEO at BNY Mellon) 44
Hedge Fund Journal 90
hedge funds 89–91 *see also* subject entry
  managers of 90–91
  regulation of 90
  strategy of different 90
HMRC 243, 244, 350–52, 453–55, 462–64, 468–70, 473, 476, 479, 491, 492, 502, 503, 501–02
  website 454, 505
Holton, G 98
Hong Kong, regulatory landscape in (and) 525–30
  background to Hong Kong financial industry 525–27
  in practice 526
  banks 527
  Futures Exchange (HKFE) 530
  Hong Kong Monetary Authority (HKMA) 527–28
  Independent Insurance Authority (IIA) 530
  'One country, Two Systems' political and legal system 526–27
  regulation of financial services sector 527
  Securities and Futures (Amendment) Ordinance (2012) 529
  Securities and Futures Commission (SFC) 95, 528–29
  in practice 529
  Stock Exchange (SEHK) 529, 530 *see also* stock exchanges
  talking points: total economic unification: a future likelihood? 535–36

Iceland 25, 187, 218
India 7, 12, 256, 539
indices *see also* FTSE indices
  DAX 150
  Domini 400
  Dow Jones EURO STOXX Sustainability 434
  Dow Jones Industrial Average 284
  Hang Seng 150, 396
  market 150
  S&P 500 150, 396, 429, 431
  Shanghai Composite 431
  Social 434
individual savings accounts (ISAs) 218, 219, 268, 290, 353, 378, 394, 476, 485
insolvency (and) 183, 214–17, 229, 251, 546
  BHS 254–55
International Monetary Fund (IMF) 32
  Financial Committee 88
International Securities Exchange (ISE) 522
Investment Association (IA) 50–54, 56
investment classes: alternative investments 327–63
  collectibles and chattels 332–33 *see also* keywords
  collective funds 352–55, 359 *see also* keywords
    fund of funds 355
    investment rusts 355
    life assurance property bonds 355
    offshore property funds 355
    property authorised investment fund (PAIF) 353, 356–58
    real estate investment trust (REIT) 354 *see also* REITs benchmarks
    unit trusts 352–53
  commodities 333–35 *see also* commodity indices *and* keywords
    as hedge against inflation and risk events 334–35
    and how they are traded 335

Index

crowdfunding 338–40 *see also subject entry*
  and general risks of investing in alternative assets 328–32
    fraud and forgery, and in practice 331–32 *see also* keywords
    lack of income 329
    liquidity 328
    regulation 330–31
    storage and insurance costs, and in practice 330
    transaction costs 329–30
    trends and fashions 329
    valuation, and in practice 328–29
  gold for direct investment 336–37
    bullion 336 *see also* legislation (EU)
    and exchange-traded (ETF) funds 337
    gold certificates 337
    jewellery and coins 336–37
  and indirect investment 337–38
    derivative investments 338
    secondary equity investing 337–38
  property 340–52, *348, 349 see also subject entry*
  stamp duty land tax (SDLT) 347, *348*
  structured products 359–62
investment classes: collective investment funds 262–94
  advantages of 264–66
    diversification of holdings 265
    ease of access 264
    economies of scale 265
    liquidity 265–66
    professional fund management 264–65
    regulation 266
  and different types of collective funds 269–93
    closed-ended funds 269, 271 *see also* keywords
    exchange-traded funds (ETF) 277–81
    investment trusts (IT) 285–88
    mutual funds 281–84
    open-ended funds 269
    open-ended investment companies (OEIC) 275–77
    real estate investment trusts (REITs) and their benefits 289–91
    undertakings for collective investment of transferable securities (UCITS): range of fund types 292–93
    unit trusts (UT) 272–75
  disadvantages of 266–69
    costs 266–67
    dilution 267
    loss of control 268–69
    in practice 269
    professional management 267
    taxes 267–68
    tracking error 268
investment classes: derivatives (and) 295–326
  derivative uses for investors 297–99
    hedging 297–98
    speculation 298–99 *see also* keywords
  determining the option premium (and) 317–22
    American-style put and call options 317–18, *317*
    equity and covered warrants: pricing – formula and premium values 319–21
    the Greeks 319
    retail contracts for difference 322
    share price volatility 318
    time to expiry; share price volatility; discount rate 318
  methods of ending a derivative contract 322–23
    in practice 323
  trading derivatives 323–24
    community pool 324
    managed accounts 324
    self-managed 323
  types of derivative 299–317
    forward contract (forwards) 299–302 *see also* keywords
    futures 302–08, *305, 306 see also subject entry*
    options 309–17, *312, 313, 315, 316*
    spread betting (spreads) 308–09
    swaps 309
  uncertainty and risk 296–97
investment classes: equity (and) 222–61
  advantages/disadvantages of equity investment 258, *258*
  effect of corporate actions on costs of buying/selling shares 245
  factors affecting share prices 255–58 *see also* share prices, factors affecting
  limited liability companies 223
  measuring returns from shares *see* shares, measuring returns from
  possible returns from holding shares as investment 245–46
  private equity and equity – the same? 258–60

investment classes: equity (and) *(Continued)*
    and indirect investment 260
    in practice 259
    risks of investing in shares *see* shares, risks of investing in
    stock exchanges *see subject entry and* London Stock Exchange (LSE)
    trading shares *see* shares, trading
investment classes: fixed-interest (debt) 176–221 *see also* bonds *and* loans
    advantages and disadvantages of investing in bonds 219, *219*
    bond issuers and bond types 180–85
    bond ownership 197–98
    bond taxation 218–19
    costs of buying a bond 198–201, *200*
    factors affecting bond prices 201–04
    identifying a bond 193–94
    maturity or other repayment of a bond 189–92, *192*
    measuring the return on a bond 209–13, *212*
    nominal or par value of a bond 185
    risks of investing in bonds 213–18
    types of coupon or interest rates payable on a bond 186–88
    understanding risk in bonds and its effect on bond prices 204–09, *207*
    when will coupon or interest be paid 188–89
    where can investors buy bonds? 194–97
investment theory (and) 130–75
    arbitrage pricing theory 158–61
        basic formula for 159
        in practice 160–61
    behavioural finance 161–62
    capital asset pricing model (CAPM) 151–58, *159*
        assumptions for 157–58
        market risk premium 154
        in practice 156
        risk-free return 153–54
        security market line 154–55, *152, 155, 156*
        time value of money 154
    efficient market hypothesis (EMH) 132–35
        in practice 134
        semi-strong form 133
        strong form 134
        weak form 133
    investment returns (and) 163–74
        annualized growth rate 165
        dividend yield 168–69
        earnings per share 170–71
        impact of fees on 167–68
        price-earnings ratio 171–73
        simple 164
        time value of money 173–74
        total 165–67
    measurement of performance under modern portfolio theory 150–51
        and portfolio weighted return 150–51
    modern portfolio theory 135–50, *136, 137 see also subject entry*
    random walk theory 131–32 *see also* Kendall, M
Italy 3, 25, 53, 110, 238
    Borsa 4, 13, 239
    and MOT market 13
Ito, T 104

the January effect 161
Japan 539
    deflation in 104
    holds US debt 13
    and increased assets under management (AUM) levels 53
Jensen, M C 146
    and Jensen's measure 146
Johnson, E C (founder of Fidelity International) 44

Kahneman, D 161
Kendall, M 131
keywords for
    financial markets
        buy-side/sell-side 19
        capital markets 10
        clearing house 14
        commodities market 15
        dark pools 26
        day trading 29
        derivatives markets 17
        fat finger trades 28
        flash crashes 27
        high-frequency trading 27
        latency 24
        market economy 3
        money markets 13
        multilateral trading facilities (MTFs) 25
        over-the-counter (OTC) 12
        traders vs investors 19
    financial regulation and supervision
        Financial Ombudsman Service (FOS) 555
        money-laundering 548

prudential scrutiny 509
stress-testing 547–48
global fund management industry
   fiscal policy 47
   fund valuation 49
   stagflation 46
   UK investment bodies 52–53
investment classes: alternative
      investments
   collectibles and chattels 332
   commodities 333
   conveyancing 349
   exchange-traded fund 337
   fraud and forgery: provenance 331
   hedging (commodities as hedge
      against inflation and risk events)
      334
   life assurance property bonds 355
   limited liability partnership 352
   property authorised investment fund
      (PAIF) 353
   real estate investment trust (REIT)
      354
   revisionary value 346
   straight-line capital allowances 351
investment classes: collective investments
   closed-ended funds 270–71
   exchange-traded funds (ETF) 277–78
   investment trust (IT) 285
   mutual funds 281
   mutual funds: investment trusts (IT)
      285
   open-ended funds 270
   open-ended investment companies
      (OEICs) 275
   real estate investment trusts (REITs)
      289
   undertakings for collective
      investment of transferable
      securities (UCITS) 91
   unit trusts (UTs) 272, 274
investment classes: derivatives
   basis point 299
   beneficial ownership and legal title
      299
   CAPM 307
   contract for difference (CFD) 322
   exchange-traded derivatives 302
   futures 302
   over-the-counter (OTC) 300
   risk-free interest rate 318
investment classes: equity
   capitalization issue/bonus issue 232
   dividends 225
   limited liability 223

open offer 238
ordinary shares 224
pound cost averaging 252
preference shares 228
rights issue 234
share or stock split 233
theoretical ex-rights share price
   (TERP) 235
investment classes: fixed-interest (debt)
   bond prices – clean and dirty 199
   coupons rate 186
   fixed security 216
   floating security 216–17
   liquidity 177–78
   Macaulay duration 206–07
   modified duration 209
   nominal value/par value 185
   registered bonds 197–98
   retail and wholesale bonds 196
   risk 204
investment theory
   alpha 138
   arbitrage pricing theory 158
   behavioural finance 161
   beta 138
   capital asset pricing model 151–52
   efficient market hypothesis (EMH)
      132–33
   information ratio 148–49
   investment returns: absolute *and*
      relative 163
   Jensen's measure 146–47
   modern portfolio theory 135
   R-squared 140
   random walk theory 131
   risk-free return 154
   Sharpe ratio 142
   Treynor ratio 144
main market participants
   central banks 72
   hedge funds 89
   insurance companies 91
   investment banks 80
   pension funds 91
   private banks 79
   private equity 82
   private investors 93
   quantitative easing 74
   retail banking 77–78
   sovereign wealth funds 84
   wholesale banking 75
portfolio management: adviser and
      client
   active management service 397
   adviser status 387

keywords for *(Continued)*
    affordability and suitability: test of 'know your client' 384
    attitude to investment risk 391
    changes in the financial environment 401
    clients' objectives or needs 386
    client referral 372
    identification of client requirements 379
    rainy-day fund 382
    standardized data questionnaire 368
  portfolio management: utilization of retail fund management products
    absolute return 430
    asset class 413
    asset class correction 412
    bottom-up equity investing strategy 420–21
    identification and setting of portfolio objectives 410
    relative return 430, 432
    selection of securities 418
    strategic asset allocation 416
    tactical asset allocation 417
    time-weighted rate of return (TWRR) 442–43
  risk
    beta/beta coefficient 124
    black swan event 109
    capital risk 117
    coefficient of variation 118
    correlation coefficient 122
    credit risk 106
    duration/Macaulay duration 125
    exchange/foreign exchange rate risk 111
    income risk 113
    inflation risk 103
    interest rate risk 102
    liquidity risk 107
    market risk 105
    political risk 108–09
    standard deviation 117
    systematic and unsystematic risk 100
    value at risk (VaR) 120–21
    variance 116
    Z-scores 119
  taxation
    tax avoidance 453
    tax years 455
    domicile 456
    double taxation treaty (DTT) 461
Kirchgaessner, S 36

Lehman Brothers, economic failure of 32, 101–02, 360, 508
legislation (EU)
  European Directive on Administrative Co-operation (DAC) 453
  gold Directive (2000) 336
  International Tax Compliance Regulations (2015) 453
  Markets in Financial Instruments Directive (MiFID) 11, 13, 25–26, 37
legislation (UK) 453
  Commonhold and Leasehold Reform Act (2002) 341
  Companies Act (2006) 225
  Data Protection Act 452
  Financial Services Act (2012) 512, 513
  Financial Services and Markets Act (2000) 322, 506, 513, 514, 555
  Money Laundering (ML) Regulations (2007) 549, 551
  Proceeds of Crime Act (2002) 452, 549, 550–51
  Serious Organised Crime and Police Act (SOCPA, 2005) 549, 551
legislation (US)
  Dodd–Frank Wall Street Reform and Consumer Protection Act 521, 522, 525
  Foreign Account Tax Compliance Act (FACTA, 2014) 453
  Investment Advisers Act (1940) 521, 522
  Investment Company Act (1940) 521
  Sarbanes–Oxley Act (2002) 521, 522
Leham, B 508
limited liability companies/partnerships 89, 223, 352
Linaburg, C 88
Lintner, J 152
Lloyds of London 337
loans 14, 76, 78, 92, 177, 178–79, 182, 215–16, 368, 370, 487
  non-performing 104
London Stock Exchange (LSE) (and) 238–41
  Borsa Italiana and Turquoise 239
  CREST 9
  group and Order Book for Retail Bonds (ORB, 2010) 13
  identifying individual shares 239–40
    in practice: Marks & Spencer plc 240
  markets 239
  potential merger with Germany Stock Exchange 238

Index

purchases 51 per cent stake in Turquoise (2010) 27
systems for trading shares on 240–41
   alternative trading systems (ATS) 241
   over-the-counter (OTC) 241
   SEAQ 241
   SETS 240–41
   SETSqx 241

Macaulay, F 125 *see also* risk, measuring
Maduell, M 88
main market participants 71–97 *see also* banks *and* monetary policy
   central banks 72–75, 74
   hedge fund(s) 89–91 *see also subject entry*
   investment banks 80–82
     typical clients of 81–82
   pension funds and insurance companies 91–93 *see also* keywords
     in practice 92
   private banks 79–80
   private equity 82–84 *see also* keywords
   private investors 93–96
     appropriate investment vehicles for 94
     in practice 95
     and regulations 96
   retail banking 77–78 *see also* keywords
   sovereign wealth funds 84–85, 88, 86–87 *see also subject entry*
   wholesale banking 75–77 *see also* keywords
Malkiel, B 131, 132 *see also* random walk theory
Markowitz, H 131, 135 see modern portfolio theory
Merrick, A 227
Mishkin, F S 104
models
   Binomial 319
   Black–Scholes pricing 309, 319
   capital asset pricing (CAPM) 124, 131, 139, 146–47, 151–53, *152*, 158, 252
modern portfolio theory 135–50, *136, 137*
   Alpha 138–39, 141
   Beta 138–39, 141
   information ratio 148–50
   Jensen's measure 146–47
   R-squared 140–41, *141*
   Sharpe ratio 142–44
   standard deviation 139–40
   Treynor ratio 144–46

monetary policy 73–75 *see also* Bank of England
   and quantitative easing 74, *74*
Money Advice Service (MAS) 52
money-laundering (and) 548–54, *550 see also* legislation (UK)
   FCA principles-based approach to prevention of 553–54
   Joint Money Laundering Steering Group 552
   Money Laundering Reporting Officer (MLRO) 452, 551
Morse, A 85
Mossin, J 152

National Crime Agency 452, 551

Okimoto, D 104
OTC agreements 14, 309

portfolio management: adviser and client 364–404
   advisory and planning process 373–90, *375*
     affordability and suitability 383–87 *see also* keywords
     identification of client requirements 376–79, *377*
     presentation of recommendations 387–90
     risk and the ability to bear losses 379–83, *380 see also* keywords
   client relationship (and) 365–73
     adviser skills 365–66
     adviser status 366–68
     client information 368–73 *see also* keywords
     remuneration of the adviser 373
   client review process 399–403, *403*
     changes in client circumstances 400–401
     changes in the financial environment 401–03, *403 see also* keywords
   investment strategies 390–99
     active management service 397–98 *see also* keywords
     attitude to risk 391–92 *see also* keywords
     discretionary fund management 398–99
     growth or income 393–96
     periodic management service 396–97
     timescale of investment 392–93

portfolio management: utilization of retail fund management products 405–50
  identification and setting of portfolio objectives 407–10
    in practice 408, 409
  implementation of appropriate investment strategy (and) 410–36, 439–49, 429
    asset allocation 411–17, *414–15*, 417
    costs and charges 435–36, 439–41, *437–38*
    management style: absolute *and* relative returns 430–31 see also keywords
    management style: active investment 427–28
    management style: passive investment 425–27, 428
    performance measurement/review and benchmarks 441–49 see also keywords
    in practice 410–11, 432, 433, 434
    selection of securities 418–25, *419*
    specific client requirements 432–34
  key steps in 406, *407*
property (and) 340–52, *348, 349*
  authorised investment fund (PAIF) 353, *356–58*
  buying and selling: transaction costs for sellers *and* buyers 346–47
  capital gains tax 351
  conveyancing 349–50 see also keywords
  indirect property investment 351–52
    limited liability partnerships 352 see also keywords
    property company shares 352
  leasehold premiums 348
    for second-home owners *and* in practice 348–49, *349*
  ownership: common hold 341–42 see also legislation (UK)
  ownership: freehold *and* leasehold 340–42
    in practice 341
  returns from 342–46
    capital: gross rent multiplier *and* capitalization rate 344–46
    factors affecting 344
    in practice 343–44
    rent 342–43
    revisionary value of leases 346 see also keywords

stamp duty land tax (SDLT) 347, *348*
structured products: deposits and investments 359–60
  buffer zone investments *and* in practice 361
  principal protected investments *and* in practice 360
  return enhanced investments *and* in practice 361–62
  taxation of property income (for) 350–51 see also keywords
    commercial property 351
    residential property 350–51
  types of 340, *340*
  taxation of property income: residential *and* commercial 350–51 see also keywords
Prudential Regulation Authority (PRA) 512, 513–14

quantitative easing 74, *74* see also keywords

A Random Walk Down Wall Street 131, 132
random walk theory 131–32 see also Malkiel, B
ratio analysis 168, 169
ratios 178, 245–46, 286 see also Sharpe ratio *and* Traynor ratio
  Alpha risk 65–66
  dividend 64
  financial 119–20
  P/E growth (PEG) 19
  price to earnings (P/E) 64, 170, 249, 261
Reilly, F K 119
REITs benchmarks for FTSE EPRA/NAREIT UK index *and* FTSE Russell 354
reports (on)
  cost of financial services regulation in UK (New City Agenda, 2016) 510
  financial planning 388–89
  Investment Outlook 2017 (Goldman Sachs) 45
  suitability report 388
research (on)
  crowdfunding regulation (European Banking Authority *and* European Securities and Markets Authority) 340
  deflation in Japan (Ito, T and Mishkin, F S) 104 see also studies
  ethical performance of companies (Ethical Investment Research Service) 434

hedge funds (*Hedge Fund Journal*, Hennessee Group) 90
relative correlations between asset classes 412
risk, measuring (and) 115–28, *115*
  Bessel's correction factor 117–18
  beta/beta coefficient 124–25
    in practice 125
  coefficient of variation 118
  correlation coefficient 122–23
    in practice 122
  duration/Macaulay duration 125–26
  inflation and investment returns 126–28
    formulae for 127
    in practice 127
  standard deviation and variance 116–18
  value at risk (VaR) 120–21
    in practice 121
  Z-scores/Altman Z-score 119–20 *see also* Altman, E
risk, types of 99–114
  black swan events 114 *see also subject entry*
  in bonds *see* investment classes: fixed-interest (debt)
  capital 112–13
  credit 106–07, *107*
  default 107
  duration 102
  exchange rate 111–12
  income 113
  inflation 103–04 *see also* Japan
  interest rate 102–03
  liquidity 107–08
  market 105
  market timing 105–06
  political and country 108–10, *109–10*
  systematic and unsystematic 99–101, *100, 101*
  systemic 101
risk (and) 98–129
  ability to bear losses 379–83
  measuring *see* risk, measuring
  types of *see* risk, types of
  uncertainty 296–97
  volatility 99
risk-profiling tools 371, 379
Ross, S 158
  and arbitrage pricing theory 158–61

S&P 500 index 284
Schliefer, A 162
Scholes, M 309
share prices, factors affecting 255–58

  chartists 257–58
  company news 256
    in practice 256
  the economy 255–56
  interest rates 256
  investor sentiment 257
  market consolidation 257
  market makers 258
  press and analysts reports 257
share register 224, 498, *498*
shares, measuring returns from 246–59
  capital 249–50
    capital growth 249–50
    enterprise value 250
  dividend measures 246–48
    cover 247–48
    in practice 247
    yield 246–47
  price and earnings 248–49
    earnings per share (EPS) 248
    earnings yield 248
    price–earnings (P/E) ratio 249
shares, ordinary (and) 224–28
  deferred dividend 228
  dividends 225–26
  dual-class 226–27
    in practice: Alphabet Inc *and* Hollinger International 227
  founder 228
  redeemable 228
  security 226
  voting rights 225
shares, preference (and) 228–30
  conversion 230
  cumulative and non-cumulative 229–30
  dividends and security 229
  participating 230
  redemption 230
shares, risks of investing in 250–55
  capital 251
  growth 251
  industry and company-specific issues 254–55
    company finances 255
    cyclicality of industry 254
    management quality 254–55
    nature of industry 254
  liquidity 250–51
    in practice 250–51
  market conditions 255
  price volatility 252–54
    and areas to be considered/understood 253–54
shares, trading 242–44
  and share purchase costs 243–44

shares, trading *(Continued)*
    cost of share 243
    commissions 243
    levy by Panel on Takeovers and Mergers (PTM) 243
    off-market transactions 244
    stamp duty reserve tax (SDRT), stamp duty – and in practice 243–44
    sources for: agents/broker *and* principal 242
    in practice 242
shares, types of 224–30 *see also* shares, ordinary
    founder 228
    redeemable 228
    and research on effect of shareholder rights on returns 227 *see also* studies
shares 223–38, 245–50
    changes in number of issued 231–37
        capitalization issue 232–33
        open offer *see* keywords
        rights issue 234–35
        share or stock split 233–34
        theoretical ex-rights share price or TERP 235–37
    effect of corporation actions on costs of buying and selling 245
    factors affecting price of *see* share prices, factors affecting
    measuring returns from 246–50
    nominal and market value of 230–31
    Plc shares available through stock exchanges in UK 223–24
    possible returns from holding shares as investment 245–46
    types of *see* shares, types of
Sharpe, W F 142, 152
Sharpe ratio 68, 138, 142–44, 148, 152, 445–46, 447, *445 see also* Treynor ratio
Sieff, K 36
Singapore, regulatory landscape in (and) 536–40
    Accounting and Corporate Regulatory Authority (ACRA) 537, 540
    legislation: Monetary Authority of Singapore Act (1970) 537
    legislation: Securities Industry Act (1973) 537, 540
    Monetary Authority of Singapore (MAS) 537–38
    Securities Industry Act 540
    Securities Industry Council (SIC) 537, 540
    Singapore Exchange Securities Trading (SGX) 537, 539, *539*
Singapore 6, 7, 226, 506, 526, 557
Sovereign Wealth Funds, International Forum of (IFSWF) 88
    and the Santiago Principles: compliance with *and* objectives of 88
sovereign wealth funds 84–85, 88, *86–87 see also* articles
    commonly observed objectives of 85
    transparency ratings 88
stock exchanges (in) 238–41
    Amsterdam (AEX) 11
    auction and electronic 31
    Canadian 7
    Chicago 6
    Germany (Deutsche Börse) 238, 519
    Hong Kong (SEHK) 11, 529, 530
    London (LSE) 4, 11, 519 *see also* London Stock Exchange (LSE)
    Mexican 7
    and NASDAQ 31, 522
    New York (NYSE) 6, 11, 522
    and error corrections 28–29
    over the counter (OTC) 31
    Shanghai 12
    Singapore Exchange Securities Trading (SGX) 537, 539, *539*
    Tokyo (TSE) 11
    United Kingdom 4
studies (on)
    deflation in Japan (Okimoto, D) 104
    effect of shareholder rights on shareholder returns (Gompers, P A and Metrick, A, 2003) 227
    Paying Taxes (World Bank and International Finance Corporation (2016) 526
    survey of investors to assess importance of trust within the industry (CFA, 2013) 365
Switzerland 79, 80, 109, *109*, 211, *212*

tables
    2008 financial crisis timeline *33–36*
    accrued coupons – summary (example) *200*
    advantages and disadvantages of alternative property investments *356–58*
    advantages and disadvantages of investing in bonds *219*
    advantages and disadvantages of investing in equities *258*
    American-style put and call options *317*

Index

change in asset allocation mix over time 403
characteristics of property assets 340
global rankings of countries 109–10
Macauley's duration: example 207
national insurance classes 472
national insurance rates for the year 2017/18 472
overseas government bond yields 212
portfolio management: retail fund management: asset allocation: in practice 417
portfolio management: retail fund management products: Sharpe ratio 445
portfolio management: retail fund management products: Treynor ratio 447
risk tolerance and investment mix for growth and income 414–15
SDLT rates for year to April 2018 348
SDLT: example SDLT payable 349
sovereign wealth fund ranks as at June 2016 86–87
tax bands 2016/17 464
tax bands ('in practice') 464
tax calculation ('in practice') 475
tax calculations ('in practice') 478
tax rates on collective investments income 469
tax rates on OEICs, unit trust and EFTs 469
tax relief reduction on property (2017–2021) 477
taxation: calculation of capital gain/allowable loss 480
and in practice (Elise) 481
taxation: calculation of CGT on chargeable assets 483
taxation: calculation of VAT – example 501–02
taxation: chargeable and exempt assets 482
taxation: dividend income – tax rates 476
taxation: inheritance tax rates 487
taxation: investment trust – tax on income 471
taxation: residency/domicile combinations for tax purposes 459
taxation: sufficient ties test 457
taxation: stamp duty/SDRT 498
taxation: tax band for SDLT 499
and in practice (Sarah) 499
taxation: using remittance basis – in practice 460
trust, types of 466
trust tax rates: accumulation and discretionary trusts 467
trusts: interest in possession trusts – tax rates by type of income 468
typical investor risk spectrum 380
typical performance of asset classes in varying economic conditions 419
typical Standard & Poor's bond ratings 107
variable rate bonds: repayment schedule 192
taxation (and) 451–505 *see also* legislation (UK) *and* HMRC
  avoidance of 453–54 *see also* keywords; legislation (EU) *and* legislation (US)
  capital gains tax (CGT) 351, 479–85
    amount and liability for charities and trusts 484
    amount and liability for collective investments 484–85
    amount and liability for individuals 482–83, *483*
    assets generating chargeable gain or allowable loss on disposal 482, *482*
    calculating chargeable capital gain/allowable loss on disposal 479–81, *480*, *481*
    and tax planning: timing of disposals and tax wrappers 485
  corporation tax 503
  HMRC 453, 468–70, 473, 476, 479, 491, 492, 502, 503, *501–02*
  income tax (and) 461–65, *464*, 464
    bands 463–64, *464*
    blind persons allowance 462
    charities 464–65
    individuals 461
    married couples/civil partners 462–63
    minors and personal allowance 462
    personal allowances 461–62
  inheritance tax (IHT) (and) 486–97, *489*
    asset valuation following death 491–93
    exemptions 488–90
    interaction with income tax 491
    planning strategies *see* inheritance tax (IHT) planning strategies
    potentially exempt transfer (PET) 486, *487*
    transfers on death 487–88

taxation (and) *(Continued)*
  transfers into/out of trusts, and on trust assets 491
  wills (invalid) and assets 494
  wills (non-existent), intestacy and assets 494–95
  wills (valid) and assets 493–94
  inheritance tax (IHT) planning strategies (for) 495–97
    borrowing to release cash 497
    jointly owned property 496
    lifetime gifts 496
    non-financial issues 497
    transferability of nil rate IHT band 496
    use of trusts 497
  investment income or unearned income tax 473–79, 477, 478
    dividend income 476, 476
    rental income: commercial property 478–79
    rental income: residential property 476–78, 477, 478
    savings income and taxation 474–75, 475
  National Insurance (NI) 471–73
    classes 471, 473, 472
    payment of 473
  residency and domicile 455–60, 459, 460
    automatic overseas and residency tests for 456–57
    and effect on amount of tax paid 458–60, 459, 460
    sufficient ties test for 457–58, 457
  stamp duty (and) 243, 321, 452, 498–99, 498
    stamp duty land tax (SDLT) 498
    stamp duty reserve tax (SDRT) 498
  tax years 454–55 *see also* keywords
  trusts 465, 467–70, 472, 473
    types of 465, 466
  trusts: liability to pay and rates of income payable (by) 467–71
    accumulation and discretionary trusts 467, 467
    bare trusts 468
    collective investments 468, 469
    equalization payments 469–70
    interest in possession trusts 467–68, 468
    investment trusts 470, 471
    open-ended investment companies, unit trusts, exchange-traded funds 469, 469

  REITs 470
  settlor-interested trusts 468
value added tax (VAT) 500–502
  calculation of 501–02, *501–02*
  charges, rates of and exemptions from 500–501
  and zero-rated or exempt supplies and sales 502
withholding tax 460–61 *see also* keywords
theories
  modern portfolio 131
  portfolio 131
  random walk (Malkiel) 131
transparency 5, 17–18, 22, 25–26, 30, 31, 80, 84, 88, 90, 93, 266, 280, 283, 303, 360, 373, 455, 508, 517–18
  lack of 26, 290, 533
Treynor, J L 144, 148, 152
Treynor ratio 144–46, 445–47, 447
Trump, D 46, 47, 69, 525, 557
Turquoise equity market 239
Tversky, A 161
types of risk *see* risk

UCITS: undertakings for collective investment in transferable securities 330
  regulated by the EU 330
United Kingdom (UK) and 4, 14, 25 *see also* stock exchanges
  banks, stress-tests for (Financial Policy Committee, 2014) 547
  business structures: sole trade, partnership *and* company 223
  Chicago Board Options Exchange (CBOE) 309
  Financial Conduct Authority 95
  GILTS, UK government index-linked 113
  Gold Sovereign 336
  issue of data availability in 84
  Retail Distribution Review (2013) 373, 439–40
United Kingdom (UK) fund management industry (2016) (and) 53–57
  allocation of assets within the industry 57
  clients 56
  effect of Brexit 57
  importance of UK asset management to the domestic economy 53–54
  importance of UK asset management within global market 53
  levels of employment in UK asset management industry 54, 54

number and size of firms in UK asset management industry 54, 55
passive vs active investing 55–56, 56
regulation 57
technology 55
United Kingdom (UK) regulatory landscape 511–15 *see also subject entries*
Bank of England 512–13
Financial Conduct Authority (FCA) 514–15
Prudential Regulation Authority (PRA) 512, 513–14
three statutory objectives 513
United States of America (USA) 93
Federal Reserve 519, 523–24
financial market in 9
first 100 days of Donald Trump's presidency of 46
gold coins: Eagle *and* Double Eagle 336
OTC markets in 31
Securities and Exchange Commission 95, 520–522
Rule 17a-4 regulation issued by 542
stress-resting in 548
and the Trump administration 557
United States of America (USA): regulatory landscape (and) 519–25

Commodity Futures Trading Commission (CFTC) 522–23
Federal Reserve 523–24
Financial Industry Regulatory Authority (FINRA) 522
Office of the Comptroller of the Currency (OCC) 520
in practice
federal reserve banks 524
focus on ensuring access to information 519
legislation 521–22 *see also* legislation (US)
talking points from current financial world (2) 525
regulatory agencies 520
Securities and Exchange Commission 520–522
Treasury Department 524–25
Vietnam 6, 508 *see also* ASEAN member states
Vishney, R 162

World Bank 526
and revision of annual global growth forecast (2016) 255
Wright, D J 119

Ingram Content Group UK Ltd.
Milton Keynes UK
UKHW010653210323
418913UK00006B/346